Dublin's Stained Glass

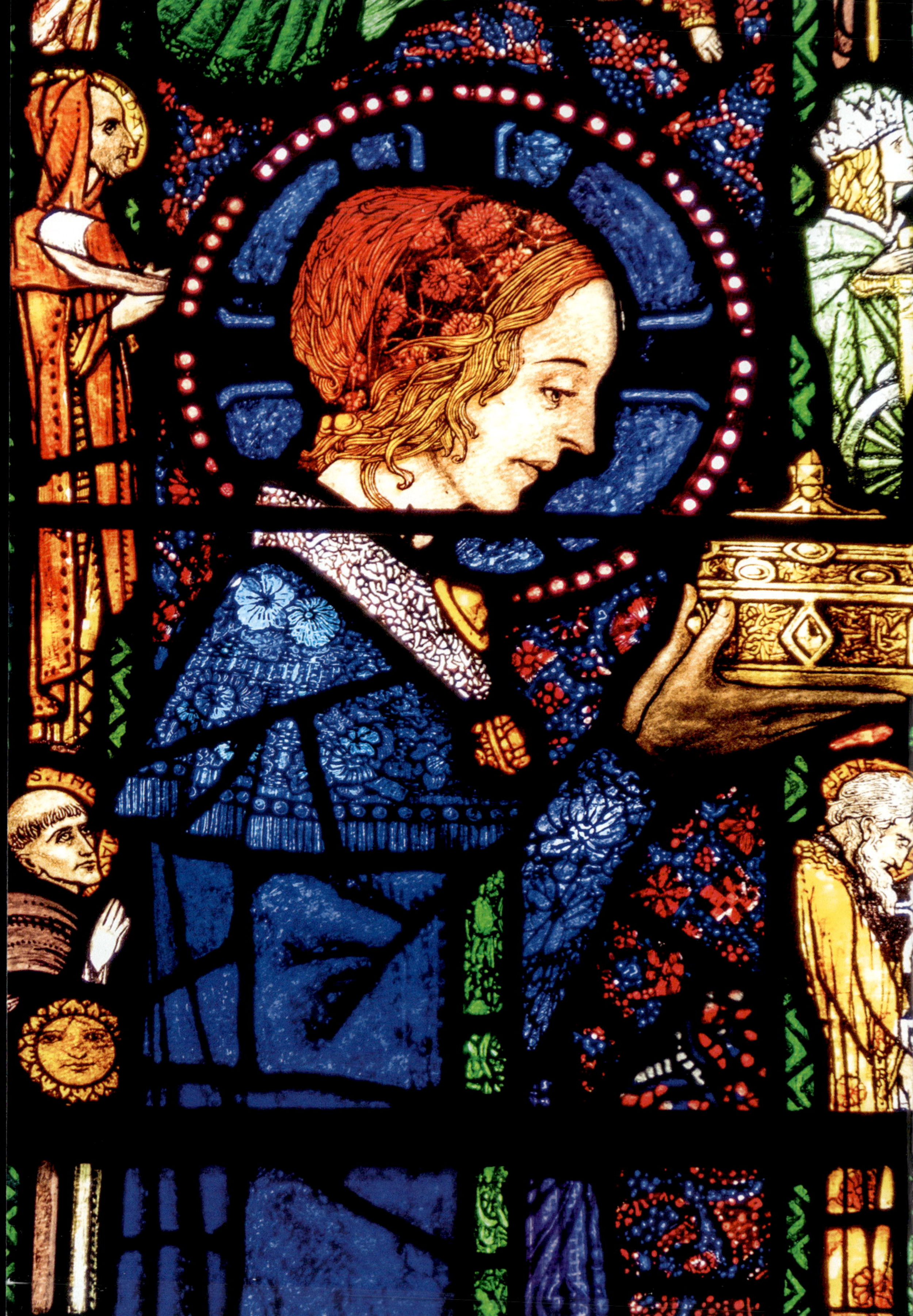

Dublin's Stained Glass

A guide to the finest twentieth-century windows

DAVID CARON

Principal photography by Jozef Vrtiel

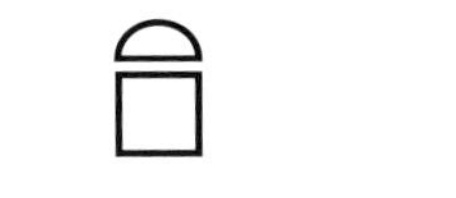

FOUR COURTS PRESS

This book was published by
Four Courts Press
7 Malpas Street, Dublin 8, Ireland
www.fourcourtspress.ie
and in North America by
Four Courts Press
c/o IPG Books, 814 N. Franklin St, Chicago, IL 60610

A catalogue record for this title
is available from the British Library.

ISBN 978-1-80151-167-4

Page ii (facing the title page), image by Harry Clarke, detail of St Margaret Mary from *The Sacred Heart, St Margaret Mary, and St John Eudes* (1919), St Peter's church (RC), Phibsborough.
Page vii (facing contents page), image by Beatrice Elvery, detail of the Prodigal Son from *The Good Samaritan and the Prodigal Son* (1908), Tullow Parish (C of I, Carrickmines).

Printed in Poland by L & C Printing Group, Krakow
Book design and typesetting by Anú Design, Tara

The publisher and author would
like to acknowledge the generous
financial assistance of
Dublin City Council
and South Dublin County Council

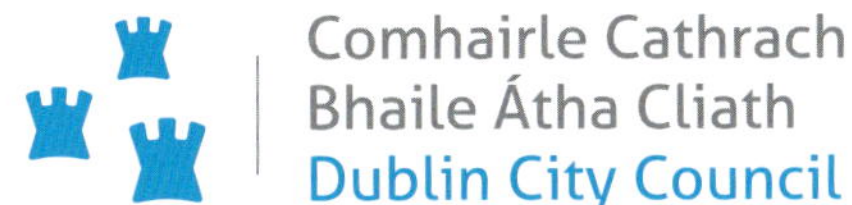

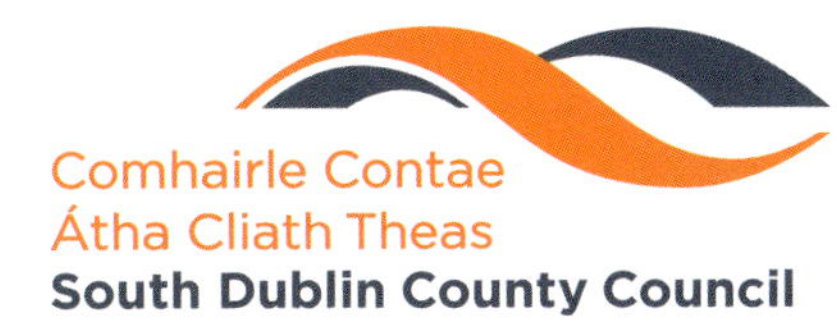

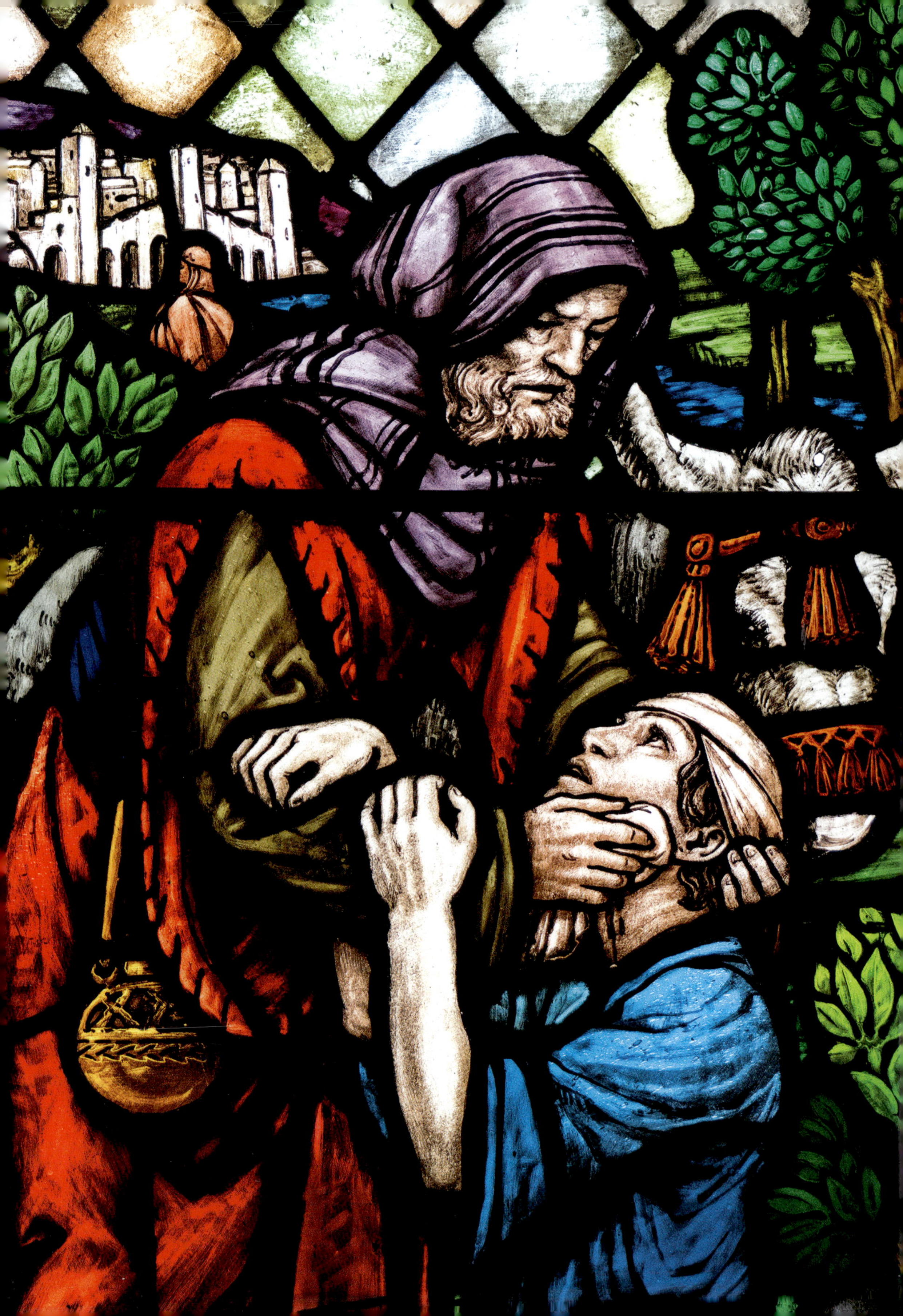

Contents

Dublin South, Suburbs and County

Abbreviations

ATG	An Túr Gloine
C of I	Church of Ireland
CSGSA	Clarke Stained Glass Studios Archives
CSIA	Centre for the Study of Irish Art
DCU	Dublin City University
DDA	Dublin Diocesan Archive (RC)
FNCI	Friends of the National Collections of Ireland
HLG	Hugh Lane Gallery
IAA	Irish Architectural Archive
NCA	National College of Art (Dublin)
NCAD	National College of Art and Design
NGI	National Gallery of Ireland
NIVAL	National Irish Visual Arts Library
RC	Roman Catholic
RCB	Representative Church Body
RDS	Royal Dublin Society
RHA	Royal Hibernian Academy
RIA	Royal Irish Academy
RIC	Royal Irish Constabulary
TCD	Trinity College Dublin
UCC	University College Cork
UCD	University College Dublin

Acknowledgments

I would like to acknowledge a particular debt of gratitude to Jozef Vrtiel for his unstinting commitment to expertly photographing Dublin's stained glass, in many instances returning several times to locations in order to capture windows under the best possible lighting conditions. All photographs in the book, including exterior shots of the buildings, were taken by him with the exception of five images kindly supplied by the National Gallery. Three individuals were of particular assistance in preparing the text – Reiltín Murphy undertook considerable online archival research on my behalf; Dr Paul Donnelly has been a tremendous help in sharing his extensive knowledge of the Clarke Studios; I relied greatly on Colm O'Brien's expertise as an architectural historian. I am also most grateful to the following for generously sharing their expert knowledge with me – Dr Joseph McBrinn, Dr Stephen Huws, Ruth Sheehy, Finola Finlay, Dr Michael Earley and Bart Felle. Jim O'Crowley's review of the text was hugely helpful. I would like to express particular gratitude to several artists who I interviewed in relation to their work: Phyllis Burke, Patrick Muldowney, Killian Schurmann, Alan Tomlin, George W. Walsh and Peter Young.

I would also like to thank Dr Jasmine Allen, Marcella Bannon, Canon Liam Belton, John Bird, Margaret Bluett, David Britton, Alan Brooks, Clare Brophy, Maura Butler, Cól Campbell, Evan Connon, Peter Cormack, Revd Dr John Cunningham, Patricia Curtin-Kelly, Susan Devane, Eleanor Donnelly, Martin Donnelly, Noelle Dowling, Vincent Downing, Fr Des Doyle, Charles Duggan, Bernard Dunleavy, Revd Alastair Dunlop, Aisling Dunne, Rosaleen Dwyer, William Earley, Friends of the National Collections of Ireland, Canon Mark Gardner, John Glynn, Brendan Grimes, Ruth Hallinan, Fr Bernard Healy, Anne Henderson, Anne Hodge, Con Hogan, Geraldine Hone, Dr Susan Hood, Dr Stephen Huws, Ken Kerr, Oliver Kerr, Stephen Kerr, Fr Michael Kilkenny, Dr Stuart Kinsella, Sarah McAuliffe, Frank McCann, Fr Joe

McCann, Dr Eve McCauley, James McCrory, Kirstin Matson, David Millar, Fr Kevin Moore, Seamus Moran, Ruby Morrow, Patrick Muldowney, Rónán Murray, Fr Ultan Naughton, Niamh O'Brien, Mons. Dr Ciarán O'Carroll, Professor Eunan O'Halpin, Fr Paddy O'Reilly, Ronan O'Reilly, Dr David O'Shea, Vincent Owen, Canon David Oxley, Louis Parminter, Eve Parnell, David Petherbridge, Revd Nigel Pierpoint, Dr Carole Pollard, Bríd Pollen, Fr Joe Poole, Lewis Purser, Fr Frank Reburn, Professor Olivia Robinson, Johnny Ronan, Dr Ellen Rowley, Ken Ryan, AnneMarie Saliba, Dr Billy Shortall, Fr Michel Simo, Logan Sisley, Shawn Talbot, Revd John Tanner, Brendan Teeling, Nora Tillman, Professor John Turpin, Fr Paul Tyrrell, Miriam van der Molen, Stephen Walsh, Rory Williams, Janienne Wood and Susanna Wyse Jackson.

Finally I would also like to acknowledge the many clergy, parish administrators, and other individuals and institutions who are custodians of Dublin's rich stained glass heritage for their assistance in making this publication possible.

Glossary

antique glass – Mouth-blown handmade glass, with the irregularity of medieval glass. Glass blown into a large cylinder that is cut, opened, and flattened into a sheet. 'Antique' refers to the technique, not the age.
aciding – Aciding (also known as acid etching) is the process where wax or similar substance is applied to flashed glass (glass with a skim of surface colour) and onto which designs are then incised. Hydrofluoric acid is used to dissolve away all or part of the coloured surface layer which is not protected by wax to achieve a variety of tones from deep colour all the way to completely clear. Clarke and Healy mastered this technique and often plated (sandwiched together, carefully registered) two layers of acided flashed glass to introduce additional colours and tones.
cames – The slender, malleable H-shaped strips of grooved lead used to hold the pieces of glass together within a stained glass window or panel.
canopy – An architectural framing device to enclose a figure or scene. Christopher Whall and A.E. Child favoured ones inspired by nature: branches, leaves, etc.
cartoon – The full-sized drawing of a stained glass window showing the exact size and shape of all the pieces of glass, their colour, the size of the lead and the support system to glaze the window.
cathedral glass – Textured translucent sheet glass made by casting and rolling, and despite the name, is unconnected with medieval cathedrals.
cinquefoil – Tracery light containing five sections, having the appearance of a flower with five petals.
clerestory – The uppermost level of windows in a church or cathedral, usually above the nave.
cullet – Small pieces of glass left over after cutting. Often employed creatively by Harry Clarke, his studio, and ATG.

cusp – Projecting point/termination within the foils in Gothic tracery.
cutlines – Lines of a cartoon indicating the outlines of the individual pieces of glass.
dalle de verre – A structural glass window/wall which uses thick slabs of glass that are cut or broken and cemented into a panel using an epoxy adhesive or cement matrix
flashed glass – A base sheet of glass, usually white, of which is overlaid a 'flash' layer of coloured glass. The coloured layer can be removed by the 'aciding' process.
flèche – Narrow slender spire on the centre of a roof.
grisaille – Painting technique by which an image is executed entirely in shades of grey.
lancet – Tall, narrow window with a pointed arch at its top.
lantern – A circular or polygonal turret with windows all round crowning a roof or dome.
leading – The web or matrix of lead cames holding together pieces of glass in a leaded window.
liturgical east – Traditionally churches are constructed so that during the celebration of the morning liturgy the priest and congregation face towards the rising sun, a symbol of Christ; however, frequently churches cannot be oriented in this manner and regardless the window behind the altar is still referred to as the east window, and the one opposite as the west window.
matting – A light, even wash of glass paint applied to glass to soften and control the light. While still wet it can be stippled or patterned to increase the textural quality.
medallion – Narrative scene or design, usually enclosed within geometrically-shaped borders often set into a window of quarries.
mullion – the vertical member between lights in a window opening.
panel – An element/unit of a stained glass window or a small autonomous piece. A single window, as a rule, comprises several panels.
plating – The doubling of one piece of glass with another, within the same lead.
pot metal glass – Glass that is coloured throughout, when molten, by the addition of one or more metallic oxides.
predella panel – Panel at the base of a window, usually featuring a narrative scene relating to the subject of the larger image above.
quarry – Square or diamond-shaped, usually of white glass. Often used in multiples to make up whole windows or as a decorative background.

quatrefoil – Small opening in Gothic tracery having four arched sides.

quoin – Dressed stones at the angle of a building, usually alternatly long and short.

reredos – Painted and/or sculpted screen behind and above the altar.

rose window – A large circular window opening, usually divided by stoned mullions, most often composed of stained glass panels radiating from the centre.

roundel – A small, usually circular, panel of stained glass, depicting a religious or secular subject.

silver stain – A stain produced by applying a silver-compound solution to the surface of the glass, which, when fired turns yellow ranging from pale yellow to deep amber.

single-light window – A window, usually narrow, usually crowned by an arch, either pointed or curved.

sketch design – A small (normally 1ft to 1in. scale) coloured design (usually in pencil and watercolour, sometimes with ink, crayon or gouache) created by the artist to show the client what the completed window would look like.

slab glass or bottle glass – A piece of glass cut from a square bottle. Of irregular thickness and intensity of colour.

snecked stone – Courses of stone which are frequently broken by smaller square stones (snecks).

spandrel – Of roughly triangular shape, usually found in pairs, between the top of an arch and a rectangular frame.

streaky glass – Glass which has been unevenly coloured in its molten state to create streaks or swirls.

tracery – The small, often ornate, openings at the top of a window, commonly found in multi-light Gothic windows.

transept – Transverse portions of a traditional cross-shaped church/cathedral.

transom – Horizontal member between the lights in a window opening.

trefoil – Small opening in Gothic tracery having three arcs.

2-light, 3-light window, etc. – Two or more lights separated by vertical mullions.

vesica – A pointed oval shape of vertical orientation.

wheel window – Circular window with tracery of radiating shafts like the spokes of a wheel, a variant of a rose window.

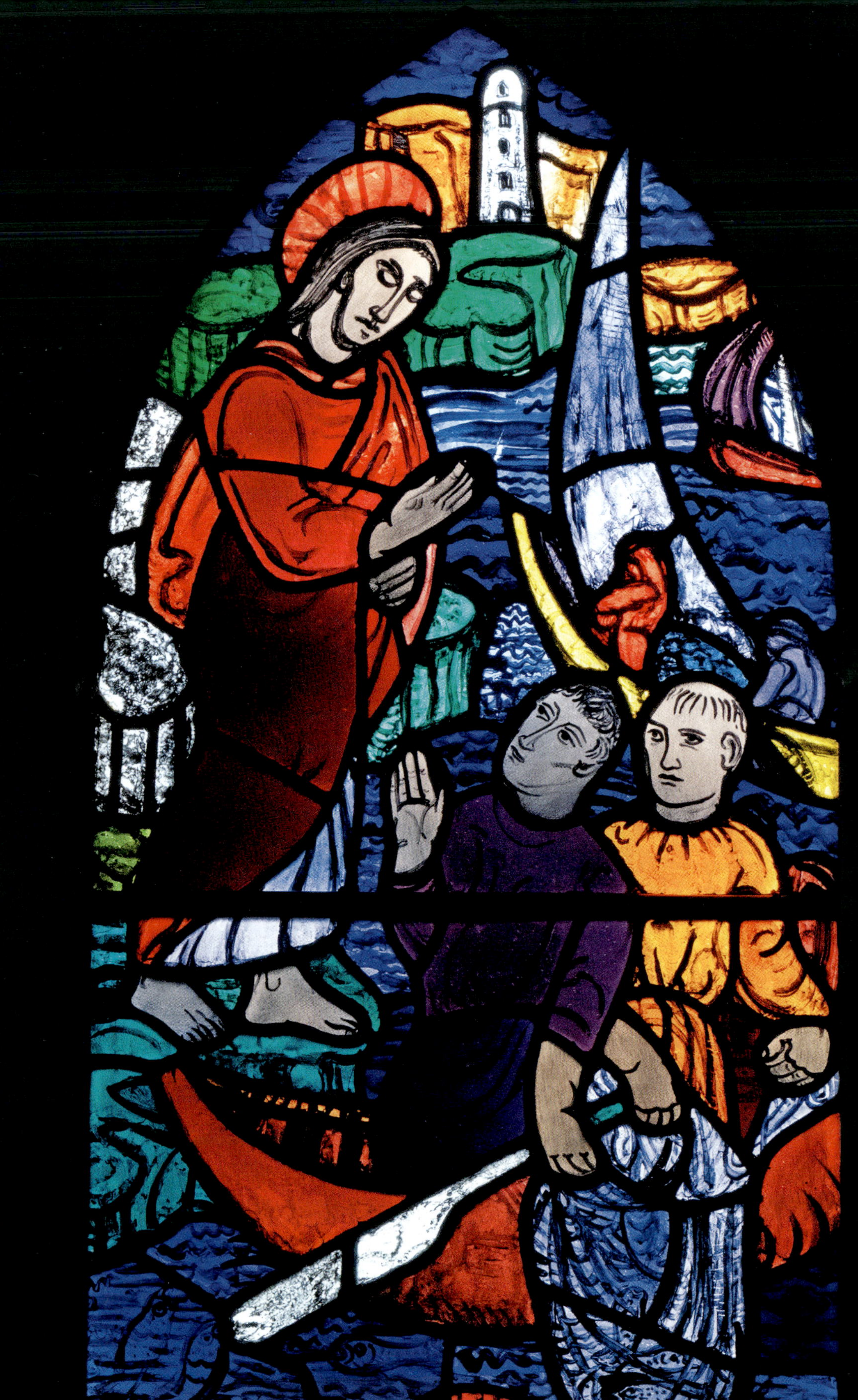

Introduction

During the twentieth century Dublin's reputation as a centre for stained glass excellence, both in terms of artistry and craftsmanship, was internationally lauded and is evidenced by the many orders placed by overseas patrons. Stained glass was the one area of the visual arts in twentieth-century Ireland that had an established school of the highest calibre, as distinct from singular talents such as Jack B. Yeats and Eileen Gray. The high point for Irish twentieth-century stained glass was the period from *c.*1915 to *c.*1980 and the leading figures were Harry Clarke, Wilhelmina Geddes, Michael Healy, Evie Hone and Richard King, all of whom trained in Dublin, worked out of Dublin studios, and so it is not surprising that the city has a concentration of first-rate stained glass by them and many others.

The main objective of this book was to select key locations in Dublin that hold significant collections of twentieth-century Irish stained glass; most of the locations are, not surprisingly, religious (cathedrals, churches and chapels), though also included are the stained glass rooms in the National Gallery and the Hugh Lane Gallery, and Bewley's café, the latter well known for its Harry Clarke windows. Consideration was given to representing all the main artists and studios, prioritizing locations with a number of windows over a single example, no matter how fine it might be. Relative ease of access was also taken into account so for instance school chapels have not been included in the selection. Although this book concerns itself with Irish glass, on occasion where deemed appropriate, a small number of non-Irish examples have been included for context and comparison. It must be stressed that the sites chosen for inclusion in the book comprise a personal selection and others would doubtless make different choices.

(opposite) Evie Hone, detail of The calling of Saints Peter and Andrew from *Scenes from the Lives of Christ and St Andrew* (1943), St Andrew's church (C of I), Malahide

Dublin's stained glass sets out to provide a holistic overview, including the artists' response to the architectural setting, the evolution of their design concepts (where known), their differing stained glass techniques, along with the key role of the clergy and donors in determining the selection and interpretation of the iconography. Some windows hold secrets such as Harry Clarke's wily use of recycled vintage glass in Lusk, and others have intriguing histories such as Sheila Corcoran's expressionist stained glass Stations of the Cross for the airport church, which were removed at the insistence of Archbishop McQuaid only to be reinstated years later, and Dun Laoghaire's Presbyterian church featuring a series of windows designed by Ethel Rhind that were commissioned by siblings before they died with, uniquely, the provision for the memorial inscriptions to be inserted retrospectively so that all five would be commemorated. The book reveals the changing styles, mores, and subject choices for windows that evolved over the course of the century; these were in part determined by artistic and architectural movements but also by seismic events such as the First World War with the consequent desire to erect war memorial windows, and by new approaches to church design resulting from Vatican II.

This book covers all of Dublin city and county, so for ease of reference it has been divided into three sections – Dublin city (defined as between the Royal and Grand canals); north suburbs and county; and south suburbs and county. For the principal twenty artists and five studios there are short entries at the back of the book.

If one were to visit all or many of the locations featured in the book, one would get a comprehensive overview of the story of twentieth-century Irish stained glass. In 1901 Sarah Purser arranged for a young Londoner, A.E. Child, who had trained under the great Arts and Crafts stained glass artist Christopher Whall, to relocate to Dublin to teach the craft at the Dublin Metropolitan School of Art and to set up and manage An Túr Gloine. Child, though not an innovative artist, was a first-rate instructor and virtually all of the artists of the first half of the century owe their training to him. Child is represented in this book in several locations, including an early window designed by Purser but executed by him, for St Patrick's cathedral, and an iconographically unique window, *Discovery, Truth, Inspiration, Love, and Work* for the Unitarian church, St Stephen's Green, which he considered to be the highlight of his career.

An Túr Gloine was never a large studio and the artists – Michael Healy, Catherine (Kitty) O'Brien, Beatrice Elvery, Ethel Rhind, Wilhelmina Geddes, Hubert McGoldrick and Evie Hone – are all represented in this book and between them there are nearly sixty windows at sixteen locations. That one small studio fostered the careers of artists of the stature of Healy, Geddes and Hone is truly remarkable.

There are examples from the studio of Joshua Clarke, created before his supremely talented son Harry began working in the medium, such as an apse window (1904) in St Augustine and St John's church, Thomas Street. Windows by Harry Clarke feature in several locations – Balbriggan, Lusk, Phibsborough, the National Gallery, the Hugh Lane Gallery, Bewley's café, Terenure and Killiney. Members of Harry Clarke's studio, specifically Richard King, William Dowling and Terry Clarke, are also represented, and in three instances (Balbriggan, Lusk and Terenure), one can view windows by Harry Clarke and also ones made at Harry Clarke Studios after he had died which provides an opportunity to compare how the studio's distinctive style evolved over time. Works by the artists of Harry Clarke Studios are sometimes looked down upon relative to those created by Clarke himself, but Kimmage Manor church with its selection of twenty-six windows by the studio demonstrates how skilled its leading artists were.

Dublin's third large studio, and the one longest established, Earley & Company, is represented in several locations by its most talented member, William E. Earley, who was responsible for developing the studio's hallmark exuberant style, which flourished between the 1920s and 1940s, largely inspired by Baroque painting with a distinctive rich and lush colour palette and often featuring an abundance of putti.

Richard King, who had been Harry Clarke's most talented apprentice, departed Clarke's in 1940 and after a lengthy interregnum relaunched his career as a solo artist working in a modernist idiom, and one of his finest windows, a monumental gable wall of glass, *Pentecost* (1967–70) for Greenhills church, is included. Among the key artists of the second half of the century are Patrick Pollen and Patrick Pye whose careers began in the 1950s, and who, like King, worked independently outside of the studio system, and are both represented in two locations.

By the mid-1960s only two of the long established studios, Clarke's and Earley's, remained and both were struggling to attract new clients, their style of stained glass now deemed outmoded and incompatible with a modern aesthetic that had emerged post-Vatican II, and which was largely driven by young architects rather than the clergy. Two new studios, Murphy-Devitt Studios and Abbey Stained Glass, capitalized on this demand, providing not only a contemporary interpretation of figurative imagery but were adept at devising dynamic abstract schemes, sometimes on challenging budgets. Johnny Murphy was the creative force behind Murphy-Devitt Studios and he also reintroduced classes in the craft at the National College of Art. Frank Ryan was the artistically-inclined manager of Abbey who had a keen eye for spotting talent and a reputation for encouraging individuality.

There were also younger independent artists vying for commissions. Helen Moloney was to some extent an outsider who developed a singular style using a repertoire of timeless Christian symbols interpreted in jazzy complementary colours. Her largest work is an enormous glazed lantern (1968) in Our Lady of Victories, Ballymun. Phyllis Burke began her career in the late 1950s and developed a fresh style often choosing a lighter palette that addressed architects' desire for brighter interiors. Her largest commission, a series of twelve figurative windows spanning the years 1990–2007, is in St Teresa's church, Clarendon Street. George W. Walsh, who had worked in the US for six years before returning to Ireland in 1963, has had a prodigious output, working for Abbey Stained Glass initially before going solo and he is represented by windows in three locations that date from three different decades. Other living artists included are Patrick Muldowney, Peter Young and Killian Schurmann, each of whom work in very different styles while responding to the architectural contexts for which their work has been commissioned.

(opposite) Michael Healy, detail of *St Patrick with Saints Eithne and Fidelma* (1914), Sacred Heart church (RC), Donnybrook

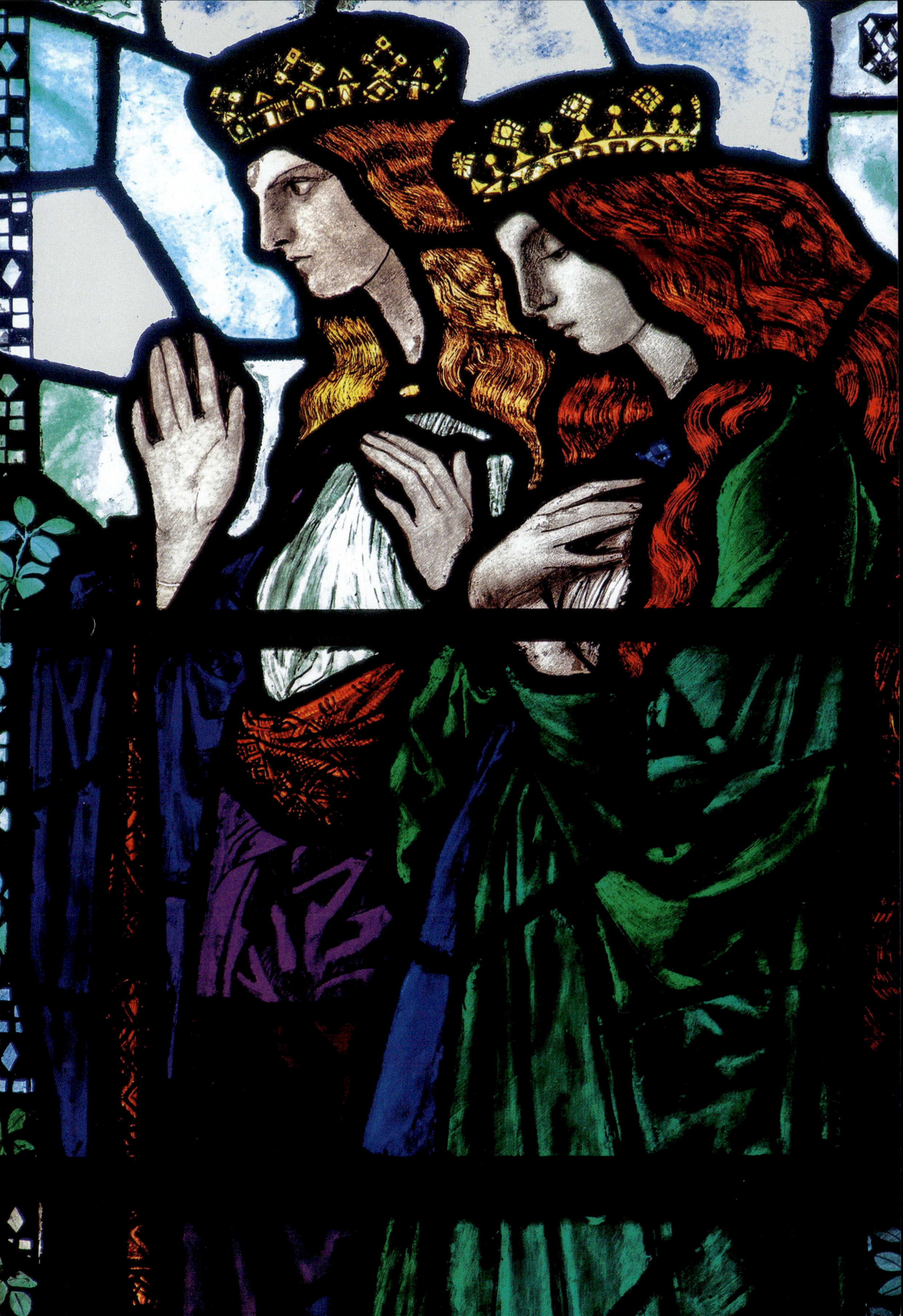

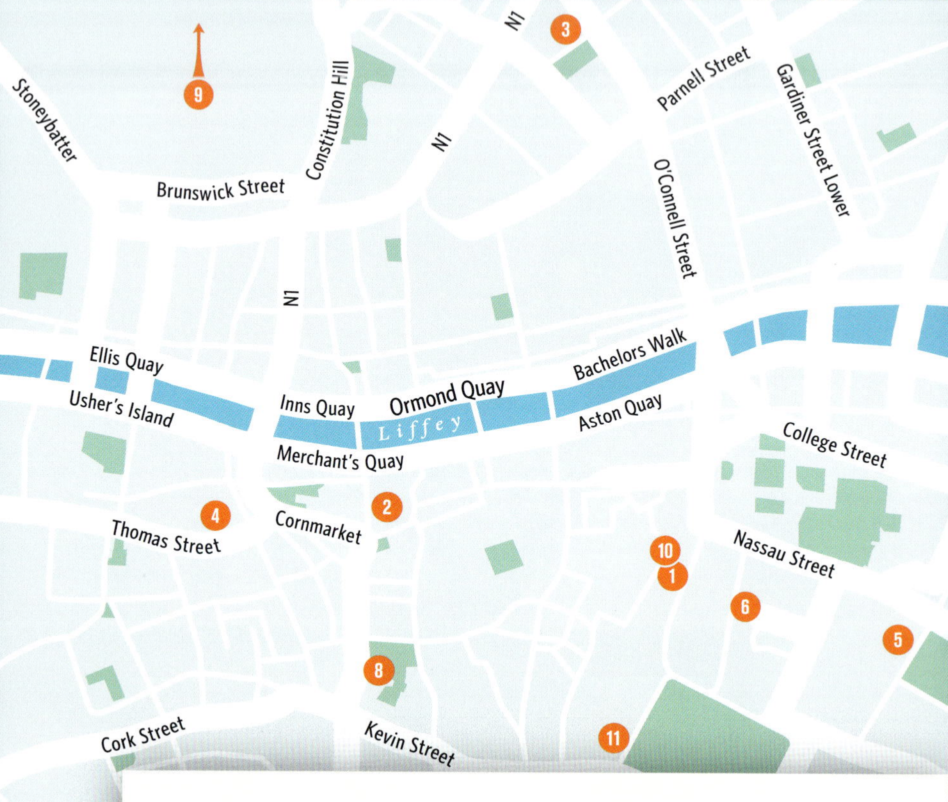

Dublin City

1. **Bewley's Oriental Café**
78–9 Grafton Street, D02 K033
2. **Christ Church cathedral (C of I) and Dublinia**
Christchurch Place, D08 TF98
3. **Hugh Lane Gallery**
Parnell Square North, D01 F2X9
4. **St Augustine and St John's church (John's Lane church) (RC)**
Thomas Street, D08 Y802
5. **National Gallery**
Merrion Square West, D02 K303
6. **St Ann's church (C of I)**
Dawson Street, D02 YV00
7. **St Catherine and St James's church (C of I)**
Donore Avenue, D08 R6YC
8. **St Patrick's cathedral (C of I)**
St Patrick's Close, D08 H6X3
9. **St Peter's church (RC)**
North Circular Road, Phibsborough, D07 FW29 (2 km NW of map coverage)
10. **St Teresa's church (RC)**
Clarendon Street, D02 XD26
11. **Unitarian church**
St Stephen's Green West, D02 YP23

Dublin City

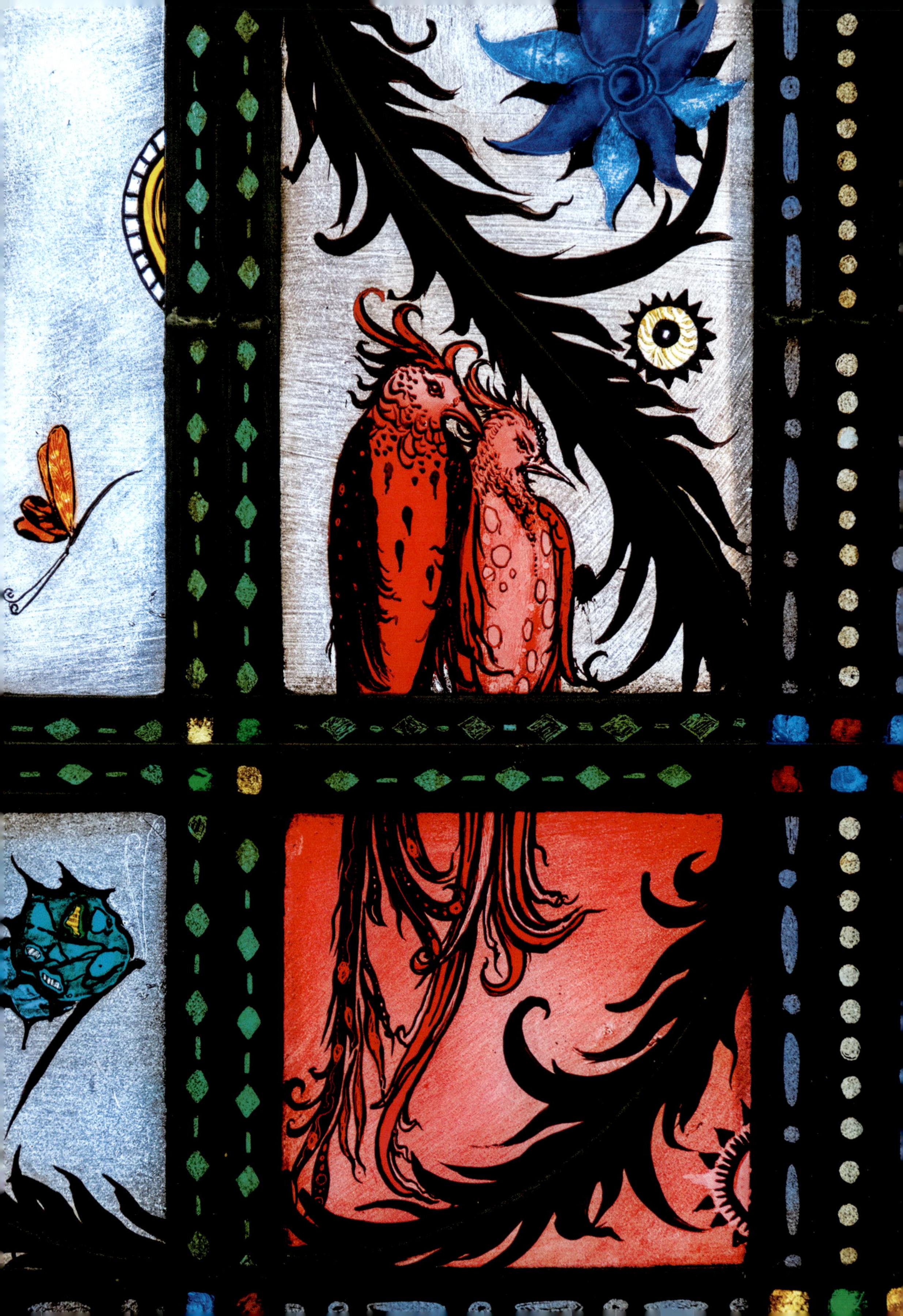

Bewley's Oriental Café

78–9 Grafton Street, D02 K033

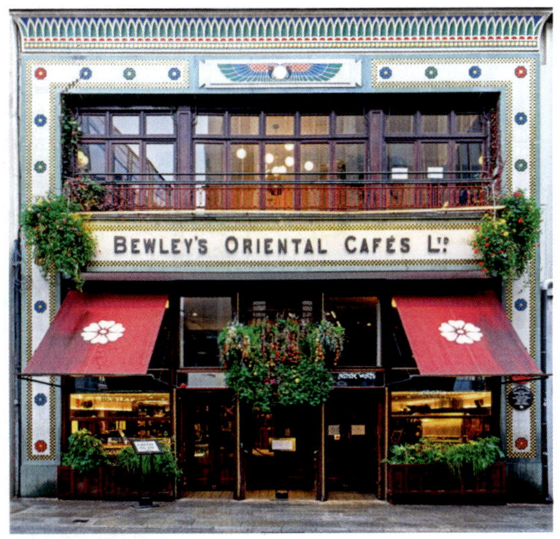

Bewley's cafés, a Dublin institution since the nineteenth century, had cafés in South Great George's Street and Westmoreland Street but when they opened a new café on Grafton Street in the mid-1920s it soon became their flagship. The Grafton Street café's distinctive façade, by Dublin architectural practice Millar and Symes, rises above the neighbouring properties, and is a rare example of the Egyptian Revival style in Ireland. The first-floor windows open onto a full-span mosaic and terrazzo balcony. The interior was much remodelled in recent decades and now few of the ground floor's original features remain, the principal exceptions being Harry Clarke's windows, the dark wooden panelling and fireplaces.

(opposite) Harry Clarke, detail of Doric Window from *The Orders of Architecture* (1928)

THE SIX RECTANGULAR windows designed by Harry Clarke for Bewley's comprised two sets of related windows positioned perpendicular to each other and located in the principal dining space on the ground floor of the café: four inspired by the Orders of Architecture (specifically the different types of capitals found at the top of classical columns), and two, facing out to Swan Yard,[1] which are essentially decorative with no specific themes. Bewley's engaged two different Dublin architectural firms during this period and both had dealings with Clarke – McDonnell and Dixon of Ely Place, and Millar and Symes of Kildare Street, and it would appear that it was the former who were principally involved in the commission of the six windows.

Harry Clarke's windows were ordered in spring 1927, begun later that year, and installed in spring 1928. There is limited surviving correspondence concerning the discussions that arose about the designs of the windows but as Bewley's, Clarke's studio, McDonnell and Dixon, and Millar and Symes were all located in the city centre it might be presumed that much of the discussion about the commission, both the artistic elements and the functional aspects, was done in person and was never formally documented. We don't know, for instance, who first mooted the idea of treating the Orders of Architecture as the theme. As Clarke was by now firmly established as an illustrator and stained glass artist par excellence it is likely he was given a lot of latitude and perhaps allowed to select the subject.

Among the early discussions held between Harry Clarke, Ernest Bewley and the architects there must have been conversations about the specific and unique functions that the windows must serve. The café space at the rear of the building is large (subsequently somewhat reduced in size) and it would have been clear that the windows must maximize potential natural light, a particular challenge because the four Orders of Architecture windows gave out to a small yard surrounded by buildings on all sides, and the pair of windows looking out to Swan Yard would also have had limited light due to adjacent buildings though had the benefit of a southerly aspect. Additionally there was the issue of ventilation; there were two fireplaces in the room, smoking had increased in popularity among women as well as men by the 1920s, and perhaps memories of the recent Spanish flu epidemic may have been a further consideration. Consequently the six windows would have to be the lightest in tone that Clarke had ever made and would require a bespoke structure to facilitate and control ventilation.

Despite the light and ventilation constrictions that would impact on his designs, doubtless Clarke would have been delighted to secure this commission, partly because his windows would be in a new Bewley's café on Dublin's premier shopping street but also because it was a secular commission. Unlike some other stained glass artists of the period there is nothing to suggest that Clarke himself was particularly religious, and tellingly all his personal work and illustration commissions were of non-religious subjects. However, not surprisingly, most of his stained glass windows were necessarily for churches as that was where the demand lay, and his only significant secular window to date had been his dark and mysterious 2-light *The Eve of St Agnes* (1924) which he had created for a private residence on Ailesbury Road, Dublin (see pp 31–6).

To facilitate the ventilation imperative, each of the six windows is composed of four hinged sashes whose dominant transoms visually divide the windows into four compartments, one on top of another; however Clarke's choice of an elegant

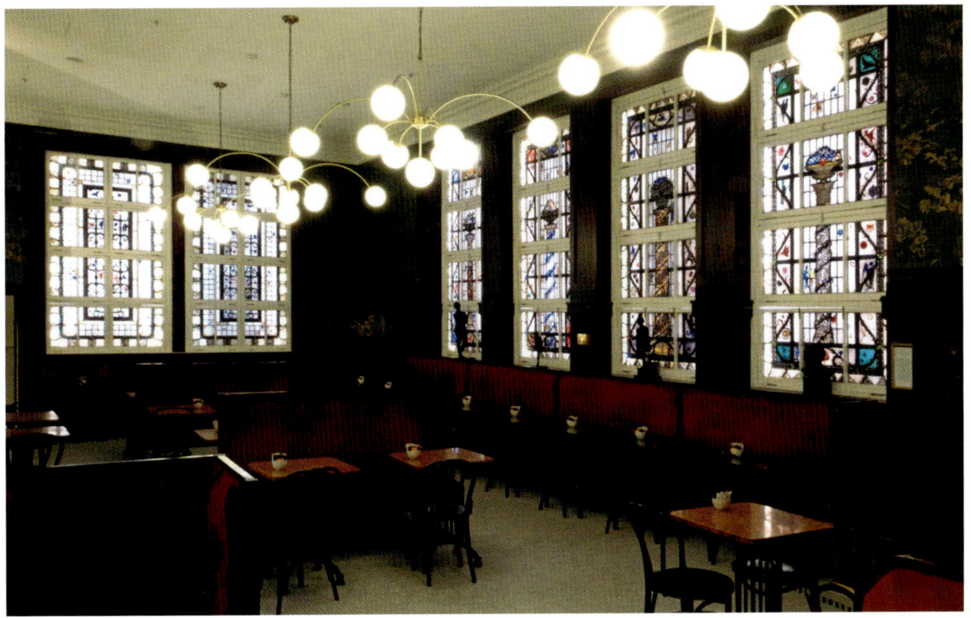

Harry Clarke, interior with *Decorative Windows* (left), *The Orders of Architecture* (right) (1928)

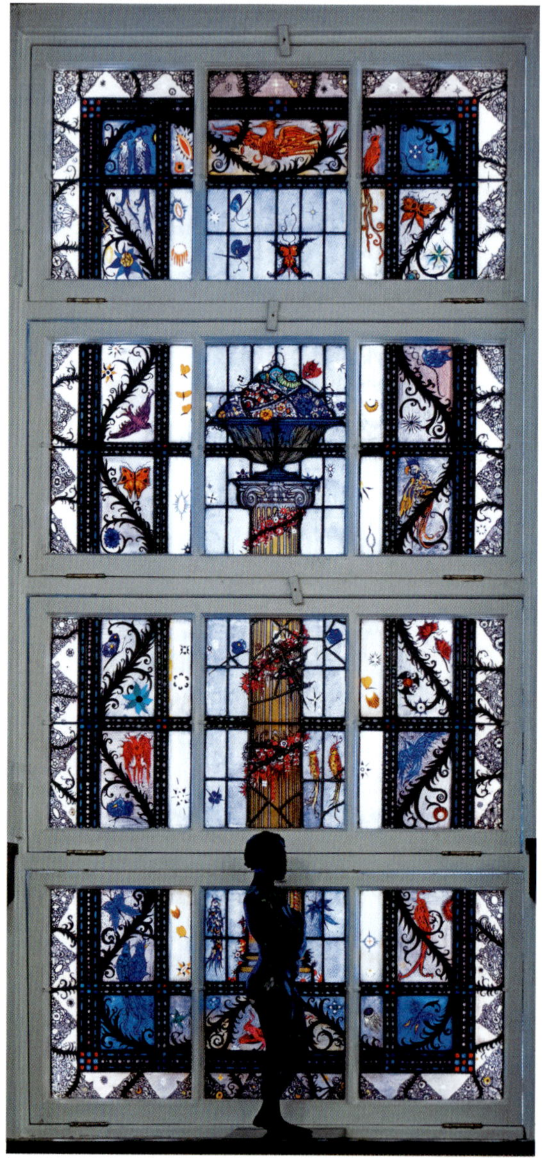

(left) Harry Clarke, Ionic Window from *The Orders of Architecture* (1928)

(opposite) Harry Clarke, detail of Ionic Window from *The Orders of Architecture* (1928)

classical column for each of the Orders of Architecture windows goes a considerable way to defy the horizontal intrusions. It is known that Clarke borrowed a book on architectural capitals, Corinthian columns and vases from W.A. Dixon (of McDonnell and Dixon) for inspiration and reference purposes.[2] Each of these windows features either a Corinthian, Doric, Ionic or Tuscan column with an associated different colour theme, all adorned with spiralling garlands of flowers, and crowned with a tazza overflowing with more blooms. Flying, perching and floating in the parchment-coloured background is a menagerie of creatures which inhabit a magical world, part aviary and part aquarium – exotic parakeets, cockatoos, butterflies, moths, jellyfish, sea anemones, sea urchins and less identifiable marine and extra-terrestrial creatures. Jet-black sinuous tendrils undulate around the perimeter of each window, acting as a frame to the columns, and skilfully disguising the leadlines, a visual device that Clarke had previously utilized in the two lunettes of his *The Eve of St Agnes*.

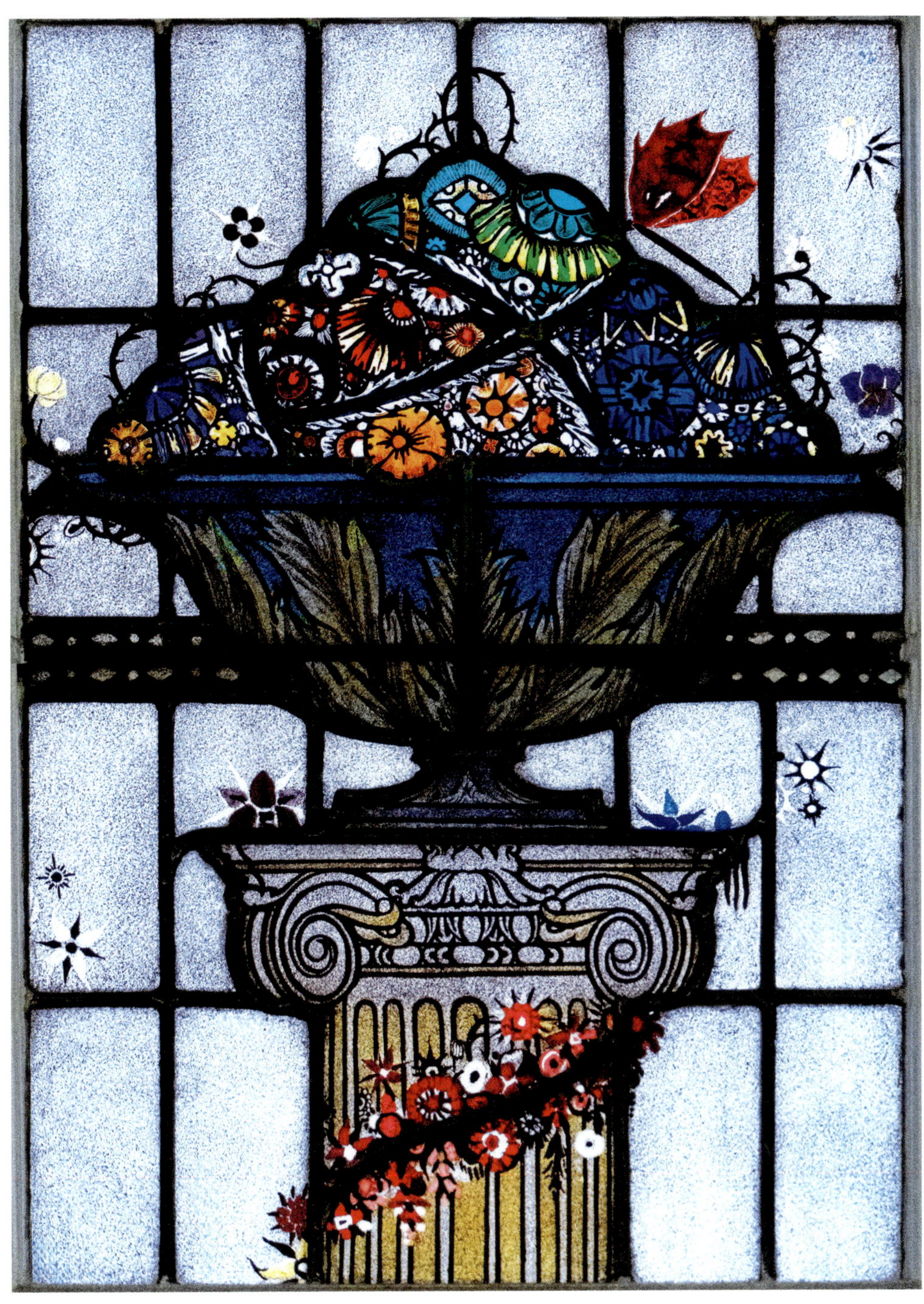

As to where Clarke sourced his imagery for Bewley's windows, a likely location he would have gone to observe, draw and be inspired was the Natural History Museum in Merrion Square, affectionally referred to by Dubliners as the 'Dead Zoo'. In addition to the predictable stuffed animals and birds, mounted butterflies and moths, the museum had (and still has, though not currently on display) a collection of over 500 eerie lifelike glass models, created by the Blaschka father-son team of Dresden, which includes sea creatures such as jellyfish and sea anemones.

Leading Harry Clarke expert, Nicola Gordon Bowe, who was the first to categorize the artist's stained glass oeuvre, a system that is still in place today, considered Clarke's six Bewley's windows to be in the 'A' category, that is in addition to having been designed by Harry Clarke, that Clarke was actively involved in part of the windows' execution, the rest being executed under his supervision in his studio.[3] She noted the considerable amount of time Clarke and his artists would have taken over the birds, insects and sea creatures, none of which is drawn to scale, and how deceptive it could appear, 'each piece of what looks like clear glass is, in fact, a piece of flashed antique ruby, blue, green, gold-pink or mauve, acided, painted and sometimes stained, so that only the bird (or whatever) depicted is left and an echo of the colour acided away. The windows are four decorative masterpieces; the leadlines and geometric design of the double row of tiny black beaded grids, set at each junction with turquoise, ruby and gold, strengthen the design of each window in an intricate and masterly resolution of what could have been exceedingly dull.'[4]

The two other windows, positioned at right angles to the quartet, are wider and comprise eight sashes each, and could be described as grisaille, as they are essentially decorative with no themes as such, but again they are populated by a selection of dainty butterflies, preening birds, sea anemones, etc. In general, although decorative, they have fewer elements and were designed to permit more daylight to enter through these south-facing windows. Gordon Bowe noted in respect of this pair of windows how Clarke made 'much use of silver stains of different intensities, of uncoloured glasses, of iron oxide painting medium and ingenious leading, which becomes a feature in itself. The only colours are tiny beads of amber, mauve, blue, green and gold-pink, set within the centre panel of painted feathery fronds, like flowers in a formal garden. Again, the linear design is surprisingly complex.'[5]

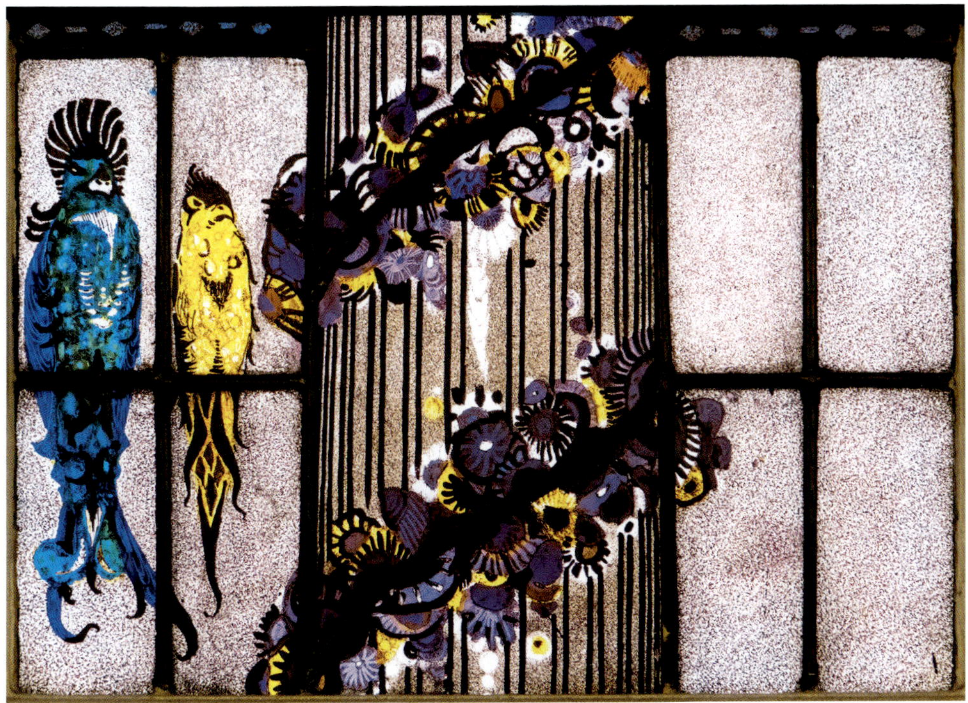

Harry Clarke, detail of Corinthian Window from *The Orders of Architecture* (1928)

Without Clarke's six windows the café's principal space could have appeared distinctly dull and uninviting, but his delightful and luminous stained glass windows transform the room, introducing a vital, sophisticated note while referencing the ambiance of classic European coffee houses. Worth noting is that although Bewley's full title, as proclaimed in brass letters on the exterior balcony, is 'Bewley's Oriental Cafés Ltd', Clarke deliberately chose to eschew any clichéd oriental references and instead created something that is refreshingly original and beguiling.

Both sets of windows have been moved and reinstalled over the years; the first time in 1940 or early 1941 for safe keeping during the Second World War when they were stored in Victor (son of Ernest) Bewley's home in Rathgar,[6] and are thought to have been the only stained glass windows in the Republic afforded this special treatment during the 'Emergency'. Artificial lighting was installed behind the windows, possibly after they were reinstated after the war and upgraded a few times; this decision meant that the windows could no longer open and close. In

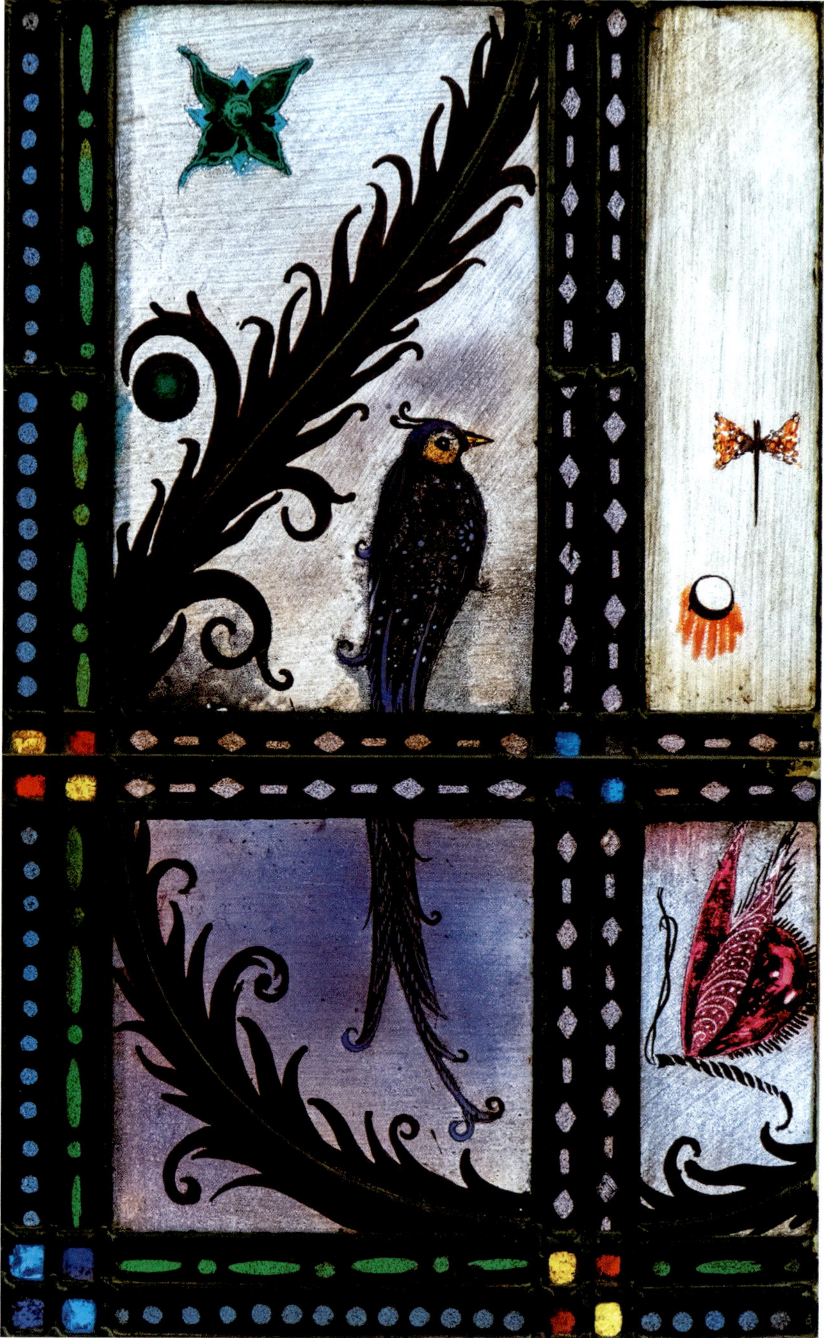

Harry Clarke, detail of Tuscan Window from *The Orders of Architecture* (1928)

1987 the south end of the room was reduced in size (to allow for the introduction of a stairwell with fire exit) and Clarke's two grisaille windows were taken out and reinstalled in a new, non-exterior, wall which necessarily altered the proportions of the room causing one fireplace to end up in the corner. The original bespoke brass hopper system that allowed the café's staff to open incrementally the top three sashes of each window for ventilation purposes by means of a lever was removed at some point; this is a shame as it is part of the fabric of Clarke's original windows and visually explains how they originally functioned, however the good news is that the brass hopper system has been stored in Bewley's and so can be reinstated.

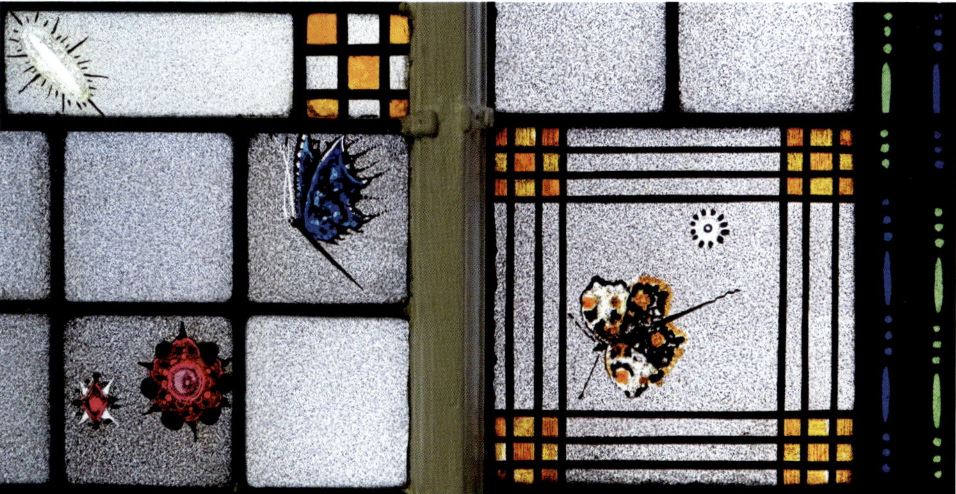

Harry Clarke, detail of right Decorative Window (1928)

The ground floor of Bewley's also features an elaborately detailed window inspired by Celtic art which was designed by Jim FitzPatrick (b.1944). It depicts *Cruitne, daughter of Lochan* and was made to FitzPatrick's designs in 1993 by Alan Tomlin of Irish Stained Glass. The window was originally created for the first-floor bay window of Bewley's café on Mary Street (since closed) and was subsequently modified to fit in its new ground-floor location in Bewley's, Grafton Street.

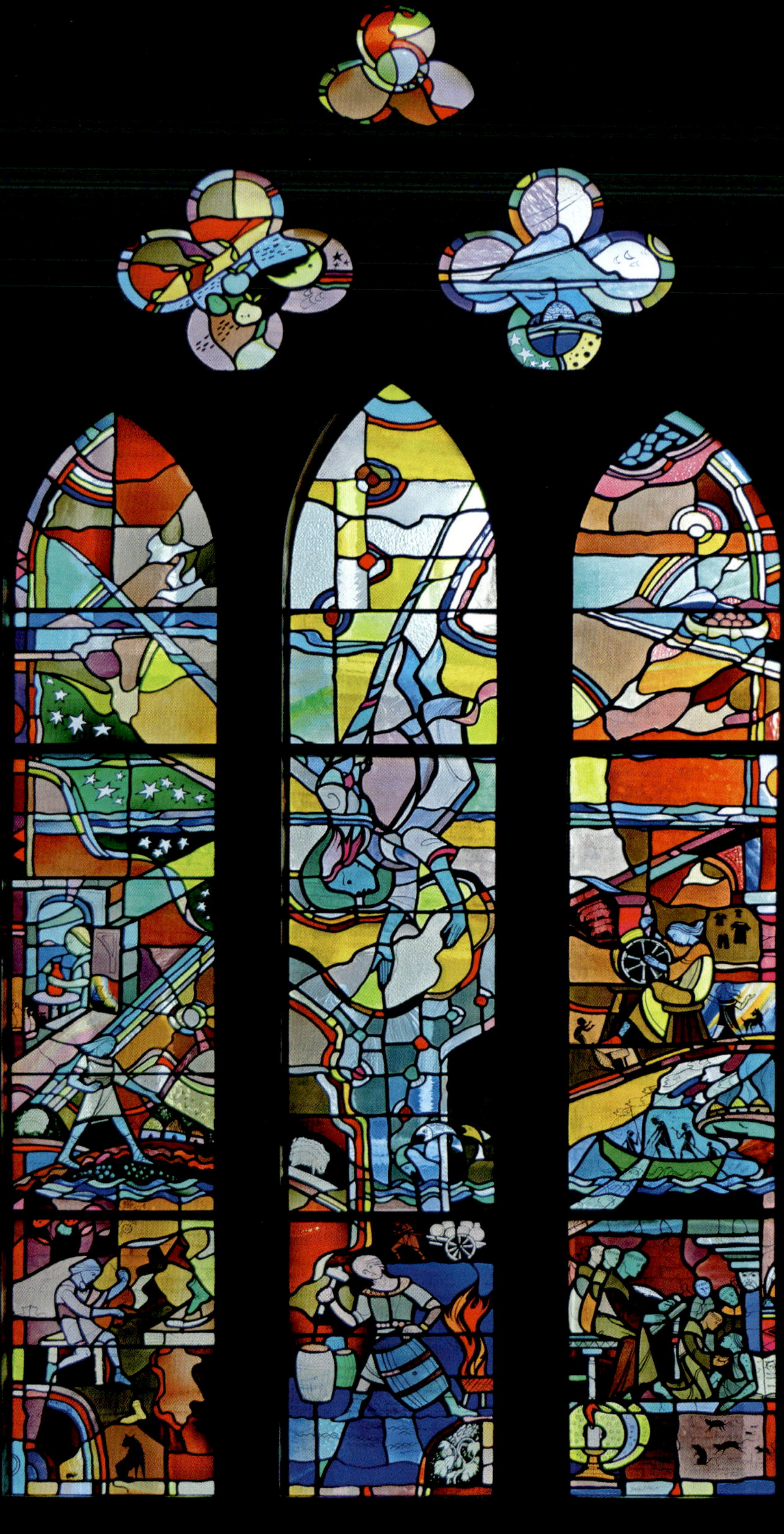

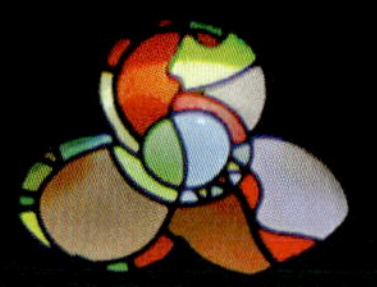

Christ Church cathedral (C of I) and Dublinia

Christchurch Place, D08 TF98

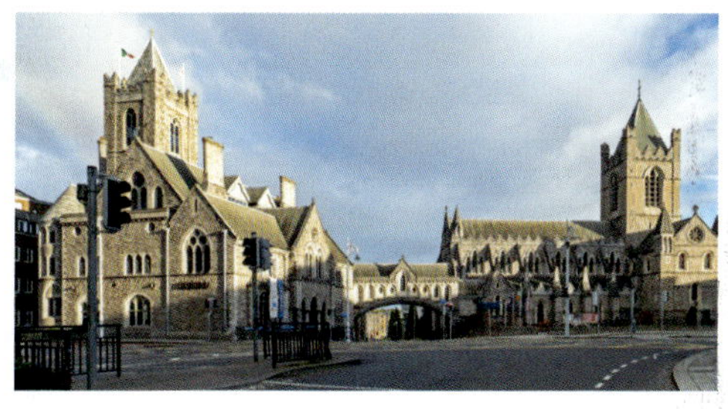

Considerably smaller than St Patrick's cathedral, Christ Church cathedral is the older of the city's two medieval cathedrals and is located in a more prominent and elevated location. Combined with the distinctive bridge over Winetavern Street, which links it to the former synod hall (now Dublinia), it is one of Dublin's most recognizable landmarks. The cathedral dates from *c.*1186–1200. By the early nineteenth century it had fallen into a sorry state but in 1871, Henry Roe, the Dublin whiskey distiller, offered to cover the cost of a complete restoration of the cathedral and the construction of the new synod hall, both under the direction of English architect, George Edmund Street. Street's 'restoration' was radical, demolishing much of the extant cathedral and removing vast quantities of medieval stone, and his interventions were not limited to the architecture; he also oversaw the interior fittings and furnishings, including the stained glass, resulting in the High Victorian expression that is visible today.

(opposite) George W. Walsh, *St Michael Surrounded by Craftsmen and Traders of the City* (1993), Dublinia

Unlike its sibling cathedral, the stained glass scheme is remarkably unified and this is due to G.E. Street's firm hand dictating the iconography and determining from whom the windows were commissioned; the majority were made by two of the pre-eminent English firms – Clayton & Bell of London, and Hardman & Co. of Birmingham, and all these windows date from *c.*1878.[1] Additionally the heraldic grisaille glass in the nave and clerestory was designed by Street himself and executed by Bell & Beckham of London.[2] As all of these windows were created in the 1870s they do not fall within the remit of this book but are well worth taking time to appreciate. In terms of twentieth-century stained glass, due to Street's comprehensive approach, there is almost none, however there is one window that is noteworthy not only for the artist who made it but also for the stained glass artist in whose memory it was erected.

When Catherine (Kitty) O'Brien died aged 82 in July 1963 she was the last surviving member of An Túr Gloine. Her stained glass career at the studio spanned a remarkable six decades, having joined in 1903 and taken over sole responsibility for the studio in 1944. She is buried in Whitechurch cemetery, County Dublin, alongside her three sisters. Miss O'Brien had a strong attachment to the cathedral having arranged the altar flowers for the major festivals since 1918 and, although of modest means, she left the cathedral a small bequest. Her only brother and last surviving sibling, Brigadier Brian Pallisee O'Brien, who lived in London, approached the cathedral for permission to have a window erected in memory of his sister and this was granted. The location provided was in the small Mothers' Union chapel in the south transept where there was an existing single-light window depicting *Saints Patrick, David, George and Andrew* which the cathedral board were content to have removed;[3] it seems likely that this location for Miss O'Brien's memorial, separate from the main body of the church, was chosen so that a modern window would not strike a discordant note with the Victorian interior.

The artist selected for the window was an obvious choice; London-born Patrick Pollen had been renting half of An Túr Gloine from O'Brien since the 1950s and in fact after her death he arranged to purchase the studio from her nephew, Timothy, who had inherited it. Pollen and O'Brien shared the same glazier, Peter Connolly, who had been with An Túr Gloine since 1916.

The subject chosen for O'Brien's memorial window was the *Virgin and Child, with St Luke*; the former with its maternal theme is obviously suitable for a chapel dedicated to the Mothers' Union,[4] and the latter was chosen because he is the patron saint of artists. Pollen treated the window in classic An Túr Gloine style, that is a full-length figure filling the window with a predella panel below. The Virgin is depicted holding the Christ Child in her hands as if presenting him to the world, both sets of their eyes looking directly at the viewer as they enter the small chapel. Below, St Luke is seated at his easel with drawing implement in hand, engrossed while working on a tonal drawing of the Virgin and Child; here Pollen is referencing the long-established tradition in art history of depicting St Luke drawing or painting the Virgin. Appropriately the drawing that St Luke is finishing is a small-scale version, in monochrome, of the Virgin and Child as they appear in the actual stained glass window. St Luke wears wire frame glasses, as did Miss O'Brien in her old age, and this feature is probably an affectionate nod to his

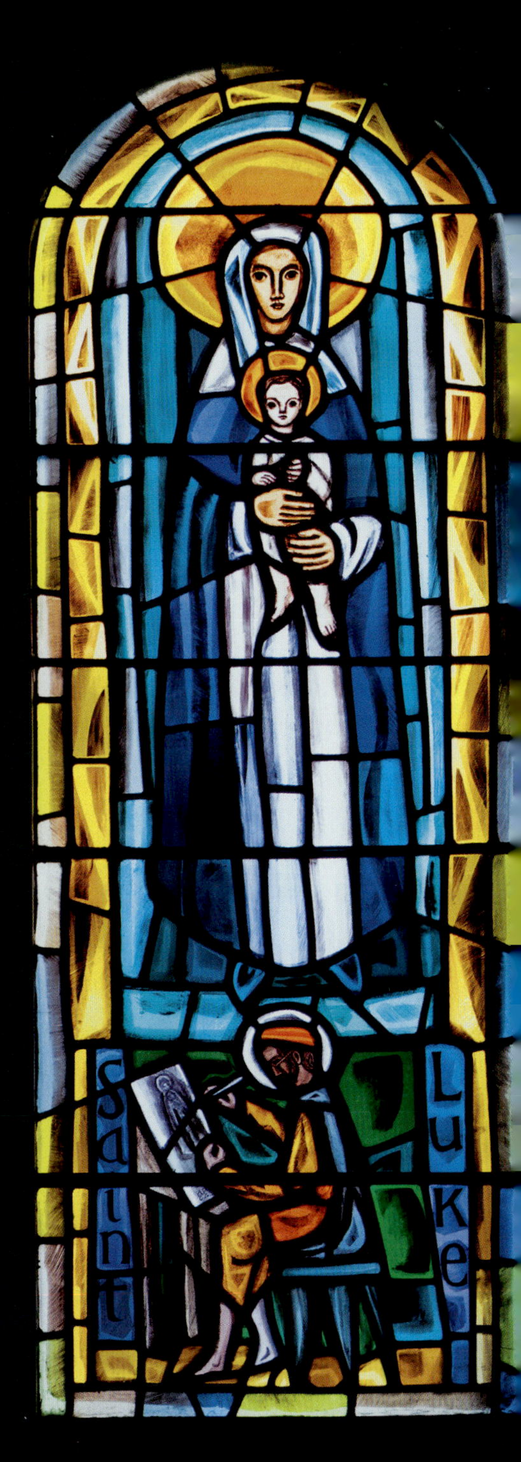

Patrick Pollen, *Virgin and Child, with St Luke* (1964), Christ Church cathedral

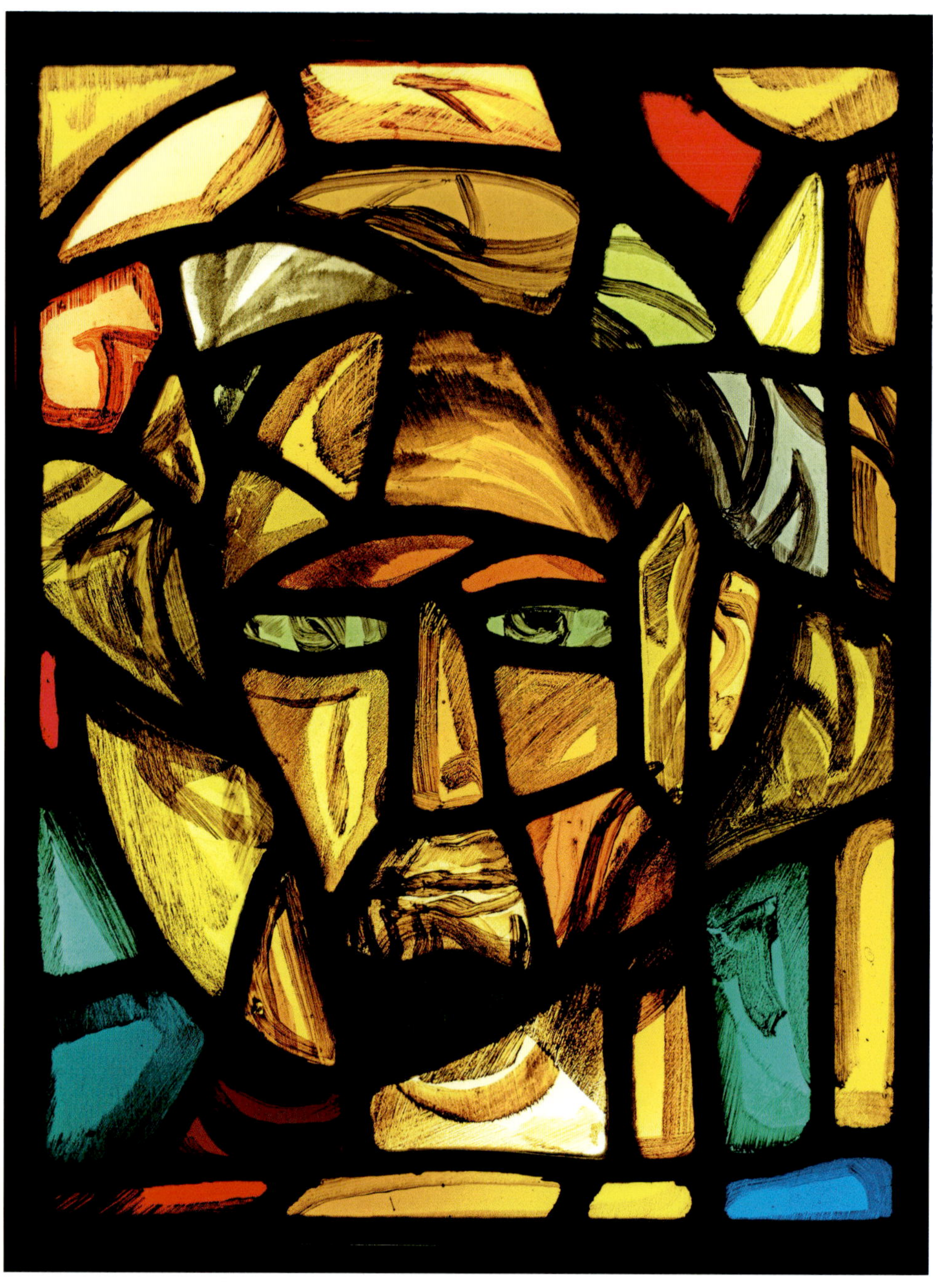

Elizabeth Rivers, *Head of Christ* (*c.*1959–60), Christ Church cathedral

late friend and colleague. Blues and golden yellows predominate and gentle washes of pale pigment soften the colours and add depth and texture. Pollen introduced a pattern around the perimeter of the window and while not of strict chevron design, it does seem to respond to the chevron pattern carved into the surrounding stone. The simple hand lettering of 'Saint Luke' looks like it could have been carved with a chisel. The resulting effect is that the whole window is harmonious both visually and in the choice and treatment of its subjects. If one looks very carefully at the drawing on the easel one can see that it is initialled and dated 'P.L.P. 64'.

On the opposite side of the nave in the north transept, in a side chapel beneath the old organ loft there is – in addition to the heart of St Laurence O'Toole – a small stained glass panel, artificially lit, titled *Head of Christ*, by Elizabeth Rivers (1903–64). It is one of a small number of panels known to have been made by the English-born artist who is best known as a skilled wood-engraver and painter who spent several years on Inis Mór, a recurring source of inspiration. Between 1946 and 1955 she assisted Evie Hone at her studio in Marlay, Rathfarnham, by scaling up her sketch designs for windows into cartoons, and although Hone inspired her artistically and religiously – she later converted to Catholicism as had Hone – there is no record of her making her own stained glass at Marlay though it remains a possibility. Rivers did however exhibit stained glass panels at the Irish Exhibition of Living Art in 1959 and in 1960,[5] and it seems probable that the *Head of Christ* panel dates from this period, and, if it was made then, it seems likely it was fired courtesy of Patrick Pollen at An Túr Gloine. A preliminary design survives for the *Head of Christ*.[6] Due to the small sizes of the individual pieces of glass it would appear that she used cullets. The stained glass panel, a dramatic contrast to her realistic and precisely executed wood-engravings, is expressionistic, painted with verve and energy, particularly evident in Christ's crown of thorns. Traditionally in depictions of Christ on the Cross his expression is often serene but here he appears to be alert and in anguish, experiencing the pain of being crucified. The panel was gifted to the cathedral by the noted conservationist, author and collector Harold Clarke.

The synod hall had ceased to be used for its intended purpose by *c.*1980 and in 1991 the Synod Hall Trust sold the building to the not-for-profit Medieval Trust who now operate Dublinia, a 'historical recreation' museum and visitor attraction

(opposite page) George W. Walsh, detail of *St Michael Surrounded by Craftsmen and Traders of the City* (1993), Dublinia

focusing on the city's Viking and medieval history. A key feature of the new museum is the pair of stained glass windows, commissioned from George W. Walsh in 1993, and which were installed in original 3-light windows, one east-facing and one south-facing, located in different parts of the building. The themes of the windows are derived from Dublin's early history; Walsh was a perfect choice for the commission, not only for his acknowledged artistry and craftsmanship but also for his track record of incorporating local references in his windows, whether for secular or religious locations.

The theme of the taller of the two windows, dramatically located at the top of a stairs, is *St Michael Surrounded by Craftsmen and Traders of the City*. Walsh has depicted the central figure of the archangel swooping downwards from heaven; St Michael has particular relevance as the synod hall and cathedral are located on St Michael's Hill and, additionally, at the core of Dublinia are remnants of the original seventeenth-century St Michael's Tower. The window exudes energy and vitality as various craftsmen and traders of the city are depicted at work. In the middle of the left light there is a potter, a reference to the many items and pieces of pottery that were uncovered during adjacent archaeological digs, and a farmer sowing alluding to the many small farms that existed within the city in medieval times. In the middle of the right light, a woman is depicted spinning for the purpose of making clothing, and below fishermen haul their laden nets from the Liffey. There are three predella panels: on the left a man is busy making footwear from leather hides, and at his feet a cat turns its gaze on a nervous rodent, no doubt a reference to the famous mummified cat chasing a rat that is on display in the cathedral's crypt; in the centre predella panel a cooper is hard at work crafting a barrel, perhaps a nod to Henry Roe's benevolence derived from his whiskey business; on the right, acknowledging the grimmer aspects of medieval life, monks are shown attending to those afflicted by the Black Death, the plague, which was transmitted by rats' fleas.

Located in what is now the café is Walsh's other window. It is titled *The Civic Window*, and it reveals aspects of the city's history and key events that shaped present-day Dublin. While the other window is bustling with energy and activity,

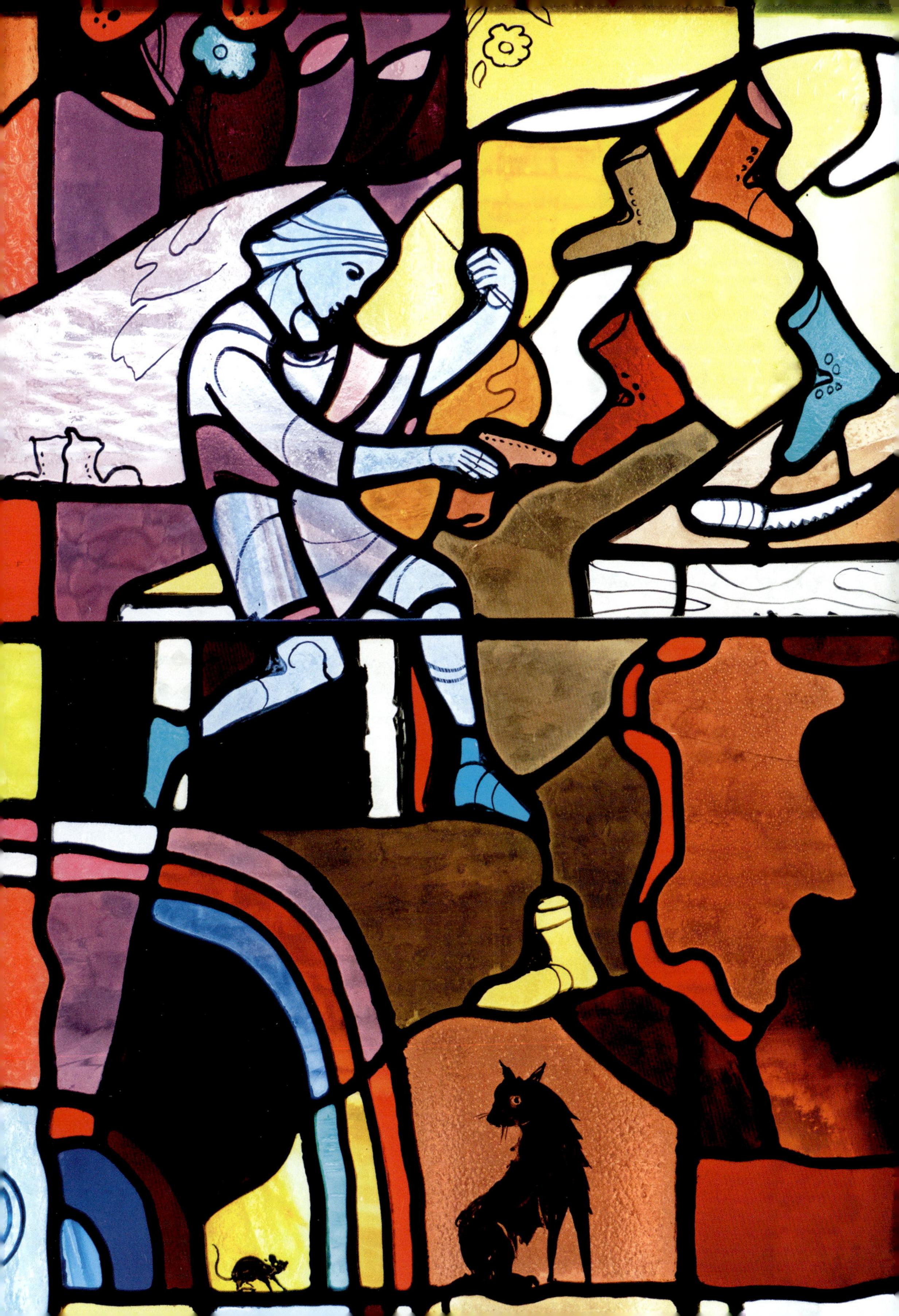

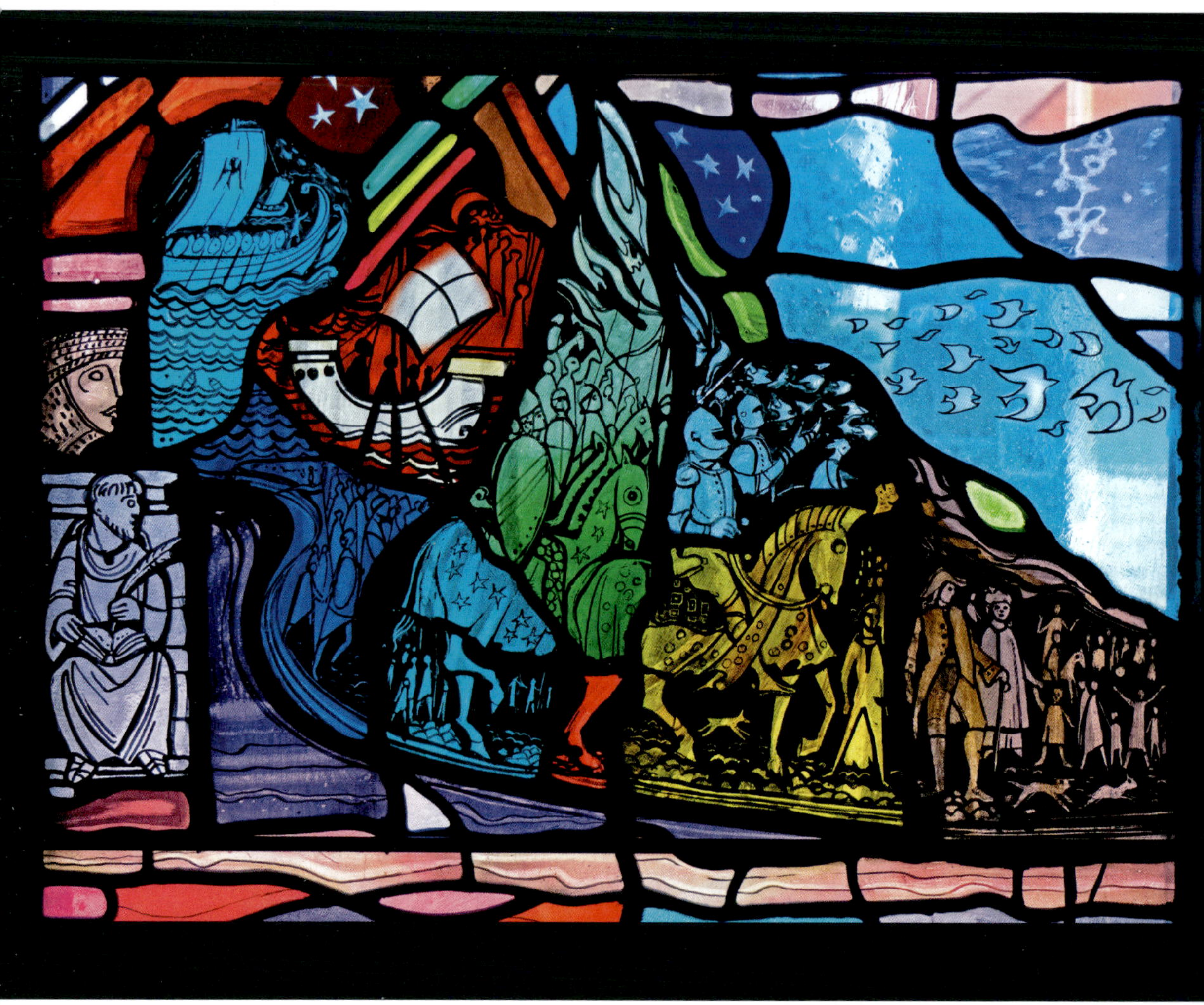

George W. Walsh, detail of *The Civic Window* (1993), Dublinia

this window has a greater sense of symmetry and gravitas. Walsh wanted to focus on the medieval administration of the city and chose rich reds and blues evocative of stained glass in the great European cathedrals.

Roundels alluding to historic events feature in each of the three lights. The central roundel, appropriately, contains the shield of Dublin depicting the three burning castles flanked by two female figures, one with a scale represents Justice (without the usual blindfold), and the other carrying a sword represents Law, while each figure also holds aloft an olive branch. Circling the roundel is the city's motto, *Obedientia Civium Urbis Felicitas*, which translates as 'The obedience of the citizens produces a happy city'. Seated below is a medieval lord mayor, and below, an original seal from the period. The left-hand roundel features a crest with three rampant lions surrounded by the text *Dubline sigielum prepositure* which translates as 'In Dublin, the seal is preserved.' The roundel in the right light depicts the Charter of Henry II of 1171–2 permitting the men of Bristol the right to live in the city of Dublin. Later charters contained grants to the city of rights, privileges and property, and taken together they form the basis of municipal law in Ireland.[7]

Traversing the three lights is the perfect arc of a rainbow containing the signs of the zodiac, included to suggest the movement of time both within a year and over the centuries. In the lower section of the window, emerging from the far left and far right, is a theatrical-style pageant of different costumed men and women through the ages – Normans, the English settlers, those who came on the armadas, etc. – each group blending into the next, conveying the continuum of constant arrivals of different peoples over the centuries. Running along the entire base is the fast-moving River Liffey, the life blood of the city and the perennial focal point of settlement. Walsh always delights in including imaginative detail, so in addition to fishermen, leaping fish, and seashells, there is – improbably – a mermaid!

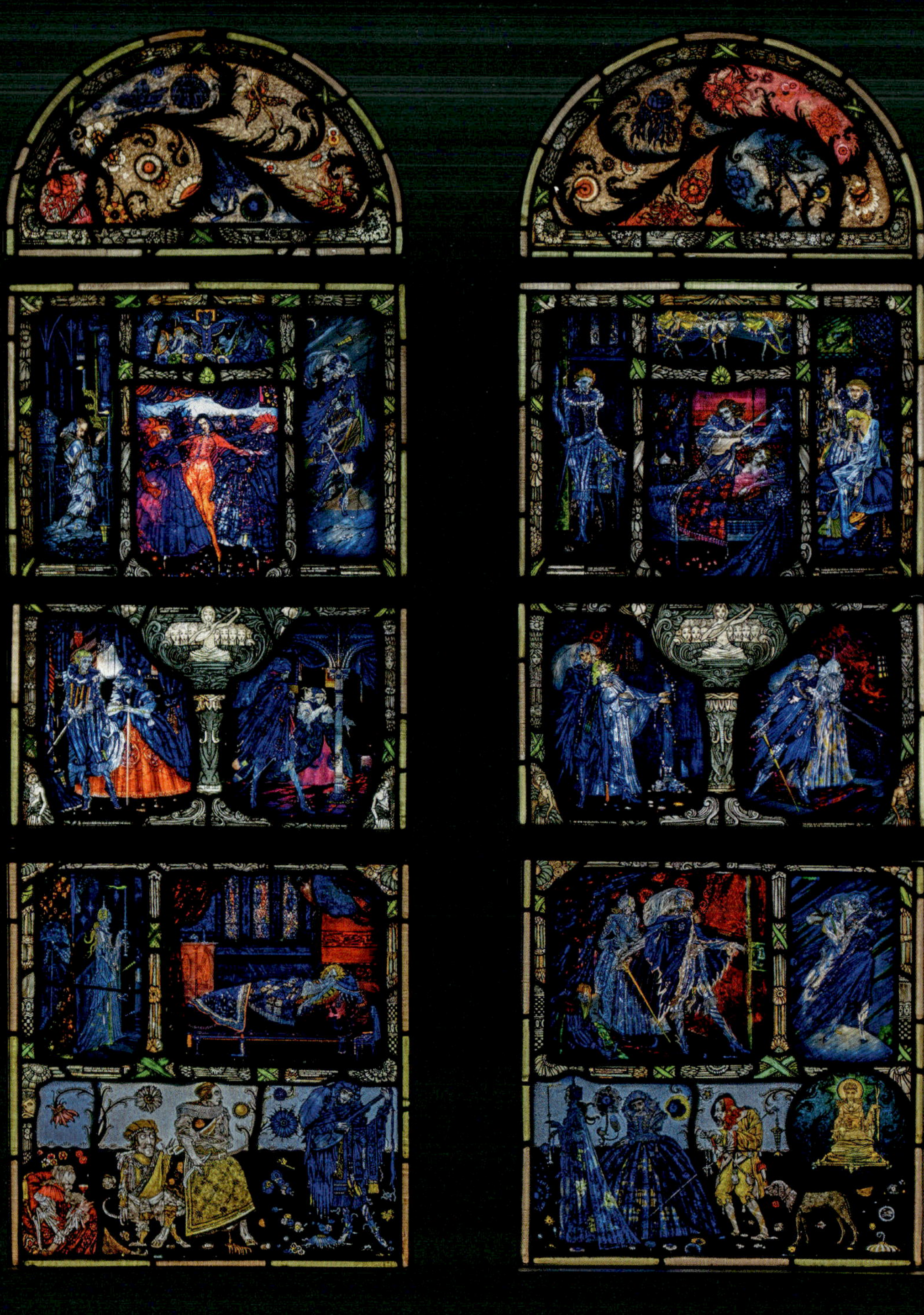

Hugh Lane Gallery

Parnell Square North, D01 F2X9

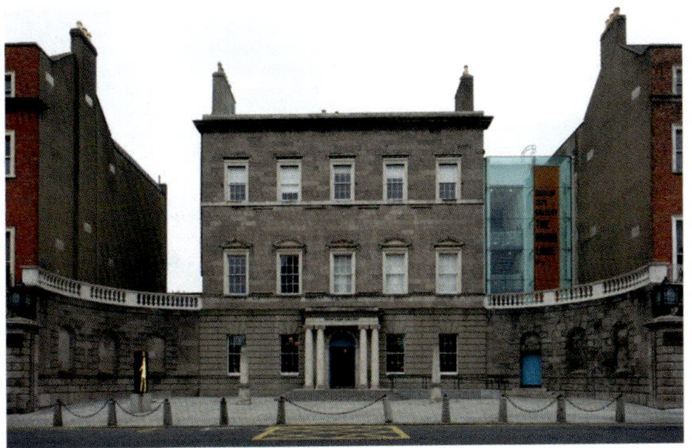

The Hugh Lane Municipal Gallery of Modern Art is housed in Charlemont House, a neoclassical palazzo designed by William Chambers and dating from 1763. In 1928 Sarah Purser – who played such a key role in the revitalization of the Irish stained glass scene – recommended to W.T. Cosgrave's government that Charlemont House, then housing a government department, should become home to the Municipal Gallery's collection; this was agreed and it was remodelled for this purpose in 1931–3 by the city architect, Horace O'Rourke.

(opposite) Harry Clarke, *The Eve of St Agnes* (1924). Collection and image © Hugh Lane Gallery

THE EARLIEST PANEL in the gallery's stained glass room is by Wilhelmina Geddes and was made in 1911. Geddes's initial conception for her *Scenes from the Life of St Colman MacDuagh of Galway* is that it would comprise three individual roundels but soon switched to a design of three separate but related rectangular panels.[1] Her *Scenes from the Life of St Colman MacDuagh of Galway*[2] is particularly significant as it is the artist's first independent work in stained glass and was made soon after she came to An Túr Gloine at Sarah Purser's invitation; furthermore it was commissioned by Miss Purser as a personal gift to her friend the playwright and philanthropist Edward Martyn who had mooted the idea of an Irish stained glass revival to her at the turn of the century. Martyn, a devout individual, was of an ancient Galway family who lived in Tulira Castle, near Ardrahan in the diocese of Galway, Kilmacduagh and Kinfenora and hence the choice of theme. Not unlike St Colman MacDuagh, Martyn lived a relatively ascetic existence choosing to sleep in the original fifteenth-century tower rather than the comfortable adjoining Victorian mansion, and Purser must have envisaged Geddes's three rectangular panels would be installed in one of the castle's small 3-light windows, perhaps in Martyn's study replacing an English artist's pretty but banal panels (1882) of historic literary figures; however Miss Purser liked Wilhelmina Geddes's outcome so much that she never parted with the panels.

Geddes chose to depict St Colman in three guises; in the centre panel as bishop carrying his crozier (now in the National Museum) and blessing the assembled faithful, his long white habit and sandaled feet illuminated by a single candle set on a carved Romanesque altar, and in the background an early stone cross. In the left panel, Geddes depicted St Colman as a hermit, barefoot with unkempt beard, his russet-coloured habit clinging to his body as he braves the elements, and oblivious to everything and absorbed in the holy book he carries. At his side, a fawn accompanies him, reflecting his love of animals. The right panel depicts an aged version of the saint when he had moved to the Burren seeking greater solitude. At his behest two men carry great limestone slabs, assisting in the construction of a beehive-style oratory.

The three panels are a remarkable achievement for an artist just starting out in the craft and demonstrate her ready confidence in painting on glass, her appreciation of how the leadlines can be used to maximum effect, and her affinity for depicting

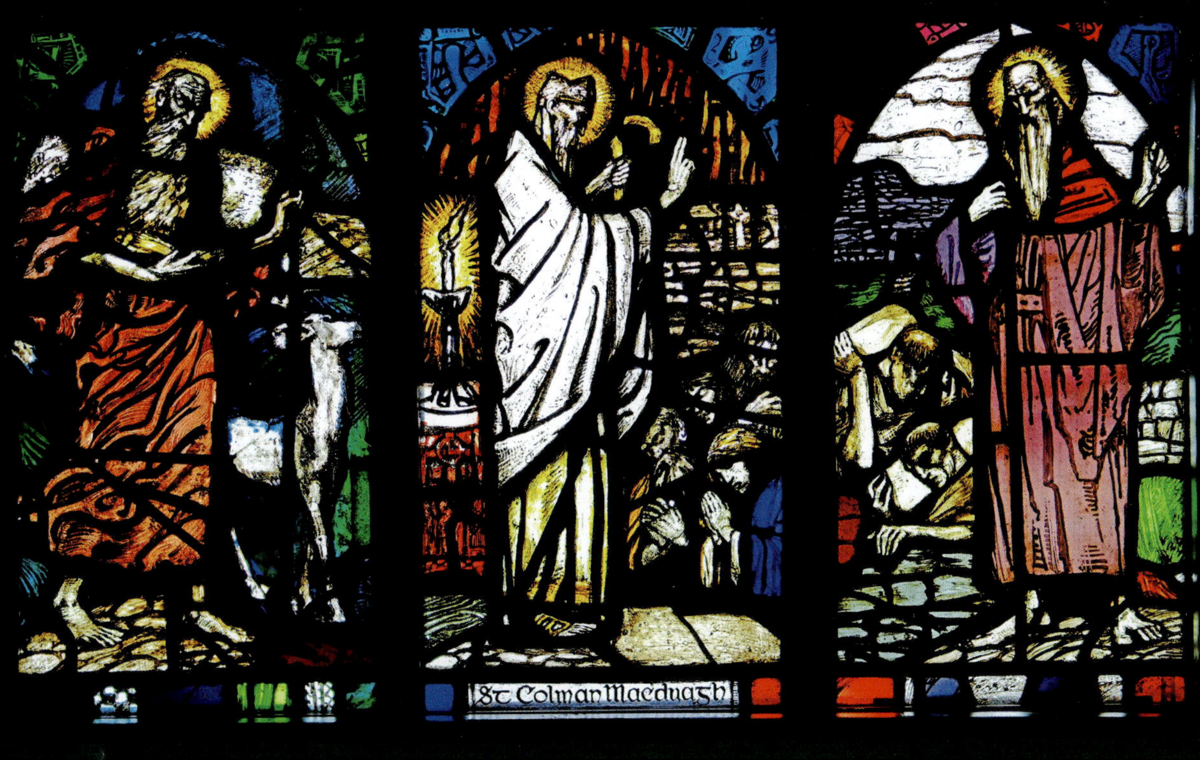

Wilhelmina Geddes, *Scenes from the Life of St Colman MacDuagh of Galway* (1911). © The Brothers Kerr. Collection and image © Hugh Lane Gallery

rugged men who are both heroic and believable. Small cullets of glass have been used to integrate little bursts of colour among the muted palette, and despite the references to Ireland's early Christian period there are modern touches too such as the abstract designs at the top of each panel.

In April 1923 Harold Jacob, scion of the famous biscuit manufacturing family, commissioned Harry Clarke to design and make a window for his parents' home, St Michaels, Ailesbury Road, Ballsbridge. The 2-light window on the main staircase landing of the substantial Victorian house was selected as a suitable location. Harold Jacob was the artistically inclined only son of George Jacob, chairman of Jacob's, and in due course Harold would assume this role. He most likely had seen some of Clarke's small cabinet panels of recent years such as *The Song of the Mad Prince* (1917) or *The Enchantment of Bottom by Titania* (1922) (see pp 56–7). Harold Jacob suggested some generic themes such as 'night and morning' or 'summer and winter', but Harry Clarke was more interested in illustrating a subject with a narrative dimension such

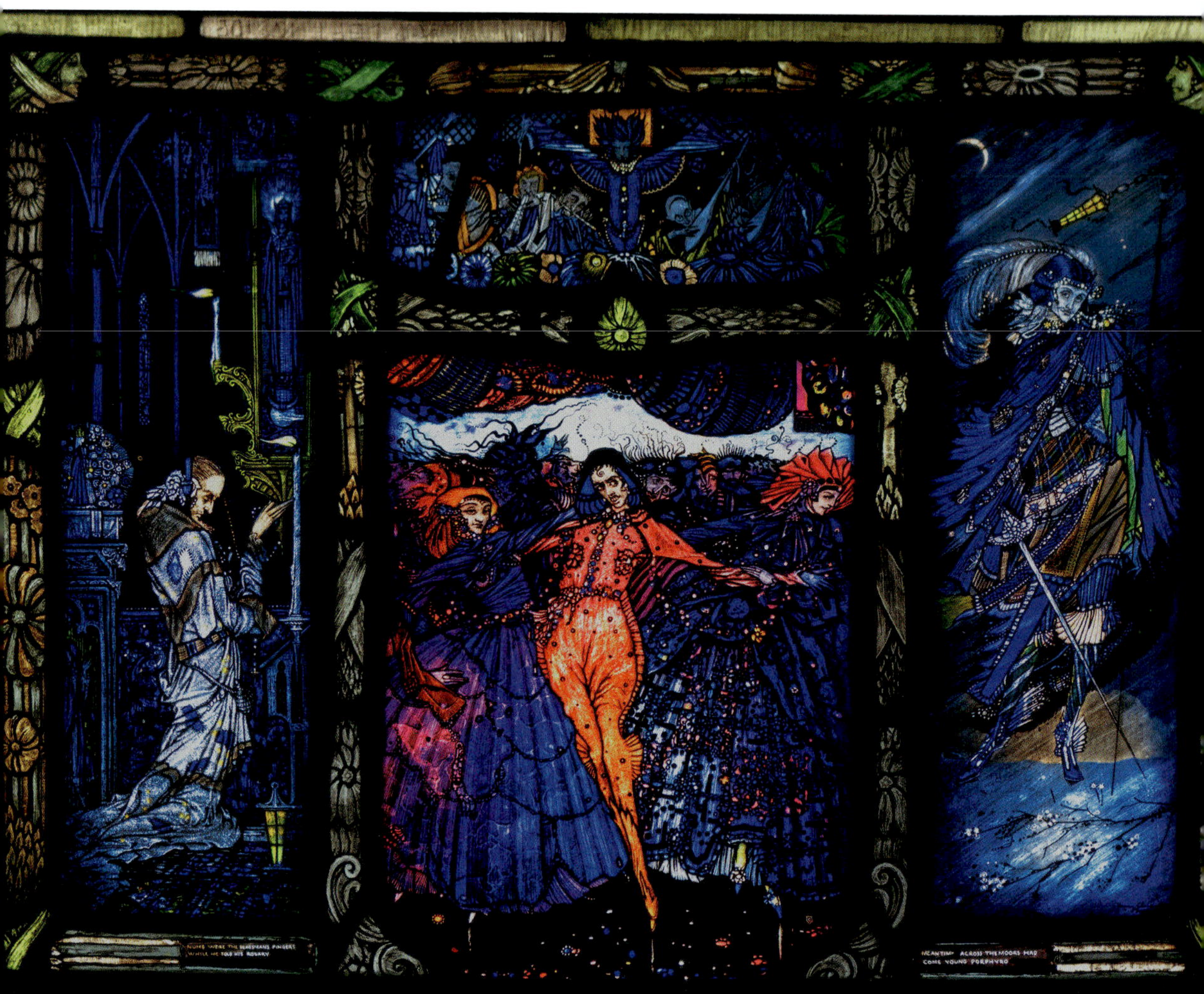

Harry Clarke, detail of the costume ball from *The Eve of St Agnes* (1924). Collection and image © Hugh Lane Gallery

as the story of Blackbeard the pirate, or themes derived from literature: the fairy tale of *Sleeping Beauty*, John M. Synge's play *The Playboy of the Western World* or John Keats's poem, *The Eve of St Agnes*, and it was Keats's poem that was agreed upon.[3] Set in the Middle Ages, Keats penned the poem in 1819 in the Gothic style and it runs to forty-two stanzas from which Clarke selected fourteen short extracts which feature in the window in minute script.[4]

St Agnes is the patron saint of virgins and died a martyr, and the poem's title refers to the evening before her feast day, 20 February, when, according to legend, if a girl performed certain religious rites her husband-to-be would appear in her dream. Despite the ostensible religious context, it is not a religious story as such – and it is worth noting neither Clarke nor George Jacob were particularly religious – and deals instead with youthful passion and forbidden love. The narrative revolves around the beautiful Madeleine, her dashing suitor Porphyro, her controlling father Lord Maurice, and Madeleine's faithful maid Old Angela.

Clarke structured the window as follows; decorative lunettes at the top of both lights, three tiers of panels comprising fourteen individual scenes along with some ancillary illustrations, and a frieze running along the bottom of both lights which functions as a *dramatis personae*; the characters depicted in the frieze are (left to right), a drunken wassailer or reveller, the dwarf Hilderbrand, Lord Maurice, Porphyro, Madeleine, Old Angela, and the beadsman with his hound. On the right is a roundel containing a golden image of the eponymous St Agnes, surprisingly seated crossed legged on a tasselled cushion, and with her lamb on her lap. The frieze also contains a self-portrait of Clarke in the border on the left as if he is sneaking a peek at the assembled cast.

The poem is set entirely at night-time and consequently it is a distinctly dark window that one needs to visually tune into; in fact it is so dark that at some point, perhaps to avoid a potential accident, the two lunettes at the top were temporarily removed to allow more light to illuminate the staircase of the Jacobs' home. The lunettes are interesting as they feature black unfurling fronds used to conceal the leadlines that would become a prominent element in Clarke's decorative windows for Bewley's café created a few years later. And similar to his Bewley's windows, small creatures float and fly about the fronds; those from the sea such as jellyfish and sea anemones, and those from the air like dragonflies and butterflies (see pp 9–17).

The first narrative panel, top left, locates the tale in a draughty castle as the beadsman – an impoverished person whose duty was to pray for his benefactor – is on his knees in the oratory saying the rosary ('Numb were the Beadsman's fingers'). The next scene, in dramatic contrast, depicts a fabulous costume ball in full sway ('With plume, tiara and all rich array...') with frenetic musicians playing in the

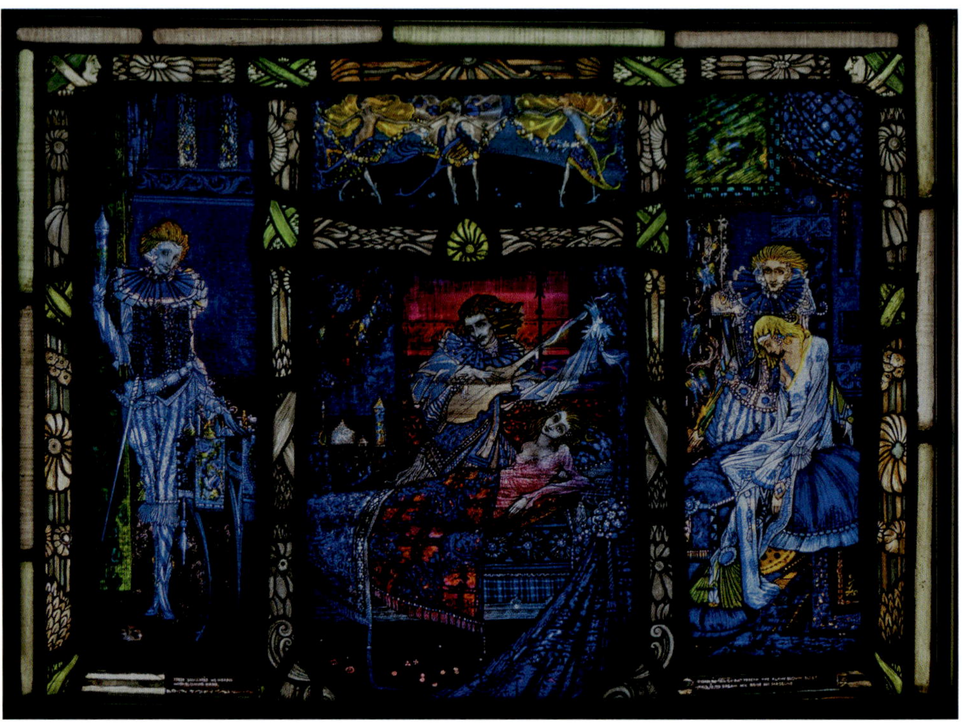

(above) Harry Clarke, detail of Porphyro serenading Madeleine from *The Eve of St Agnes* (1924). Collection and image © Hugh Lane Gallery

overhead minstrel gallery. Then we are introduced to the hero emerging from a gale ('Meantime, across the moors, had come young Porphyro …'). The second tier down features Old Angela as she encounters Porphyro who has snuck into the castle. This is followed by a panel depicting her guiding Porphyro to follow her before Lord Maurice kills him. The bottom tier introduces ethereal Madeleine, wearing a silvery nightgown and holding an unbelievably long candle as she glides towards her bedroom ('With silver taper's light, and pious care …'). The final panel in the left light has Madeleine asleep in her bedchamber, softly illuminated by moonlight filtered through a stained glass window, and beside her bed, a prayer book.

The second light starts at the point when Porphyro encounters Madeleine; he steps out of the small room he has been sequestered in to get a glance of his beloved, carrying with him a gift of fruit and spices whose aromas fill the room. He then enters her bedchamber, takes her lute and serenades her with *La Belle Dame*

Sans Merci hoping to wake her gently. Meanwhile Madeleine, dreaming of her suitor, begins to waken. In the next panel Porphyro reassures her ('This is no dream, my bride, my Madeleine …'). In the eleventh panel he encourages Madeleine to flee with him from the castle ('Awake! Arise! My love and fearless be, for o'er the moors I have a home for thee …'). With the storm still raging outside, and all asleep within the castle, they hasten down the staircase. In the penultimate panel the couple arrive at the castle's great door to find the guardsman in a drunken stupor ('The key turns, and the door upon its hinges groans …'). Their escape is a success and in the final panel they pause to embrace before continuing across the moors ('… ages long ago these lovers fled away into the storm').

What is perhaps surprising is that although Hildebrand and Lord Maurice feature in Keats's poem (the former referred to only fleetingly), and are depicted in Clarke's *dramatis personae* frieze, they do not appear in any of the fourteen narrative scenes.

Throughout the 2-light window Clarke chose to employ extensive aciding, the technique using wax resist and hydrofluoric acid that he had become so expert in exploiting; most of the narrative scenes and parade of characters were created on acid-etched, flashed blue glass, and in several instances he carefully registered, or 'plated' together, a second layer of glass, this time of acid-etched, flashed gold-pink or ruby glass, and this allowed him to achieve a mesmerizing range of blues, purples, violets, reds and pinks, which recall his earlier cabinet panels referred to above. Additionally, Clarke applied silver stain to introduce yellow highlights and to colour the costumes of some of the characters portrayed in the frieze, but the overwhelming impression of this window is a symphony of blues.

The Eve of St Agnes is Harry Clarke's finest multi-panel window, and artistically superior to his controversial *Geneva Window* (1930) of similar scale; it excels in technical virtuosity, exquisite draughtsmanship, imaginative characterization of the costumed characters, and visual storytelling that captures mood, atmosphere and dramatic tension. It cost the client £160 *7s. 6d.* and before the window was installed in his home it was exhibited that August at the Aonach Tailteann art exhibition where it caused a sensation and won the gold medal for arts and crafts and art industries. The following year, 1925, the Crawford Art Gallery, Cork acquired Clarke's nineteen preliminary pencil, watercolour and gouache drawings for the window. In 1977,

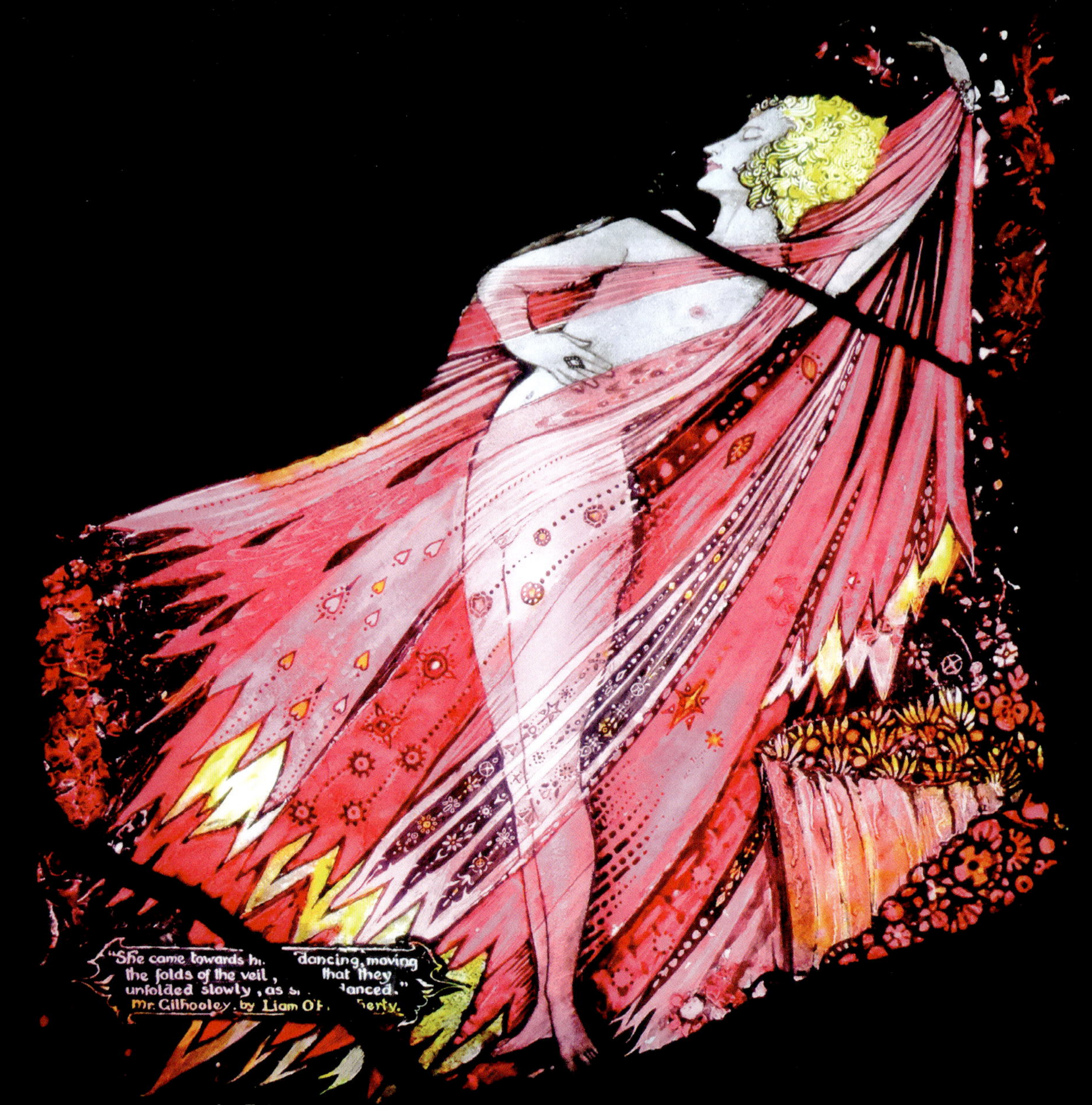

(above) Harry Clarke, *Mr Gilhooley by Liam O'Flaherty* (1929). Collection and image © Hugh Lane Gallery.
(opposite page) Evie Hone, *The Entombment* (*c.*1953). Collection and image © Hugh Lane Gallery

Nicola Gordon Bowe, the leading Clarke expert, discovered that the window was in the possession of Alison King, widow of stained glass artist Richard King, and proposed to the Hugh Lane Gallery that it be purchased, which it was, in 1978.[5]

The stained glass room also contains a small panel of painted, stained and etched gold-pink flashed glass by Harry Clarke, *Mr Gilhooley by Liam O'Flaherty*

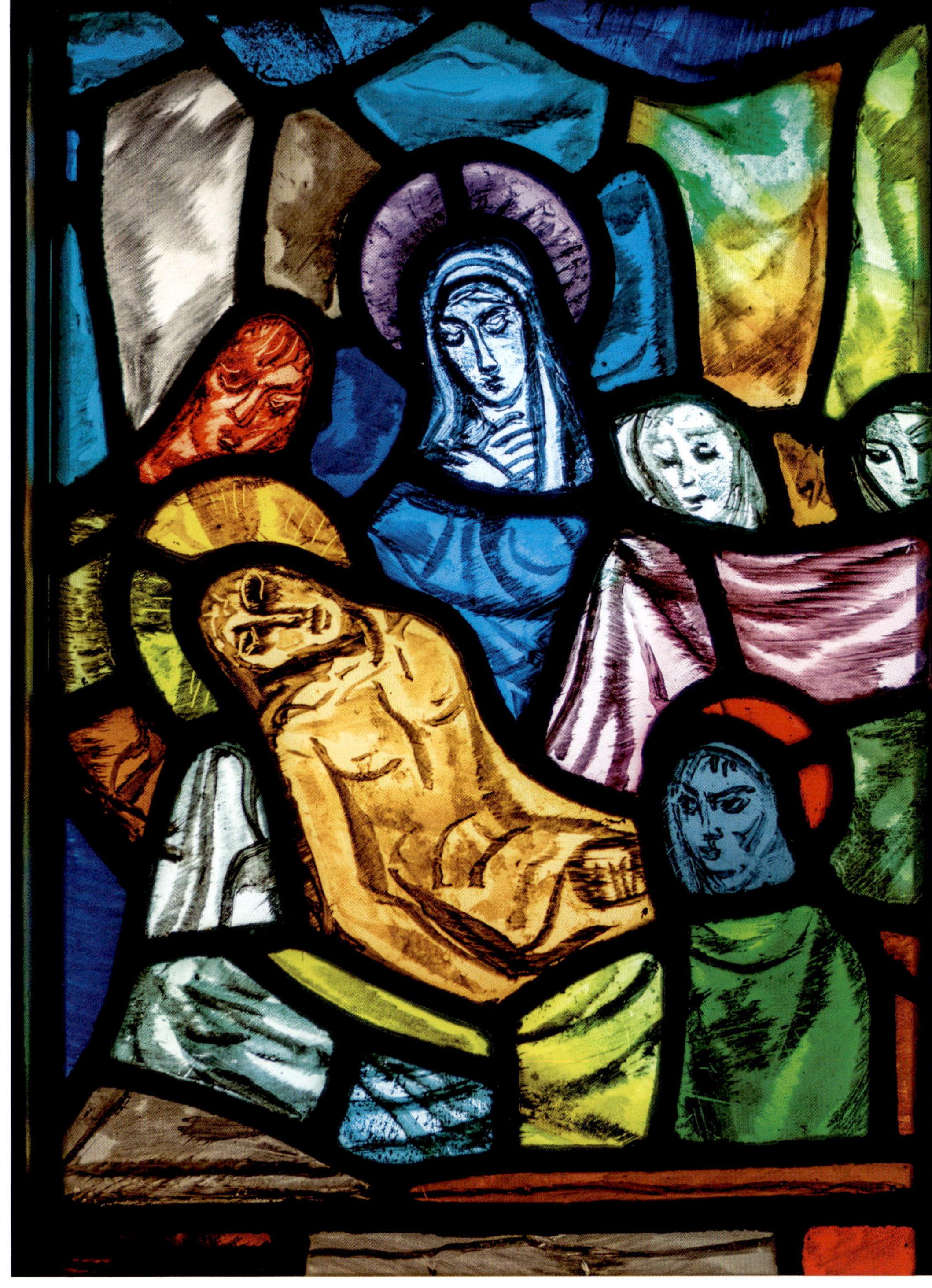

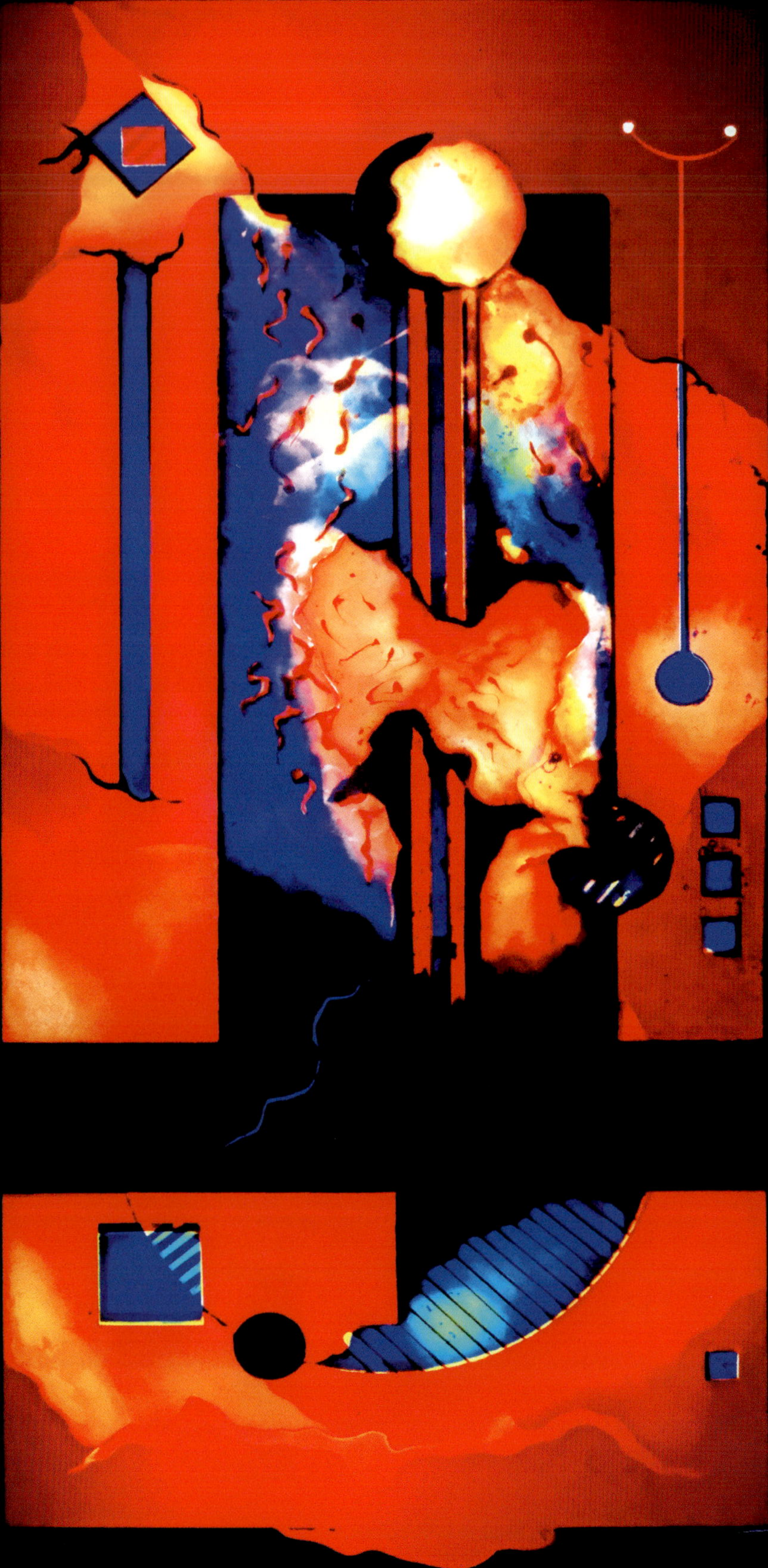

(opposite page) James Scanlon, *Study no. 2 by Miró* (1985). Collection and image © Hugh Lane Gallery

(1929), which had been made for his *Geneva Window* but cracked in the firing and was rejected by Clarke; the design of the gallery's repaired version is similar to his replacement panel comprising a sheet of gold-pink flashed glass plated on top of a sheet of blue flashed glass. The *Geneva Window* had been intended as a gift from W.T. Cosgrave's government to the International Labour Court in Geneva and Clarke was given considerable freedom in terms of subject matter. He chose to depict a series of vignettes inspired by (mainly) contemporary Irish writers, some of whose publications, such as those of Liam O'Flaherty, would soon be banned by Ireland's Censorship of Publication Act. Clarke's Gilhooley panel was among several images in the window deemed controversial; it would seem partly due to the semi-naked figure but also the other section of the complete vignette – absent in this version – which included the inebriated Gilhooley as he gazed lecherously at his lover, Nelly. Cosgrave, who appreciated Clarke's artistry, singled out the Gilhooley panel as problematic and asked the artist to replace it. Clarke, by then gravely ill, offered to produce alternative designs but insisted on retaining his choice of text. Ultimately his window was never sent to Geneva due to persistent unease about how it might be perceived; it is now in the collection of the Wolfsonian Museum, Florida.[6]

Also on display, the gallery has a late panel (*c.*1953) by Evie Hone, a tender depiction of *The Entombment*, the final Station of the Cross. The *St John* panel by the French artist, Paul Bony (1911–82), is also associated with Evie Hone as she knew the artist personally and acquired it for her collection; painterly in execution and atmospheric in mood, it was created from a sheet of painted, stained and etched blue flashed glass. Both panels were gifted through the FNCI.

Study no. 2 by Miró (1985) is by Kerry-born stained glass artist James Scanlon (b.1952). The theme was prompted by the Catalan painter's Constellation series and is made from two sheets of painted, stained and acided ruby and blue flashed glass plated together.

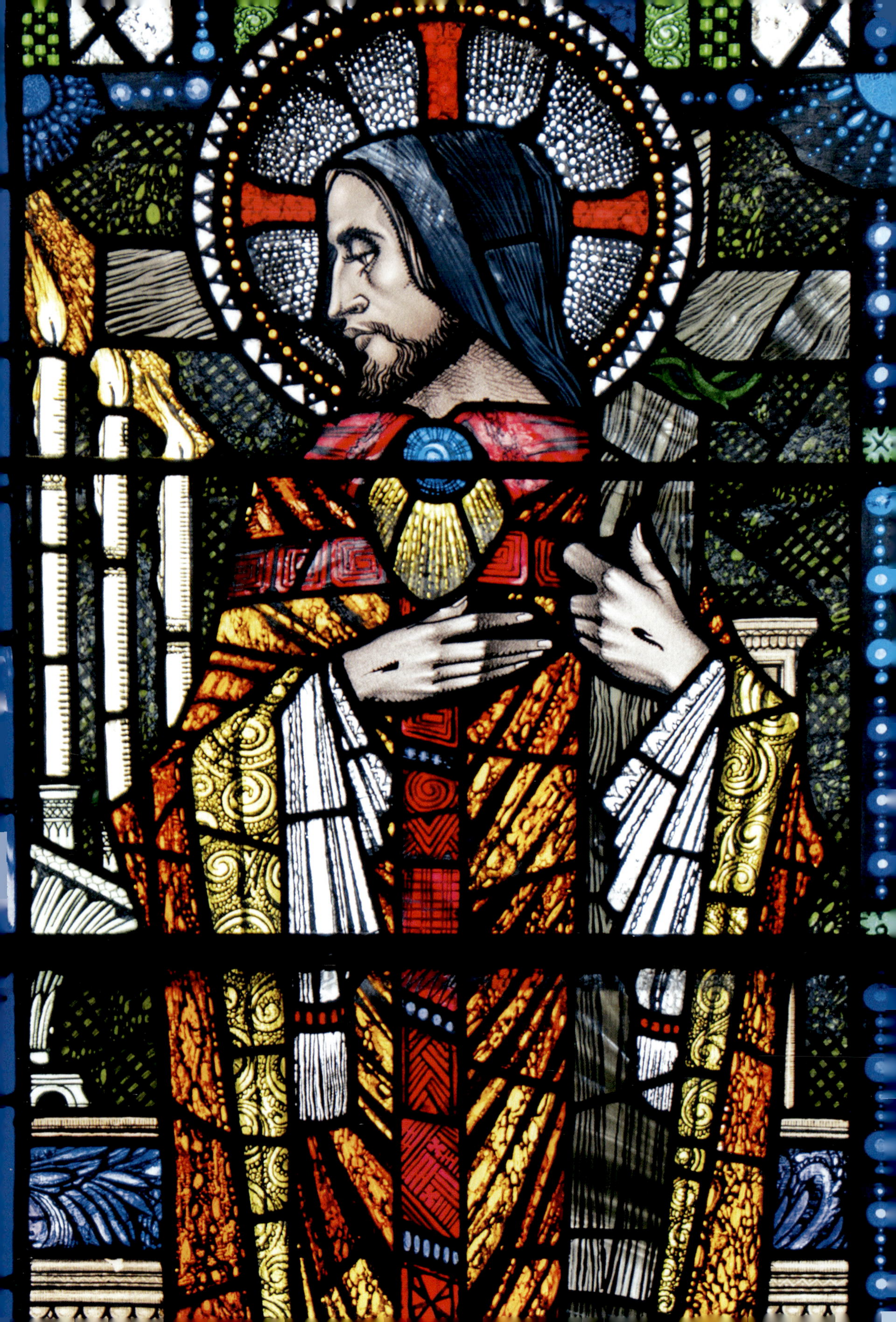

St Augustine and St John's church (John's Lane church) (RC)

Thomas Street, D08 Y802

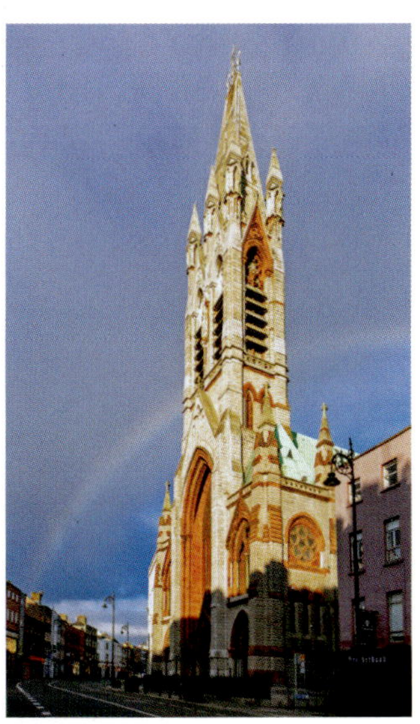

Positioned on an elevated site high above the Liffey, the Gothic revival church of St Augustine and St John – colloquially known as John's Lane church – seems like it was always destined for prominence but the soaring chisel-faced spire makes it a particularly distinctive landmark on the capital's skyline. It was designed by Pugin and Ashlin in 1866–92, with an apse added by William Hague in 1895, the same year it opened, and with side chapels following in 1899. The exterior comprises an attractive combination of rock-faced granite, red sandstone and grey limestone, while the main façade features great arched portals, along with steeply tapered roof profiles.

(opposite) Harry Clarke Studios, detail of Christ from *St Clare of Montefalco's Vision of Christ with His Cross* (1934)

On passing through the entrance vestibule one is struck by the vastness of the interior, more akin to a cathedral than a parish church. As with most churches, among the first windows to be installed were those in the sanctuary; it appears that four in the apse are by Mayer of Munich. The fifth one on the far left, *St Patrick Blessing the King of Cashel*, was ordered from Joshua Clarke and Sons by Fr Edward Mooney in September 1904.[1] Fr Mooney and another Augustinian priest had previously spent six years in Australia fundraising for the construction of the church.[2] As all the windows in the church are located up high, binoculars are recommended.

St Patrick Blessing the King of Cashel was almost certainly designed and painted by either Englishman James E. Pope or Dubliner William Flood Nagle. Harry Clarke ranked Pope very highly and he learnt the basics of the stained glass craft from Nagle.[3] At this stage Harry was aged fifteen and had left Belvedere College the previous year following his mother's death to start working in his father's business. In general terms the composition of the window is not dissimilar to the adjacent apse windows by Mayer for whom Joshua Clarke acted as an agent at this stage. However, this window has much more character and the Irish theme has been taken up with gusto: plenty of elaborate Celtic-style interlacing feature top and bottom,[4] and Aengus, the King of Cashel, is accompanied by a mighty band of soldiers, all with walrus-style moustaches or untamed beards. Cashel, off in the distance, is visible beneath a rich blue sky. Two kneeling acolytes who flank St Patrick carry tall candles, the flames of which are dramatically blown sideways by the breeze, a feature that Harry Clarke would, in time, include in several of his windows. The window was erected in memory of Alicia White (d.1903), the wife of a prominent organ builder, John Patrick White,[5] who had died tragically when she threw herself out of an upstairs window at their home on York Street.[6] There are several aspects of this window that are perplexing: the subject is decidedly masculine with sixteen men, mostly warriors, included, which makes it a curious choice to commemorate the tragic death of a middle-aged woman; a window depicting a baptism would be an unusual subject for the sanctuary; the decision to eschew the Gothic style present in the four Mayer companion windows in favour of overt Celtic revivalism. It is not known if it was John P. White or Fr Mooney, or both, who were responsible for these decisions.

The next windows of interest were all made within a ten-year period, 1929–39; three created at Clarke's and one made at An Túr Gloine by Michael Healy. The earliest two Clarke windows are located on the north side, that is 'liturgical north', not true north, and the other two are opposite on the south side. Traditionally most churches are built on an east–west axis though John's Lane church is built on a north–south axis.

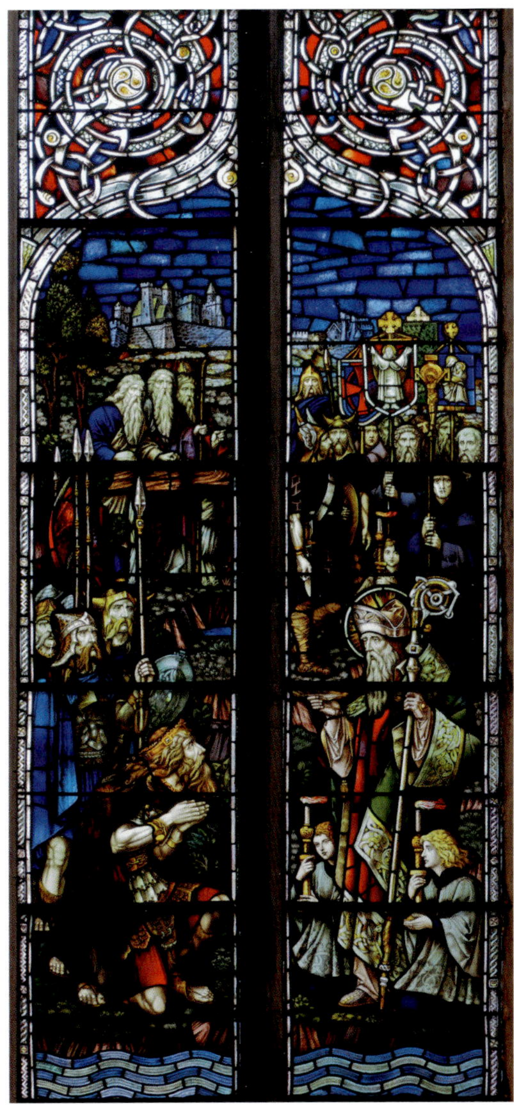

Joshua Clarke & Sons, detail of *St Patrick Blessing the King of Cashel* (1904)

The first window, *Scenes from the Life of St Rita of Cascia: St Rita and her Two Adult Sons; St Rita in Conversation with St Augustine, St John the Baptist and St Nicholas of Tolentino*, was ordered, at a cost of £310, from Joshua Clarke & Sons in March 1929; the studio still retained Joshua's name even though he had died eight years earlier. 1929 was a tough year for the studio and a horrendous year for Harry Clarke personally as his tuberculosis, which was evident throughout the previous year, required him to move to Switzerland for treatment, and on 18 March he departed for a sanitorium in Davos where he remained for fourteen months. During this period the studio was managed by Philip Deegan (when not in hospital with his own

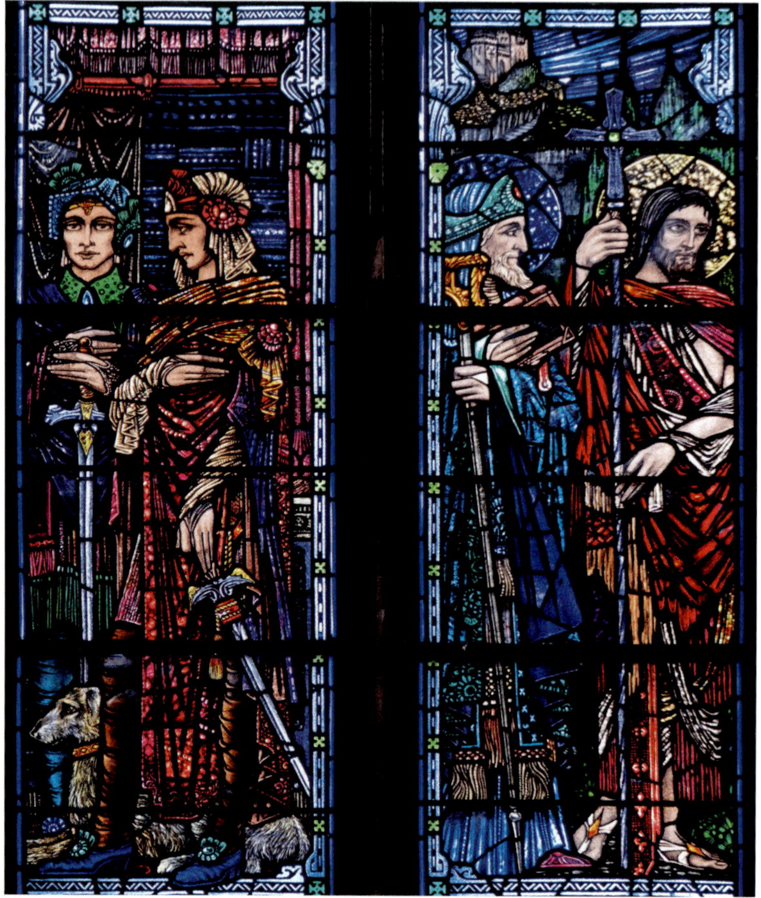

(left) Joshua Clarke & Sons, centre two lights from *Scenes from the Life of St Rita of Cascia* (1929–31)

health issues), and by Harry's siblings, Walter and Florence (Dolly). In April 1930, the same month he left Switzerland to return home, Harry Clarke sent a sketch for the window to the prior, Revd John Stokes, apologizing for the delay, which he put down to 'business reorganization'. He also offered for Cecil B. Simmonds, the newly appointed manager, to call to discuss the job if required. Although the St Rita window certainly shows Harry Clarke's influence, it was almost certainly designed and definitely painted by other members of the studio; at this stage there were about twenty staff of which fewer than half were artists. The studio maintained a strict policy of not disclosing which particular artist may have been involved with any particular window, and an erroneous impression was projected that all were designed by Harry Clarke himself. Although some clients knew that Harry Clarke was abroad in a sanitorium it was in the studio's interest to keep this secret.[7] Given the size of the window it is likely it was completed sometime in 1931.

St Rita (1381–1457), who was born in Umbria, endured a difficult marriage to an abusive husband and when widowed became an Augustinian nun. She was canonized in 1900 and at the ceremony was proclaimed 'Patroness of impossible causes', and so became a popular figure for veneration, particularly in Augustinian churches. At a glance the 4-light St Rita window appears to depict, in frieze-like formation, a single group of seven figures but in fact two quite separate scenes are represented, each taking up two lights; on the left is *St Rita and her Two Adult Sons*, and on the right is *St Rita in Conversation with St Augustine, St John the Baptist and St Nicholas of Tolentino.* So St Rita appears twice,[8] almost functioning as bookends to the composition, both times wearing a distinctive oversized halo surrounded by flowers, though surprisingly not roses which are particularly associated with her. In the left scene Rita is shown holding aloft a crucifix to dissuade her sons from seeking revenge for their father's murder. The two men, improbably dressed in exotic headgear and lavish garments, have their silver swords drawn while an Irish wolfhound obediently rests at their feet. In the right lights the four figures seem disengaged from each other and in general the quality of the draughtsmanship falls short of the studio at its best.

In June 1933 Revd Stokes placed an order for a new window, this time from Michael Healy of An Túr Gloine. It would cost more than twice Clarke's *St Rita* window of the same size, coming in at £760, and would in fact make it Healy's single most expensive window. In this instance the funds came from a Mr Murphy,[9] the brother of a deceased former prior, Revd Dr James Murphy (d.1923). The decision to erect a window to Revd Murphy's memory had been agreed back in June 1929 and it is not known what caused the delay though the high cost of Healy's window may have been a factor. This commission must have been important to Healy personally as he had been born in the locality and still had no large window by him in his native city, having been disappointed when a major commission for St Patrick's cathedral fell through a few years earlier.[10] It appears that Healy believed he was designing his window for the west wall (liturgical north) of the church, to be placed next to *St Rita* and prepared a detailed sketch design for it, utilizing some diamond patterns and

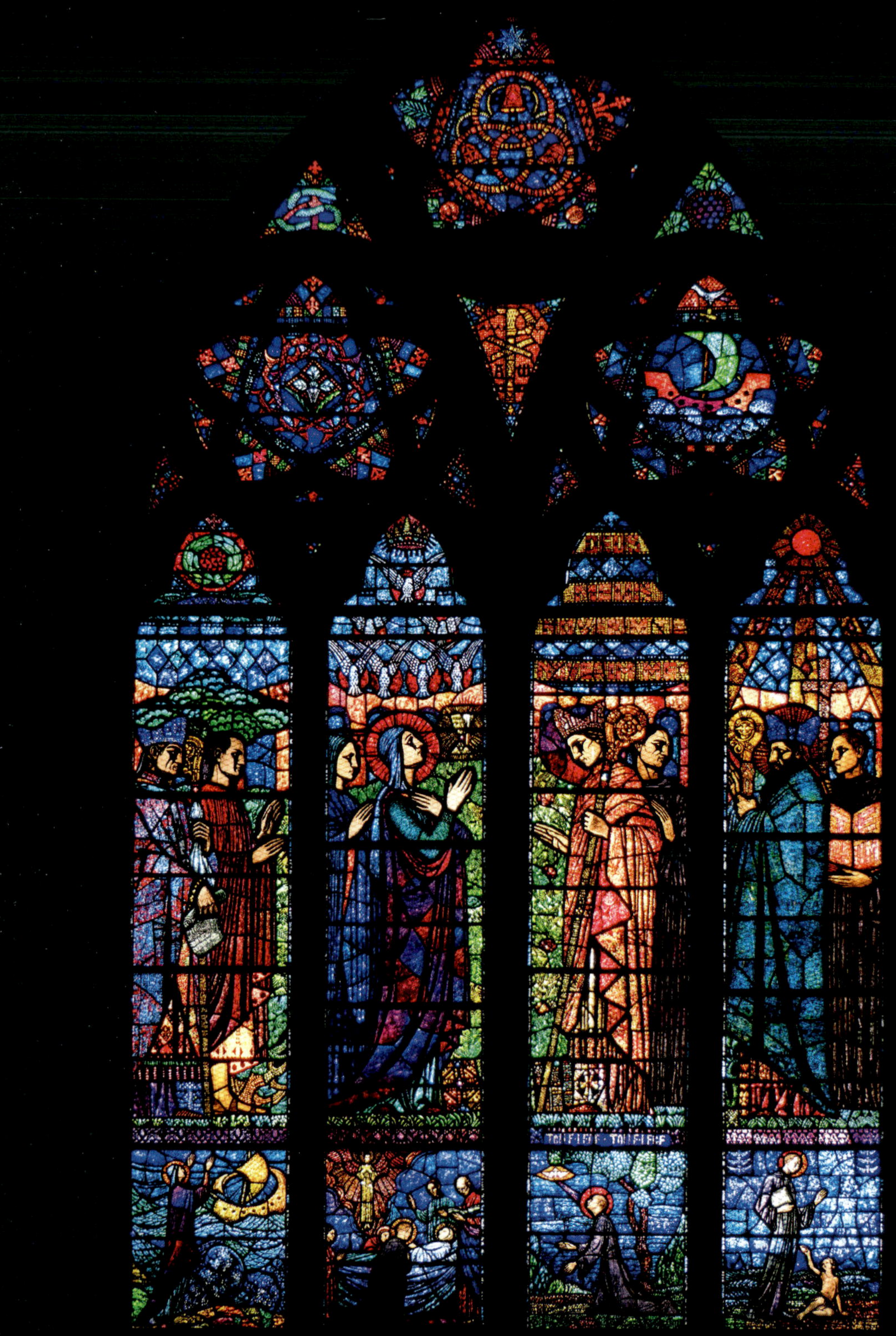

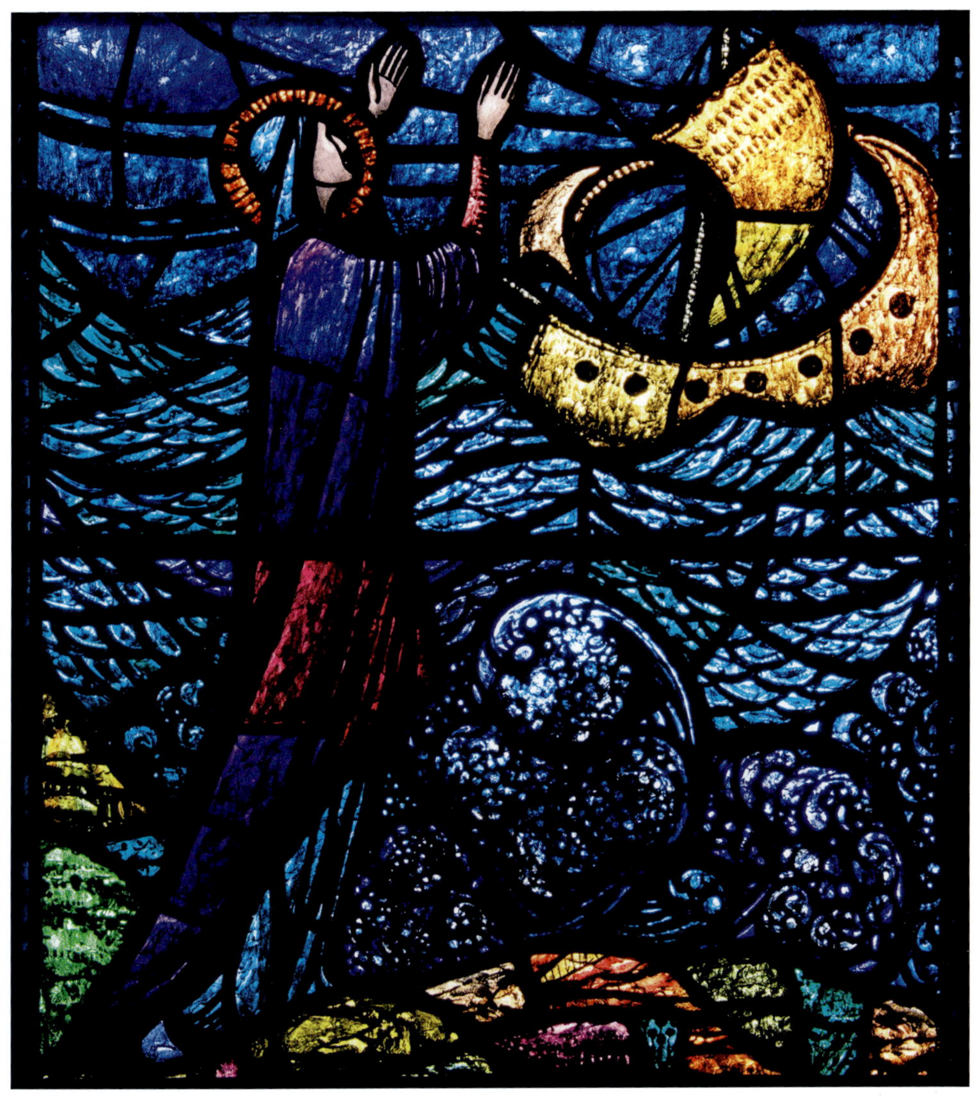

(above) Michael Healy, St Monica waving farewell to St Augustine from *St Augustine and St Monica* (1933–4); (opposite) Michael Healy, *St Augustine and St Monica* (1933–4)

including two central predella panels just as Clarke's had done in order to harmonize the composition of the two windows.[11] The sequence of events is not clear but when Clarke's received an order in March 1934 for another window, they understood it was for the same location. The error appears to have been Healy's as the tracery details noted in the An Túr Gloine order book had been for the window on the wall *opposite* and not beside the *St Rita*, and so his initial design required modifications, though one benefit is that he got to include four figurative predella panels rather than two; however the window is decidedly dark – it is best viewed in early morning light – and this may be explained partly by the confusion over its location.

The theme of the window relates to mother and son, St Monica and St Augustine, two stalwarts of Augustinian devotion, and it is arguably one of Healy's most beautiful and monumental windows.[12] The distinctive colour palette is dominated by turquoise, peacock green, purple and orange and the complexions of the protagonists remind the viewer that both Augustine and Monica were Christian Berbers from North Africa. The main section of the window features eight figures in a flat frieze-like arrangement, from left to right they are St Alipius and Nebridius; St Monica with her daughter Perpetua; St Augustine with his son Adeodatus; St Ambrose with an acolyte who carries a volume inscribed *Te Deum*, a hymn traditionally ascribed to both Augustine and Ambrose. Although the focal point is Monica meeting Augustine, her attention is drawn not to him but to a chalice which hovers above in a golden aureole which may be a reference to her dying words to Augustine, 'All I ask of you is that wherever you may be, you will remember me at the altar of the Lord' (i.e. the Eucharist), words which often appear on Catholic memorial cards. Healy has treated the figures' faces in a crisp graphic Art Deco style with no intermediate tones, whereas the rich brocades and embroidered fabrics they wear, along with the background, have been extensively acided.

The four narrative predella panels illustrate key incidents from Augustine's life, left to right: Monica waving farewell to her son; Augustine praying at Monica's deathbed in Ostia; Augustine seeking spiritual guidance; Augustine and the parable of the Trinity. In the extensive tracery Healy has included a variety of images or symbols; contained in one of the three large cinquefoils is one of his favourites, an ark with a billowing sail and a little dove atop its mast. The other cinquefoils feature Christ's crown of thorns, and three interlinking rings with three bells symbolizing the Trinity. Smaller spandrels contain the Chi Rho monogram, the tree of life and the pomegranate, the latter having multiple interpretations. The labour intensive aciding technique has been utilized extensively throughout the window to create a work that, as the external light changes, becomes animated and sparkles.

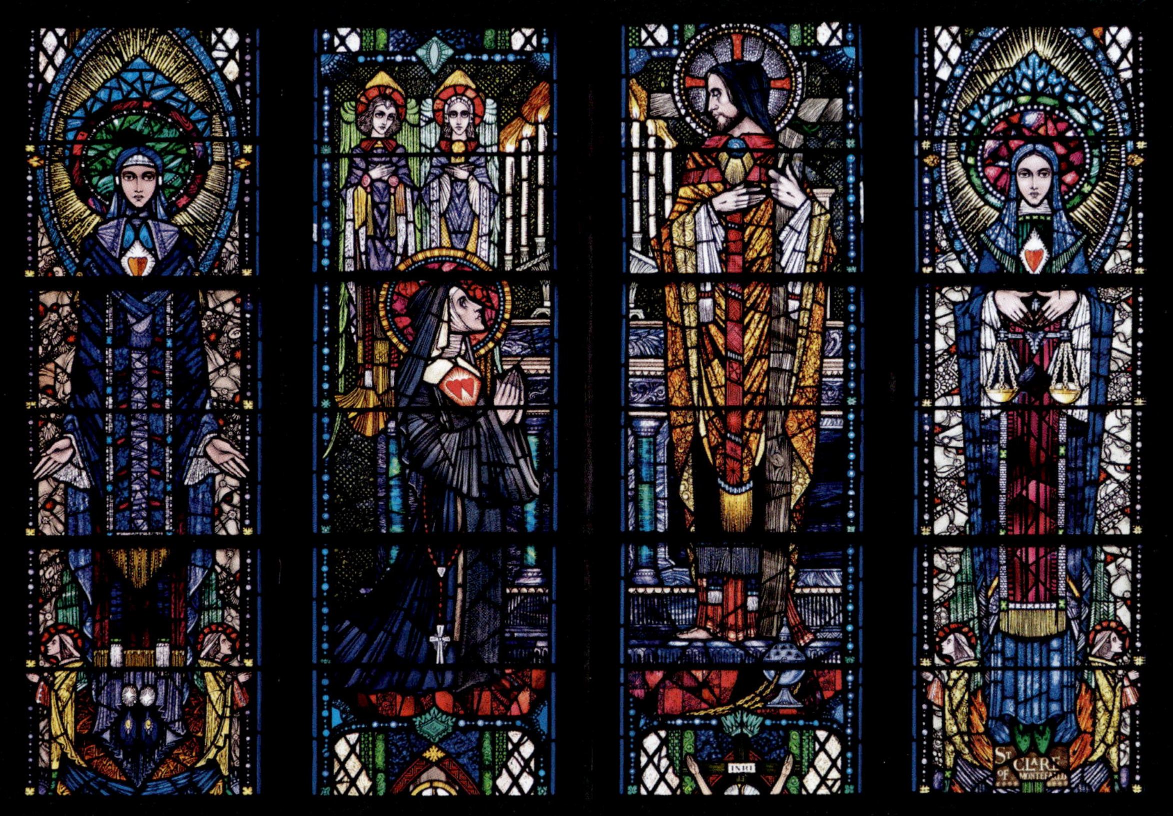

Harry Clarke Studios, detail of *St Clare of Montefalco's Vision of Christ with His Cross* (1934)

The next Clarke window, *St Clare of Montefalco's Vision of Christ with His Cross*, was ordered in March 1934, three years after Harry Clarke had died, and it depicts a pivotal episode from the life of another Umbrian Augustinian nun who was elevated to sainthood. At a cost of £350, it is not known who in the studio designed it but it would appear to have been either Richard King or William Dowling, both of whom had joined in early 1928. Both of these artists quickly assimilated the distinctive Harry Clarke aesthetic. After Clarke's death their style evolved, but did so in sync and distinguishing one artist's work from the other can be challenging. Resembling the composition of many standard treatments of *The Apparition of the Sacred Heart to St Margaret Mary*, Christ is depicted standing while the saint kneels at a prie-dieu.

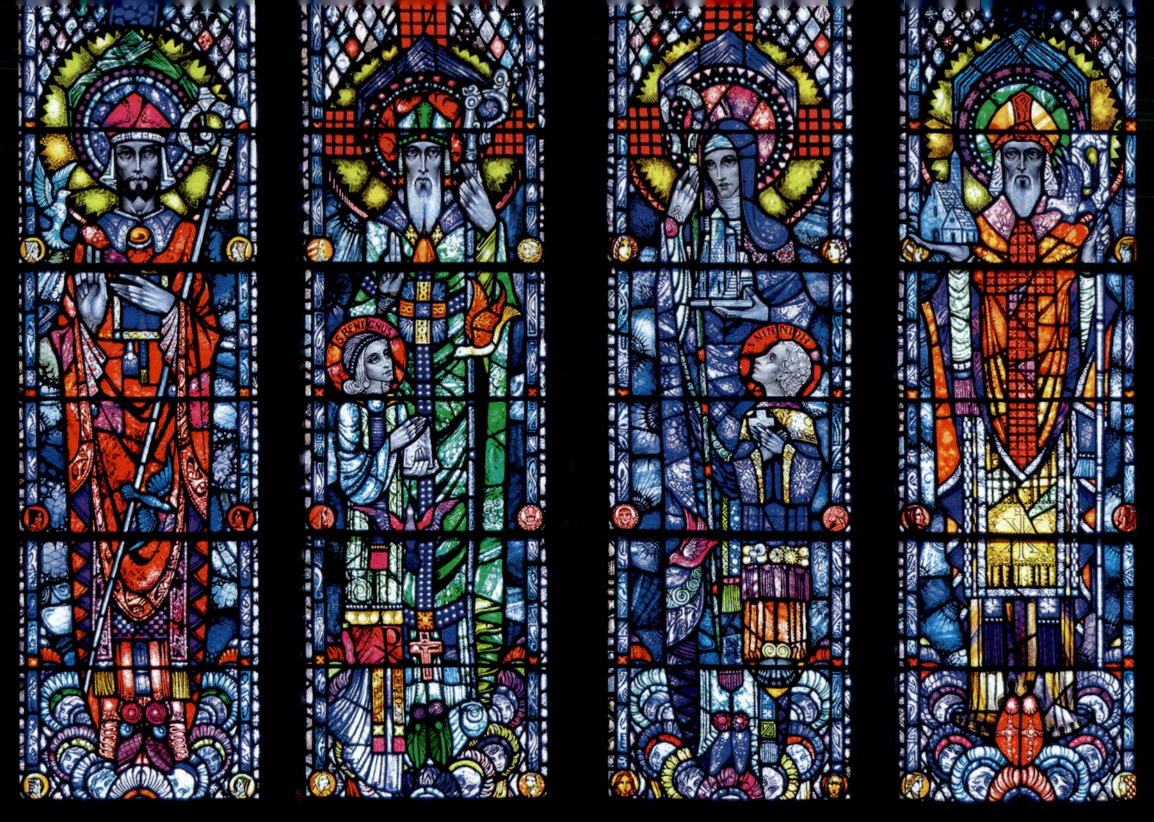

William Dowling (Harry Clarke Studios), detail of *Saints Lawrence O'Toole, Patrick, Brigid and Kevin* (1938–9)

Almost indiscernible initially is the grey-brown cross that Christ carries upright which merges into the grisaille background. St Clare, eyes focused intensely on Christ, has a double heart pinned to her chest, a reference to Christ implanting his cross in her heart. Notably their hands are of normal proportions compared with the long tapered, often splayed, fingers that Clarke favoured and which were a key component of his signature style. Between the two figures but divided by the central stone mullion of the window is an altar candelabra with, curiously, the flames of the tall candles blowing both left and right, as if perhaps to convey the supernatural energy that passed between Christ and St Clare. Two vesica-shaped vignettes below show Christ in classic *Ecce Homo* pose being mocked, and the Crucifixion; elsewhere various symbols associated with his Passion are included.

In September 1937 a series of six decorative diamond-paned 4-light windows featuring symbols associated with Christ and Our Lady were ordered from Clarke's which would fill all the remaining windows with the exception of one opening on the south wall which was reserved for a final pictorial window to complete the set of four windows featuring saints. There were clearly budgetary concerns and these decorative windows were made from cheaper manufactured glass mainly utilizing glass with a 'hammered' (bumpy) texture. Shades of blue and off-white predominate with accents in ruby, and it is likely these were completed in late 1937 or early 1938.

The third and final pictorial window from Clarke's, *Saints Lawrence O'Toole, Patrick, Brigid and Kevin*, was ordered in October 1938, by which point Richard King had assumed management of the studio, though he would choose to leave in 1940; he was succeeded by his friend William Dowling, and this window is attributed to him.[13] The Studios had depicted Patrick and Brigid many, many times before; St Kevin of Glendalough less so, and St Lawrence O'Toole, although principal patron of the Dublin archdiocese, was a surprisingly infrequent subject.

Dowling incorporated the diamond-patterned background which featured prominently in the two earlier Clarke pictorial windows, as well as the decorative windows, but this time the diamonds are of greater colour variation and so more fully integrate with the figurative elements of the window. Blues and reds predominate, two colours particularly associated with medieval stained glass. The three male figures appear to stare straight ahead with detached impassiveness, conveying a cold quality to their countenances that is emphasized by the choice of grey glass as the base colour for flesh, something Harry Clarke would never have considered, combined with a much more tonal rendering of the facial features which evokes a smooth stone-like quality. In fact, the studio's faces of this period often resemble the medieval statues found on the exterior of the great cathedrals. However not all the figures in the window convey a chilly absence of humanity, boyish St Ninnidh of the Pure Hand (as distinct from Ninnidh of Inismacsaint) gazes attentively up at St Brigid whom, legend states, he would attend on her deathbed. St Patrick's companion, the equally youthful St Benignus – a male saint though one would not think it from this depiction – is lost

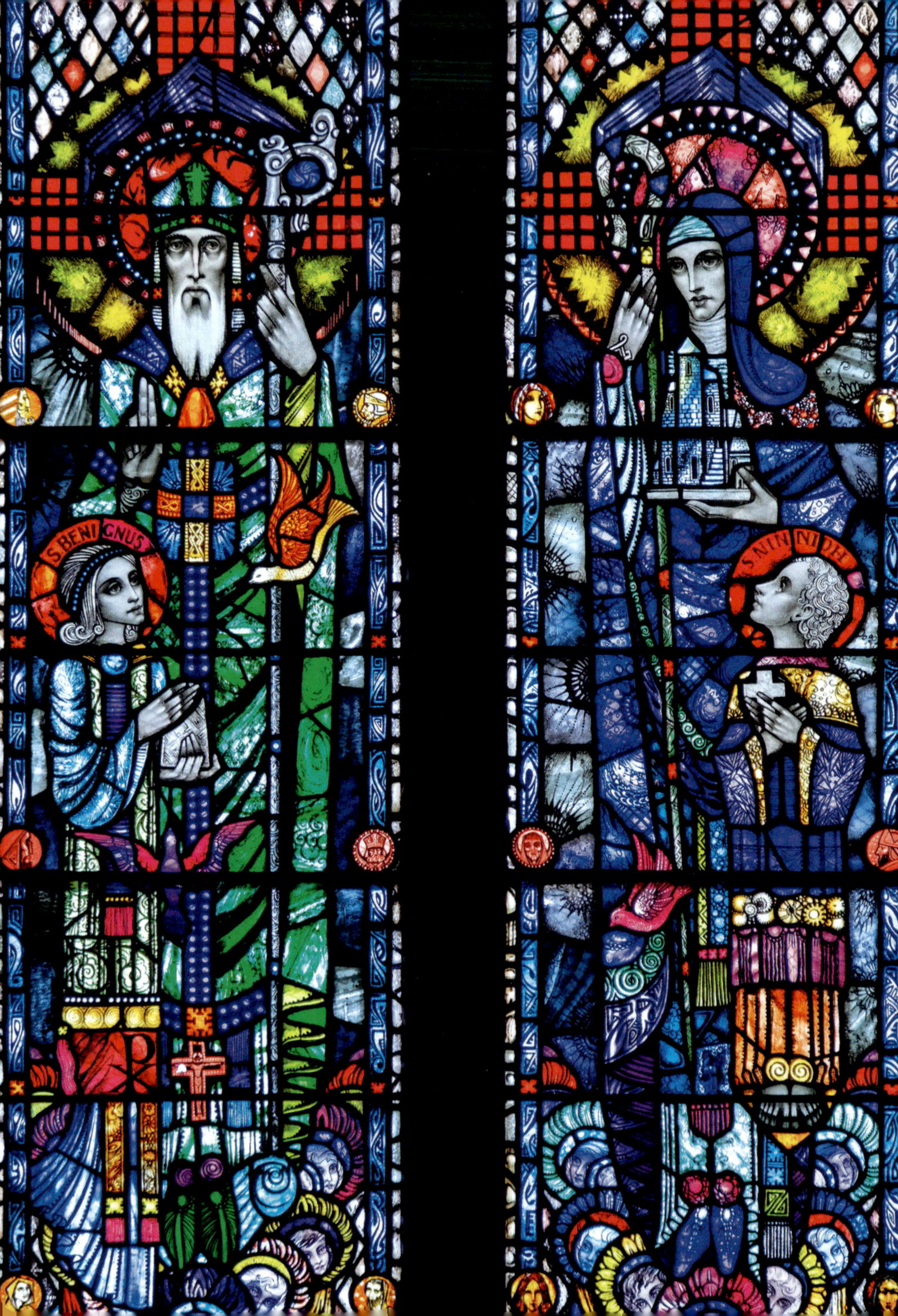
S BENIGNUS
S NINNIDH

(opposite) William Dowling (Harry Clarke Studios), detail of St Patrick with St Benignus and St Brigid from *Saints Lawrence O'Toole, Patrick, Brigid and Kevin* (1938–9)

in his reverie as he carries the shrine that holds St Patrick's bell; a depiction of the bell itself which has been carefully copied from the actual object in the National Museum is featured in the apex of this light. There are lighter touches too, such as the flotillas of putti that support the severe looking saints – though these are not conventional putti as such, having the features of attractive bright-eyed and full-lipped young girls with perfectly coiffed hair. In addition, the six birds that gaily flutter about, all of different colours, are a whimsical inclusion of which Harry Clarke would surely have approved of and are perhaps an affectionate nod to his popular Bewley's windows made by him a decade earlier. Additionally, and these can only be seen with binoculars, there are forty tiny circular medallions in the borders of each light featuring caricatures of faces recalling the playful and grotesque marginalia found in Celtic manuscripts. Of all three Clarke windows, this is the one that offers the most visual rewards for those who take the time to study it. The window cost £375 and although the Clarke order books do not record the date of the window's installation, given its size, it must have been some time in 1939.

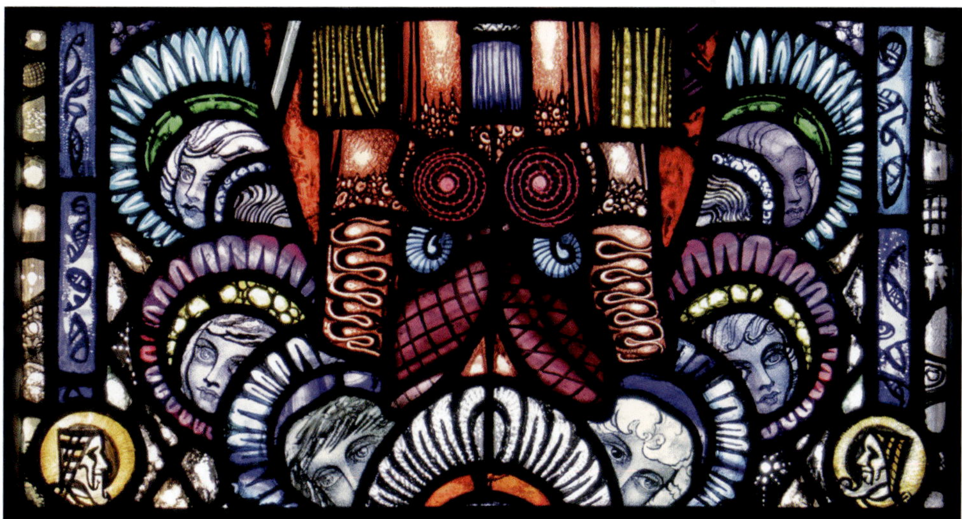

William Dowling (Harry Clarke Studios), detail of base of St Lawrence O'Toole from *Saints Lawrence O'Toole, Patrick, Brigid and Kevin* (1938–9)

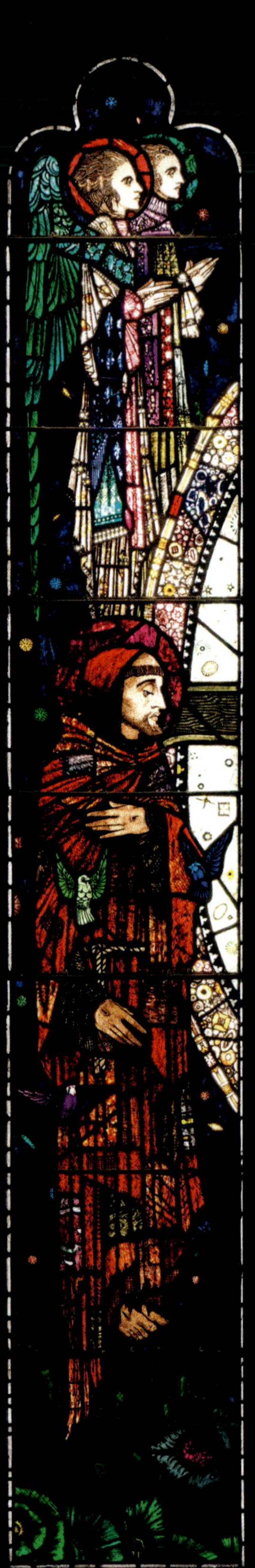

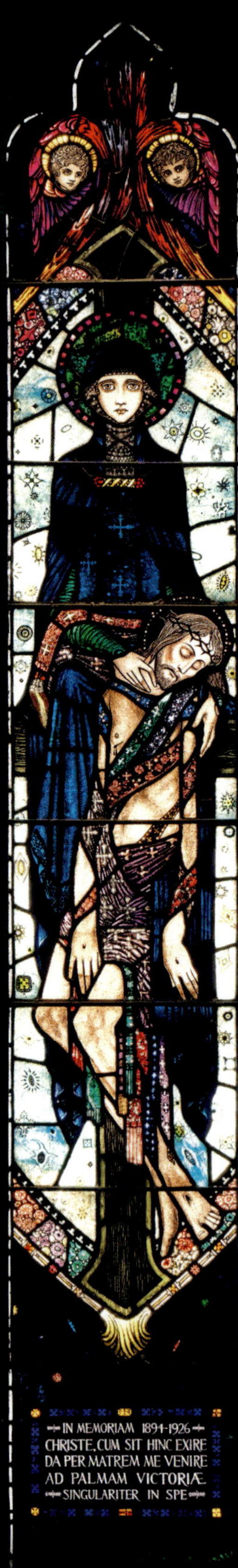
IN MEMORIAM 1894-1926
CHRISTE, CUM SIT HINC EXIRE
DA PER MATREM ME VENIRE
AD PALMAM VICTORIÆ
SINGULARITER IN SPE

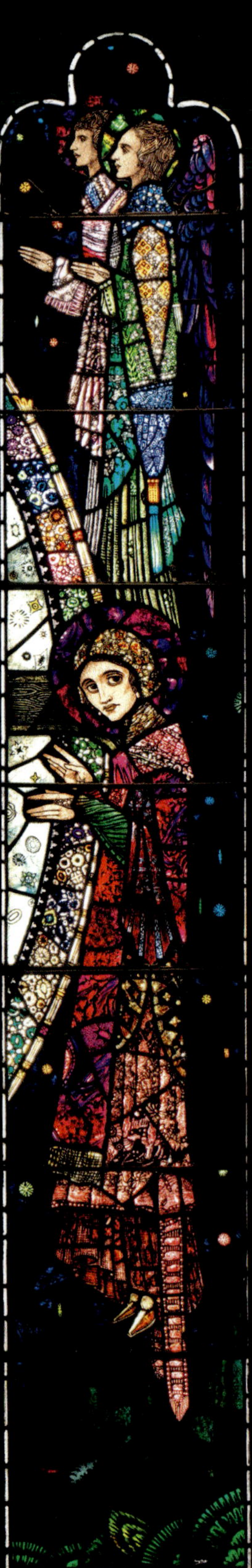

National Gallery

Merrion Square West, D02 K303

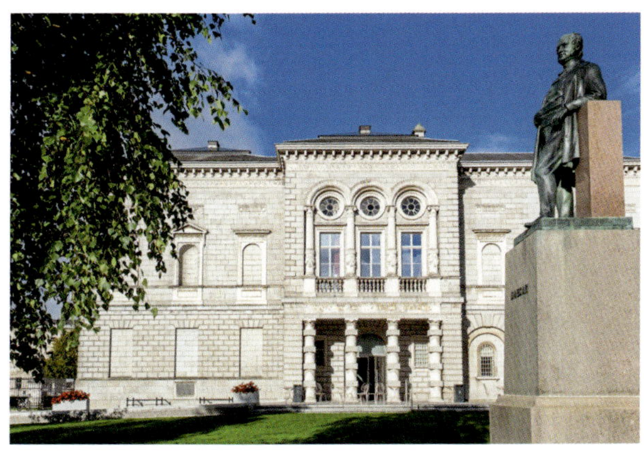

The National Gallery's stained glass collection is housed in the Milltown Wing, designed by Thomas M. Deane in 1900–3. It can be found in the final of a series of ground-floor rooms (room 20) that are dedicated to Irish art. As this is a windowless room all the windows/panels are displayed in lightboxes. Although essentially a cube, the room's subdued ambient lighting distracts from any architectural elements and allows viewers to focus on and appreciate the windows in an atmosphere that approximates the lighting level in historic places of worship.

(opposite) Harry Clarke, *The Mother of Sorrows* (1926). Photo © National Gallery of Ireland

HARRY CLARKE IS REPRESENTED by three works in the gallery's stained glass room, two of which demonstrate his ability to work in minute detail with sheets of stained and painted, acid-etched flashed glass (one ruby, one blue), which were 'plated', or registered, one on top of the other to create a myriad of shades. The first panel, *The Song of the Mad Prince*, was inspired by Walter de la Mare's short poem of that name and made in 1917 at the request of his friend, Thomas Bodkin, who would later become director of the gallery. The nostalgic poem is a meditation on life, death and the passage of time, with Clarke's consumptive-looking prince, centre stage, gazing at the viewer, while his parents in profile behind him, seem self-absorbed and remote. The prince wears a richly embroidered tabard and, bizarrely, holds a crucifix-shaped dagger in one hand and a fan in the other. The prince's enigmatic expression hinting at melancholia draws one in and invites reflection. Bodkin had the panel mounted in a bespoke walnut cabinet made by James Hicks with an electric bulb behind a sheet of opaque glass providing diffused illumination.

The second cabinet panel is in landscape format and was created in 1922 for Sir Robert Woods who was one of a social set in Killiney who befriended the young Clarke and championed his work, both in stained glass and book illustration. *The Enchantment of Bottom by Titania* was inspired by act IV, scene I of *A Midsummer's Night's Dream*. In the foreground the protagonists lie together in semi-slumber while mischievous naked fairies, Peaseblossom, Cobweb, Moth, Mustardseed and King Oberon, cavort in the lush glade, playing with a long daisy chain. It is likely that Clarke's depiction of the fairies was influenced by the 'Cottingley fairies', whose photographs, promoted by Arthur Conan Doyle, had been a *cause célèbre* a few years earlier.[1] The suggestion of soft spotlights highlighting the besotted couple and a painted backdrop convey the sense of a theatrical production; significantly Clarke was an enthusiastic attender of theatre and ballet in Dublin and London. The level of illustrated detail is so fine in this panel that one strains to see it with the naked eye.

The Enchantment of Bottom by Titania again features the aciding technique that Clarke pushed to its limits; and sometimes beyond its limits, as Clarke's first effort resulted in the fragile ruby flashed glass shattering in the kiln. Clarke creatively used

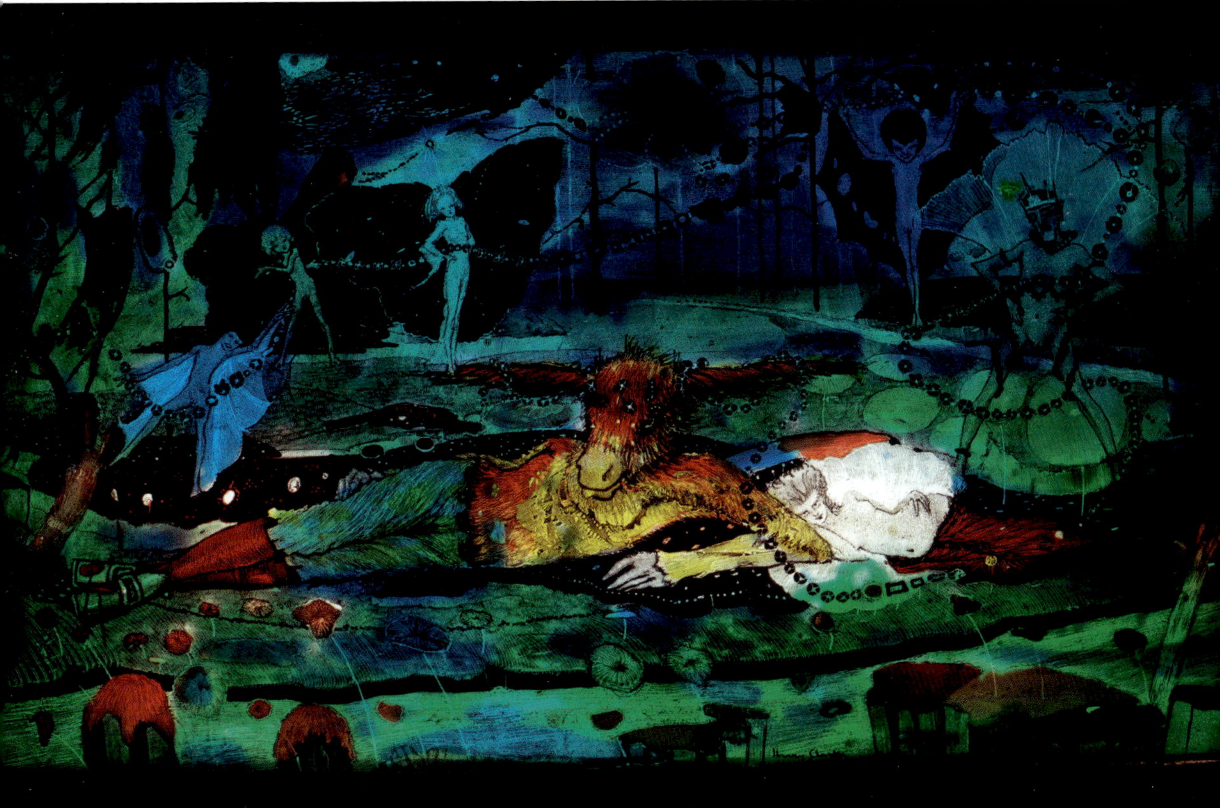

Harry Clarke, *The Enchantment of Bottom by Titania* (1922). Photo © National Gallery of Ireland

lead cames to reconfigure the broken panel and Sir Robert liked the end result so much that he bought it along with the second version for a total of £40. He had the latter encased in a mahogany cabinet made by James Hicks and this work was acquired by the Gallery in 2023. For a panel that is comprised of plated ruby and blue flashed glass, there is remarkably little red visible and Clarke has used extensive silver stain, painted in different strengths on the blue glass to achieve the dominant shades of aquamarine.

The stained glass room is dominated by a large 3-light window, Harry Clarke's *The Mother of Sorrows*, and one could be forgiven for assuming that it was made in Ireland for an Irish church, but in fact Clarke made it in London for a convent chapel in Glasgow. It was the second 3-light window, both costing £450, that had been

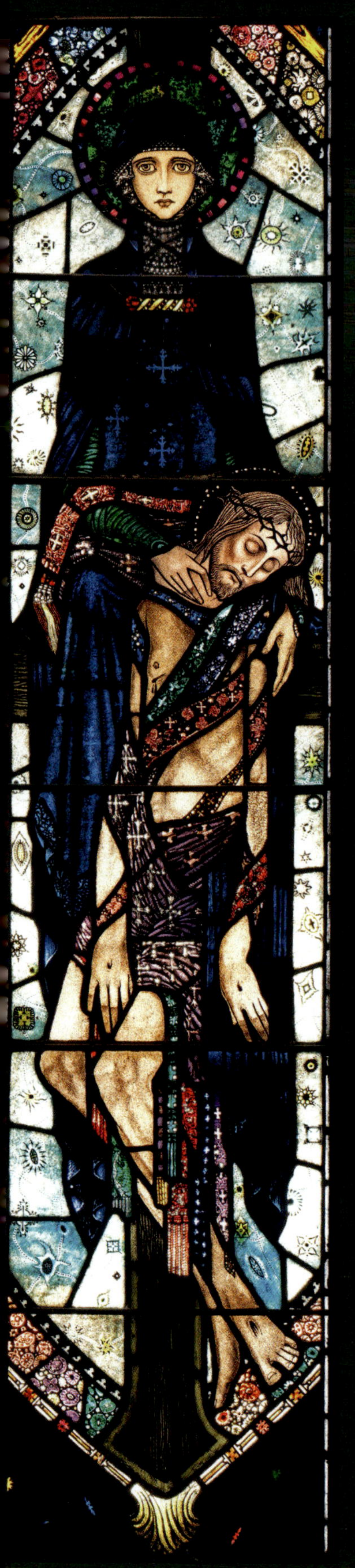

commissioned by Sr Mary of St Wilfrid, retired principal of Dowanhill teacher training college; Clarke had been recommended to her by Sir Bertram Windle, president of UCC.[2] He created *The Mother of Sorrows* in 1926 as a companion window for his *The Coronation of the Blessed Virgin* (1923), now on display in Glasgow's Kelvingrove Museum. It was conceived as a war memorial, as had his earlier window, and this time the theme was to be the Pietà, a subject to which Sr Mary was devoted but which Clarke had not tackled before and was dubious about its suitability for a window.[3]

The composition of *The Mother of Sorrows* is unified by an enormous almond-shaped vesica, a shape favoured by Clarke that he featured regularly, though usually on a much smaller scale, and here Mary and Jesus are contained within it. Our Lady is remarkably youthful, almost girlish, and she gazes with profound sadness at the viewer. Christ's dark wooden cross is T-shaped, and in an unusual departure from convention, Mary is seated atop the horizontal bar, while gently lowering the limp body of her son so that the image is less the standard Pietà pose and more that of *The Deposition* (also referred to as *The Descent from the Cross*). Two Italian saints, St Francis of Assisi and St Catherine of Genoa, hover either side, both chosen for their connection to Sr Mary, and the bar of the cross appears to nominally rest on their shoulders. Clarke depicted St Francis in

Harry Clarke, detail of *The Mother of Sorrows* (1926)

a tattered and patched brown and russet habit, the stigmata on his hands and feet clearly visible, and accompanied by three fluttering birds, while St Catherine of Genoa, a Franciscan nun of noble birth, is depicted in a sparkling garment fashioned from shades of pink glass. Most of the vesica features pale glass in tones of blue and grey-green and floating within are tiny organisms and some geometric forms too, all of which appear as if magnified thousands of times. This visual treatment bears a close resemblance to his series of decorative windows for Bewley's café, made about the same time, however in this instance one is left wondering if there is a particular meaning or significance to the choice. The upper reaches of the window contain a pair of praying angels in each of the side lights awaiting to receive the soul of the dead Christ, and two seraphim in the centre light look down as interested observers.

Although the entire scene is set in the celestial realm, earth is indicted too at the very bottom. Clarke has included some lush emerald green fronds and behind them, also in shades of green, is what appears to be a futuristic urban skyline full of windowless tower blocks – another example of Clarke including visual elements that leaves one intrigued and speculating.

Harry Clarke made the window at the Glass House, Fulham, where it was exhibited in January 1927 before being dispatched to Glasgow. Unfortunately Sr Mary died a few months later and a decision was then made that it should become a memorial to her personally rather than a memorial to those who died in the First World War. The inscription includes her favourite stanza from the *Stabat Mater*, the thirteenth-century hymn reflecting on Mary's suffering at the crucifixion, and included below is Sr Mary's family motto, *Singulariter in spe* (Hopeful in unity).[4] In 1997 the window was relocated to Notre Dame College of Education, Bearsden, Glasgow, and then in 2002 it was sold at Christie's, London, minus the seven pieces of tracery, when it was acquired by the National Gallery.[5]

Clarke created a total of four windows for the chapel at Dowanhill. Sr Mary had commissioned two lancets prior to her untimely demise and he made them in 1927, again at the Glass House in Fulham; one is now in Britain's Stained Glass Museum in Ely, Cambridgeshire, and the other one, *The Blessed Julie with Two Children, and the Visitation of Our Lady to St Elizabeth*, happily is on permanent display in Staunton's Hotel, St Stephen's Green, Dublin.[6]

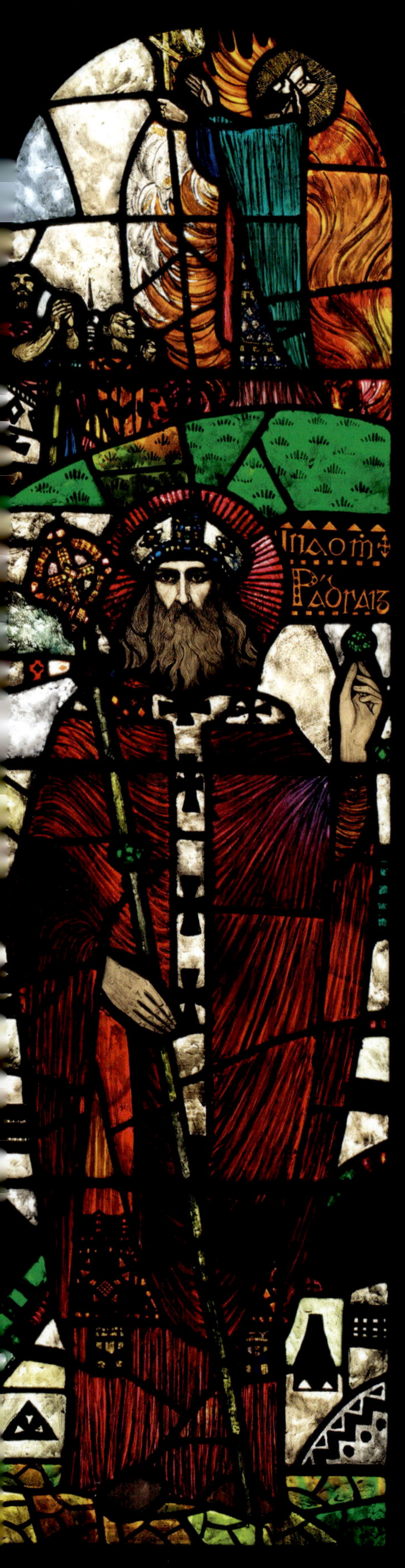

Michael Healy, Clarke's contemporary who worked at the rival An Túr Gloine studio, has a set of five windows on display in the gallery, and these too had been made for a convent chapel, just one year before *The Mother of Sorrows*. The architect who placed the order was Rudolf Maximillian Butler who was also an enthusiastic patron of Harry Clarke. In addition to being a practising architect, Butler was professor of architecture at UCD and long-time editor of the *Irish Builder and Engineer*, a popular trade journal, that regularly promoted An Túr Gloine via short articles about the studio's latest windows.

Healy's five windows were designed for the tiny curved sanctuary of the Sisters of Mercy convent chapel, Ballyhaunis, Co. Mayo, in 1925, and as originally placed, *The Good Shepherd* was located in the centre with a male and female Irish saint either side. It is clear that Healy was eager to instil the figures in each window with a particular mood or personality – *The Good Shepherd* is sombre and meditative; St Patrick, severe

(left) Michael Healy, *St Patrick* (1924–5). Photo © National Gallery of Ireland
(opposite) Evie Hone, *St Christopher* (1944). © Geraldine Hone, Kate Hone and the Friends of the National Collections of Ireland. Photo © National Gallery of Ireland

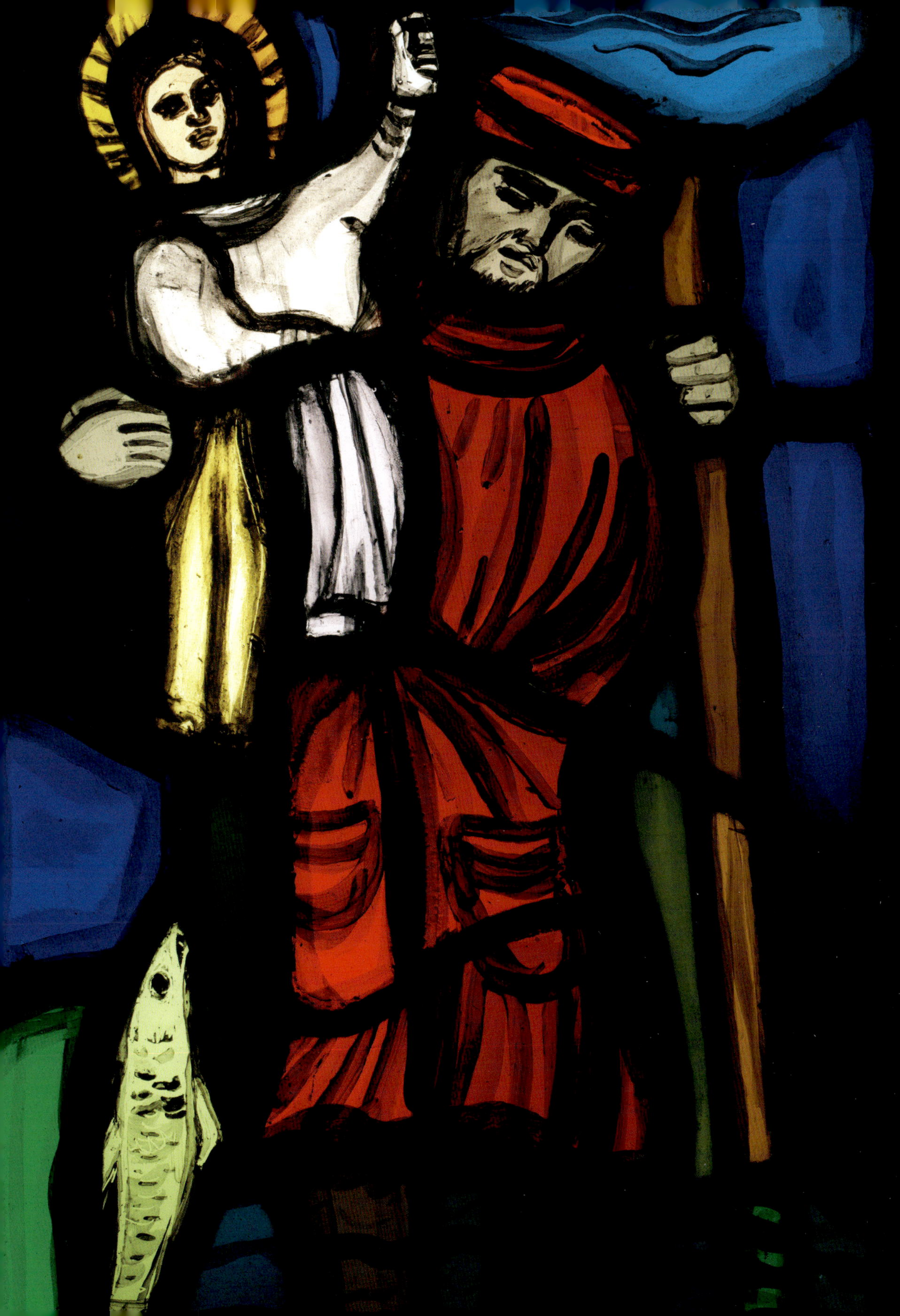

and patriarchal; St Brigid, wistful and serene; St Ita, motherly and compassionate (as she looks down at the young St Brendan in her charge); and St Colmcille, proud and resilient. Each window features a thematically related vignette in the curved apex – Christ calming the storm; St Patrick lighting the paschal fire at Slane; a huge oak

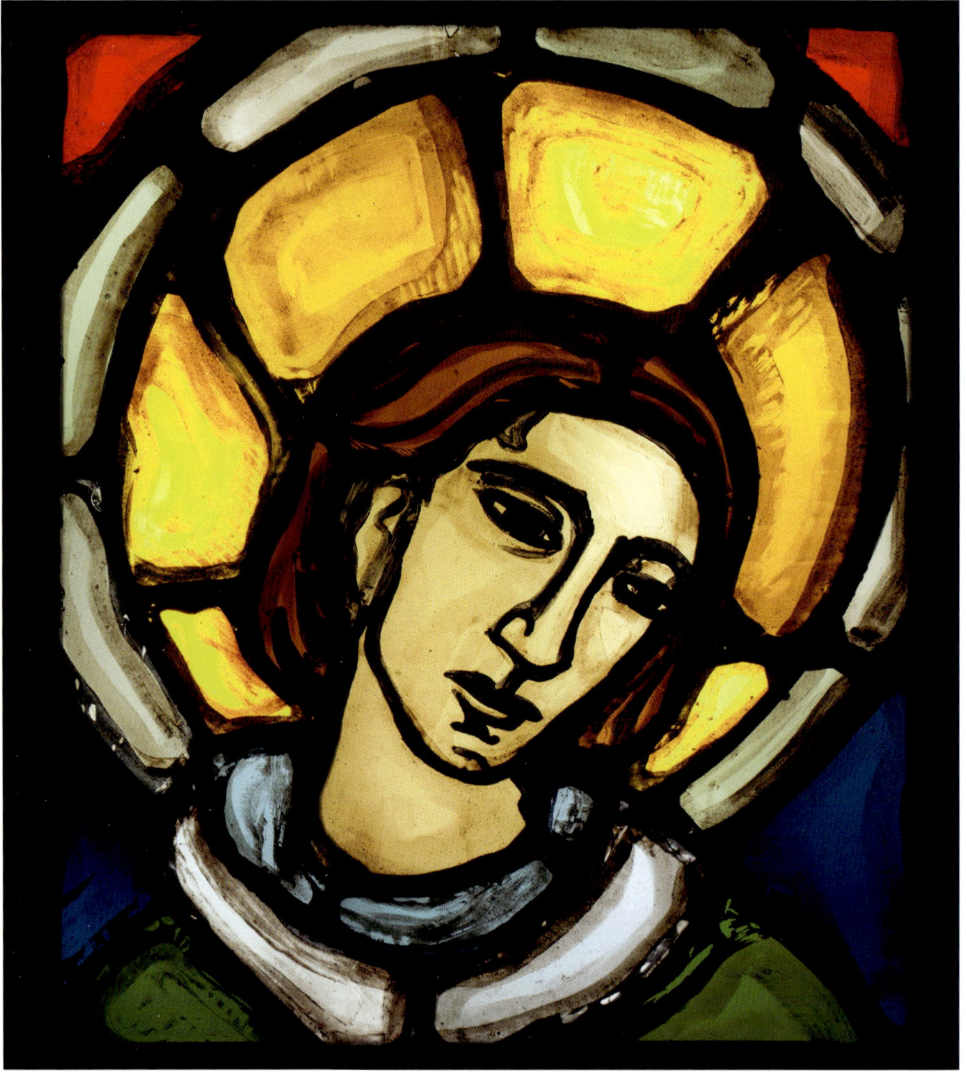

Evie Hone, *Head of St John* (*c*.1949). © Geraldine Hone, Kate Hone and the Friends of the National Collections of Ireland. Photo © National Gallery of Ireland

tree to represent Kildare (*Cill Dara*, meaning 'church of the oak') where St Brigid founded her convent; St Colmcille departing for Iona; St Ita's dream of receiving three precious stones which represent the Trinity. The rich colours of the windows are tempered by the lightly matted quarries used for the background and Healy took particular interest in the hand-lettering for each saint's name. Before being dispatched to Ballyhaunis the windows 'were exhibited on loan by special request in New York and Boston, and excited much interest in the minds of competent judges in America including Ralph Adams Cram, the world renowned ecclesiastical architect ...'[7]

Evie Hone, who was mentored by Healy at An Túr Gloine, is represented by five small panels; these come from approximately 150 panels which she created throughout her highly productive twenty-year stained glass career, in addition to about fifty or so large schemes created for architectural contexts.[8] Three of the panels were conceived as autonomous works of art, the earliest of which is *St Christopher* (1944) and which is based on a medieval carved stone panel in Jerpoint Abbey, Co. Kilkenny. It was presented to the gallery through FNCI in memory of Dr Michael Wynne, keeper of the gallery and a pioneering researcher of Ireland's stained glass heritage who was a particular enthusiast of Evie Hone. *The Cock and the Pot*, also known as *The Betrayal* (1945), may look like a piece of tracery but is also an autonomous panel. *Resurrection* dates from *c.*1947 and significantly Hone did not mean the title to indicate the resurrection of Christ, but the general concept of re-birth.[9] The other two panels featuring heads are studies or tests for larger windows which Hone made for English locations: *Head of St John* (*c.*1949) is a study for *The Crucifixion, with the Blessed Virgin Mary and St John* in St Mary's church, Downe, Kent, and *Heads of two Apostles* (1952) is a trial piece for two of the disciples in her magnum opus, *The Crucifixion and Last Supper*, in Eton College's chapel, Berkshire.[10]

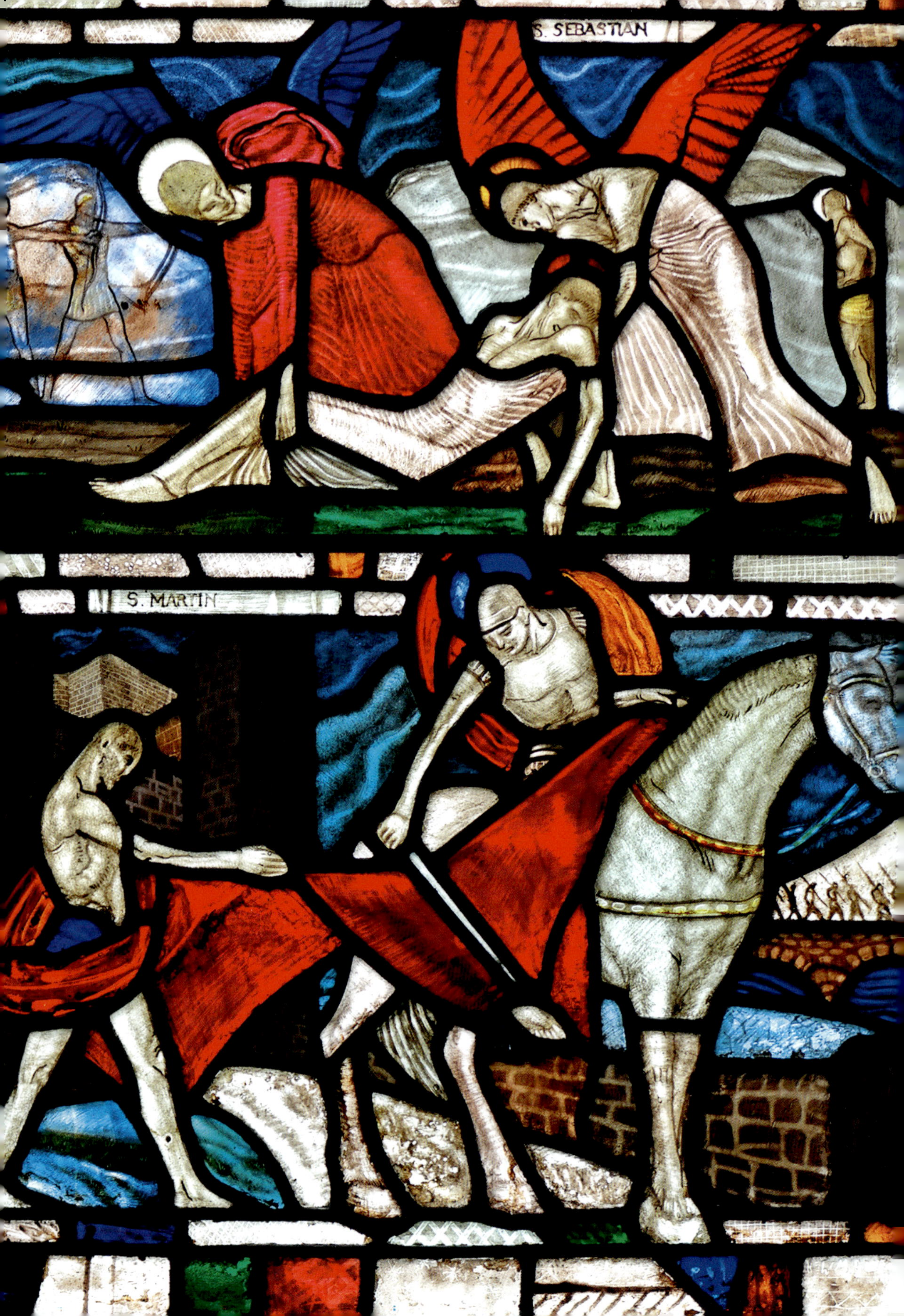
S. SEBASTIAN
S. MARTIN

St Ann's church (C of I)

Dawson Street, D02 YV00

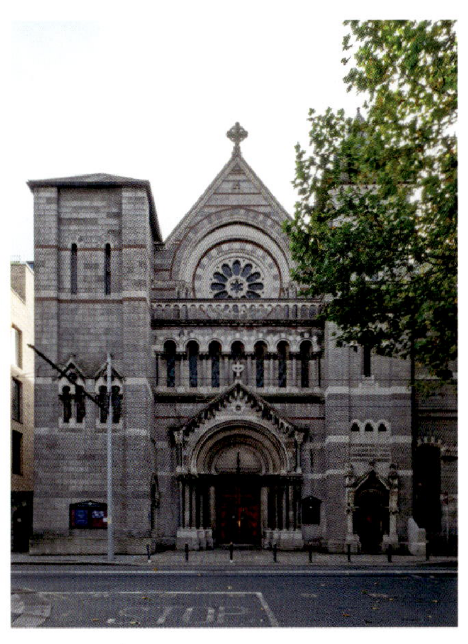

While the interior of the church dates to 1719, it gained its exuberant Lombardo-Romanesque façade 150 years later courtesy of architect Thomas Newenham Deane. The exterior, best appreciated when approached via South Anne Street, is composed of Wicklow granite with dressings of grey limestone, Portland stone and distinctive red sandstone. Two sturdy towers flank the entrance portal surmounted by an arcade and above it, a wheel window. Beyond the lofty entrance vestibule one enters the early eighteenth-century galleried hall, which aside from some fine stained glass, features excellent woodcarving and novel features such as the bread shelves in the apse where fresh loaves are placed in accordance with Baron Butler's enduring bequest of 1723.

(opposite) Wilhelmina Geddes, detail of St Martin and St Sebastian panels from *Archangels Raphael, Michael and Jacob's Angel, with Joshua, Gideon's Vision, David and Jonathan, Saints Longinus, Sebastian and George* (1918). © The Brothers Kerr

As St Ann's was one of Dublin's most well-to-do churches, which originally housed canopied pews reserved for the archbishop of Dublin and the duke of Leinster, it is not surprising that the stained glass is generally of a high order. The largest windows are all at gallery level, ten in total and with a further three in the apse, mostly created in the mid–late nineteenth century by the London firms of Heaton, Butler & Bayne, William Warrington & Son, and O'Connor, though one window from the 1860s is by Dublin company Earley & Powell, and there is also a 1970s replacement window.[1]

In terms of twentieth-century stained glass, the most interesting windows in St Ann's are undoubtedly those made at An Túr Gloine, particularly two designed and made by Wilhelmina Geddes, a small window by Ethel Rhind, and one which the two artists jointly created; these were all made between 1913 and 1918 and they can be found under the galleries. Wilhelmina Geddes had attended the Belfast School of Art, as had Rhind, her senior by ten years. They both gravitated to Dublin, Rhind in 1906 and Geddes five years later, and both attended A.E. Child's stained glass classes at the Dublin Metropolitan School of Art and joined An Túr Gloine, of which he was manager, and where it seems they probably first met and in time would become firm friends.

When one of St Ann's parishioners, Miss Charlotte Dooner of Orwell Road, died aged 100 her nephew, Col. William Toke Dooner, decided he would erect a window to her memory and approached An Túr Gloine probably in late summer 1913. Sarah Purser, who had founded An Túr Gloine and was pivotal to its continued success, would match up artist with patron, and chose Geddes to undertake the commission, and maybe as Miss Dooner had been a generous benefactor to St Ann's, *Charity* was deemed an appropriate theme. Geddes prepared a small-scale sketch for the window and on 20 October the vicar presented the sketch to the vestry for approval which was forthcoming. This would be Wilhelmina Geddes's first window for a Dublin church and she began making it on 15 November. Like the majority of windows beneath the galleries it is a small window, just 3ft 10⅝in. high by 5ft 6¾in. wide, and the cost, reflecting the modest scale, was £40.[2]

The enthroned woman in the centre is an allegorical figure representing Charity

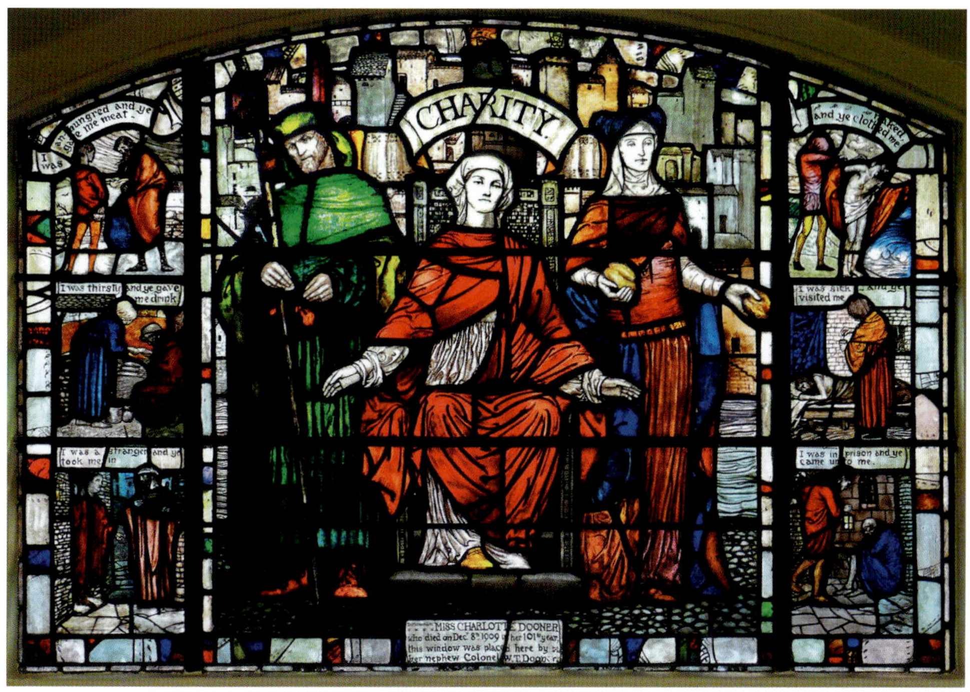

Wilhelmina Geddes, *Charity* (1913). © The Brothers Kerr

and she is a commanding presence with arms outstretched, perhaps in a gesture of giving but also, it would appear, to demonstrate her precedence over the Good Samaritan and the Virtuous Woman who flank her.[3] With her inscrutable appearance it is difficult to ascribe a particular age to her, though one would not guess that her features are actually based on those of Geddes's 20-year-old sister, Florence. Noteworthy is that the Virtuous Woman is depicted distributing loaves of bread, no doubt a reference to the real loaves that are a constant presence on the bread shelves in the apse. The three figures' costumes and the urban cityscape behind them evoke a medieval context, and either side are three small panels which collectively illustrate six of the seven Corporal Works of Mercy (Matthew 25:34–6), and the relevant quotations are inscribed in archaic lettering on parchment-like scrolls. There is a didactic aspect to the window with each of the six panels depicting two figures; one administering a practical application of charity and the other receiving its benefit. The colour palette of the window is restrained with plenty of pale quarries, reds and

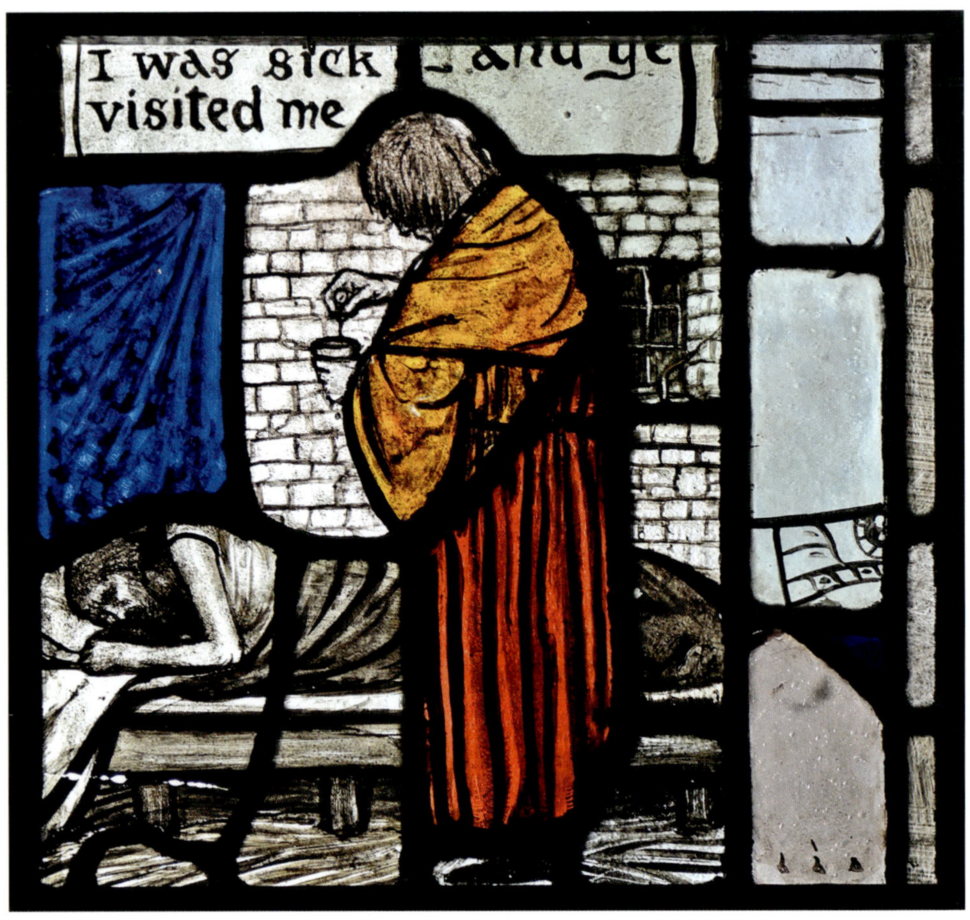

Wilhelmina Geddes, detail of *Charity* (1913). © The Brothers Kerr

ochres with accents of midnight blue and deep green. Ultimately, the expressions of the figures and their activities convey that this is a serious window created to convey the obligations of Christian duty without any associated hint of personal reward. Geddes completed the window by mid-December 1913 and it was fixed in place in early January; subsequent to the window being installed, external construction in recent decades necessitated it be artificially lit.

In summer 1915 Misses Olave Charlotte, Mary Dorothy and Harriet Emily Reed of Lansdowne Road, the three daughters of Sir Andrew and Dame Elizabeth Mary Reed, approached An Túr Gloine with a view to ordering a window for St Ann's in

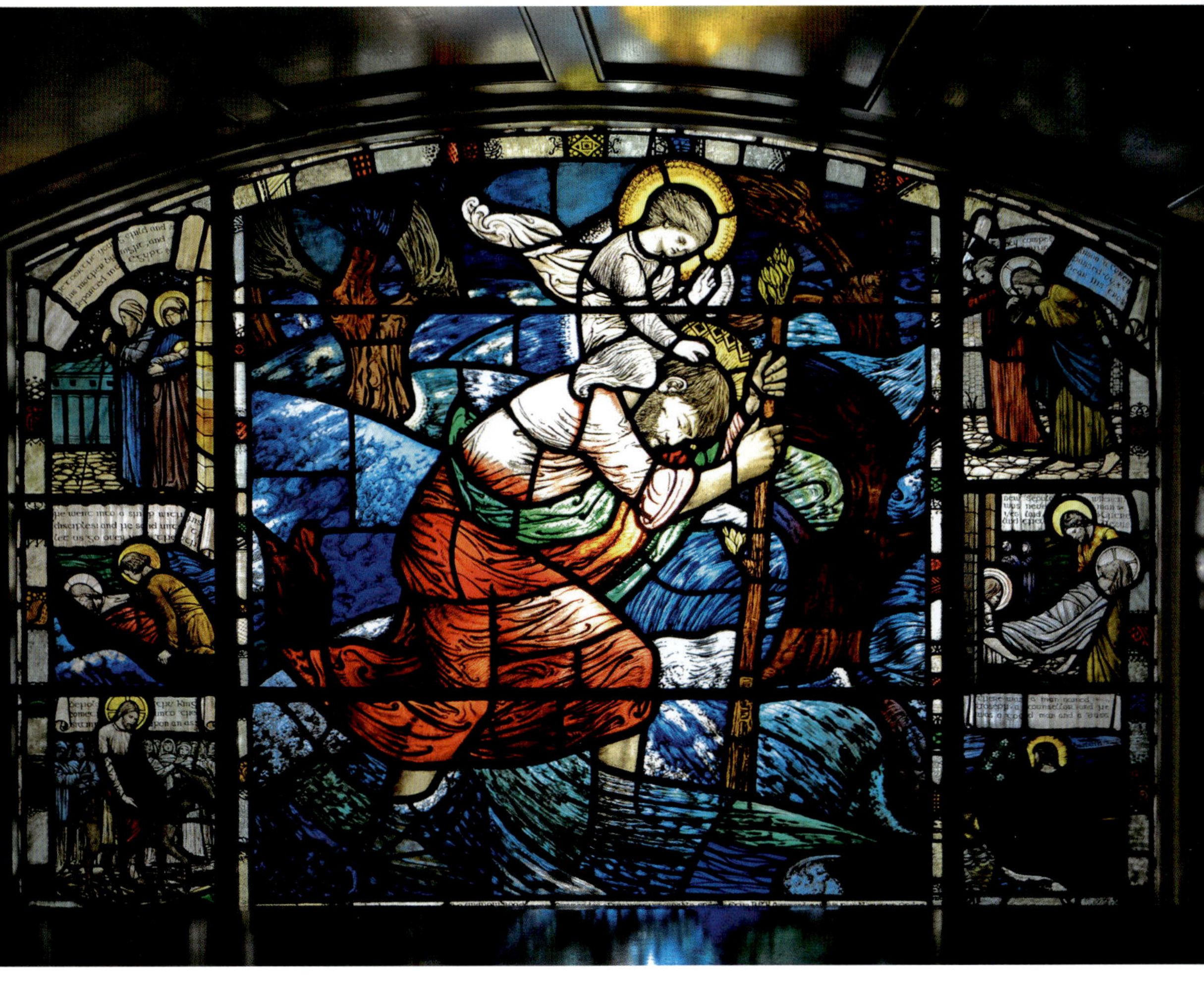

Wilhelmina Geddes (with Ethel Rhind), *St Christopher* (1916). © The Brothers Kerr

memory of their late parents, parishioners who had also been married in the church, and Sarah Purser again entrusted the commission to Wilhelmina Geddes. The subject selected was St Christopher carrying the Christ Child, and so this window continued the general theme of Charity and would also be erected in the south wall adjacent to the earlier window. Sir Andrew Reed, a former vestryman of St Ann's, was one of the pivotal figures in Irish police history known for his hands-on approach who had risen to the rank of inspector-general of the RIC and Geddes's depiction of St Christopher

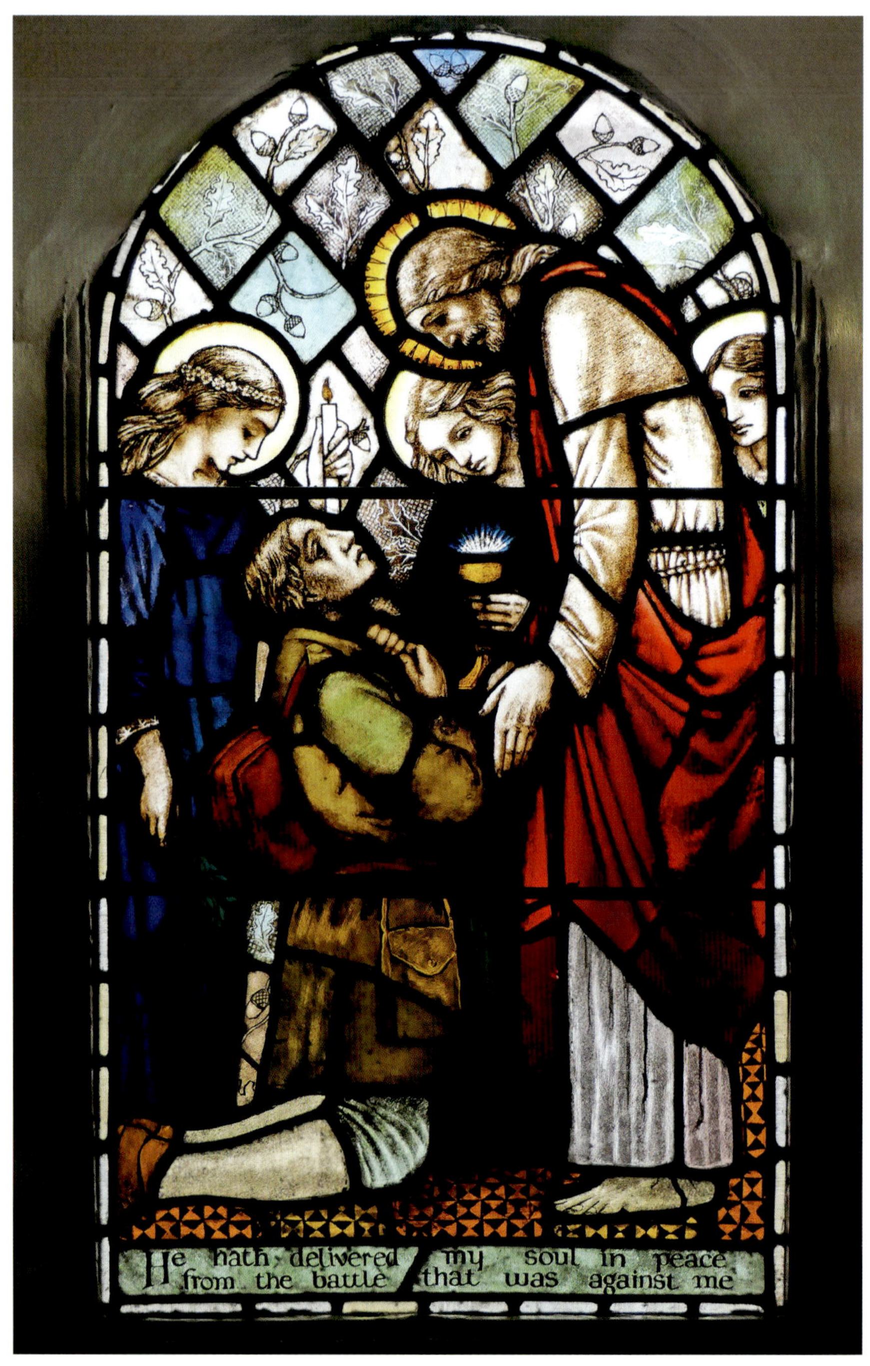
He hath delivered my soul in peace
from the battle that was against me

carrying the Christ Child while he strides across a raging torrent with the tiny infant clinging to the saint presents an image of masculine determination and heroism.

The overall composition of the window echoes that of *Charity*, with three smaller panels either side that illustrate the general theme of serving Christ. In a letter written to Sarah Purser from Belfast, Wilhelmina Geddes explained the choices: 'The last of the six, St Joseph going to Britain, stands for a sort of missionary idea. As for the rest, the other St Joseph is taking Christ into Egypt, St Peter ferrying him in his boat, the Donkey carrying him, St Simon carrying his cross, St Joseph of Arimathea lifting him into his tomb; and they are all carrying him, or something belonging to him, like St Christopher.'[4]

Throughout much of 1915 Geddes had been unwell; mental and physical health issues dominated much of her life and she would regularly retreat back to her family in Belfast for support though paradoxically the home environment could often be fraught. On 18 January 1916 the Misses Reed received approval for their parents' memorial window from the vestry, and in addition to this commission Geddes was committed to two substantial orders for Presbyterian clients – completing a 3-light for Christ Church in Rathgar, Dublin, and a making a 4-light for the Presbyterian Assembly Hall, Belfast. However, as her health began to buckle under increasing strain exacerbated by the recent death of her father, Ethel Rhind took over responsibility for *St Christopher*; using Geddes's sketch design she drew up the full-scale cartoon and painted all the glass. The figures in the six side panels lack Geddes's ease of gesture and ability to convey mood, which are evident in the equivalent panels in *Charity*, and instead Rhind focused more on detailed facial expressions. Likewise, whereas Geddes's hand lettering appeared organic and natural, Rhind's treatment of the text in a precise lower-case Celtic style has a certain sterility. Most of all, the figure of St Christopher with the Christ Child lacks the physicality and drama that Geddes could impart when painting her figures.

The window was dedicated on 2 August and it was reported in the press as being the work of Miss Rhind, which is fair as her hand is definitely much more evident

(opposite) Ethel Rhind, '*He Hath Delivered my Soul in Peace from the Battle of War that was Against Me*' (1916)

than Geddes in the end result.[5] The following day Mary Dorothy Reed, the middle of the three sisters, got married in St Ann's to the Revd John Powell, rector of Howth. It is worth noting that the window was originally sited where the door in the south wall is now (inserted *c.*1970s), and unfortunately the window being slightly larger than the ope into which it was relocated, the bottom line of the inscription now presents a challenge to the viewer.[6] Like *Charity*, the window is now also artificially lit.

In late February 1916 Annie Bell of Morehampton Road requested permission from the vestry to erect a window in memory of her only son Ray Lancaster Bell, second lieutenant in the Royal Dublin Fusiliers, who had been killed in action near Ypres seven months previously. Alfred and Annie Bell were of relatively modest means and the window selected, either by the Bells or the vestry, was the smallest one in the church; located in the north-west corner, it is a mere 3ft 6in. high by 21½in. wide. The permission came with a condition: while Ethel Rhind's coloured sketch was approved it was 'subject to the substitution of a khaki tunic for the woolcoat on the soldier.'[7] Rhind's window depicts a kneeling soldier being comforted by Christ while three young women, all with halos, gather close, one offering the soldier a chalice, and another illuminating the group with a candle. The face of the soldier is a likeness of Ray Bell, and with his britches and small leather knapsack he looks like a teenager, which he was, though he was 6ft 5in. tall which may account for Rhind's depiction of him kneeling. In the background Rhind included finely drawn acorns and oak leaves on the pale quarries, the kind of nature-inspired details that the studio manager, A.E. Child, would have taught her and approved of. Ray Bell's memorial window was fixed in place on 24 June 1916 and cost the couple £17.

When two members of the congregation, law graduates Ernest Lawrence Julian and Robert Hornidge Cullinan, died from sniper fire at Gallipoli on the same day in August 1915 their friends decided to erect a window to their memory and chose the last available window in St Ann's, the south-west corner under the gallery.[8] Wilhelmina Geddes was again called upon to prepare a small-scale design and this was submitted to the vicar and approved by the vestry on 1 February 1918. This is undoubtedly her finest window in the church, one of several war memorials that she created during these years. The first of these had the most prestigious client and location, the duke of Connaught and the 3-light was destined for St Bartholomew's, the parish church of Government House in Ottawa, and she laboured on it over four years. Her window for Dawson Street would be her first Irish war memorial, followed soon after by a trio of lancet windows for All Saints, Carysfort Avenue, Blackrock. Sarah Purser clearly recognized Geddes's suitability for war memorial windows as she had the ability to depict heroic male figures whose features could be subtly idealized yet would be completely believable and could transcend time so that Geddes's saints and archangels with their cropped hair looked modern and vital, even when decked out in medieval armour.

Geddes titled her window *Archangels Raphael, Michael and Jacob's Angel, with Joshua, Gideon's Vision, David and Jonathan, Saints Longinus, Sebastian and George*, though the principal figure is that of Archangel Michael who dominates the window. Although the composition is similar to her designs for the two adjacent windows, this time she allowed much more space for the side panels so that their width actually exceeds that of the central panel which may explain why the archangel is singularly tall and slim. Geddes depicts him as an assured, athletic young man, firmly clasping his unsheathed sword having vanquished the serpent at his feet. Dressed in ruby and indigo over silver armour and chain mail, his wide wings, poised as if for further action, project into the top two side panels with dramatic effect. Geddes expert, Nicola Gordon Bowe, noted that 'for the first time in glass, Geddes has freely interpreted her studies of Romanesque, Gothic and Byzantine art in her own idiosyncratic idiom.'[9] Surrounding the archangel, as if to emphasize his commanding status, are diminutive military and missionary martyrs, two of which are dressed in khaki to represent the deceased soldiers.

The side panels are a particular triumph, reliant on bold gestures to convey the narrative, each one is a carefully considered gem. Noteworthy is the depiction of St Sebastian whose limp corpse is lifted by two angels while the scene that led to his death, archers firing arrows as he is bound to a stake, plays in the background. Below it is a scene of Roman soldier St Martin of Tours on horseback who has halted to divide his cloak in two for the benefit of a naked beggar, and in the background one can see his fellow soldiers marching in lockstep across a bridge oblivious to his charitable deed.

In this memorial window Geddes incorporated richer tones than in her previous windows, though as in *Charity*, glowing red still dominates. She also used plenty of

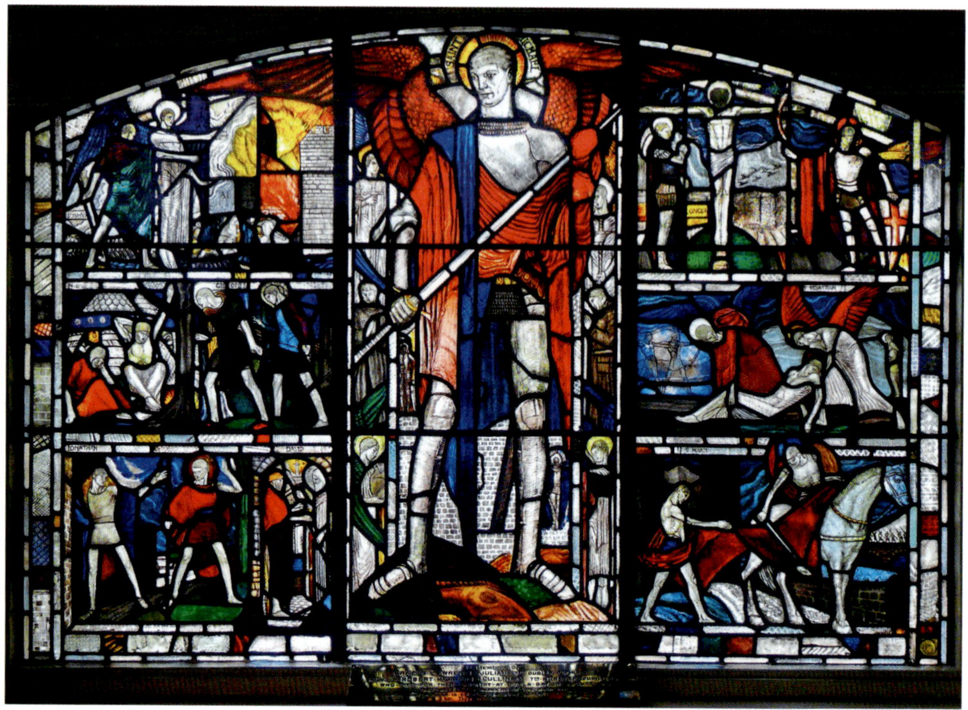

(above) Wilhelmina Geddes, *Archangels Raphael, Michael and Jacob's Angel, with Joshua, Gideon's Vision, David and Jonathan, Saints Longinus, Sebastian and George* (1918). © The Brothers Kerr; (opposite) Wilhelmina Geddes, detail of St Michael from *Archangels Raphael, Michael and Jacob's Angel, with Joshua, Gideon's Vision, David and Jonathan, Saints Longinus, Sebastian and George* (1918). © The Brothers Kerr

white glass, subtly matted, which Child and his mentor Christopher Whall favoured; this may have been partly due to adjacent buildings that reduced the amount of natural light. In the very bottom right corner of the window Geddes' initials are visible, something she did not regularly include but perhaps an indication of her satisfaction with the outcome. Beside it, but difficult to discern, is the circular *Déanta in Éirinn* (Made in Ireland) trademark that Purser championed. When Geddes received a cheque from Purser after An Túr Gloine was paid £84 in early December 1918, she thanked her and added she 'really [did] hope to lead a better life next year',[10] perhaps a reference to overcoming the health issues that had plagued her in recent years.

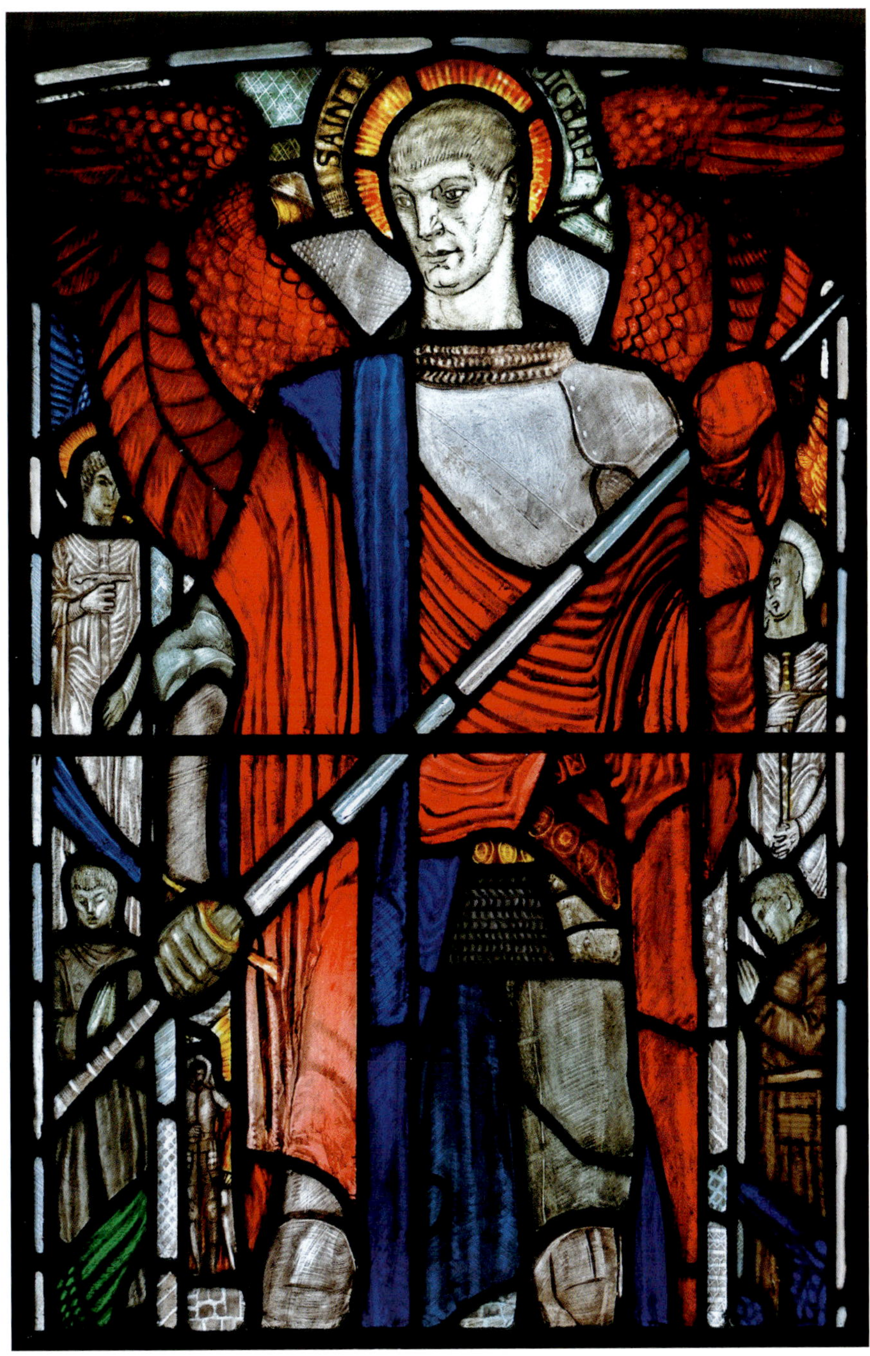

ST ANN'S CHURCH (C OF I), DAWSON STREET

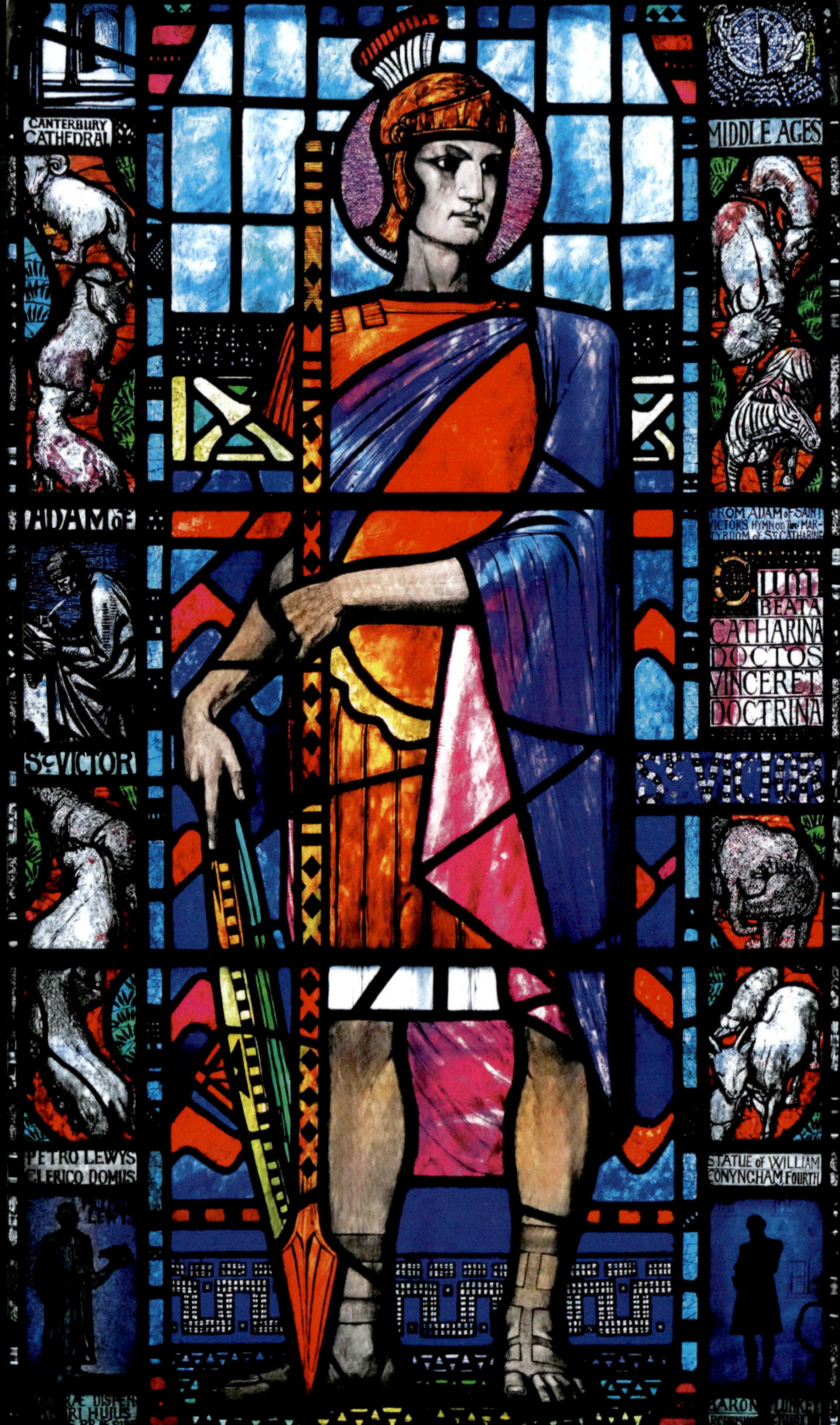

CANTERBURY CATHEDRAL
MIDDLE AGES
ADAM OF
FROM ADAM OF SAINT VICTORS HYMN ON THE MARTYRDOM OF St CATHARINE
CUM BEATA CATHARINA DOCTOS VINCERET DOCTRINA
St VICTOR
St VICTOR
PETRO LEWYS CLERICO DOMUS
STATUE OF WILLIAM CONYNGHAM, FOURTH

St Catherine and St James's church (C of I)

Donore Avenue, D08 R6YC

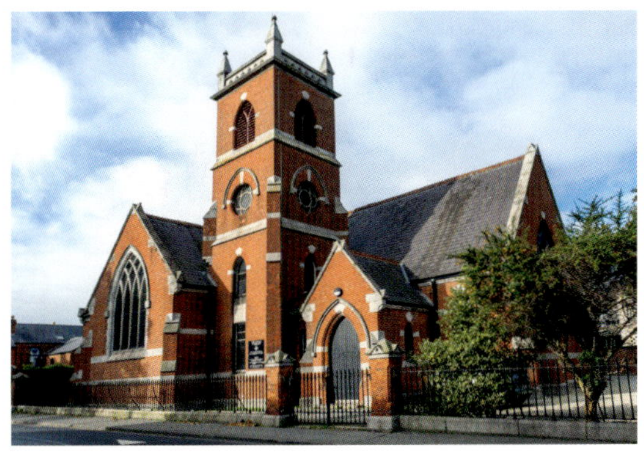

This unassuming red-bricked structure with dressings of granite ashlar and a low tower was designed by Robert Stirling in 1896 as a chapel of ease to St Catherine's in Thomas Street; it was also named St Catherine's though two successive name changes followed in due course. The church's low scale fits comfortably with the late Victorian and Edwardian red-bricked houses in the vicinity.

(opposite) Michael Healy, detail of *St Victor* (1930)

THE HIGHLIGHTS OF St Catherine and St Jame's church are three lancet windows by Michael Healy which span a decade-and-a-half of the middle period of his stained glass career at An Túr Gloine. All three windows were erected in memory of local teachers and it is understood that the incumbent, Revd (later Canon) Hugh Walter Brownlow Thompson, was instrumental in the selection of Healy as the artist; he had previously been curate at Holy Trinity church, Rathmines, and while there Healy created a large 4-light window (1909) for the church which had presumably impressed him.

Revd Thompson departed Rathmines to become rector of St Catherine's in 1912. Two years later he enlarged the church with the addition of a chancel and transepts, and by November of the same year Michael Healy had started making his first window for the church; the subject was an allegorical figure representing *Spes* (Hope) and it was in memory of a former teacher, Mrs Frances Day. Healy depicted Hope as a woman resting against an anchor, the symbol of hope which is grounded in faith. Robed in emerald green, her attention is focused on a single bloom at the end of the dry spindly twig she holds, and at her feet crocuses and other small flowers bloom suggesting the promise of spring.[1] A broad border of decorative architecture surrounds the figure – a fanciful confection of turrets, pink-tiled roofs, crenelations, arches and windows – which is in marked contrast to the restrained, low-key architecture of the actual church. The end result conjures up a medieval cityscape, and one wonders if this reflects some input from Revd Thompson who was known for his keen interest in Dublin's history.[2]

In 1923 following the sudden death of Miss Jane Elizabeth Matthews, assistant teacher in St Catherine's Day and Sunday School, there was a public subscription to erect a window to her memory to be placed directly opposite *Hope* on the north wall. The subject was St Catherine of Alexandria, and Healy has depicted her as a handsome woman with her traditional attributes, a crown to reflect her royal status and a large wheel on which she was martyred by evil Emperor Maxentius. Into her outstretched hand a dove drops a morsel of bread referencing the period she spent imprisoned by Maxentius when it was her only sustenance. In contrast to the elegant dove depicted mid-flight, Healy has included, either side of it, a long,

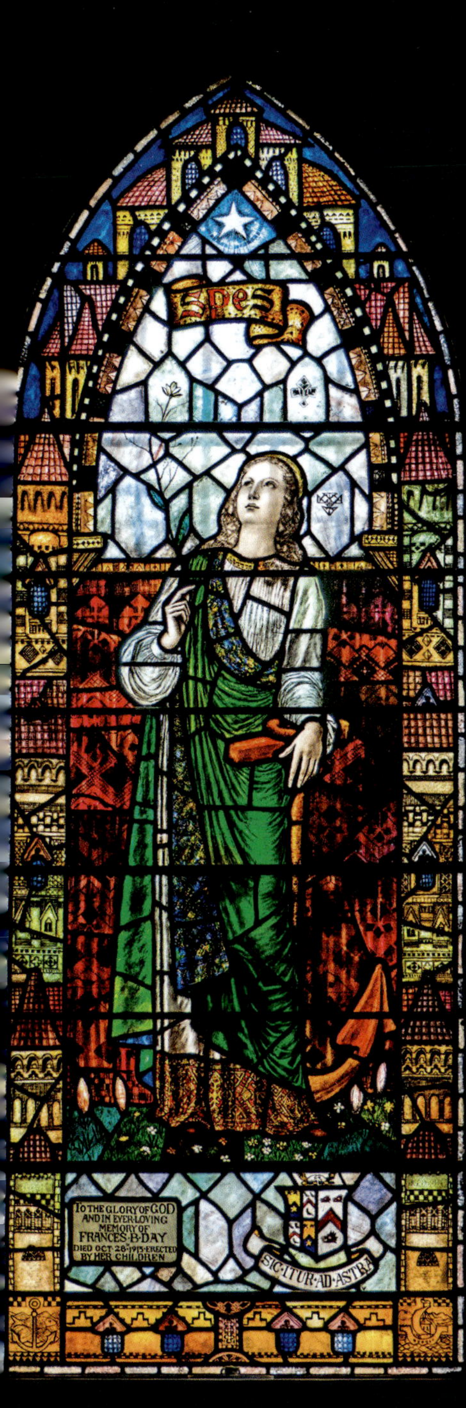

Michael Healy, *Hope* (1915)

scaly serpent ('the spiritual adversary of the saints of God'),[3] skilfully fashioned from two layers of acided, painted and stained flashed glass that have been plated together. Seated at the base of the window is a young boy holding an open volume – perhaps referencing Elizabeth Matthew's role as a teacher, or of St Catherine's study of philosophy – though his attention is distracted from his studies and poignantly he appears to be focused on the large metal-studded wheel with rope attached, the object of Catherine's martyrdom. In the apex of the lancet Healy has depicted a trio of solicitous angels carefully laying out the saint's shrouded corpse, ahead of transporting her earthly remains to a monastery at the foot of Mount Sinai.

As with many of Healy's windows, in addition to the principal narratives, there are small vignettes to which the eye is irresistibly drawn. In this instance they mainly fall into two categories. There is a series of five border panels stained and painted to resemble beaten bronze repoussé work which tell the story of the Victory of the Cross, including a kneeling soldier representing the spread of Christianity among the emperor's army, a rhetorician on the left, and a philosopher on the right.[4] Contrasting with these are four border panels featuring a blue river with steep

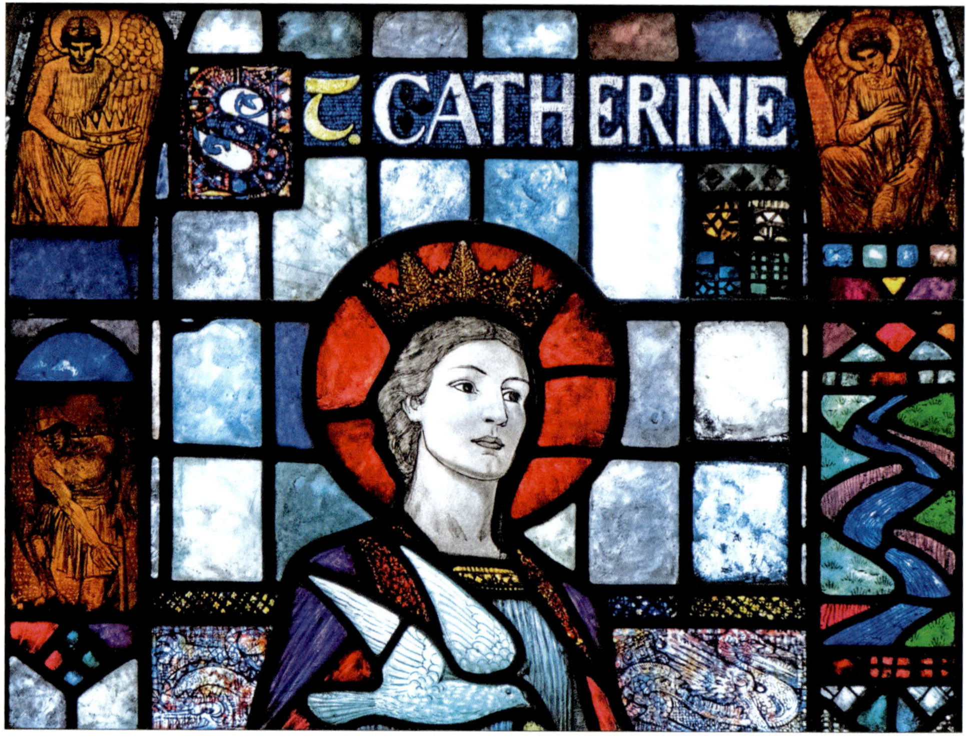

Michael Healy, detail of *St Catherine* (1923)

pink and mauve banks, meandering through lush, verdant vegetation. The obvious assumption would be that this represents the Nile given St Catherine's association with the port city of Alexandria but Revd Thompson, with his passion for local history, had an entirely different intention: the winding river actually represents the Poddle, one of Dublin's ancient and largely invisible waterways that passes underground adjacent to the church. Fittingly, the blue glass was sourced by An Túr Gloine in Dublin, almost certainly at one of the bottle manufacturers in Ringsend, and most likely the type of glass used for bottles marked 'poison'. In case the Poddle reference was perceived as too secular or parochial, Revd Thompson pointed out that the four panels also had a theological basis; the four flowing rivers are an early Christian symbol of the writings of the Evangelists whose words fertilize and enrich human life.[5]

Two other small panels are worth noting. Behind the boy is the tree of knowledge with a serpent coiled around its broad trunk symbolizing the Fall of Man. Opposite

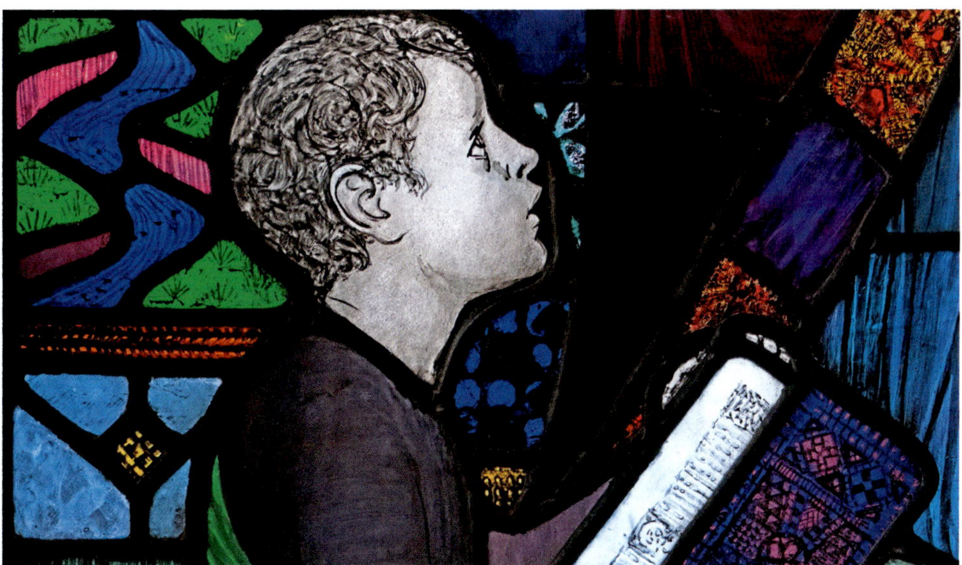

Michael Healy, detail of *St Catherine* (1923)

is an elegant queen in profile, dressed in mint green, who is almost certainly Valeria Maximilla, wife of Emperor Maxentius. She visited Catherine in prison and castigated her husband who then had her put to death.

Healy completed *St Catherine* at the end of November, less than three months after he had received diocesan approval for his preliminary sketch design, which would suggest he worked on it very intensively. The cost of the 8ft tall window was £103 and it was dedicated two days before Christmas 1923. The following year Revd Thompson was appointed editor of the *Church of Ireland Gazette*, a role he would combine with his clerical duties, and in which he would regularly feature short articles lauding An Túr Gloine's latest achievements. These articles almost suggested an official endorsement of the studio and contributed to An Túr Gloine's success in securing orders throughout the island from Church of Ireland clerics and laity.

When Mrs Hannah Bailey, the former principal of St Catherine's School, died in 1929 it was hardly surprising that a decision was made to erect a window in her memory as had been done for her two former colleagues. The location chosen was in the north wall and would be located next to *St Catherine*. The choice of the subject this time was St Victor to whom the church had been rededicated at Revd

Thompson's instigation in order to revive a link with the twelfth-century abbey of St Thomas located near Thomas Street which was administered by the canons of St Victor. The parish's select vestry approved Michael Healy's preliminary design on 30 March 1930 and it subsequently received sanction from the archbishop of Dublin on 23 May.[6]

St Victor of Marseille was a Roman soldier who suffered martyrdom for his steadfast Christian faith. Healy depicted him with helmet, spear and shield utilizing a combination of orange, streaky purple and expensive gold-pink glass which contrast with the saint's light brown skin tone, a reference to his north African origins. Beneath him, in chunky decorative san serif letters painted on etched and stained ruby flashed glass, are the words *Fight the Good Fight* (from *St Paul's First Epistle to Timothy*) which is also the title of a popular hymn.

Echoing the overall design of *St Catherine*, Healy has introduced plenty of small panels in the broad border surrounding St Victor and again they fall into two main categories: the first is a series of animals, both wild and domestic, forming a cavalcade led by a carefree young child which is inspired by a quotation from Isaiah ('The wolf shall dwell with the lamb and the leopard will lay down with the kid, and the calf and the lion and the fatling together, and a little child shall lead them'), and second a series of vignettes related to the history of the parish which almost amounts to a visual explanation for why the church had been rededicated to St Victor. This latter selection is the more intriguing and conveniently Revd Thompson has left an account of their significance.

Mid-way up the left border Healy has depicted in wood-cut fashion 'Adam of St Victor', quill in hand, who was the abbot of the abbey of St Thomas in 1290. In the opposite border Healy has included an extract from Adam's *Hymn on the Martyrdom of St Catherine* – 'Cum beata Catherine doctos vinceret doctrina' – which harks back to Healy's earlier window.

Higher up on the left side there is a small monochrome vignette depicting the Becket chapel in Canterbury cathedral, which alludes to the fact that St Thomas's abbey was named in memory of St Thomas à Becket, archbishop of Canterbury. The vignette in the right border opposite shows two angels spinning an armillary sphere (a model of the presumed orbits of the sun and planets). It is titled 'Science

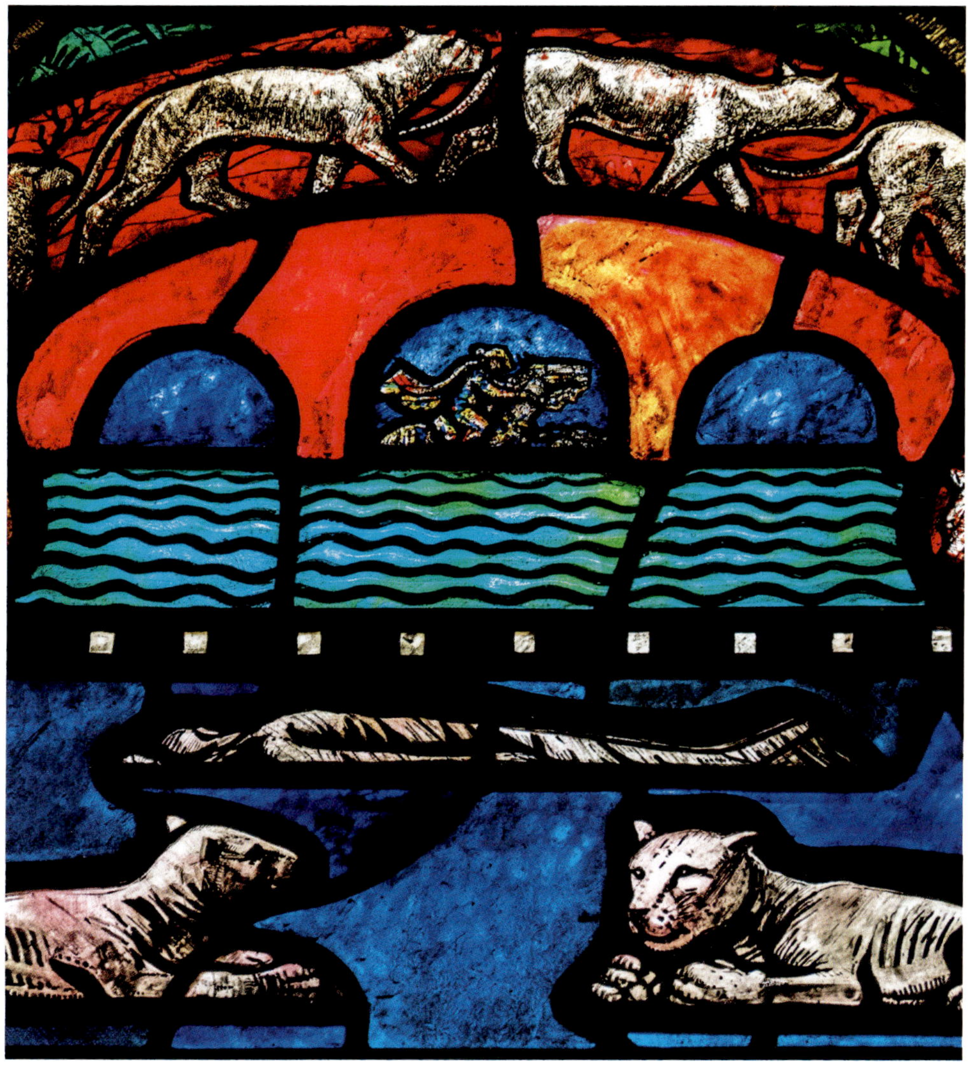

Michael Healy, detail of *St Victor* (1930)

of the Middle Ages' and references the fact that the Congregation of St Victor were renowned for their scientific erudition during this period.

Also on the left side, Healy has included an image of Sir Peter Lewis, the first post-Reformation vicar of St Catherine's, and Revd Thompson, who was the thirty-third incumbent of the same position, had a particular interest in Lewis and lectured on the subject.[7] Healy's depiction of Lewis is based on two carved stone panels of the cleric that were removed from the old Bridge of Athlone and deposited in the National Museum where Healy would have received permission to sketch them. Lewis is shown displaying an animal, thought to be a rat, on the palm of his hand. The scene at the apex of the lancet window is a stylized depiction of the nine-arched Bridge of Athlone that Lewis built over the Shannon in 1566–7. Lewis was an accomplished architect and master mason and in addition to this bridge is also credited with rebuilding the crypt of Christ Church cathedral. Beneath the bridge's centre arch there is a tiny figure on horseback wading across the Shannon which is the Dutch general Godard van Reede who was commander of the Williamite forces in Ireland. Below the Shannon are two lionesses guarding the body of St Victor.

At the base of the window Healy has included a little scene featuring the neo-classical sanctuary of St Catherine's church, Thomas Street, which was Donore Avenue's parent church. Almost opposite Healy included a silhouette of the statue of Archbishop Plunkett in Kildare Street as it was he who laid the foundation stone of the Donore Avenue church; additionally the Church of Ireland training college where Mrs Bailey and her colleagues had trained had been based in Kildare Place, Kildare Street. Behind the statue Healy has painted the door and windows of a since demolished Georgian house.

An Túr Gloine sent the bill (£108) for the window on 28 November 1930 indicating that it had been completed by this date. Unfortunately Revd Thompson never got to see the finished window as he died suddenly in April of that year, and so the window into which he poured so much of his own extensive knowledge of the parish's history became a memorial to him as well as to Mrs Bailey.

Over two decades later, in 1952, Revd Thompson's son and daughter commissioned a window in memory of both their parents to be situated in the south wall opposite *St Victor*.[8] At this stage Healy was dead eleven years and the only remaining artist at An Túr Gloine was Catherine O'Brien so she undertook the job. The subject was St Colmcille and while the overall design nods to *St Victor*, O'Brien's window lacks Healy's finesse and his painterly skills, however her strong colour palette and simplified style has a charming folk art quality. The main feature of the window is the standing

Catherine O'Brien, detail of *St Columba* (1952)

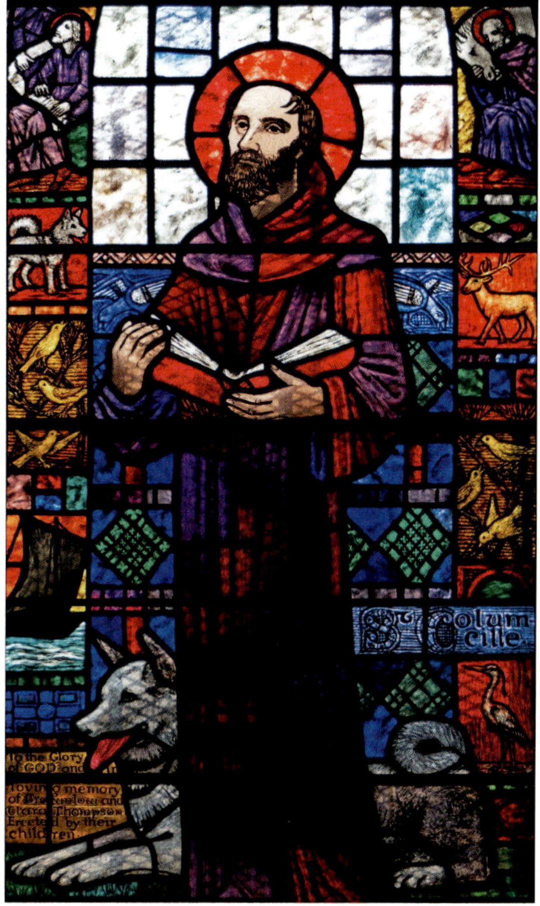

figure of St Colmcille holding an open volume, perhaps his famous *Cathach*, and lost in reverie.

There are some interesting images that are contained in the window which were requested by the donors, specifically the large Norwegian elkhound resting at the saint's feet and two small border panels featuring three canaries in each; one might assume that these were cherished pets which belonged to Canon Thompson and his wife but there is no way of knowing.[9] A standing elkhound and a stag also feature separately in two of the border panels.

The vignette at the base of the window has an unusual theme, it illustrates an incident before St Colmcille's birth when an angel appeared to his mother and presented her with a cloak richly embroidered with spring flowers. O'Brien has depicted the cloak as comprising patch-work, and floating over Ireland and Scotland, the scenes of the saint's labours.[10] The upper section of the design features the saint three times: in his role translating the gospels, with the white horse that foretold his death, and in the centre, performing his last meditation in his cell.

St Catherine and St James's church also contains another work created at An Túr Gloine; an opus sectile mosaic panel, *Charity* (1928), by Ethel Rhind that was originally made for St Peter's church, Aungier Street (since demolished).

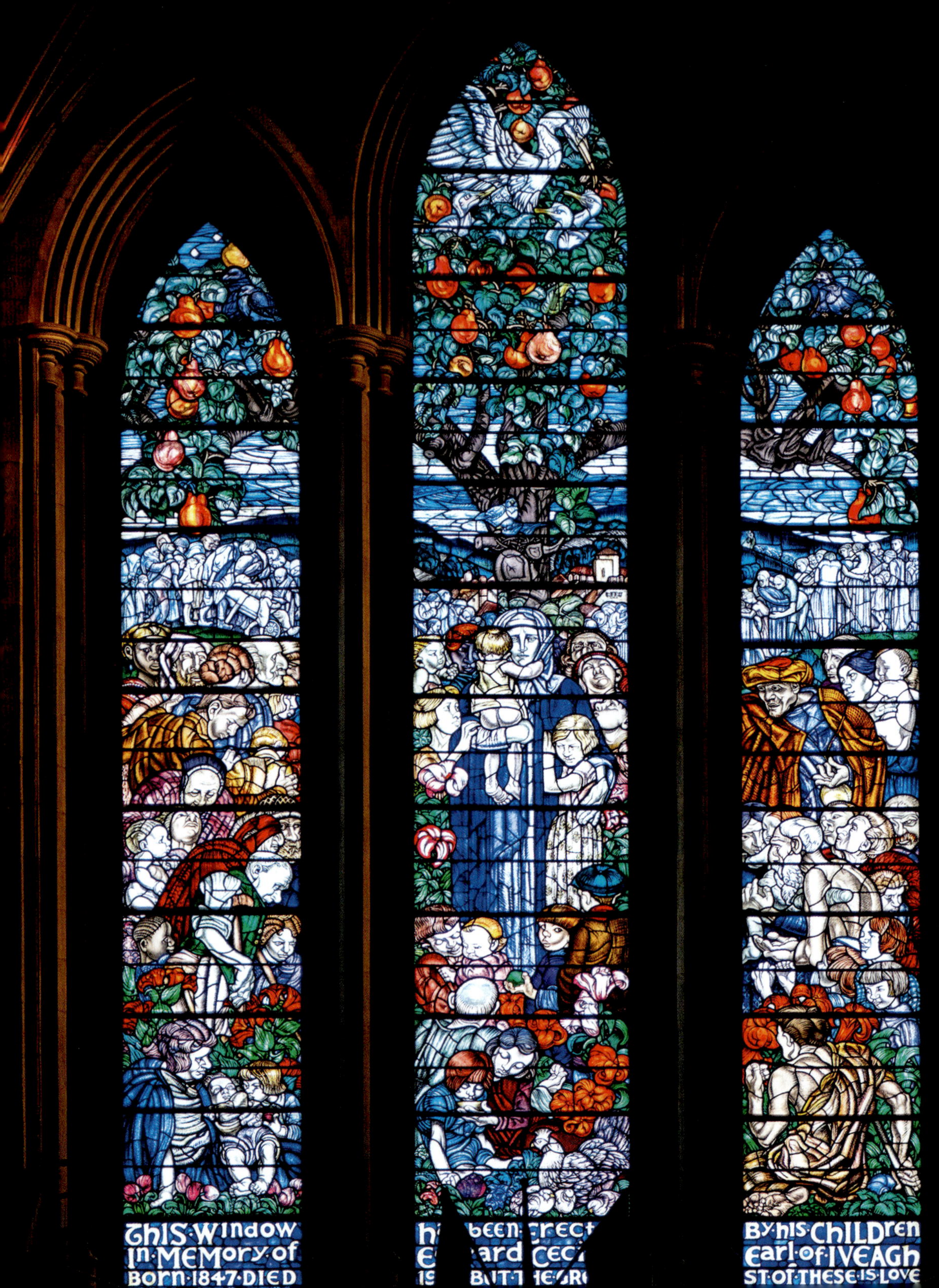
THIS·WINDOW
IN·MEMORY·OF
BORN·1847·DIED
BY·HIS·CHILDREN
EARL·OF·IVEAGH
ST·OF·THESE·IS·LOVE

St Patrick's cathedral (C of I)

St Patrick's Close, D08 H6X3

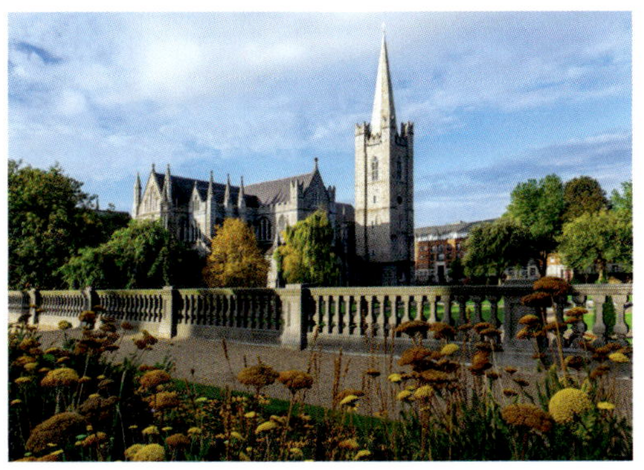

Construction of Ireland's largest cathedral, built on a grand European scale, occurred between 1220 and 1260 though its Gothic features have been much modified over its long life, including the addition of its spire in the mid-eighteenth century. A substantial restoration programme was undertaken in the 1860s, funded by Sir Benjamin Lee Guinness, which is largely responsible for the cathedral's present appearance. The adjoining St Patrick's Park, laid out by his son, the first earl of Iveagh, provides a pleasant setting for the cathedral. The cathedral's interior contains Ireland's largest and richest collection of funerary monuments, though relatively few from the medieval period.

(opposite) Frank Brangwyn, *Charity (Iveagh Memorial Window)* (1937)

St Patrick's cathedral contains a diverse collection of stained glass from a multitude of studios, the vast majority of which dates from a fifty-year period commencing in the mid-1860s. Most of these windows came from prominent London firms such as Clayton & Bell, Heaton, Butler & Bayne, James Powell & Sons and Kemp & Co., though regional firms are also represented including William Wailes of Newcastle-upon-Tyne, Hardman & Co. of Birmingham, and James Ballentine & Son of Edinburgh. Dublin is also represented by Casey Bros., and Barff & Co.[1]

The most interesting twentieth-century stained glass can be found mainly in the north transept which features a preponderance of memorials in stained glass, brass, stone and marble to those who died in various wars. The earliest window of note is, however, not a war memorial but was erected in memory of the Right Hon. Hugh Law, sometime lord chancellor of Ireland, who had died in 1883. The subject is *St Columba*, presumably chosen for his strong Ulster associations as Hugh Law was born in Co. Down and died in Co. Donegal. It was made in 1905 by the English artist Louis Davis (1861–1941) who had trained under the great Arts and Crafts stained glass artist and educator, Christopher Whall. *St Columba* was most likely made at Lowndes & Drury's premises in Park Walk, Chelsea, and either painted by Davis himself or, possibly, by pupils of Whall.[2]

Clean-shaven St Columba, more commonly depicted with a big beard, is accompanied by two pretty ruby-winged angels of identical features; one carries a model of the cathedral bearing his name in Derry (Hugh Law entered parliament as MP for Londonderry), the other a bound volume, the saint's *cathach*, the oldest surviving Irish manuscript. The central trio is completed by two kneeling angels, mirror images of each other; the one below positioned on a patch of verdant grass labelled *Ireland*, and one above on a rocky outcrop labelled *Iona*. Compositionally they are linked together by a flock of mauve doves that have been released from a wicker basket by the 'Irish angel' (which has a replacement head, due to later damage presumably), and in a serpentine line they fly upwards to be warmly greeted by the corresponding angel in Iona, reflecting St Columba's journey as a missionary. The delicately inscribed Latin text *Ecce salutiferam Christi fert nuntia pacem* translates as 'Behold the salutary peace of Christ'.

On the opposite side of the transept is another lancet window, *Cormac of Cashel*, made in 1906–7. The artist was Sarah Purser, and her pencil and watercolour small-scale sketch design for it survives,[3] however it is understood A.E. Child drew up the full-scale cartoon and painted the glass. Ordered by the cathedral's dean from An Túr Gloine at a cost of £100, it was erected 'in memory of the officers, non-commissioned officers and men of the Royal Irish Regiment who fell in the South African War, 1899–1902.' As for the choice of subject, the *Evening Irish Times* noted that Cormac of Cashel was 'equally famous as king, warrior, archbishop and scribe' and that 'the headquarters of the regiment are in Clonmel, in the diocese of Cashel, so that the choice of subject is very appropriate.'[4] Miss Purser's original design had the saint carrying a standard bearing the cross of St George and this was replaced in the actual window by a more appropriate fire-breathing dragon illustrated in the manner of marginalia from manuscripts such as the Book of Kells. Cormac, wearing armour and clutching a bejewelled holy book, appears decidedly middle-aged and forlorn as if his best fighting days are behind him. The predella panel features an angel mourning those deceased while clasping the arms of the regiment. The inclusion of the vignette of the sphinx is curious as there is no obvious association to the Boer War but may allude to the Royal Irish Regiment's participation

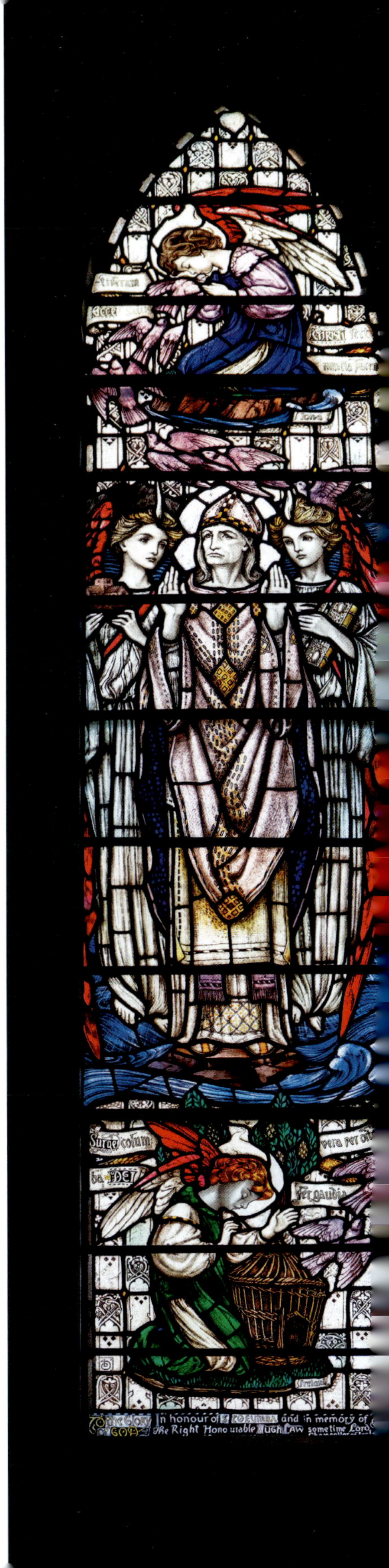

Louis Davis, *St Columba* (1905)

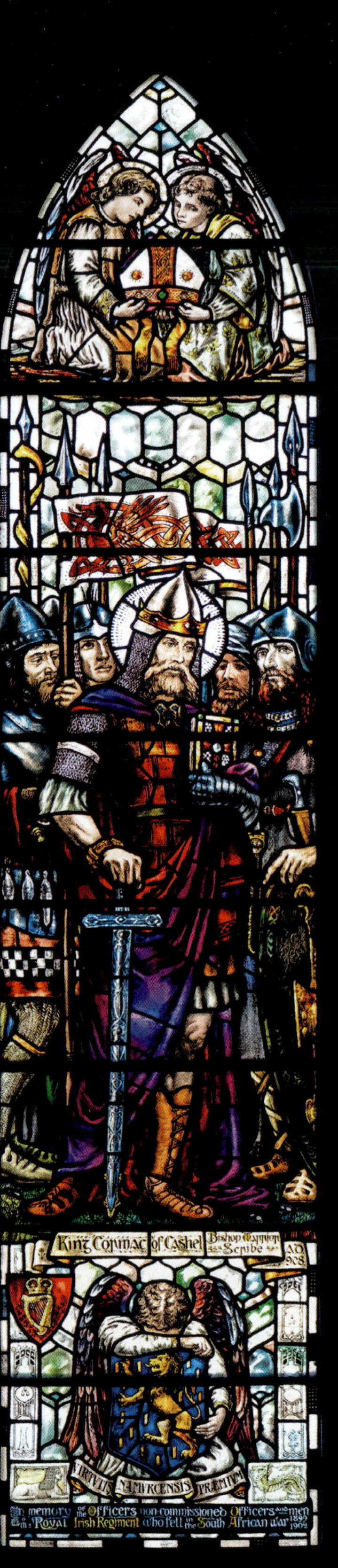

in the earlier Anglo-Egyptian War. Worthy of note is the inclusion at the base of the window – and so small it would be easy to miss – the *Déanta in Éirinn* (Made in Ireland) logo, an initiative of the Irish Industrial Development Association of which Sarah Purser was a council member for decades and was on the selection committee for the logo design in 1906.

Proceeding chronologically, the next window of note is across the nave, and located above the south door. It was designed and made by Beatrice Elvery at An Túr Gloine. A charming window, it depicts angel musicians, and was erected in memory of Samuel Dobbin, vicar choral, by his wife and children. Ordered in September 1908, it was completed the following year at a cost of £72. The window features seven angels engaged in singing or playing various instruments: bells, a violin, a harpsichord, and a decorative lyre. Several of the angels have similar feminine features and it is possible that some at least are based on Elvery's sketches of her own sisters, something she was in the habit of doing. Angel musicians have been subjects in art over the centuries though the actual scriptural basis for angels singing or playing musical instruments is slight.

Reverting back to the north transept, a war memorial window was commissioned in 1917 by a Dublin solicitor and his wife,[5] to be located left of *St Columba*. The artist was William MacBride who

Sarah Purser, *Cormac of Cashel* (executed by A.E. Child) (1906–7)

had trained under A.E. Child at the Dublin School of Art and subsequently worked for Joshua Clarke & Sons until late 1918 but fell foul of Clarke when he discovered MacBride was undertaking external commissions, and as there is no record of this window in the Clarke order books it would appear to be one of those which was made elsewhere.[6] Titled *Chivalry*, it depicts a knight and was erected in memory of two brothers, Lt Charles Stockley French and Capt. Claude Alexander French, and their half-brother, Capt. Bernard Digby Johns, all of whom served in different regiments and who died in 1915 or 1916.

When the window was installed, the *Church of Ireland Gazette* noted in an article penned by one of the cathedral's canons that it was 'not intended to allow any more stained glass into the clerestory, and in the ground floor no window remains plain. This window is therefore, the last window of its kind which St Patrick's can accept.'[7]

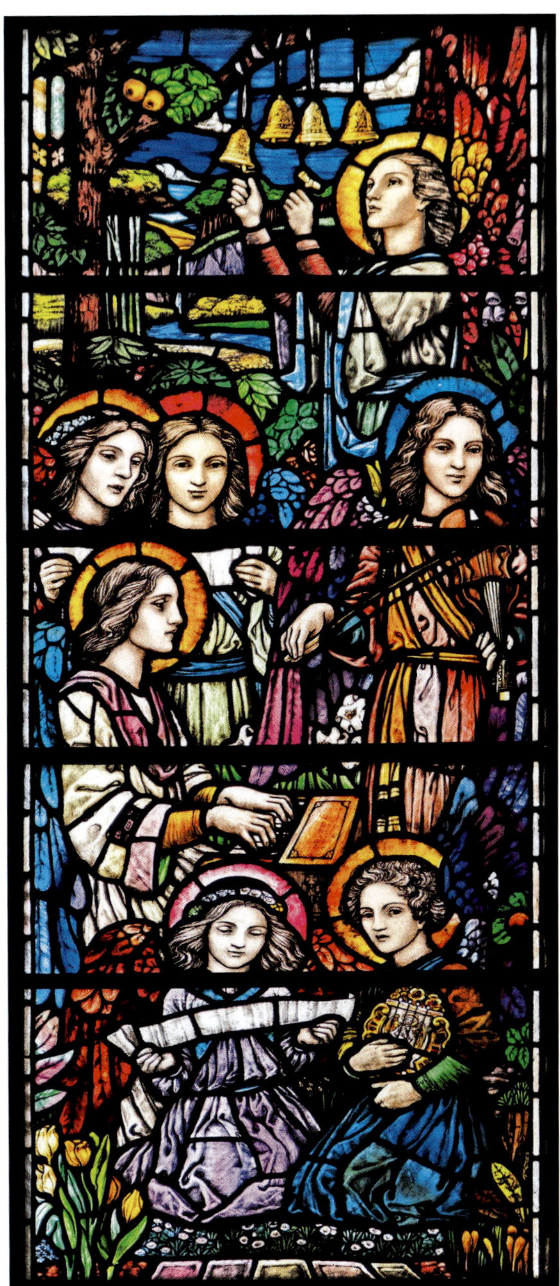

Beatrice Elvery, detail of *Angel Musicians* (1909)

MacBride depicted the handsome young knight with large penetrating eyes staring resolutely ahead, both hands upon the hilt of his great two-handed sword and carrying a shield on which is inscribed *Pro patria* (For the fatherland). A rich mantle falls from his shoulder, whose crimson shades are in brilliant contrast to the steel blue of his armour. Above, two angels in profile are depicted deftly weaving wreaths of honour. The arrangement is entirely symmetrical, something that MacBride appears to have often favoured. The *Church of Ireland Gazette* article drew attention to an interesting feature which would otherwise go unnoticed: just below the knight's feet there is a small shield-like shape comprising five fragments of grisaille glass that came from Ypres cathedral – two of the brothers had died at Ypres – and somehow these fragments were brought back to Dublin. In the predella panel a comrade is shown comforting a wounded soldier, while in the background refugees pour from a burning town. The window was dedicated in February 1917, one of a relatively small number of memorial windows that were erected during the war. In 1918 MacBride created a virtually identical window, minus the predella, for St John's Church of Ireland church, Malone Road, Belfast.

With all the available windows filled with stained glass, when a powerful individual or family wanted to install a window the only option was to have an existing window removed, and this is what occurred when the three sons of Edward Cecil Guinness, the first earl of Iveagh, wished to erect a memorial to his memory. They had a certain authority to do so, however, as it was their grandfather, Benjamin Lee Guinness, who had donated the window that would be taken out, *The Ascension* by Barff & Co.[8]

The earl of Iveagh had died in 1927. At one point he had been the richest man in Ireland and also a noted philanthropist, with a particular interest in slum clearance and its replacement by quality social housing including in the area close to the cathedral. The year after his death An Túr Gloine was approached and Michael Healy created a design but for reasons unknown his submission never proceeded beyond the initial stage, much to his disappointment.[9] The progression of the memorial window appears to have stalled for a few years until a decision was made to offer it to the versatile Welsh-born artist Frank Brangwyn (1867–1956) who had been a

(opposite) William MacBride, detail of *Chivalry* (1917)

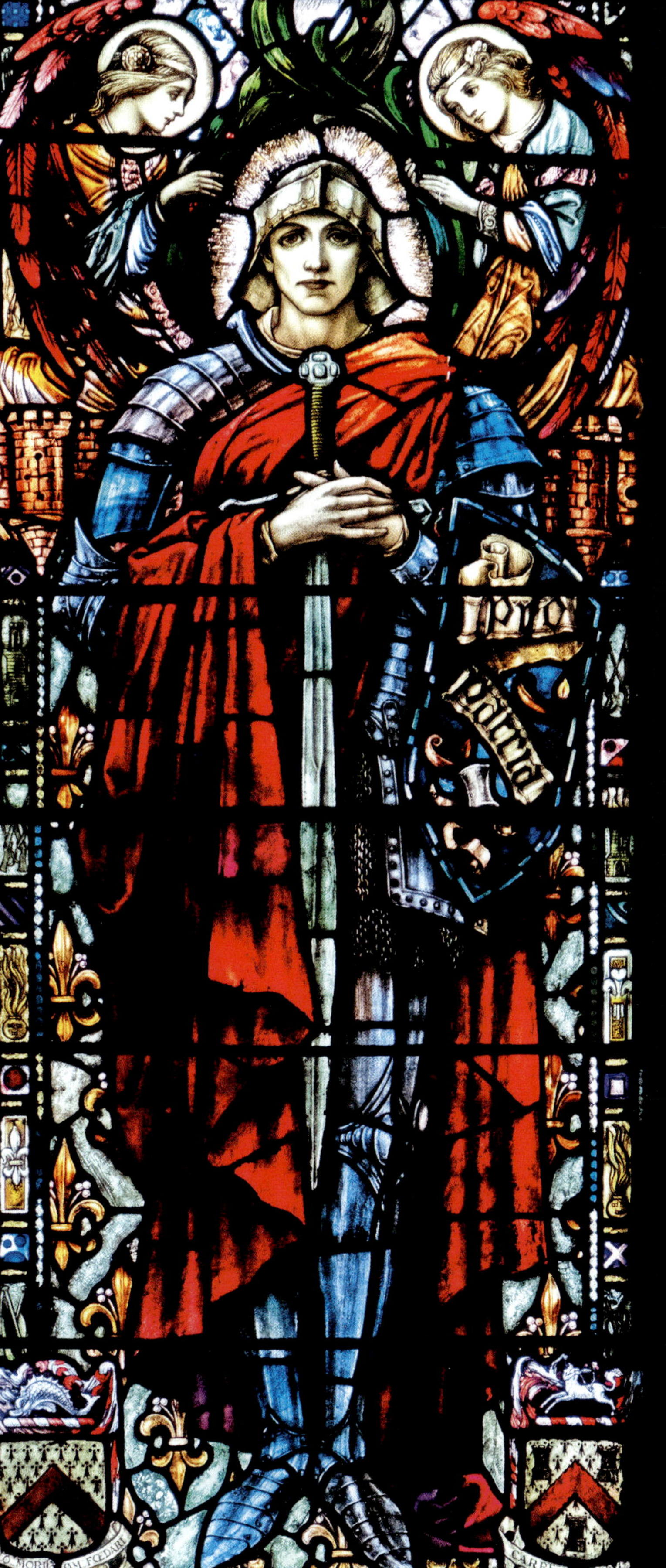

friend and admirer of the late earl. Brangwyn was then best known as a muralist who worked on a grand scale though over the years he had designed, though not personally made, several stained glass windows.

The Guinness family decided that Charity would be a suitable theme for Brangwyn's monumental 3-light window (centre light 27 feet tall). Different small-scale colour iterations by Brangwyn have survived showing varying thematic approaches, though all teeming with men, women and children, and one of which closely resembles the window as executed.[10] *Charity* was made in Edinburgh in 1937 by Alexander Strachan, brother of Douglas Strachan, Scotland's most distinguished twentieth-century stained glass artist.

In his window Brangwyn chose to personify *Charity* as a matronly figure who is positioned centre stage in the middle light. Robed in shades of blue, she could possibly be viewed as a modern Madonna although the toddler she carries strikes an irreligious note by showing its bare bottom. Staring straight ahead with a stoic if slightly under siege expression, she is surrounded by jostling figures, mainly female, including two young girls who cling to her for protection. Continuing the mothering theme other women tend to their children and at the window's base a hen is depicted with its clutch of chicks. Men feature too, but less so, and mainly elderly, including three with crutches. Costumes are mainly contemporary but one man inexplicably appears to be in medieval garb. In the background huge numbers of additional destitute and displaced individuals appear to converge towards the central figure. Of the very many figures, no one appears happy. David Lawrence has suggested that the images of suffering in the window reflect not only the Iveaghs' 're-imagining' of a medieval Dublin quarter but are also a comment on the First World War in which one of the earl's sons had been in service.[11]

Behind and above the figure of *Charity* there is a tree whose boughs traverse the three lights and are heavy with luscious ripe pears yet no one is picking them or eating them. At the highest point a pelican nests with its brood of three youngsters; traditionally the bird was believed to have pecked on its own flesh to feed it to its starving chicks and consequently became a symbol for Christ because he feeds believers with his body and blood in the eucharist, though unlike most representations in art history this pelican is not pecking at its breast.

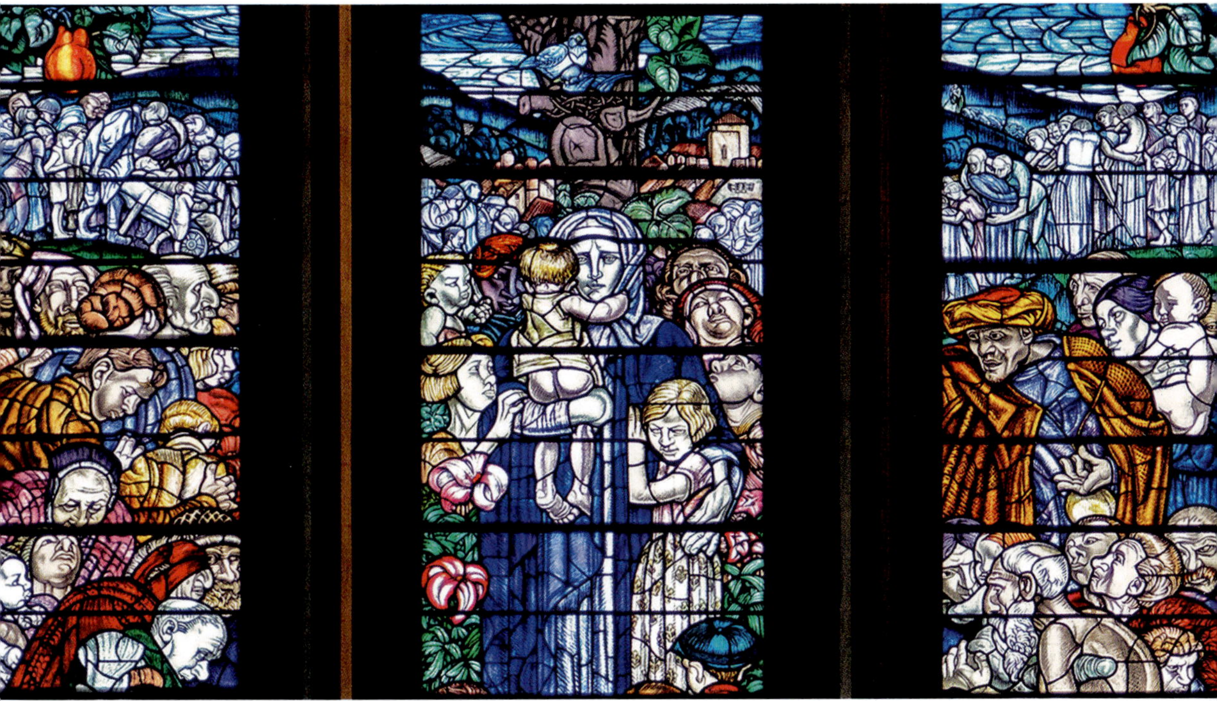

Frank Brangwyn, detail of *Charity (Iveagh Memorial Window)* (1937)

The same year as *Charity* was installed in St Patrick's, a smaller 4-light window, also in memory of the earl, and also designed by Brangwyn, was unveiled in the parish church of Elveden, Suffolk, the location of the Iveagh's English estate.[12] The theme of Charity was again chosen, along with Education, and the window includes depictions of Saints Andrew and Patrick to whom the church is dedicated. Children abound in a bucolic scene and it was Brangwyn's intention to convey their happiness,[13] perhaps to redress the general sense of despondency pervading his major opus in St Patrick's cathedral.

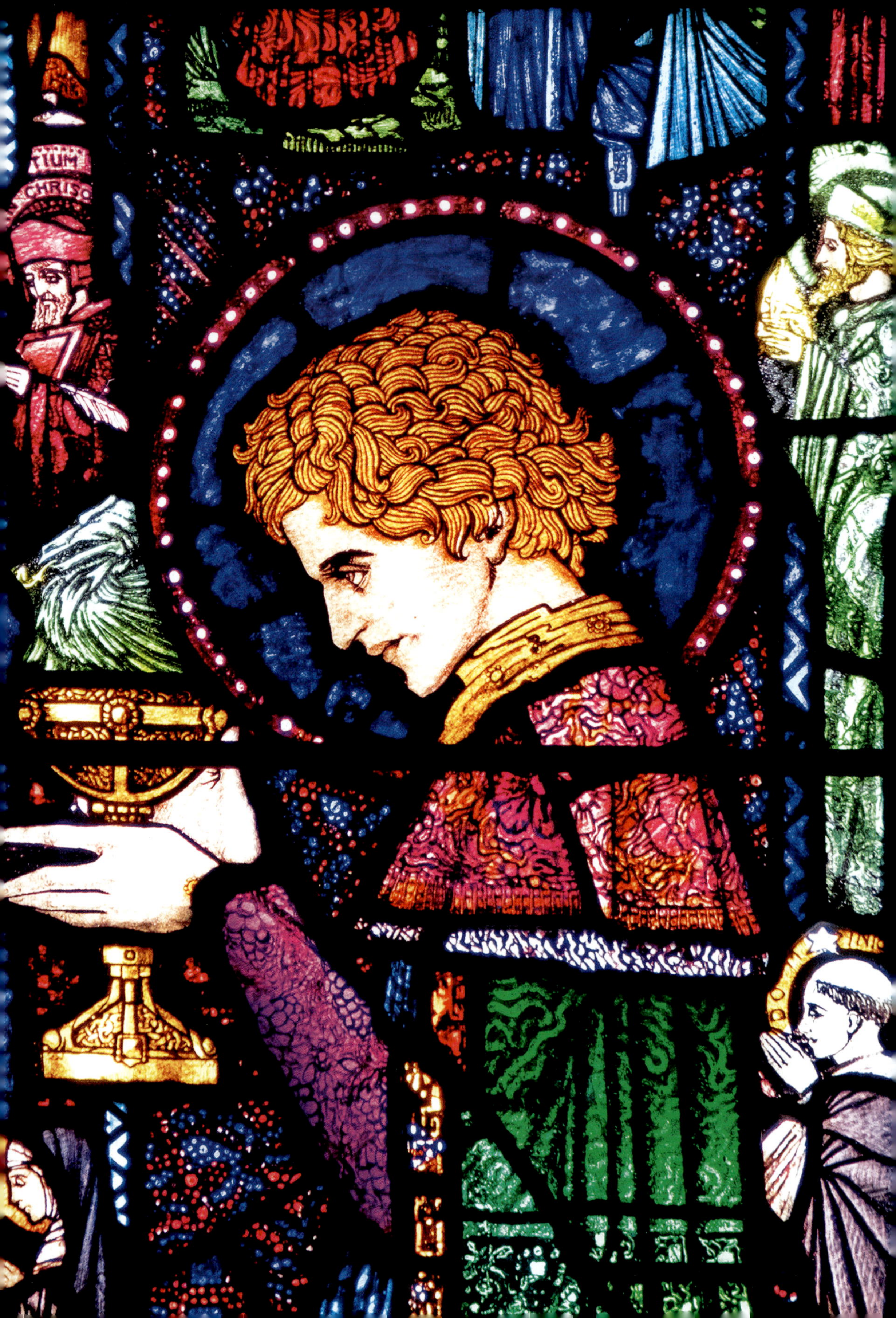
TIUM
CHRISO

DUBLIN CITY

St Peter's church (RC)

North Circular Road, Phibsborough, D07 FW29

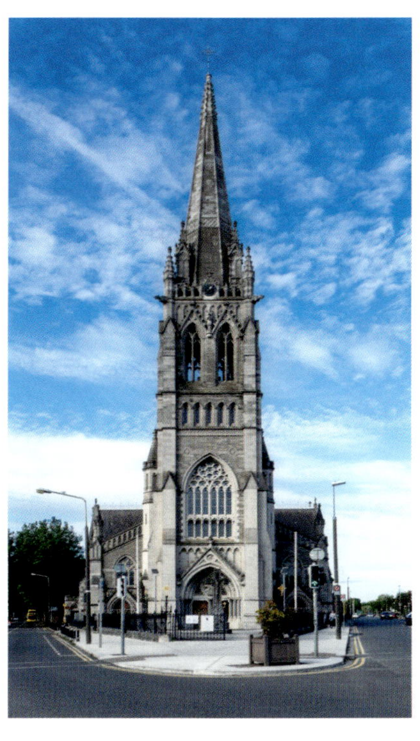

St Peter's church (Vincentian Fathers), located at the junction of North Circular Road and New Cabra Road, is distinguished by its soaring spire, one of the tallest in Dublin, which dominates the northern edge of Dublin's inner city, though the actual church fits snugly into a tight wedge-shaped plot. Gothic Revival in style, it was constructed in several phases with Ashlin & Coleman making a major contribution in unifying the structure.

(opposite) Harry Clarke, detail of St John Eudes from *The Sacred Heart, St Margaret Mary and St John Eudes* (1919)

This commodious church includes several windows by Lobin of Tours (such as the south transept rose) and a good 3-light window made in 1935–6 by William E. Earley, *Our Lady with St Vincent de Paul and St Catherine Labouré* (note the inclusion of the miraculous medals), but the undoubted highlights are two contributions by Harry Clarke and though created only five years apart, are quite different in style, technique and imagery. The first was a 3-light window, one of Clarke's early masterpieces, depicting *The Sacred Heart, St Margaret Mary and St John Eudes*, which was commissioned by Revd Edmund Comerford in 1918. The church, including some of the windows, had been damaged two years previously during the Easter Rising when the railway bridge on the North Circular Road was blown up on 25 April 1916 and a large piece of masonry fell on the church roof and presbytery.[1] It appears that Fr Comerford used the insurance money to fund his new window.

Christ revealing his sacred heart (centre light) is a stalwart of Catholic devotional imagery and this was the first time Clarke treated this subject. The choice of the two saints, both French, reflects their roles as ardent proponents of the Sacred Heart of Jesus, and when Clarke prepared his designs for this window both Margaret Mary and John Eudes had recently been beatified and were on their way to being canonized.[2] Significantly, St Peter's church was, and remains, home to the Arch-Confraternity of the Sacred Heart in Dublin so the choice of theme for the window was unsurprising.

When viewing this window, it is necessary to realize that it no longer appears as Clarke had designed or intended; he originally created it to face north-east in the north wall of the nave but it was subsequently moved to a side chapel (Chapel of Adoration) and it now faces south-west.[3] Alterations were necessary to make it fit: the original tracery was removed and replaced with an inferior and dissimilar substitute, sections were cut out of each of the side lights to shorten them, and a mauve border – which strikes a discordant note – was introduced to compensate for the wider openings. Fortunately the sketch design and cartoons survive so one can see Clarke's original vision for it.[4] As Clarke expert Nicola Gordon Bowe states, 'Despite the adverse conditions of light, structure and design, what remains

(opposite) Harry Clarke, *The Sacred Heart, St Margaret Mary and St John Eudes* (1919)

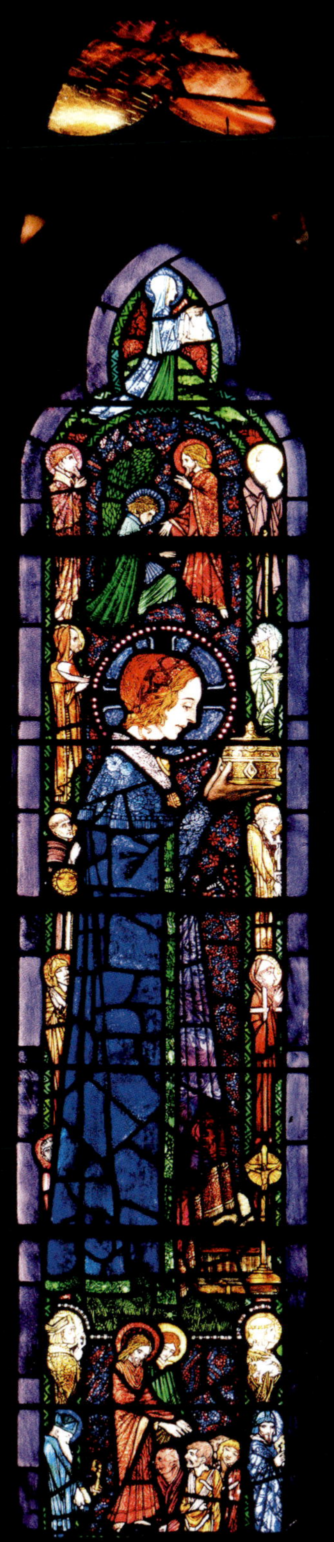
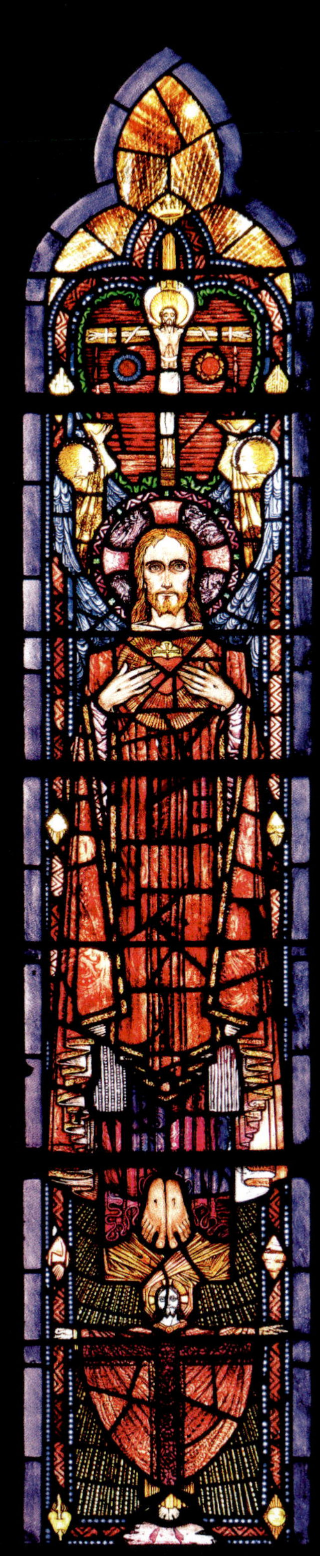
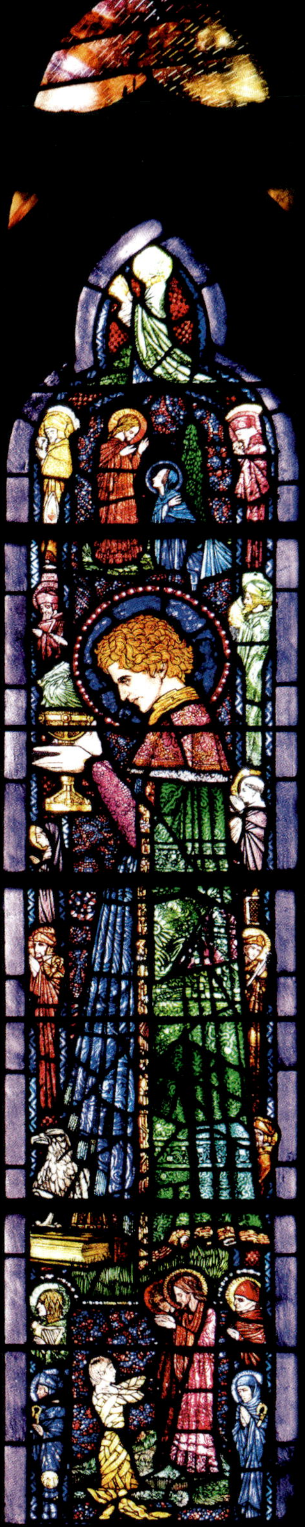

of Harry's window is still a wonder.'[5] She was of the view that *The Sacred Heart, St Margaret Mary and St John Eudes* with its deep, rich and sumptuous colours was on a par with Clarke's remarkable series of windows for University College Cork's Honan chapel (1915–17), which had effectively launched his career.

While Christ, with penetrating eyes, stares straight ahead, St Margaret Mary and St John Eudes are both depicted in profile and with heads bowed – she reflective, he intense – and holding golden objects; in her hands a delicately fashioned casket containing the Eucharist, and in his, a large chalice tooled in intricate Celtic decoration. Directly above the figure of Christ revealing his sacred heart, Clarke has included a miniature Crucifixion; note the blood dripping from Christ's hands, caught in two tiny golden bowls, held aloft by a pair of angels.

In addition to the main figure of Christ and the principal saints there is a multitude – twenty-seven in total – of attendant miniature saints, some half hidden as they peek out from behind the heavy damask cloaks worn by Margaret Mary and John Eudes; each is distinct and full of character, and Clarke has conveniently identified most by delicately inscribing their names on their halos – though binoculars may be needed to read the names and also to appreciate fully Clarke's beguiling details. The predictable Irish saints are present – Patrick and Brigid are accorded preferential status in the apex of each light, but there are also some less frequently featured saints including Fachtna, Malachy, Enda and Columbanus. Additionally there are European saints, again featuring the familiar and also the less-well known such as Francis de Sales, Bonaventure and John Chrysostom. At the base of the left and right lights there are predella panels, both depicting Christ in ministering roles – on the left he is accompanied by St John blessing the deformed, crippled and destitute; and on the right Christ, accompanied by an unidentified saint, blessing a young man swathed in bandages.[6] The window, which warrants generous time to relish fully the myriad details, is signed 'H. Clarke. Aug 1919' and was installed the following month.[7]

Clarke's second commission for the church, ordered in 1924, again by Fr Comerford, was to supply windows for the new mortuary chapel; these are similar in design and conception to nine small sanctuary windows that Clarke had made for the Catholic church in Lusk earlier the same year and which had charmed Fr Comerford when he saw them in Clarke's studio.[8]

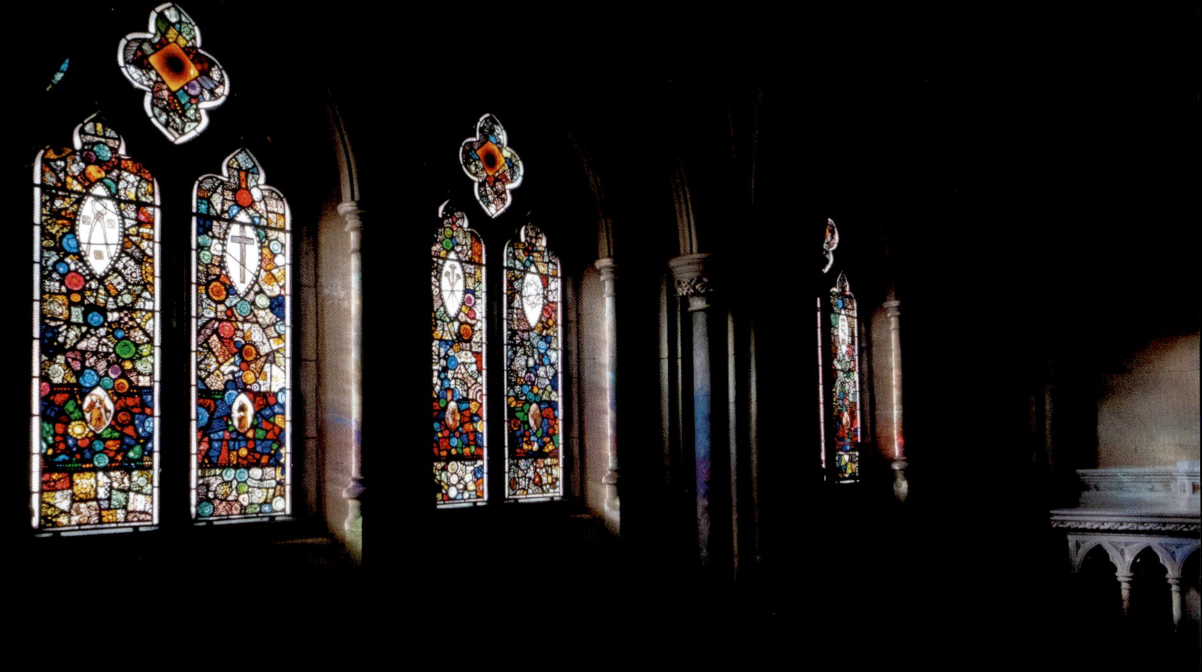

Harry Clarke, *Arma Christi* ('weapons of Christ') mortuary chapel window (1924)

St Peter's mortuary chapel can be accessed from within the church and also directly through double-doors via the North Circular Road side. This intimate, groin-vaulted space is in dramatic contrast to the spaciousness of the church. It comprises a set of four 2-light windows with quatrefoils above, and – easy to overlook – a fanlight comprising a rose with spandrels above the exterior door. The mortuary chapel provided Clarke with one of his first opportunities to create all the glass for a single, albeit very small, space and it has a cohesiveness of intent. The set of 2-lights punctuate the west wall and can be viewed as a sequence of eight. One is struck by a sea of 'Floral Ornament', a feature invented and favoured by Clarke, which was created mostly from 'cullets' (discarded off-cuts of glass) and painted with simple floral motifs. The thick, irregular pieces of glass, even including the bottoms of bottles, have been leaded together in an organic manner to create a richly jewelled effect that exudes a sense of joyous delight in colour, texture and form which transforms this otherwise grey stone space, one which has the most sombre of functions – to receive a coffin and provide a brief home for it overnight prior to the funeral the following day. Nicola Gordon Bowe described these mortuary windows as 'perhaps the most successful Floral Ornament windows Harry ever did and he was justifiably proud of them.'[9] But these windows are not solely an exercise in Floral Ornament, each light contains two vesica-shaped panels, a favourite shape Clarke utilized, both in his stained glass and his graphic illustrations.

The top series, eight vesica panels in total, depict *Arma Christi* ('weapons of Christ') or commonly referred to as the Instruments of Christ's Passion (left to right: whip & lance; ladder & reed with sponge; pincers with dice & cross; nails and crown of thorns; column with pillar of flagellation). These have been painted in a very precise, almost diagrammatic manner, crisp black on white glass, which cast the instruments of torture in a cold, harsh light, quite in contrast to the exuberance of the colourful background. The smaller vesica panels are at eye level, highlighted by a band of even more richly coloured floral ornament, and subtly linked to the top vesica panels by a series of larger, floating circles of rainbow-coloured glass. These vesica panels are painted in a much looser manner with silver stain,[10] in a range of hues from burnt sienna to palest lemon, recalling Netherlandish stained glass. While the image nearest the external door depicts God the Father enveloping the crucified Christ in his robes, the other images are – rather surprisingly – all unrelated to the Passion and are mostly associated with Christ's earlier years, depicting (left to right): the Baptism of Christ; the Flight into Egypt; Our Lady with the young Christ and John the Baptist; the Presentation in the Temple; the Three Shepherds; the Wise Men; the Visitation.

The striking feature of the quatrefoil above each of the four windows is a large Norman quarry slab, set on the diagonal, and so thick as to give the sense of a deep brown orb throbbing at its centre.[11] Clarke had first employed a similar slab in a small abstract lancet window for the earl of Wicklow in his parish church and was obviously pleased with the outcome,[12] and he repeated the feature in his Lusk windows (see pp 207–9). St Peter's set of windows, costing £160, was installed in March 1925 and must surely be the finest windows to be found in any mortuary chapel in Ireland.

(opposite) Harry Clarke, *Arma Christi* ('weapons of Christ') mortuary chapel window (1924)

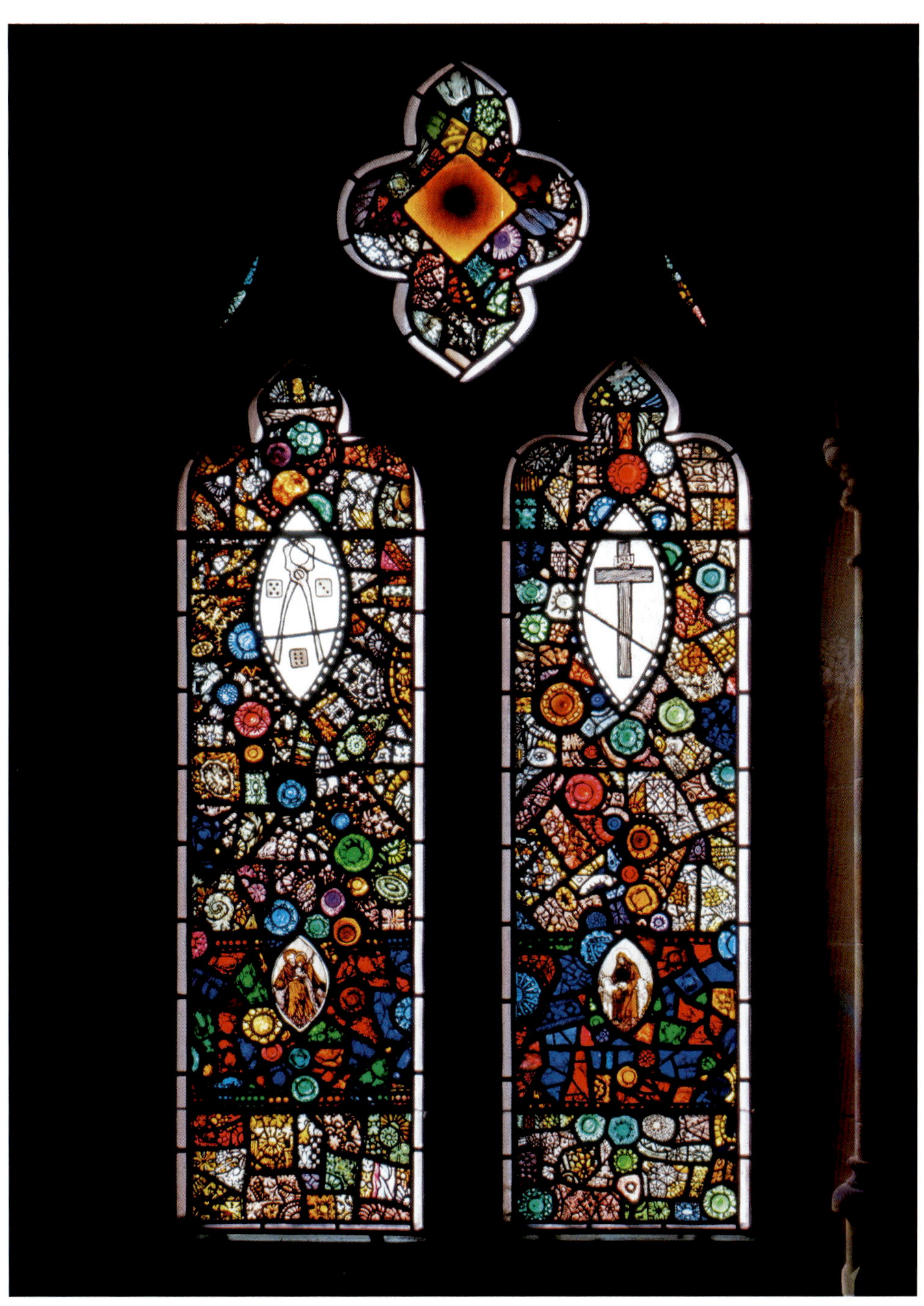

ST PETER'S CHURCH (RC), NORTH CIRCULAR ROAD

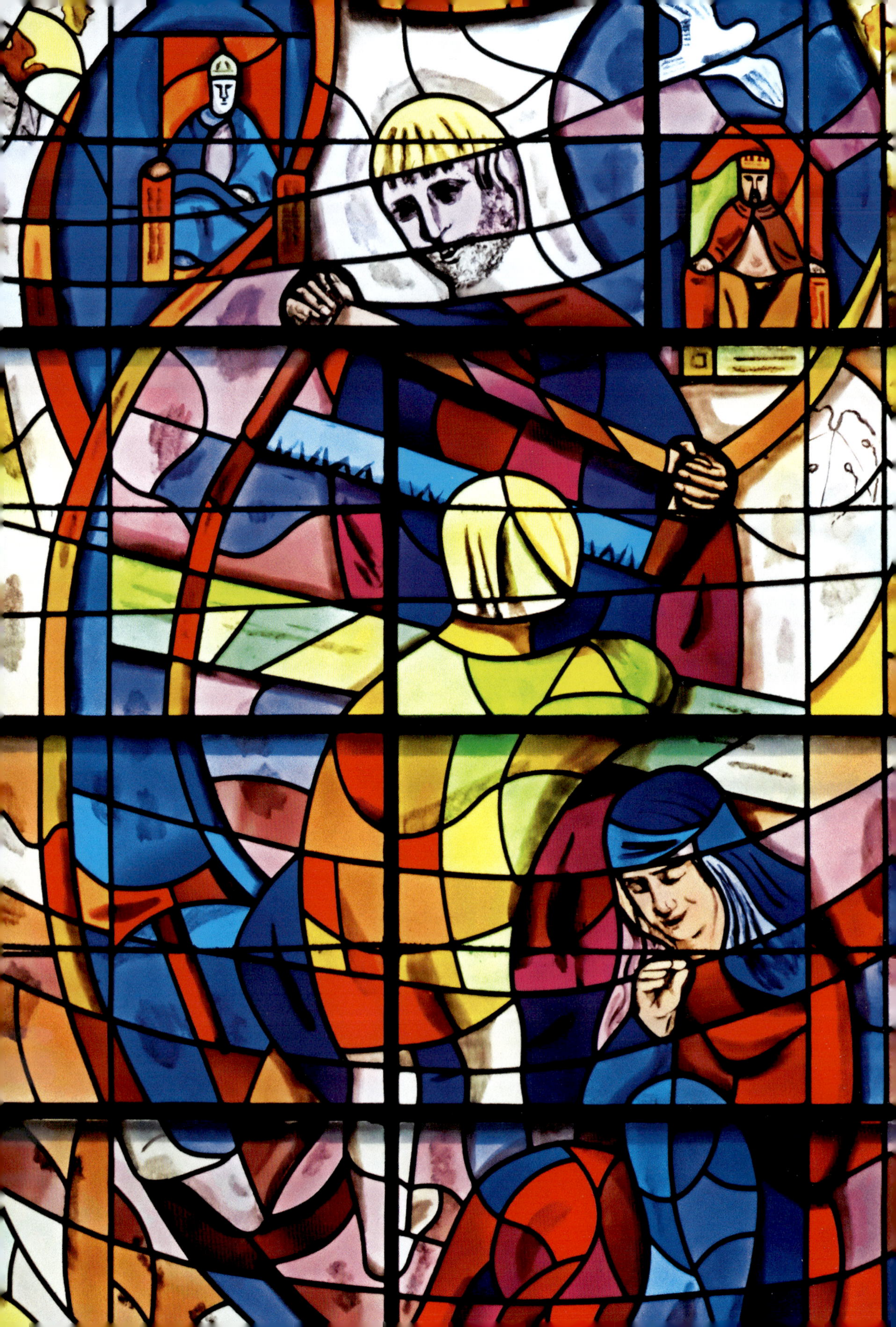

St Teresa's church (RC)

Clarendon Street, D02 XD26

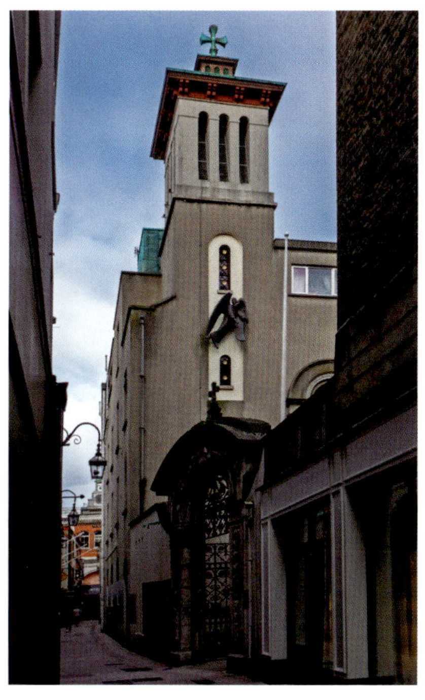

Possibly Dublin's most frequented church, though one which is to a large degree tucked away from view, St Teresa's Carmelite church – often referred to as Clarendon Street church – is one of the oldest Catholic churches in Dublin city. Built 1793–1810, the original entrance was off Wicklow Street. The Lombardesque west façade on Clarendon Street is constructed of ashlar and rock-faced granite with Portland stone dressings. The church was extensively reworked during the late nineteenth century and the sanctuary embellished 1880s–90s, with oratories and chapels added throughout the first half of the twentieth century.

(opposite) Phyllis Burke, detail of *St Joseph* (1990)

In terms of stained glass, the main features in this church are two series of windows; those in the sanctuary designed by William E. Earley (in 1936) and those designed by Phyllis Burke (in 1990–2007). However the 'oldest' window now in the church, made *c.*1900–10, also by Earley's, is also the most recent addition;[1] it is the large rose in the south transept and the stained glass in the petals was removed from the former Carmelite chapel at Avila, Donnybrook, *c.*2017 and modified so as to fit into the existing rose window.[2] As the Clarendon Street window has two extra petals, bringing the number to ten, two new Carmelite saints were introduced which were painted by Brendan Mullins of Abbey Stained Glass Studios – St Elizabeth of the Trinity and St Teresa of the Andes.

The five sanctuary windows by William E. Earley replaced earlier windows made in 1877 by the same family-run company.[3] The subjects of William E. Earley's windows relate to Our Lady and prominent Carmelite saints. Visually the windows form an ensemble piece and are situated within a triple-arched logia-like frame supported by pairs of Corinthian columns. The high altar features a Venetian 3-light window with, on either side, a single light and, at some distance above, a roundel. The centre light of the Venetian window depicts *Our Lady of Mount Carmel, with the Christ Child on her Knees, bestowing the Scapular to St Simon Stock*. *Elijah* and *St John of the Cross* occupy the smaller round-headed windows either side. The window above the left side altar depicts *The Betrothal of Mary and Joseph*, and the one above the right side altar depicts *The Ecstasy of St Teresa of Avila*. As with all of William E. Earley's windows, harmony of colour and composition take precedence, with shades of pinks and blues predominating, but in this instance he has also introduced a warm ochre for the Carmelite habits. No space is left unadorned, and angels and putti abound to contribute to a lush fully orchestrated effect. A small rose, also by William E. Earley, which depicts *St Anne Teaching the Virgin*, can be found in the Lady Chapel. Similar in style and technique to the sanctuary windows, the subject has an intimate quality befitting the smaller space.

In 1988 the Carmelite Fathers engaged the services of Wilfrid Cantwell (1921–2000), an architect who specialized in the design and re-ordering of churches (taking into account Vatican II recommendations), to advise on their stained glass; both to provide an assessment of the existing windows in St Teresa's and recommendations

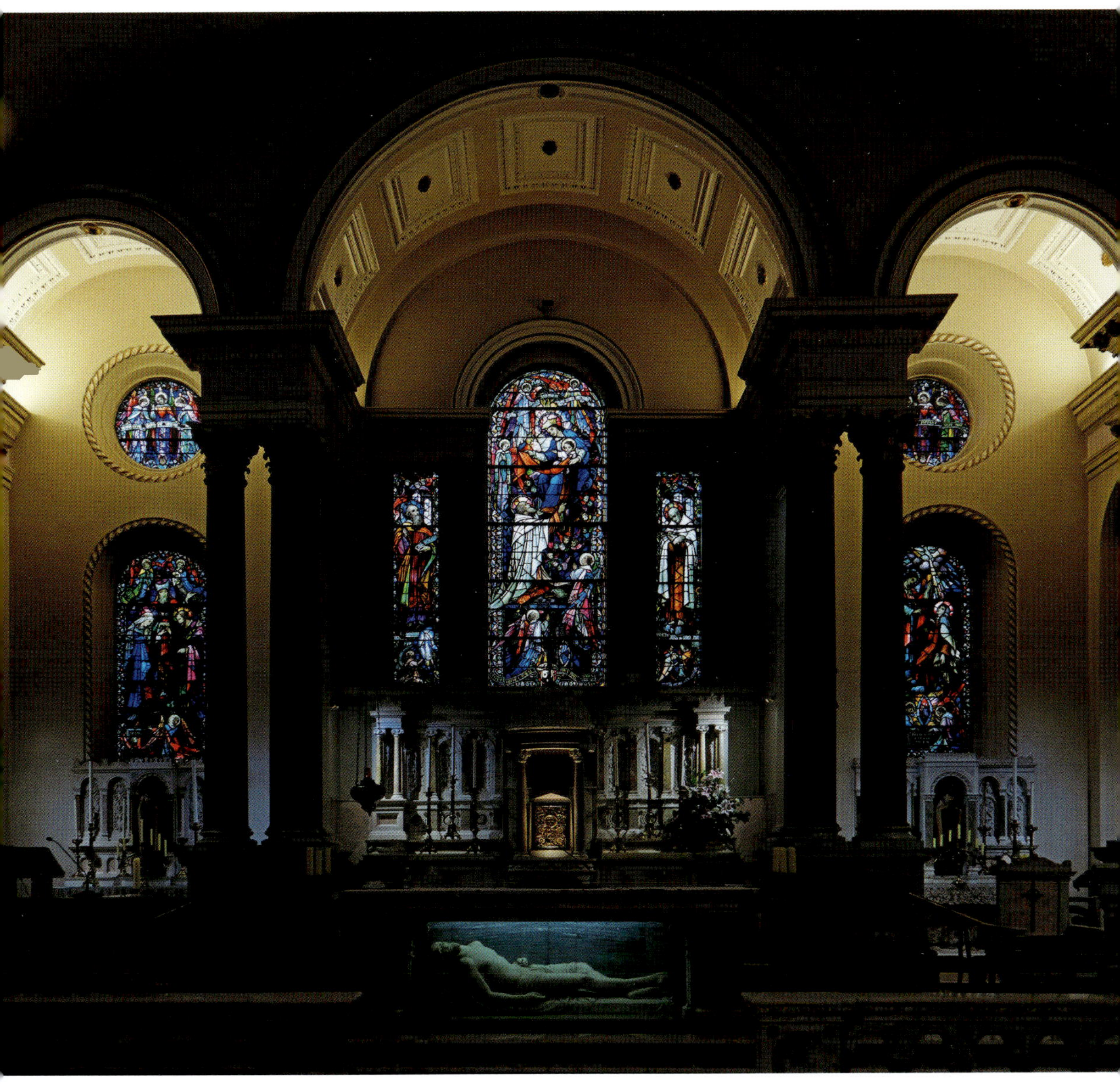

William E. Earley, *Sanctuary Windows* (1936)

concerning the commission of a new series. By summer of the following year the subjects for seven (subsequently eight) clerestory level windows had been chosen and a few months later short-listed artists including Phyllis Burke, Patrick Pye, Frances

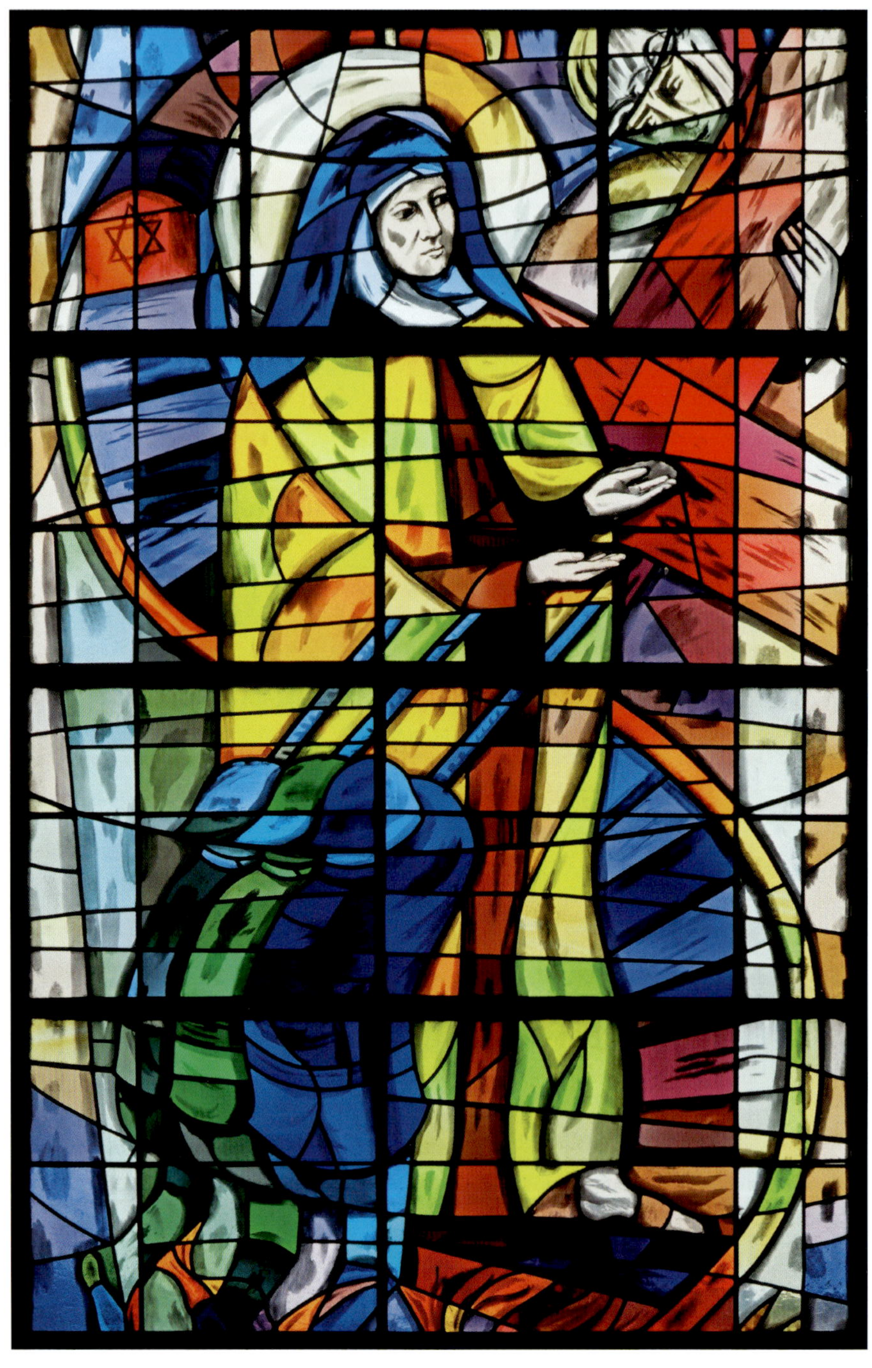

Biggs and Helen Moloney were interviewed, with Phyllis Burke being selected.[4] This was a significant commission for the artist due to the popular city-centre location of the church and the large size of the windows (15ft 4in. x 5ft 9in.). Phyllis Burke was presented with detailed briefing notes containing recommendations prepared by the Carmelite Fathers on how to treat the nominated subjects.

As an independent stained glass artist Phyllis Burke had a studio in her house, complete with small kiln, where she would create her designs, draw the cartoons, paint and fire the glass but the windows were fabricated by her long-term glazier, Dermot McLoughlin, at his facility in Arbour Hill. Phyllis Burke's main source for her sheets of glass was Saint Gobain, located south of Lyon, and she travelled there to choose the glass.

The first of the clerestory windows depicts *St Joseph* (1990) and as Phyllis Burke later recalled, 'I knew the first window would be very important as the other ones would have to follow suit. I was conscious that the windows needed to allow plenty of light in and couldn't use dark glass. I always had to be very aware of the rotation of the sun but Clarendon Street church was unusual as there were adjacent tall buildings, some of which bounced light off them in an unexpected manner and that brought additional light into the nave. I remember when I finished the *St Joseph* window, Fr Christopher [Clarke] brought me up to view it after it had been installed. With a large window you never see it all together until it is erected in position and I would hold my breath in anticipation. Until that happens the window is still mine, and then it is put in and when I see it, it goes from me. And I get so depressed. Fr Christopher was surprised and said but you've got all the other nave windows yet to do!'[5] Phyllis Burke represented St Joseph as a young father (as advised by the briefing notes) in contrast to most depictions of the saint as an elderly man. While he is engaged in carpentry work, Mary is busy sewing and the young Jesus has, unexpectedly, his back to the viewer as he faces his father. Three small crowned and enthroned figures are a reminder that Jesus was, through Joseph, a 'Son of David' and two doves reference Jesus's presentation in the temple. (For fun a playful cat fascinated by a ball of wool is also introduced.) The strong narrative element

(opposite) Phyllis Burke, detail of *St Teresa Benedicta of the Cross* (Edith Stein) (1990)

in this window and a desire for a fresh alternative to conventional iconographic interpretations is maintained throughout the entire series.

By December 1992 four of the windows had been installed and a reassessment of the other subjects was under consideration with the intention to replace 'out of context' subjects such as St Patrick and St Brigid with some more recent Carmelites saints such as Edith Stein (St Teresa Benedicta of the Cross).[6] The Edith Stein window, the final of the eight clerestory windows to be installed (in 2006), is a subject Burke had previously treated in stained glass though this is a more unusual representation as the Carmelite nun, a convert from Judaism, is depicted before a firing squad at Auschwitz.[7]

Two of the most charming windows by Phyllis Burke in the church, and also her final ones, are the pair below the choir balcony which both depict interpretations of *Psalm 41/42* ('Like the deer that yearns for running streams, so my soul is yearning for you, my God'); they feature deer, waterfowl and colourful doves drinking from a fountain.

Despite the seventeen-year gap between her first and final windows in St Teresa's church, there is a stylistic consistency throughout with an emphasis on translucent colour, particularly in shades ranging from palest yellow to deepest purple, combined with soft smudges of pigment to modulate the light. The subject of light is one felt keenly by Burke who opined, 'Light is very important: a sculptor's medium is stone, wood or metal, a musician's is sound, a glassblower's is glass – but a stained glass artist's medium is light and glass is their tool. It carves, moulds, directs the light which is never static, even on a clear day light changes, however gradually. It is good to have a tree – at a reasonable distance – as its branches and leaves moving give life to a window. A bird flying past, even for a second, can bring a window to life. So a window is always changing – constantly being recreated, I like to think.'[8]

In addition to the above windows, there is also a striking 3-light: *Resurrection*, or *The Risen Christ*, which was designed by George W. Walsh and made at Abbey Stained Glass Studios in 1968. This dynamic, modernist 3-light window is located above the Johnson's Court entrance (north transept) and features a figurative representation of Christ with completely abstract side lights. The glass is mainly limited to tones of the three primary colours, blue, yellow, and to a lesser extent

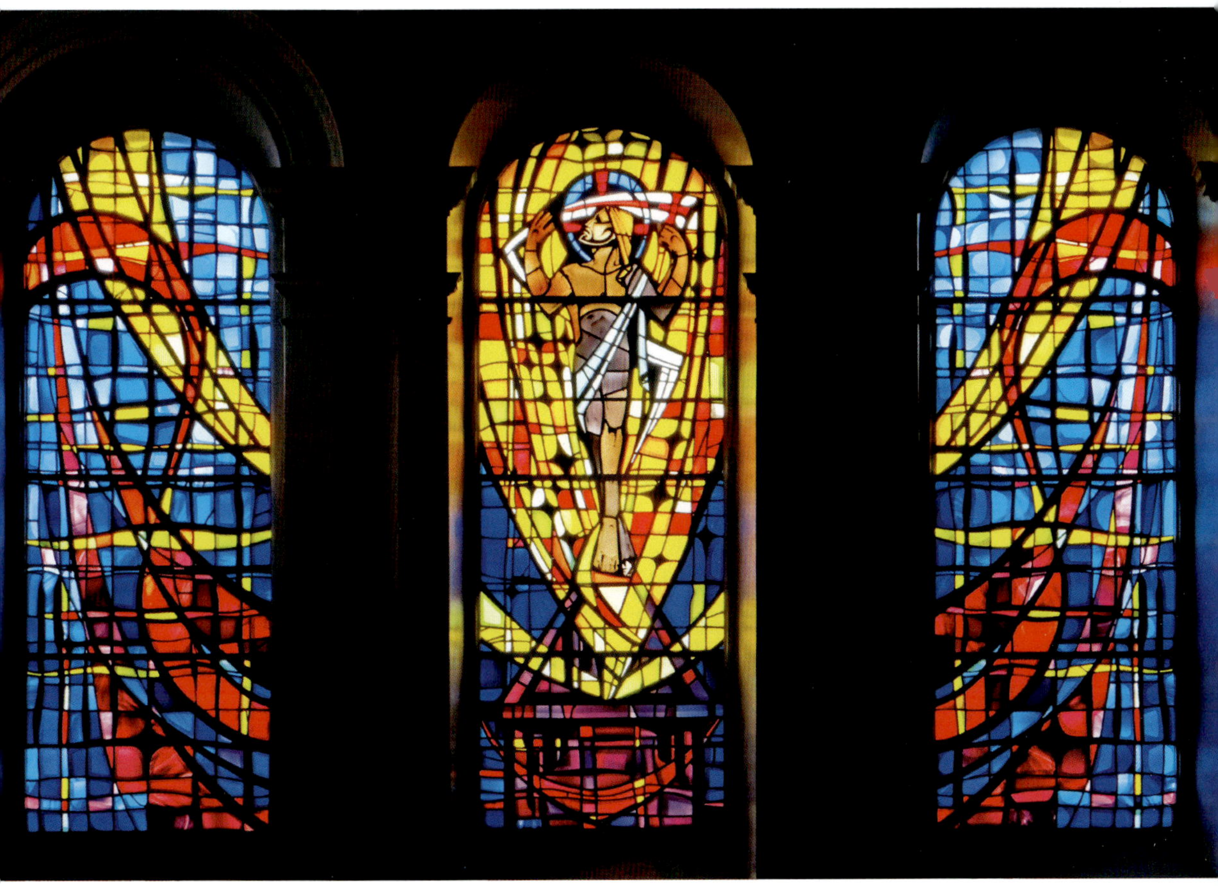

George W. Walsh, *The Resurrection* (1968)

red, though noteworthy is the distinctly dark-skinned Christ as he soars upwards, carrying the Flag of the Resurrection and in an unconventional pose for this subject, with his feet firmly positioned, one on top of the other, recalling Christ's crucifixion. At the same time as this window was made, George W. Walsh and his friend and colleague at Abbey Stained Glass Studios, Willie Earley (grandnephew of William E. Earley), created a series of Stations of the Cross for the church which were made from antique glass set on a background of polished granite.

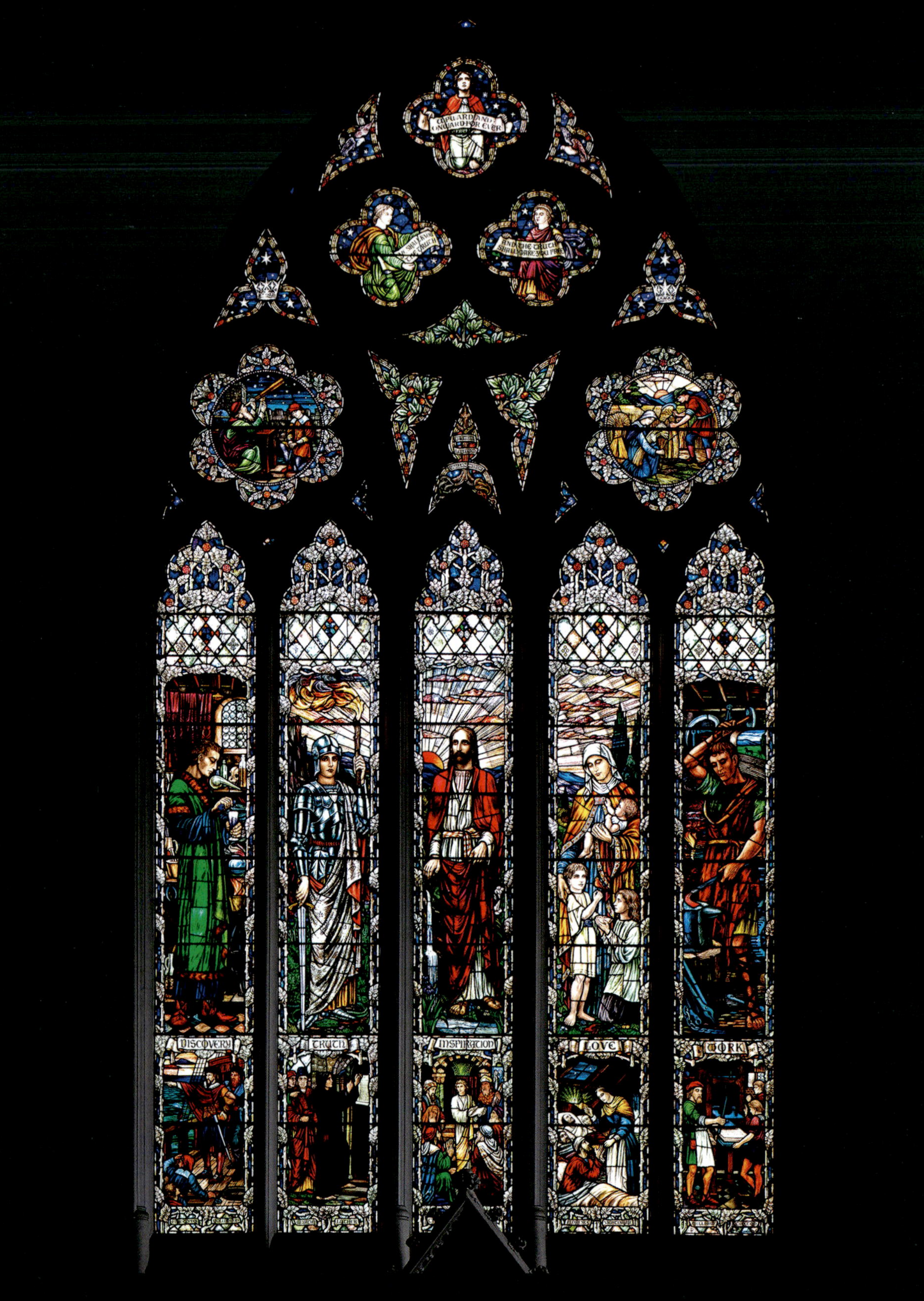
UPWARD AND ONWARD FOR EVER
DISCOVERY
TRUTH
INSPIRATION
LOVE
WORK

Unitarian church

St Stephen's Green West, D02 YP23

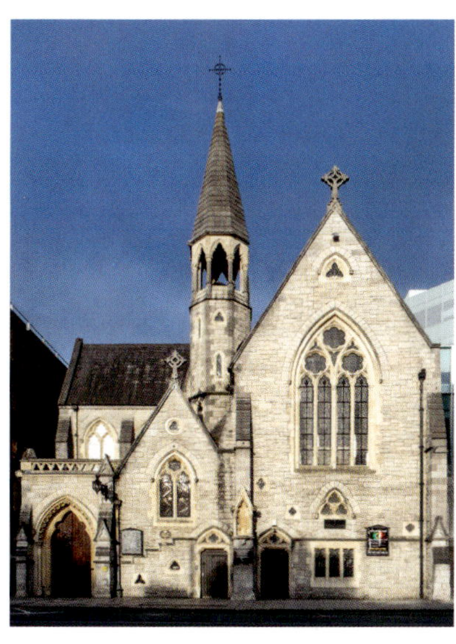

Formerly attached, now freestanding, this Gothic Revival church on St Stephen's Green West is constructed of uncoursed squared quarry-faced granite walls with sandstone dressings. It was designed by architects Lanyon, Lynn & Lanyon of Belfast and built in 1861–3. The church has an unusual L-shaped plan, and reflects a clever approach to a restricted site with a narrow street frontage. The interior arrangement is particularly notable; a flight of stairs, parallel to the street, leads one into the church, and separately a school, meeting rooms and caretaker's apartment are located in the under-croft below.

(opposite) A.E. Child, *Discovery, Truth, Inspiration, Love, and Work (Wilson Memorial Window)* (1917–18)

While the church features several fine nineteenth-century windows by Lobin of Tours, what are of particular interest are three windows made at An Túr Gloine between 1917 and 1943. The first of these is the largest, a 5-light window with extensive tracery; it is arguably a singularly unfortunate window as the two previous windows in this location, both also by Lobin, were destroyed by fires, first in 1892 and again in 1916, the latter blaze unconnected to the Easter Rising.[1] All three windows were devised as memorials to Thomas Wilson (d.1857), a significant benefactor of the church though his charitable reputation has been overshadowed in recent years by research which revealed he was a major slave owner.[2] It should be stated though that when the rector of the Unitarian church, Revd Ernest Savell Hicks, came to An Túr Gloine to order the replacement window in 1917 the church's congregation would have been unaware of Wilson's connection to the slave trade.[3]

Revd Savell Hicks and A.E. Child, the artist (and An Túr Gloine's manager) to whom the commission had been entrusted, seem to have established a rapport straight away. Savell Hicks wanted a window that would not only be beautiful but also didactic. With its dominant position above the altar it would serve as a constant reference point for his congregation in respect of the key tenets of Unitarianism – or, more specifically, his own philosophical interpretation of them. For Child, the attraction would have been the scale of the window – the largest he would ever make – and the fact it was for a prestigious city centre location. The cost of the window was £550 and it took him sixty weeks to complete.

The *Wilson Memorial Window* is also known by its five themes, *Discovery, Truth, Inspiration, Love, and Work*. Each light comprises a personification of the themes and all but one is represented by allegorical figures; Inspiration, in the centre light, is represented by Jesus Christ. In a predella panel beneath each of the figures is a vignette which espouses the theme above.

Christopher Whall, who was A.E. Child's mentor, was a keen proponent of utilizing nature as a source of inspiration; specifically, he regularly incorporated canopies of boughs and foliage in his designs into which he placed figures and in Child's window he uses this structural device to surround the five principal figures and also to separate

A.E. Child, detail of scientist in *Discovery, Truth, Inspiration, Love, and Work (Wilson Memorial Window)* (1917–18)

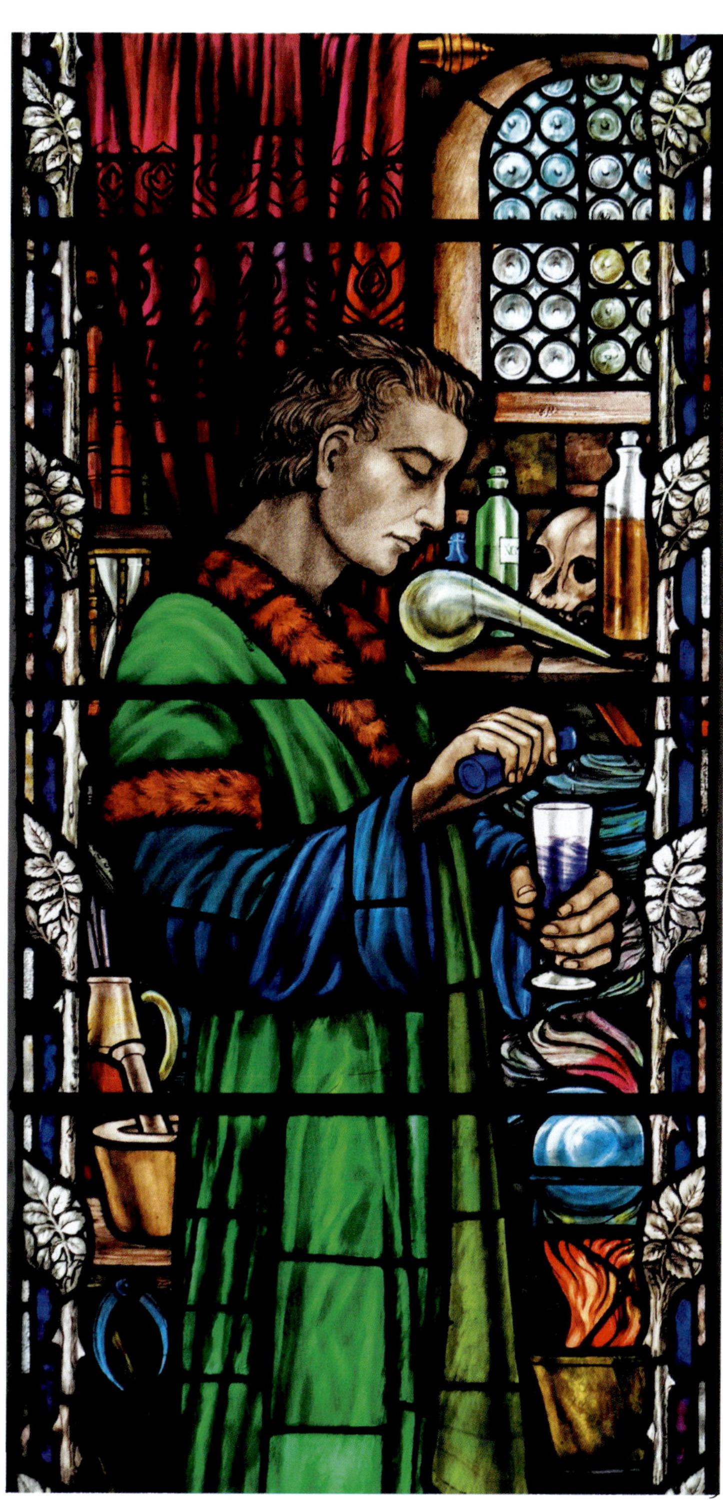

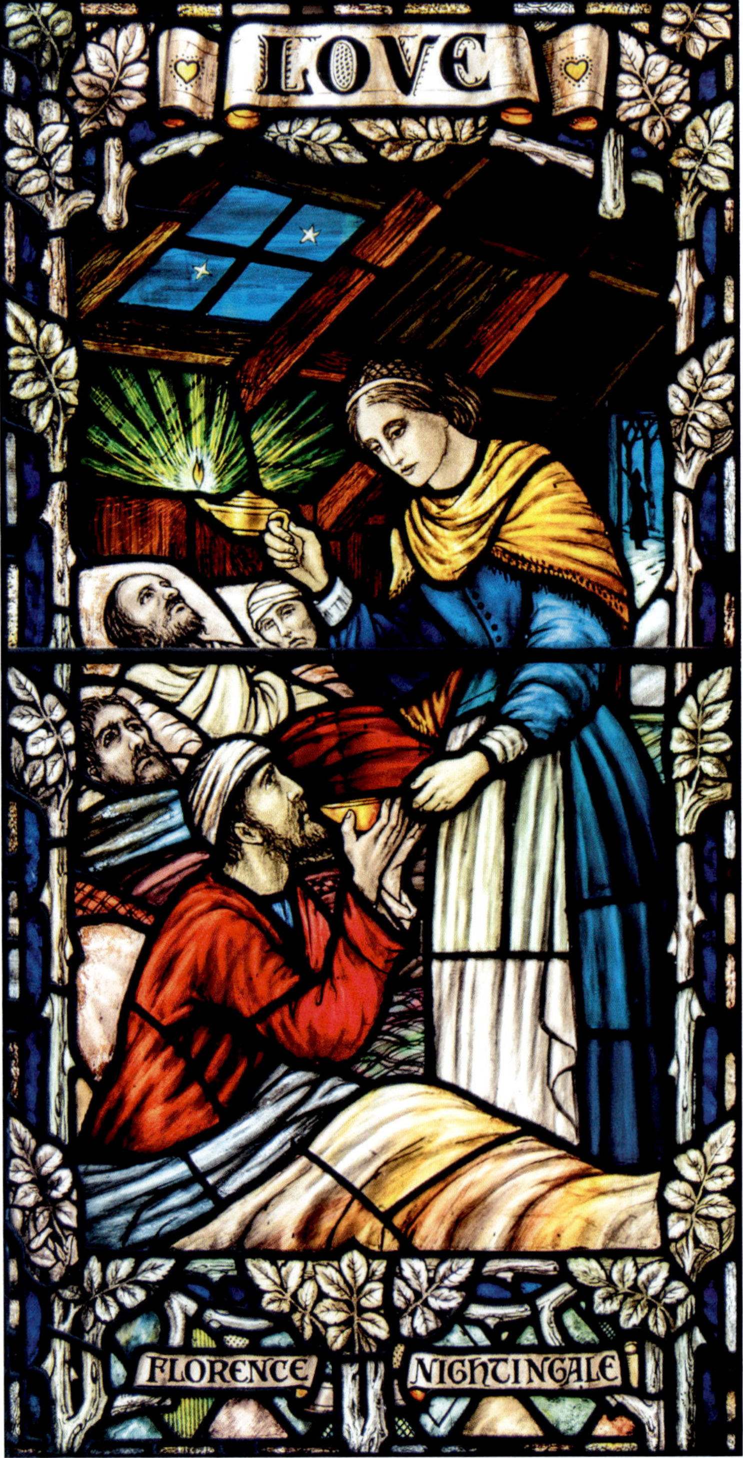

A.E. Child, detail of Florence Nightingale in *Discovery, Truth, Inspiration, Love, and Work (Wilson Memorial Window)* (1917–18)

them from the corresponding predella panels below. Also, like Whall, he utilized many pale translucent quarries which would allow for increased light to be transmitted to the church's interior, a particular issue for this north-facing window.

It is fortunate that the window's dedication sermon delivered by Revd Savell Hicks in June 1918 survives as he goes into considerable detail concerning many aspects of the choice and treatment of imagery, not all of which might be readily apparent. For instance, the figure of Christ, with dawn breaking in the background, is meant to be set in Gethsemane on the morning of the crucifixion though there are no visual clues to indicate this.[4]

To the left of Christ is a female figure representing Truth, clad in armour head to heel, who for Revd Savell Hicks was 'a symbol of intellectual honesty, integrity in action, and veracity of speech.'[5] At this stage, having created several war memorial windows, Child had had plenty of practice capturing the cool sheen of metal armour. To the left of Truth is a figure representing Discovery, personified as a scientist, described by Revd Savell Hicks as one who 'dares to think, to seek, to search out the hidden mysteries, and to grope in the danger and difficulty of the unknown forces and possibilities of the world.'[6] To the right of Inspiration/Christ is a female figure representing 'Love, the mother-instinct of humanity clasping the child, the symbol of the future, to her breast, while at her feet two elder children carry on the same thought in attitude and action; the elder offering a bowl of food to the younger, and the younger intending to share it with a tame robin which perches on her hand.'[7] We know from Child's daughter that he often used his children as models so it's likely that some feature in this window.[8] The fifth figure, a blacksmith toiling at a forge, represents Work, as he 'seizes the raw material of the earth and welds it to shape and use; which grows strong and stalwart in the process, which grapples with and overcomes difficulties … it may serve to remind us that all human accomplishment, all wealth, all civilization is built by Work.'[9]

In the predella panels below the five figures, Child has created illustrative vignettes to support the principal themes: Discovery is represented by Christopher Columbus on board with his crew; Truth represented by Martin Luther nailing his theses to the church door at Wittenberg; Inspiration by Jesus among the doctors in the temple; Love by Florence Nightingale; and Work by William Caxton at his

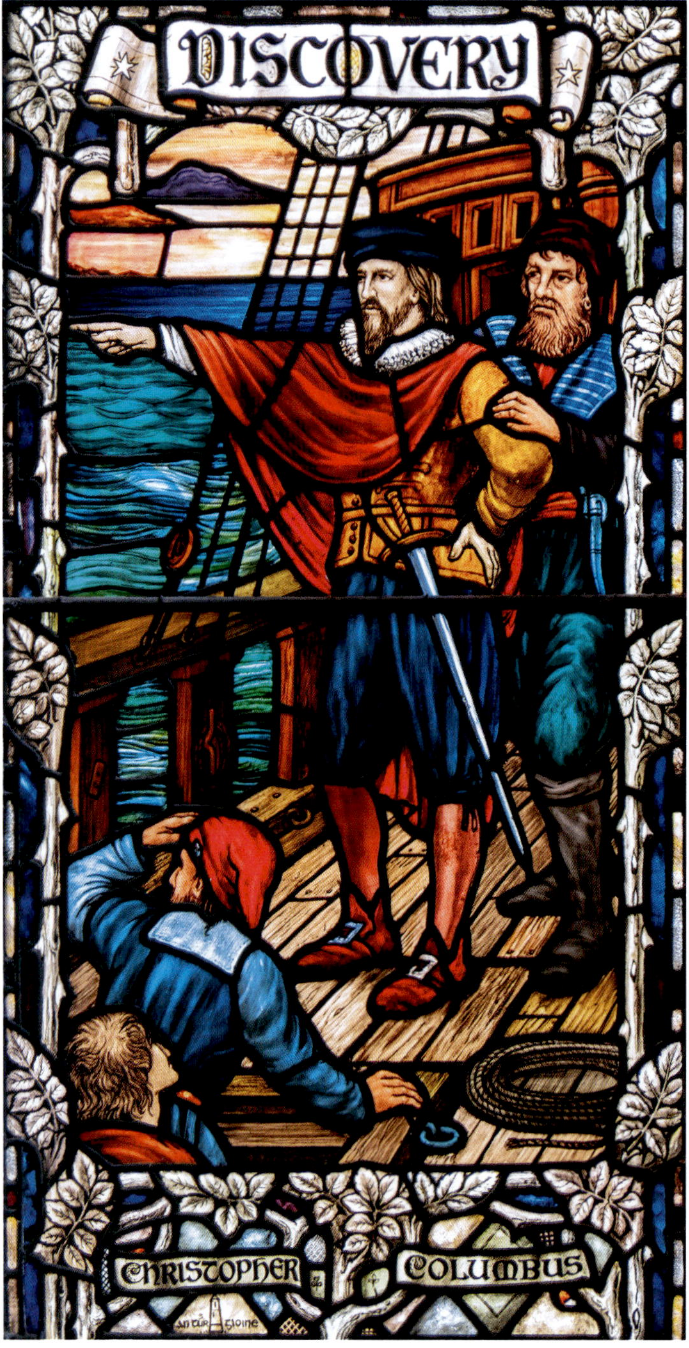

A.E. Child, detail of Christopher Columbus from *Discovery, Truth, Inspiration, Love, and Work (Wilson Memorial Window)* (1917–18)

printing press. In many respects these smaller scenes are more successful than the larger figures as they allowed Child to dramatize events, create moods, and add more expression to the figures as they interact. It is worth noting that Florence Nightingale, who came from a Unitarian family herself, had died only a few years previously. Her inclusion, depicted ministering to wounded soldiers, would have had a particular resonance for the Unitarian congregation in St Stephen's Green as they lost several young men in the First World War.

Above the five lights there is extensive tracery which comprises two large six-petaled roses, and, higher still, a trio of smaller ones at the apex, along with various trefoils and spandrels, all visually united by a deep blue sky sparkling with stars. The main themes that are addressed in the five lights are revisited in the rose windows. One of the tenants of Unitarianism are that reason, rational thought and science coexist with faith in God and so in the large rose to the left, above Discovery and Truth, Child combined these two themes in 'the figure of an astronomer, directing his instruments towards the distant stars, and bringing back to us the revelation which sets our thoughts towards vaster causes and greater issues than those of this small world – the revelation of an infinite Universe.'[10]

In the equivalent rose window on the right, Child combined the themes of Love and Work to illustrate a man and woman harvesting, 'a symbol at once of the labour of man, the never-failing providence of God, and the eternal promise of ever-renewed growth ... the glad earth yielding golden store of produce as the magic of their touch directs and concentrates its vast energies'.[11] It is worth noting that off in the distance of the field Child has included a tiny third worker, almost invisible to the naked eye. It is one of several details that are included throughout the window which add an additionally rewarding experience for those who take the time to explore it. At the base one can see a charming little An Túr Gloine logo and the national trade mark *Déanta in Éirinn*.

In his dedication ceremony address Revd Savell Hicks noted 'the great pains he [Child] has taken to give expression to what it was desired to convey in the design of the window, our very sincere appreciation of the loving care he bestowed upon it, and the never-failing courtesy with which he received, considered, and where possible acted upon, any suggestion made to him as work progressed. The association with him during the past year has been a pleasure ...' We also know from Child's daughter that of all the windows he made it was this one for the Unitarian church which he considered to be his best.[12] The newly constructed adjacent building, although considerably higher than the one it replaced, has been designed in such a way to allow increased daylight to benefit the window.

The next An Túr Gloine window to be made for the church was the work of Ethel Rhind, one of her final windows, and it was made in 1937. *The Good Samaritan* was ordered and paid for by a wealthy American, Miss Elizabeth West of New York and Massachusetts, and erected in memory of her parents, Albert Sargent West, a banker, and his wife, Martha Ann (née Sargent) of Massachusetts. Curiously, neither the West nor Sargent families had close Irish connections and it is not known why Elizabeth West chose Dublin's Unitarian church as the location for her parents' memorial. It is recorded that Elizabeth West visited An Túr Gloine, accompanied by Revd Savell Hicks, in May 1936 when she placed the order.[13]

The 2-light window principally comprises two scenes; the left light depicts the young traveller after he has been set upon by thieves, stripped of clothing and beaten, and who is being assisted by the kindly Samaritan who stopped to help, and the right light depicts the two protagonists again but this time it is an interior scene with the Samaritan paying an innkeeper to care for the traveller, now recuperating. Traversing the background of both lights Rhind has included a mountainous landscape featuring exotic trees below an azure sky with scorching sun. In the distance, on the steep twisting road, the Levite and Jewish priest, both of whom had ignored the injured traveller's plight, are seen making their way to Jerusalem. In the cusps of the two lights, in the middle, and at the base, Rhind has included decorative passages in shades of blue; what appears to be abstract designs but on close inspection (visible only with binoculars) feature leaping dog-like creatures and birds of paradise, both surrounded by floral designs reminiscent of blue and white middle eastern pottery and ceramics.

The single large piece of tracery above the two lights features a cherub's face framed by a profusion of crimson angel wings. The cherub's inclusion bears no connection to the parable depicted below and one wonders if it was possibly intended to commemorate Louise Caroline West, Elizabeth's elder sister who died aged one, the year before Elizabeth was born.[14] It is recorded that Elizabeth West returned to Ireland in spring 1938 when she presumably viewed her window in the church.

It is perhaps surprising that Sarah Purser who had not only established An Túr Gloine (with Edward Martyn) but had also funded the enterprise from the outset, and for nearly four decades liaised with the patrons, assigned jobs to the individual artists, and promoted the studio tirelessly, only ordered a single church window herself, and that was in the year she died, 1943. It was in memory of Margaret Huxley (1855–1940), a kindred spirit who like Purser was a pioneering, independent woman; in the case of Miss Huxley, her principal life's mission related to the professionalization of nurses' training, and she was also a champion of improved housing for the poor.[15] The window was designed by Catherine O'Brien, who by 1943, along with Evie Hone, were the only artists still working at An Túr Gloine. The window comprises three irregularly-shaped trefoils, and in addition to the

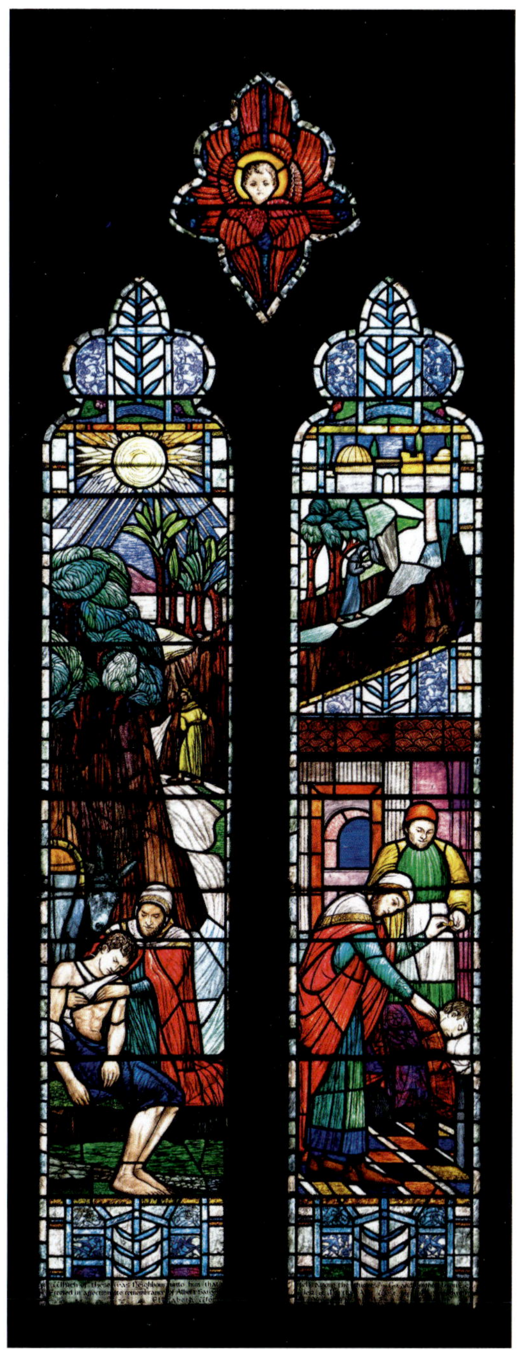

Ethel Rhind, *The Good Samaritan* (1937)

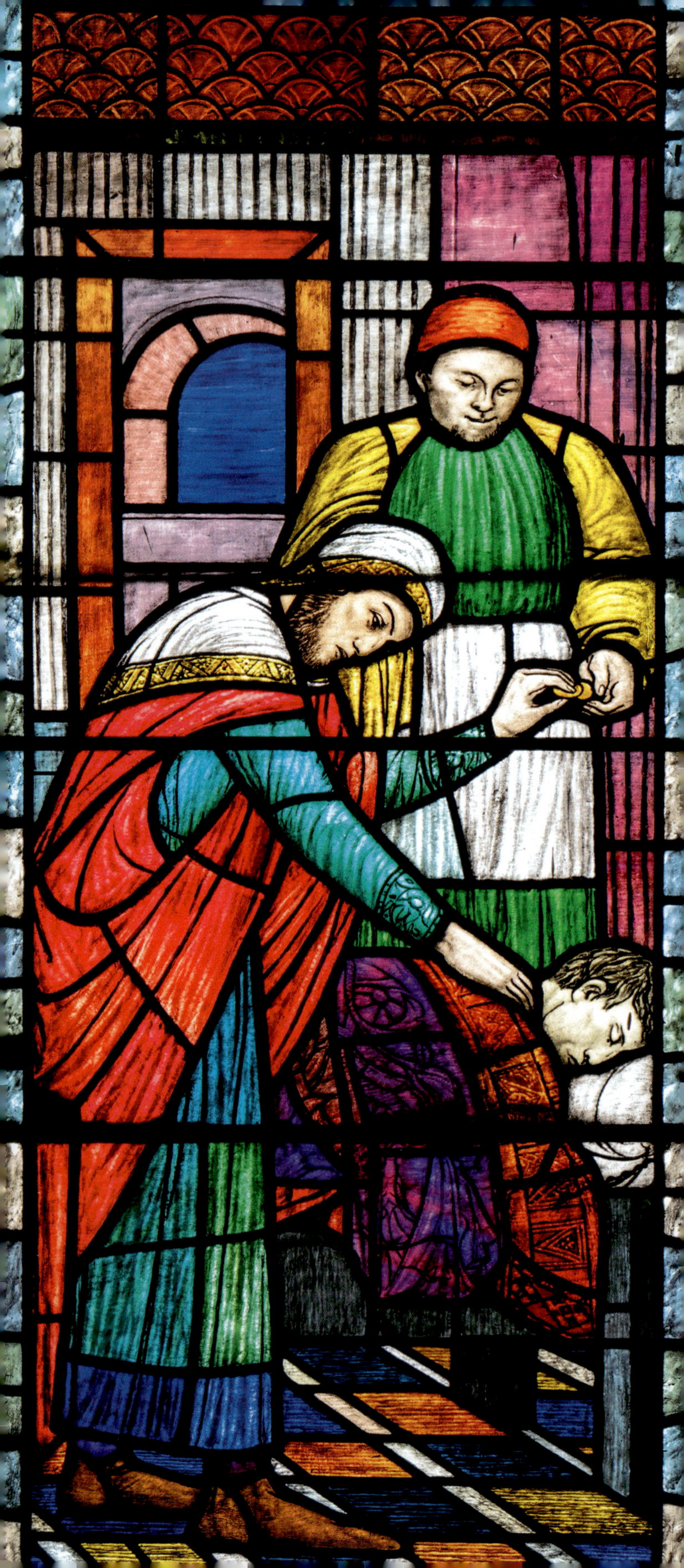

succinct exhortation 'Remember Margaret Huxley, a great woman', Purser chose three words that encapsulated Huxley's personality and character to feature on a scroll in each of the trefoils – 'courage', 'efficiency' and 'kindness' – qualities that could have been applied to Miss Purser too, indisputably another 'great woman'. O'Brien's cheerful window brims with swirling foliate forms, mainly utilizing blue, red, green and gold, a colour palette reminiscent of medieval glass such as those of the great French cathedrals that O'Brien and Purser had visited together decades earlier.[16] Sarah Purser died unexpectedly following a stroke on 7 August 1943 and the dedication service for Miss Huxley's window, officiated by Revd Savell Hicks, took place on 19 September so sadly it is virtually certain Miss Purser never got to see the window in situ.[17]

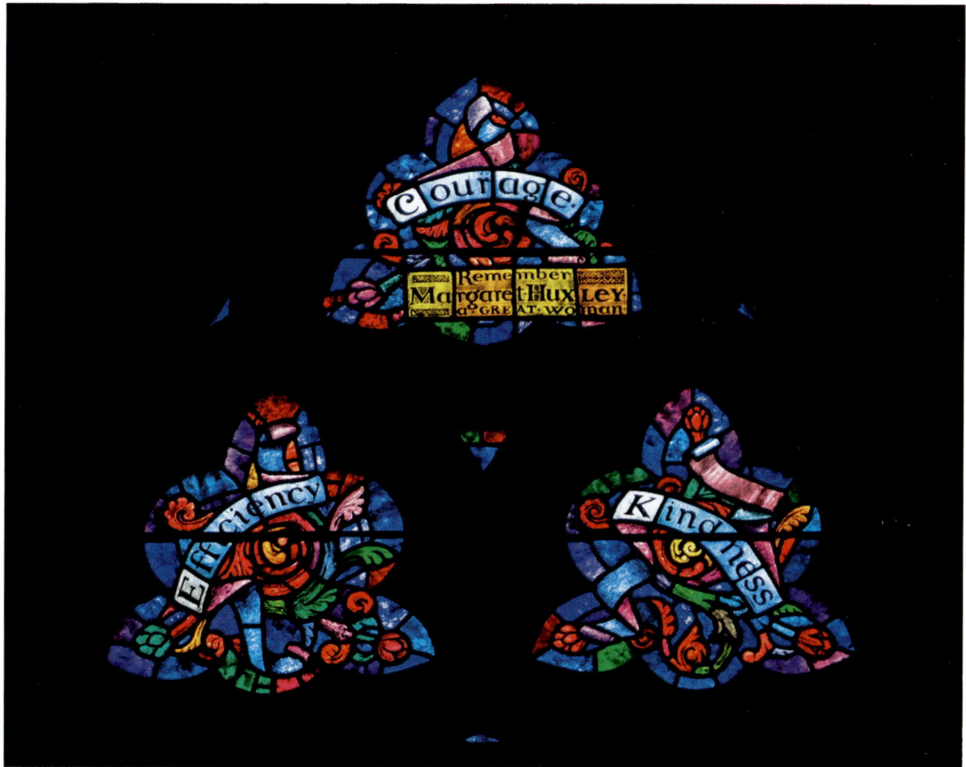

(above) Catherine O'Brien, *Courage, Efficiency, Kindness (Huxley Memorial Window)* (1943)
(opposite) Ethel Rhind, detail of *The Good Samaritan* (1937)

Dublin North, Suburbs and County

12 Artane
St John Vianney church (RC),
Ardlea Road, D05 TH79
Our Lady of Mercy church (RC),
Brookwood Grove, D05 FH28

13 Balbriggan
Saints Peter and Paul's church (RC),
Dublin Street, K32 YW77

14 Ballymun
Our Lady of Victories church (RC),
Ballymun Road, D09 Y925

15 Dollymount
Manresa Jesuit Centre of Spirituality,
Clontarf Road, D03 FP52

16 Donnycarney
Our Lady of Consolation church (RC),
Malahide Road, D05 XN22

17 Drumcondra
Our Lady Seat of Wisdom chapel (RC) and 'Quiet Space',
St Patrick's Campus (DCU),
Drumcondra Road Upper, D09 YT18

18 Dublin Airport
Our Lady Queen of Heaven church (RC),
K67 HX98

19 Howth
St Mary's church (C of I),
Howth Road, D13 V259

20 Lusk
St MacCullin's church (RC),
Chapel Road, K45 TY26

21 Malahide
St Andrew's church (C of I),
Church Road, K36 HE33
Presbyterian church,
Dublin Road, K36 PE80
St Sylvester's church (RC),
Main Street, K36 HR63

22 Santry
St Pappin's church (C of I),
Santry Villas, D09 W597

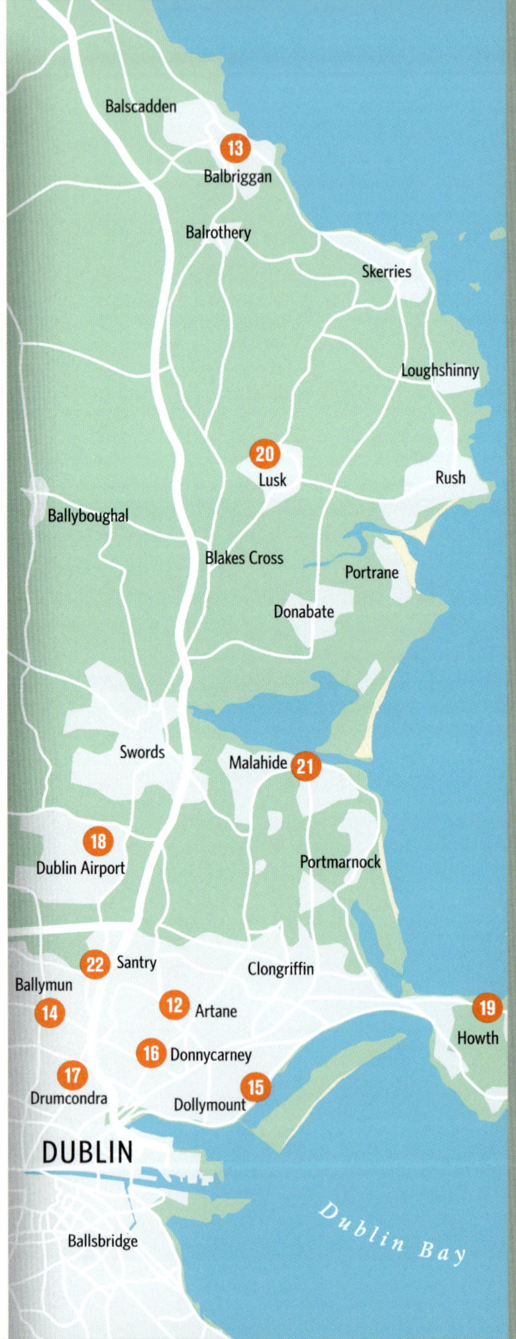

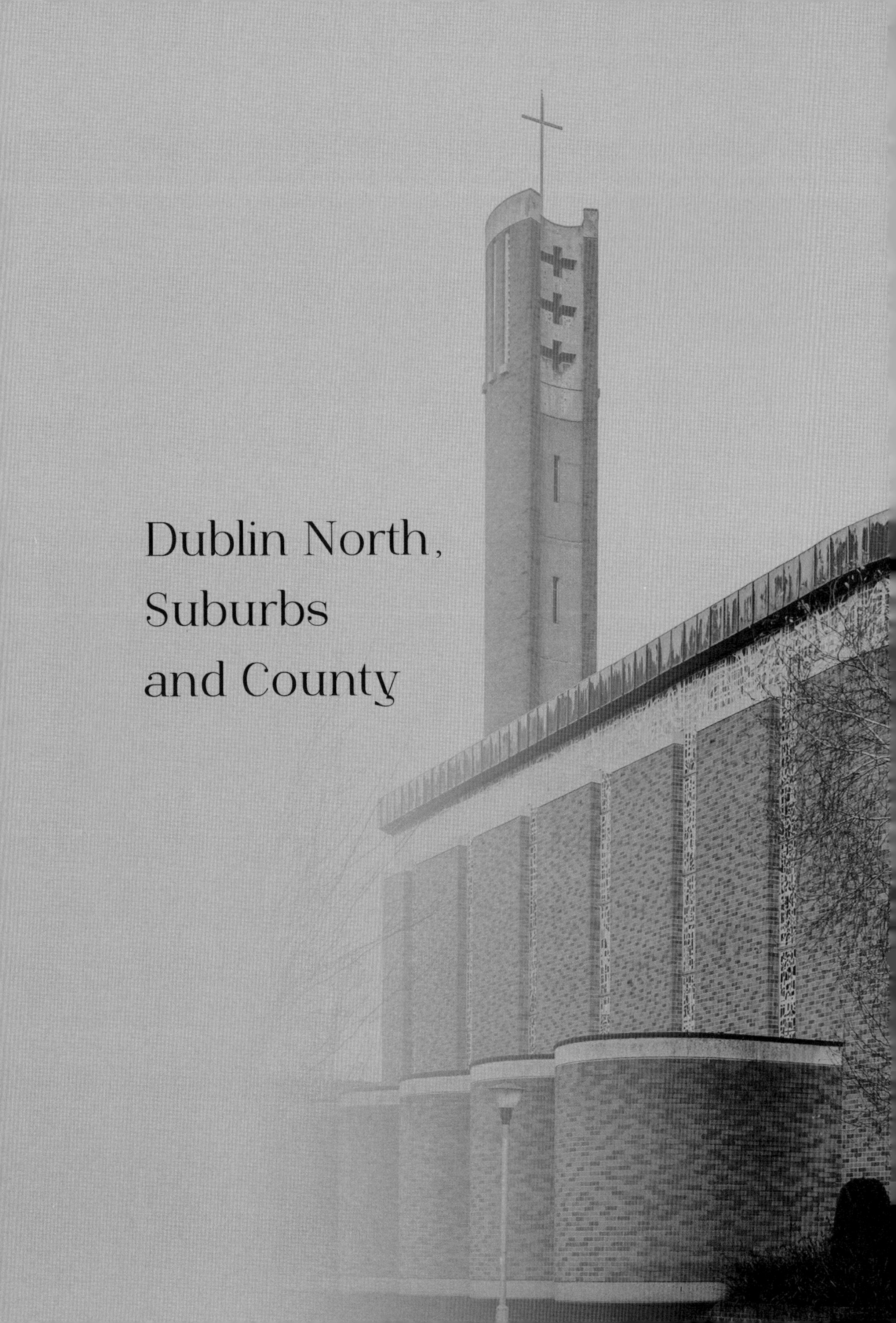

Dublin North, Suburbs and County

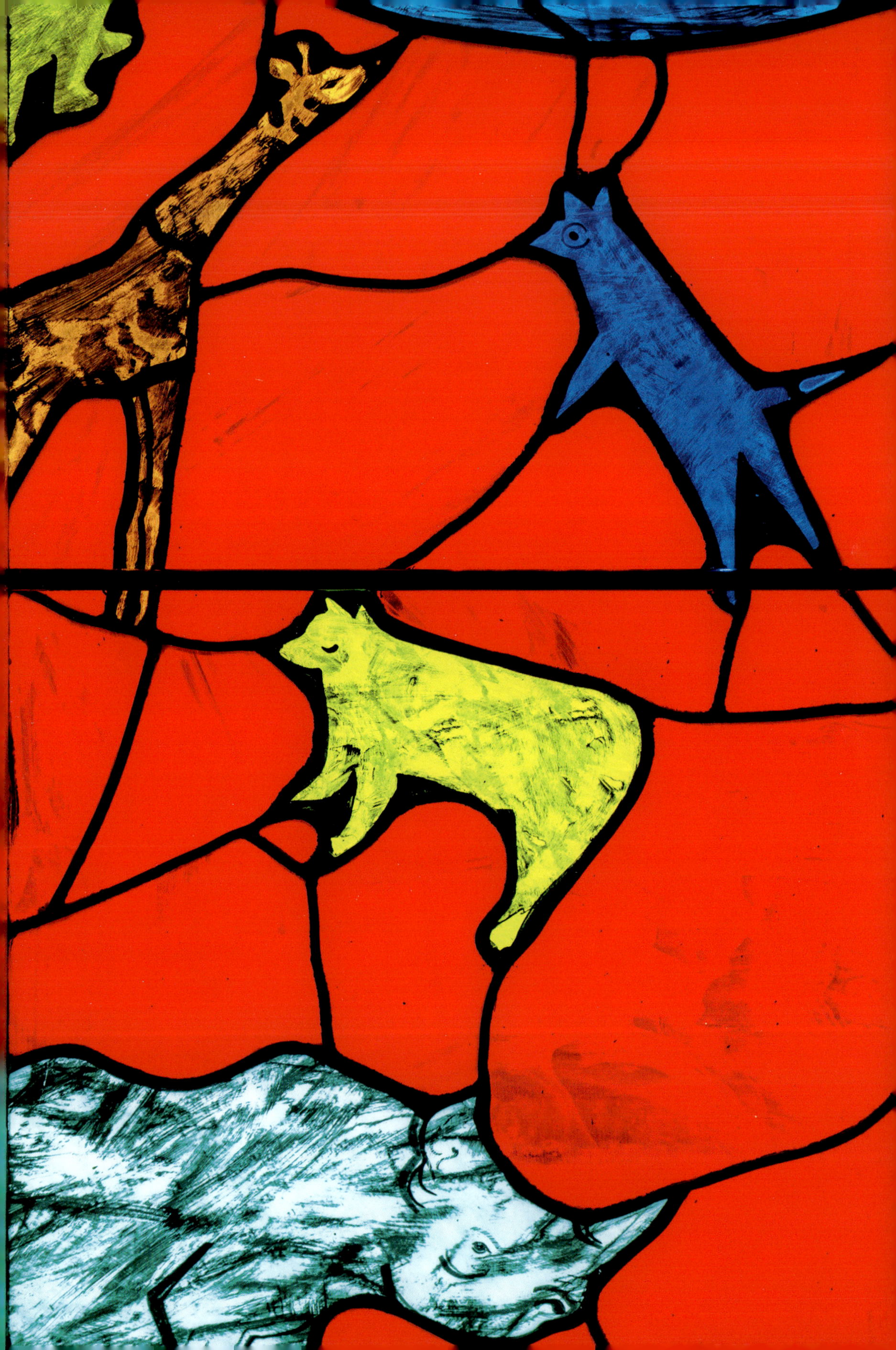

ARTANE

Two churches in Artane, St John Vianney and Our Lady of Mercy, contain interesting collections of stained glass so both are included here.

St John Vianney church (RC)

Ardlea Road, D05 TH79

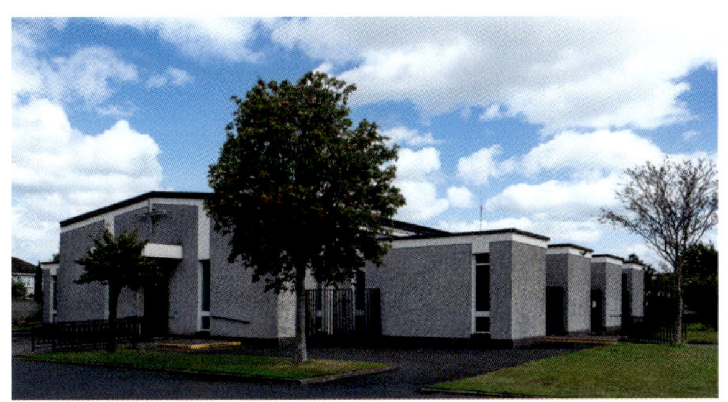

St John Vianney's church came about when the priest assigned to the new parish, Fr Joseph Newth, decided that 'rather than build one grandiose church at an astronomical cost, I propose that we build two simple, solid, serviceable churches – one in Ardlea and one in Greencastle',[1] and so two identical utilitarian buildings costed at £45,000 each were built 2km apart in 1969 with designs prepared by Edward W. Brady. The architect's proposed sketch which was pitched to the parishioners in a brochure indicated there would be stained glass windows but in reality the original budget proved insufficient for this embellishment.

(opposite) Patrick Muldowney, detail of animals from Noah's ark caught in a sea storm in *Jubilee Windows 3* (*c.*2000)

In 1993 the parish priest, Fr Michael Walsh, commissioned a modestly-sized stained glass window for the right side of the church's entrance lobby – an area originally assigned to be the baptistry – from Kilkenny-born Dublin-based artist, Patrick Muldowney (b.1955), who had trained under Johnny Murphy at NCAD. The rectangular window comprises five panels depicting (top to bottom) *Dove, The Miracle of Loaves and Fishes, The Crucifixion, The Last Supper, Agnus Dei.*

As the year 2000 approached, Pope John Paul II promoted it as the Great Jubilee heralding the beginning of the third Christian millennium. In the parish of St John Vianney, Fr Andrew Ryder, the then parish priest, decided to mark the event by commissioning a series of stained glass windows, collectively titled *The Jubilee Windows*, and again Patrick Muldowney was called upon. Lengthy discussions ensued until they both were satisfied that Muldowney's visual concepts matched Fr Ryder's interpretations of a key quotation he had selected for each pair of windows from either the Old or New Testaments. Muldowney then retreated to his studio on the Greek island of Leros where he developed preparatory watercolours with a palette drawn from the turquoise sea and inspired by the icons and frescoes of the little hilltop churches that surrounded him.[2] When the first pair of windows was completed in 1999 they were installed on the north wall but the limited light dulled Muldowney's vibrant colours and following encouragement from him they and the remaining pair of figurative windows – made over the following years as funds became available – were installed on the south wall.[3] Fr Ryder erected four small panels to accompany each pair of windows which contained the quote he had selected and his personal reflections upon it, and this commentary helps the viewer to understand the disparate selection of subjects and treatment of imagery.

Jubilee Windows 1 was inspired by a quote from Exodus, 'I am the Lord, your God, who brought you out of the land of slavery', and features in the left light Moses as an infant in his wicker basket being whisked by his sister out of the swirling waters of the turquoise Nile, colours perhaps inspired by the Aegean Sea. The companion window features the adult Moses, though youthful and without the stereotypical grey beard, clasping the Ten Commandments to his chest, above him the burning bush, and beneath him the golden calf, a reminder of the worship of false gods.

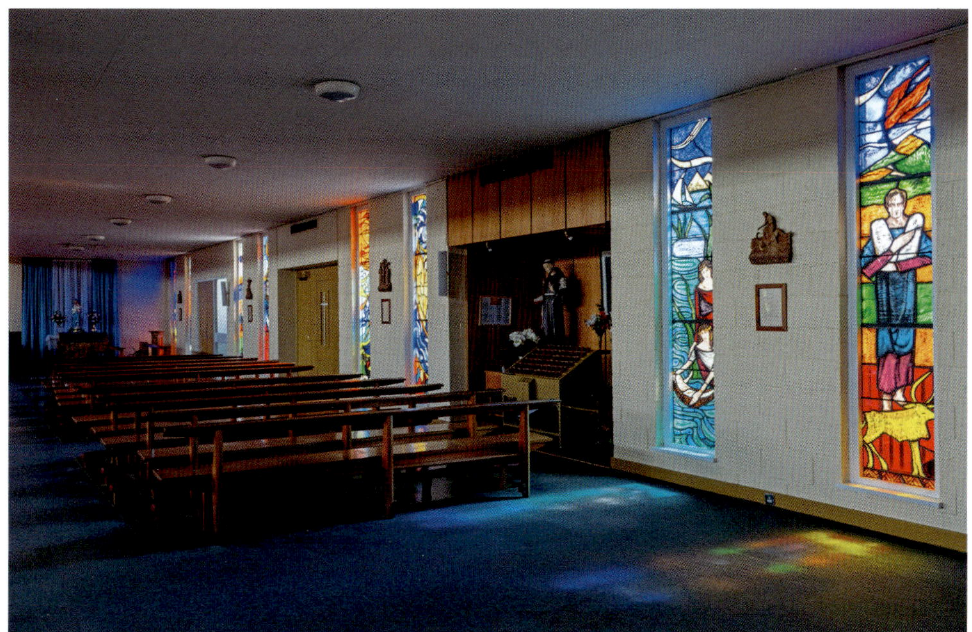

Patrick Muldowney, south wall featuring *Jubilee Windows 1 – 4* (1999–2001)

Compositionally an azure blue sky links both scenes with the pyramids on the left echoed by the striking profile of Mount Sinai on the right.

The quote which inspired *Jubilee Windows 2* comes from Hebrews 13:8, 'Jesus Christ is the same yesterday, today and tomorrow', which was challenging to represent due to its conceptual nature. The two lights present contrasting images; the left light reflects human frailty and failure, perhaps a salutary warning of how the future could be: a sun consumed by a ball of fire, a youth pierced by a sword and brought to his knees, gazing down in despair at an open grave. By comparison, the right light represents the past, the moment of creation; the figure of Christ bestows a blessing on the faithful while above five white doves circle around an olive wreath symbolizing the hope of peace.

Jubilee Windows 3 features what appears on the surface to be two incompatible images: St Brigid and Noah's ark. Fr Ryder was keen to include the saint not only to reference Ireland's contribution to the first two thousand years of Christianity, but also her love of animals and link it to the animals saved on the ark. Muldowney has

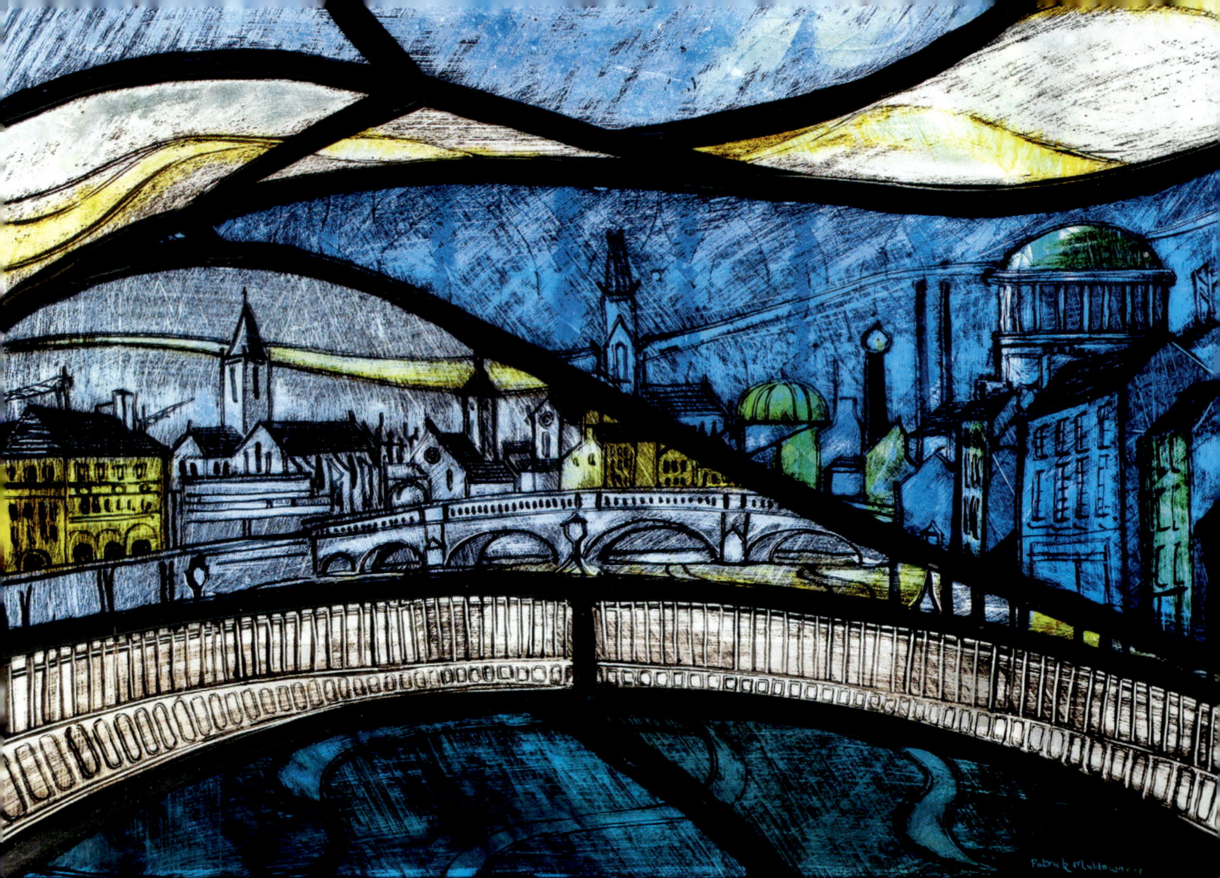

Patrick Muldowney, detail of Dublin from *Jubilee Windows 4* (2000–1)

depicted a serene St Brigid accompanied by a deer and a dog, the model for the latter being one of the artist's own dogs. The companion light has the ark caught in the eye of a violent sea storm, and below the animals have been flung about against a bright red background. However, there is cause for optimism; a rainbow and above it a dove carrying a sprig of olive to indicate that the waters were receding and land was nearby.

The pair of windows nearest the altar, *Jubilee Windows 4*, depict the Angel Gabriel in the left light and Our Lady in the right light, but this is no conventional representation of *The Annunciation* as the right light depicts the coming of the Holy Spirit at Pentecost. According to Fr Ryder's notes, Our Lady's prayers will bring the Holy Spirit's gifts and 'these blessings will enable us to give witness to Jesus Christ in our city and our world', and below the Pentecost scene there is a charming vignette of Dublin as viewed, appropriately, from the Millennium Bridge.

Our Lady of Mercy church (RC)

Brookwood Grove, D05 FH28

Our Lady of Mercy church, located on Brookwood Grove and Gracefield Road, is a large monolith designed by Downes, Meehan & Robinson in 1967–8 and constructed of cheerless grey concrete brick. Our Lady of Mercy was one of many churches dedicated to the Virgin Mary during the reign of Archbishop McQuaid. The uninviting brutalist exterior does not prepare one for the colourful interior; an example of the transformative effect of stained glass. The church used to be significantly longer but in the early 2000s a decision was made to hive off the final third, erect a new sanctuary wall, and behind it create a parish hall and ancillary rooms.

On entering the lofty space, one cannot escape the washes of colour cast by the six (originally nine) full height windows on either side of the nave, each made from hundreds of rectangles of pot metal glass in different shades of a chosen colour creating a spectrum effect. Walking towards the altar and turning around one encounters a vast square window above the choir gallery, titled *Our Lady of Ransom*, which was designed by Christopher Campbell (1908–72). The origin of the devotion dates back to the 1200s when a religious order was founded for the redemption of captives seized by the Moors in Spain and on the seas, and the clerics sought donations to raise the funds to pay ransoms. The name of the feast day dedicated to Our Lady of Ransom was changed post-Vatican II to Our Lady of Mercy.

Christopher Campbell initially trained at Harry Clarke's studio in the 1930s,[4] and was back working at Clarke's from 1954 to 1963,[5] though almost certainly as a glass painter rather than a designer. In his earlier years he certainly created some designs for stained glass windows in the style of Harry Clarke but the few extant windows

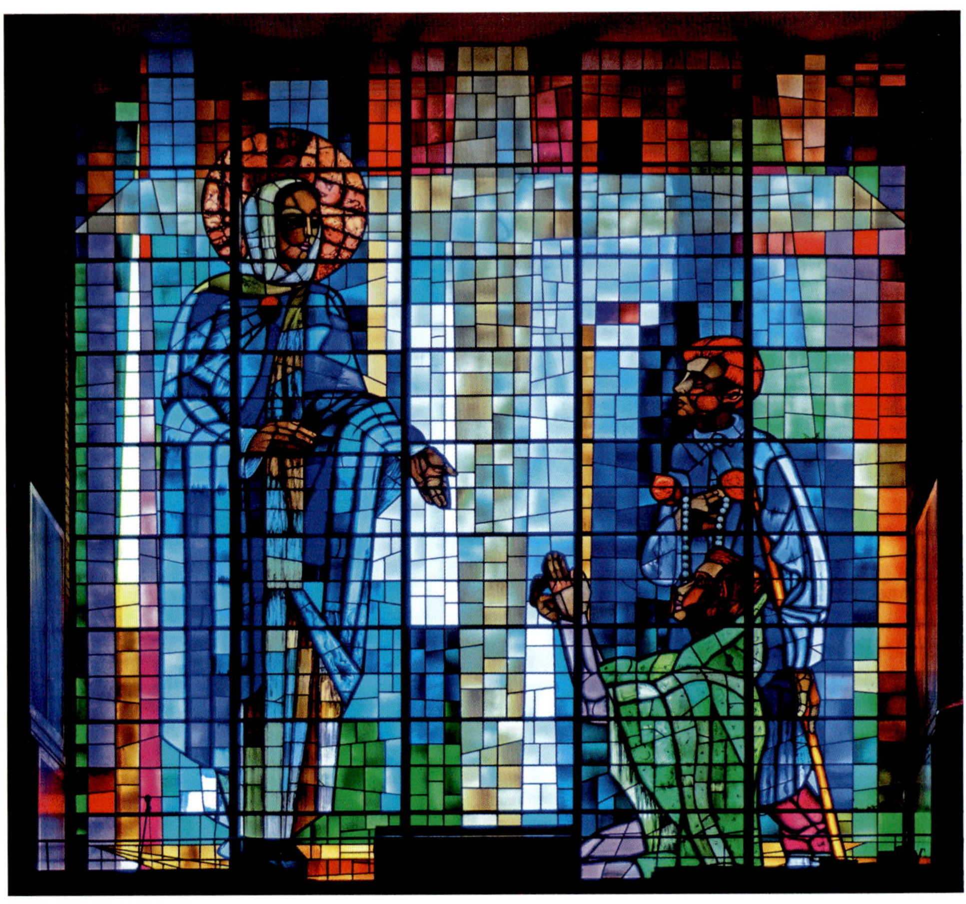

Christopher Campbell, *Our Lady of Ransom* (*c.*1968)

that have been identified by him are decidedly modern and the antithesis of Clarke. In this instance Campbell has depicted Our Lady comforting two young men, one with crutches and rosary beads, the other on his knees; it is not the standard iconography associated with Our Lady of Ransom which usually shows her giving shelter under her cloak or dispensing bags of coins (ransoms), or a scapular. Significantly, all three figures are depicted with distinctly dark skin tones, presumably to reference Our Lady of Ransom's association with the Moors. The figures, set against a flat though colourful background that evokes mosaic tesserae, features a subtle cross shape in the exact centre of the composition.

Either side of the choir balcony are two full height figurative windows, also by Campbell: on the left *The Risen Christ*, and on the right *The Baptism of Christ*, located in alcoves that were originally conceived to function as mortuary chapel and baptistry respectively. Unfortunately, in recent years a store room was constructed at the base of the former and a toilet at the base of the latter so it is now impossible to appreciate fully what would appear to be dramatic windows drawing on disparate stylistic influences. However, it is still possible to view the top and bottom halves of the windows separately which is worth doing even if it presents an odd experience encountering Christ's soaring feet in the store room, and two giant disconnected legs and fish when entering the lobby of the toilet. Noteworthy is Campbell's expressionist treatment of St John the Baptist, depicted with wild red hair and beard and who bears some resemblance to Luke Kelly of The Dubliners. Campbell signed his name at the base of both windows, followed by 'I.A.G.'[6] It is not known where Campbell had his large windows fabricated. Campbell was a regular exhibitor in Dublin and there are two oil paintings by him in Our Lady of Mercy.

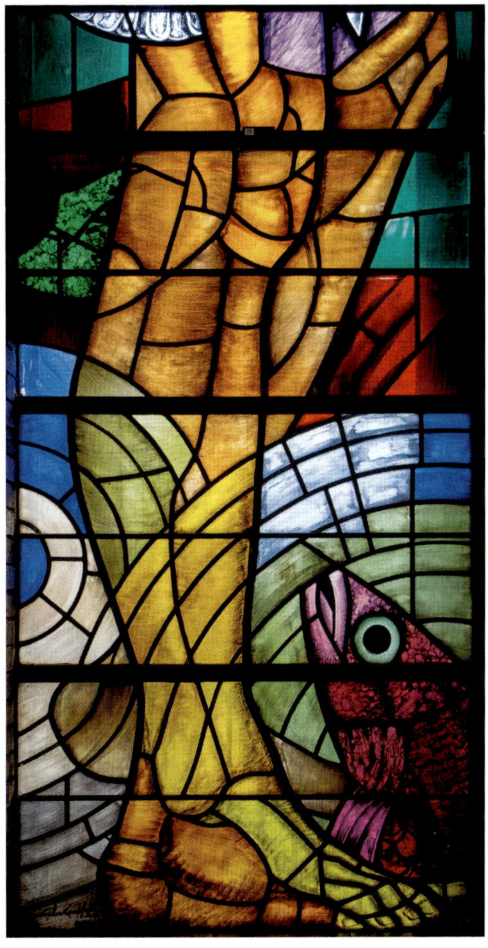

Christopher Campbell, detail of lower section of *The Baptism of Christ* (*c.*1968)

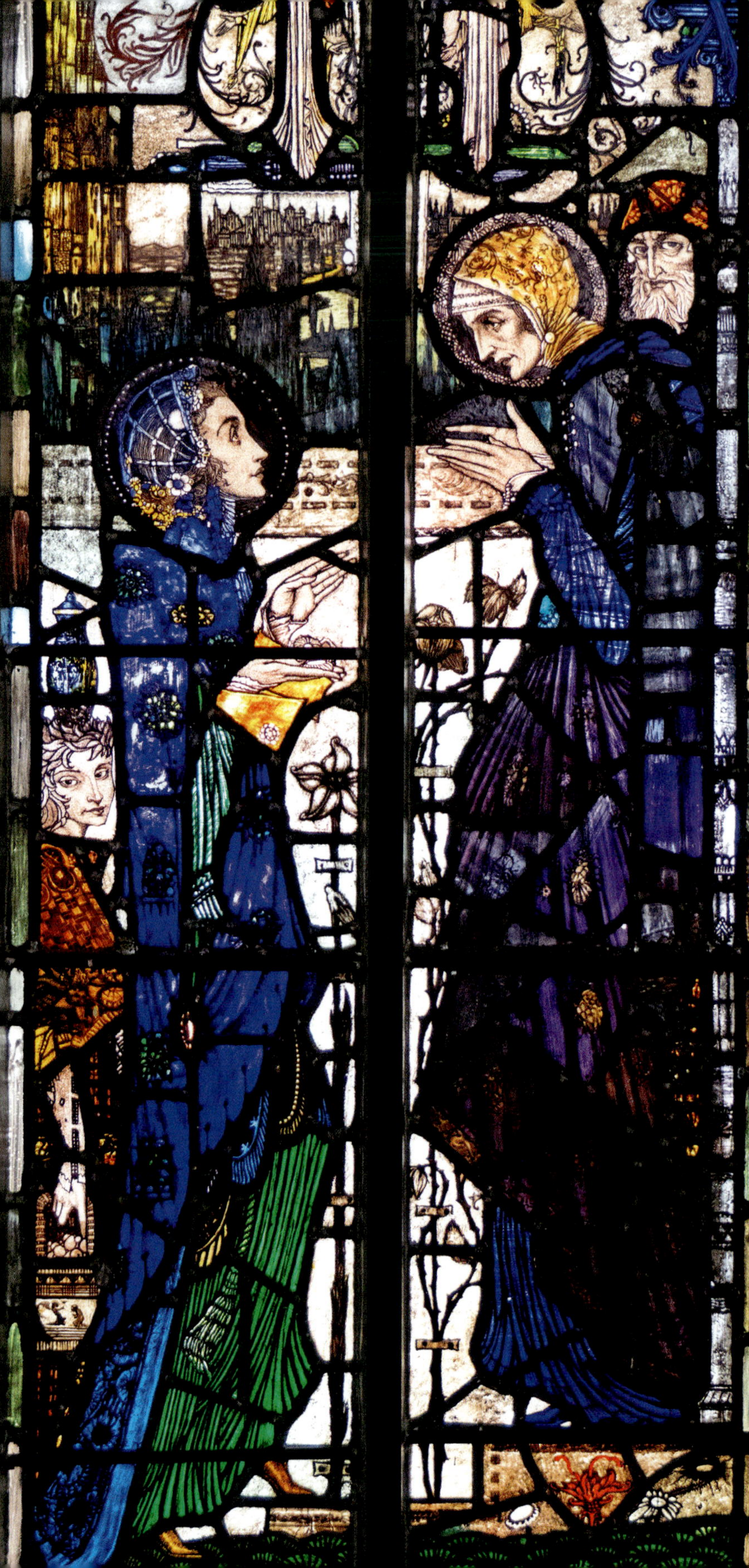

Saints Peter and Paul's church (RC)

Dublin Street, K32 YW77

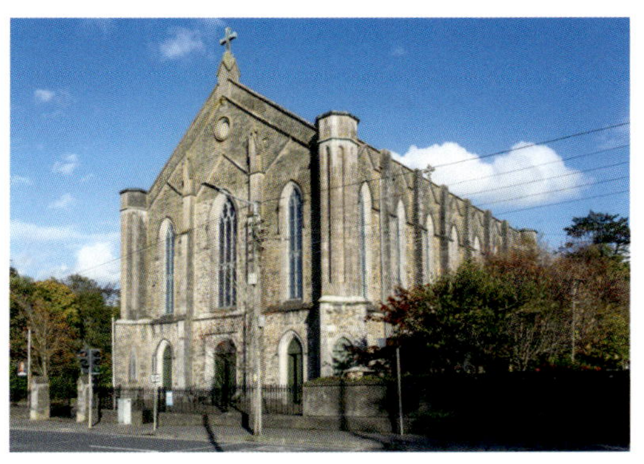

An imposing Gothic edifice of eclectic design and constructed of coursed limestone rubble with ashlar limestone quoining, the church of Saints Peter and Paul opened in 1842. Patrick Byrne has been identified as the possible architect and it was later remodelled in the mid-1890s by George Coppinger Ashlin who added the sanctuary, Gothic vaulting, sacristy and an organ gallery. High and wide inside, it is principally lit by two rows of clear glazed, double lancet clerestory windows which makes for an exceptionally bright nave, usually not ideal conditions to appreciate stained glass. Subdued lighting conditions within a building (with artificial lights preferably turned off) allows the stained glass to 'sing' without any distraction from reflected internal light.

(opposite) Harry Clarke, detail of *The Visitation* (1924)

If one wants to visit a single church that contains some exceptional stained glass by Harry Clarke, and excellent windows by his two best assistants, Richard King and William Dowling (both of whom became successive managers of his studio after he died), then one of the places to visit is the church of St Peter and Paul in Balbriggan, to view fifteen windows in total. Many stained glass enthusiasts will doubtless be eager to see the two windows by Harry Clarke first, which are the earliest Irish windows in the church and both were made in 1924; they can be found facing each other in the north and south walls adjacent to the two side altars.

In April 1923 the parish priest, Canon Eugene D. Byrne, wrote to Harry Clarke confirming the order: 'With much pleasure I give you the commission for the erection of two stained glass windows measured by your brother [Walter] last Saturday. The subjects you submit are admirable [*The Widow's Son* and *The Visitation*]. May I suggest for the altar beside the Sacred Heart, The Widow's Son and for the altar beside Our Lady's altar *The Presentation* or *Visitation of the BVM* [Blessed Virgin Mary] – whichever you prefer.'[1] Worth noting is that Canon Byrne was happy to give Clarke an element of free rein in selecting the subject matter, perhaps a reflection of the status Clarke had by then attained. The windows were to be erected in memory of two deceased parishioners, retired school teacher Marcella Rogers who died in 1921, and Kathleen Cumisky, a woman of some means, who died in 1922, the latter leaving £100 to Canon Byrne for the church and which would go most of the way to covering the cost of £116 for both windows.

In April also, Harry Clarke was commissioned to undertake what would become one of his most famous secular works, *The Eve of St Agnes* (see pp 28, 31–6). By now there was considerable pressure on Clarke who was juggling several orders including his *The Coronation of the Virgin in Glory* for St Joseph's, Terenure (see pp 337–40). While Clarke had drawn the Balbriggan cartoons in fine detail and with coloured washes by November he had previously agreed with Canon Byrne that the completed *The Visitation* would have been installed by then. The following March he wrote to the priest stating that he felt 'utterly ashamed' of himself for the delay. This was partly due, he explained, because of the studio being moved to a larger premises on the opposite side of North Frederick Street. However the good news was that 'the windows are drawn, the glass cut, the heads and hands painted and the bulk of the work should be through in say another six weeks.'[2] Sadly a few weeks later Canon Byrne died after a short illness and a further delay with the windows ensued.

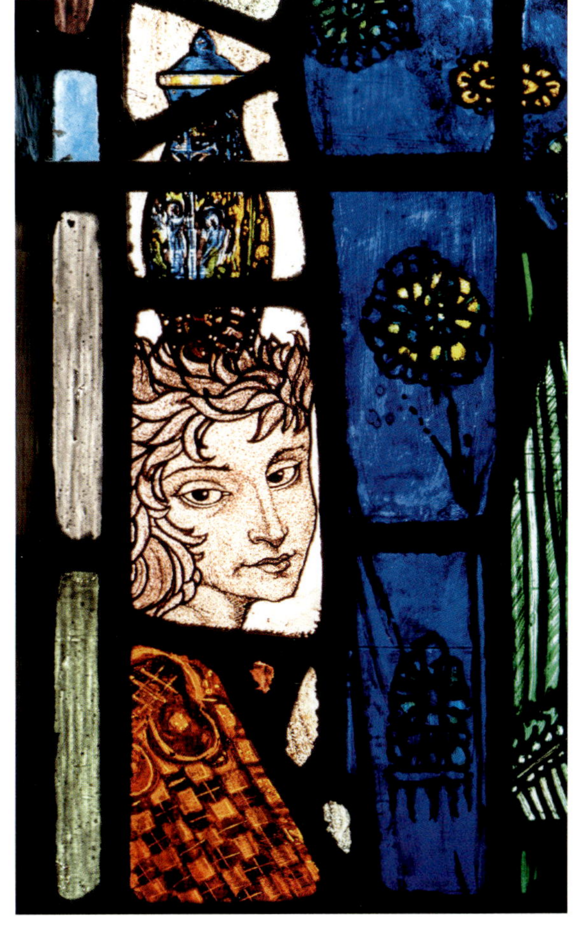

Harry Clarke, detail of Our Lady's attendant in *The Visitation* (1924)

Both *The Visitation* and *The Widow's Son* are located near eye level and so the detail is easy to appreciate but because the windows are deeply recessed it is not possible to get really close to inspect them.

Occasionally Harry Clarke is critiqued for creating works that are excessively decorative and ultimately vacuous but in *The Visitation* there is a remarkable intensity in the interaction between the young Virgin Mary and her much older cousin, Elizabeth, both with eyes locked together. The scene takes place as Mary enters Elizabeth's house in Judah, and in the background Clarke has depicted the city as a vertiginous concoction of tall towers and off in the distance is Nazareth, from where Mary came, looking distinctly central European with a plethora of turrets and spires. Elizabeth's husband, Zacharias, stands close to his pregnant wife and seems to observe us, the viewers, warily as if we are intruding on a private moment.

There is another figure too, a young girl at Mary's side who gazes out also but in a more distracted manner, probably an attendant who accompanied her on the long journey to Judah, and although not having any scriptural origin there are art historical precedents for including an attendant.[3] The girl is carrying a basket, which has a silhouetted Annunciation scene emblazoned on it, referencing that that event foreshadowed the Visitation. The basket is filled with what appear to be mushrooms and possibly pears, presumably sustenance for the journey. At the same time she is somewhat bizarrely balancing a beautiful glazed ceramic urn on her head that has two figures, difficult to discern, painted on it, and one could speculate that the urn or its contents are a gift from Mary to Elizabeth. Anna Brownell Jameson, a noted Victorian art historian, whom Harry Clarke is known to have admired, in her writing referenced some versions of *The Visitation* in which Mary's handmaid carries a basket on her head, so perhaps this is where he got the idea and substituted an urn.[4] Ultimately it seems that Clarke is being somewhat whimsical, and relishing the opportunity to introduce secular elements with decorative potential into a standard religious narrative. Mary inexplicably also seems to have a few mushrooms in the open palm of her hand (though a glazing bar partly obscures this detail).

The upper portion of the two lights features four little angels in white gowns amid delicate unfurling fronds, hinting towards the thicker black furry fronds which will feature prominently in Clarke's *The Eve of St Agnes,* and also in his Bewley's windows. There is also the capital of a classical pillar on which sits a blue tazza and which provides a roost for two cockatoos, and again these elements provide a foretaste of the Orders of Architecture windows in Bewley's (see pp 8–14).

At the base of both lights, instead of predella panels there are two vesica shapes, each containing a vignette: the Nativity on the left, and the baptism of Christ by St John the Baptist on the right; two scenes that are a natural progression from the story of the Visitation. The vignettes are skilfully fashioned from painted and stained blue flashed glass.

Clarke's *The Widow's Son* is situated directly opposite and depicts the story of Christ's arrival at the village of Nain during the burial ceremony of a widow's only son. She had previously lost her husband, and touched by the woman's plight, Christ raised the young man from the dead. Clarke has depicted seven mourners pressed in around Christ witnessing the man, as if in a trance, sit upright while his mother lowers her head in a mixture of reverence and nervous awe. Clarke often enlarged

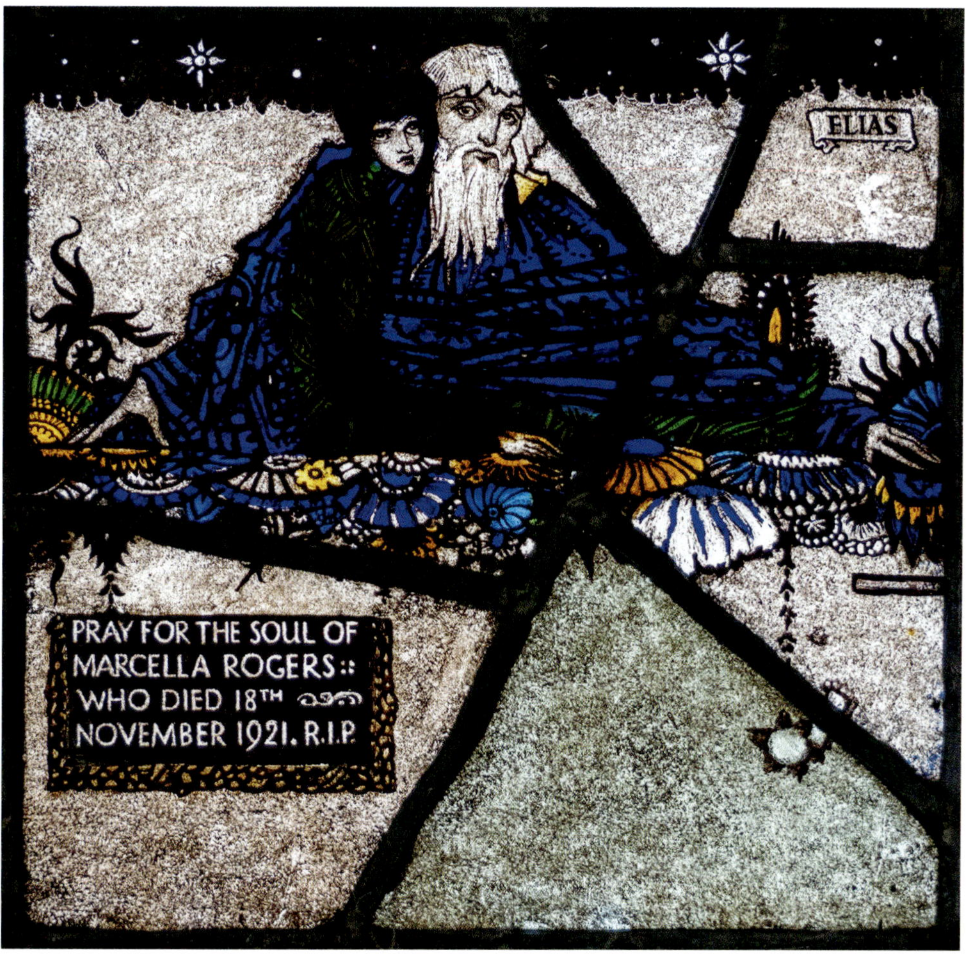

Harry Clarke, detail of Elias (Elijah) who raised the son of the widow of Zarephath in *The Widow's Son* (1924)

the eyes of his subjects, but particularly so here, and it is as if Christ and several of the mourners are welling up with tears so moved were they by the sadness of the occasion. Each face, full of individual character, is drawn with precision almost as if it were done with a fine pen on parchment, some recalling Dürer, another Botticelli.

At the head of each light there is a glamorous angel who appears to have emerged from between decorative clouds, which have been trimmed with fine beading, as if making a dramatic entrance. Fine black fronds swirl about in a symmetrical but organic manner, some magically sprouting flowers. These flights of fancy owe more

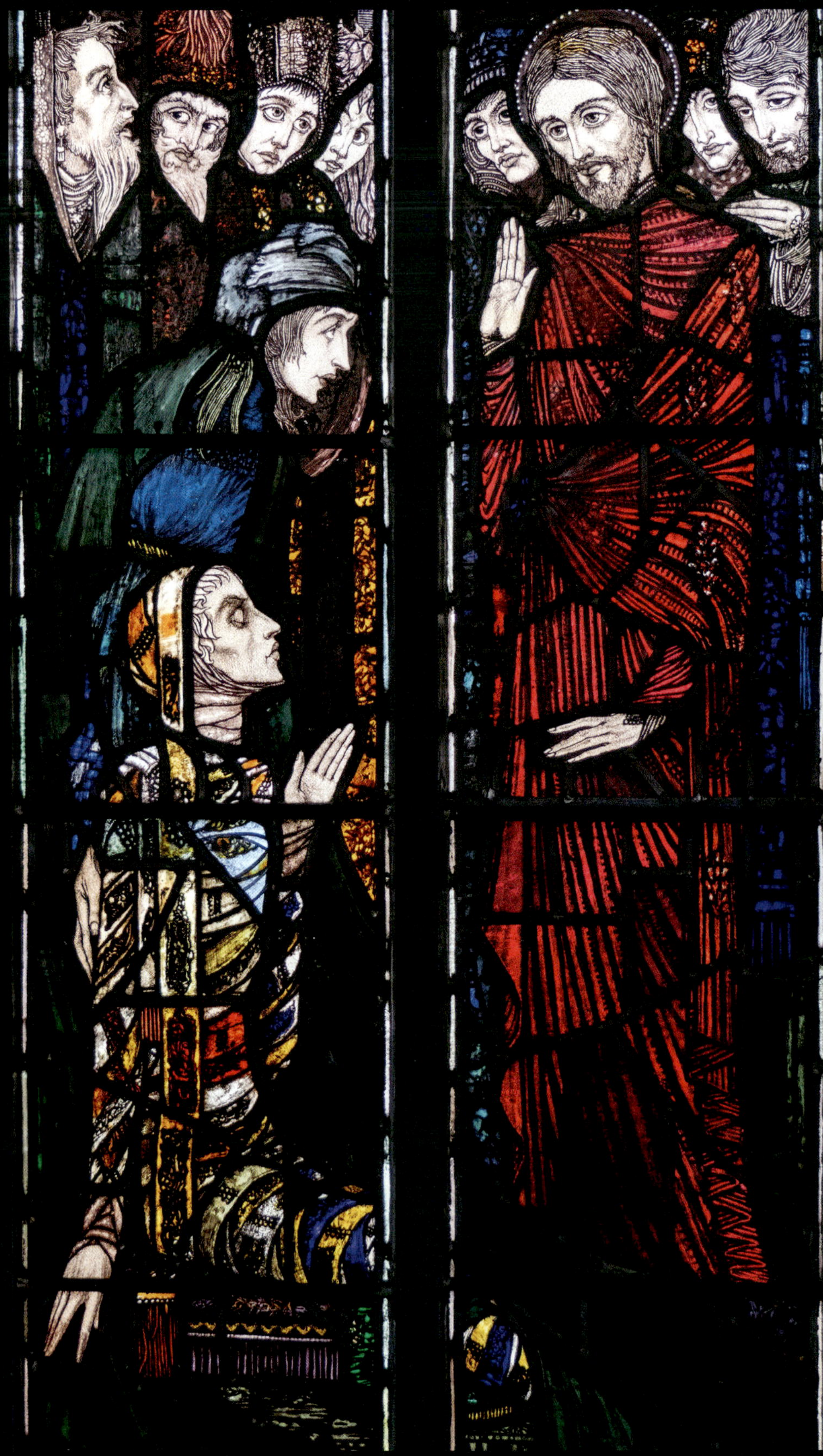

to whimsical fashion illustrations than to conventional pious depictions of angels, and although a delight to the eyes are startingly at variance with the solemnity of the principal scene below.

The subject of the window's main scene is echoed in the two vignettes at the base fashioned from acided, painted and stained flashed glass, one ruby, one blue; in them Clarke has reprised the theme of someone being miraculously raised from the dead. He rejected the more obvious tale of Lazarus or the raising of the daughter of Jairus and instead chose two less familiar incidents from the Book of Kings in the Old Testament. On the left is the prophet Elisha who successfully resuscitated the son of a rich lady of Shunem. The red-haired, bearded prophet leans over the dead blond-haired boy who rests on a bed of tasselled cushions and flowers. The right vignette depicts the prophet Elias (Elijah) who raised the son of the widow of Zarephath, which is the first instance of raising the dead recorded in scripture. Here the white-haired, bearded prophet seems almost to envelop the drowsy boy, their heads close together, while Elias gazes out at the viewer. Both images are decidedly unconventional treatments of the subjects.

Following on from Clarke's windows it appears two windows designed by William E. Earley of Earley and Co. were installed, *The Apparition of the Sacred Heart to St Margaret Mary* and *The Nativity*, the latter since moved to create a side door and can now be viewed when ascending the south staircase to the gallery.

In 1936 Canon Byrne's successor as parish priest, Canon Joseph Hickey, ordered four very tall 2-light windows from Harry Clarke Studios, two for either side of the sanctuary wall. The cost was £300 for each window and collectively they were erected in memory of the deceased priests of the parish. The artist was Richard King, by now holding the position of manager of the studios. The left side features *Blessed Virgin Mary and St Joseph*, alongside Mary's parents, *Joachim and Anna*. The right side has *St Brigid and St Patrick*, and an unlikely coupling, *St Philomena and Blessed Oliver Plunkett*. Subsequent to King making these windows St Philomena was demoted,[5] and Oliver Plunkett was elevated to sainthood. The dominant colour of all the windows is deep blue and King has eliminated any depth of field so that

(opposite) Harry Clarke, detail of *The Widow's Son* (1924)

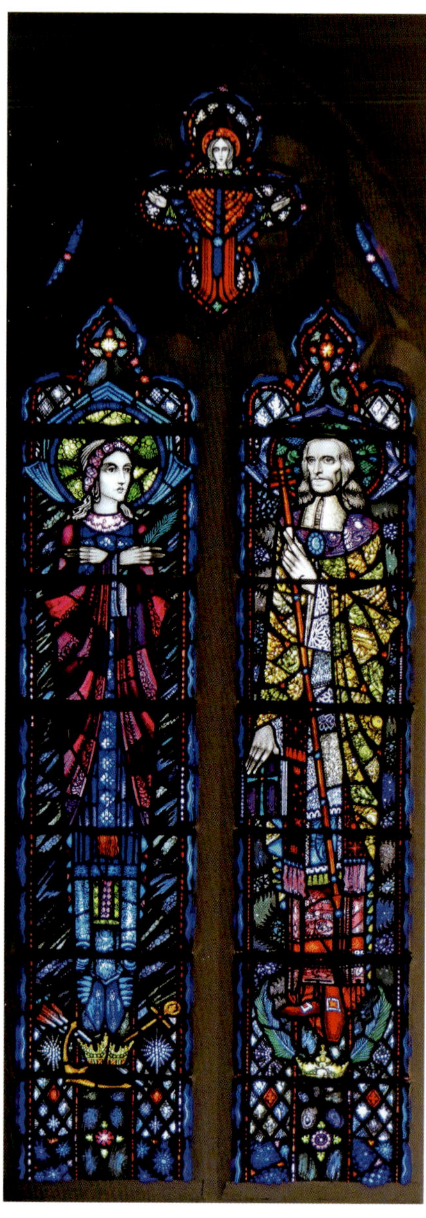

(above) Richard King, detail of *St Philomena and Blessed Oliver Plunkett* (1936–7)

(opposite) William Dowling (attributed), detail of *The Presentation in the Temple* (1944)

the focus is entirely on the interplay of patterns, many geometric and jazzy, quite different to Harry Clarke's preference for floral ornament and cursive lines.

In 1944 Canon Hickey embarked on an ambitious project: to seek sponsors so that he could place an order at Harry Clarke Studios for all the remaining nave windows, a total of ten 2-lights, as well as a pair of lancets for the mortuary chapel. A spectrum of people from the parish committed to the project, among them owners of a small chair factory in the town, the proprietor of a drapery, and farmers. Money was most likely scarce as Ireland was now in the fifth year of 'The Emergency'. By now Richard King had departed Clarke's and was on an extended sabbatical from stained glass. His successor as principal artist and manager of the studio was William Dowling; both had originally joined the studio in spring 1928 and had trained under Harry Clarke himself. All the new windows, with one possible exception, have been attributed to William Dowling.[6]

Thematically the windows on the south wall all depict scenes from the period before Christ's birth or the early years of his life, taking their cue from the fact that Harry Clarke's *The Visitation* and Earley's *The Nativity* were already in place; to these were added *The Annunciation, The Presentation in the Temple,* and *The Finding in the Temple*.

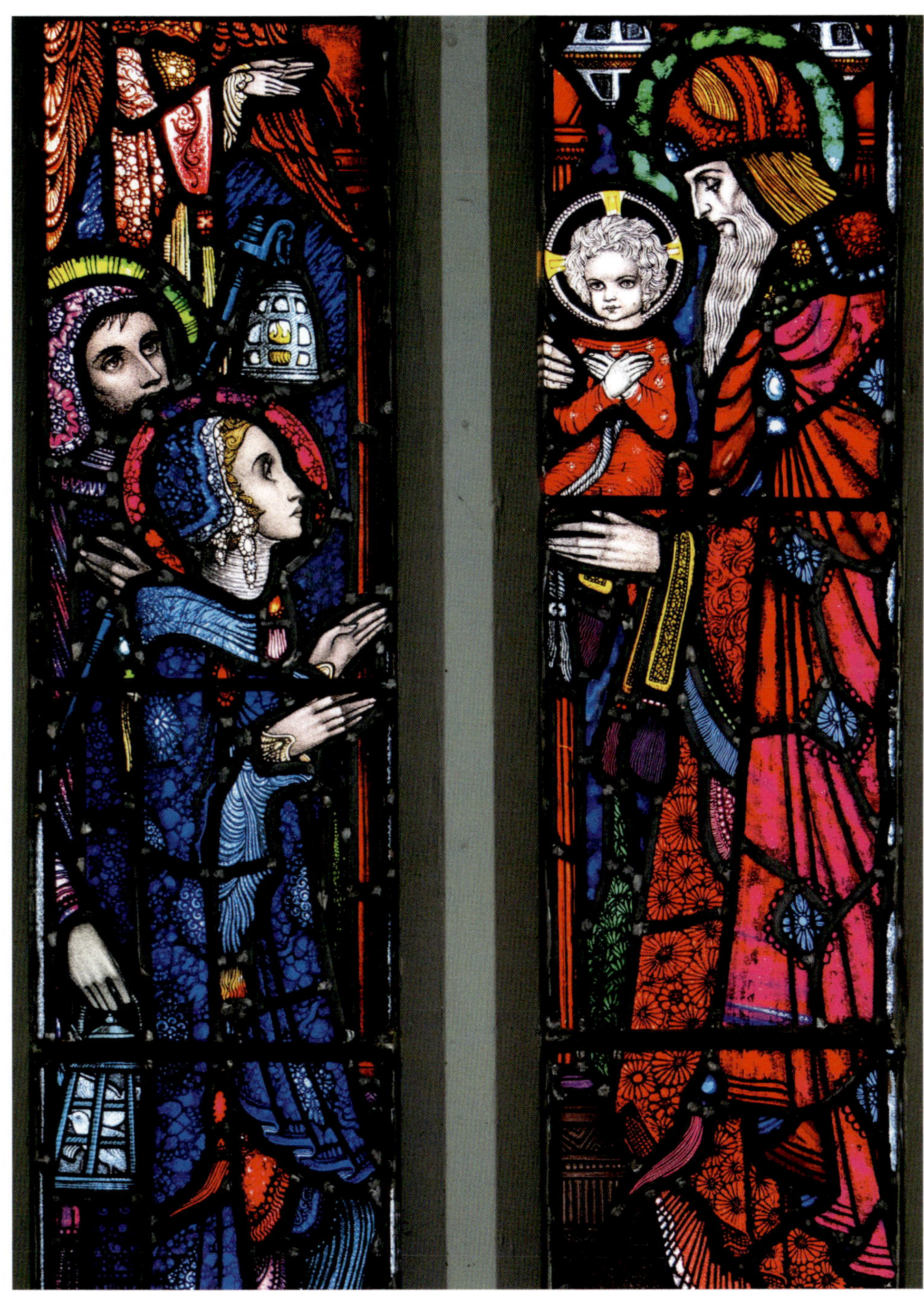

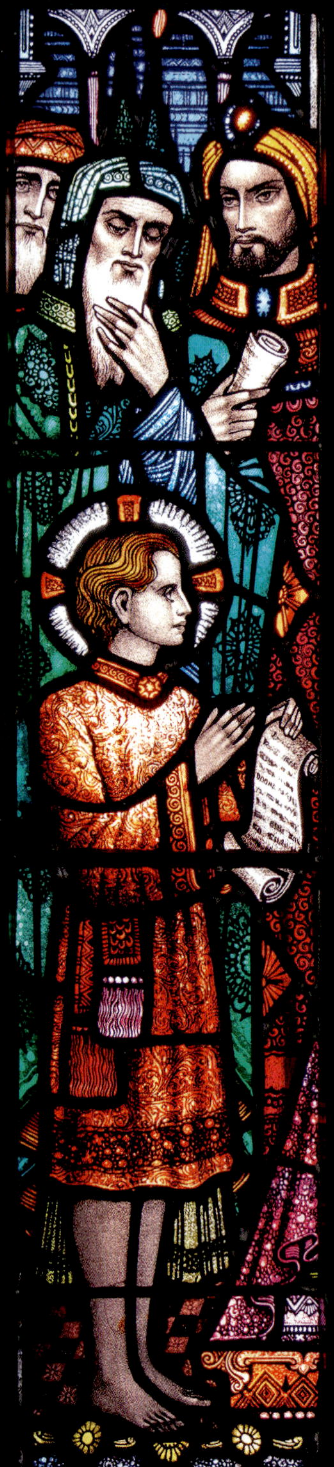

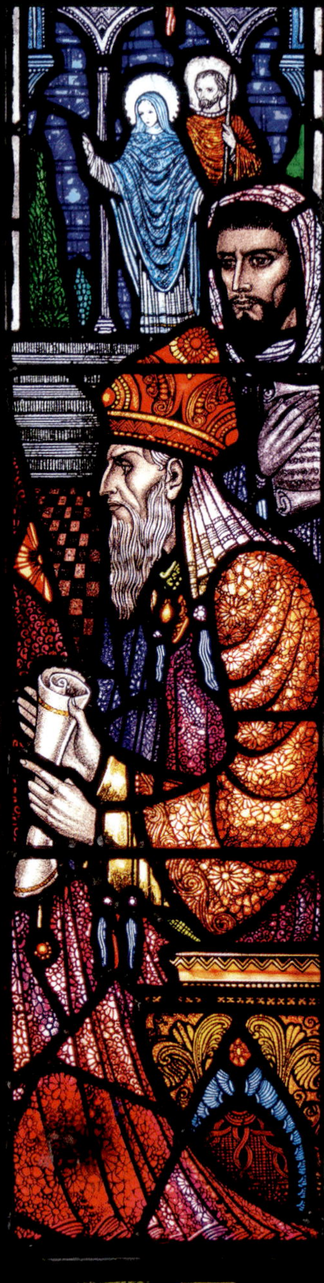

William Dowling (attributed), detail of *The Finding in the Temple* (1944)

The subjects of the new windows on the north wall of the nave, with one exception, are derived from miracles performed by Christ, taking their cue from Clarke's *The Widow's Son*. They are *The Miracle of the Loaves and Fishes, Christ Healing Lepers* and *The Healing of the Woman who Touched the Hem of Our Lord's Garment*, the latter being a relatively obscure miracle that has rarely been treated in art. The odd one out in which no miracle is involved is *St Patrick and the Princesses*, and this window, using a somewhat different colour palette and with less detail in the faces and drapery, may have been designed by, or had some input from Terry Clarke, son of Walter and nephew of Harry.[7]

What is immediately striking about the series of ten windows is that the colour palette is much richer and varied than Clarke's pair of windows, which used a lot of clear glass, muted colours and passages painted in the grisaille technique. Some of Dowling's windows are more eye-catching than others; *Christ Healing Lepers* features ghoulish, deformed characters, which Clarke revelled at the opportunity to include, but Dowling's preference was generally for much more wholesome, prettier representations. In this case perhaps Dowling took his inspiration from Harry Clarke's depiction of lepers that can be seen in his *St MacCullin* lancet in nearby Lusk Catholic church (see pp 204–7). Dowling's depictions of the Virgin Mary in *The Annunciation* and in *The Presentation in the Temple* are the ones in which his master's influence is most apparent in the treatment of the faces, hands, and lithe figures dressed in elaborately decorated fabrics. The placement of the figures in the latter also echoes Clarke's *The Visitation*.

Canon Hickey's final order, also in 1944, was for two lancets for the (former) mortuary chapel costing £60 each. They depict *The Resurrection* and *The Raising of Lazarus*, and are both by William Dowling, though not as visually interesting as his nave windows. It is worth noting that the vesica shape, so loved by Harry Clarke, features in all the windows designed for Balbriggan church by his former assistants, Richard King and William Dowling. Those by Dowling contain finely painted narrative scenes and those by King contain illustrated symbols.

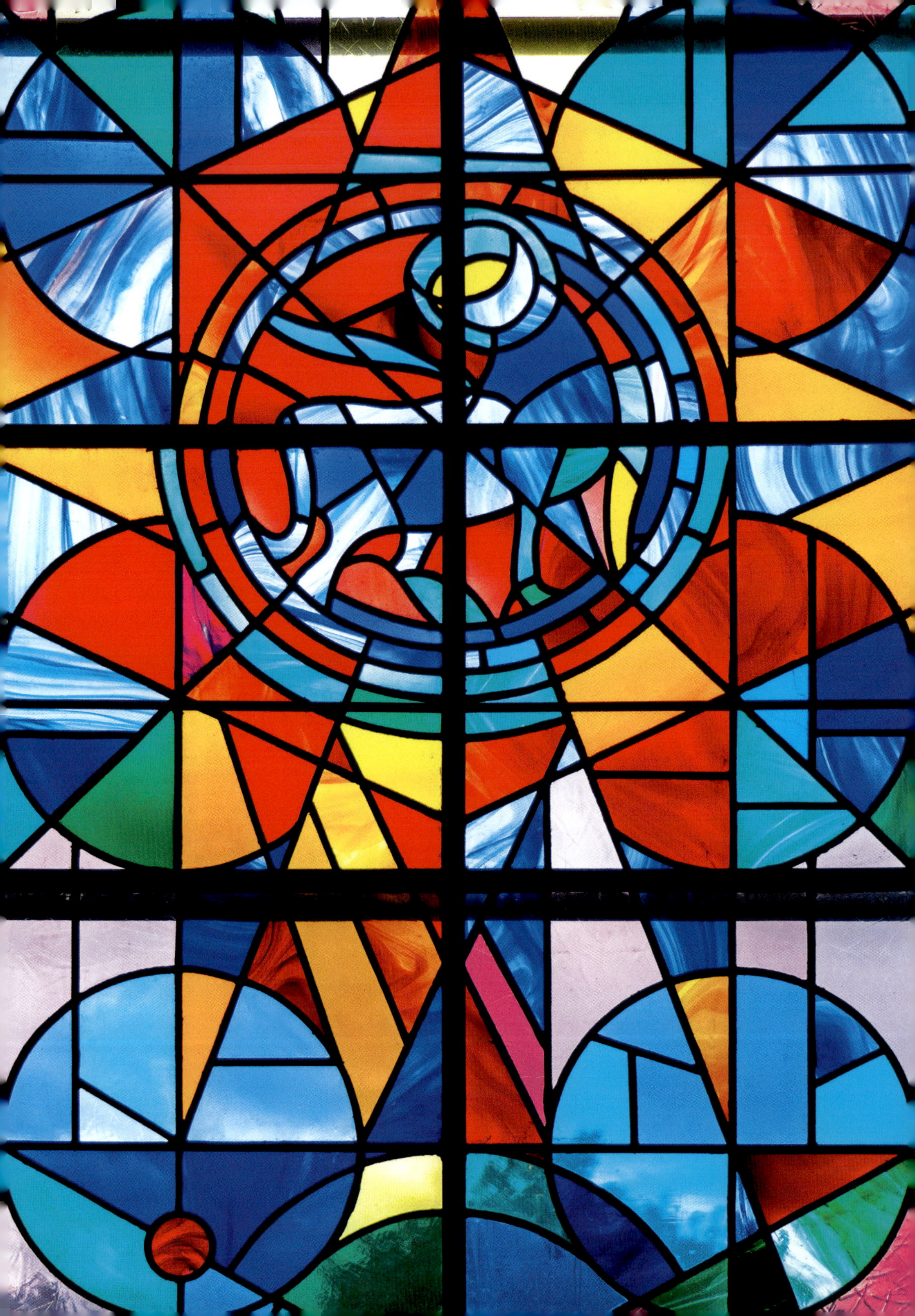

BALLYMUN

Our Lady of Victories church (RC)

Ballymun Road, D09 Y925

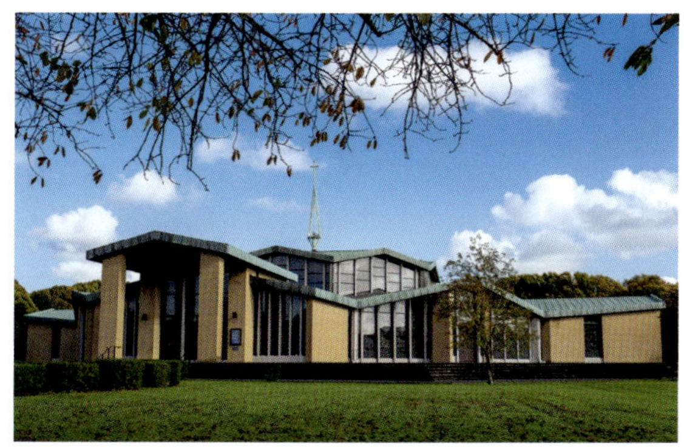

Our Lady of Victories, Ballymun Road was designed by Patrick V. Moloney of Guy Moloney & Associates in 1967–8 and the architect's brother was the parish priest, Fr James F. Moloney. Our Lady of Victories was one of the first batch of six churches in the Dublin diocese that were built in the five years immediately after Vatican II, and which takes into account the guidelines of the council. The design comprises an irregular polygonal plan built for a congregation of 1,900 and was constructed of yellow brick with copper-clad multi-pitched roofs. The most striking interior feature is the substantial central raised octagonal lantern above the altar plinth. The church was dedicated by the archbishop of Dublin, John Charles McQuaid, on 2 February 1969 on which occasion the homily was preached by Bishop Joseph A. Carroll, who described the church as 'modern but not eccentric'.

(opposite) Sheila Corcoran, *Winged Ox, Symbol of St Luke* (1968)

THREE STAINED GLASS ARTISTS, Helen Moloney, George W. Walsh and Sheila Corcoran, were engaged concurrently to contribute to Our Lady of Victories which was an unusual arrangement, and while the three aesthetic approaches differ, all the stained glass for the church was fabricated at Abbey Stained Glass in Dublin.

The outstanding feature of the church is the massive octagonal stained glass lantern which features Helen Moloney's designs. It seems likely that Patrick Moloney – who was not related to the artist – became aware of the continuous abstract band of intensely coloured stained glass she created the previous year for Liam McCormick's iconic St Aengus's church at Burt, Co. Donegal; perhaps he recognized how Moloney would have the ability to create a dynamic visual solution that would also be continuous, even if in this instance it was faceted and not circular.

Although it comprises eight sides or 'windows' (each composed of five panels), Helen Moloney created just two different designs for the windows; from these she made four different colour versions and these were duplicated to create the eight different windows. Despite the fact that there are essentially just two designs and she chose a deliberately restricted colour palette, this repetition is hardly apparent and instead one experiences an almost overwhelming sense of intensely zinging complementary colours enlivened by punchy graphic symbols. Moloney used only the best of mouth-blown glass in a selection of rich colours including red, blue, yellow, purple, violet, orange, green and aquamarine, and although she has included different shades of these, mostly they are full strength for maximum visual impact.

Moloney chose a series of classic symbols, some of which she put her own twist on, to enhance or modify their symbolism, several of which she would return to again in her work. Most of the symbols have ancient origins such as the fish as a symbol of Christ or Christianity which dates from the second century, and the Chi Rho symbol to represent Christ is from the third century. Design 'A' features the following symbols: the Cross and five wounds as a symbol of the Crucifixion; the dove as a symbol of the Holy Spirit; flames to represent Pentecost; the Lamb of God; a snake to represent The Fall. Design 'B' also features the Cross and five wounds as a symbol of the Crucifixion; a crown to represent victory; the crossed keys to represent the kingdom of God; an anchor as a symbol of hope and steadfastness;

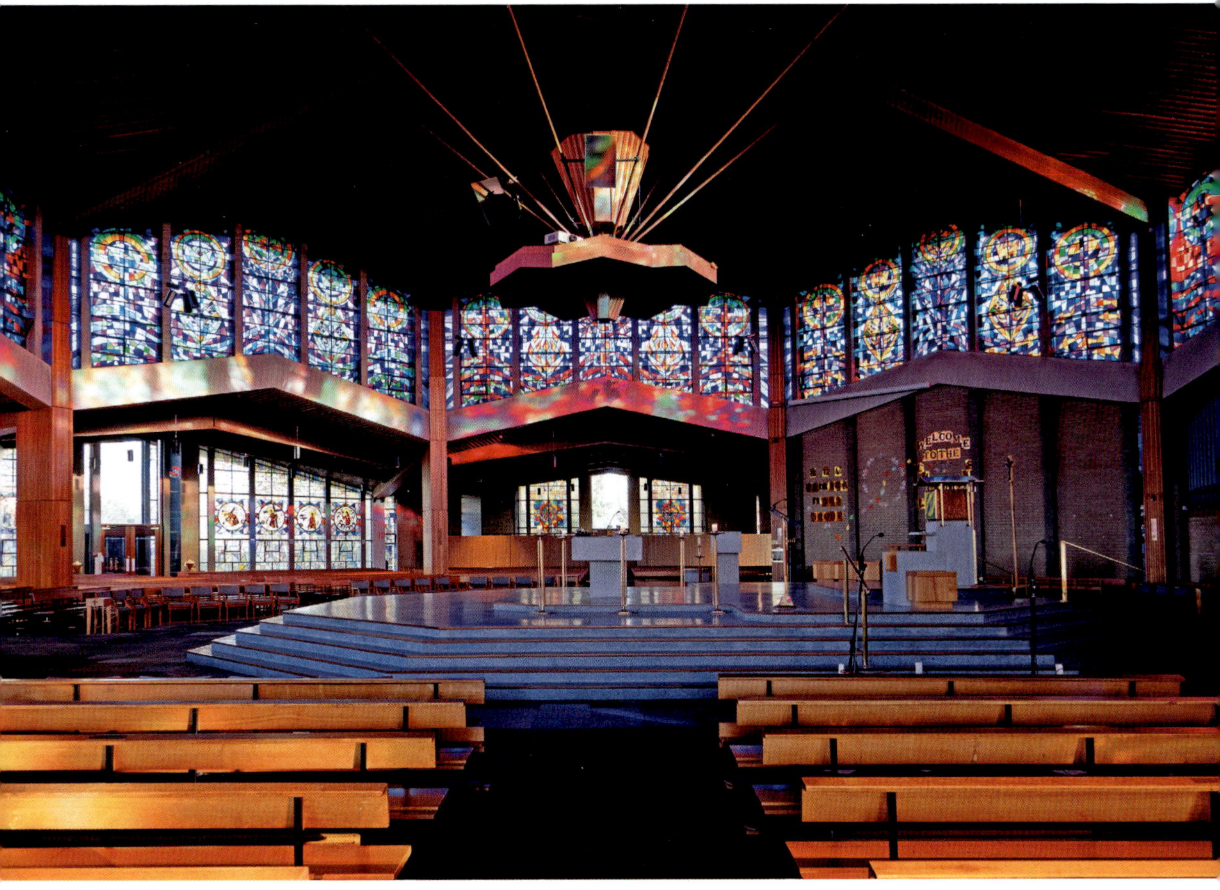

Interior with Helen Moloney's lantern and George W. Walsh's *Stations of the Cross* (1968)

a fish with Chi Rho symbol symbolizing Christ; the Tree of Jesse to represent the Virgin Mary.[1] One symbol appears sixteen times: that of the Cross which includes five small abstract shapes in complementary colours that represent the crown of thorns, the nails in Christ's hands and feet, and the wound from the soldier's lance. In many ways Moloney was more of a designer than an artist and this becomes particularly evident in the skilful way she has combined the crossed keys with an anchor which, if taken in isolation, almost has the quality of a logo.

At the base of all eight windows she incorporated a unifying motif of an undulating body of water populated by many swimming fish which forms a

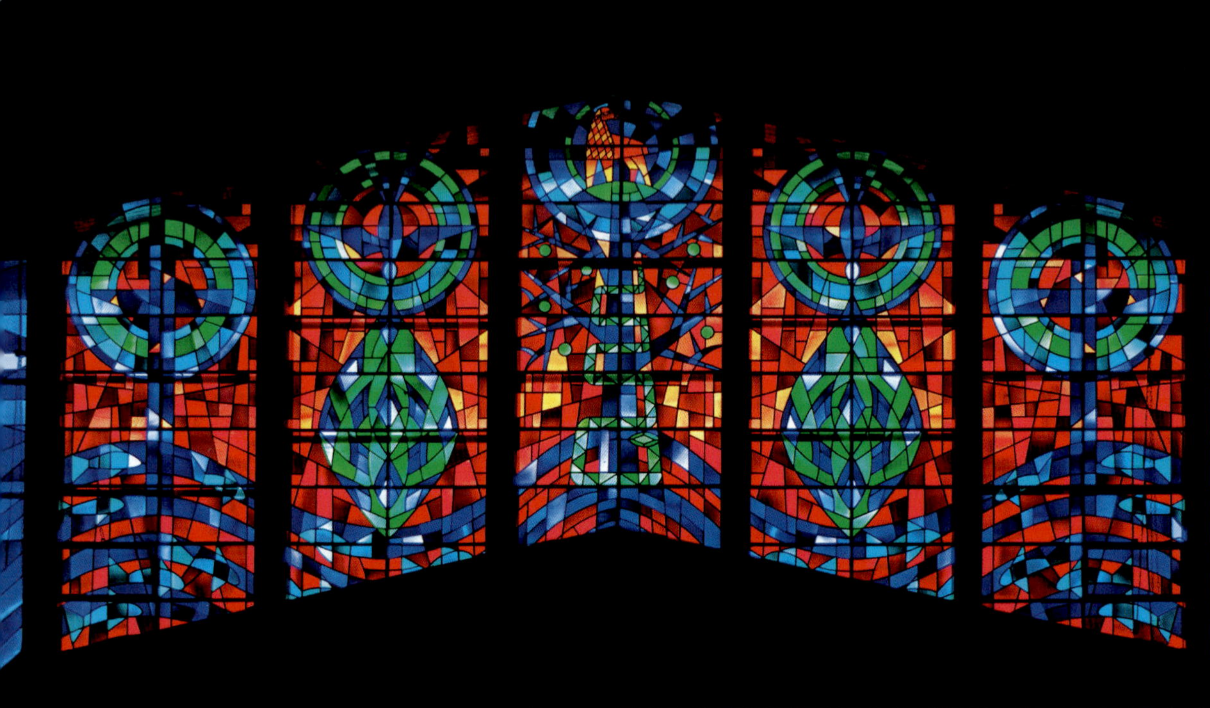

Helen Moloney, one side of *Octagonal Lantern with Christian Symbols* (1968)

continuous loop. Moloney explained her intention for this: she viewed water as a symbol of purification, washing away sins, and fish as a symbol of Christians, and when combined together in this manner she felt that they created a symbol of baptism.[2] Noteworthy is that throughout the eight windows there is no painting or staining whatsoever, all the images have been achieved relying purely on colour and skilful use of leadlines to communicate clarity of meaning and impact.

Sadly Moloney lacked confidence in her work and having attended the official dedication of a church would never revisit, an exception being Our Lady of Victories when she attended a grand-nephew's confirmation and afterwards remarked to fellow artist Margaret Becker that she was pleased with it.[3]

In 1969 Guy Moloney & Associates designed another octagonal structure, the Edmund Rice Memorial Chapel, for the Christian Brothers at Callan, Co. Kilkenny, and once again Helen Moloney was engaged to design the stained glass. She revisited several of her favourite symbols, this time for floor-to-ceiling windows, and the outcome is more fluid and less disciplined than the approach she adopted in Our Lady of Victories.

At ground-floor level most of the windows feature large circular medallions set into colourful squares depicting the Stations of the Cross which were designed by George W. Walsh. Devotion to the Way of the Cross began in earnest in the 1300s though it was not until 1730 that Pope Clement XII set the number of Stations at fourteen. Vatican II recognized the importance of popular devotions such as the Stations of the Cross and so they continued to be incorporated in newer churches. One thing that is unusual about the Stations in Our Lady of Victories is that a fifteenth Station has been included. This practice was not commonplace in the 1960s; it became somewhat more popular when Pope John Paul II, whose papacy began in 1978, encouraged the addition of the fifteenth Station depicting the Resurrection.

George W. Walsh, who unlike independent artists Moloney and Corcoran, was then a full-time artist at Abbey Stained Glass Studios of Middle Abbey Street; during this period the studio was managed by Frank Ryan, an artistic and enlightened businessman who drew in a cohort of artists such as Walsh, Willie Earley (of the Earley stained glass dynasty), and the established painter George Campbell. Walsh had spent several years in the US with his father, the stained glass artist George Stephen Walsh, and returned to Dublin with fresh ideas and experience of techniques such as *dalle de verre*. His Stations for Our Lady of Victories are unusual as the figures have been created out of copper sheets and into which details have been cut, something he had seen done in the US, which almost gives the appearance of a stencil.[4] The effect is graphic and reduces the Stations to their essence. For these and the other ground-floor windows a mixture of glass has been utilized; limited use of the more expensive mouth-blown glass and larger amounts of lighter coloured factory-made glass with a straw texture. This selection of glass not only controlled the cost of a very large job but the pale coloured straw-textured glass, often used in a domestic context, allows greater light to pass through it. Walsh also created two straightforward figurative windows, one of St Joseph and one of St Patrick, and at an upper level in the crying room – set aside for parents with young children, a new innovation in church design – he created an image of the Madonna and Child,

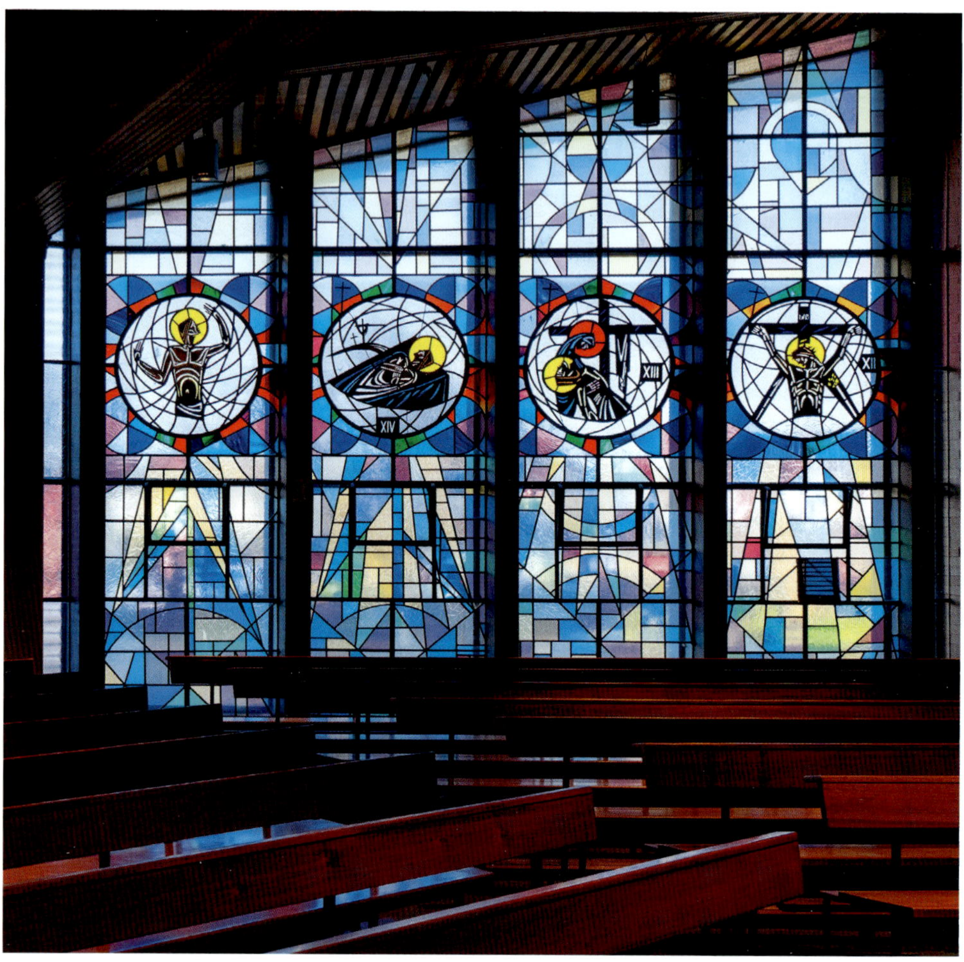

George W. Walsh, *Stations of the Cross, XII, XIII, XIV and the Risen Christ* (1968)

which is unusual in that they are depicted in profile and in conversation with each other, perhaps an acknowledgment that this was a soundproof room where it was permissible to converse.

Sheila Corcoran's contribution to Our Lady of Victories was radically different to her sole previous stained glass commission for a Dublin church – her expressionist Stations of the Cross for Our Lady Queen of Heaven at the airport which Archbishop McQuaid could not abide (see pp 180–9). This time her approach was more akin to Helen Moloney's, with a use of simplified shapes and strong colours though her style was more pictorial and detailed compared to Moloney's preference for elemental shapes. Like Moloney, this time she eschewed any use of paint. The main body of the church features her *Four Evangelists*, St Matthew and St Mark either side of the entrance on the north wall, and St John and St Luke either side of the entrance on the south wall. She also created images of *Christ the King* for the former Sacred Heart chapel and *Madonna and Child* for the former Our Lady's chapel, both spaces now used for other purposes. Perhaps her most interesting image is the one she created for the former baptistry which features a streamlined dove that looks like it is about to break through the sound barrier as it speeds to earth; Corcoran's design perhaps was influenced by the developments in space exploration that came to the fore in the 1960s. Unfortunately her designs for Our Lady of Victories seem to be the last stained glass commission she undertook and there is no record of any further artistic pursuits by her which seems a shame for someone who was patently trying to work in a modernist manner, injecting energy and vitality into Irish ecclesiastical stained glass.

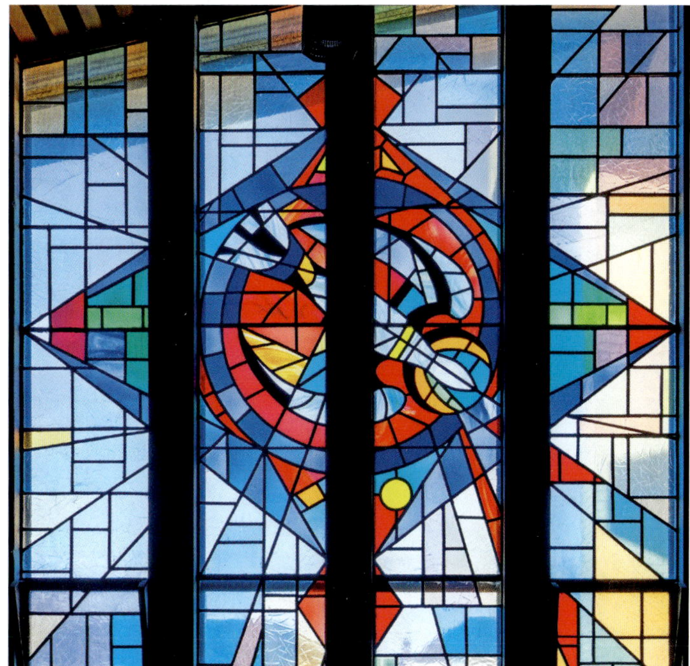

Sheila Corcoran, detail of *The Holy Spirit* (1968)

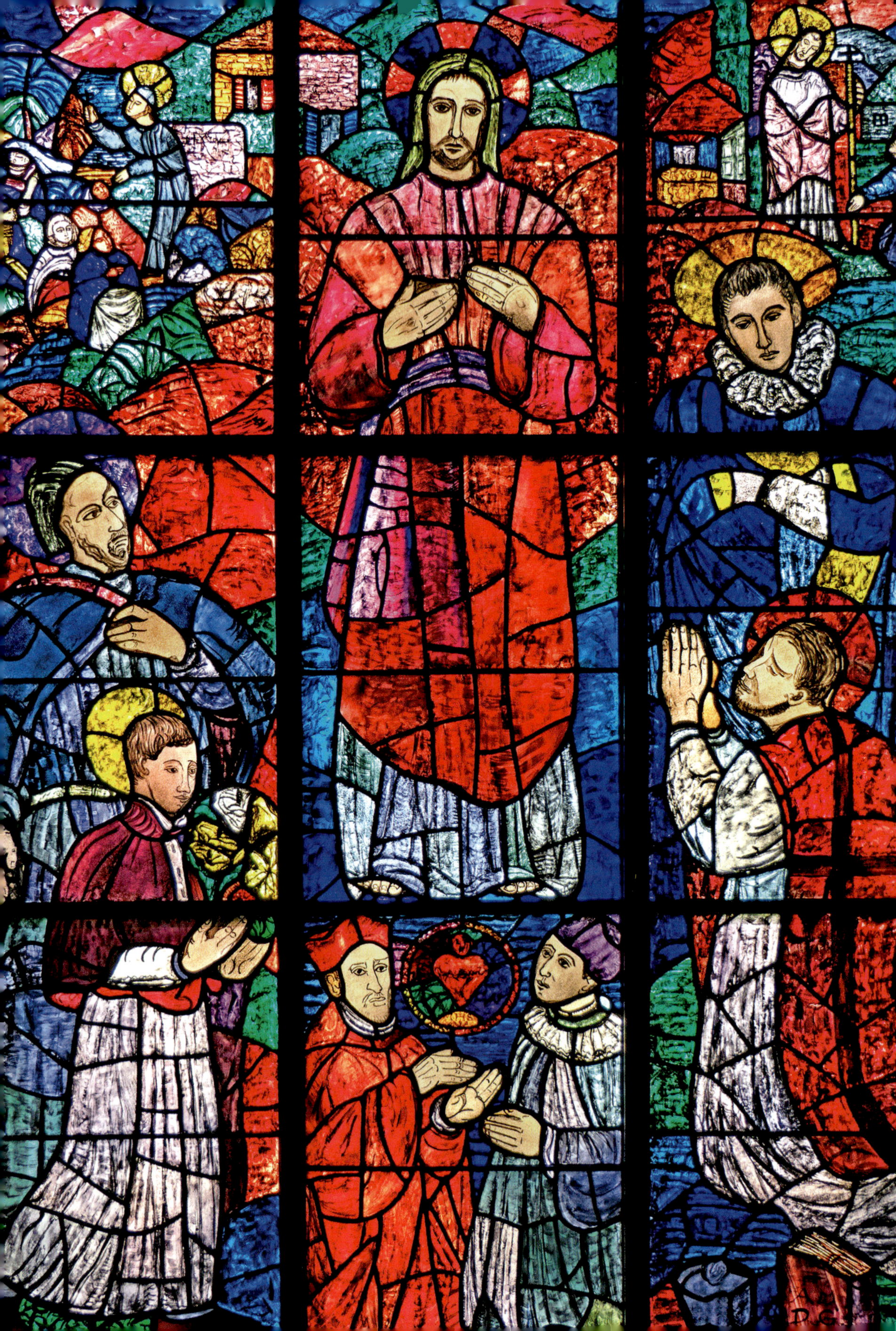

DOLLYMOUNT

Manresa Jesuit Centre of Spirituality

Clontarf Road, D03 FP52

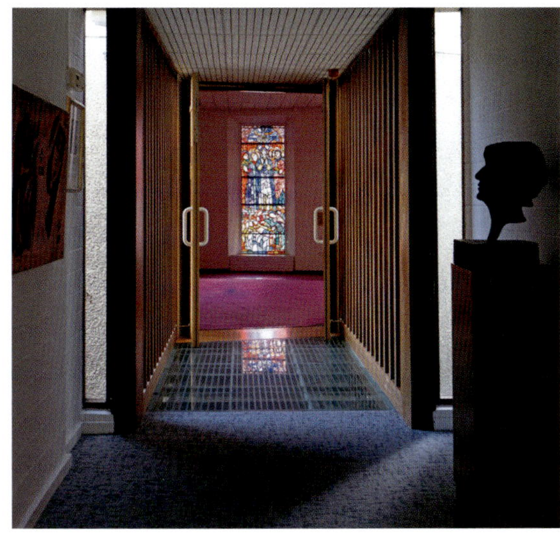

In 1948 the archbishop of Dublin, John Charles McQuaid, asked the Jesuit order to establish a spirituality centre in the Dollymount area, so they bought a substantial Georgian house and named it Manresa House after the city in Catalonia associated with St Ignatius of Loyola, the founder of their order. In addition to this original building, the complex includes a retreat house and a modernist chapel designed in 1966 by Andrew Devane of Robinson, Keefe & Devane (RKD); this serene space based on a spiral contains no stained glass though it features Stations of the Cross by Richard Enda King. In 1992 a prayer room designed by Roderick McCafferty, also of RKD, and linked to Devane's retreat house was built to house five windows by Evie Hone.

(opposite) Evie Hone, *The Sacred Heart and Jesuit Saints* (1945)

ONE OF THE CHALLENGES for custodians of stained glass windows is how to find or create appropriate new homes for works when there is a necessity to move them from their original location. This was the situation confronting the Jesuit fathers in St Stanislaus's College, Tullabeg, Rahan, Co. Offaly, in 1991 when a decision was made to close the retreat house, formerly a novitiate (and now derelict) and relocate five particularly fine windows by Evie Hone. The windows had been created in 1945–6 for the 'domestic chapel' which was located on the third floor of the Georgian building. The rector, Revd Donal O'Sullivan SJ, later director of the Arts Council, had appointed Michael Scott, pioneering architect of the modern movement, to design the chapel. Scott was already well acquainted with Hone and her stained glass as he had commissioned her *My Four Green Fields* for the Irish Pavilion in the New York World's Fair of 1939,[1] and Fr O'Sullivan also was familiar with her three *Dolour* (Sorrows of Our Lady) stained glass windows created in 1941–2 for the chapel of Clongowes Wood College, Co. Kildare.

The chapel at St Stanislaus's was rectangular with high ceilings, and had four somewhat narrow windows (10ft x 3ft 5in.) facing east and a larger rectangular window (10ft x 7ft) facing south. The cost was £1,050, over twice the bequest that had been put aside to cover the cost so additional fundraising was necessary.[2] Michael Scott's architectural intervention was minimal, creating an apse that accommodated the altar above which was positioned a large crucifix, carved from sycamore, by Lawrence Campbell (brother of Christopher who worked in stained glass). However in 1991, forty-five years after the windows were installed, St Stanislaus's closed permanently; intriguingly the Jesuit priest and writer on art Anthony Symondson noted that 'neither O'Sullivan nor Hone believed that Rahan would be the windows' permanent destination. Hone believed that subsequent removal was possible and to some extent this is said to have influenced her designs.'[3]

Upon closure there were many applications to receive Hone's five windows, notably Mullingar cathedral and the Jesuit-run Milltown Institute, Dublin. Serious consideration was given to reinstalling them in the parish church at Rahan, the Marian shrine at Knock, housing them in Clongowes, or a prominent secular location, the Irish Museum of Modern Art in Kilmainham.[4]

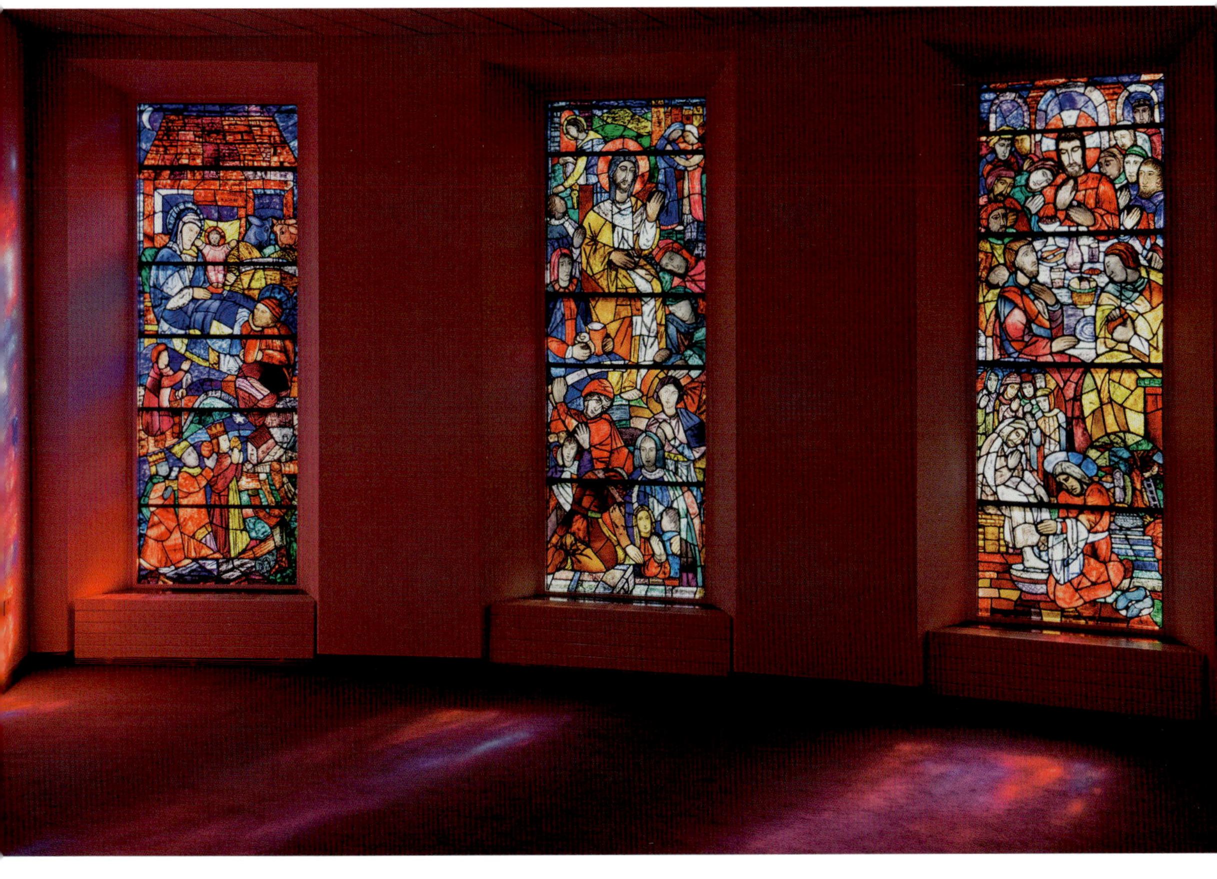

Evie Hone, interior with *The Nativity* (1945), *The Beatitudes* (1946), *The Last Supper* (1946)

The final decision was that they be installed in a new prayer room at Manresa in Dollymount. Roderick McCafferty designed a small single-storey fan-shaped building which is approached by a narrow corridor – where one initially encounters Oisín Kelly's bust of Hone on a plinth – and proceeds over a short bridge with glazed floor below which is a narrow pool with low fountains. One enters the room at its highest level, and at a halfway point three curved tiers lead one down to ground level; facing is the long south wall designed in the form of an extended arc into which Hone's windows are placed at intervals in the same sequence as they had appeared in St Stanislaus's: *The Nativity, The Beatitudes, The Last Supper, Pentecost,* and *The Sacred Heart and Jesuit Saints*. Due to the fact that the windows are now positioned

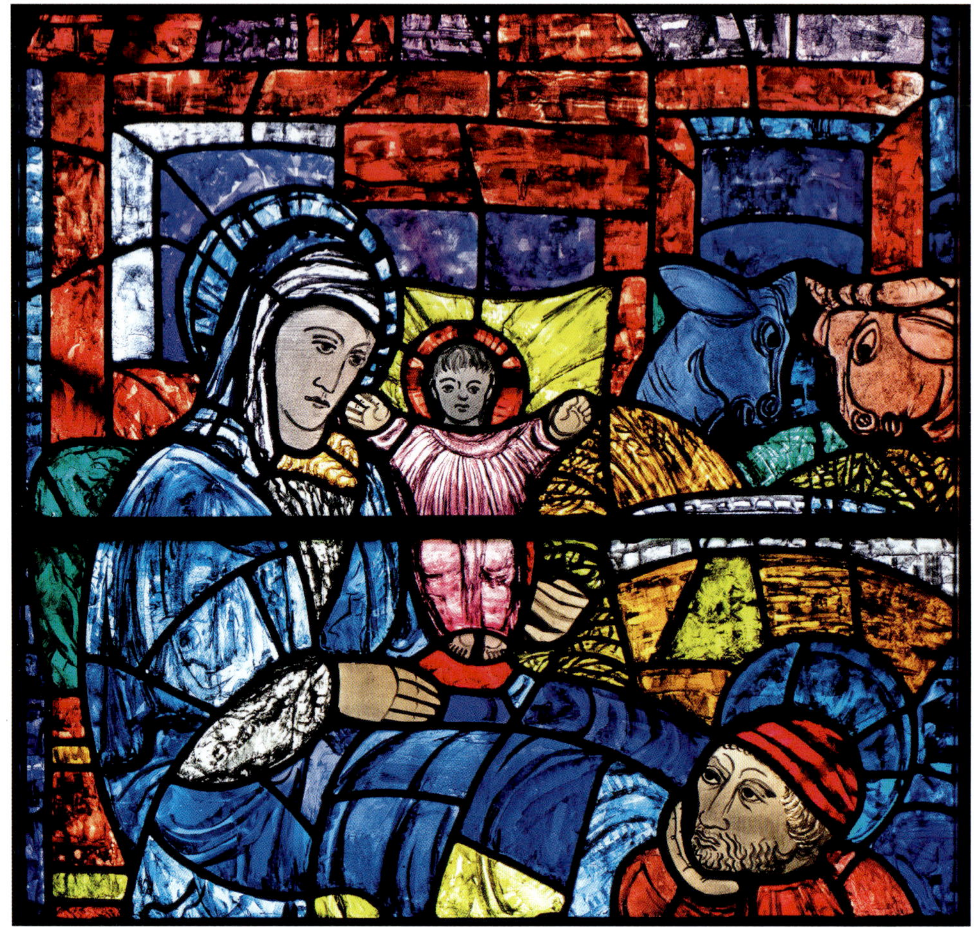

Evie Hone, detail of *The Nativity* (1945)

lower down than in the original chapel one views them from a somewhat different vantage point to how they were conceived to be appreciated. Dark purple carpet and a small amount of light filtered by slim wooden slats at ceiling level ensures that the interior light level is permanently subdued allowing Hone's deeply luminous windows to sing, though depending on the time of year foliage on adjacent tall trees can impact on the viewing experience.

This was a significant commission for Hone as it came in 1944, the year she left An Túr Gloine to establish her own studio at Marlay in Rathfarnham, and presented a welcome opportunity to create an ensemble of windows for a discerning and appreciative client. By the summer Hone was busy working on small-scale coloured sketches for all five windows. Her stock of richly coloured glass came from James Hetley & Co. of London, and as she had yet to acquire a kiln she availed of the services of Harry Clarke Studios who supplied the necessary lead and undertook the firing for the first three windows.[5]

The first window she executed was *The Nativity* and like most of the five windows depicts more than one narrative in an idiosyncratic manner. The scene(s) is set at night, in the top section Mary, Joseph and the infant Jesus are in the stable, below a single shepherd waves in their general direction, and below him are the three kings, bearing gifts, following the guiding star. Leading authority on Hone, Joseph McBrinn, has noted the influence of two of the finest windows in Chartres, composed of pulsating blue and ruby, that Hone is known to have studied intensely when she visited the cathedral nearly a quarter of a century previously, and has identified a diverse range of influences from different countries, in varied media, and spanning many centuries of art and architectural history, 'ancient Irish stone carving, illuminated manuscripts and penal crosses, Italian primitives, Russian icons, Byzantine mosaics, Romanesque sculpture and French stained glass of the twelfth and thirteenth centuries.'[6] Hone has managed to synthesize them all within a composition that appears effortless, instilled with an almost child-like, magical charm, yet conveying profound sentiment and depth. When James White, the art critic and later director of the National Gallery, came to Marlay to view the completed window he was overwhelmed and pronounced that it marked a new level of achievement in the craft of stained glass, as well as in the career of Evie Hone.[7]

Following on from *The Nativity*, the next window that Hone made, *The Sacred Heart and Jesuit Saints,* was completed in summer 1945. The Sacred Heart of Jesus is one of the most widely practised and well-known Catholic devotions, wherein the heart of Jesus is viewed as a symbol of God's boundless and passionate love for the human race. Hone has placed Christ in the centre, gesturing with both hands to his heart, but it is not present, and instead it is below him, contained within a circle like a sacred relic and is being venerated by Saints Robert Bellarmine and Claude la Colombière. Four more Jesuit saints are either petitioning Christ or are lost in prayerful reverie; on the left Saints Francis Xavier and Stanislaw Kostka (after whom the novitiate was named), and on the right Saints Aloysius Gonzaga and Ignatius of Loyola. At the top of the window, left and right, are two small independent scenes depicting key episodes from Jesuit history.

The next window Hone made was *Pentecost* and it was installed in early 1946. The top two-thirds of the window depicts the event when Mary, in the company of the apostles, witnesses the descent of the Holy Spirit, depicted in the guise of a dove. In Christian tradition Pentecost represents fulfilment of the promise that Christ will baptise his followers with the Holy Spirit symbolized by tongues of fire. The *Acts of the Apostles* states that the event occurred in a house (or temple or sanctuary) and Hone has the compact group situated under a curved stone arch to convey this. The apostles are surprisingly youthful in appearance with only one bearded, perhaps depicted in this manner so as to be relatable to the young novices. Hone's depiction of the scene suggests both transformation and unity. With the descent of the Holy Spirit, the apostles were given power and guidance to begin their mission to preach the gospel to all nations and to heal the sick, and it is the latter aspect that Hone has represented in the bottom panel. While the depiction of Pentecost conveys energy and drama, by comparison the bottom scene presents one of quiet tenderness and devotion.

The fourth window, *The Last Supper*, was completed and installed in July 1946. In addition to the principal scene it includes two smaller narrative scenes which took place the same evening. The Last Supper scene occupies the upper half of the window and shows, as is the tradition, the moment that Christ blesses the bread and wine in the presence of his apostles gathered around a table. The youngest apostle, John, has his head resting on Christ's shoulder perhaps anticipating what lies ahead, and while all the other disciples are seated, Judas, the betrayer, is visible hovering at the back, ready to make his exit. In the lower left section of the window a profoundly sad Christ washes the feet of one of the apostles in a display of his humility and servanthood in forgiving sinners. Behind, the other apostles observe the ritual and wait their turn. To the right, there is a vignette contained in a circular shape depicting a very small Judas as if by now he has retreated to some distant spot. Hone shows him dead, swinging from

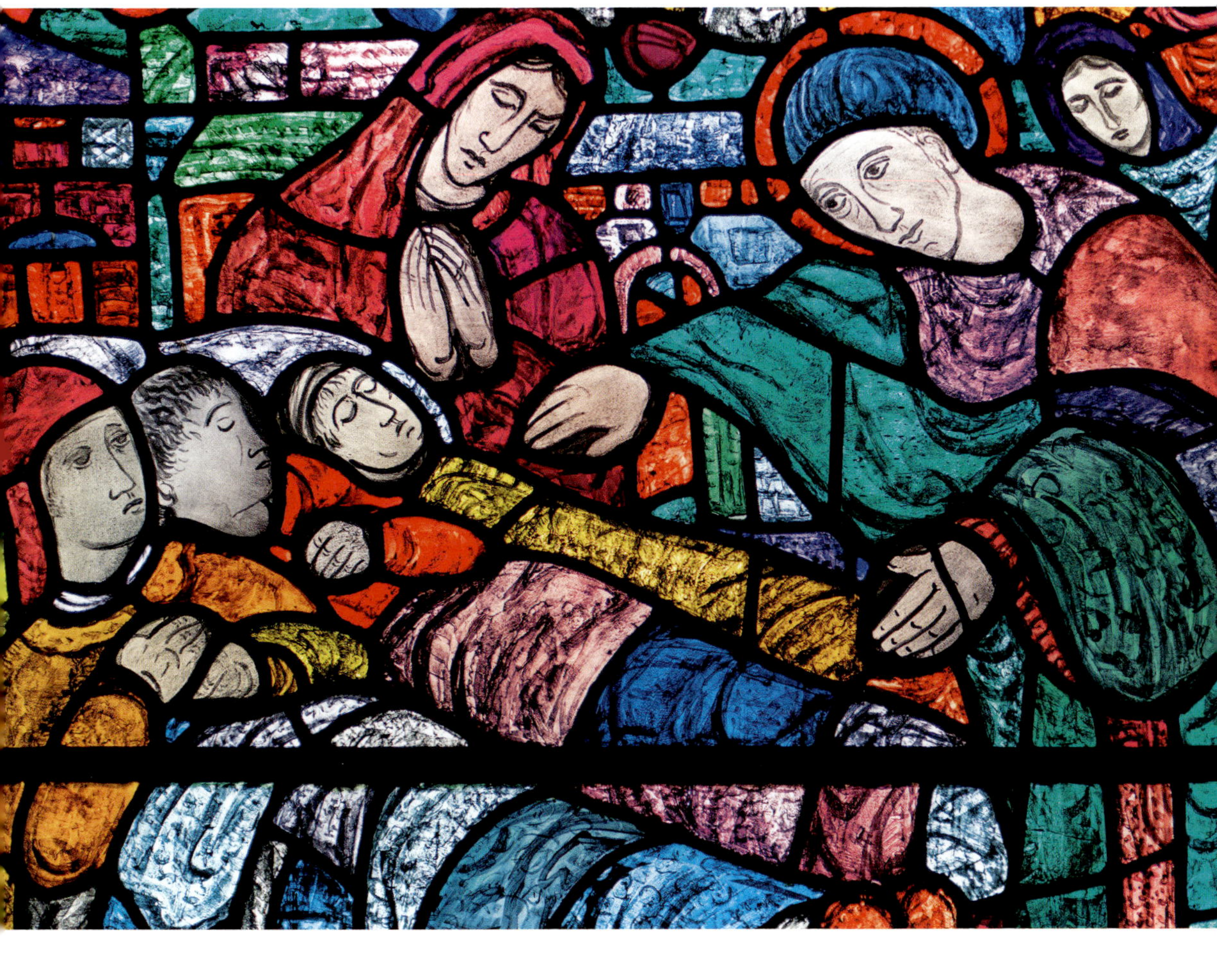

Evie Hone, detail of apostles caring for the sick in *Pentecost* (1946)

a noose which he had attached to a sturdy tree – a ladder propped against the trunk reveals how he tied it there – and scattered at his feet are the thirty pieces of silver.

The final window of the series, *The Beatitudes*, was her favourite and immediately considered the finest of them.[8] *The Beatitudes* are blessings recounted by Jesus ('Blessed are the poor in spirit, for theirs is the kingdom of heaven…') within the *Sermon on the Mount* in St Matthew's gospel, and four in the *Sermon on the Plain* in St Luke's gospel. Hone depicts a seated Christ dressed in a golden robe and making a gesture of blessing as he is surrounded by the eight different Beatitudes interpreted by a total

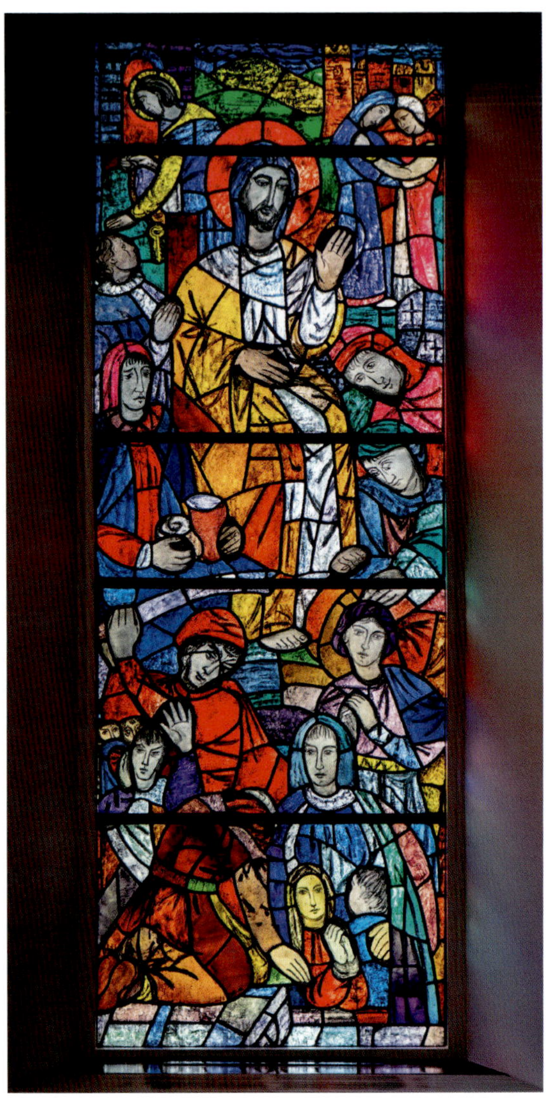

(left) Evie Hone, *The Beatitudes* (1946)
(opposite) Evie Hone, detail of *The Last Supper* (1946)

of sixteen figures. It is a complex but harmonious composition in which Christ stands out yet is fully integrated. It was completed in August 1946 and when James White returned to Marlay and viewed both it and *The Last Supper* he declared them to be masterpieces and the scheme, 'the finest piece of religious art produced in Ireland in our time'.[9] Following Hone's death in 1955 these two windows were loaned by St Stanislaus's College for inclusion in a major retrospective exhibition of Hone's work which took place in Dublin in 1958, and in London the following year.

In addition to Hone's five magnificent windows in the prayer chapel, Manresa holds a sizable collection of framed sketch designs and cartoons by Hone, as well as some small stained glass panels by her, most of which are displayed in the retreat building.

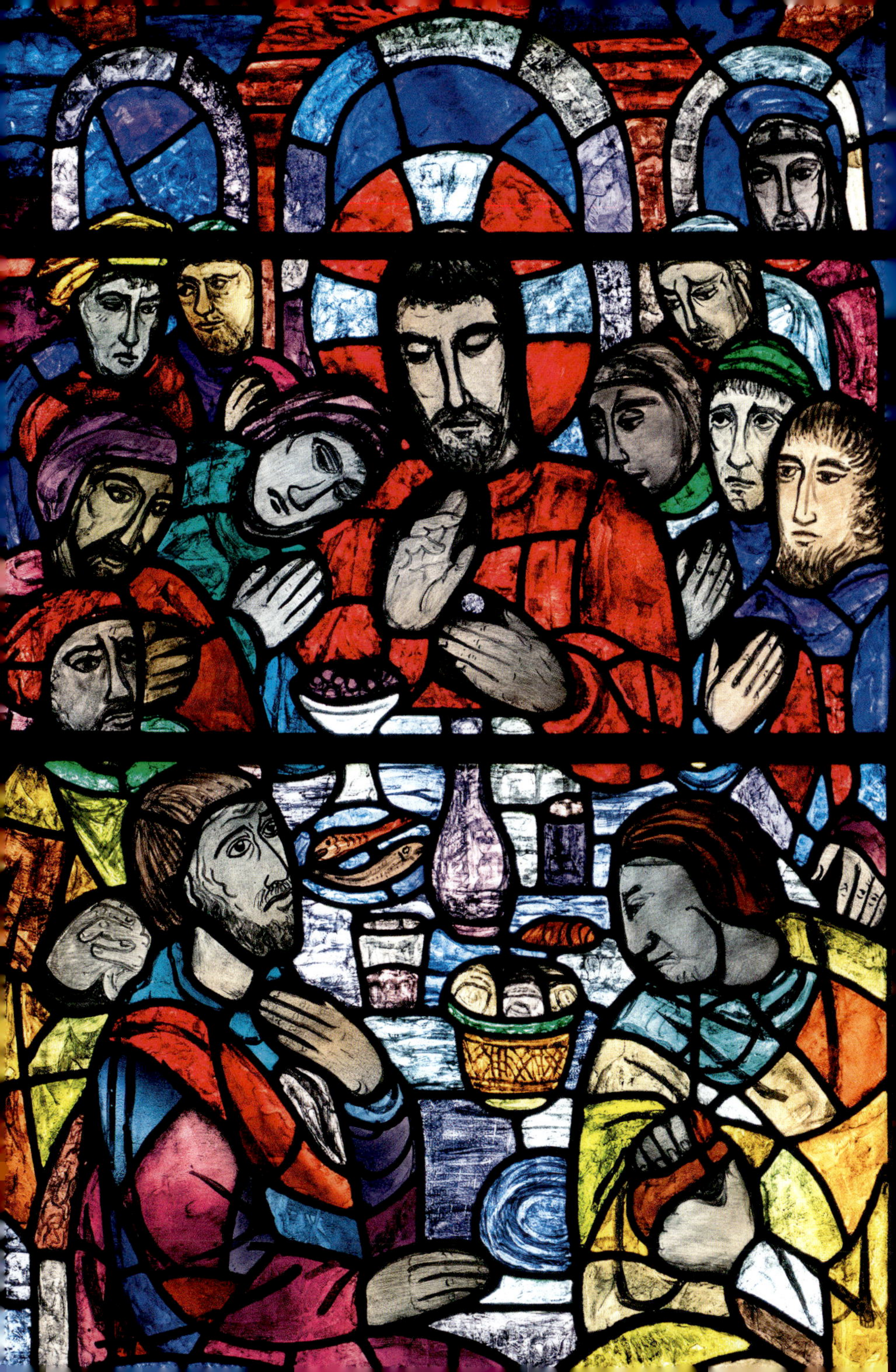

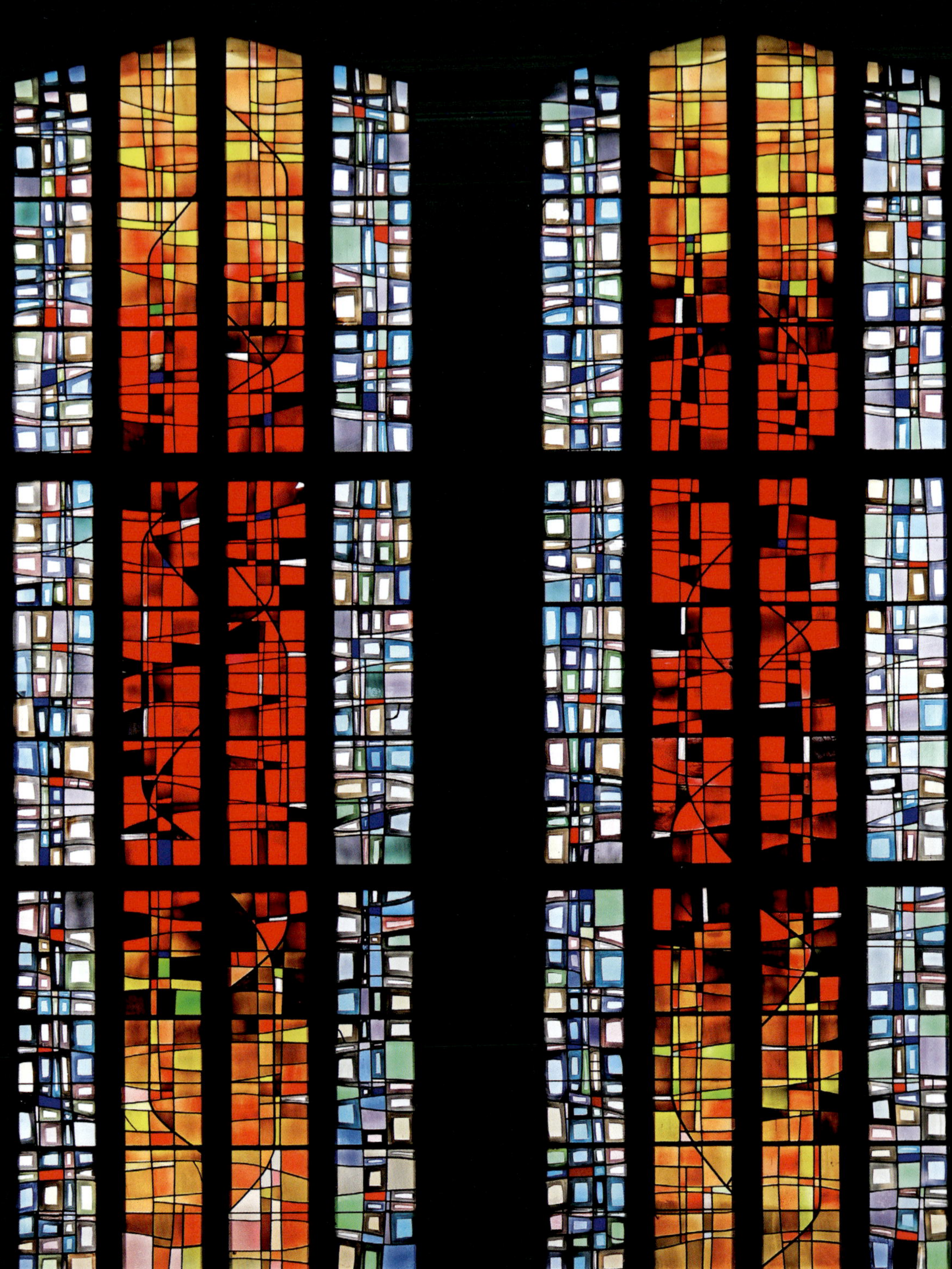

DONNYCARNEY

Our Lady of Consolation church (RC)

Malahide Road, D05 XN22

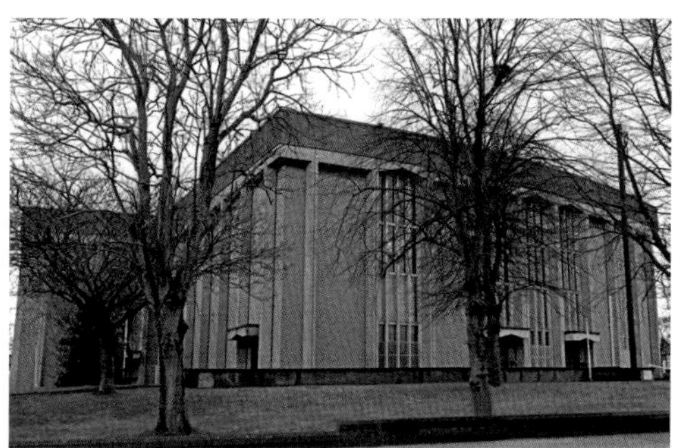

Located at the junction of Malahide Road and Collins Avenue East, this austere structure was designed by modernist architect Thomas Paul Kennedy, best known as an architect of hospitals. Replacing a temporary galvanized church ('the tin chapel'), it had a lengthy gestation with Kennedy being involved in its design by 1955, however its foundation stone was not laid until 1967 and it was completed in 1969[1] – the same year that Kennedy served as president of the Royal Institute of Architects in Ireland. A reinforced concrete-frame of cruciform plan with fan-shaped nave, it was constructed of fair-faced block and pale yellow brickwork infills.

(opposite) Murphy-Devitt Studios, *Abstract* (1968)

OUR LADY OF CONSOLATION was one of the last large suburban churches built during the episcopate of Dr John Charles McQuaid, Dublin's archbishop from 1940 to 1972; a traditionalist, he was reluctant to embrace many of the changes brought in by Vatican II (1962–5), which from an architectural perspective, included a fresh approach to the design of churches so that priests faced the congregation and barriers such as altar rails were discouraged.[2] Although he personally provided the abstract and cubist artist Evie Hone with instruction when she wished to convert from Anglicanism to Catholicism, his own taste in art and design was unwaveringly conservative – for which he made no apology – and combined with his controlling personality and instinct for micro-managing he resisted moves to incorporate contemporary art and design features in his churches.

Murphy-Devitt Studios (MDS) supplied all the stained glass for Our Lady of Consolation; the windows were designed by Johnny Murphy and the glazing was overseen by master glazier, Des Devitt, helped by a small number of skilled assistants. The cost was £10,000, out of the total construction budget of £260,00. The funding of Our Lady of Consolation had always been a struggle for the parish despite valiant fund-raising efforts by the parishioners, and as abstract stained glass was significantly cheaper than figurative windows, it may be that Murphy-Devitt's essentially abstract scheme was given the go-ahead on purely pragmatic grounds.

At the time of its dedication, May 1969, Our Lady of Consolation was described as 'a modern interpretation of Gothic style'[3] and although there is little to convey this from the exterior, upon entering this vast space, with a capacity for 2,000, one can glean the reference in the design of the nave and transept's principal windows; large, soaring windows with pointed tops, though the angle of the top – a motif repeated elsewhere in the interior – is too shallow to be of true Gothic proportions. The main colours of the nave and transept windows are blue and red, the two colours most associated with medieval stained glass, though here Murphy has essentially chosen to keep them separate and assign the red-themed windows to the transepts whereas the nave and sanctuary are all in shades of blue. Keeping the red and blue distinct draws attention to their traditional associations – the shades of blue of

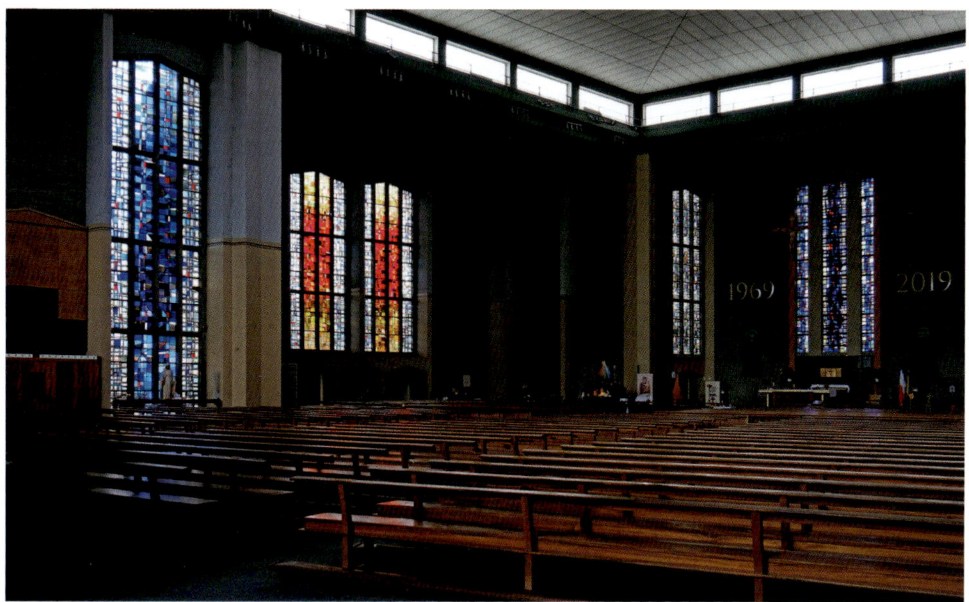

Murphy-Devitt Studios, nave and north transept (1968)

course associated with the Blessed Virgin, to whom the church is dedicated, and the transept windows with their wide, vertical bands of deepest, pulsating shades of red, emerging from gold, could be seen to reference Christ of the Sacred Heart.

All the nave and transept windows comprise a combination of two types of glass; expensive mouth-blown glass purchased from the famous French company of Saint Gobain, and much cheaper commercially produced straw textured cathedral glass;[4] MDS regularly utilized both types of glass in various proportions, particularly when budgets had to be stretched. The nave and transept windows, specifically the lighter coloured glass, feature a signature style of Murphy's when it came to abstract glass; that is a wash of grey translucent pigment applied around the perimeter of each piece of glass with a broad brush, a technique which adds depth and modulates light penetration.

The sanctuary, elevated by a series of low-rise steps, features a single narrow *dalle de verre* window in the centre, with a large crucifix suspended some distance in front of it above the altar. *Dalle de verre*, a popular technique in continental Europe, was slow to catch on in Ireland and the only two studios who used the technique were MDS and Abbey Stained Glass Studios. The technique utilized slab glass (which was

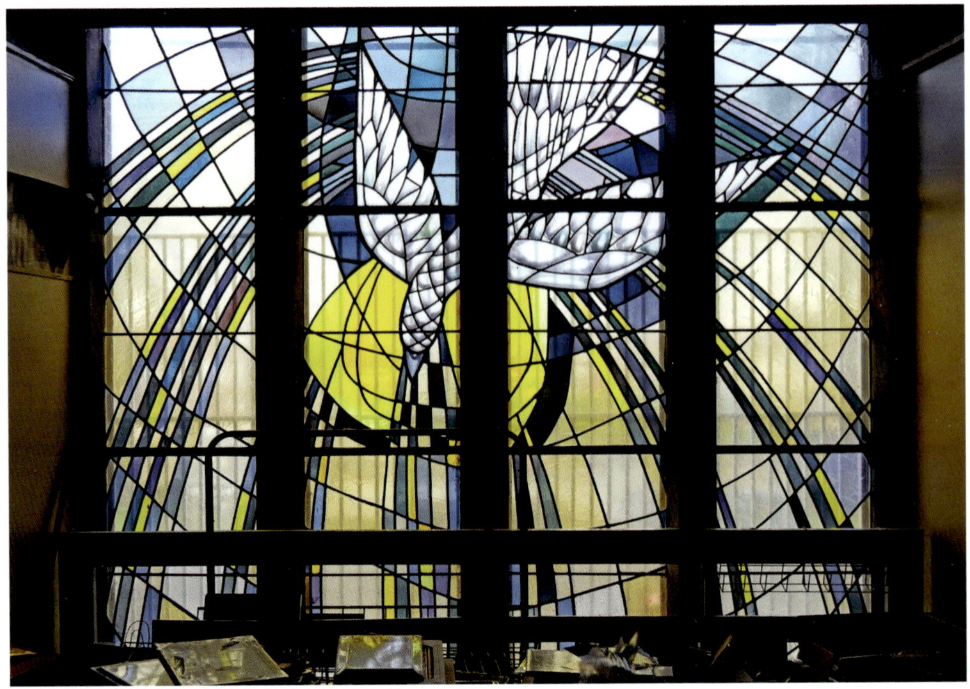

Murphy-Devitt Studios, *Holy Spirit* (1968) (in former baptistry)

also manufactured at Saint Gobain); a much thicker type of glass that was blown into square moulds and cut into small panels afterwards. Once the artist had created the design, drawn up the full sized cartoon, and selected the glass, each piece of glass, cut to size, was then spalled – chips were broken off the edge to increase the level of refraction – and set into a frame, and resin then poured in to the level of the glass. Like a conventional stained glass window, *dalle de verre* windows were made in sections and then the entire window was assembled on site.

MDS first used *dalle de verre* for a window in Lowertown church, near Schull, in 1967, a year ahead of Donnycarney and in both instances the matrix comprised only resin; thereafter Johnny Murphy experimented with a mixture of resin and concrete, which did not always respond favourably to the damp Irish climate, with sometimes calamitous results. In Donnycarney's *dalle de verre* window Murphy also added a three-dimensional element by attaching simple star shapes, twenty in all, of various sizes; these were made of fibreglass with a ribbed effect achieved with corrugated card. The resin was covered with what appears to be flakes of vermiculite to provide a contrasting texture, and then both stars and resin painted black which adds an additional layer of contrast to the luminous slab glass.

Directly facing the sanctuary, slotted snugly between the pair of main entrance doors to the church, is a baptistry, the baptismal font no longer present, and currently used as a shop. The main visual feature, thankfully untouched, is a wall-to-ceiling window designed and painted by Johnny Murphy which depicts a vigorous dove, dramatically swooping downwards, a metaphor for the Holy Spirit entering the soul of the one brought forward for baptism. Again both mouth-blown glass and cathedral glass have been combined judiciously to great effect. The image of a dove was Murphy's favourite motif and appeared in many iterations in his stained glass windows created from the late 1950s onwards, though by this time these enormous doves increasingly became the principal feature of baptistries such as in Ballyroan church of 1967 (see pp 325–31).

There is a small amount of MDS stained glass elsewhere in the church, a 3-light abstract in a side chapel and two 4-light windows, also abstract, adjacent to each of the front doors, though what is surprising is the large amount of clear glass (some of which was originally textured)[5] in the large expanse of windows on the front façade and those at clerestory level where, it seems, the likely aspiration was that they too would also feature stained glass but that the budget simply did not permit. Also of note is a large painting, *St Lawrence O'Toole* (1974), by Patrick Pye which features the saint against the Dublin skyline.

At the time that MDS were fulfilling their order for Donnycarney, the other large Dublin studio, Abbey Stained Glass, was supplying a similar amount of stained glass for another of Archbishop McQuaid's massive new churches, also named in honour of the Blessed Virgin, Our Lady of Victories Church, Ballymun (see pp 146–53).

By the late 1960s MDS were no longer experiencing the same demand; the staff were aware of it and there was a sense that they were winding down, and that the Donnycarney church would be their final big job – that is until the Catholic church in Dún Laoghaire burned down and they secured that tender too[6] (see pp 272–80). More jobs followed for the next two decades, though none on the scale of Our Lady of Consolation.

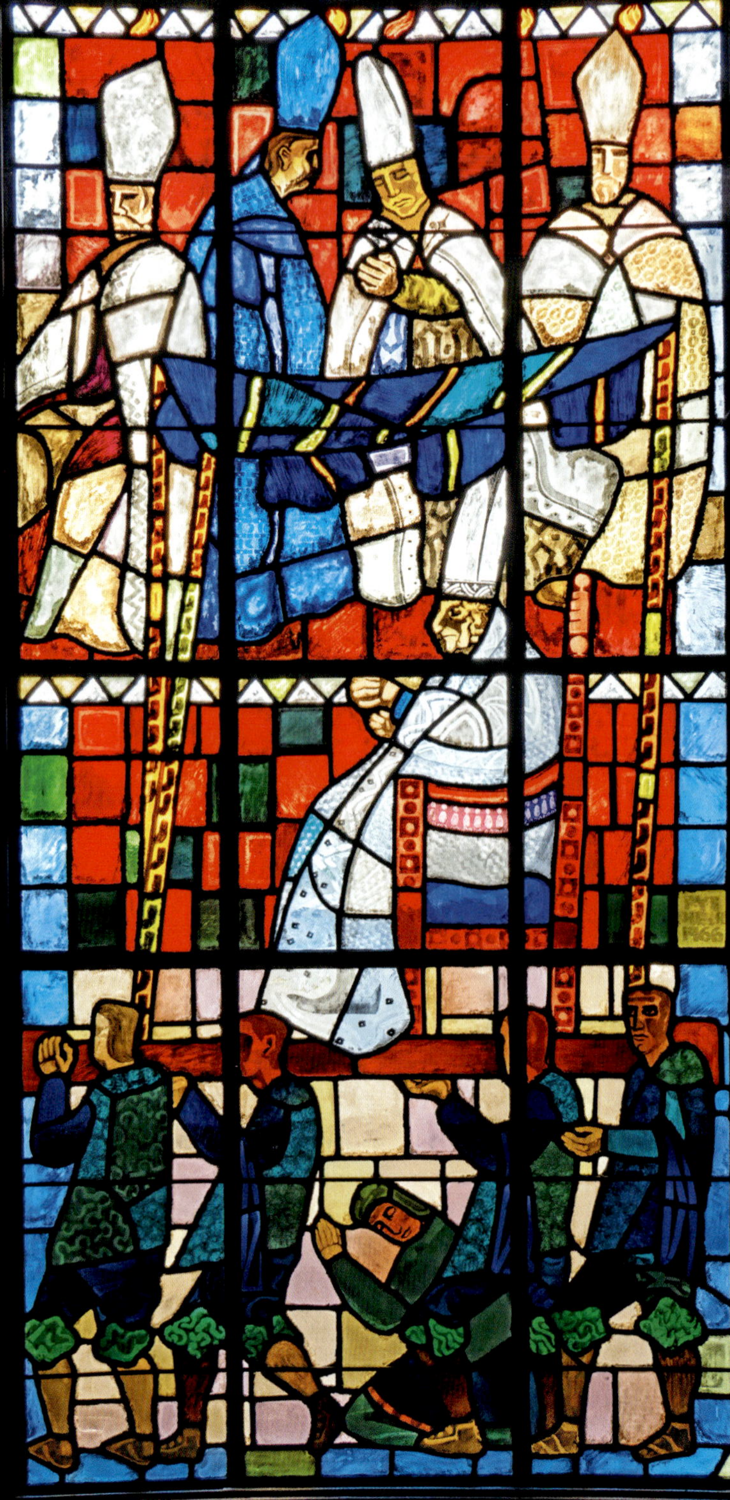
1966

Our Lady Seat of Wisdom chapel (RC), and 'Quiet Space', St Patrick's Campus (DCU)

Drumcondra Road Upper, D09 YT18

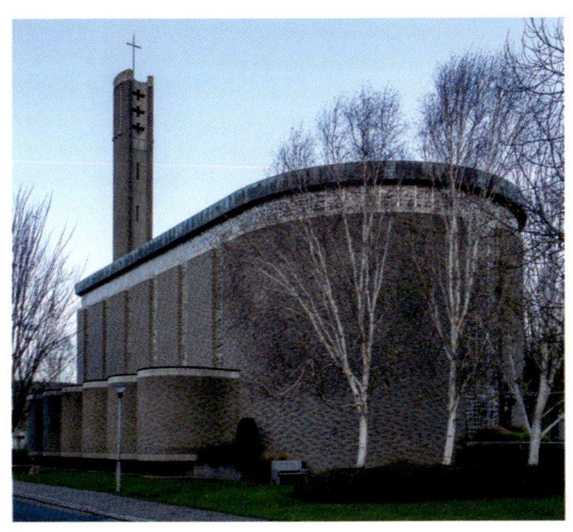

Our Lady Seat of Wisdom was designed by Andrew Devane of Robinson, Keefe & Devane in 1964–5 as a chapel for the students attending St Patrick's College, Drumcondra, which was then the largest primary teacher training college in Ireland. The chapel was constructed of concrete bricks of different shades of grey and taupe and features a slim concrete tower. Six cantilevered side chapels, which resemble mini-versions of the main structure, protrude in a row from the south wall.

(opposite) Patrick Pye, detail of *The Holy Spirit in the Form of an Angel Guiding Vatican II, with the Arrival of Pope John XXIII* (1966) in 'Quiet Space'

ST PATRICK'S COLLEGE was operated by the Vincentian order, and from the mid-1950s to mid-1970s the president was Fr Donal Cregan who oversaw an extensive building plan which was designed with the intention that it would foster greater freedom and nurture independent thinking, judgement and decision-making among the students.[1] Adjacent to the chapel is the gym and restaurant, also designed in brick by Devane, which were arranged to form a cloister-like space (now a car park) while the chapel remained the fulcrum. Devane's student accommodation blocks were arranged in a loose open circle recalling early monastic settlements and, as if to emphasize this, bear names such as Clonmacnoise and Glendalough.[2] One can see why Cregan chose Andrew Devane, a reflective architect tuned into Ireland's early Christian past but working in a contemporary idiom who also was deeply committed to his Catholic faith.

When designing Our Lady Seat of Wisdom chapel, Devane decided to employ *dalle de verre* instead of conventional stained glass, his only time to do so. *Dalle de verre* utilizes large pieces of very thick glass set into a matrix of concrete or epoxy and which is made in large panels, and these are then assembled together on site. It is a technique that originated in Paris in the 1930s and which became popular on the Continent though was slow being introduced to Ireland. For Our Lady Seat of Wisdom, Devane sought out the world leader working in *dalle de verre*, Gabriel Loire, who had his studio in Chartres, and the deep blues and reds of the city's cathedral often permeate his work. Loire used glass that was approximately one inch thick and was deliberately chipped and spalled around the edges to maximize the refraction potential. His suite of windows for the Drumcondra chapel, made 1964–5, would be his second work on the island; in 1962 he had created five large windows for the chapel of the Dominican sisters, Falls Road, Belfast.

Due to the intrinsic nature of *dalle de verre*, complex figurative imagery can be challenging to introduce so artists often opt for symbols and exploit the expressive power of colour and shape to communicate themes and concepts, and this was Loire's principal approach in Drumcondra. As one enters the chapel one immediately sees the largest of the windows which acts as a backdrop to Michael Biggs' monolithic granite altar. The top section reveals the Trinity – the Hand of God, the Dove, and

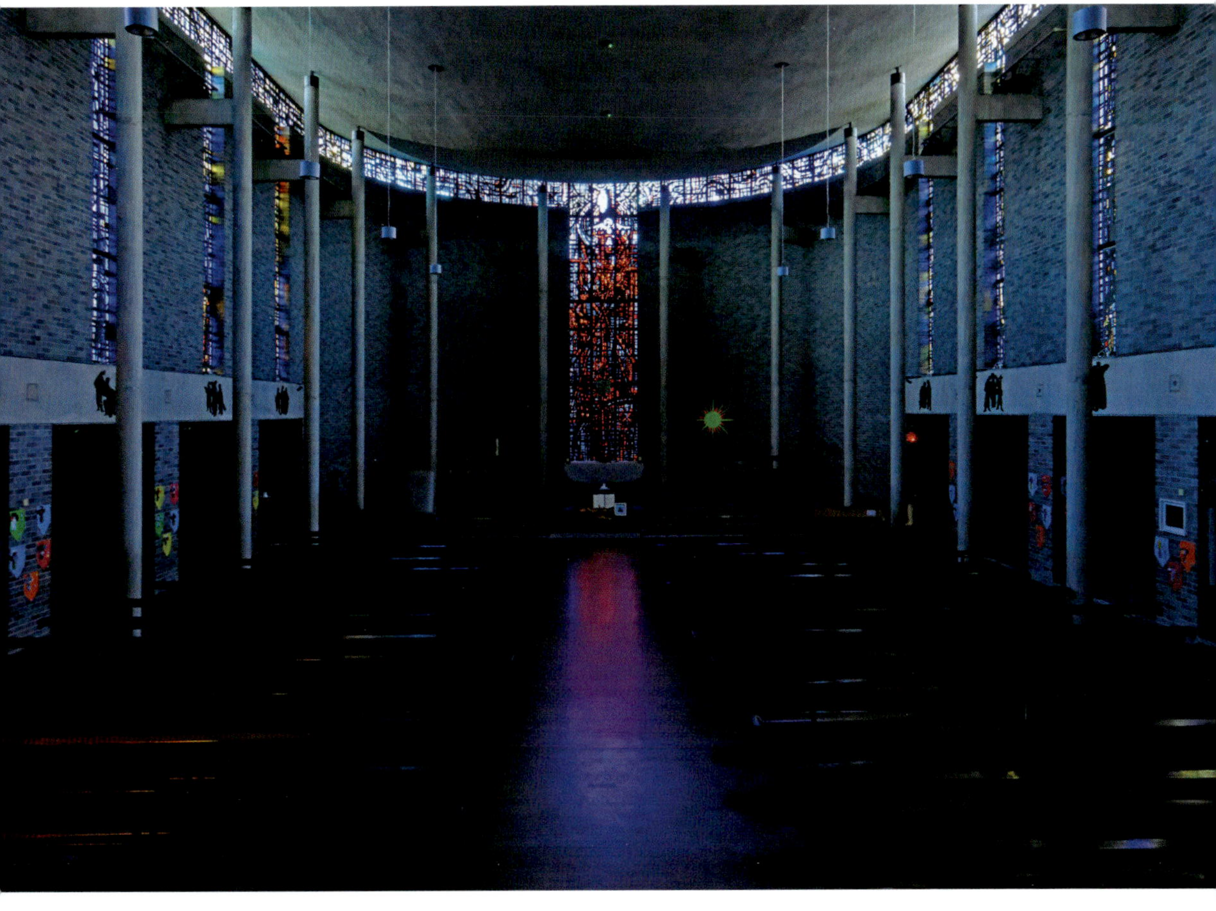

Gabriel Loire, interior with *dalle de verre* scheme in Our Lady Seat of Wisdom chapel (1964–5)

Chi Rho symbol to represent Christ – then shades of blue merge into shades of red and one can discern instruments associated with Christ's Passion, among them the spear, the pole with the sponge, the cock, the crown of thorns and the nails. Emanating left and right from the top of the window is a clerestory band of *dalle de verre*; this is intended to represent a river of grace flowing from the Godhead around the chapel.[3] A dozen vertical windows, six each side, descend from it.

On the south side (right as one faces the altar), the six themes relate to Our Lady – fleur-de-lis; The Annunciation with the Holy Spirit descending; The Nativity represented by the Star of Bethlehem and the yellow straw of the manger; Jesus's

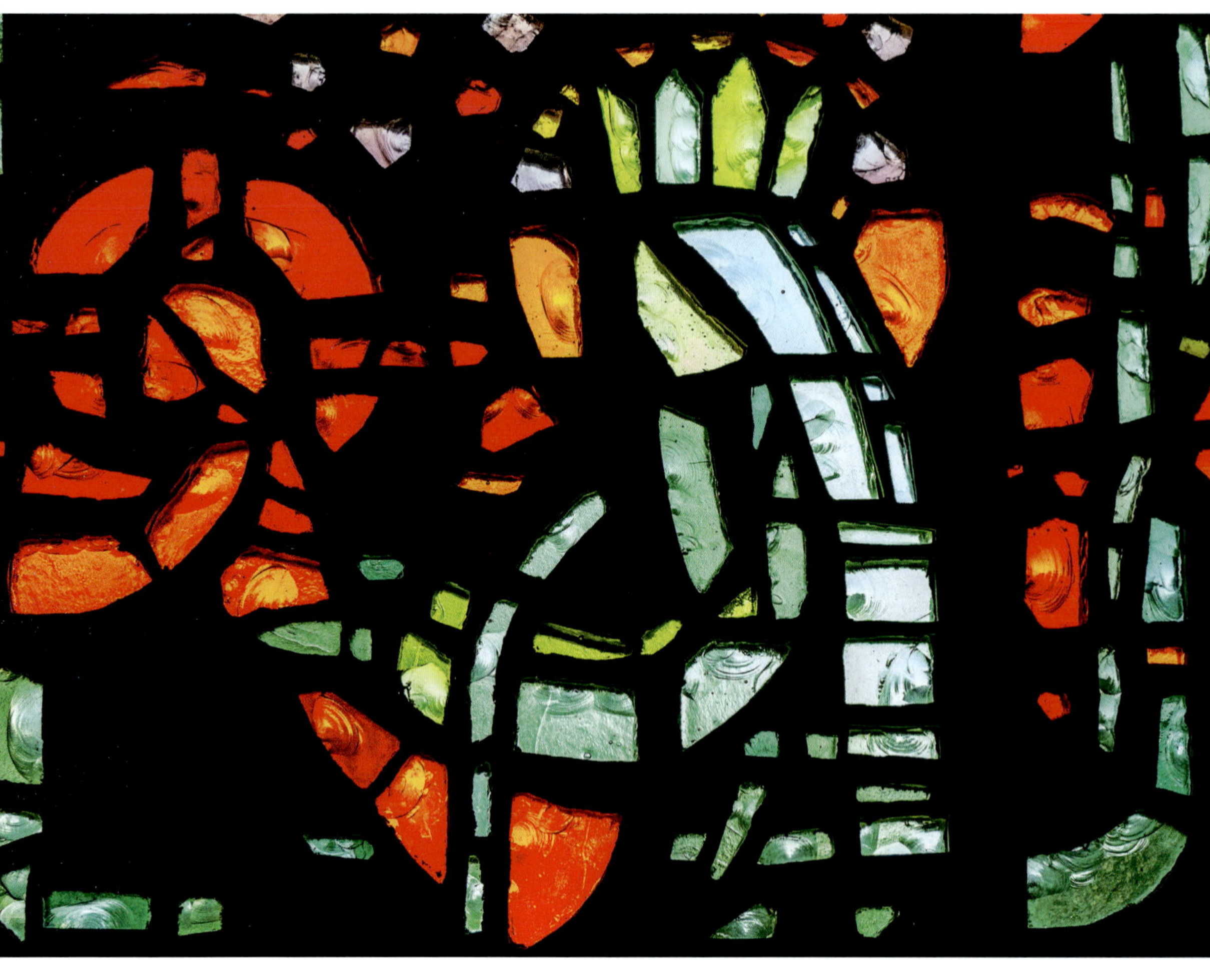

Gabriel Loire, detail from window in the chapel's south-west entrance vestibule (1964–5)

early life represented by the tools of a carpenter; the marriage feast at Cana evoked by water jugs and entwined rings; The Assumption and Coronation of Mary conveyed by the upward flow of light and a crown. The six windows on the north side relate to St Patrick – the Sun of Truth; the overthrow of idols; the spread of St Patrick's evangelization of Ireland; the spring of living water and the cross; St Patrick's crozier and a snake; the defeat of paganism with Satan in red.[4] Shades of blue dominate all twelve windows, even those associated with St Patrick's side of the chapel where one might expect significant use of green.

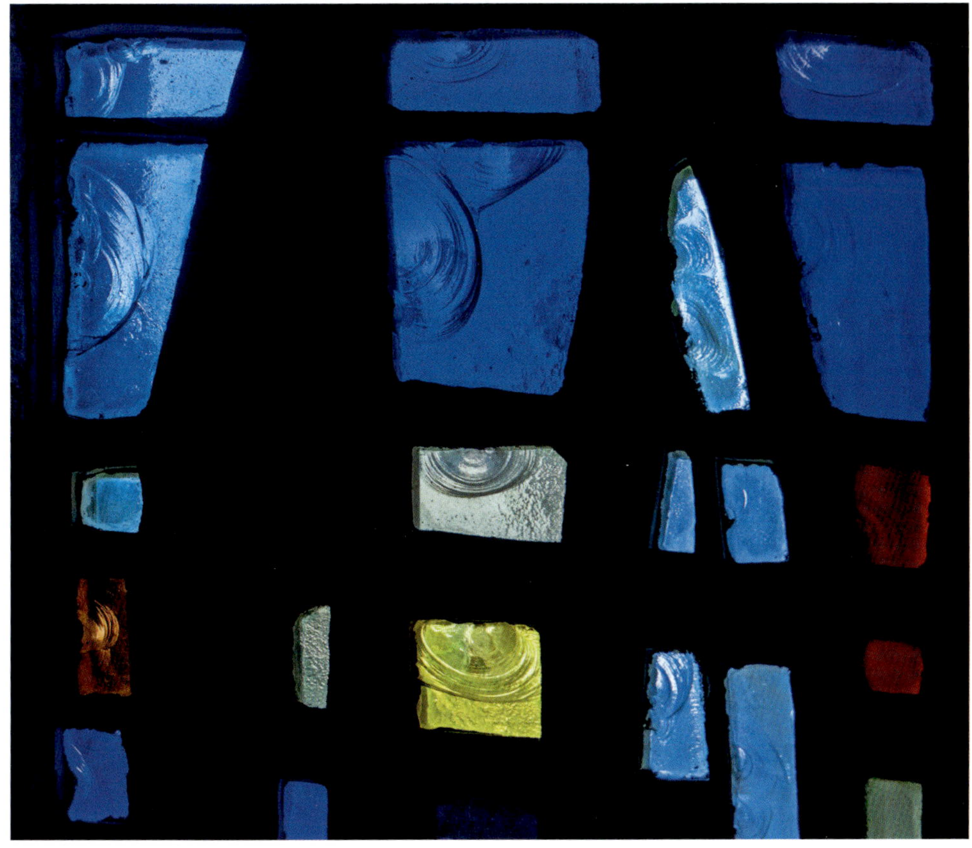

Gabriel Loire, detail of *dalle de verre* technique using thick spalled glass set in resin (1964–5)

Apparently, the windows installed on the south wall were intended for the north wall, and vice versa, and when Gabriel Loire visited the chapel after they were installed and saw the error he was greatly distressed and attempted to darken the windows on the south side with black pigment to diminish the amount of light that passed through them, however much of what he applied flaked off in time.[5]

Each of the side chapels features a narrow *dalle de verre* window with symbols that relate to the eucharist – chalice; vine and grapes; wheat; Chi Rho monogram; incense; alpha and omega. The windows either side of the organ represent Prayer (left of organ) and Silence (right of organ). In the entrance lobby (south-west corner) there is a large rectangular wall of glass which features an abstracted St Patrick on the left and the remaining two thirds is inspired by the *Book of Revelation* 12:1–6. Our Lady crowned is depicted presenting 'the child to an angel to be taken straight up to God and to his throne.' Also discernible is the defeated seven-headed dragon.[6]

The best time to view Loire's *dalle de verre* in the chapel is the early morning when it benefits from maximum light that passes through the east window, however the chapel remains a distinctly dark space, perhaps deliberately so in order to evoke the subdued lighting found in the great medieval cathedrals, which would have been illuminated only by candles, and which arguably creates an atmosphere that is more conducive to prayer and contemplation.

Separate from the chapel, the Vincentian fathers had their own first-floor oratory – now known as 'Quiet Space' – in what was the priests' residential building, which was also designed by Andrew Devane. The oratory is a perfect circle and features two floor-to-ceiling windows which face each other and which dominate this double-height space, and both are the work of Patrick Pye. There is no record of Devane having been involved in this commission so it would seem likely that it was Fr Cregan who engaged Pye directly. As the audience for the oratory's windows would be the Vincentian fathers and not the young students who would worship only in the chapel, an entirely different approach could be taken.

Patrick Pye, a Catholic convert, was a deeply spiritual individual who rarely depicted standard Christian iconography without adding his own imprint, often with idiosyncratic results. The subjects of Pye's two windows are *The Holy Spirit in the Form of an Angel Guiding Vatican II, with the Arrival of Pope John XXIII* which was made in 1966, and *The Holy Spirit in the Form of a Dove Coming Down on the Apostles as they Head out into the World* which was made in 1967.

It is not known to what degree Fr Cregan liaised with Pye but one can imagine that both would have had a keen interest in the deliberations and directives of Vatican II which had just concluded the year before Pye made the first of his two windows. Noteworthy is that the Holy Spirit features in both windows, and that Vatican II recognized the significant role the Holy Spirit had in not only guiding the

(opposite) Patrick Pye, detail of two cardinals from *The Holy Spirit in the Form of an Angel Guiding Vatican II, with the Arrival of Pope John XXIII* (1966) in 'Quiet Space'

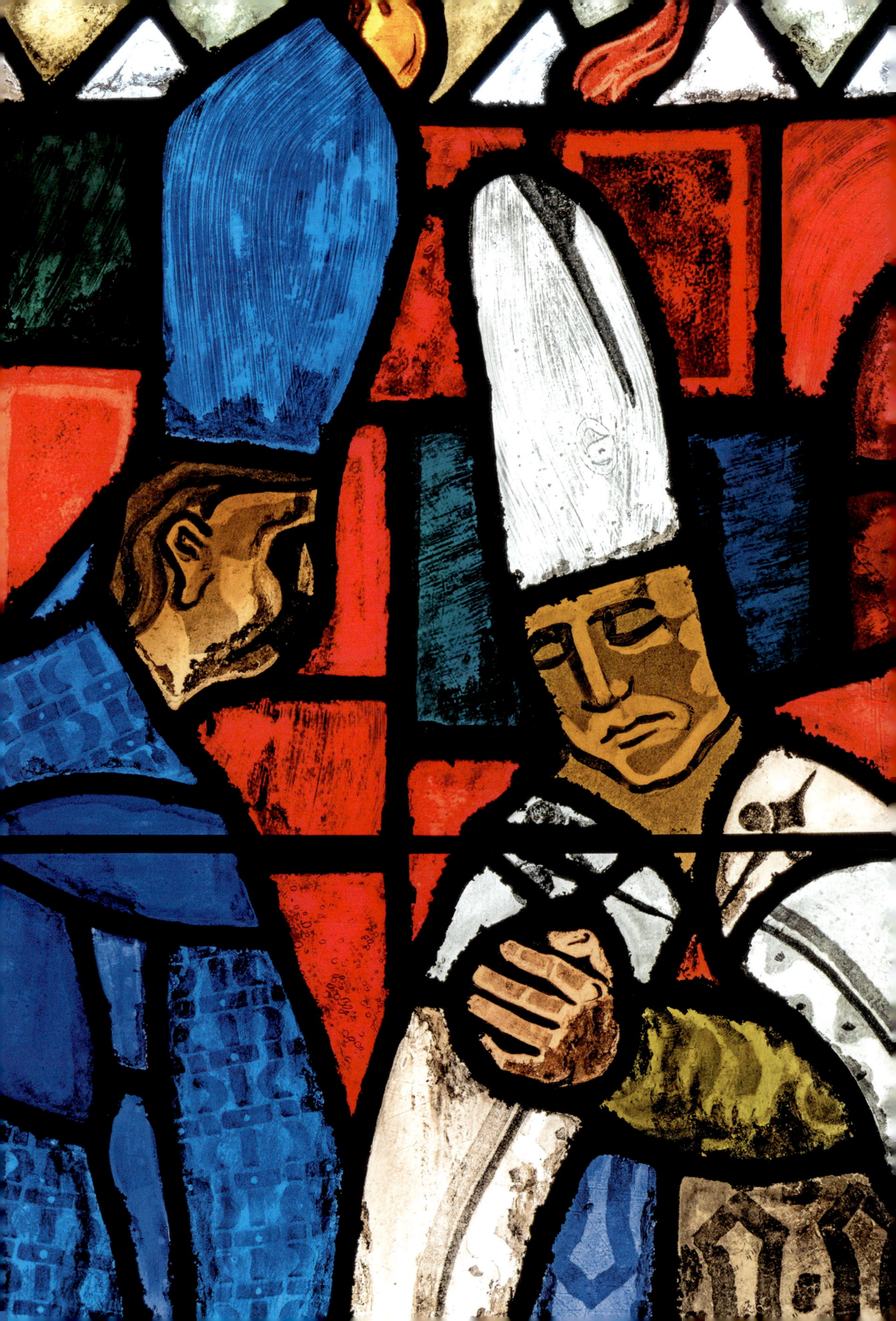

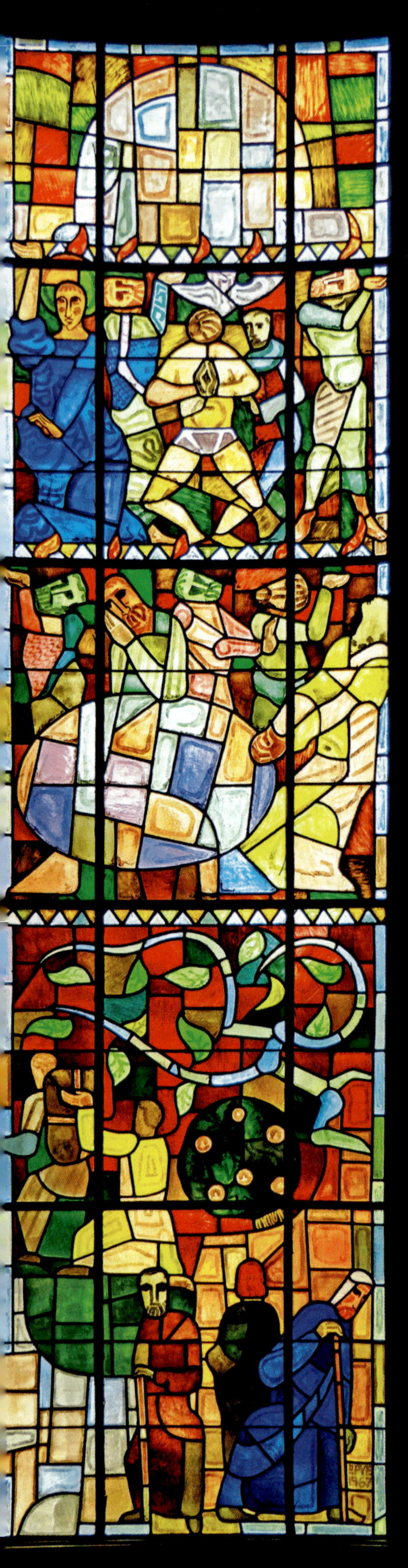

Council but informing all aspects of the faithful's spiritual life.

In the first window Pye depicted Pope John XXIII, recognizable by his distinctive profile, carried aloft in a *sedia gestatoria* by five men and processing with pomp and ceremony through St Peter's Basilica where various cardinals are already assembled. At the very top, the Holy Spirit in the guise of an angel, darts in from the right, holding a slim sceptre as if to direct the proceedings. On either side of the angel, Pye has included two of the distinctive helical columns of Bernini's baldachin that hold the canopy above the altar in St Peter's. Above the heads of the cardinals and the pontiff are tongues of fire to indicate that the Holy Spirit is at work. Rich colours feature, particularly in the scarlet background referencing the colour traditionally associated with cardinals' clothing, though in this instance they are dressed in pastel colours, perhaps so as not to detract attention from the

Patrick Pye, *The Holy Spirit in the Form of a Dove Coming Down on the Apostles as they Head out into the World* (1967) in 'Quiet Space'

pope. Pye has also added plenty of texture in the form of lightly matted pigment to all the fabrics to suggest brocade and embroidery, and convey a general sense of pageantry.

The top section of Pye's second window depicts Pentecost, the event that occurred after Christ's resurrection when the apostles were assembled together 'And suddenly there came from the sky a noise like a strong driving wind, and it filled the entire house in which they were. Then there appeared to them tongues as of fire, which parted and came to rest on each one of them. And they were all filled with the Holy Spirit and began to speak in different tongues, as the Spirit enabled them to proclaim.'[7] Most depictions of Pentecost since medieval times include Our Lady – though she is not directly referenced in the Acts of the Apostles – however Pye has looked back to pre-twelfth-century examples in art history when the norm was only to depict the apostles. In these earlier depictions of Pentecost, St Peter was positioned in the centre, and we can assume that it is he who Pye has placed in the middle and in a state of undress as if taken by surprise. All the apostles appear to be twisting this way and that as if trying to establish the source of the unidentified 'noise like a driving wind'. Echoing his earlier window, Pye has included tongues of fire above the heads of all those present.

Fr Cregan paid particular attention to the manner in which the students attending St Patrick's were instructed in how to teach religion and this probably explains the choice of subject in the bottom section of the window; Pye has depicted the apostles heading forth to spread the gospel and one easily can draw an analogy with the nascent primary school teachers embarking on careers that would involve teaching the tenets of Catholicism to generations of Irish children.

Although by the mid-1960s Patrick Pye had undertaken important stained glass orders for churches or chapels in counties Limerick, Galway, Donegal and Tyrone, these two windows for St Patrick's College were his first commission for a Dublin location. His next stained glass order was for a 3-light window for St Ninian's Church of Ireland church, Convoy, Co. Donegal; it was commissioned by the distinguished art historian, Professor Anne Crookshank of Trinity College, and it seems likely that she placed the order with Pye on the basis of having seen these two windows made for Drumcondra.

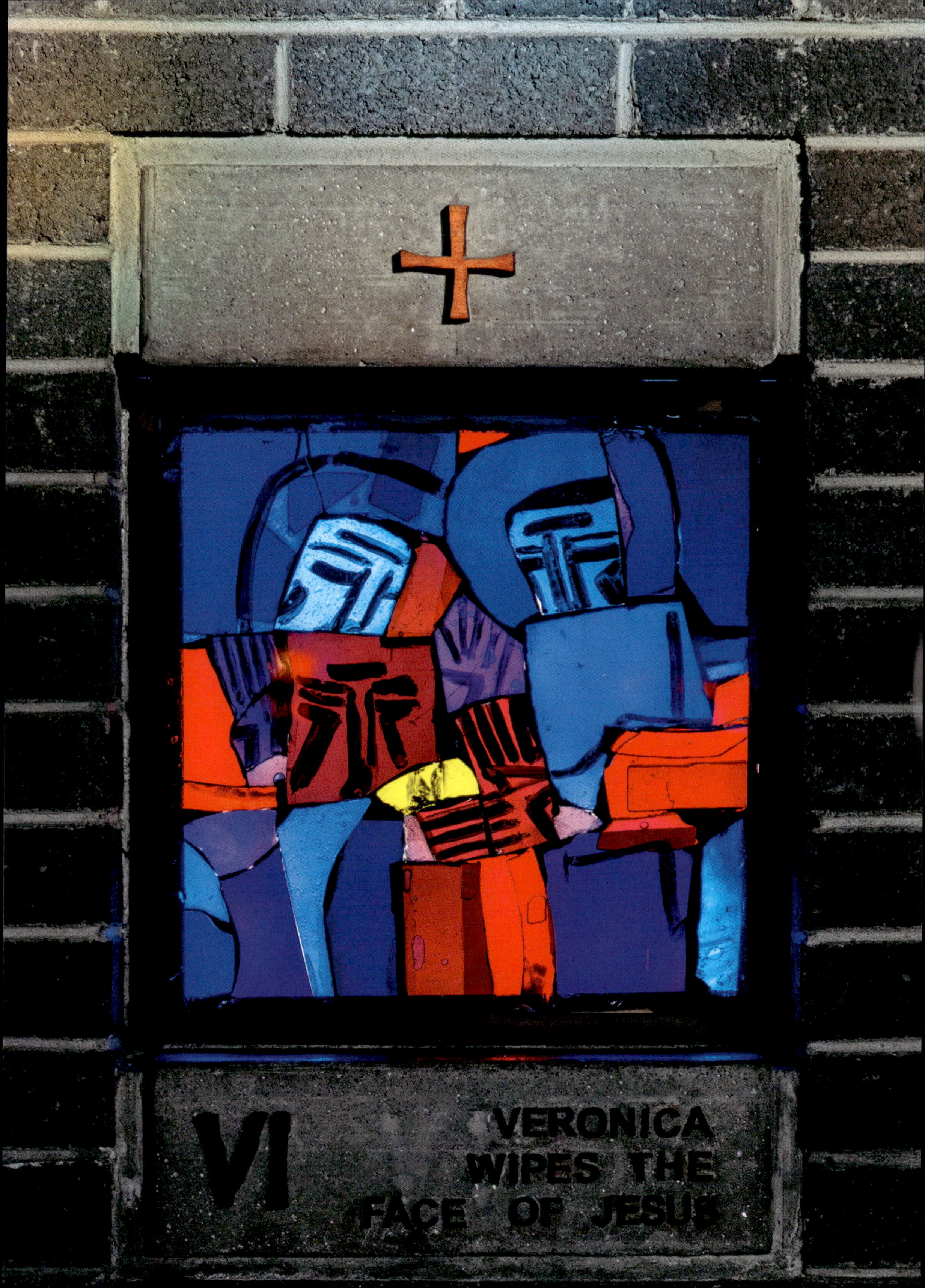
VI
VERONICA
WIPES THE
FACE OF JESUS

DUBLIN AIRPORT

Our Lady Queen of Heaven church (RC)

K67 HX98

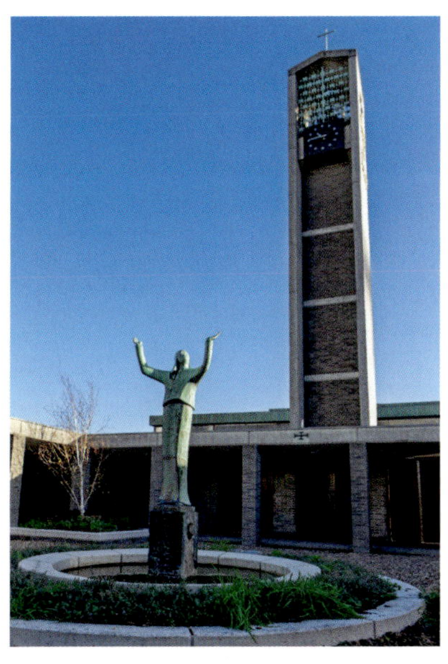

Generally considered to be Dublin's first Modernist church, the church of Our Lady Queen of Heaven (1964) was designed by Andrew Devane, who had studied under Frank Lloyd Wright in the 1940s. Returning to Ireland he became a partner in Robinson, Keefe & Devane and is recognized as one of Ireland's most accomplished mid-twentieth-century architects. Our Lady Queen of Heaven is one of several Dublin churches designed by Devane in the 1960s and 70s during the episcopate of the redoubtable Dr John Charles McQuaid. The church is signalled by a slim tower and is accessed via a cloister-like atrium. The materials and aesthetic of the church are both spare and sparse; the nave, a rectangular hall constructed of cool grey concrete bricks offset by the ceiling and sanctuary wall clad in warm cedar sheeting.[1]

(opposite) Sheila Corcoran, *Station VI, Veronica Wipes the Face of Jesus* (1964)

In terms of stained glass, Our Lady Queen of Heaven features two types, simple, understated leaded clerestory and side sanctuary windows of geometric pattern in muted colours by Michael Dunne which were designed to complement the architecture and allow plenty of soft light to filter in,[2] and the *pièce de resistance*, a set of dramatic, visually intense – and for their time, radical – Stations of the Cross by Sheila Corcoran.[3]

Dublin-born Sheila Corcoran, about whom little is known, had initially won a scholarship to the National College of Art and studied stained glass under Johnny Murphy, head of the college's small but vibrant glass department (Murphy was concurrently the principal artist at Murphy-Devitt Studios). Corcoran attended the college from 1960 to 1963, and in the summer of her final year she was one of a group of Murphy's students who put on a public exhibition of their work.[4] She displayed four pieces; an angel, two described as 'abstract', and one as a 'laminate panel', the latter probably being made of two or more pieces of glass laminated or fused together with epoxy resin. It is possible that it was at this exhibition where Devane first encountered her work and on this basis approached her about the potential commission. He wrote formally to her in February 1964, enclosing architectural plans of the church, then under construction, while Corcoran, still aged only 20, was on a Royal Dublin Society travelling scholarship attending art college in London.

Before proceeding with the set of fourteen, Devane suggested to Corcoran that she should first make two trial Stations for his consideration, and for which he was happy to pay regardless of whether the commission proceeded.[5] What is clear from the extant correspondence is that Devane was very supportive of the young artist and eager to mentor her ('Fused glass would be wonderful – I would much prefer it to leading, and I shall await your sketches with interest'), was happy for her to experiment, encouraged her to increase the payment she suggested, and stressed that she must not feel rushed. He was also conscious that they had an uphill battle ahead: 'For my part here, the next step is to obtain approval from the Parish Priest [Fr Donal O'Leary] and the Archbishop. This will not be easy, but keep your fingers crossed and say a painter's prayer.'[6]

The square Stations (only 40cm x 40cm) are made of mouth-blown pot metal

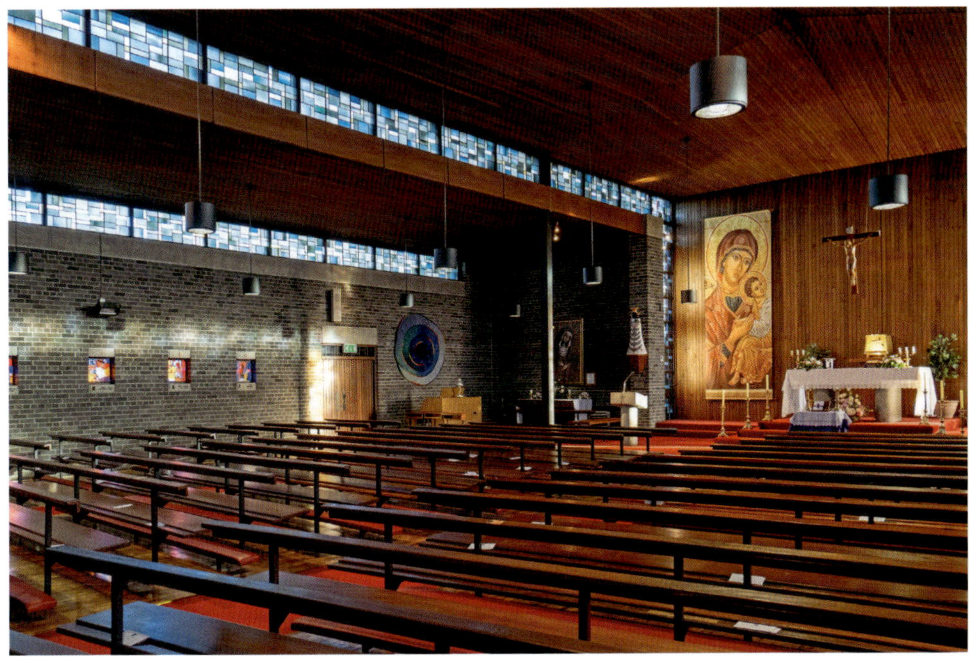

Our Lady Queen of Heaven church featuring *Stations of the Cross* (1964) by Sheila Corcoran and abstract glazing (*c.*1964) by Michael Dunne

glass in a limited range of colours, essentially tones of red, yellow, blue, green, pink and maroon – with minimal painting and no leading whatsoever – and set into slim, hinged metal frames. Behind each Station is the actual window of clear translucent glass which weather-proofs the building, and a fluorescent light bulb was accommodated in the space between stained glass and the clear glass to allow for evening illumination; possibly the first instance in Ireland of an architect setting out to incorporate artificial lighting as part of the viewing experience.

In order to make the windows Corcoran had arranged to access facilities in her London college though it seems she may have relied to some degree on cullets (discarded off-cuts of glass) when making these small windows. The individual shapes in each of the Stations are simple – with a conscious focus on silhouettes – all slotting together, and the separate pieces of glass were glued with epoxy resin (Araldite) onto clear glass, sometimes with additional small pieces adding another layer. Fine cement was used to fill any gaps so that no clear light penetrates to

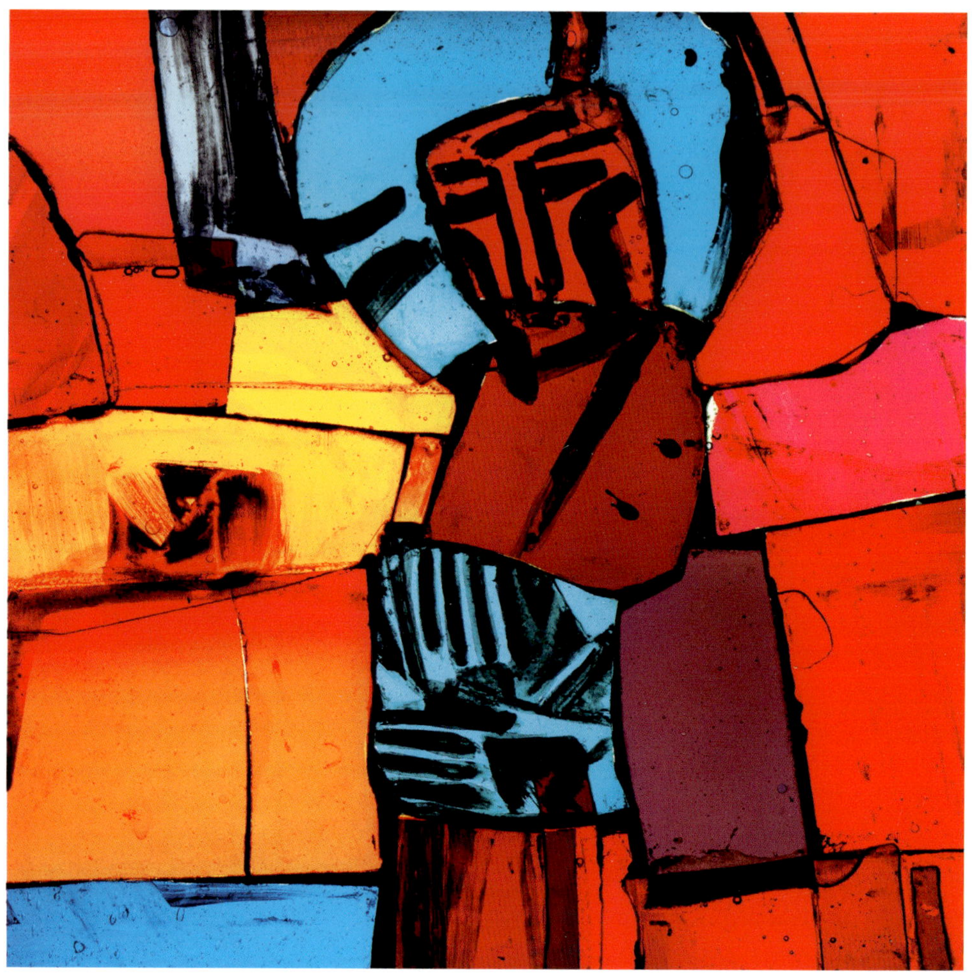

Sheila Corcoran, *Station II, Jesus Carries His Cross* (1964)

undermine the visual intensity of the experience. On occasions when dissatisfied with a Station Corcoran made a second version, as with *Station III (Jesus Falls the First Time)* where the second version shows Jesus in the act of falling forward with greater clarity and heightened drama,[7] and in *Station VII (Jesus Falls the Second Time)* where she has changed the colours for greater impact.[8] Corcoran's painting style varies somewhat over the fourteen Stations; the records show that they were undertaken over many months and in several of them – Stations I, II, III, IV, VI, X – the dark brush strokes appear primal, even harsh, befitting the theme of Christ's passion, the others are more translucent and applied with a lighter touch.

Corcoran had the first few Stations – perhaps as many as five – finished by June 1964, in time for the church's July dedication by Archbishop McQuaid. Over the next few months she made the remaining windows and had them transported to Dublin in small numbers, sometimes by her father, so that all had arrived by the end of the year. Devane's concern that the windows might not be well received was well founded and before the year was out Archbishop McQuaid instructed Fr

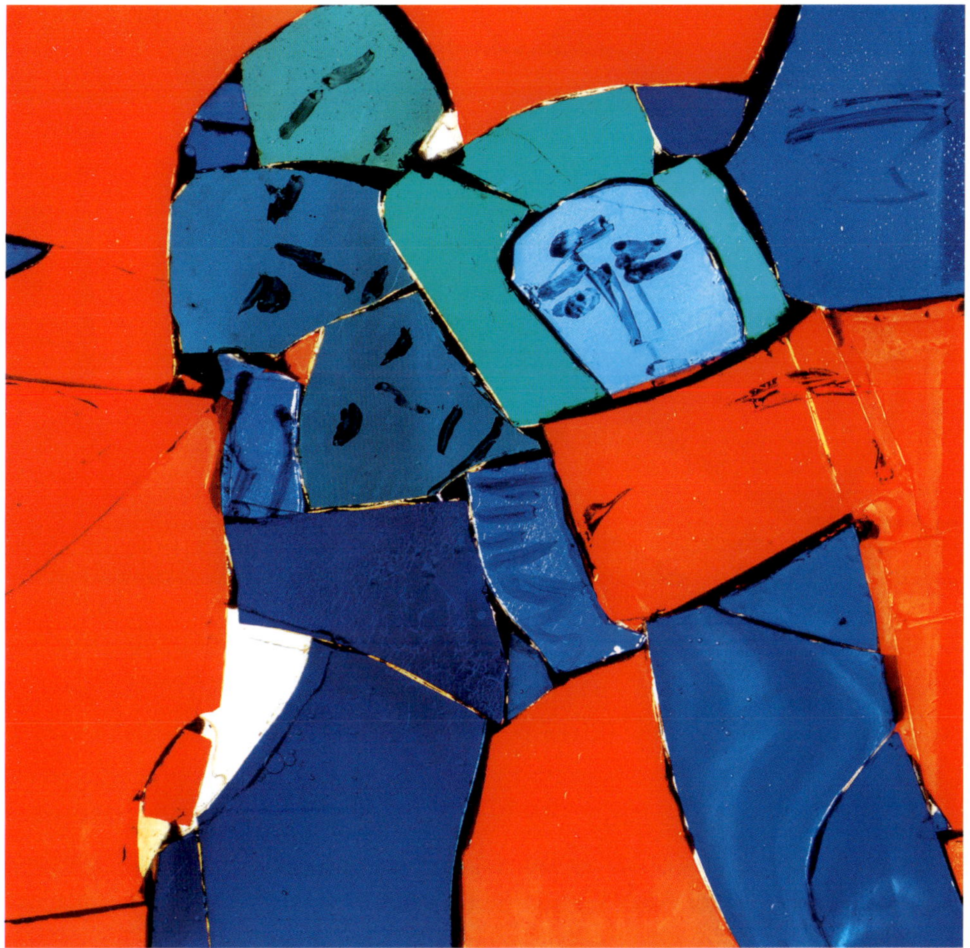

Sheila Corcoran, *Station VIII, Jesus Speaks to the Women of Jerusalem* (1964)

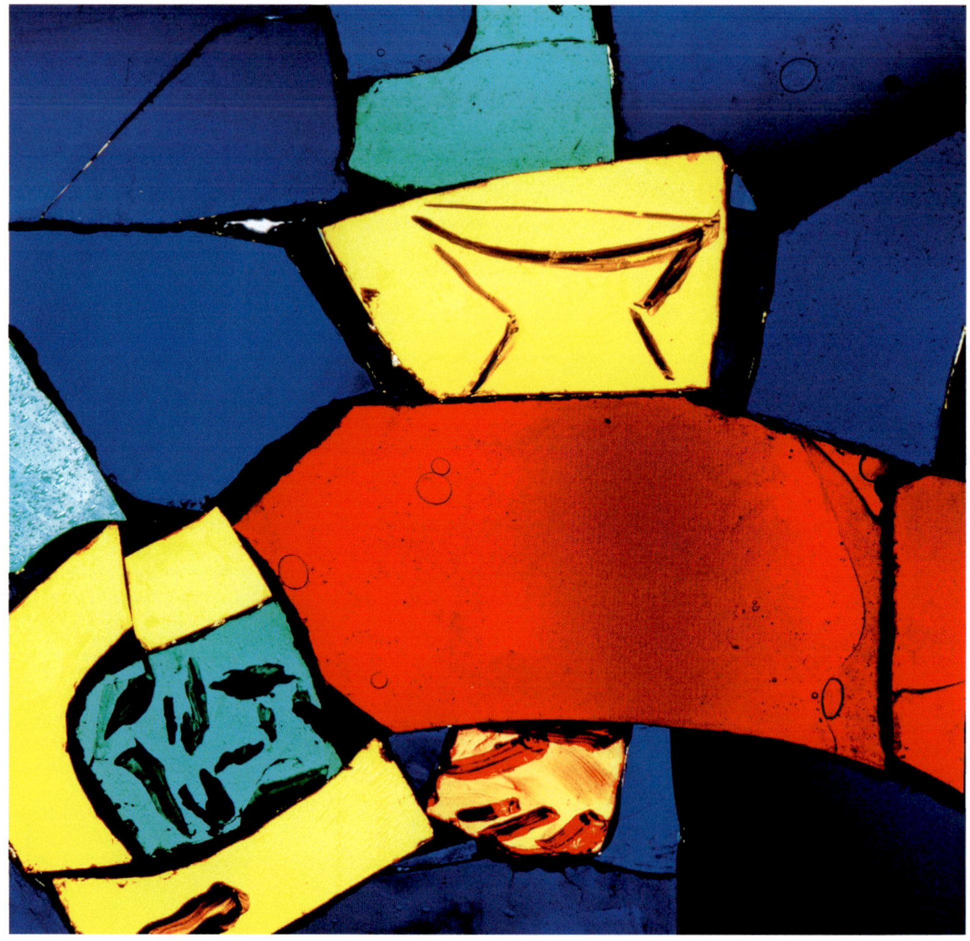

Sheila Corcoran, *Station IX, Jesus Falls the Third Time* (1964)

O'Leary that both Corcoran's windows and a modern Christmas crib designed by sculptor/craftsman Fergus O'Farrell be removed.[9] The crib in particular incurred his ire '... figures which are beneath the level of human dignity, in that they are not human. No reference, I regret to say, was made to me concerning this crib. I must require the removal of this crib. It is an offence against the Canon Law and the prescriptions of the Holy See to offer for public veneration figures which are purporting to be sacred, without the previous sanction of the Archbishop ...'[10] The press had a field day, though they were much more focused on the offending crib than the Stations; this was probably due to a combination of the following – Dr McQuaid had singled out the crib for his stinging criticism, photographs of the crib were available to reproduce, and Fergus O'Farrell was willing to be interviewed.[11]

It appears that Sheila Corcoran, back in London after Christmas holidays at home,[12] was notified by family or friends of the debacle, and she wrote to Dr McQuaid straightaway, explaining her motivation and intention:

> Working in the medium of stained glass, I tried to depict a simple image of Christ that would not amaze or outrage by its form, and that would follow in the form and tradition of all true Irish Christian art. Every new creative work of art is necessarily unusual and people in the diocese of Dublin would find these Stations a little strange at first, not having any in the medium of stained glass. I had hoped that strangeness would quickly disappear. Whether I have failed, in that the figures appear in any way incongruous or undignified, is of course, now for others to decide. I did not deliberately force any ideas on this work, but tried to the best of my ability, to work within the framework laid down by the Church, and to try to express the suffering and the dignity of the way of the cross.[13]

Dr McQuaid replied:

> Dear Miss Corcoran, I thank you for your very courteous note. I fear that you are somewhat in error: I was never afforded a chance of even studying your Stations. And I never judge, except on evidence that I have examined. What I saw of evidence of one Station in my brief visit to the Airport Church for other purposes, did not give me an opportunity of studying and evaluating the Stations. I did not see any figure such as you say you have delineated.[14]

His reply does raise the question as to why, if he saw only one Station which he said he did not have the opportunity to study, he had so swiftly instructed Fr O'Leary to remove the set of Stations, along with the crib.

The controversy rumbled on and by February 1965 Corcoran, still a student in London, was making new versions of the fifth and sixth Stations that were to be reviewed by Dr McQuaid. Devane wrote to Corcoran's father of being conscious that the new Vatican II liturgical guidelines may have some bearing on the situation.[15] (Devane, a devout Catholic, was a member of the Committee on Sacred Art and Architecture advising the Episcopal Liturgical Commission of Ireland at Maynooth.) Ultimately the new Stations did not garner Dr McQuaid's approval and by April they were consigned to the basement of Robinson, Keefe & Devane.

It seems that in August 1967 Andrew Devane arranged for their reinstatement in the airport church, though without first consulting Dr McQuaid, with whom it appears he had a generally good rapport. In reply to a letter from the archbishop Devane wrote:

> My Lord Archbishop … about the Stations of the Cross – I now realise how silly it was of me to suggest such a cloak-and-dagger arrangement, but I wanted so much for you to see them, in sequence in their proper setting – because the truth is they look terrible in isolation – and most surprisingly right and beautiful in situ. I shall leave them in to you with this letter, but I fear greatly that you will not like them – all the more so, as what you said in your letter is certainly valid. I really don't know how far – in sacred art and in our time representation can be subordinate to imagination – so much depends on the mind and eye of the beholder – and, more especially, on the soul and the ability of the artist (the bridgeless gap between a Picasso and a Rouault). I suppose in all of these things, time alone will provide the measured answer – long after our time! And all we can do now is to act on what we believe to be right and good, – as I know you do – and as I hope I do …[16]

Whether Dr McQuaid acquiesced at this stage or not is not clear,[17] but at some stage Sheila Corcoran's Stations were reinstated though possibly not until after the archbishop retired in January 1972, or more probably until after his death the following April.

Ultimately several of the Stations are challenging due to their abstraction, something that Devane had cautioned Corcoran about early in the design process

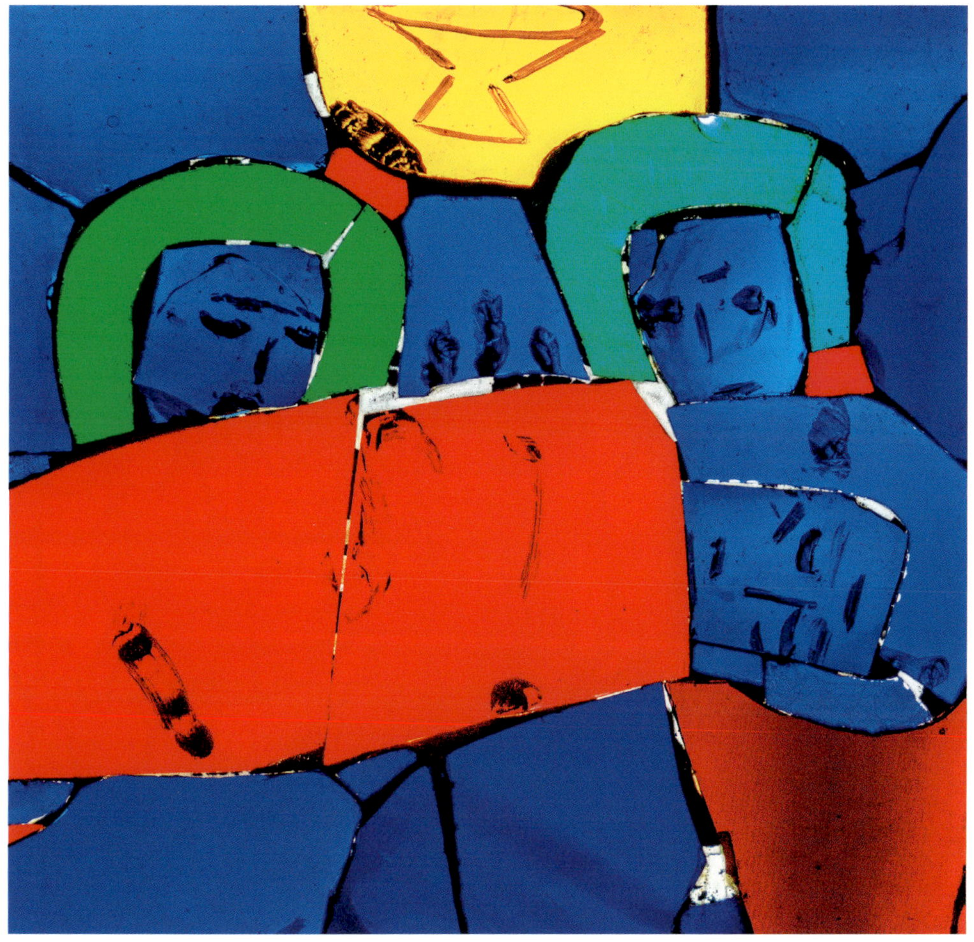

Sheila Corcoran, *Station XIV, Jesus is Laid in the Tomb* (1964)

'One point which is important – the Stations must be representational – they are didactic, i.e., their purpose primarily is to teach – to remind people of Christ's passion and death …'[18] Devane's original intention was that each Station would only be identified by a simple bronze cross and roman numerals but at a later stage titles/ descriptors were added beneath each Station, presumably a concession to those, like Dr McQuaid, who struggled to interpret the images. Despite any shortcomings in their ability to communicate, coupled with their diminutive size, Corcoran's fourteen Stations add a vital visual note in Devane's understated interior.

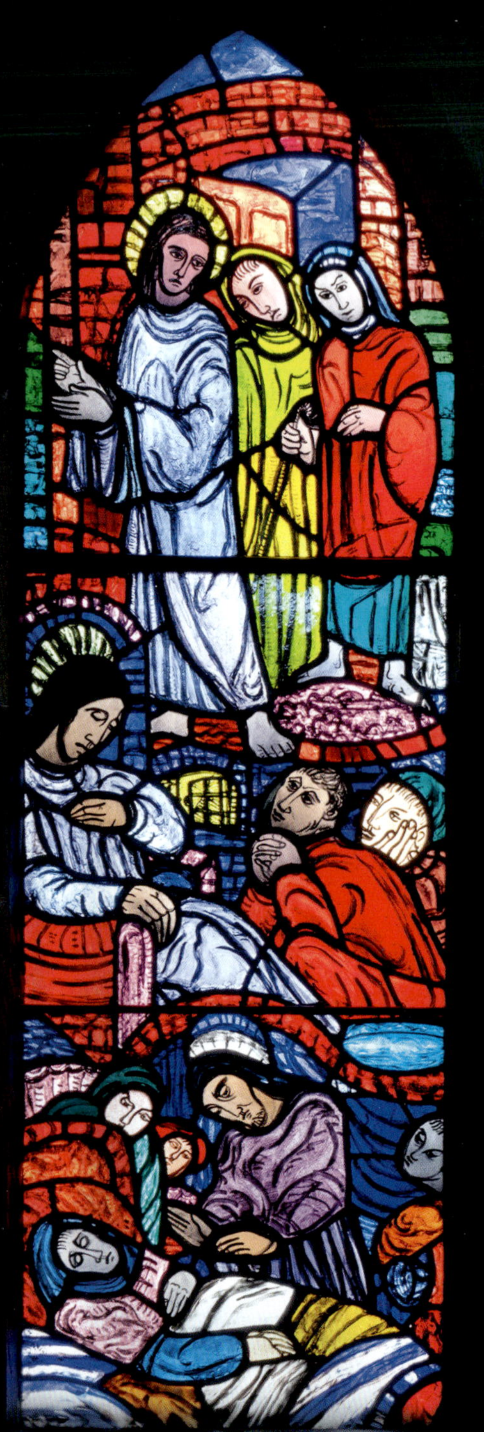
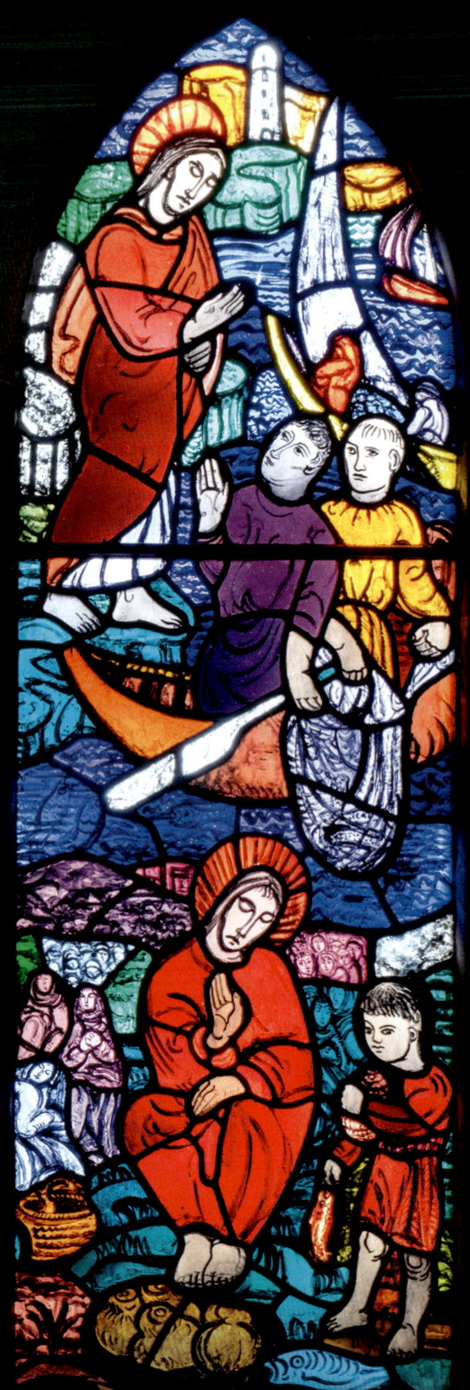

St Mary's church (C of I)

Howth Road, D13 V259

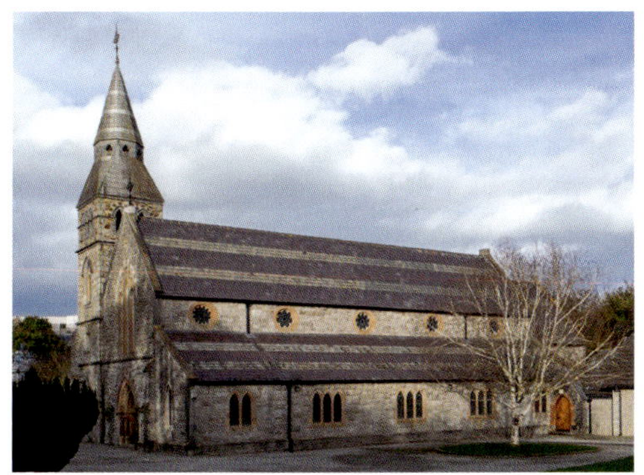

St Mary's church on the Howth Road is situated on an elevated site near the entrance to Howth demesne and castle, the home for many centuries, until recently, of the earls of Howth and their descendants, the Gaisford St Lawrence family. Designed by J.E. Rogers, a student of Benjamin Woodward, it was built in the Gothic style in 1866 and constructed of rock-faced granite laid in random courses with quoin dressed corners. The slate roof retains its original terracotta ridge tiles, and the four-stage tower, topped by a spire, rises to 80ft and is terminated by a wrought iron gilt finial.

(opposite) Evie Hone, *Scenes from the Lives of Christ and St Andrew* (1943)

St Mary's has the character of a charming village church, which of course it was when it originally opened, and most of the windows are of modest proportions, the largest of which is the 3-light east window behind the reredos. More often than not the first stained glass window to be erected in a church of this age (often replacing the original diamond-paned clear glass) is the east window in the chancel as it is in the most sacred space of the church and the focus of the congregation. In this instance, the first window to be installed, *Faith, Hope and Charity*, in 1905, was a small window in the south wall. This location may have been selected because there were insufficient funds for the east window, or the fact that it was commemorating a mere churchwarden, but it is likely that what was also taken into account was that the last earl of Howth, then aged 78, was deserving of the prime location given that his family had been the church's benefactors.

Sarah Purser, the co-founder and unofficial manager of An Túr Gloine, is credited with having designed *Faith, Hope and Charity*,[1] which was erected in memory of local businessman, Samuel Smalldridge, who, as the inscription states, 'was five times churchwarden and for 22 years a member of the Select Vestry of this church.' It is a fairly simple window, each of the female allegorical figures clearly identified by their name inscribed in Latin on a scroll. Additionally Faith carries a torch to light the way, Charity dispenses sustenance to a barefooted child, and Hope holds a dry branch from which a flower blooms while resting on an anchor, a symbol of hope which is grounded in faith. *Faith, Hope and Charity* is one of the first windows designed by Purser – who designed only about twenty windows in total – and the studio's order books would suggest that it was mainly painted by A.E. Child, assisted by Catherine O'Brien, and with some painting possibly done by Hugh Barden.

The colour palette of the *Faith, Hope and Charity* is muted, mainly mellow greens and golden browns, the reason being that most of the background glass came from Irish-manufactured rectangular bottles which had been cut down into slabs. When An Túr Gloine opened in January 1903 Miss Purser had already paid for a large consignment of the very best mouth-blown glass in a wide variety of colours from a major English supplier; however An Túr Gloine was eager to gain a competitive edge over their main rivals, Clarke's and Earley's, so after a year or so they tried

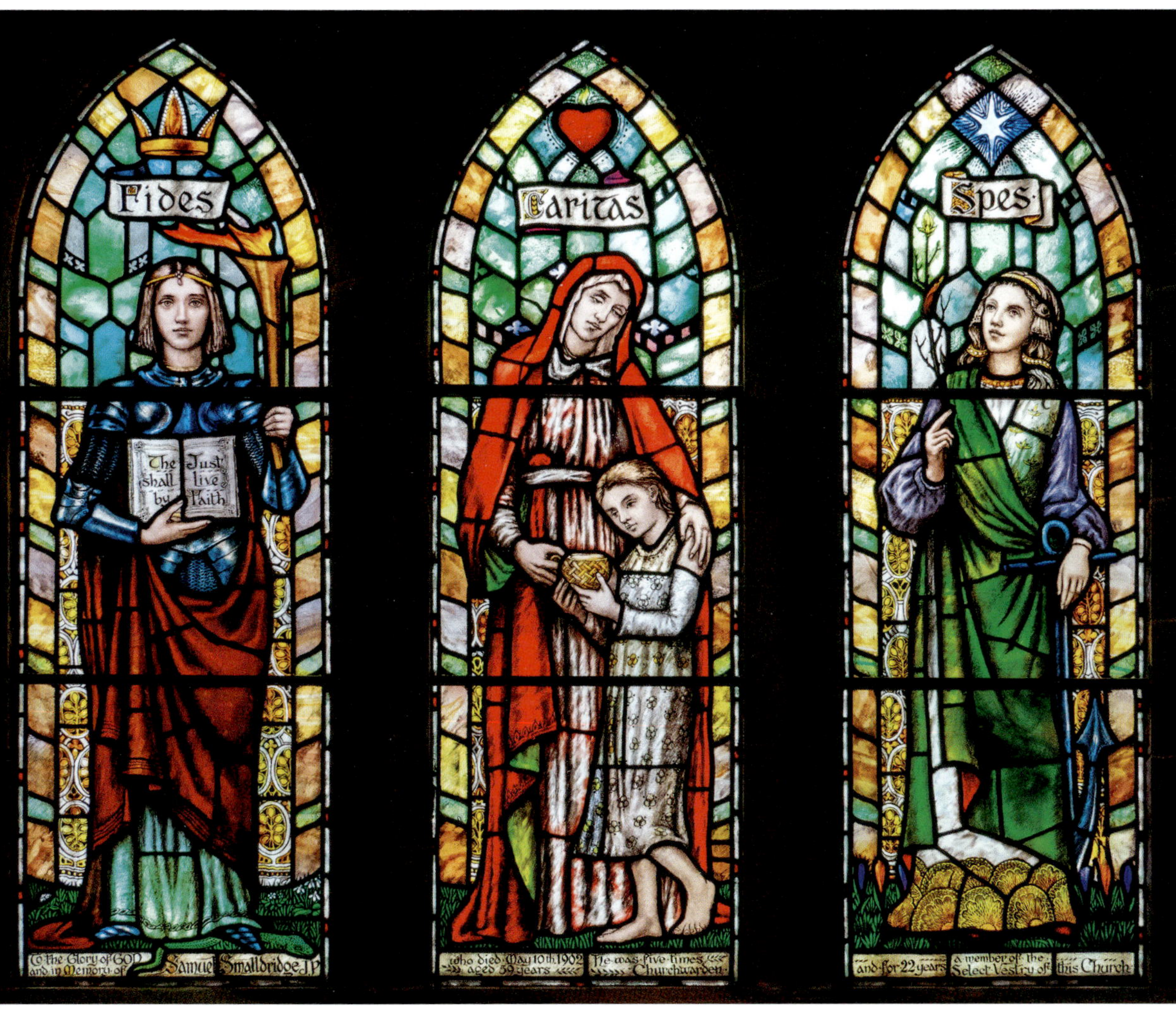

Sarah Purser (painted by A.E. Child, assisted by Catherine O'Brien), *Faith, Hope and Charity* (1905)

to utilize local glass when possible, and pointedly advertised this fact. However in the context of pictorial windows, the few available colours of Irish-manufactured bottle glass was creatively limiting so after trying it in a few windows, *c.*1903–5, they reserved its use solely for decorative leaded lights.

In 1909 Mary Guinness,[2] a wealthy resident of St Nessan's, Howth, placed an order at An Túr Gloine for a small lancet window. Titled *Fortitude*,[3] it was erected in memory

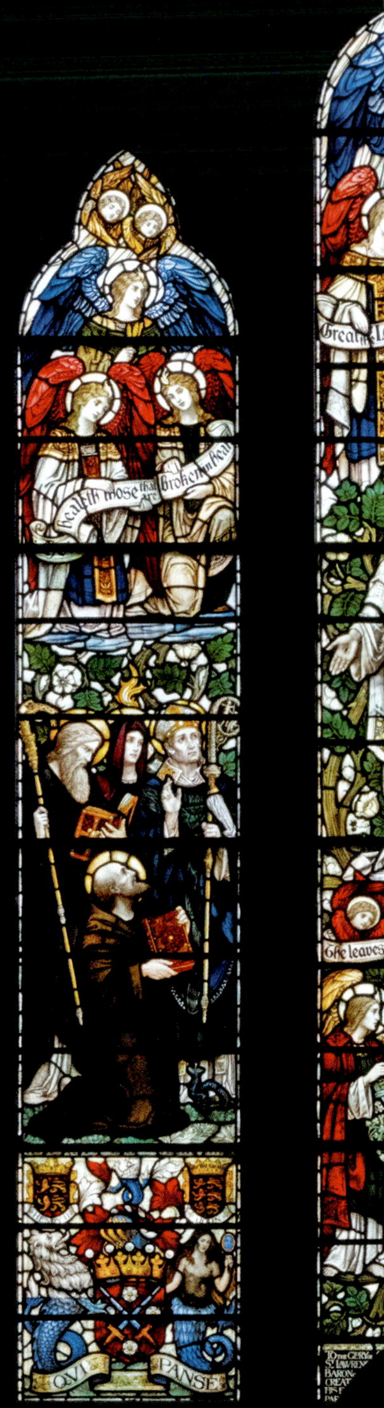
healeth those that are broken in hea
QVI PANSE

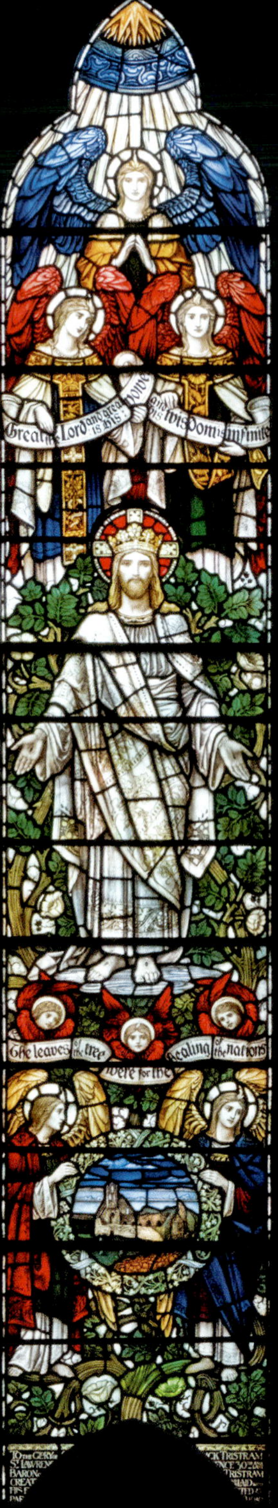
Great is the Lord and great is his power and his wisdom is infinite
The leaves of the tree were for the healing of the nations

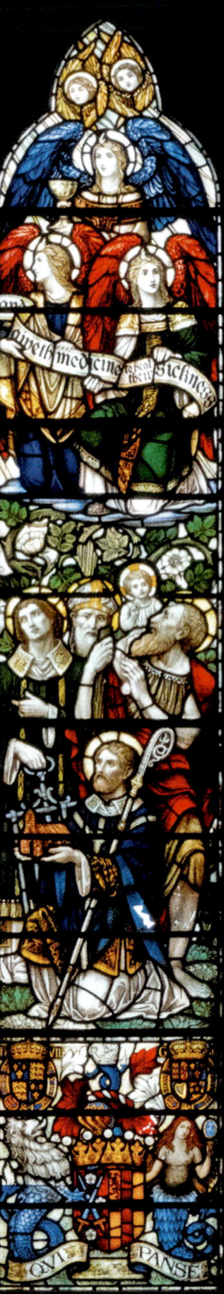
giveth medicine to heal their sickness
QVI PANSE

of fellow Howth residents, Henry MacDougall (d.1893) and Henrietta MacDougall (d.1909) of Drumleck who were her uncle and aunt.[4] Ethel Rhind's lancet depicts a somewhat androgynous full-length female figure staring impassively ahead, wearing a silver helmet and two-toned golden armour across her chest, below which is a flowing garment decorated with pretty little flowers which goes someway to offset her formidable countenance. Both hands, fingers interwoven, rest on the hilt of a long upright sword. The figure appears to have successfully emerged through a narrow opening in a steep rocky outcrop of an inhospitable landscape into a verdant glade which possibly can be interpreted as a visual metaphor for some challenges one or both of the MacDougall siblings overcame with strength of mind or courage. Costing £30, it was dedicated by the archbishop of Dublin on 26 June 1910.

Also dedicated on the same day was the large 3-light east window made in London by the prominent studio of James Powell & Sons. The cartoonist of this elaborate window was John Humphries Hogan,[5] who had trained under Christopher Whall whose personal guidance and his Arts and Crafts philosophy had greatly informed Sarah Purser when she was establishing An Túr Gloine. The prominence of branches, foliage and flowers in Hogan's window may owe something to Whall's enthusiasm for drawing from nature as a source of inspiration but their curvaceous forms also suggest an influence of art nouveau.

Hogan's window was erected in memory of William Ulick Tristram St Lawrence, fourth earl of Howth, and is titled *Christ in Majesty with Saints*, a principal theme being Christ the healer of mankind, illustrating the motto of the Howth family 'Qui panse' (old Norman French for 'which heals') which features in a heraldic form in both lower side lights.[6] Angels and putti also bear scrolls alluding to Christ's healing power. Positioned in the centre, the figure of Christ dominates the window, his hands inviting all to come. Standing on the left are Saints Brigid, Columba and Patrick, and standing on the right are saints associated with the Howth family, Saints Christopher, Lawrence and Nicholas. Two local saints kneel in front of both groupings, St Nessan displays his book, *The Garland of Howth*, and St Fintan holds

(opposite) John Humphries Hogan of James Powell & Sons, *Christ in Majesty with Saints* (1910)

a model of his church. In the lower section of the centre light two angels hold a roundel featuring the ruins of Howth Abbey, a precursor to St Mary's church.

Clearly Hogan did his research when designing this window and a contemporary newspaper article noted that St Patrick's crozier and other details in the window were based on artefacts in the Science and Art Museum (National History Museum).[7] Three years after designing the Howth window John Humphries Hogan was promoted to the position of chief designer at Powell's, and remained with the company throughout his career becoming managing director in 1933 and finally chairman in 1946.

The First World War took a grave toll on the majority of Church of Ireland parishes and many erected a memorial to those from the parish who had perished; in the case of St Mary's, fourteen men died. In late 1919 or early 1920 the rector, Revd Powell, placed an order at An Túr Gloine for a 3-light war memorial window. The artist selected was Ethel Rhind once again, and the subject of the window was *Saints Killian, Michael and George*. The choice of Michael and George, both warrior saints usually depicted overcoming Satan, seems obvious but with St Killian, a Cavan-born saint best known as a missionary bishop who spread Christianity in northern Bavaria, the reason is less apparent. The clue to his inclusion is in the words beneath the three saints: 'Victory' and 'Duty' are under Michael and George respectively, and 'Sacrifice' beneath Killian; this alludes to the fact that St Killian was martyred for his missionary work.[8] Rhind depicted St Michael as youthful, handsome and resolute, blond tresses blowing in the wind, and with wide burnished golden and copper wings, which spread across into the two side lights. Bearded and reflective St Killian holds aloft a Celtic cross, a symbol of his missionary zeal, with both his feet firmly planted on a sword, a symbol of his beheading. St George determinedly lances a scaly dragon, and behind him a castle surrounded by a moat suggests his role as patriotic protector. An Túr Gloine undertook many war memorial commissions in the years after the First World War and the studio was so busy that they took on another full time artist, Hubert McGoldrick, to cope with the demand.

In 1943 a new window was commissioned from the studio. Sarah Purser and Ethel Rhind had by now retired from stained glass but as the patron was the painter Harriet Kirkwood, a cousin of Evie Hone's, it was no surprise that she asked her;

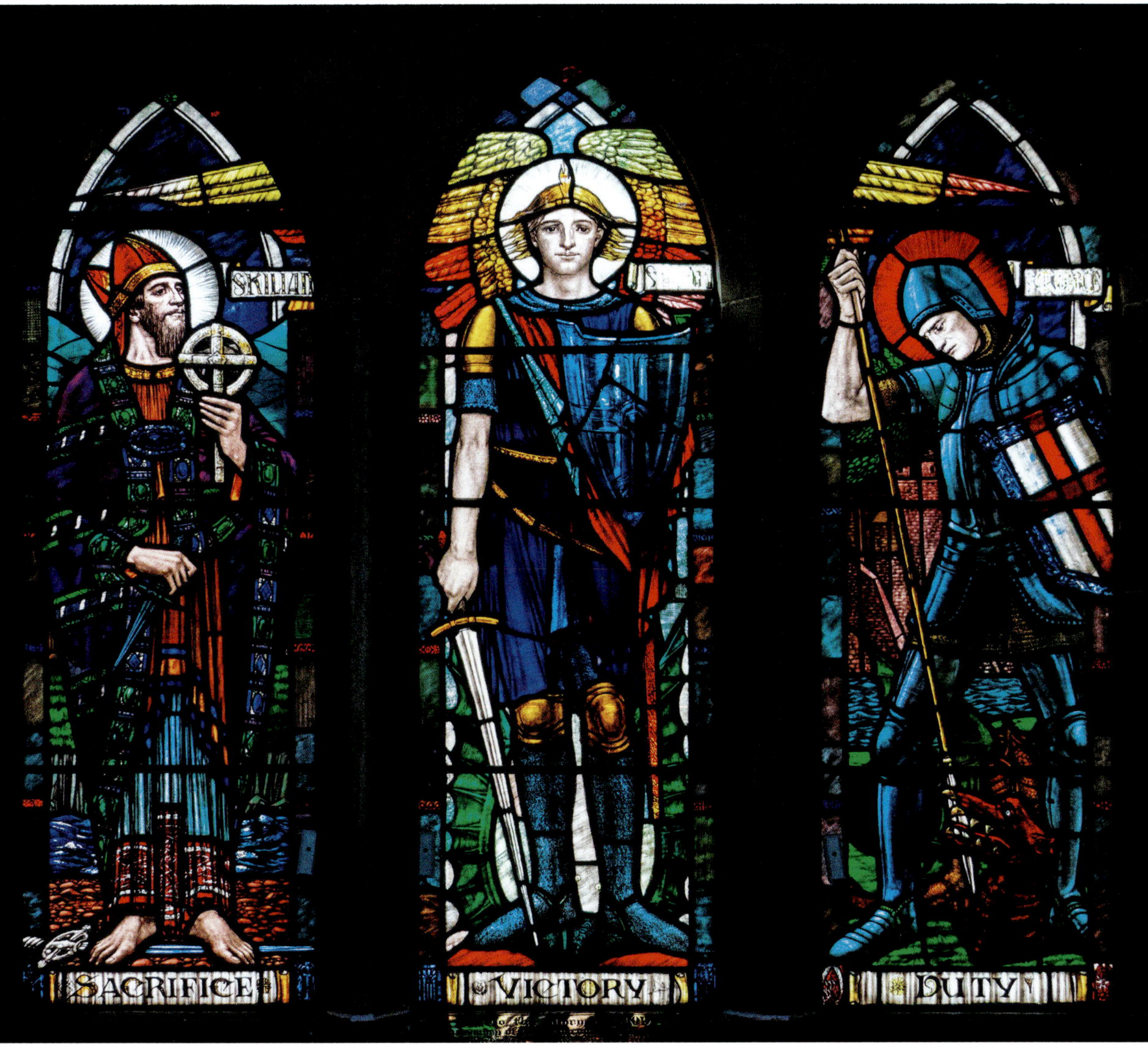

Ethel Rhind, *Saints Killian, Michael and George* (1920)

previously Kirkwood, along with her husband, had commissioned a window from Hone early on in her stained glass career in memory of her father-in-law.[9] This time the window was in memory of Kirkwood's late father, Andrew Jameson, who had been a member of St Mary's select vestry, and was a well-known figure in Irish

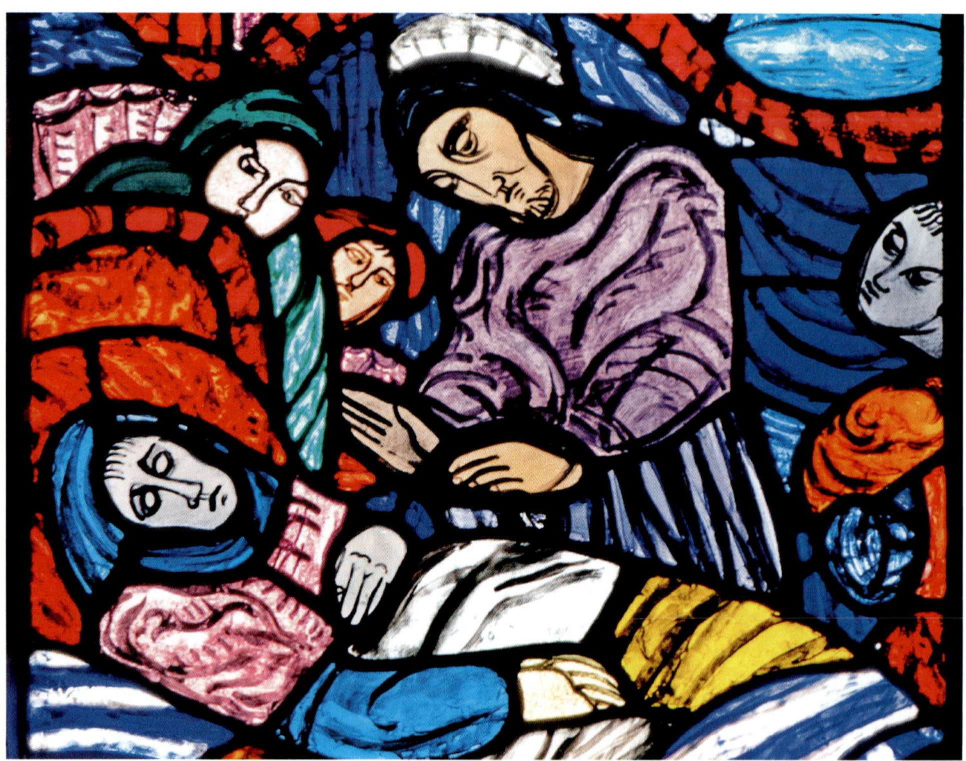

Evie Hone, detail of the healing of Simon Peter's mother-in-law from *Scenes from the Lives of Christ and St Andrew* (1943)

business and politics; he had been chairman of the Jameson whiskey business and the Irish lighthouse authority, and a member of both the Senate of Southern Ireland and subsequently Seanad Éireann.

The principal theme of Evie Hone's window is Christ performing miracles and it is a window which is brimming with exuberant, joyous colour. Costing £84, it is not a large window with each light less than 5ft high, however more than sixteen individuals as well as a large crowd and distant fishermen are included. The left light focuses specifically on miracles related to Christ's healing ministry and so links back to the main theme of Powell & Sons' large east window. In the left light Hone included three scenes (top to bottom) – *Restoring Sight to Two Blind Men; Jesus Heals the Ear of a Servant*; and *The Healing of Simon Peter's Mother-in-law*.[10] The right light depicts just two scenes – *The Calling of Saints Peter and Andrew*; and *The Miraculous Draught of Fishes*. Both having an obvious fishing theme and Howth being a working port ties them together nicely. In the top scene, *The Calling of Saints Peter and Andrew*, a lighthouse features, possibly a visual allusion to the Bailey Lighthouse on Howth Head, and of course the inclusion of St Andrew references Andrew Jameson. Hone has utilized a strong palette, with deep blue and primary red dominating, supported by green and golden yellow, and with smaller amounts of pink, brown and other colours. The window is believed to have been made from scraps of glass due to the war-time shortages.[11] Collectively the two lights present a visually busy, vibrant melange of images, suggestive of a driven Christ performing one miracle after another, after another.

By the mid-1940s all the artists at An Túr Gloine had either died or retired, with the exception of Catherine O'Brien who soldiered on into her eighties. In 1960 a new order came to the studio placed by the rector, Canon Frank Blennerhasset, for a 2-light window commemorating his predecessor, Canon J.J.L. Armstrong, who had been rector 1935–60. The subject combined two baptismal narratives, one a standard, *The Baptism of Christ by John the Baptist*, and the other one, very rarely depicted, *The Baptism of the Ethiopian Eunuch by Philip*, which is in fact the only window of this theme in a Church of Ireland church, or perhaps in a church of any denomination in Ireland.[12] It is also one of the rare representations of a person of colour in stained glass in Ireland with the exception of Balthasar, one of the Magi.

It is a particularly brightly coloured window, distinctive for the azure blue used for both sky and water. Although there is a separate narrative in each of the lights, O'Brien has treated the water (the River Jordan in the case of Jesus, and that which the Ethiopian is about to enter, thought to be the Dhirweh fountain near Halhul, Palestine) as a single entity, perhaps to convey that the eunuch was inspired by Christ's example, and indeed he, Philip, and the small group accompanying them are all pointedly focused in the direction of St John as he baptizes Christ. The quote inscribed at the base of the window, 'How beautiful are the feet of them that preach the gospel of peace …' (Romans 10:15), refers to whomever is the bearer of Christ's message and hence responsible for its dissemination which would have a particular resonance for a parish rector. The window was paid for by the congregation and was dedicated by Archbishop Simms in December 1960. At the time the baptismal font was positioned adjacent to the window but has since been relocated to the front of the church.

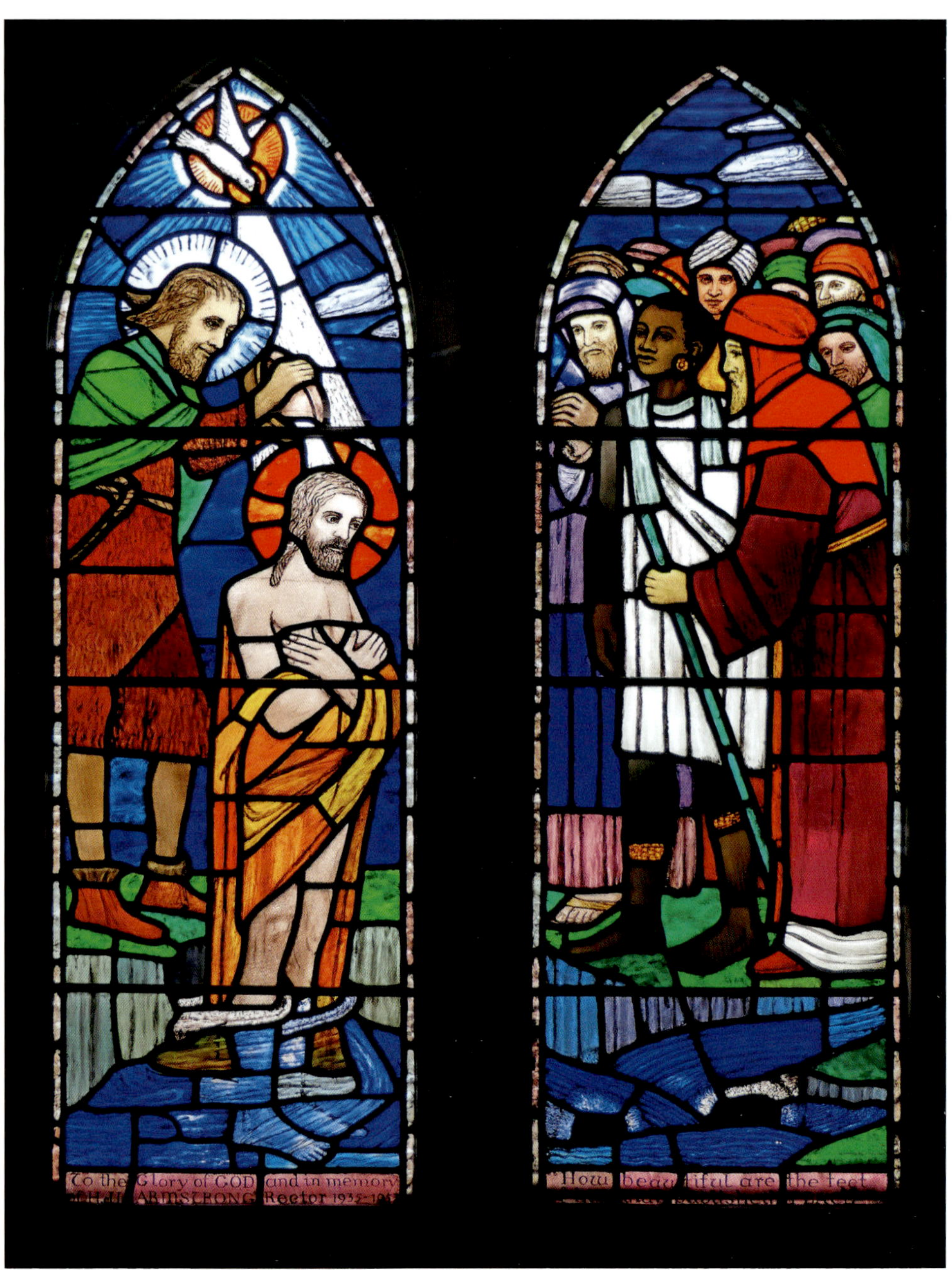

Catherine O'Brien, *The Baptism of Christ by John the Baptist and the Baptism of the Ethiopian Eunuch by Philip* (1960)

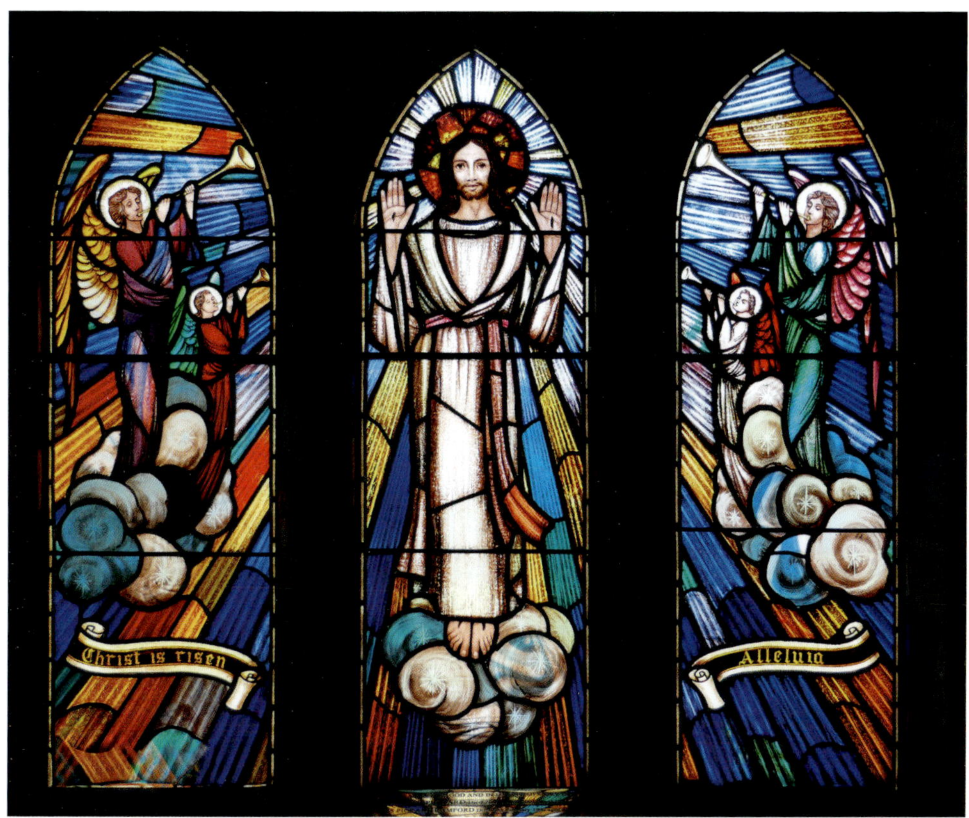

Alan Tomlin, *The Risen Christ with Angels* (2004)

Two more windows were installed subsequently. The first, a 3-light, depicts the Blessed Virgin Mary, and was made in 1973 by father and son, Stanley and Alan Tomlin of Irish Stained Glass. The realistic treatment of Mary and the dove is in dramatic contrast to the abstract background comprising of shades of blue. The composition of the window is almost identical to another one made by Alan Tomlin around the same time for Holy Trinity church, Garvary, Co. Fermanagh, though in that instance tones of turquoise predominate. It was erected in memory of Hugh Usher and his son Howard. In 2004 Alan Tomlin created a 3-light window, *The Risen Christ with Angels*, in memory of Ron Pickard and Tess Bamford Pickard. Tomlin depicted Christ displaying the stigmata on his hands while his whole body exudes multicoloured rays of light and trumpeting angels heralding his resurrection.

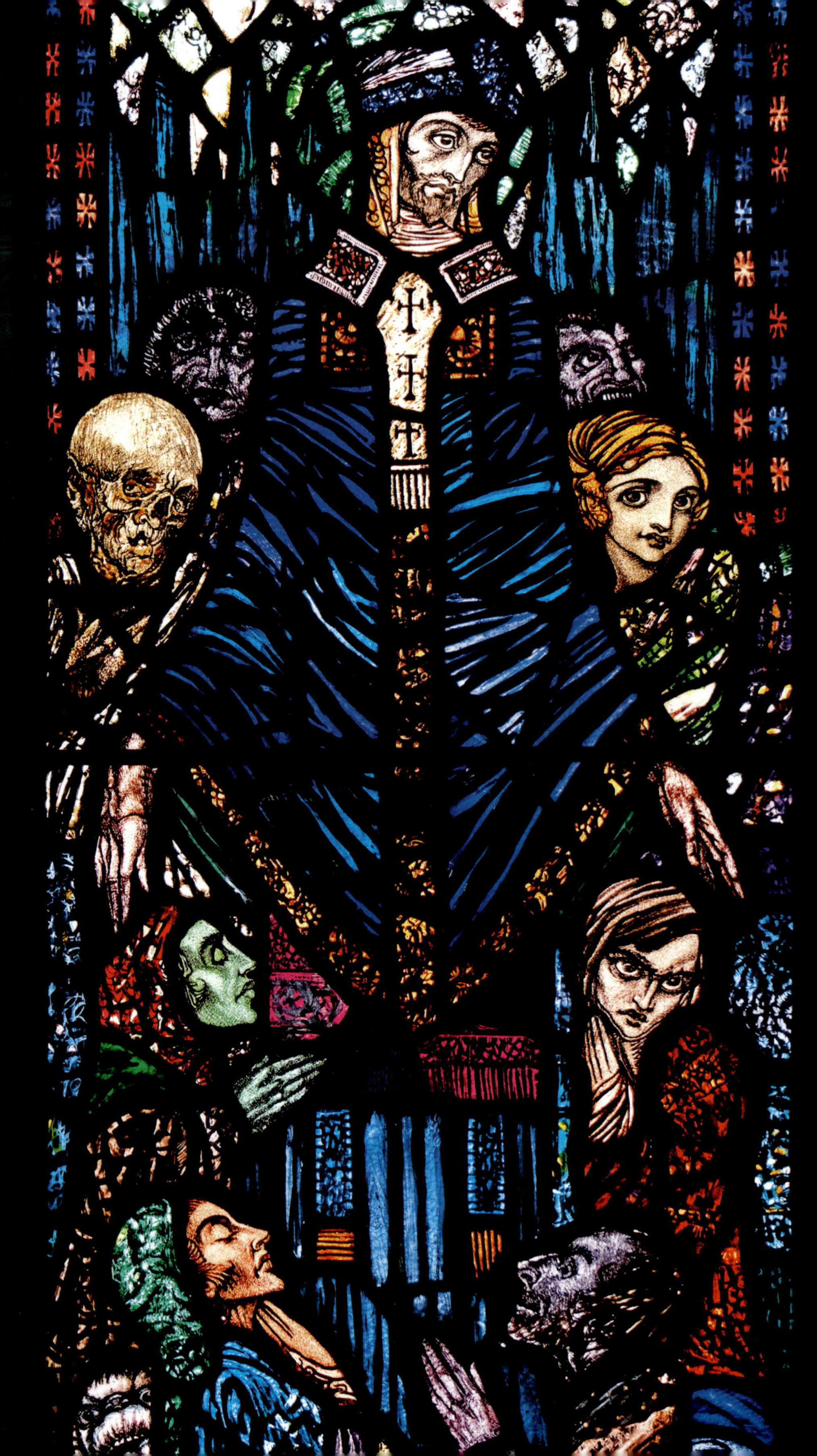

LUSK

St MacCullin's church (RC)

Chapel Road, K45 TY26

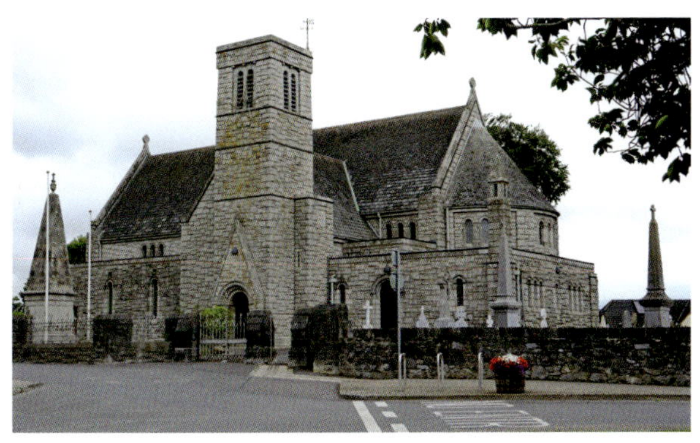

Lusk's St MacCullin's Catholic church is a charming Hiberno-Romanesque structure built of rock-faced granite and surrounded by a graveyard.[1] The foundation stone was laid in 1922 and it was designed by John Joseph Robinson, a favourite architect with the Catholic hierarchy, who in this instance drew on several historic references – the south doorway recalls those at Killeshin and Roscrea; the bell-tower, the steeply pitched gables and the plaster barrel vault in the nave were inspired by Cormac's Chapel; and windows are copies of those in the round towers of Cashel and Monasterboice, among others.[2] In 1929 Robinson became a founding member of the [Irish] Academy of Christian Art, which interpreted its mission to further 'Christian and catholic' artistic concepts as a defence of historic revival styles against the creeping infection of modernism.[3]

(opposite) Harry Clarke, detail of *St MacCullin* (1924)

Robinson paid great attention to detail and craftsmanship when designing St MacCullin's so it is no surprise that windows of the highest order were sought for the church when it was under construction. Two orders were placed with Harry Clarke, initially a single light depicting St MacCullin was commissioned in December 1923, and subsequently a series of decorative sanctuary windows was ordered in June 1924.

The *St MacCullin* window presents a surprise if one enters, as most do, via the south side door at the base of the bell-tower facing the road. It is only when one is within the nave and turns 180 degrees that the exceedingly slim and tall round-headed window becomes properly visible. Its extreme proportions are unlike any other window Harry Clarke tackled previously or subsequently. Visually the window is divided into three figurative sections buffered by areas of luminous diamond-patterned quarries which provide a pleasing counterpoint to the rich colours deployed in the figurative areas.

The main scene depicts a full-length depiction of St MacCullin in his role as patron and first bishop of Lusk, holding aloft a little model of Robinson's church and drawn from such an angle that Clarke's sanctuary windows could be included. In his other hand he holds a slender staff or crozier. The saint, with Clarke's characteristic over-sized eyes, stares impassively ahead. His dainty feet stand on a writhing double-headed creature, with scrawny necks and vulture-like malevolent appearance which represents the monster from whom St MacCullin is said to have delivered his people.

Above the saint, floating in the sea of quarries, is a golden bell, a symbol of the call for the faithful to worship, whose shape and decoration recalls the well-known shrine of St Patrick's bell in the National Museum. Above the quarries there is a mass of spaghetti-like Celtic interlacing; this is not characteristic of Clarke, who, although associated with the Celtic revival movement and known for his depiction of early Irish saints, such as his celebrated series in Cork's Honan chapel that essentially launched his career, rarely included significant passages of Celtic decoration unlike, for instance, some of his rivals at An Túr Gloine.

At the very top section of the slender window Clarke has included five elegant angels, one holding a navigation compass divider, another an unfurled map, and

Harry Clarke,
St MacCullin
(1924)

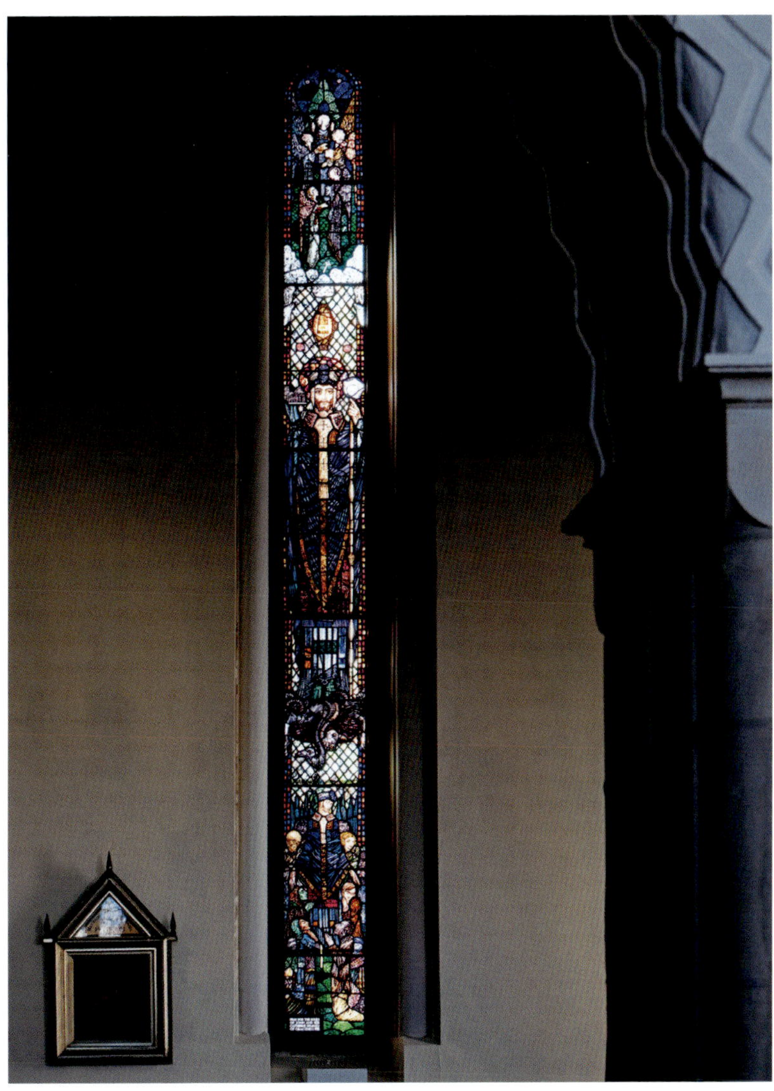

engaged in what Clarke's friend Thomas Bodkin identified as 'blessing the ancient graveyard site on which the church was to be built'.[4] While the angels hover in the deep blue sky attending to their task, below in the lush grass one can see a few little crosses which mark burial sites.

In the bottom panel, again separated by diamond-patterned quarries, St MacCullin features again, this time no longer impassive and detached, but looking somewhat lost and overwhelmed, surrounded by a closely-packed, disparate group of lepers, ghoulish figures, the pious, the destitute and the deformed, and two pretty young girls have been added into the mix. Unmistakably among the group is a self-portrait of Harry Clarke appearing intense and haunted. The majority, hands pressed together in prayer, are imploring the saint to heal them from whatever their afflictions may be. One can only guess what Clarke's burden was but he was certainly under intense pressure from work, often plagued by health issues, had three very young children at home, was trying to establish his career in London, and about to begin a new book illustration project, that of *Faust*.

The window's inscription states that it was erected in memory of John and Catherine Dempsey; they were a local farming couple living in the townland of Gracedieu and who had both died of TB, he in 1916 and she three years later. In her will Mrs Dempsey left a generous bequest of £237 for a stained glass window.[5]

Although leading Clarke expert Nicola Gordon Bowe categorized *St MacCullin* as in the 'A' category, that is windows designed by Clarke 'in which he was actively involved in their execution, the rest being executed under his supervision in his studio', she did have reservations as to whether he actually had any hand in painting the window as it was done during his absence in London.[6]

As an aside, it is worth noting that six years after the window was completed, in the summer of 1930, Evie Hone sought to buy the cartoon when she saw it hanging in Clarke's studios; interestingly this was when she was immersed in cubism and abstraction, and it would still be a few years before she embarked on her own career as a stained glass artist.[7]

Six months after the order for *St MacCullin* the studio received a second order for Lusk church; a series of nine small decorative windows for the sanctuary. These windows, arranged in groups of three, are positioned at clerestory level in the semi-circular apse. They mainly comprised Floral Ornament (or 'F.O.' as it was shorthanded in the studio) made from cullets, or discarded offcuts retained for their rich colours, and onto which simple floral designs were painted, something that junior staff would be well capable of executing under instruction. When the nine windows were removed for conservation by Evan Connon in 2024 they revealed an intriguing 100-year-old secret; most of the glass used for the F.O. were not cullets

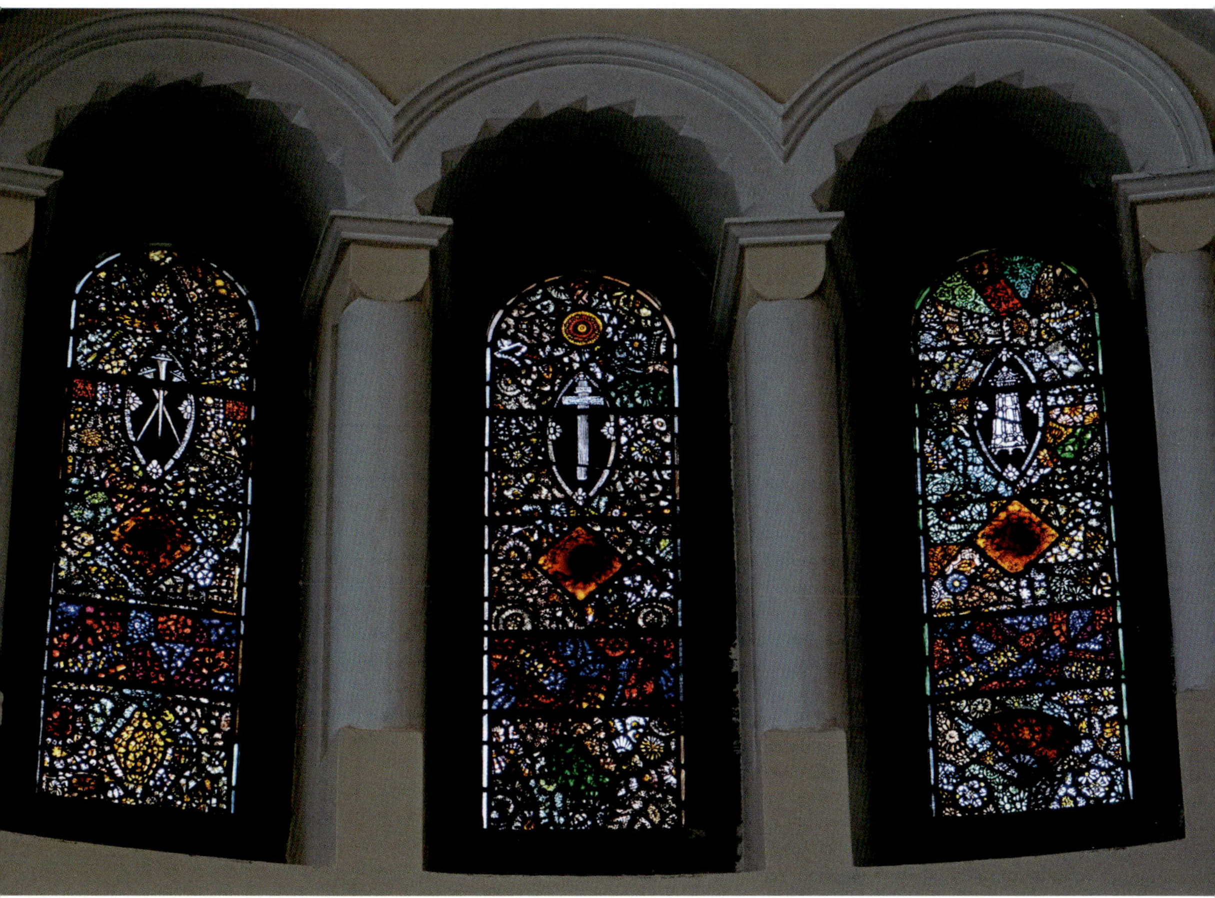

Harry Clarke, *Arma Christi ('weapons of Christ')* sanctuary windows (1924)

of new glass as presumed but instead a mixture of recycled glass from different sources, with some featuring pieces of heads, as well as at least fifteen sections of an inscription from a window made in 1862 by Messrs J. and D. Casey of Dublin for St Mary's church, Haddington Road, Dublin, which had been part of a memorial for a young curate.[8] Clarke and/or his assistants painted the F.O. on the reverse side of the old glass before the window was leaded.[9]

Each of the nine windows also incorporated an illustration of one of the instruments associated with Christ's Passion, or *Arma Christi* ('weapons of Christ'). From left to right, the first set of three depicts three nails, the cross, and lantern;[10]

the second set depicts pliers and dice, ladder and reed with sponge, and the pillar of flagellation; the third set depicts a hammer, a lance and whip, and the crown of thorns. Each image is set into a vesica shape, surrounded by a sea of multi-coloured cullets and as part of his design Clarke introduced a band of red and blue cullets that provided structure to the composition, choosing colours that recall the windows of the great medieval cathedrals. The other element Clarke introduced into each window was a large amber Norman quarry slab, set on the diagonal, and thicker at its centre that imbued it with a mysterious glowing quality.[11] Later in the same year Clarke created another series of *Arma Christi* that were inspired by the Lusk set, this time for the mortuary chapel in St Peter's church, Phibsborough; in fact the priest there got sight of the Lusk windows when visiting Clarke's studio and decided he must have similar ones (see pp 101–3).

These nine *Arma Christi* sanctuary windows were fixed in place in October 1924, while his *St MacCullin* window, though ordered earlier, was a more complex window to execute and was installed a month later.

In the first half of the 1940s more orders were placed at Clarke's, first in 1941 for a lancet for the mortuary chapel. Harry Clarke died a decade earlier and this time the job went to his nephew Terry, son of his late brother Walter. Of the eight children that Harry and Walter had between them Terry, then aged twenty-four, was the only one to pursue a long-term career as a stained glass artist.[12] The principal subject was to be the Risen Christ emerging from the tomb, something that the artists in Clarke's studio created several variants of during this period (see p. 341). At the base of the window Terry Clarke included a predella panel depicting the arrival of Peter and John (with misaligned head) at Christ's tomb after Mary Magdalene had informed them that Christ's body was gone.[13] The window was paid for from a bequest made by the late Miss Jane Dodd, a nonagenarian, originally from the townland of Thomondtown, south of Lusk, who had died a few years earlier in Dublin.

In 1943 and 1944 orders were placed at Clarke's to fill the three clerestory windows located either side of the apse, identical in size to Clarke's *Arma Christi* series. The first set of three windows, which has been designed as a 3-light window, is attributed to William Dowling who had been appointed manager in 1944 as well as being the studio's main artist.[14] The subjects are *The Virgin Mary, Christ Child with the Holy*

Spirit, and St Joseph. The richness of the colours and background floral decoration harmonize with Clarke's apse windows. The donor was Jane Dodd again so clearly her bequest had been sufficiently generous to fund a second window.

The following year Terry Clarke designed *St Brigid, St Patrick and St Colmcille*, positioned directly opposite. The donor was a local cattle dealer, Thomas Bell of Horestown House, Lusk, and it was erected in memory of his late wife and son, Patrick J. Bell, the victim of an accidental shooting during the War of Independence.[15] Terry Clarke has depicted St Brigid holding a model of a church; usually this is one with a round tower to recall St Brigid's cathedral, Co. Kildare, but in this instance it is of Lusk church, possibly an affectionate reference to his uncle Harry who had done the same in his *St MacCullin* window. St Patrick is depicted wearing very long, snugly fitting gloves which gives the disconcerting impression that his hands have been coloured bright green; in fact in medieval and renaissance paintings saints are often shown wearing gloves when performing sacred rites or in the presence of the divine, and in this instance St Patrick is holding aloft a

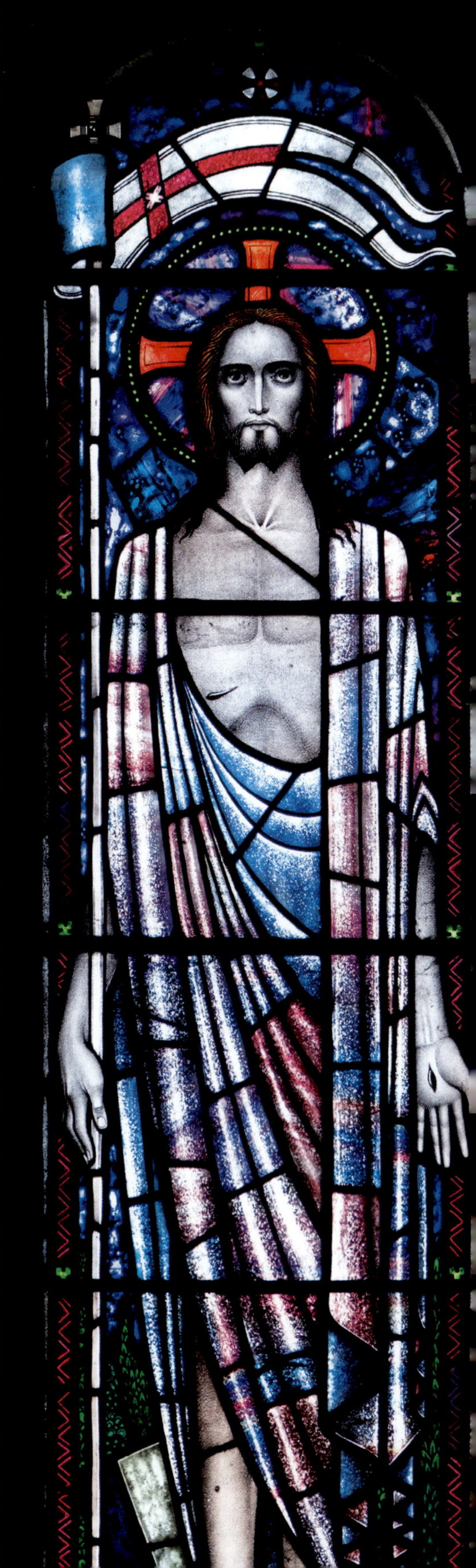

Terry Clarke, detail of *The Risen Christ* (1941)

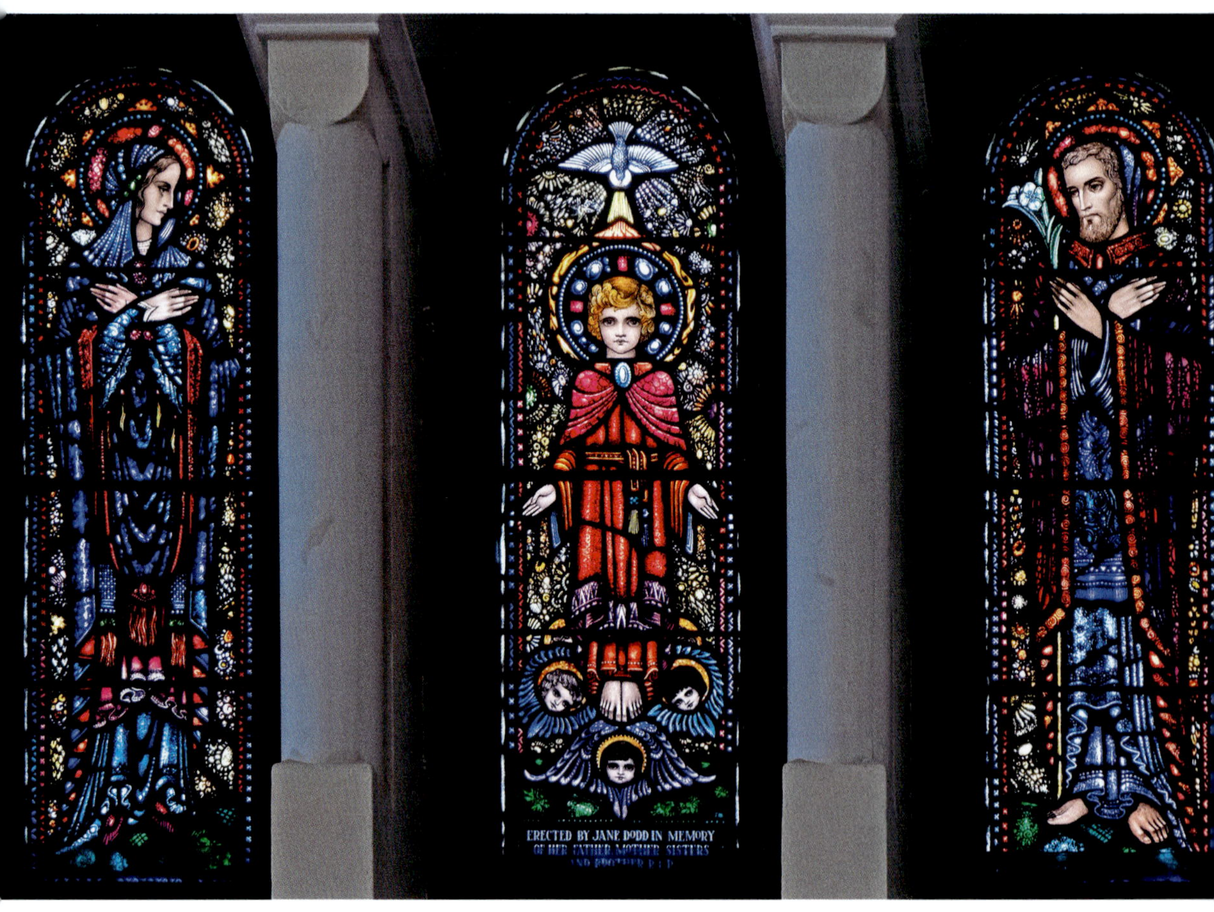

William Dowling (attributed), *Virgin Mary, Christ Child with Holy Spirit above, and St Joseph* (1943)

shamrock symbolizing the Holy Trinity. As with Dowling's companion window, Clarke has included plenty of floral decoration in the background.

In 1957 or 1958, the architectural firm of Robinson, Keefe & Devane ordered a *Baptism of Christ* for the small baptistry; this was the company that J.J Robinson had co-founded decades earlier and since 1945 had been reconstituted with the addition of a new partner, Andrew Devane. Rather than go to Clarke's (which might have seemed the obvious choice), a decision was made to commission the lancet – one of two small lancets in the church, all the rest are round-headed windows – from a then little-known artist, Patrick Pollen, who had arrived in Dublin from London a few years earlier, fired with enthusiasm for Evie Hone, having been inspired by her monumental window at Eton College. Pollen rented space in An Túr Gloine, Upper Pembroke Street, as by then it was a larger facility than Catherine O'Brien, the last surviving of the original artists, required. Together they used the same kiln and the services of the same glazier, the highly experienced Peter Connolly who had worked there since 1916.

Pollen's *Baptism of Christ* shows the influence of his mentor, Hone, in its freshness, directness and vitality. The narrow lancet didn't permit much scope in terms of composition but Pollen has effectively integrated the hand of God the Father, the Holy Spirit in the form of the dove, as well as the disembodied hand of John the Baptist pouring water on Christ who is immersed up to his waist in the choppy waters of the River Jordan.

Additionally, worth viewing in the locality is a series of nine beautiful windows made in 1990–3 by George W. Walsh for the new church of St Maur, Rush.

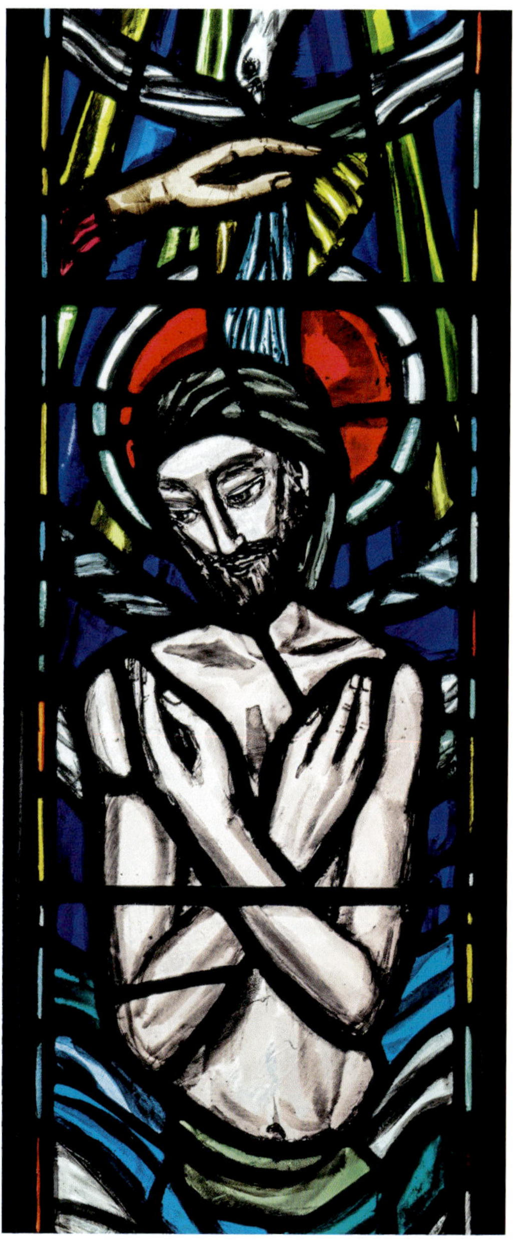

Patrick Pollen, detail of *The Baptism of Christ* (1957–8)

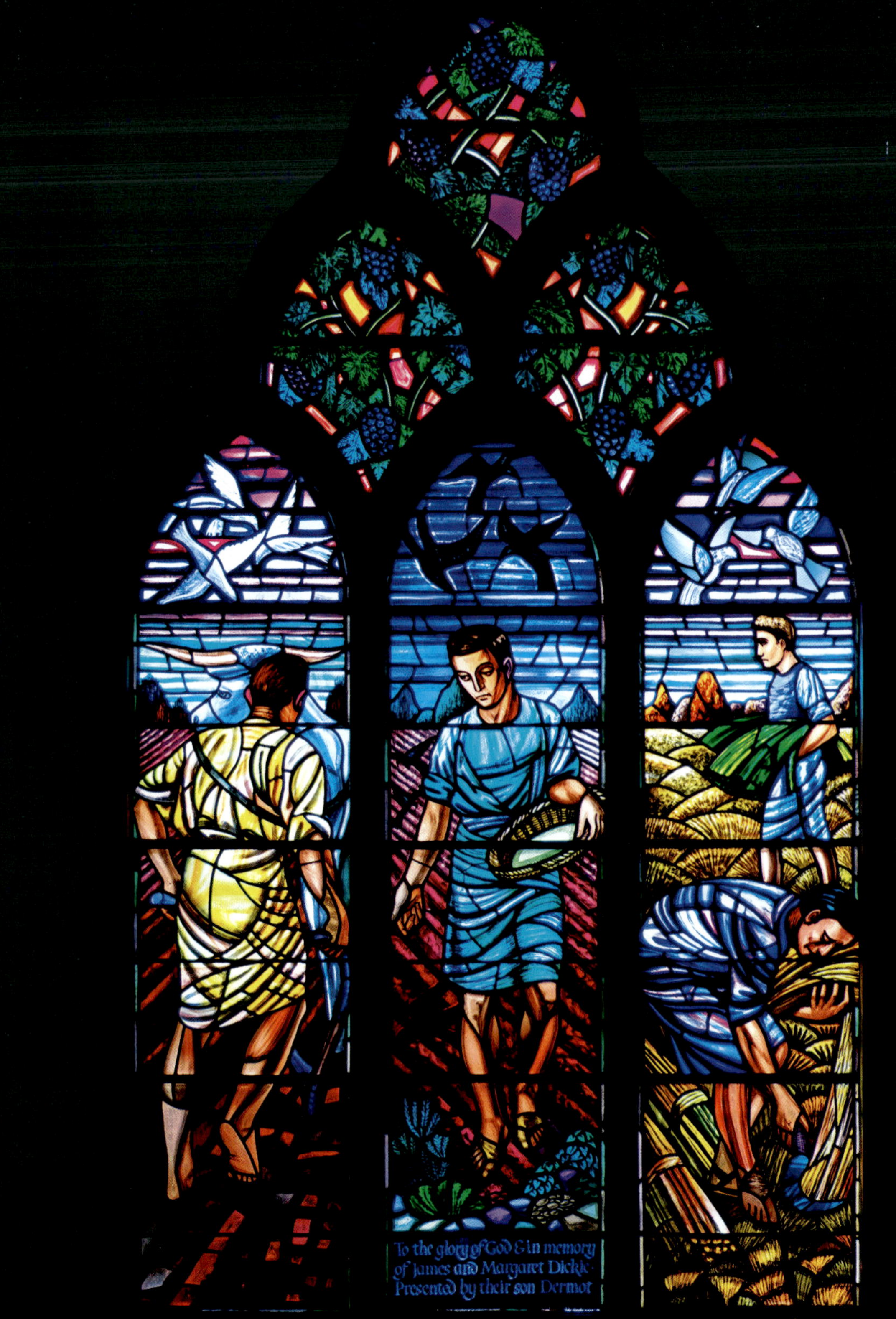
To the glory of God & in memory
of James and Margaret Dickie ·
Presented by their son Dermot

MALAHIDE

Interesting and varied stained glass can be found in three of Malahide's churches, all serving different denominations, and all located within close proximity, so rather than exclude any, the entry for Malahide includes all three.

St Andrew's church (C of I)

Church Road, K36 HE33

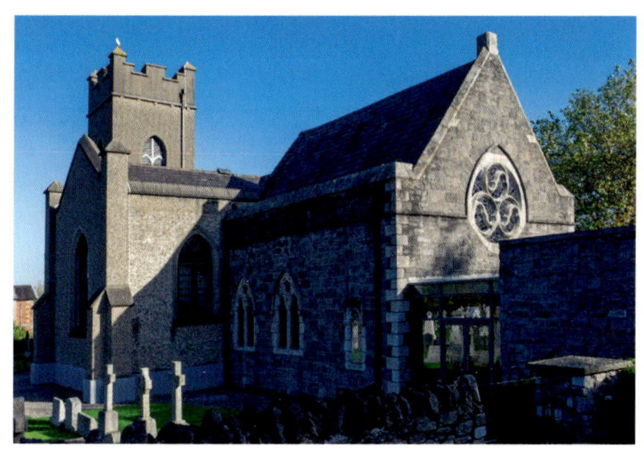

St Andrew's church on Church Road was designed in the Gothic revival style based on a cruciform plan. The exterior features an ashlar cut-limestone nave, which contrasts with the pebble-dashed transepts and crenelated tower. The church was expanded in 2004 with the addition of St Marnock's chapel, as well as providing a new entrance and porch to the building. St Andrew's church is nicely situated in its surrounding graveyard that holds the tombs of several Lords Talbot de Malahide, as well as the graves of the distinguished architect Frederick George Hicks and Flora Mitchell, the artist who recorded much of Dublin's decaying architecture in the 1950s and 60s.

(opposite) Johnny Murphy, *Sowing and Reaping* (1956), Malahide Presbyterian church

After several windows had been commissioned from prominent English firms (Heaton, Butler & Bayne, and Shrigley & Hunt), local civil servant James Franks ordered a porch window from An Túr Gloine in 1927 depicting St Andrew, an appropriate choice of subject as the church is dedicated to him. Ethel Rhind's depiction of the saint emphasizes the fact that he was a fisherman, with the quote 'Follow me and I will make you fishers of men' encircling his ruby halo. The rugged saint is shown with both a handful and a net full of fish, and above in the apex of the window, there is a wicker basket containing yet more fish. With the inclusion of so many fish and with his bare feet firmly planted on the grassy edge of a body of water, Rhind's depiction would seem calculated to reference Malahide's maritime location. This relatively small window cost £48, and following church alterations it is now artificially lit.[1]

In 1950 Lady Joyce Talbot de Malahide commissioned a 2-light window at a cost of £205 from Catherine O'Brien of An Túr Gloine in memory of her husband, James Boswell, 6th Baron, who had died two years earlier. The subject chosen was a popular theme in Church of Ireland churches and one which O'Brien treated eight times, *Christ Blessing Children*; in this particular version there are many children, a total of ten, all making their way, some eagerly with arms outstretched, towards a very paternally depicted Christ, which could be viewed as somewhat poignant considering the Talbots themselves had no children, and consequently left no direct heir to the baronetcy. At this point in her artistic career, O'Brien usually opted for a more folk-art approach to designing her windows, with brighter colours, flatter planes, and less detail. Sometimes they can appear a bit rudimentary though in this instance the window exudes a certain charm. The same year as Lady Talbot commissioned the memorial window she departed Malahide for a house in Killiney named *Marino* which has strong associations with Harry Clarke, including works by him.[2]

In 2006 (which of course is technically outside the remit of this book) St Andrew's commissioned several stained glass windows from George W. Walsh; particularly striking is the wheel window in the gallery which features curvaceous masonry into which Walsh has skilfully introduced several spirited scenes of maritime imagery.

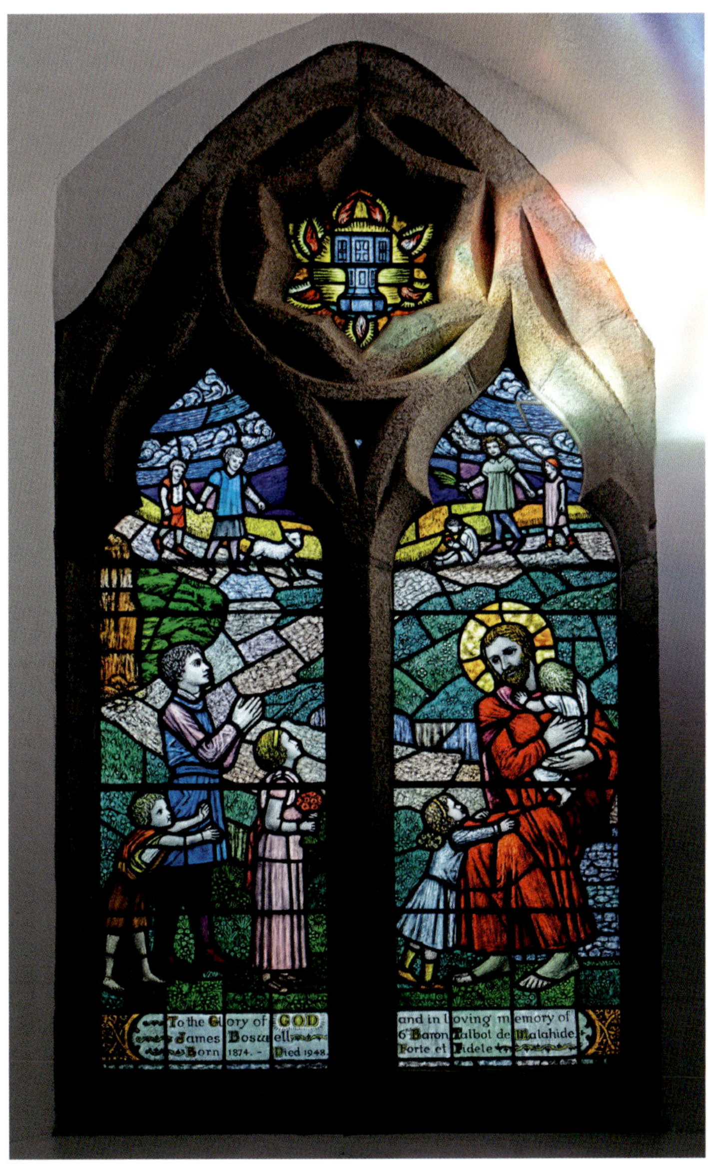

Catherine O'Brien, *Christ Blessing Children* (1950), St Andrew's church

The overall theme is the sea as a symbol of healing and renewal, and included are a lighthouse representing guidance, the Creator's hands, along with images of the Eucharist and the Holy Spirit. Continuing the maritime theme, Walsh designed a lancet window to flank the new entrance door that would act as a companion

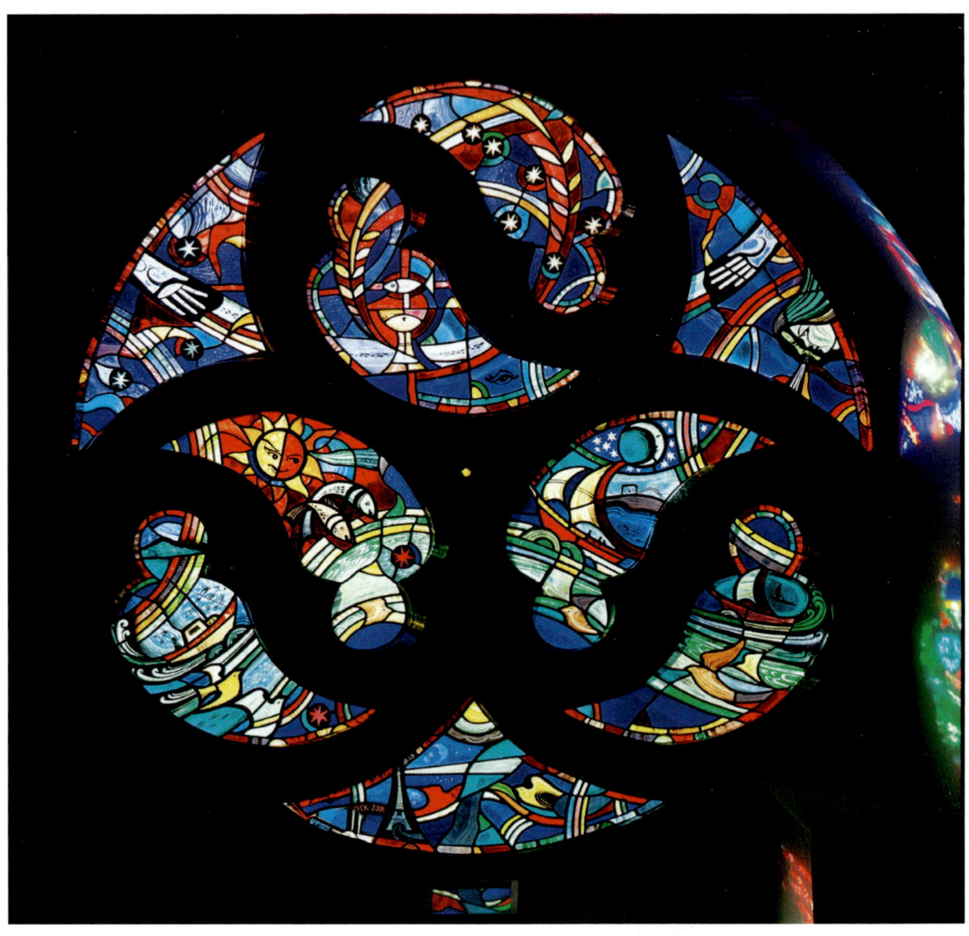

George W. Walsh, *The Sea as a Symbol of Healing and Renewal, the Creator's Hands, Eucharist, Holy Spirit, Lighthouse as Symbol of Guidance* (2006), St Andrew's church

window to Rhind's *St Andrew*; its title is *Fishers of Men* and is a vibrant and dynamic depiction of Christ summoning the apostles, all who are intently focused on hauling in their nets heavy with fish, to follow him. Adjoining the new entrance lobby is the small chapel of St Marnock, which has a series of five linear windows, also by Walsh, at ceiling level. These feature over-arching themes such as the creation and the arrival of Christianity to Ireland, and celebrate individuals associated with Malahide including St Oliver Plunkett and St Marnock, as well as lively depictions of local secular festivals.

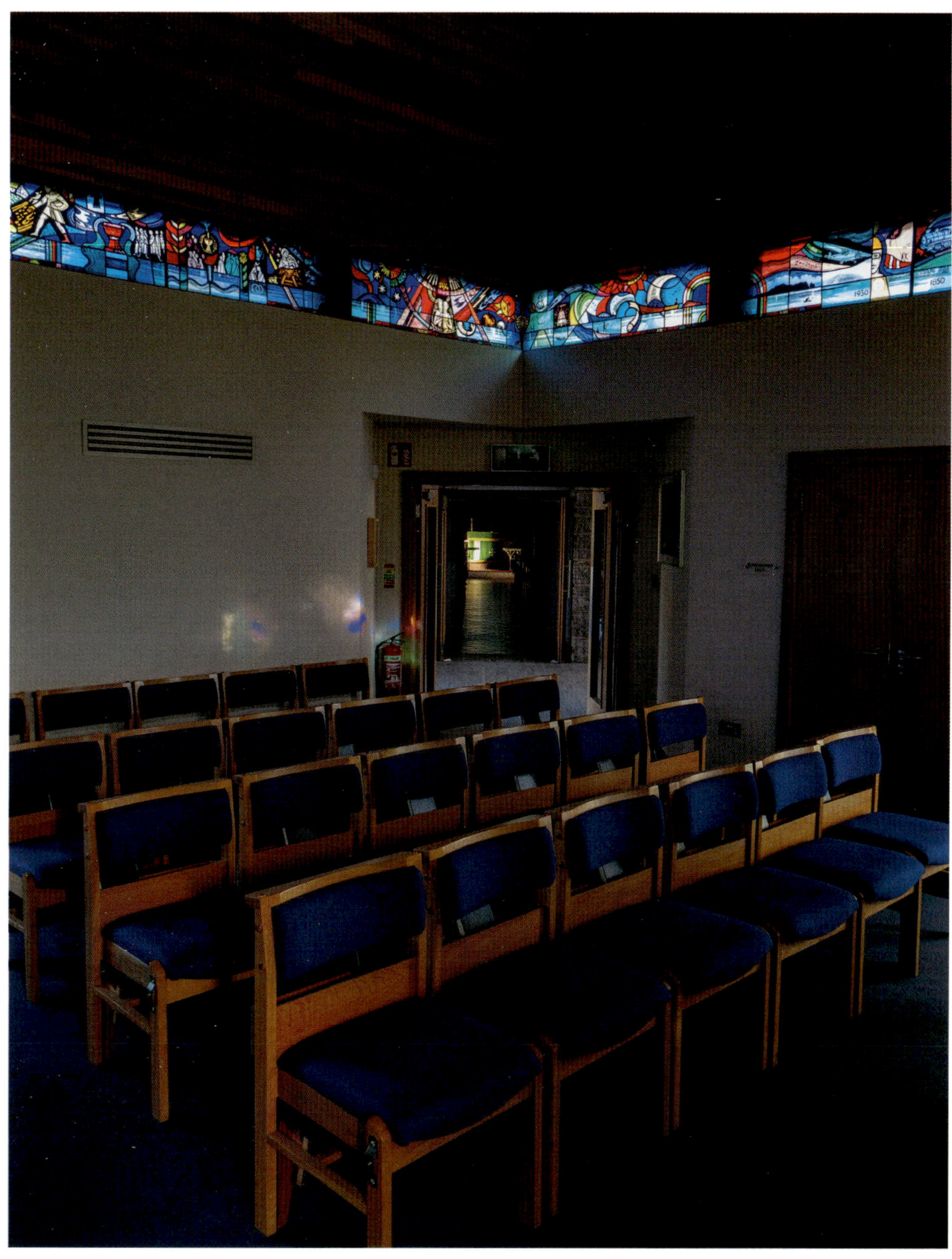

George W. Walsh, *The Creation, History, Events and Individuals Relating to Malahide including St Oliver Plunkett, St Marnock, and Local Festivals* (2006), St Marnock's chapel adjoining St Andrew's church

Presbyterian church

Dublin Road, K36 PE80

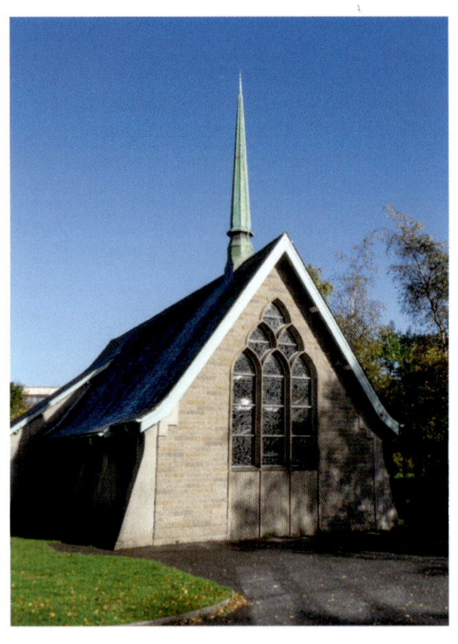

Malahide's Presbyterian church, Dublin Road, was designed by architect William (Bill) Baird, a member of the congregation, and it was the first Presbyterian church to be built in the Republic in the twentieth century. It is the only church Baird designed; he is best remembered as a restorer of Georgian mansions such as Russborough House. Malahide church was dedicated in November 1956 and cost £9,400 to construct.

The church's stand-out feature is the dominating east window, the only stained glass and the church's only artistic feature. *Sowing and Reaping* was designed by Johnny Murphy the year the church was built, ahead of when he and Des Devitt would formally establish Murphy-Devitt Studios. It was his first window for a Dublin church, and possibly his first window for anywhere in Ireland.[3] It is not known why Baird would have chosen an unknown stained glass artist for this job, though Baird's wife had attended the National College of Art and so he may have met Murphy through mutual artistic friends.

The donor of the window was Dermot Dickie whose family lived in the distinctive adjacent property, *Casino*, a commodious though mainly single-storey house (*c.*1750) which is notable for its thatched roof.[4] His father James was the driving force in Malahide's small Presbyterian community and early on church services were held in *Casino*, and *Sowing and Reaping* was erected in his and his wife's memory.

Murphy's 3-light window, which features unusual shaped tracery, depicts male figures toiling in the fields; in fact the model for all four men was the same individual, Micky Watson, who assisted the glaziers at Clarke's, and who would in a few years depart Clarke's for the nascent Murphy-Devitt Studios where he remained for many decades.[5]

The theme of sowing and reaping occurs in several instances in the Bible but the best known is the Parable of the Sower in St Mark's gospel in which Jesus tells of a farmer who sows seed indiscriminately; some seed falls on the wayside with no soil, some on rocky ground with little soil, etc. but when it falls on good soil, it grows and yields many times over. The seed represents the Gospel and the sower represents anyone who proclaims it, and the various soils represent people's responses to it. However for the Dickie family the choice of theme had a particular resonance – *Casino*'s lovely thatched roof was supplied with rye straw specially grown on the Dickie farm at the top of the Broadmeadow estuary and in the right-hand light Murphy depicted Watson collecting recently harvested bundles of golden straw.

Although the three main figures who are engaged in the activities of ploughing, sowing and reaping do so in different terrains, all three scenes share the same horizon line, and beyond which is Dublin Bay. In this richly coloured window turquoise, golden yellow and shades of violet and purple predominate, with vibrant green mainly reserved for the tracery. Birds circle above the working men; in the left and centre light they resemble seabirds referencing Malahide's coastal location, but in the third light, they are white doves. The shapes of the groupings of birds recall some of the graphic illustrations of M.C. Escher. In the tracery the agrarian theme continues and it features abundant vines heavy with grapes which has many biblical connotations.

The calligraphic inscription in memory of James and Margaret Dickie is the work of the distinguished letterer and stone carver, Michael Biggs, who like Johnny Murphy, was starting out in his career, though by 1956 had undertaken a few carved inscription commissions and produced illustrations and typography for books.

St Sylvester's church (RC)

Main Street, K36 HR63

The original austere Gothic Revival single-cell (nave, no transepts) structure located on Main Street was built during the famine period, with a tower added at the turn of the nineteenth century. All the windows are plain diamond-paned with the exception of the nineteenth-century 3-light above the altar, *The Sacred Heart with the Immaculate Conception and St Joseph*, which may be of French origin.

St Sylvester's underwent a significant conservation and building programme in 2012–14 overseen by Sean Harrington Architects, and among the additions were a parish centre and prayer chapel. It was decided that stained glass would be a feature of both and there was an open competition with Dublin glass artists Peter Young (b.1962) and Killian Schurmann (b.1962) being successful, and although the works they created are outside the time frame of this book it would be a shame not to highlight them. At the outset it was determined that Young would contribute a large rectangular window to the parish centre, and Schurmann a series of twenty-two small windows to the circular chapel. As the project progressed the artists felt that in fact they might be better suited to swap their respective commissions and this is what happened. Young felt that the chapel would offer him the opportunity to include a narrative dimension to his stained glass and also felt he could better respond to the intimacy of the meditative space compared with the bustling vibrancy of a parish centre.[6]

The prayer chapel is a circular space, close to, but separate from the main church.[7] Peter Young created the series of windows – reduced from twenty-two to fifteen after consultation with the architects so that they could each be wider

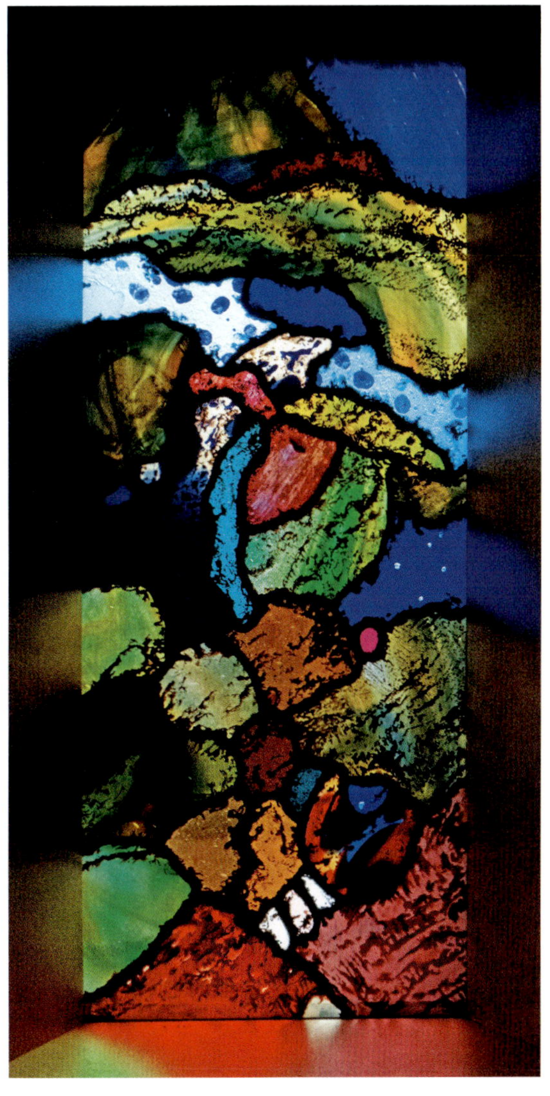

Peter Young, *Eden I: The Creation with Elemental and Celestial Guardians* (2014), prayer chapel adjoining St Sylvester's church

– which are deeply recessed and punctuate the curved wall at three levels, and are arranged in three thematic groupings, Seasons, Creation, and Eden. A very large plate glass window opposite gives a view of the meditation garden which resonates with Young's three themes; and though an attractive feature this window also floods the space with light which arguably reduces the effectiveness of Young's windows, which like most stained glass, greatly benefit from being viewed in an environment with subdued internal light.

The subjects of the top four windows are derived from two themes which would seem to be disparate but which Young has cleverly combined: the seasons and the evangelists, the latter inspired by images from the Book of Kells. Matthew, the winged man, is linked with winter, and represents incarnation, humanity, and reason; Mark, the winged lion, is linked with spring, and represents the resurrection, royalty, and courage; Luke, the winged ox, is linked with summer, and represents passion, sacrifice and strength; and John, the eagle, is linked with autumn, and represents the ascension, the spirit and divine nature.

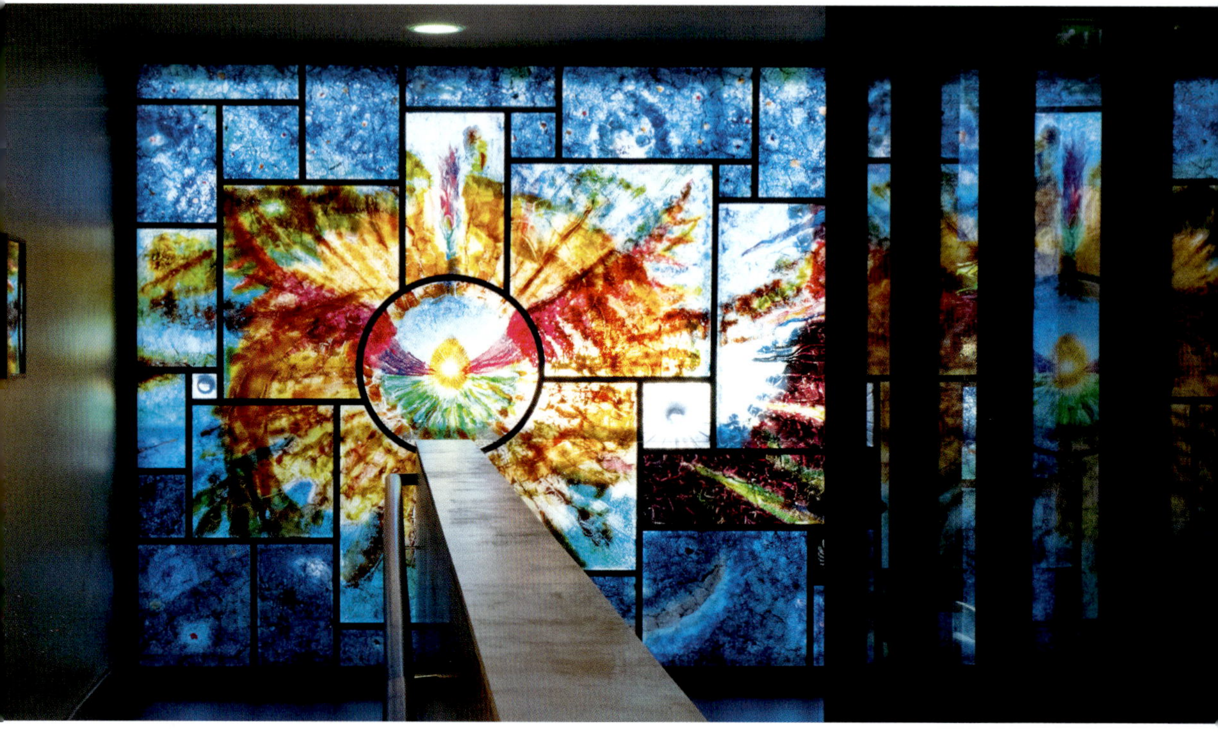

Killian Schurmann, *Resurrection* (2014), parish centre adjoining St Sylvester's church

The eight middle row windows loosely interpret the creation as described in Genesis 1, but taking a more contemporary, scientific and ecologically inspired approach, starting with one titled Beginning, and progressing through Nebula, Organization of Matter, Marine, Molecular Level, Primordial, Rainforest, Islands. Several of these are amorphous images, like slides viewed under a microscope where scale is turned on its head. In one window for instance, a delicate little sea horse is depicted bobbing in the ocean while dwarfed by enlarged molecules of water.

The final grouping of three windows, those at the lowest level, have the overarching theme of Eden, and continue the creation theme while depicting the interconnectivity of life forms. The biblical subjects of the Tree of Life, and Madonna and Child are included, and Young's interpretation of the latter conveys a sense of nurturing, which relates back to the natural world, and how it nurtures us, and our responsibility to care for and nurture it in return. This chapel, which is often empty, is a wonderful space to visit, observe, experience and reflect.

The parish centre is approached from the opposite side of St Sylvester's church and on entering one immediately sees, at some distance, Killian Schurmann's large installation – a wall he created from painted/stained and fused glass. At an early stage the architects suggested that the work should convey an explosion of colour, which it certainly does; and with an intense, almost vortex-like centre it both draws the viewer in while simultaneously 'exploding' outwards. Each section of glass, some 10–15mm thick, is set within the dark metal grid-like frame that provides a visual structure echoing the parish centre's modernist architecture, while the overall work itself has a distinctly painterly quality with soft washes of translucent colours; golden yellow dominating the centre with passages of magenta and turquoise which evolve into myriad shades of blue at the outermost points.

Each glass section within the frame has been created from several layers of glass that were individually stained/infused with pigment, sometimes with glass threads added, and then sandwiched together, and once fused at a high temperature in the kiln where chemical reactions occur, everything is sealed for eternity and it becomes one solid piece.[8] There is something very elemental about the process and the actual installation itself. The title it has been given is 'Resurrection', though it will probably mean many things to those who encounter it, conveying thoughts such as creation, energy, and the spirit.

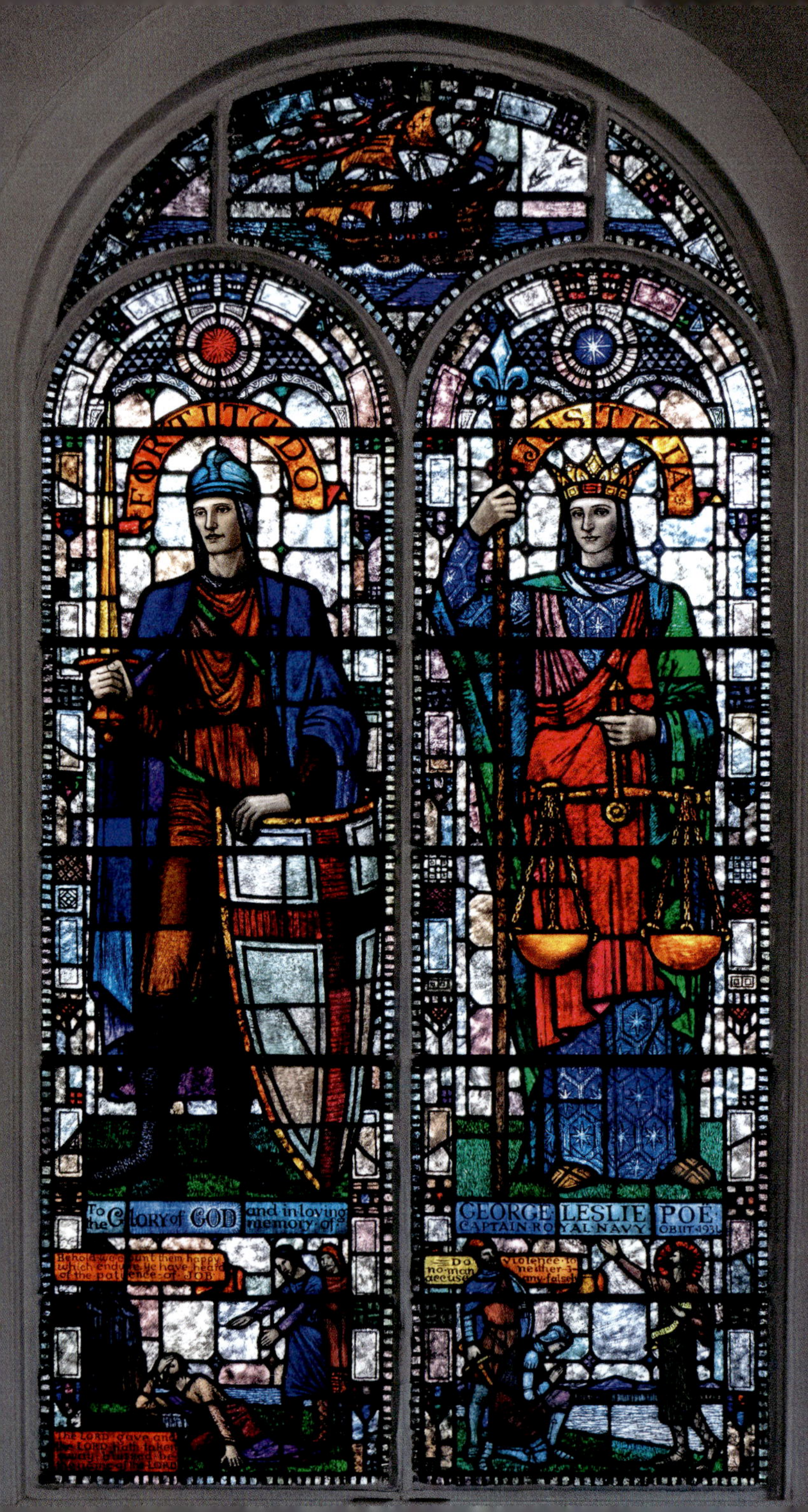
FORTITUDO
JUSTITIA
To the GLORY of GOD and in loving memory of
GEORGE LESLIE POE
CAPTAIN ROYAL NAVY
OBIIT 1931

SANTRY

St Pappin's church (C of I)

Santry Villas, D09 W597

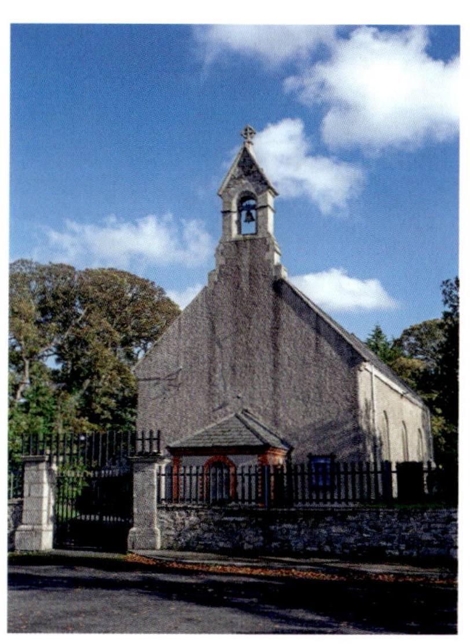

St Pappin's church is named after a local fifth-century saint (also spelt Pappan and Papán). The modestly proportioned church with roughcast cement-rendered walls and red-brick quoins was built in 1709 on the ruins of an earlier church and was modified with improvements three times in the final decades of the nineteenth century. The church is located adjacent to the former demesne of Santry Court, home to generations of the Domville family and latterly their relatives the Poës, some of whom are buried in the wooded graveyard that surrounds it. The church and the graveyard provide a tranquil oasis in an area of intense suburbanization.

(opposite) Catherine O'Brien, *Fortitude and Justice, with Job and St John the Baptist* (1935)

ST PAPPIN'S CHURCH contains three windows by An Túr Gloine's artists. Before these were commissioned it appears that in terms of stained glass there was only one very basic mid-nineteenth-century decorative window erected in memory of Sir Compton Domville's widow. The majority of the Domville family had, over the years, chosen to erect plaques, mainly of marble, to deceased relatives and these adorn the unpretentious interior.

Of the three An Túr Gloine windows, two are by Hubert McGoldrick and one by Catherine O'Brien and all three were erected in memory of members of the Poë family. The family, headed by Capt. George Leslie Poë, a retired captain in the Royal Navy, resided in Santry Court from at least 1893 and it appears the Poës rented the mansion from their wealthier kinsmen, the titled Domvilles.

In 1889 the architect John Franklin Fuller undertook restoration and improvements in St Pappin's church which included works relating to two windows in the east wall, located either side of the impressive carved reredos; these were most likely filled with simple diamond-paned glazing when first installed. In 1922 the first of the windows received a stained glass window commemorating four local casualties of the First World War: Captain and Mrs Poë's eldest son, Capt. Charley Vernon Leslie Poë,[1] gunner Edward Harris, and privates John Dugdale and Stephen Rose.[2]

Although the commission for the memorial window was placed by St Pappin's rector, Revd Richard Archdale Byrn, it appears that the cost (£80) was covered by Capt. George Poë who was active in his parish and held the post of people's churchwarden. It is likely that the suggestion to order the window from An Túr Gloine came from John (Jack) E. Geoghegan who was a member of the select vestry and was Sarah Purser's favourite nephew; he would have been acutely aware that his aunt was constantly on the lookout for potential stained glass patrons. Two years previously a window by another An Túr Gloine artist, Wilhelmina Geddes, was erected in All Saints church, Blackrock, Co. Dublin, to Jack Geoghegan's younger brother, Lt William Geoghegan, who had been killed in the Great War,[3] so Jack would have definitely been familiar with the quality of the stained glass which An Túr Gloine produced as well as his aunt's eagerness to secure orders.

Due to the number of soldiers who died in the First World War, An Túr Gloine received approximately thirty orders for war memorial windows, virtually all for churches of Protestant denominations, and these largely accounted for a dramatic increase in the studio's output, particularly in the 1918–22 period.[4] An Túr Gloine became so busy that a new artist was invited to join the studio and he was Hubert McGoldrick who started in early 1920, or perhaps late the previous year.

The subject of McGoldrick's tall window (9ft 9in.) was St Michael, the most popular saint to feature in First World War memorial windows,[5] as it gave the opportunity to portray, in dramatic manner, a heroic male figure standing over a serpent, a dragon, or the defeated figure of Satan (all of which could be equated with the oppressor), whom he sometimes is shown piercing with a lance. In this instance, McGoldrick has essentially depicted a medieval-style knight with helmet, armour, chainmail, a cape revealing midnight blue lining and, critically, wings, as otherwise he would simply be a knight. He stands resolute, and at his feet the vanquished emerald and turquoise scaly serpent with blood red mouth, nostrils and tongue. With the deed

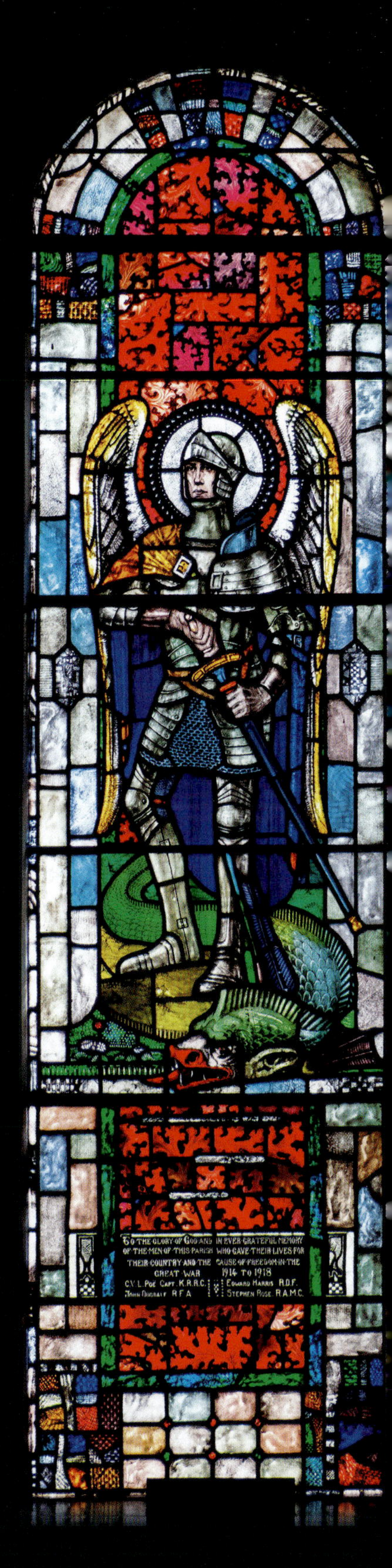

Hubert McGoldrick, *St Michael* (1921–2)

ST PAPPIN'S CHURCH (C OF I), SANTRY

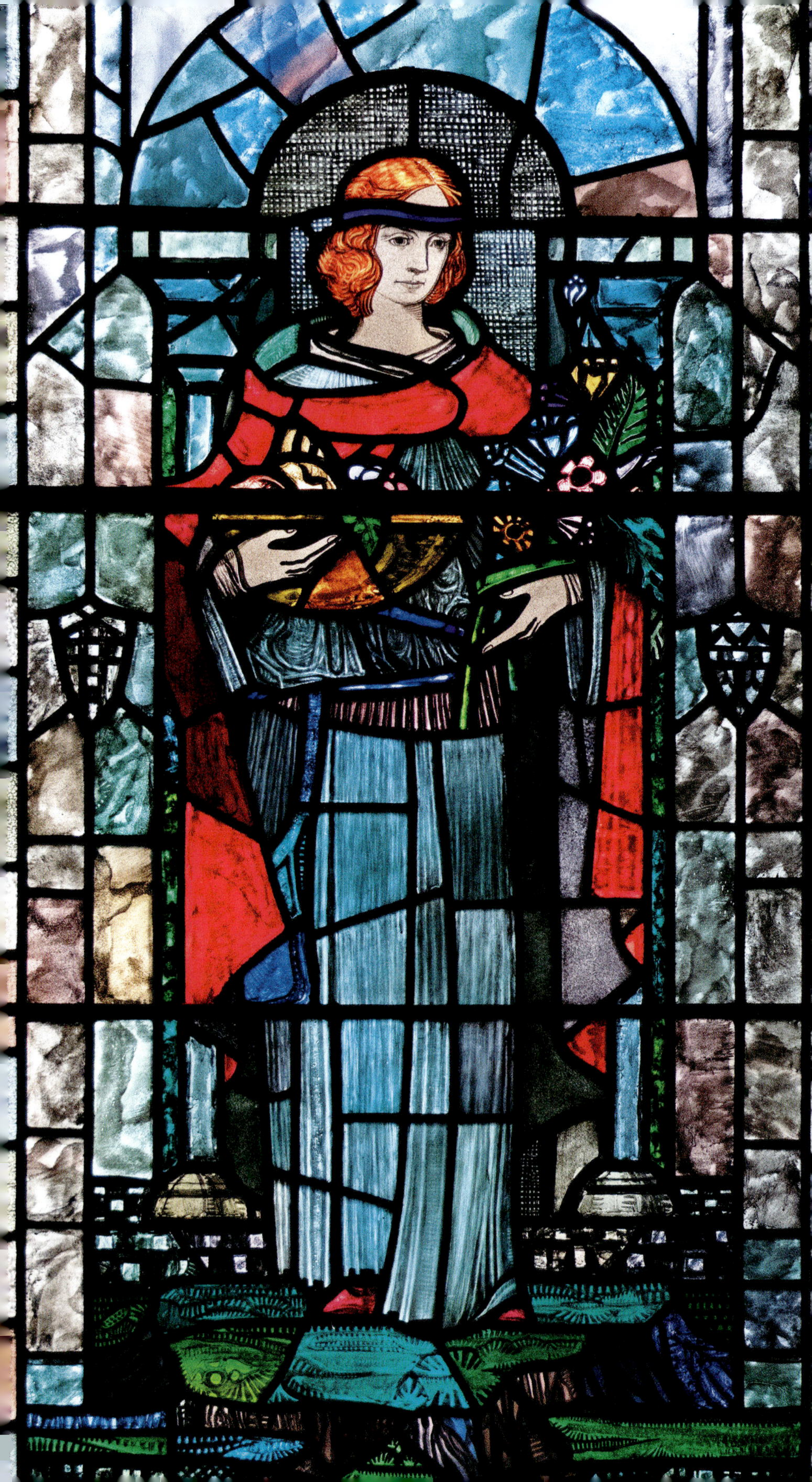

accomplished, St Michael is depicted nonchalantly sliding his sword back into its scabbard. Due to the slim proportions of the window the figure of St Michael only takes up about half the height, with sections above and below allowing McGoldrick the opportunity to introduce decorative passages. In particular he has featured a curly-shaped leaf motif. Mostly they are ruby red in colour and so convey the impression of flames and the colour echoes the use of red in the serpent's head. In other areas he has used a selection of colourful cullets and painted them with a variety of textures; it is decoration purely for the pleasure of it. McGoldrick has matted the background quarries in order to soften the light entering the chancel and modify any discordant contrast between the richly coloured areas and the milky-white quarries.

In November 1924 Capt. George Poë's wife, Mary Caldecott Poë (née Domville), died, though for reasons unknown it was not until five years later that their daughter, Muriel Gladys Poë, placed an order on behalf of the family for a memorial window at An Túr Gloine, and again the artist assigned to the job was Hubert McGoldrick, which made sense as it is very much a companion window to *St Michael*. The subject selected was Phoebe, a fifth-century Christian woman mentioned by St Paul in his Epistle to the Romans ('A succourer of many'). Phoebe is not classified as a saint so has no halo and is a highly unusual subject in Irish stained glass; the window is one of only four depicting Phoebe in windows in Church of Ireland churches.[6] McGoldrick presents Phoebe as both Roman matron and modern woman with shortish golden hair styled in a contemporary wavy manner accessorized with a mauve flapper-style headband. Mrs Poë was known for her charitable endeavours and McGoldrick depicts Phoebe as a pensive Lady Bountiful-type figure carrying a tasteful rustic floral arrangement in one hand and a bowl filled with loaves and fruit in the other, presumably ready to dispense the latter to all those in need as would be appropriate for a benevolent chatelaine. Aside from Phoebe's golden hair and her ruby slippers and mantle, the principal colours in the window are tones of blue, ranging from deep cobalt to icy pale blue, a counterbalance to the intense red passages in *St Michael*. As with *St Michael*, McGoldrick has liberally matted the

(opposite) Hubert McGoldrick, detail of *Phoebe* (1929)

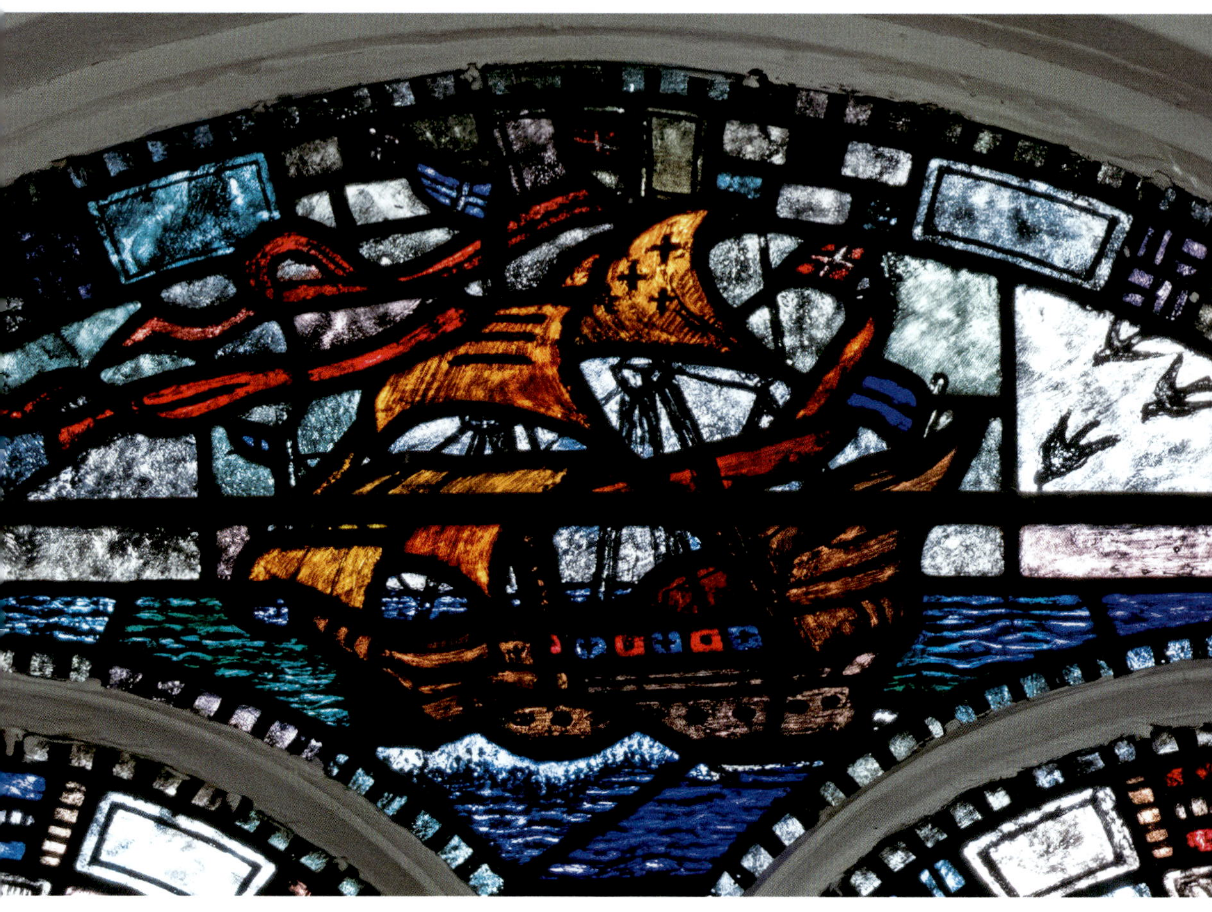

Catherine O'Brien, detail of galleon in *Fortitude and Justice, with Job and St John the Baptist* (1935)

quarries and utilized handfuls of jewel-like cullets to add visual interest. The cost for *Phoebe* was £100, an increase of £20 which was perhaps reflective of a rise in the cost of materials.

In 1935 Muriel Poë placed an order for a third and final window for Santry, this time for a location on the south wall nearest the chancel. Muriel Poë had, unlike her older married sister, pursued a life of independence and public service. In 1916 she worked for the Voluntary Aid Detachment base at the St John's Ambulance emergency hospital, 40 Merrion Square, and in 1921 she was awarded the British war medal, the victory medal and an MBE for her work in the First World War with the VAD. She also received the title Lady of Grace of the Order of St John of Jerusalem.[7]

In this instance Hubert McGoldrick did not undertake the job and the order went to Catherine O'Brien. This window was also round-headed but of different proportions to McGoldrick's pair of windows as it was approximately a foot shorter and nearly two feet wider. Being comparatively wide, it seems it was considered desirable for stability reasons to employ an iron frame to divide it vertically in two and also to separate the main tracery and spandrels either side.

The window was erected in memory of Capt. George Leslie Poë who had died, aged eighty-seven, the previous year. The principal subjects of his memorial window are two allegorical figures, one male, *Fortitude*, and one female, *Justice*, and both have their faces, which are almost identical, slightly inclined towards the altar table. *Fortitude* and *Justice* are two of the four cardinal virtues of mind and character in both classical philosophy and Christian theology, and were presumably chosen as qualities associated with the late Capt. Poë's character.

Unlike McGoldrick's windows, Catherine O'Brien introduced a predella panel beneath each of the two figures. The predella on the bottom left beneath *Fortitude*, includes quotes from both James,[8] and Job,[9] the former alluding to the famed 'patience of Job'. The panel depicts Job, he of impeccable moral character, slumped on the ground as he endures pain while two onlookers appear to berate him. The text in the Book of Job is considered difficult to interpret so artists have a wide range of options when depicting the story, however in O'Brien's depiction one can see the link between Job's enduring patience and the theme of fortitude. The predella beneath *Justice* is accompanied by a quote from Luke, 'Do violence to no man, neither accuse any falsely' (3:14). St John the Baptist is identifiable because of the scroll wrapped around him inscribed with his words 'Behold, the Lamb of God.' With his arm outstretched he addresses two knights, one with his sword drawn, the other kneeling in prayer before the saint. The connection between the figure of *Justice* and the scene below is unclear.

The central tracery piece features a charming Elizabethan galleon in full sail coursing through the cobalt blue and turquoise ocean, a trail of swallows in its wake, and O'Brien has continued the horizon line into the two spandrels either side.

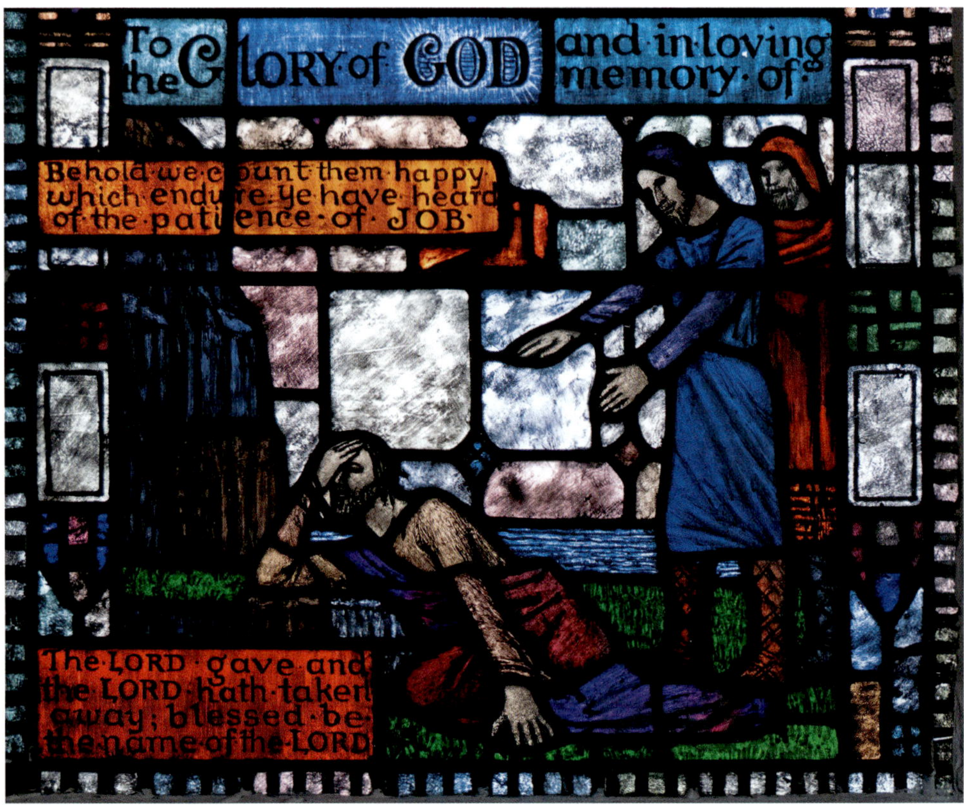

Catherine O'Brien, detail of left predella panel in *Fortitude and Justice, with Job and St John the Baptist* (1935)

The image was surely chosen to reflect the fact that Poë was a retired navy captain and perhaps the old-style galleon to allude to the family's lineage which they traced back to Anthony Poë (1540–1612) of Nottinghamshire.[10]

Although the window was ordered by Muriel Poë, it was given by both of Captain Poë's daughters (his younger son by now was also deceased) and a large number of his friends.[11] A note in the An Túr Gloine workbook indicates that the payment for the window (£130) was given in notes by Jack Geoghegan and it seems probable that he was involved in collecting the donations for the window. *Fortitude and Justice* was unveiled and dedicated by the archbishop of Dublin in June 1935. Unfortunately the perspex installed for protection in bygone years has now discoloured and has become less translucent which reduces the amount of light illuminating these beautiful windows.

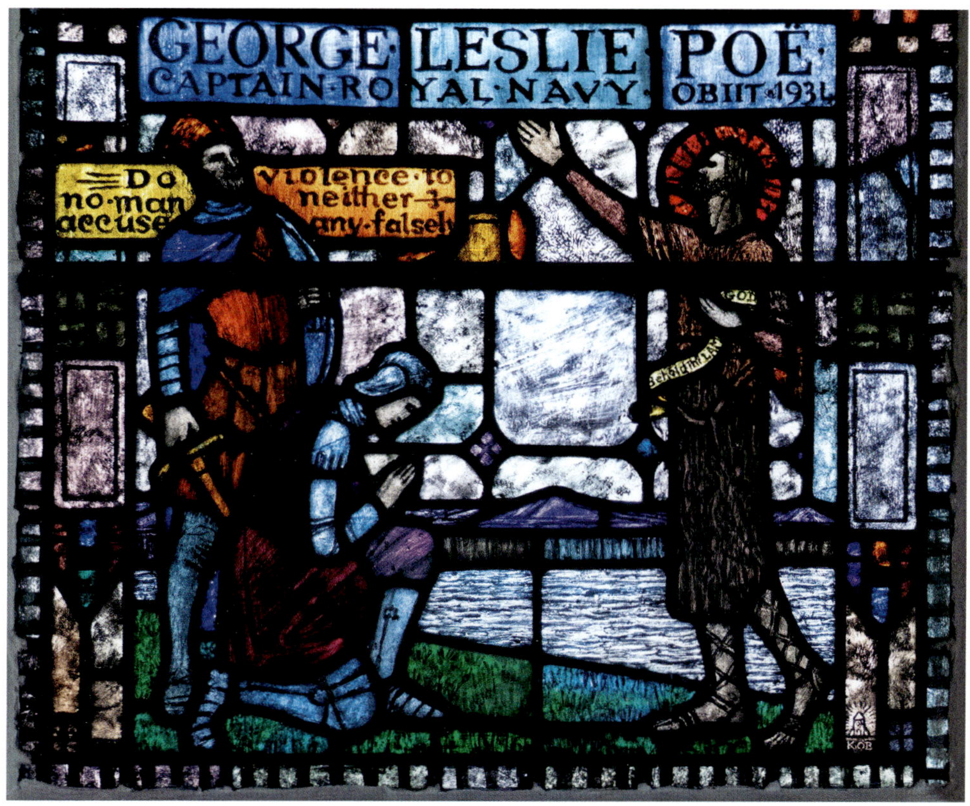

Catherine O'Brien, detail of right predella panel in *Fortitude and Justice, with Job and St John the Baptist* (1935)

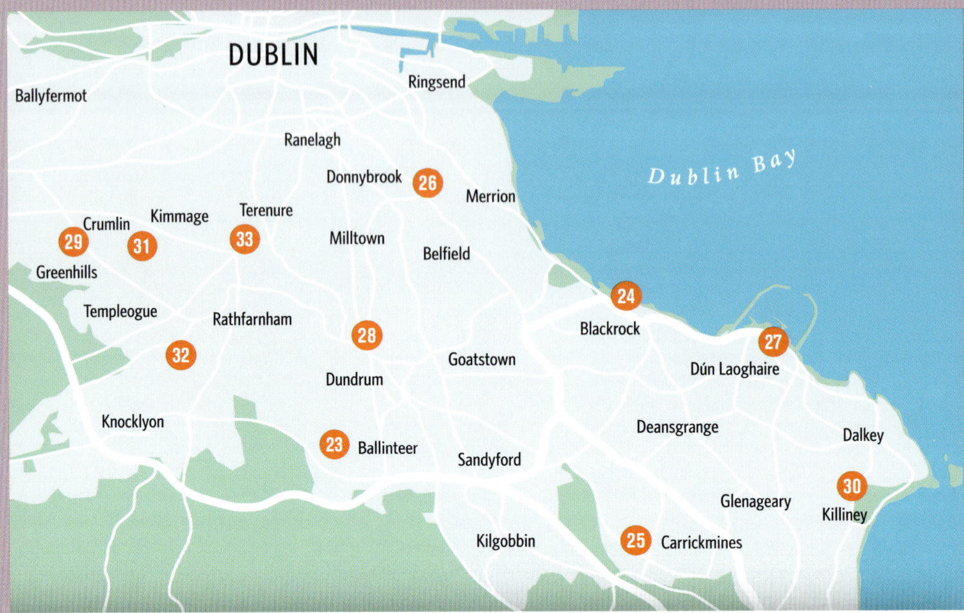

Dublin South, Suburbs and County

23 Ballinteer
St John the Evangelist church (RC),
Ballinteer Avenue, D16 VK27

24 Blackrock
St John the Baptist church (RC),
Temple Road, A94 YP08

25 Carrickmines
Tullow church (C of I),
Brighton Road, D18 RF79

26 Donnybrook
Sacred Heart church (RC),
Stillorgan Road, D04 HW82

27 Dún Laoghaire
St Michael's church (RC),
Marine Road, A96 RC98
Presbyterian church,
York Road, A96 D529

28 Dundrum
St Nahi's church (C of I),
Churchtown Road Upper, D14 V381

29 Greenhills
Holy Spirit church (RC),
Limekiln Lane, D12 YY0X

30 Killiney
Holy Trinity church (C of I),
Killiney Hill Road, A96 D990
St Stephen's church (RC),
Killiney Hill Road, A96 EY61

31 Kimmage
Holy Spirit church (RC),
Kimmage Manor, Whitehall Road, D12 WP44

32 Rathfarnham
Holy Spirit church (RC) (Ballyroan Parish),
Marian Road, D14 VR68

33 Terenure
St Joseph's church (RC),
Terenure Road East, D06 CX23

Dublin South, Suburbs and County

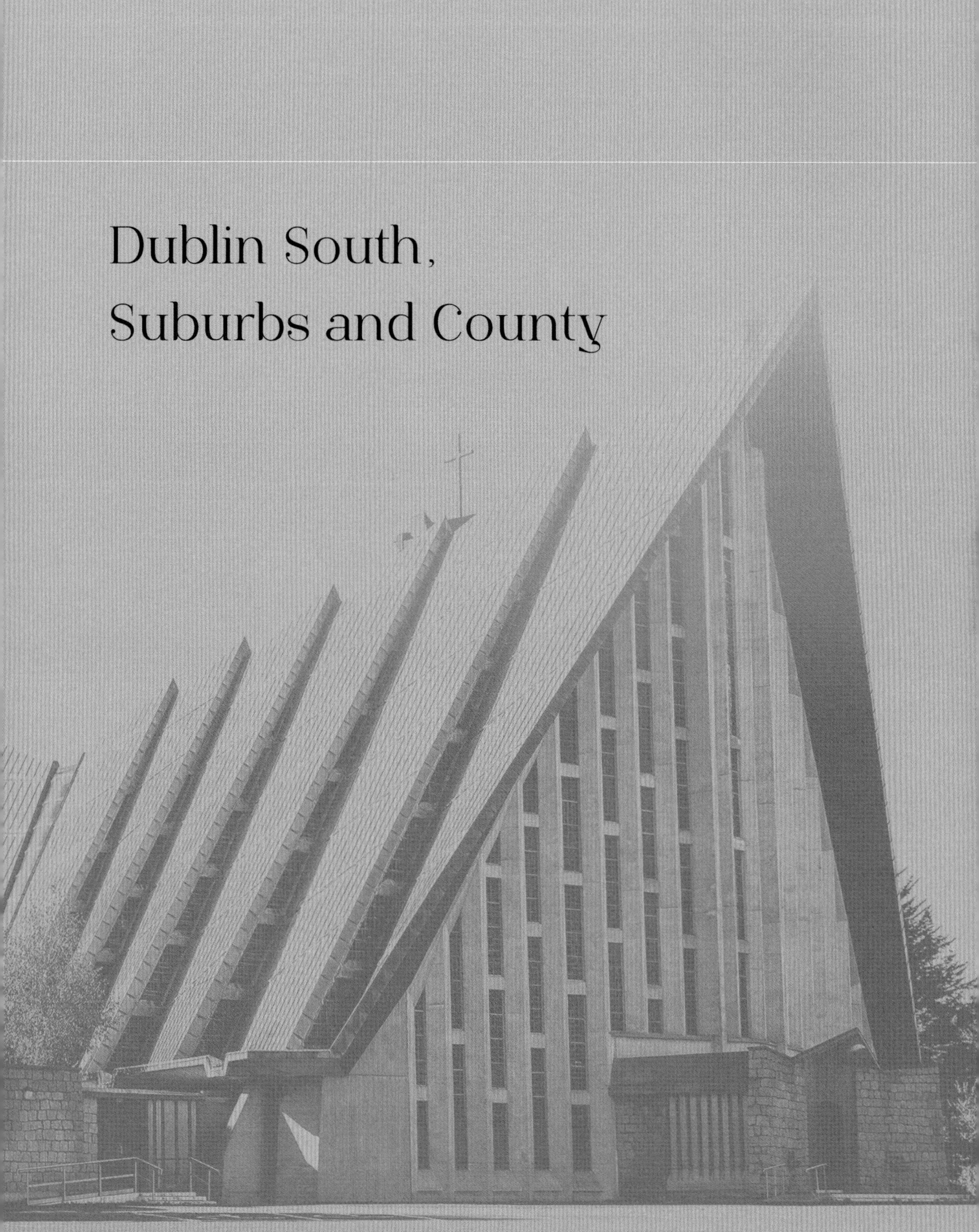

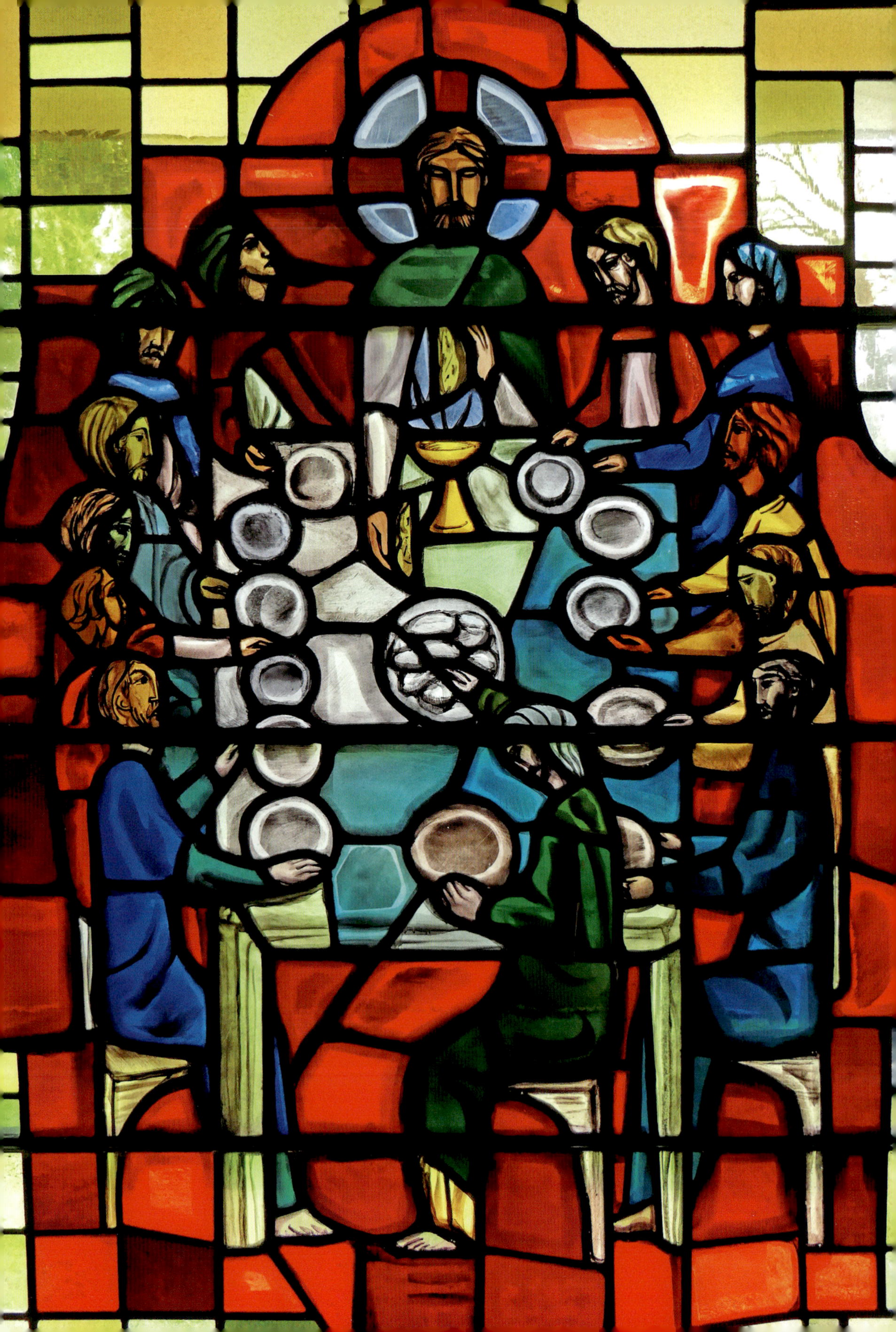

BALLINTEER

St John the Evangelist church (RC)

Ballinteer Avenue, D16 VK27

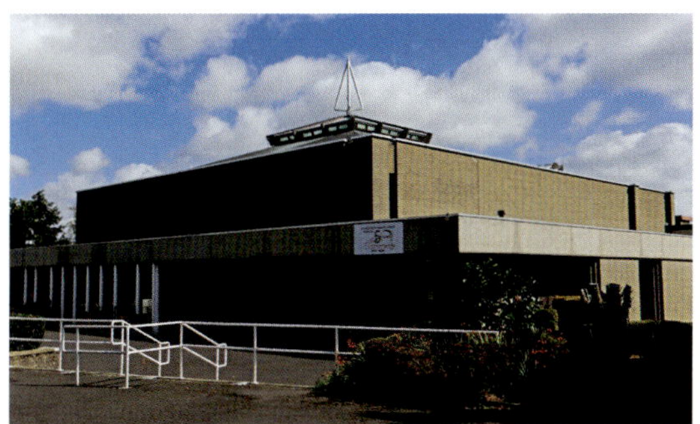

The church of St John the Evangelist, located on Ballinteer Avenue, was designed 1972–3 by architect Brendan Morris of Morris & McCullough & Associates. A square building of concrete brick and pre-cast panels construction, it features a pyramidical roof surmounted by a small *flèche*. The church's scale renders it relatively unobtrusive in its suburban location.

(opposite) Patrick Pollen, detail of *The Last Supper* (1973)

When the church was being built, the London-born stained glass artist Patrick Pollen was engaged to supply the stained glass windows which were all made in 1973: four rectangular windows for the south wall, another rectangular window for the north-west corner of the building, and a narrow floor-to-ceiling window containing symbols for the sanctuary. Pollen had married the sculptor Nell Murphy in 1963 and had set up home in Sweetmount Avenue, Dundrum – not far from Ballinteer – where in time he built his own stained glass studio in the back garden in which he made the windows for St John the Evangelist.

The south wall of St John the Evangelist is punctuated at regular intervals with Pollen's quartet of four rectangular stained glass windows depicting key episodes from Christ's life: *The Nativity, The Last Supper, The Crucifixion* and *The Resurrection*. Each of Pollen's four scenes is set into a generous background of abstract glass composed of small rectangles that visually echo the grey bricks of the church's interior.

Thematically Pollen's four windows bear some relationship to the set of four episodes from the life of Christ that his mentor, Evie Hone, designed in 1944–6, which are now in the Manresa Jesuit Centre of Spirituality in Dollymount (see pp 154–63), though they share only two episodes in common, *The Nativity* and *The Last Supper*. Hone's windows were made several years before Pollen relocated to Dublin but he definitely would have seen two of the series loaned to the major retrospective of Hone's work held in Dublin in 1958 (the set at that point was still housed in St Stanislaus's College, in Tullabeg, Co. Offaly). Although differing in composition and treatment, there are parallels with, for instance, *The Nativity*, in the manner in which the infant Jesus has his arms outstretched as if to embrace the world. Pollen's tender interpretation is quite straightforward with just Joseph, Mary and Jesus, and overhead an enormous star illuminating the manger.

The next in the sequence, *The Last Supper*, is arguably the finest of the set. Within an irregular-shaped space composed of different shades of deep red, Pollen has depicted the scene which defies traditional perspective as the rectangular table around which all are seated is shown from a bird's eye view. Christ at the

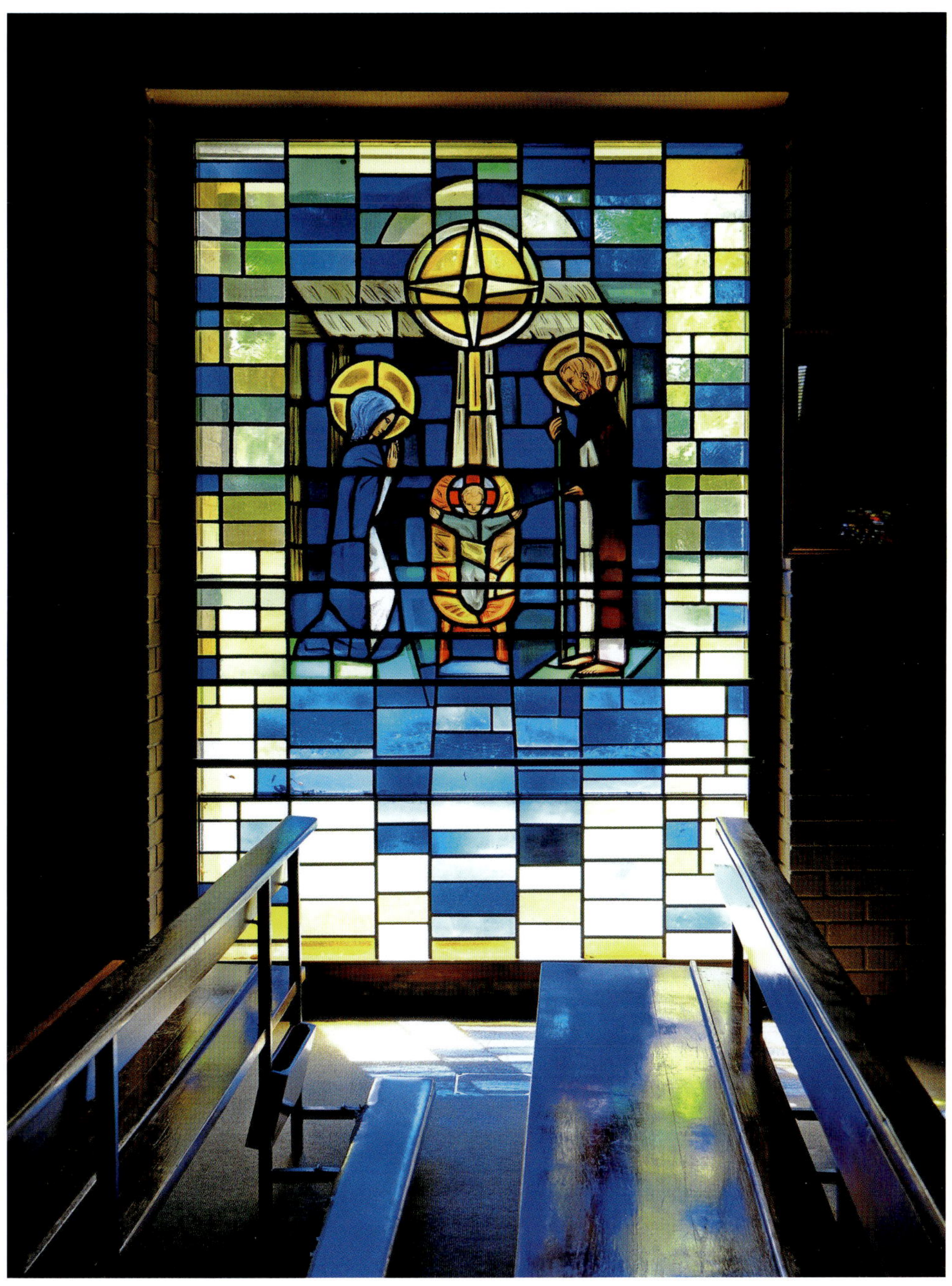

Patrick Pollen, *The Nativity* (1973)

top of the table is about to celebrate the Eucharist. All the apostles, empty plates in front of them, are seated with grave expressions, while at the bottom of the table Judas sneakily stretches forward to snatch some bread from the communal plate. Pollen is often compared to Hone and of course there are some striking similarities but when it comes to painting faces, as exemplified in this window, he generally favoured a more considered approach introducing soft washes of pale pigment providing tonal variation, whereas Hone's background as a painter is always apparent, revealed in confident, intuitive brushstrokes with minimal use of tones.

Pollen chose to replicate the powerful red background in *The Last Supper* again in the next window, *The Crucifixion*, as if to make a visual statement of how one event closely followed the other. Christ on the cross looks down at Our Lady while St John gazes up from the other side. The expressions on all three faces are understated; the window presents an image that invites contemplation so that the individual viewer can draw their own interpretations of the private anguish that all three are experiencing. Compositionally it is a very simple classic arrangement that has many precedents in art history going back to the 1400s if not further.

For the fourth window, *The Resurrection*, Pollen chose to depict Christ in a serene manner, standing on top of a box-like sarcophagus and bearing a standard with the cross of resurrection, a white flag with a red cross which is a symbol of Christ's victory over death. While this manner of depicting the Resurrection was particularly popular around the twelfth century it was gradually supplanted by Christ hovering above

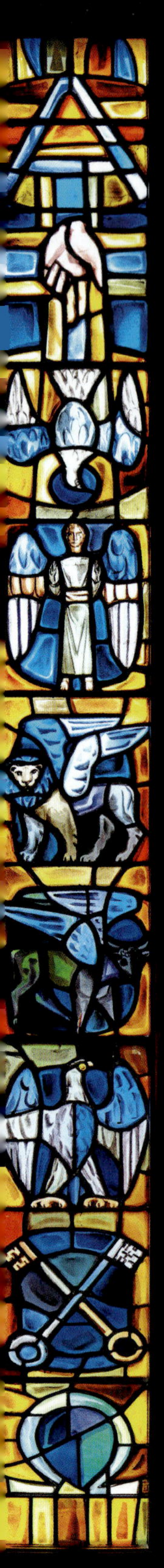

Patrick Pollen, *Hand of God, Symbols of the Evangelists, Alpha and Omega, Crossed Keys* (1973)

the sarcophagus, and over time developed further so that he was surrounded by a mandorla or floating on a cloud, and later again is infused with more action, sometimes with Christ bursting forth from a tomb.

In 1992 an internal clear-glazed and wood structure running the length of the church was designed by Brendan Morris in order to create a separate space, the Blessed Sacrament Oratory, and Pollen's four windows are now located here rather than in the main body of the church, though they can still be seen from it.[1]

Pollen also designed a full height, narrow window for the sanctuary comprising of multiple images stacked on top of each other (from top to bottom) – the symbol for alpha; the hand of God; dove (Holy Spirit); angel representing St Matthew; lion representing St Mark; calf representing St Luke; eagle representing St John; two crossed keys symbolizing St Peter's authority; the symbol for omega. The glass Pollen selected for the entire window is in opposing shades of either blue or golden orange, which creates a very harmonious effect, and the overall treatment indicates what a strong design sensibility Pollen could bring when depicting symbols.

The final window is located in an unusual position, the north-west corner of the church, and is quite unlike the other windows. The theme is the Creation, though it appears to be quite a personal interpretation; geometry underpins the composition with circles and a large triangle containing a variety of images. The hand of God descends from above in the act of creation, superimposed on the sun, and below the large triangle are two circles, one containing stars, the other a crescent moon. Contained within a large circle are various images relating to nature such as birds in flight, clouds, trees and foliage. There are also images relating to man harnessing nature including a bushel of hay, a woman at a spinning wheel and a man at work with a spade. There are also images of bygone centuries such as a galleon, and contemporary development including a factory and a segment of an urban map. Within the triangle, but outside the confines of the circle are three different species of fish, and on the other side, a lion, elephant, and a herd of cattle. It all amounts to a very idiosyncratic selection that if inspired by Genesis, takes a very liberal approach. Pollen chose to depict many of the little images in a fluid, sketchy manner, uncharacteristic of his usual controlled style, perhaps to stress the 'hand of the artist' in the creation process.

The church has some noteworthy artistic features in addition to Pollen's stained

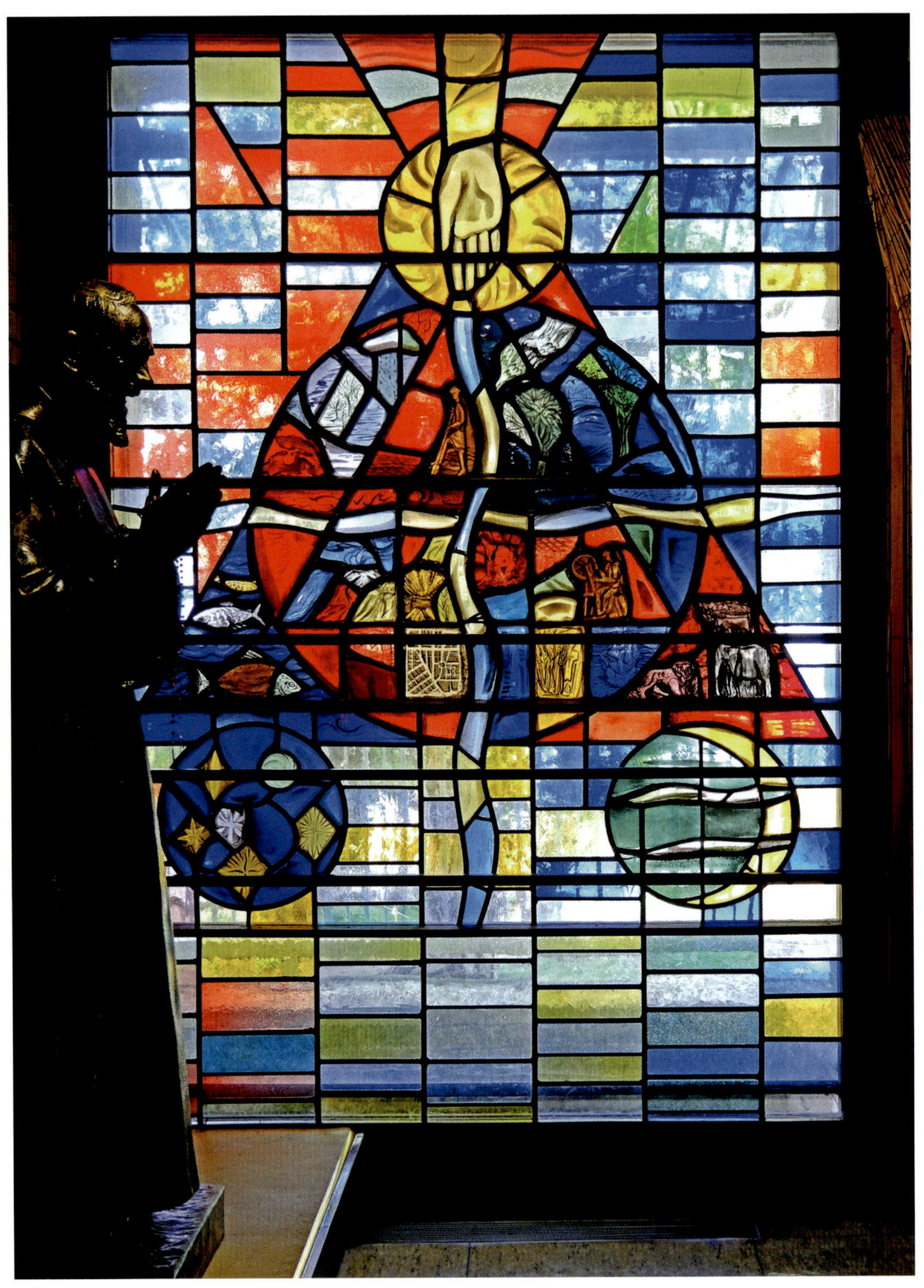

glass. First, there are two sets of Stations of the Cross which incongruously have been arranged in parallel with each other on the north wall of the church. The larger, original set date from 1973 and were designed in pairs to form an elongated frieze, and are the work of Cecil King (1921–86).[2] Fashioned out of beaten copper and focusing on Christ's face and hands, they tell the narrative of Christ's journey to Calvary and his crucifixion. They are so far removed from the type of crisp, abstract geometric oil painting that King is well known for that it is difficult to imagine him working on this subject, in this style and using this technique. Interspersed with this set are small black and white pen and ink illustrations by William Dowling, better known as principal artist and manager of Harry Clarke Studios. They were drawn by him in 1943 and given as a gift to Fr Matthias Bodkin SJ for display in the chapel of a British Army naval base in Derry where Fr Bodkin was chaplain. They were installed in the church *c.*2010.[3] Another feature in the church is the large symbol of the eagle up high on the back wall by David King (1948–2003), son of stained glass artist Richard King, and which he created in 1989.

(opposite) Patrick Pollen, *The Creation, with Symbols and Vignettes including Animals, Agricultural Activities, Maps and a Galleon* (1973)

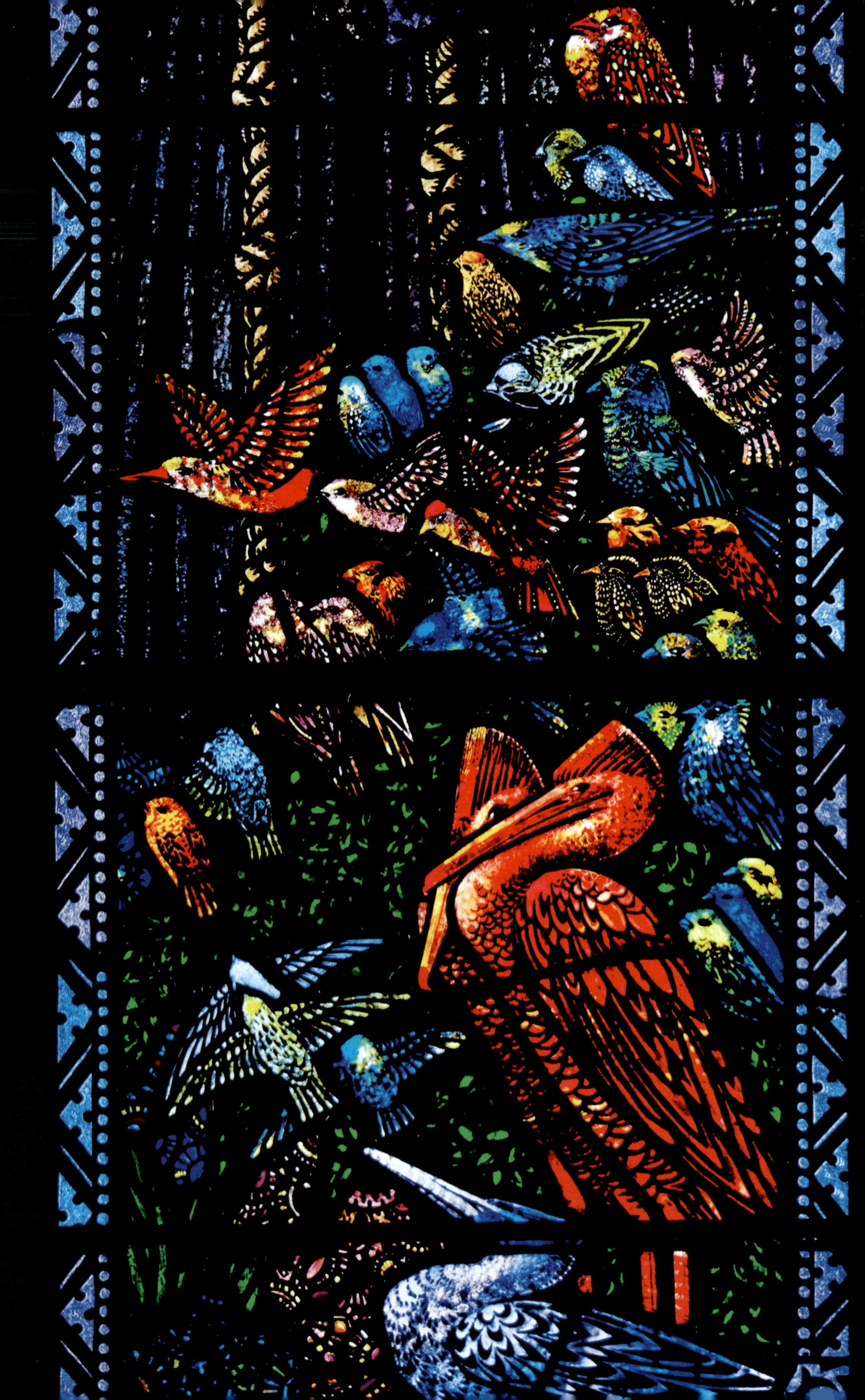

BLACKROCK

St John the Baptist church (RC)

Temple Road, A94 YP08

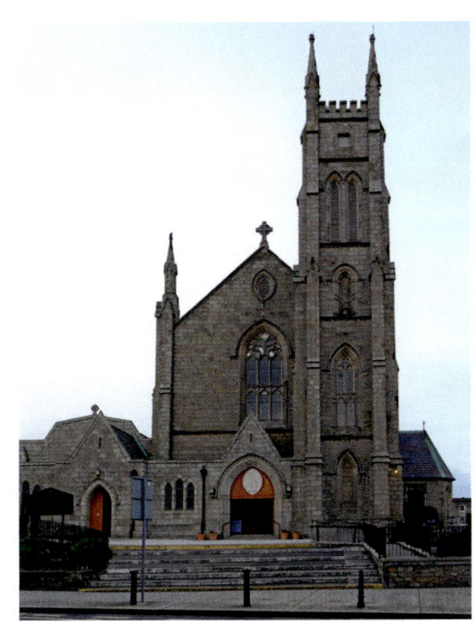

St John the Baptist church, located on Temple Road, Blackrock, is situated one street back from the coast. It was built in the mid-1840s by architect Patrick Byrne in the Gothic revival style. Initially comprising a nave, sanctuary and bell tower, in the following decades an aisle, baptistry, vestry, and chapel in honour of Our Lady were added. A further aisle was added in the 1930s.

(opposite) Joshua Clarke & Sons, detail of *St Francis of Assisi Receiving the Stigmata, and St Francis with Followers Preaching to the Birds* (1926–7)

When the church first opened it had several fine sanctuary windows in situ, including a huge rose, by the workshop of William Wailes of Newcastle, one of England's largest and most prolific stained glass producers. The choir gallery windows opposite were made by John Casey of Moore Street, Dublin, and prominently feature, in a sea of shamrock, the arms of the donor, Lord Cloncurry. The choir gallery also contains two windows, dated 1898, with the themes of the sorrowful and joyful mysteries made at the studio of Joshua Clarke.[1]

However in terms of stained glass, what will probably interest visitors most are examples of twentieth-century Irish stained glass; windows by three of Ireland's leading studios/artists – Clarke Studios, Earley & Company, and Evie Hone, which between them span four decades.

The first of these to be commissioned was a pair of 2-light windows by Clarke Studios, made in 1926–7, when the studio was still called Joshua Clarke & Sons (though Joshua had died in 1921), and before the official name change to Harry Clarke Stained Glass in 1930, a year before Harry died. During the time span that these windows were made Harry was the chief artist though there were extended periods when he was either ill or away attempting to establish his career in London, and this pair of windows would seem to have been designed and made at the studio with little or no direct input from Harry Clarke himself. It may be that two or more of the studio's artists worked on the windows which would explain some variations in style and painting technique. The windows are high up at clerestory level (and binoculars are recommended to appreciate the detail); had the commission arrived a few years later the donor would have had a choice of better, eye-level, locations in a new – yet to be constructed – side aisle.

The two windows were erected in memory of John Murphy (d.1924) of Avoca Avenue, Blackrock, by his son, Joseph Xavier Murphy, both of whom were partners in the Palgrave Murphy shipping company. Although no inscription appears in the windows it would seem that rectangular areas were left for this purpose, but perhaps due to their height it was apparent that any text would be illegible from below and instead they were filled with Clarke's signature Floral Ornament ('F.O.').

The structure of these 2-light windows, which face each other across the nave, is unusual; Gothic in style, they are two-tiered and so both feature two scenes, one above the other. The window on the right-hand side of the nave is dedicated to St Francis of Assisi. In the top scene the pale body of the crucified Christ is depicted with wings, referred to as a 'seraph', with St Francis, kneeling below, about to receive the stigmata.[2] The two attendant angels and the flotilla of wide-eyed cherubs are very much in the manner of Harry Clarke while the depictions of Christ and St Francis, less so. The scene in the two lights below shows St Francis, accompanied by fellow monks, engaging with birds, over forty in number, of varying species and colours, the largest of which appear to resemble storks; this charming proliferation of birds prefigures the inclusion of several exotic birds in Harry Clarke's famous decorative windows for Bewley's Cafe designed in 1927.

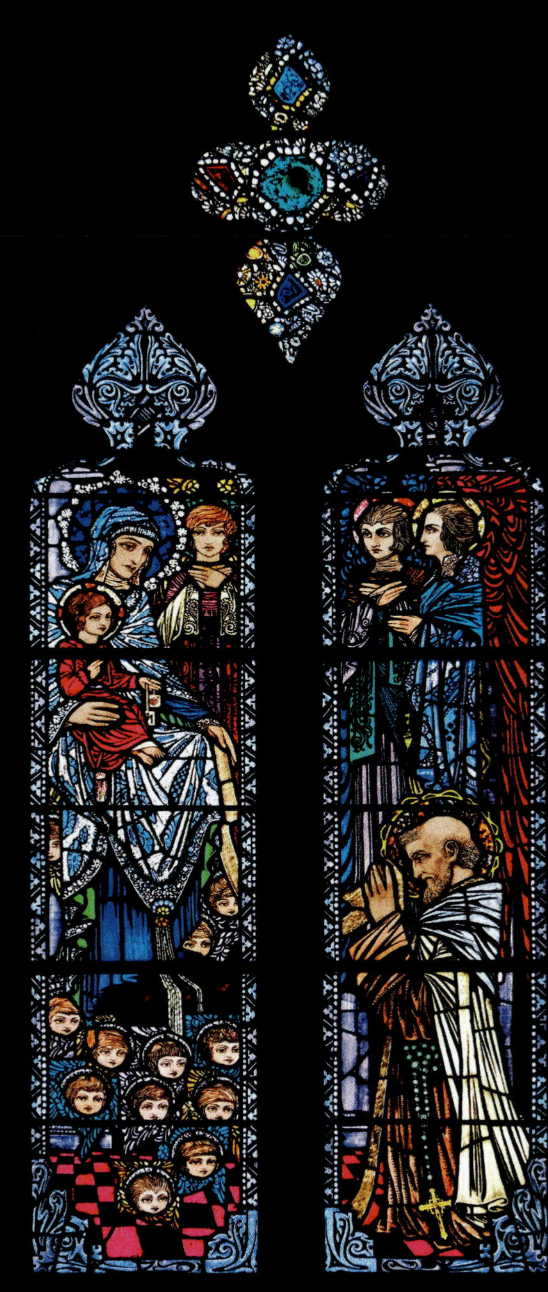

Joshua Clarke & Sons, detail of *Our Lady of Mount Carmel Presenting the Scapular to St Simon Stock, and the Death of St Angelus at the Hands of Count Berenger* (1926–7)

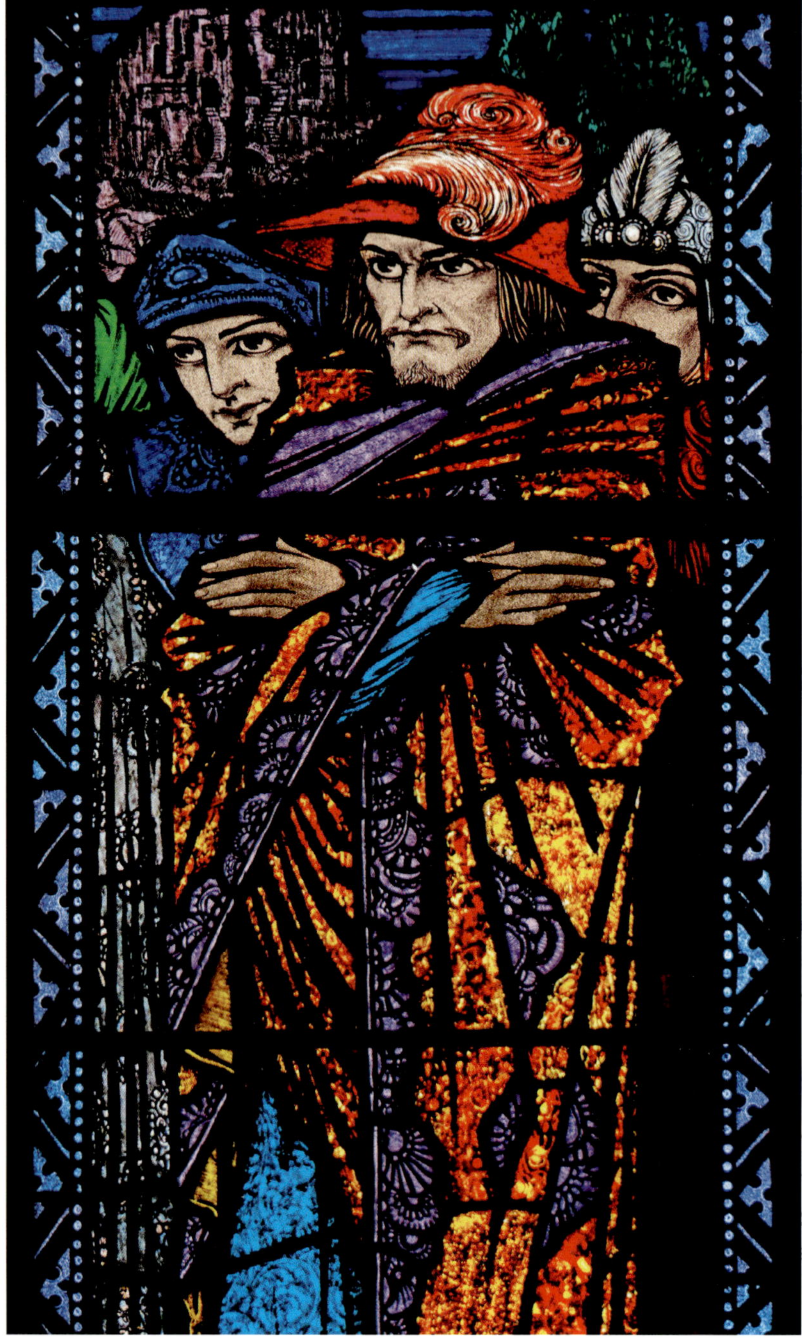

Joshua Clarke & Sons, detail of *Our Lady of Mount Carmel Presenting the Scapular to St Simon Stock, and the Death of St Angelus at the Hands of Count Berenger* (1926–7)

Opposite the St Francis themed window is one honouring the Carmelite order, and tellingly it is recorded that John Murphy had a particular devotion to the Carmelites.[3] The top scene depicts the Blessed Virgin with the infant Jesus presenting the scapular to St Simon Stock, whose kneeling pose to a degree mirrors that of St Francis opposite. All the faces, with the exception of St Simon Stock, are executed in typical Harry Clarke mode. The scene below is relatively obscure; it depicts the martyrdom of St Angelus, also a Carmelite, at the hands of a Sicilian knight, Count Berenger. There is an interesting thematic association connecting the two Clarke windows as St Angelus and St Francis were contemporaries, and when St Angelus met St Francis he told the saint that he would receive the stigmata, while St Francis foretold St Angelus's premature death. St Angelus is shown strung up on a tree, slowly expiring from a hail of arrows. The count is depicted, somewhat like a pantomime villain, in a richly brocaded golden robe with decorative violet trim which he has drawn about himself, his hat featuring a prominent plume (as if it had been plucked from one of the birds in the window opposite). In the background one can see the fortified Sicilian town of Licata, where St Angelus succumbed to his wounds and was buried.

Both windows feature not only Clarke's trademark Floral Ornament but also art nouveau flourishes top and bottom of each light, along with a linear chevron border pattern redolent of art deco; all going to show that during this period Clarke and his studio comfortably drew on various decorative influences. The windows were installed by Clarke's in February 1927 at a cost of £545. While thematically interesting, and featuring some attractive passages such as the menagerie of birds, both windows lack the compositional flair and lightness of touch associated with Harry Clarke himself, and the painting of several of the faces particularly jars.

In December 1932 the *Irish Times* published details of bequests contained in the will of a wealthy Blackrock widow, Mrs Anne Daly of Sydney Avenue, and the largest amount, £700, was for the erection of a window in St John the Baptist church in her memory and that of her late husband, solicitor, Charles Daly, and her will specified that the window should represent St Anne and scenes from her life.[4] Around this time a new side aisle and chapel were being built – and Mrs Daly had also left a separate £500 to the parish building fund – so it was an obvious decision that the

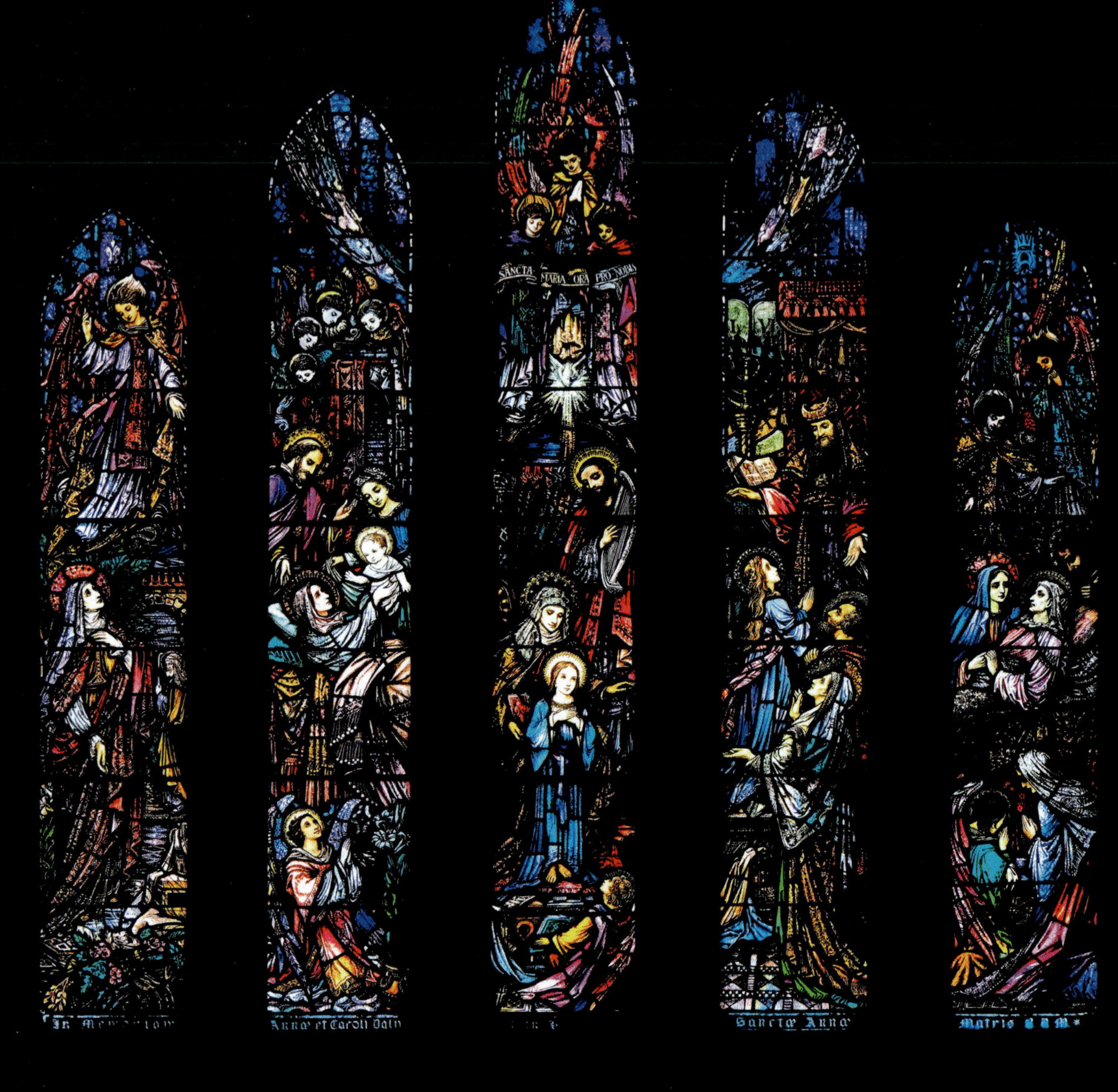

William E. Earley, *Scenes from the Life of St Anne* (1933)

Daly memorial window would be deserving of the prime spot in the new chapel dedicated to St Anne. Harry Clarke had died the previous year and this may have been a factor in the parish choosing the long-established Dublin studio of Earley & Company in placing the order for the Daly memorial window.

William E. Earley undertook the commission; a third-generation artist of the stained glass dynasty, and by the time he designed *Scenes from the Life of St Anne* he had been the studio's manager and chief artist for two decades. A prolific designer, although many of his windows were single lights and variations of standard subjects such as *The Annunciation*, when he had the opportunity – coupled with a generous budget as in this instance – to treat a multi-light window incorporating a demanding narrative, he would pull out all the stops and create a lush and lyrical extravaganza.

St Anne was the mother of the Blessed Virgin and this window focuses exclusively on her role as wife and mother without any reference to her role as the grandmother of Jesus. From left, the first light depicts an angel telling Anne that she would conceive after years of barrenness. In the distance is her husband Joachim, standing under the Golden Gate where the angel instructed them to meet. The next light shows a woman, possibly St Anne's sister, Sobe (here acting as midwife), presenting her with her new born daughter, Mary. The centre light has St Anne, guiding the young Mary, with Joachim behind, playing a harp, referencing his descent from the line of David. Significantly, books alluding to education are visible, as variations on the theme of St Anne teaching the young Mary are among the most popular representations of St Anne in art. The fourth light depicts the presentation of the young Mary in the temple before a high priest, and the fifth scene represents the dormition of St Anne, comforted by Mary and Joachim. As with many of William Earley's windows he liberally utilized angels and putti as a compositional device to create movement, fill gaps, and provide visual interest. Like Harry Clarke he relished detail for the sake of it, loved including rich fabrics and a variety of textures but his faces are always painted in the tradition of classical painting and have none of the distinctive characteristics that became Clarke's trademark.

If William Earley's windows could be faulted for being excessively pretty or overly sentimental, these remarks could never be directed at Evie Hone. The subject of her window for Blackrock church, one of her last, is the Virgin and Child, with Saints Patrick and Brigid, the two saints not chosen for their premier positions in the pantheon of Irish saints but because the window was in memory of Brigid Patricia McGuire (d.1953) of Newtown Park, Blackrock. It was erected by her husband

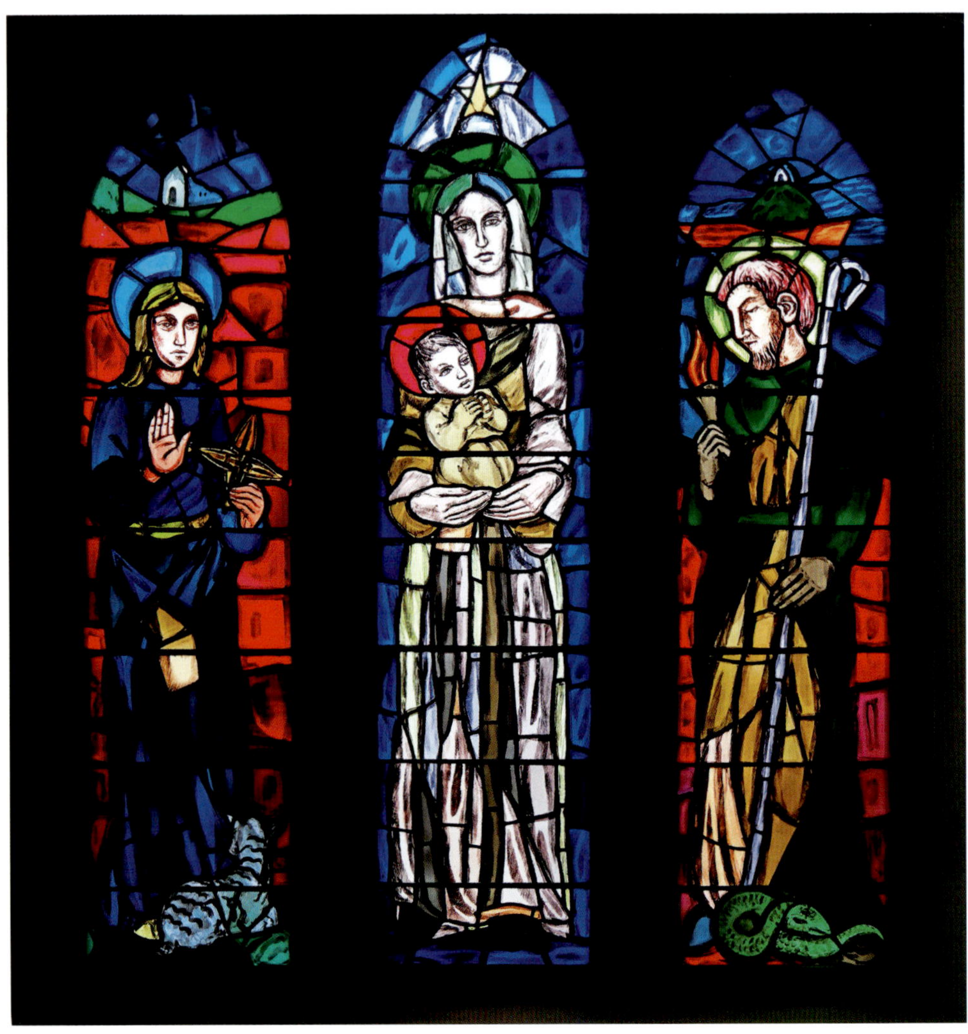

Evie Hone, *The Virgin and Child, St Brigid and St Patrick* (1954–5)

Senator Edward Maguire (1901–92), a well-known businessman, politician, amateur artist, and astute art collector.[5]

Hone started working on the window in 1953 and her friend and assistant Elizabeth Rivers drew up the cartoon.[6] Iconographically it is a fairly straightforward window to read with a few exceptions – the little church above St Brigid does not resemble St Brigid's cathedral, Kildare, as one might expect, so it may depict a church (or ruin?)

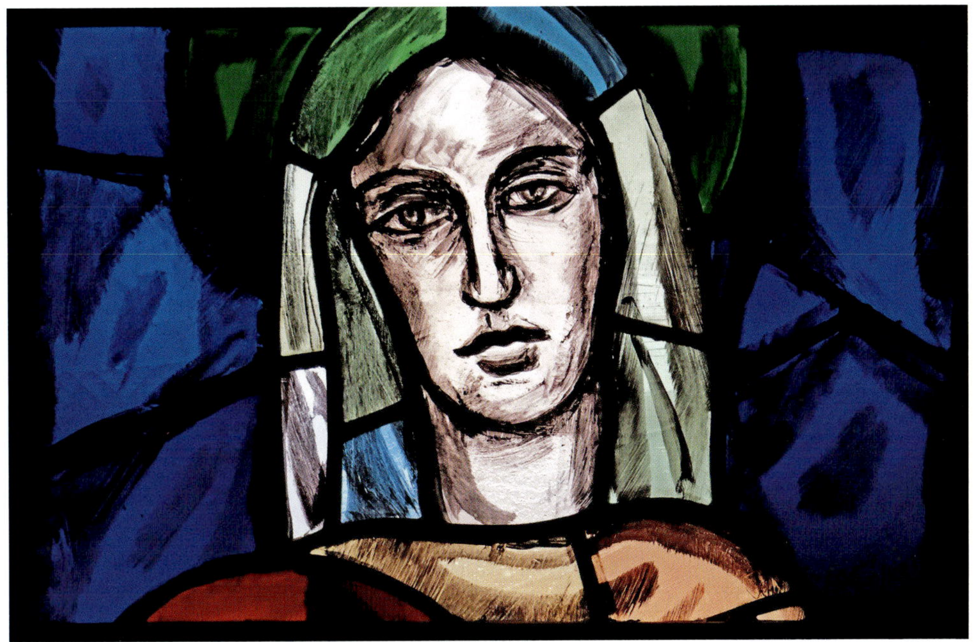

Evie Hone, detail of Mary from *The Virgin and Child, St Brigid and St Patrick* (1954–5)

elsewhere, or perhaps is a generic church to represent the many Brigid founded. In the opposite light St Patrick carries the flame to light the Paschal fire on Slane, and above him is not the hill at Slane as one might assume but what appears to be Croagh Patrick with its little chapel and in the distance Clew Bay.[7]

The Virgin and Child, with Saints Patrick and Brigid was originally installed in the window in the north aisle nearest the side altar dedicated to St Anne but some years later a decision was made to relocate it – presumably because an adjacent building was limiting the illumination of Hone's window – to the far end of St Anne's aisle which benefits from increased natural light. The window it was moved to is of identical proportions in all respects except that the two side lights are somewhat taller; consequently it was necessary to add more glass, mainly sky, to the apex of Hone's side lights and this was done with skill and sensitivity.[8]

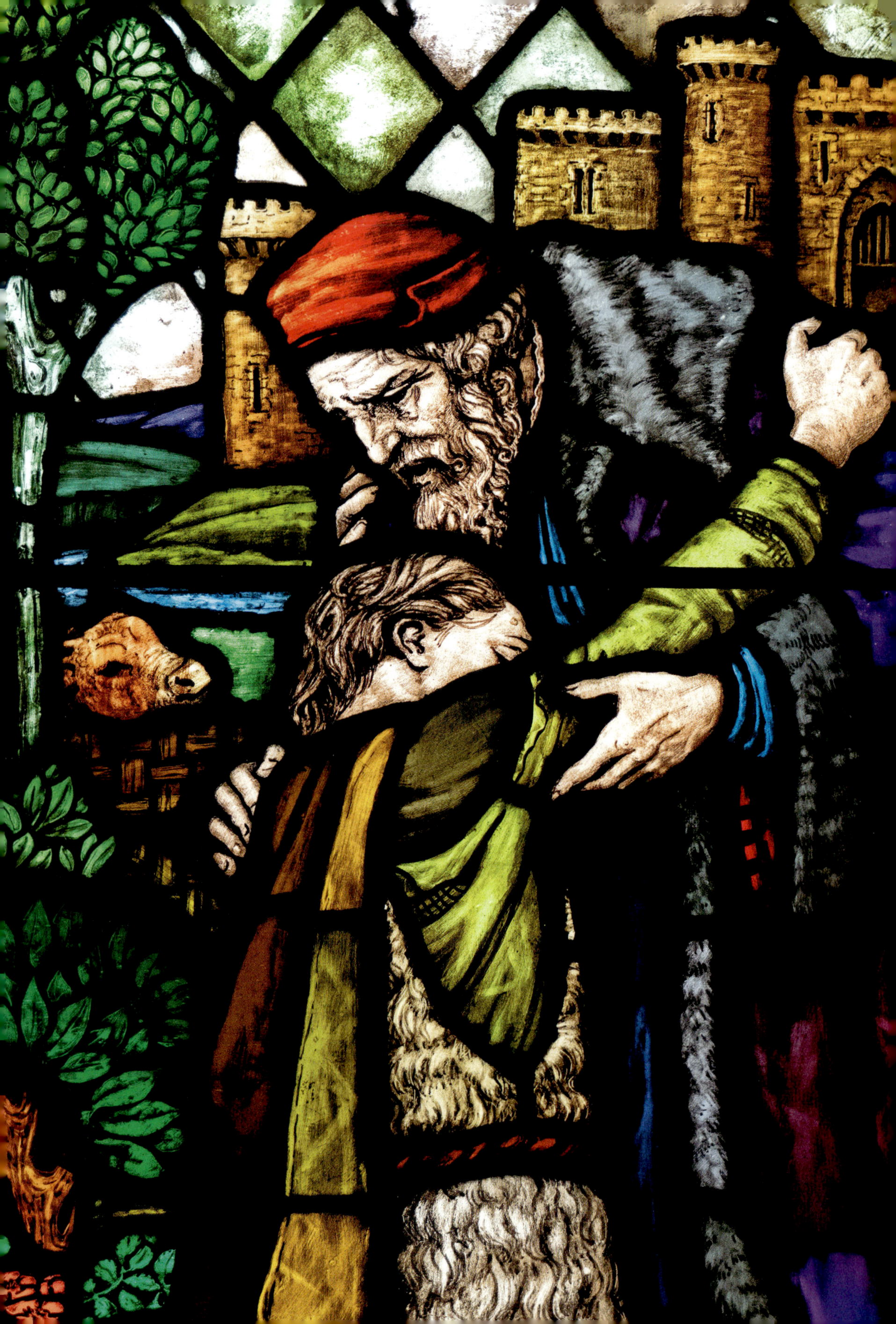

CARRICKMINES

Tullow church (C of I)

Brighton Road, D18 RF79

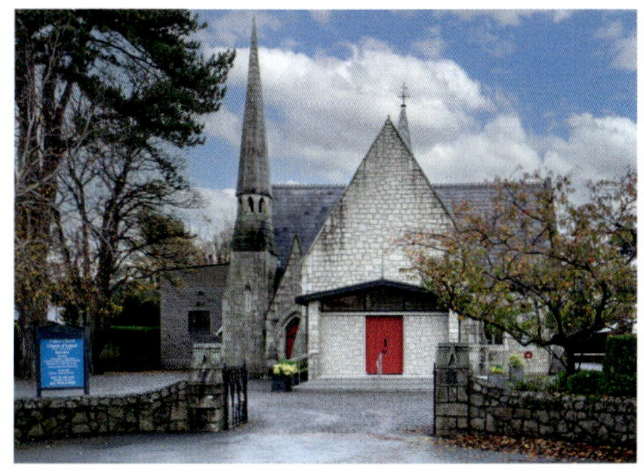

Located on Brighton Road, Carrickmines, and set in landscaped grounds approached through handsome granite ashlar entrance piers, Tullow (or Tully) church was designed in 1862 by Welland & Gillespie, architects to the Ecclesiastical Commissioners. In 1904 J.J. Fuller enlarged and re-oriented the structure so that the existing nave became the transepts and consequently the 'liturgical east' window above the altar is now north-facing. The exterior of the building is composed of granite rubble offset by silver-grey dressings with a slender polygonal spire and the bright interior features a timber-panelled, scissor-brace truss roof. A new entrance front for the church was created in 1964.

(opposite) Beatrice Elvery, detail of *The Good Samaritan and the Prodigal Son* (1908)

OF THE SIX STAINED GLASS windows in Tullow church, five are by An Túr Gloine artists, two windows by Beatrice Elvery and three by Catherine O'Brien. While O'Brien joined An Túr Gloine as a stained glass artist in 1903, when Sarah Purser invited twenty-one-year-old Beatrice Elvery to An Túr Gloine the following year it was not initially as a stained glass artist but to avail of a small corrugated iron studio adjacent to the studio where she could make busts; this she did for some time, and it seems that during this period she made a plaster cast for a bronze art nouveau-inspired lectern for Tullow church. By the end of 1904 Purser had encouraged Elvery to attend A.E. Child's part-time stained glass classes and start working in stained glass at An Túr Gloine as 'orders were pouring in'. In 1905, in addition to creating windows, Elvery designed an oak prie-dieu with matching bench seat for Tullow church,[1] both of which feature bas-relief panels of fruit and foliage and share similarities with the type of nature-inspired designs that A.E. Child, influenced by his mentor Christopher Whall, favoured in his windows.

Following the death of one of the parishioners, James Mayne in 1907, his widow and daughter sought to erect a stained glass window to his memory. His widow, Alice, was an amateur painter who had studied at the Académie Julian, as had Sarah Purser, and the Maynes and Elverys would have known each other through church activities so it is easy to see why Beatrice Elvery was asked to undertake the 2-light window. It depicts two popular parables, both from the gospel of St Luke, *The Good Samaritan* and *The Prodigal Son*. Although all the figures are male, Beatrice Elvery's artistic younger sister Dorothy posed for some of them and her youngest sister, Marjorie, was the model for the angel in the cinquefoil above the lights.[2] Elvery has cleverly created visual links between the two parables, in both cases the bearded old men – who appear to have near identical features – provide physical and emotional support for a vulnerable or reckless youth, with beautifully drawn hands featuring prominently to convey connection, care and compassion. In the background of both lights are cities or buildings; on the left is Jerusalem where the Samaritan came from, and on the right the castle from which the father emerged to embrace his errant son. The Gothicized canopies above each light evoke a certain medievalism and on close inspection one can see tiny mice carved on the capitals, reminiscent of the

Catherine O'Brien, detail of soldiers from bottom panel of *Christ in the Home of Martha and Mary* (top) *and Faithful Warrior* (bottom) (1917)

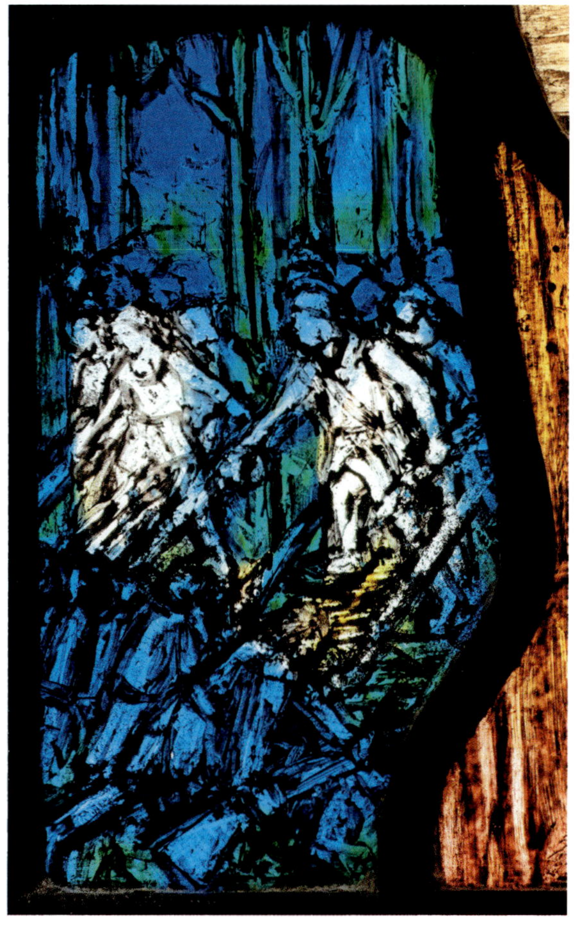

playful mice and other animals which feature on the windows of Dublin's Kildare Street Club, a building Elvery would surely have been familiar with due to its proximity to the School of Art. The diamond-shaped quarries in the background of the two scenes are likely to have come from one of the bottle factories at Ringsend; although An Túr Gloine imported most of their glass from England, as did the other Irish studios, they experimented with using local glass but the range of colours available was severely limited. Beatrice Elvery's window was dedicated on 8 March 1908, along with a new reredos and arcading by her friend and fellow parishioner Richard Caulfeild Orpen (brother of artist William) and an embroidered poplin altar cover by the Dun Emer Industries.[3]

The church's entrance porch features a slim lancet window signed 'K. O'B. 1917' which was relocated from the original porch in the mid-1960s. It features two panels of different sizes of unrelated subjects set within a background of abstract glass. It appears that one or probably both of the panels were made in 1917, though Miss O'Brien's records indicate that she did not actually make the window to contain them until 1959.[4] It is possible that the panels were made for exhibitions or as samples to show prospective patrons when they visited An Túr Gloine. The

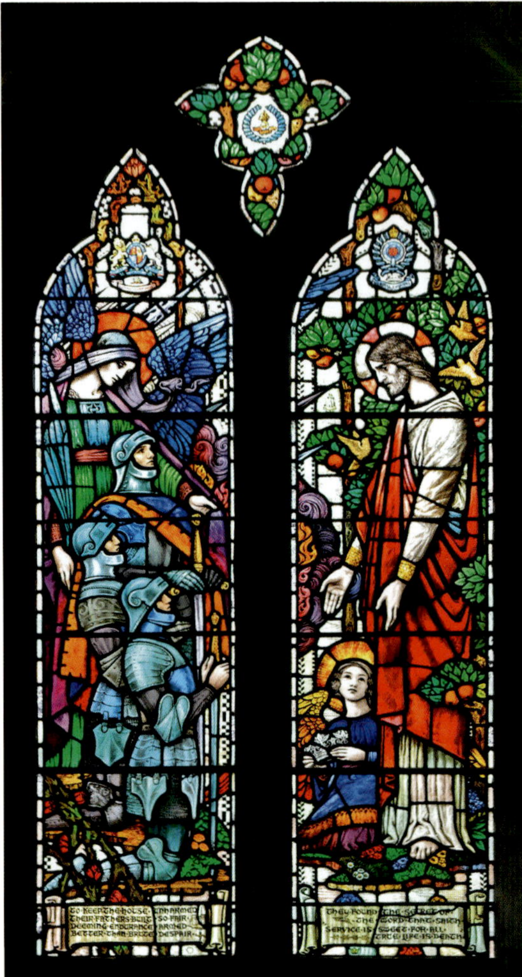

Beatrice Elvery, *Crown of Life* (1919–20)

smaller top panel depicts *Christ in the Home of Martha and Mary* and the larger panel has been titled *Faithful Warrior* and depicts Christ and the Holy Spirit, the latter in the form of a dove, welcoming a slain warrior. Although the golden-haired warrior wears armour and carries a sword, one's eyes are drawn to a vignette in the lower left foreground which depicts a company of soldiers marching through a forest at night, illuminated only by moonlight, while another group of soldiers huddle in the shadows, ready with their rifles. This chilling little scene has been created on a single piece of painted, stained and acided flashed blue glass.

In 1919 Beatrice Elvery designed a war memorial window for the church in memory of three local brothers who were personally known to her and who had died in the war, Charles, Arthur and George Wilson. In the intervening years since her earlier window Elvery had left An Túr Gloine, had married and moved to London, and it appears she returned to An Túr Gloine specially to make the window at the request of the bereaved father, William Wilson of Carrickmines House. The left light depicts three knights, one standing and two kneeling, wearing armour and large helmets which partially obscure two of their faces, but enough is visible to see that Elvery has attempted to portray

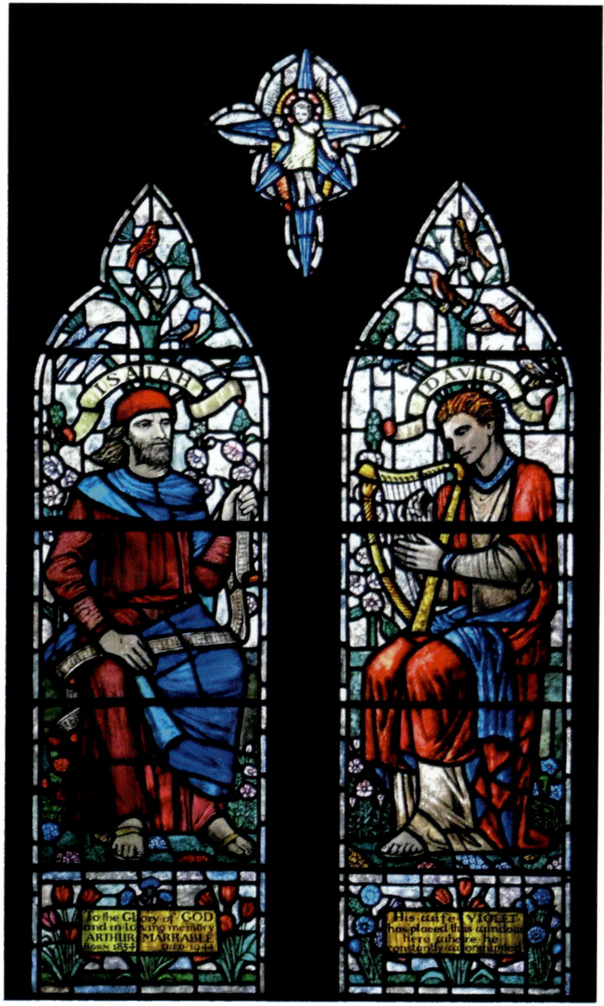

Catherine O'Brien, *David and Isaiah, with the Divine Child* (1945)

three idealized heroes with similar features. An elegant angel standing behind opens its wide purple cloak as if to receive the three brothers and remove them from the inhospitable landscape of thorny briars. Christ in the right light gestures to a young angel to hand him a crown to pass to them, a reward for making the ultimate sacrifice. Although the window is beautifully crafted it lacks the humanity that was so evident in her earlier window. Curiously the dead men's names are not included in the window but appear on a brass plaque beneath and instead the text at the base of the window features the middle stanza of Sir Henry Newbolt's poem *Farewell*, that honours the sacrifices of those who have fallen in battle. The window was dedicated on 28 March 1920.

It was twenty-five years before Tullow church received its next stained glass window. This time the deceased parishioner to be commemorated was Arthur Marrable, an active member of the congregation who read lessons and sang in the choir. By 1945 An Túr Gloine had been dissolved as a cooperative and only Catherine O'Brien remained working at the studio so when Mrs Violet Marrable came to place the order it obviously fell to O'Brien. The subject chosen was *David and Isaiah, with the Divine Child* (in the tracery) and the window cost £120. Arthur Marrable's love of music would seem to be reflected in the choice of King David playing his harp and in the upper sections of both lights O'Brien has included trees on which songbirds perch. A profusion of flowers fills the background and foreground of both lights which may suggest Mr Marrable had a love of gardening. Some of the flowers appear to be violets, acknowledging his widow's name. Although the quality of the drawing may lack finesse, such as the hands and feet, O'Brien manages to instil a certain charm.

In 1958 Catherine O'Brien, aged 77, began work on her final large window which would be a 4-light with tracery for Tullow church. At this stage she was sharing An Túr Gloine with the young English artist, Patrick Pollen. A disastrous fire broke out that October; fortuitously a few days previously O'Brien had taken down the cartoons for her Tullow window and they were only slightly damaged, however the two lights of the window that she had already completed were destroyed. The wooden studio was damaged beyond repair so a decision was taken to rebuild a larger studio in concrete and steel, which took some months, and by June 1959 the *Irish Times* reported that the glass had been cut for three of the lights for O'Brien's Tullow window and she was beginning to paint it in advance of firing.[5] Each of the lights depicts a separate scene, *The Annunciation, The Nativity, The Crucifixion,* and *Our Lord Appearing to St Mary Magdalene*. The tracery features three roundels depicting symbols representing the Trinity: *Dove, Hand of God the Father,* and *Lamb of God*. It appears that while O'Brien was progressing with making the four lights some members of the select vestry were exercised by the placement of the roundel featuring God the Father's hand and queried if it should become the top roundel, taking the place of the Holy Spirit; her views were sought as was the opinion of the archbishop of Dublin, George Otto Simms. The outcome is that while the Holy Spirit remained in the uppermost roundel, the visual treatment of the hand is totally different to the way it appears in O'Brien's original ink and watercolour sketch design.[6]

As the window is north-facing O'Brien included plenty of pale quarries. Of this window the art critic (later director of the National Gallery), James White, noted that 'Miss O'Brien has always been distinguished for the clear manner of her portrayal. At the same time she respects the values of colour in glass. Her present work is

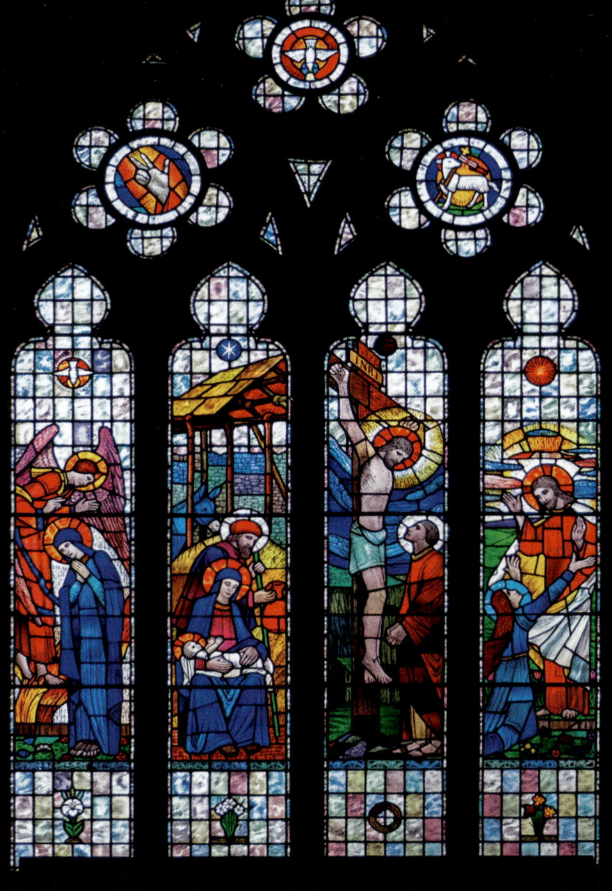

Catherine O'Brien, *The Annunciation, The Nativity, The Crucifixion, and Our Lord Appearing to St Mary Magdalene* (1958–9)

vivid in reds, blues and purples and yet there is an amount of daylight penetrating through the surrounding glass, mottled lightly in mauves and blues. No doubt the artist had to accommodate her work to the needs of the church.'[7]

Catherine O'Brien's window was paid for by Tullow's parishioners and was erected in memory of former worshipers. The cost, which included two opus sectile mosaic inscription plaques by the artist, and the small porch window (referred to above), was £557 11*s*. 0*d*. The window and the porch window were dedicated by Archbishop Simms on All Saints Day, 1 November 1959.

A final window, *Jesus among the Children*, was made by Alan Tomlin of the Irish Stained Glass studio in 1995. It was erected in memory of a parishioner, Mrs Florence Parsons, by her family and they supplied the artist with a photograph of a picture that belonged to the deceased for his use as visual reference.[8]

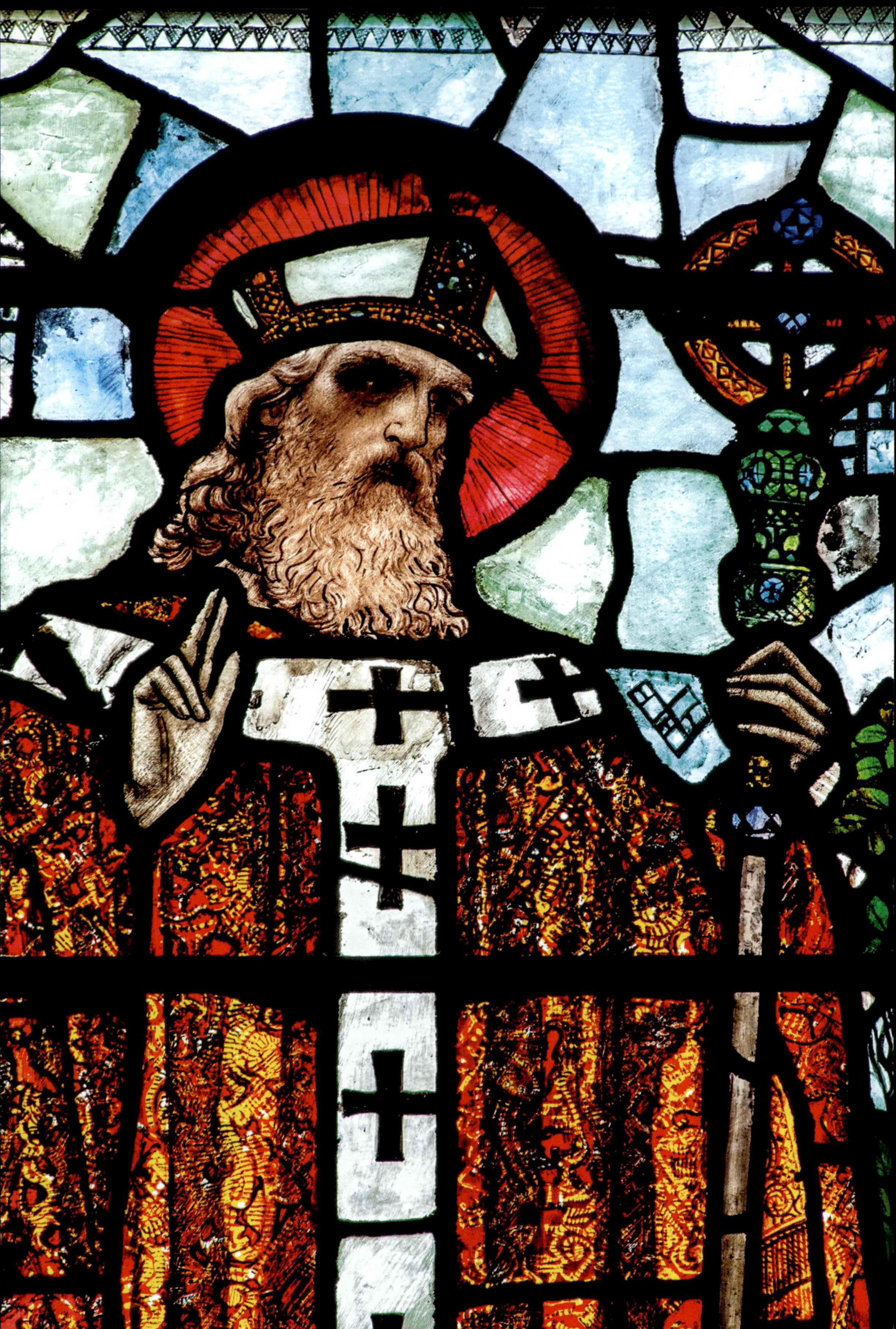

DONNYBROOK

Sacred Heart church (RC)

Stillorgan Road, D04 HW82

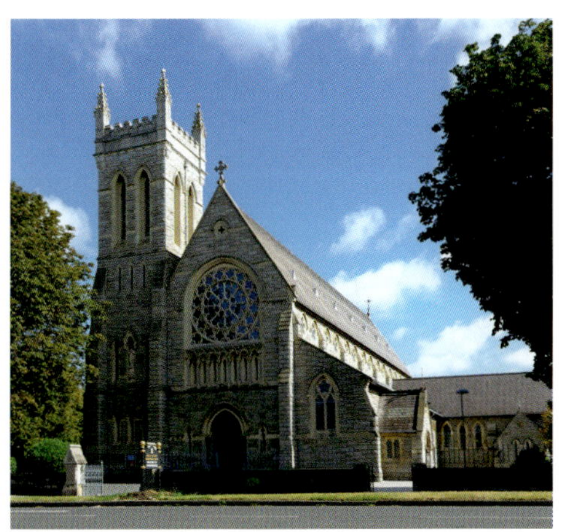

Originally conceived by octogenarian architect Patrick Byrne, the design and construction was taken over by Pugin and Ashlin and the foundation stone laid in 1863. Sacred Heart church, which was designed in the early French Gothic manner, was constructed of granite with Bath stone dressings. It never got its intended spire due to financial reasons and instead pinnacles were added to the tower *c.*1912. The church was significantly and seamlessly extended in 1936 with the addition of transepts, a new baptistry and a mortuary chapel.

(opposite) Michael Healy, detail of *St Patrick with Saints Eithne and Fidelma* (1914)

THE CHURCH'S STAINED GLASS windows that are of most artistic significance are a 2-light by Michael Healy, two lancets by Harry Clarke and a single lancet by William MacBride, all created between 1914 and 1924. There is also a 2-light attributed to William Dowling of Harry Clarke Studios made in 1946.

In 1914 a local Donnybrook resident, Roger Sweetman of Herbert Park, ordered a stained glass window for Sacred Heart church.[1] He had recently received a legacy and wished to mark his gratitude for life up to that point by gifting a window to his parish church.[2] Sarah Purser, unofficial manager at An Túr Gloine, was a friend of the Sweetman family so it was no surprise that he chose that studio, and it is most likely that it was Miss Purser who assigned Michael Healy to the job. The window selected to receive Healy's stained glass was in the original baptistry which has open access directly from the south-west corner of the nave so regular worshipers would have the benefit of viewing it, unlike many baptistries which are separate, closed-off spaces.

This was Healy's sixth time to date depicting Ireland's patron saint, and this is by far the most visually interesting of them as it features St Patrick baptizing Eithne and Fidelma, the two pagan daughters of King Laoghaire, by the stream of Lebach. The princesses have luxuriant Pre-Raphaelite-style hair, one flame coloured and one blonde,[3] and above their heads two doves fly upwards towards a richly jewelled crown, most likely representing the departing souls of the sisters, who after receiving the Eucharist, expired instantly.

In the cinquefoil panel above the two lights St Patrick holds aloft the Cross of Salvation and behind his head a circle of flames alludes to the paschal fire on the Hill of Slane. Kneeling at his feet in fear or supplication are two men from King Laoghaire's camp – a warrior with a spear and an elderly man with a scroll who is possibly a Celtic druid. Healy was so pleased with this cinquefoil panel that he made a second version that was exhibited and in due course was purchased by Charles Connick, the leading American arts and crafts stained glass artist of his day, and is now in the Cranbrook Academy of Art and Museum, Michigan.[4]

As with many of Healy's works, the delight is in the detail, sometimes not readily apparent, such as the scaly serpents in the two small spandrel-shaped pieces of tracery

Michael Healy, *St Patrick with Saints Eithne and Fidelma* (1914)

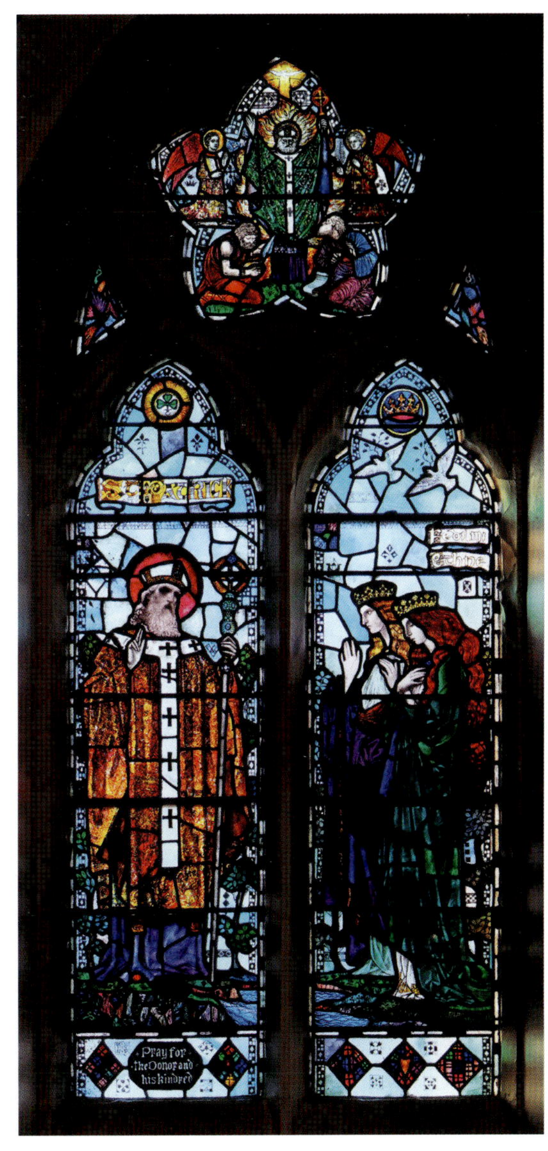

referencing St Patrick's reputation of ridding Ireland of snakes.[5]

Thomas McGreevy, Healy's friend of his later years (and later again, director of the National Gallery), was particularly impressed and moved by this window which he described as 'a masterpiece of religious art – in space, composition as well as in drawing, and colour and, as a matter of course since the artist was Michael Healy, in devotional feeling.'[6]

In 1923 two widows, a mother and daughter, Mrs Catherine Egan and Mrs May Angela Martin (née Egan), enquired about each commissioning a window by Harry Clarke; these would be erected in memory of their deceased husbands, wine merchant Edward Denis Egan (d.1907) of Merrion Square, and timber merchant Bernard John Algernon Cyril Martin (d.1916), formerly of Eglington Road, Donnybrook. Although the two men had been dead for some years and Mrs Martin since had departed the parish for a residence on St Stephen's Green, the fact that Donnybrook church had been finally consecrated in 1923 may have prompted the two women to order the memorial windows that year. However it would appear

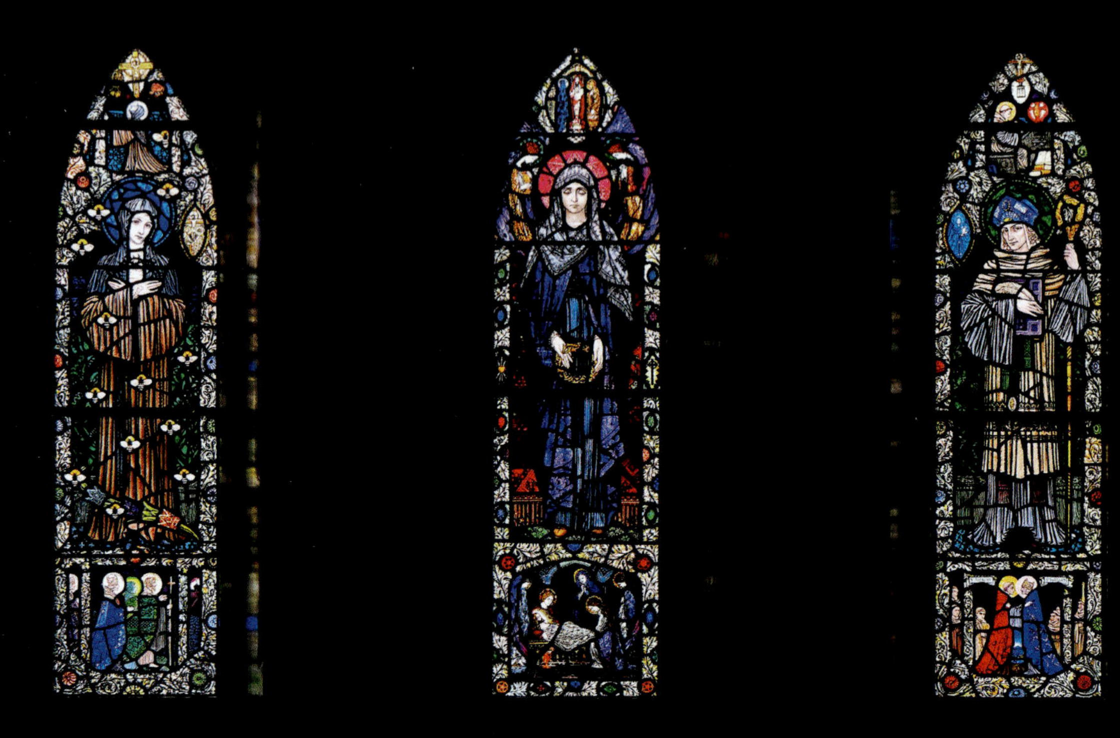

Harry Clarke, *St Rita* (1924), William MacBride, *Our Lady of Sorrows* (*c.*1924), Harry Clarke, *St Bernard* (1924)

that it was not until the following year that Harry Clarke actually attended to designing the two lancet windows, *St Rita* and *St Bernard*, and although they were initially conceived and designed by Clarke himself, they were not executed by him, but by his assistants under his close supervision.[7] By this stage Clarke was at the peak of his career, both stained glass and illustration, however, as Harry Clarke expert Nicola Gordon Bowe has observed, his health was beginning to deteriorate due to pressure of work, the death of his father, and the upheaval related to the physical reorganization of the studio and employment of additional artists.[8]

St Rita of Cascia was a fifteenth-century Italian who, following her husband's death, became an Augustinian nun. She was canonized in 1900 and is recognized as the patron saint of widows, and may be an apposite choice given the status of the donors. St Rita is most usually depicted carrying a large crucifix, sometimes holding a thorn (a symbol of her penance and stigmata), a rose, or bunch of roses. Clarke's depiction of St Rita is unusual; although she holds a crown of thorns close to her chest, the main visual feature is the thirteen large hovering bees which surround her. The choice of bees relates to an incident at her baptism when a swarm of bees was observed flying around the sleeping infant. Miraculously the bees peacefully entered and exited her mouth without causing her any discomfort or injury. Why Clarke has chosen to depict St Rita in this manner is not known but it may be that he wanted to reprise the striking visual effect of a swarm of bees which featured prominently in his celebrated *St Gobnait* window (1916) for the Honan chapel, University College Cork.[9]

The predella panel features four figures in profile – St Rita in green with arms outstretched, accompanied by her three patron saints whose names are helpfully inscribed on their halos, St Nicholas of Tolentino, St Augustine and St John the Baptist. The trio is depicted accompanying her to the monastery of St Mary Magdalene in Cascia (on the extreme right) where she remained sequestered until her death.

The subject of the companion window is *St Bernard of Clairvaux* who was a monk and mystic, and a major leader in the reformation of the Benedictine order through the nascent Cistercian order. Clarke has depicted him as a youthful abbot with a sensitive, enquiring expression, and clasping a bejewelled volume and plumed quill. The predella panel features St Bernard in later years embracing his close friend St Malachy, archbishop of Armagh, on the latter's arrival in Clairvaux with an expanse of choppy sea in the background indicating the distance he has travelled. Clarke's depiction possibly represents Malachy's final visit to Clairvaux in 1148 when he was en route to Rome but fell ill and died in Bernard's arms. In due course Bernard would later write his friend's biography and the two saints were buried in adjacent tombs at Clairvaux.

The principal figures in both windows are fairly subdued in terms of colour due to the fact that both St Rita and St Bernard are dressed in their respective Augustinian and Cistercian habits. Noteworthy is the lively art nouveau-influenced borders composed of unfurling leaves and tendrils enlivened with occasional brightly coloured abstract flowers made of cullets.

The cost of the two memorial windows was £45 10*d.* 0*s.* each with bills sent by Walter Clarke, Harry's brother and manager of the studio, to both Mrs Egan and Mrs Martin in June 1924. However the story did not end there as Catherine Egan promptly decided to order a third window; this was probably because each bay in the nave comprises three lancets and there must have been a realization that a third window composed of the existing basic coloured glass would strike a jarring note beside the new pair of jewel-like windows. Walter replied to Catherine Egan's enquiry stating that it would be impossible for the studio to complete a third window in under twelve months 'as there are so many orders here before it, and they of course must be taken in rotation.'[10] This left the mother and daughter in a dilemma, to wait their turn or seek another artist, and they pursued the latter course of action and approached William MacBride, probably at Harry's or Walter's recommendation. MacBride had trained under A.E. Child at the School of Art and worked at Clarke's for several years before departing for The Craftworkers Ltd (sometimes referred to as the Craftworkers Guild) on Harcourt Street in 1918 or 1919.

It seems likely that when MacBride agreed to create a third window in a manner to harmonize with Harry Clarke's windows, a decision was made that it should be placed in the centre with Clarke's *St Rita* and *St Bernard* flanking it. The subject of MacBride's window was *Our Lady of Sorrows*, no doubt chosen as the donors were two grieving widows.[11] In terms of stylistically integrating his window with the other two, MacBride achieved an excellent outcome, so much so that some viewers have been under the misapprehension that all three were designed by Clarke. MacBride depicted Our Lady in the period immediately after Christ's crucifixion with eyes downcast, holding his crown of thorns. Slightly taller than *St Rita* and *St Bernard*, her robes are richly coloured in shades of deep purple. MacBride has included two subordinate narrative scenes, in the apex and at the base, which represent two of the Seven Dolours (or Seven Sorrows) of Our Lady; the apex depicts the *First Dolour, The Presentation in the Temple*, and the predella panel at the base depicts the *Seventh Dolour, The Burial of Jesus*. MacBride took great care in his attention to detail throughout the window, not only in the painting of the figures, but also with the less important aspects such as the border which comprises similar leaves to Clarke's but executed with greater precision. Despite the ease with which *Our Lady of Sorrows* harmonizes

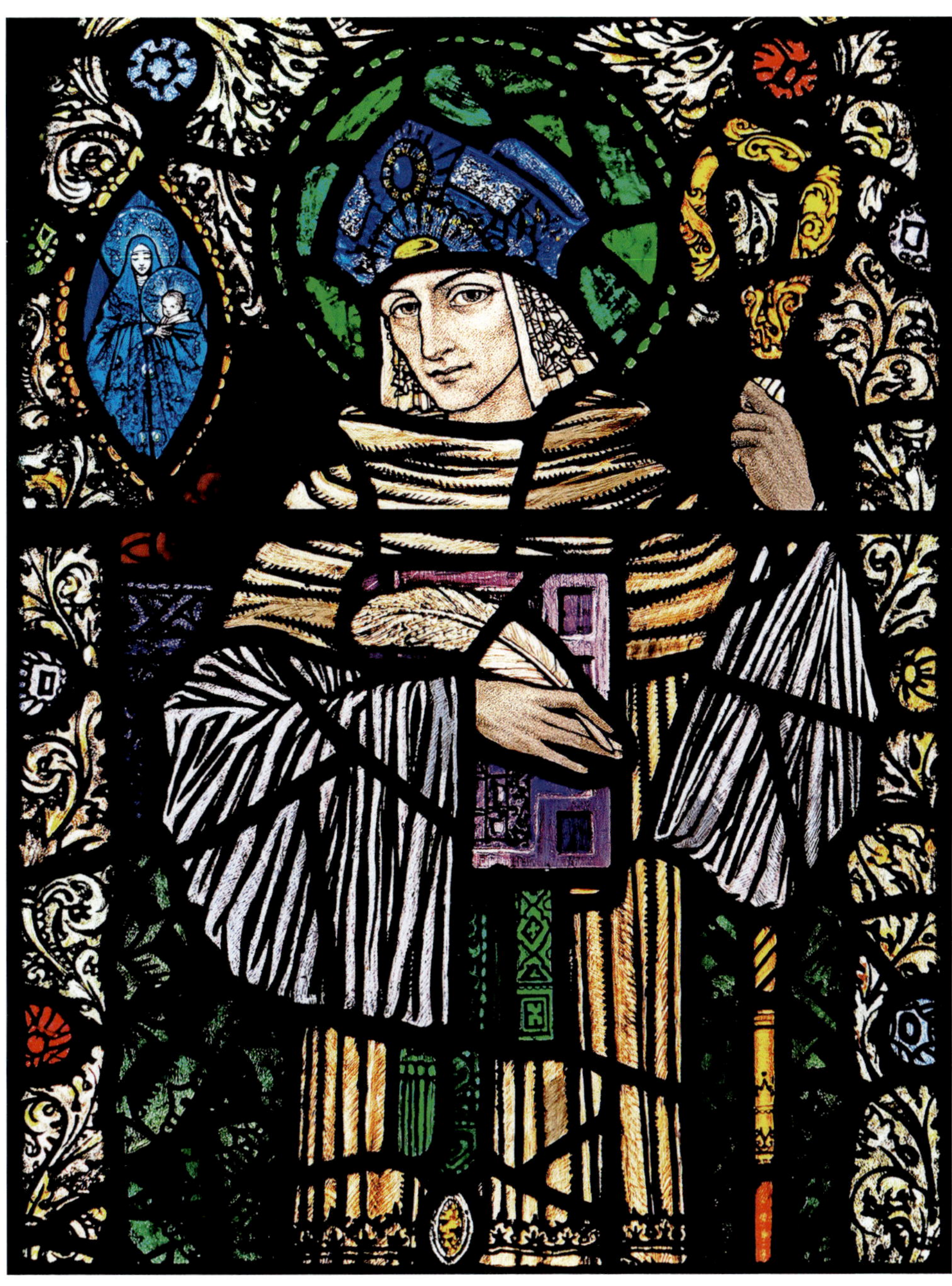

Harry Clarke, detail of *St Bernard* (1924)

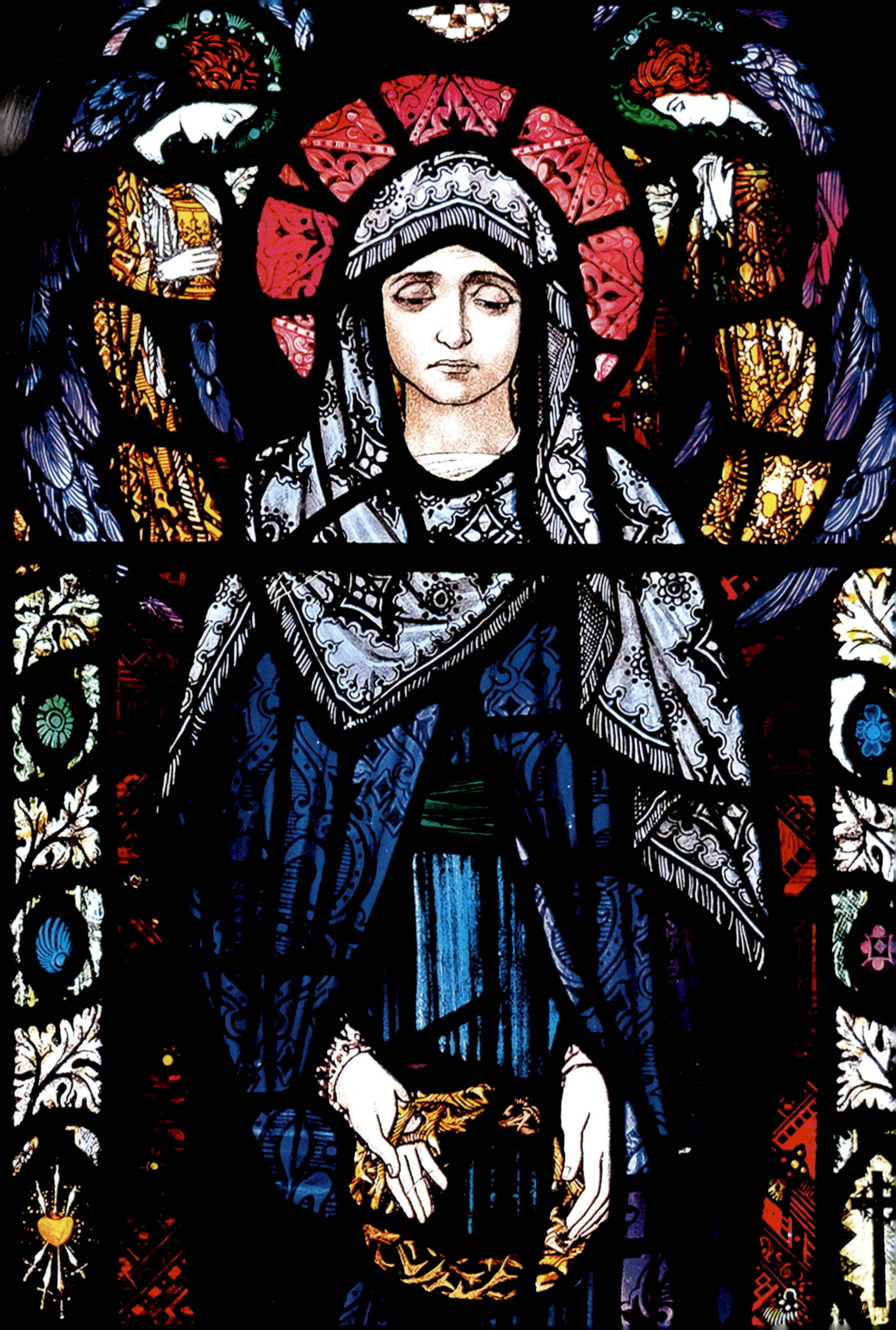

with *St Rita* and *St Bernard*, on close inspection it is clear that MacBride did not seek to imitate Clarke's signature style of gaunt, ascetic figures with doe-eyed features and slender fingers but opted for a more conventional representation.

In 1946 a final window was commissioned for the church, a 2-light depicting *The Baptism of Our Lord* which was ordered by the parish priest, Monsignor Daniel Moloney,[12] for the new baptistry (now the parish repository), part of the extension he had overseen in the mid-1930s. Previously Canon Moloney had been curate in the parish when the windows by Healy, Clarke and MacBride were commissioned. By now both Michael Healy and Harry Clarke were deceased and it appears that William MacBride had ceased working in stained glass. Monsignor Moloney decided to approach Harry Clarke Stained Glass Ltd which continued to trade successfully under Clarke's name following his death in 1931. The manager and principal artist of the studio at this stage was William Dowling; he had trained directly under Clarke and it is understood that he designed *The Baptism of Our Lord*. Sadly his interpretation of the scene is conventional and uninspiring. It is best viewed in early morning light.

(opposite) William MacBride, detail of *Our Lady of Sorrows* (*c*.1924)

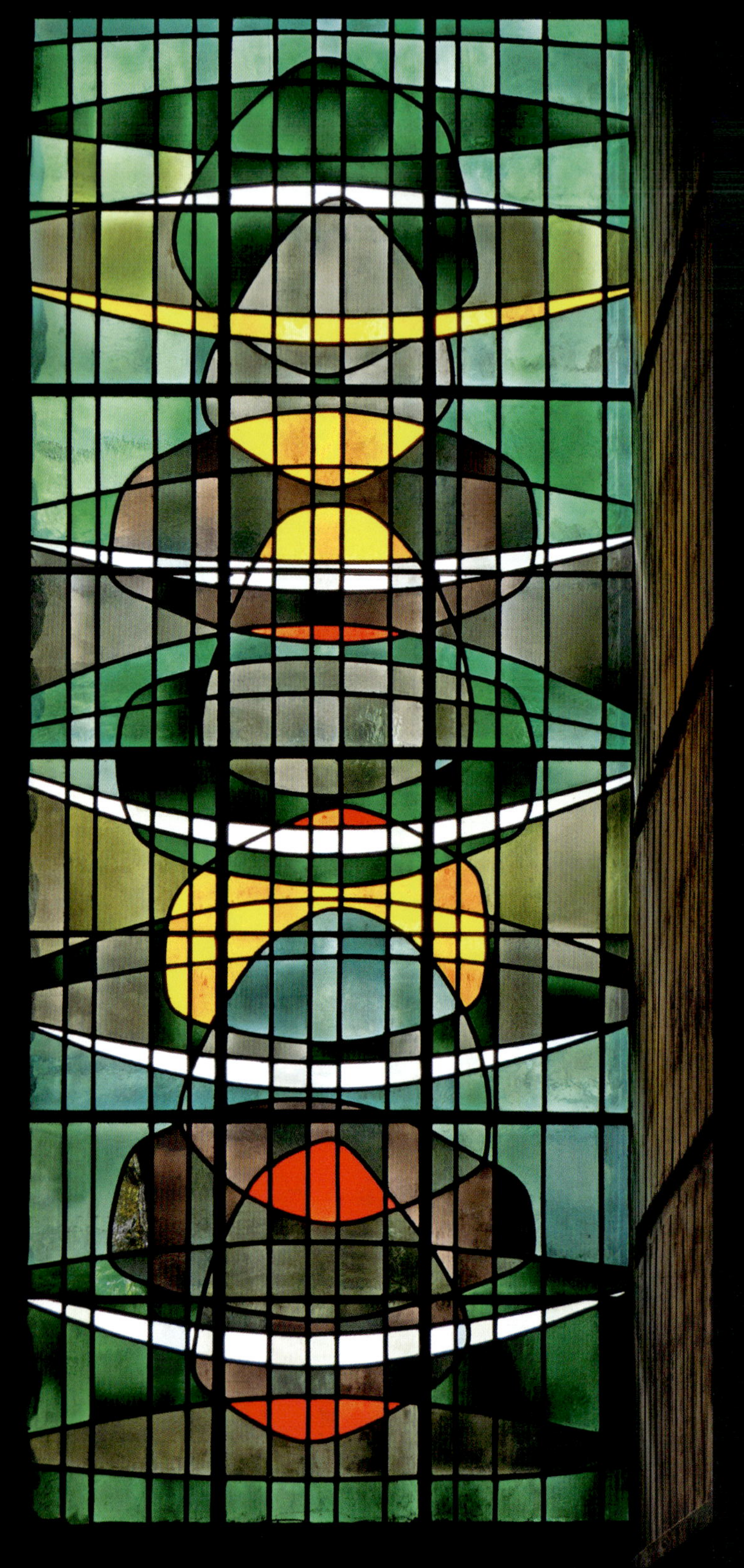

DÚN LAOGHAIRE

Dún Laoghaire has several churches, or former churches, containing interesting stained glass – Christ Church C of I with a window by A.E. Child, and the former Mariners' church (now National Maritime Museum) that houses Peadar Lamb's Dún Laoghaire Diptych, *but the two churches with the best collections of stained glass are St Michael's and the Presbyterian church, discussed below.*

St Michael's church (RC)

Marine Road, A96 RC98

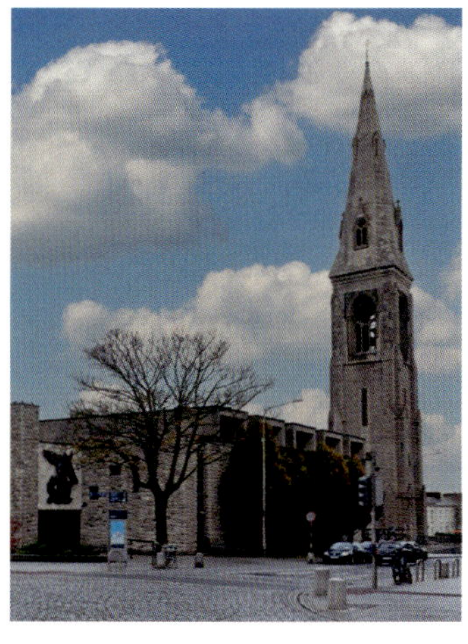

St Michael's church has the distinction of being Dublin's most brutalist church, though the use of rock-faced granite on the two principal elevations tends somewhat to soften the external appearance. It was designed by Pearse McKenna and colleagues between 1968 and 1973 to replace a nineteenth-century church on the same site. The adjacent fine four-stage tower with spire is all that remains of the original structure and it still functions as a landmark and seamark, soaring above the modern squat successor to the original Gothic-style church.

(opposite) Murphy-Devitt Studios, *Abstract* (1971–3), St Michael's church

When a fire broke out in the organ gallery of the original St Michael's in July 1965 it rapidly spread through the building destroying the interior and all the original stained glass windows; among those which are known to have perished are several from Clarke's studio – a 2-light, *St Peter and St Paul*, made in 1906 when the studio was known as Joshua Clarke & Sons (though Harry Clarke and his brother were then still teenagers), and four 2-lights made after the studio's name had changed to Harry Clarke Stained Glass Ltd. These were made subsequent to Harry Clarke's death in 1931 and date to 1932–7; one is attributed to William Dowling, *Archangel Michael and St Andrew*, and another thought to have been designed by either Richard King or William Dowling, *The Sacred Heart of Jesus and Pope Pius XI*.[1]

The devastation of the fire was so severe and so immediately apparent that the archbishop of Dublin, Dr McQuaid, called on the 85-year-old parish priest, Monsignor Patrick Boylan, the same afternoon with a donation of £1,000 towards a new church.[2] The short-term solution was a temporary church on the site of the parochial hall, which was designed by Pearse McKenna who had grown up in the parish. He was assisted by two colleagues, Sean Rothery and Naish O'Dowd, and this same team led by McKenna designed the permanent replacement church that would present a radical architectural addition to Dun Laoghaire's fundamentally Victorian core.

McKenna recognized that a new-build church, with a different orientation to the original church in order to overcome the narrowness of the site, would afford him the opportunity to build a structure that effectively responded to the liturgical directives of Vatican II.[3] Reflecting on the completed interior, McKenna felt that it relied for its effect on 'the simplicity of the space created and the dignity of the proportions. The austerity of slender columns, great beams and enclosing screen walls, all in naturally finished concrete is relieved by delicate stained glass windows and recessed tinted roof lights ...' Despite the intended restraint, there is also an element of theatre with the substantial raised, stage-like sanctuary plinth that assertively projects forward so that it is surrounded by the rows of pews on three sides. There are also deep square shafts in the concrete ceiling which admit natural daylight – though the source remains invisible – and which have the effect of

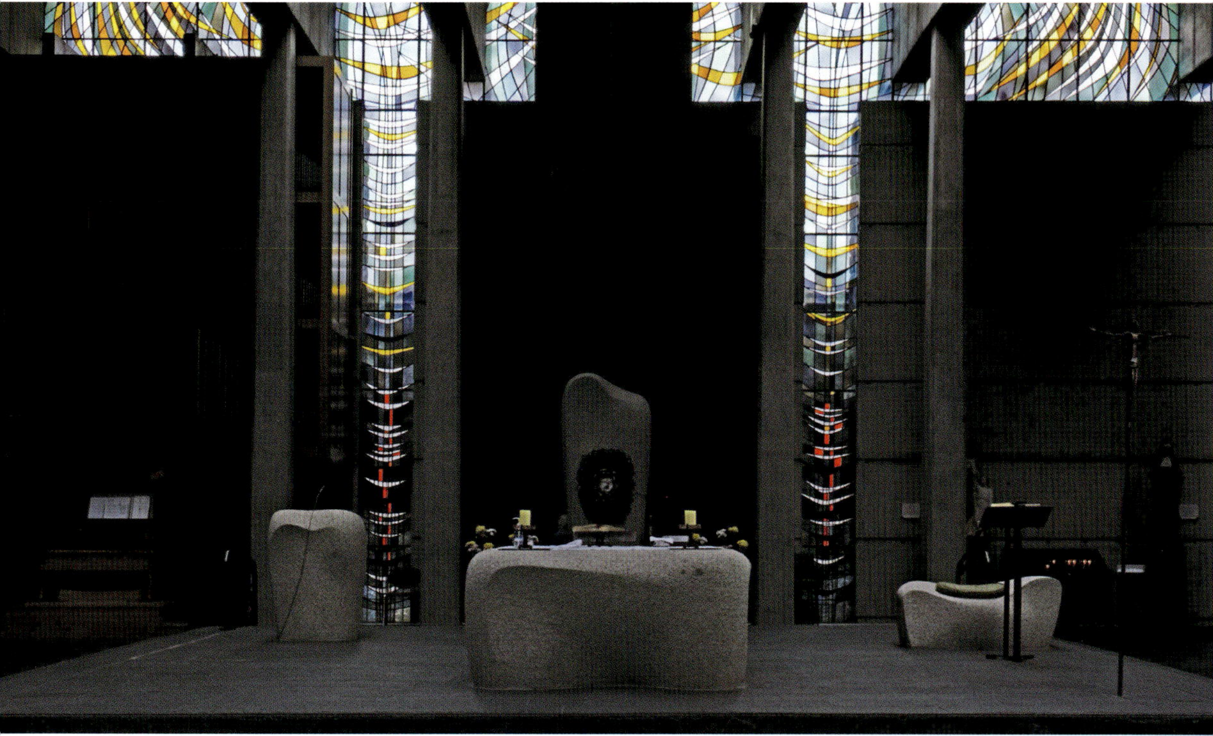

Murphy-Devitt Studios, *Abstract Sanctuary Windows* (1971–3) with altar furniture by Michael Biggs, St Michael's church

spotlighting the altar, the tabernacle and the baptistry. A continuous linear stained glass window at the point where the walls meet the ceiling appears to make the latter float, defying its obvious weight, and adding additional drama.

McKenna stressed that 'the works of art which embellish [St Michael's] church are not "post factum" applied decoration but are integral parts of the function of the building conceived organically with the overall design' and he noted that the essentially abstract stained glass by Murphy-Devitt Studios was 'a big factor in creating the atmosphere of the environment'.[4] McKenna had previously commissioned stained glass from Johnny Murphy, initially a set of Stations of the Cross in 1957 (a year before the formal foundation of Murphy-Devitt Studios) for a cathedral in Nigeria.[5] The commission for the windows in St Michael's was particularly valued by Johnny Murphy and Des Devitt as sizable orders were becoming a rarity by the

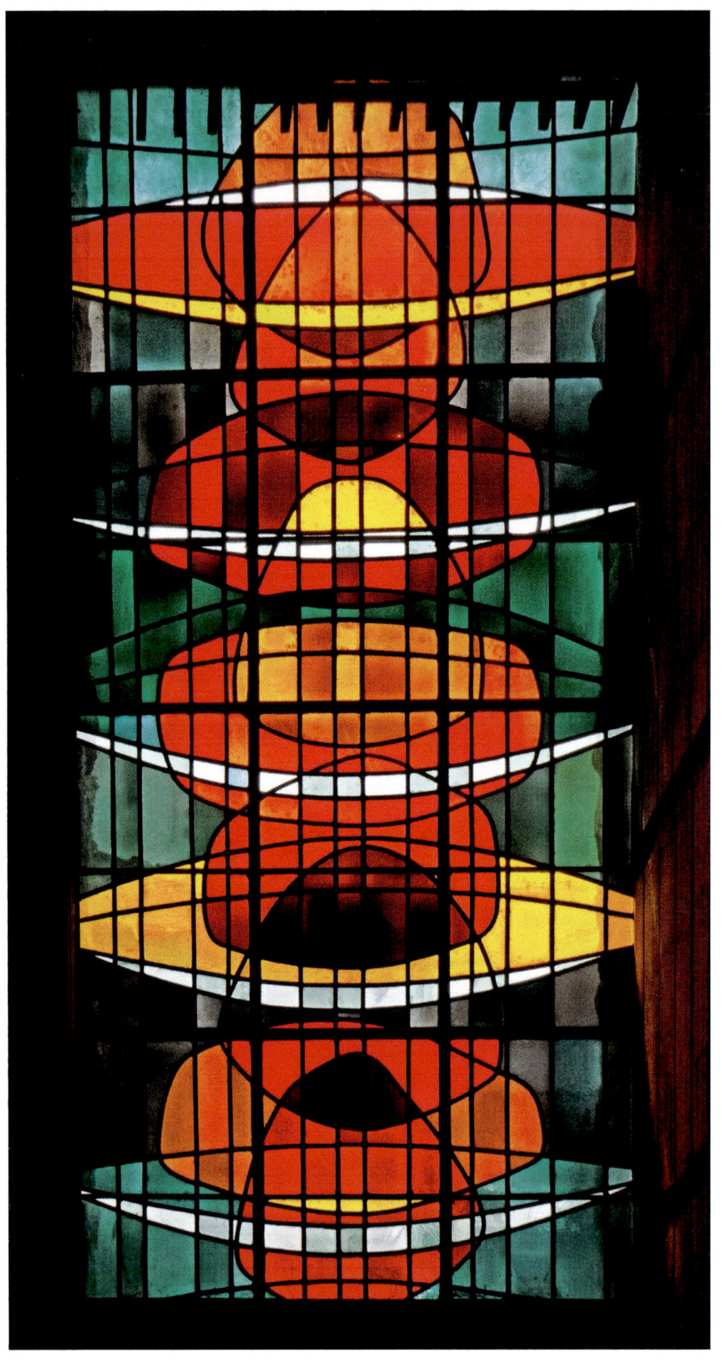

Murphy-Devitt Studios, *Abstract* (1971–3), St Michael's church

late 1960s, and in fact this would be the studio's last big job. Murphy-Devitt supplied their estimate (£7,581) in April 1969 and were making the windows by summer 1971.[6]

It is important to note that Murphy-Devitt's stained glass in St Michael's church is not 'stained' or painted as such, it derives its impact and beauty from the skilful design of the leadlines, from using only the best quality mouth-blown glass, and from the sensitive selection of colours. As with all of the windows created at Murphy-Devitt Studios, but particularly the ones which contain no painted elements, the role of master glazier, Des Devitt, was key. He and his small team would achieve, without any seeming effort, organic, fluid leadlines – actual straight lines rarely feature in any Murphy-Devitt windows – which were entirely true to Johnny Murphy's vision. All the glass in St Michael's was sourced in France.[7]

While Murphy-Devitt's stained glass in St Michael's will not readily appear to be either representational or symbolic to the majority of the church's visitors, McKenna stated that 'the windows symbolized the tree of life intertwined in the fabric of the building.'[8] The subject of the tree of life first appears in *Genesis* as the source of eternal life in the Garden of Eden. In the windows designed by Johnny Murphy, as the notional leaves and branches reach the top of the tall and narrow windows they join the horizontal band of glazing at ceiling level; at this point the shapes begin to change direction and, some at least, appear to metamorphose into flocks of wide-winged birds in flight, perhaps a reference to the many seabirds that frequent Dún Laoghaire's coastal location.[9] Recalling the job in 2003, Des Devitt said that 'the abstract design [of the windows] relates to the soaring spirit.'[10]

Johnny Murphy also designed four rectangular windows for St Michael's; two glowing in intense shades of red, orange and yellow, and two in paler tones with watery greys and greens predominating. These four windows appear to be entirely abstract, each featuring large overlapping rounded forms whose shapes were perhaps devised by Johnny Murphy to reference the granite altar, ambo, seat and baptismal font which are equally organic in appearance and are the work of distinguished sculptor (and typographer), Michael Biggs.

Murphy-Devitt Studios also made two tall, thin floor-to-ceiling windows in *dalle de verre* for St Michael's church; one for the main entrance lobby on Marine Road and one for the smaller south-facing lobby. In this instance the rectangular-shaped

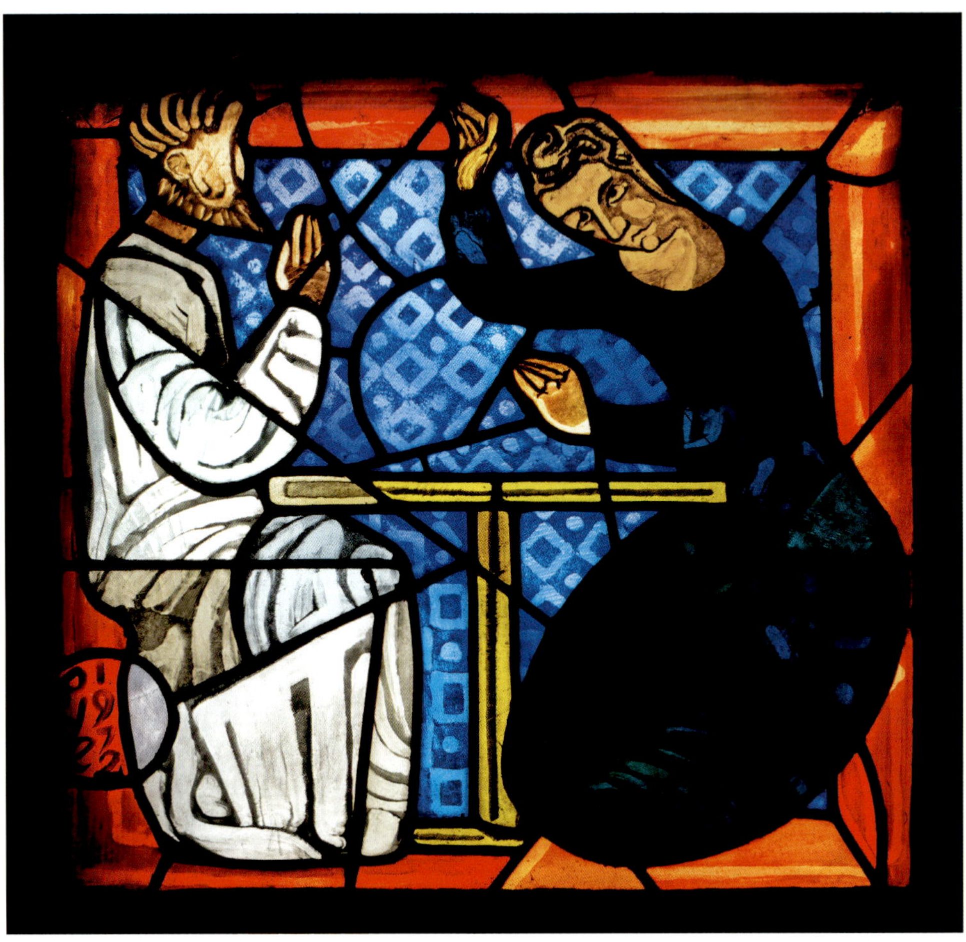

Patrick Pye, *Our Lady Teaching St John* (1972), St Michael's church

pieces of one inch thick French 'antique' glass were spalled (chipped or faceted) to give them a more textured finish – and refract more light – and then laid out in a regimented manner which echoes the blocks of granite of the church's exterior. Around the same time as work on St Michael's was underway, Pearse McKenna commissioned Murphy-Devitt Studios to create a large wall of abstract *dalle de verre* for a church he was designing in Sligo though the composition of the resin mixture in that instance was flawed and in time it became structurally unsound and had to be demolished; happily no such technical issues arose in St Michael's.[11]

In addition to Murphy-Devitt Studio's significant stained glass contribution, Pearse McKenna also commissioned four relatively small figurative windows from Patrick Pye. These windows comprise a grouping of three which are deeply recessed in the thick concrete of the north wall, all depicting themes relating to the Virgin Mary, and separately, a slim horizontal window (12.6in. x 39in.), *The Baptism of Christ*, for the baptistry. Pye submitted his sketch designs for the windows to Pearse McKenna in December 1969 with his proposed fee (£575), though the windows were not made until 1972 at Pye's little studio in Piperstown at the foot of the Dublin mountains.

Pye's Marian-themed windows depict *The Annunciation, Our Lady Attending to the Infant Jesus*, and *Our Lady Teaching St John*. Pye was a spiritual individual with an interest in theology and was inspired by many diverse artists and movements. His treatment of themes in his art, whether in paintings, etchings or stained glass, is often a deeply personal take on the subjects and not always readily apparent to the viewer.

All three of the Marian-themed windows dispense with conventional realism and perspective. Pye told McKenna in advance that 'what I am aiming for is Radiant domesticity with a capital R!'[12] Three decades after making them he recalled his intentions, 'The first window is *The Annunciation*, the theme of most theological weight in the series. The disposition of the angel's entry into the picture may be awkward but was arrived at to emphasize the inwardness of Our Lady's assent. He seems to come from above and behind, interrupting her winding of some wool. The setting is humble domesticity.' Of the *Virgin and Child* he wrote, 'The Madonna lies on a sofa attending the Child. Again an atmosphere of simple and absorbed domesticity.' His intention for the third window, *Our Lady Teaching St John*, takes place in John's house and 'is the most hieratic of the windows. Here Our Lady is our teacher (our first teacher) and John the humble servant. What is our disposition to the extraordinary grace that the Father has bestowed on us in the Son.'[13]

Pye's fourth window, *The Baptism of Christ*, is located in the north wall of the large sunken baptistry. Whereas the trio of Marian windows is up high, this one, also deeply recessed, is at eye level. Pye positioned Christ in the exact centre, immersed to his waist in the River Jordan. St John the Baptist is standing on an adjacent boulder, a bit unsteadily as he stretches across to pour water on Christ's head. There are also other figures, six in total, including a man who waits beside Christ, bearing a towel

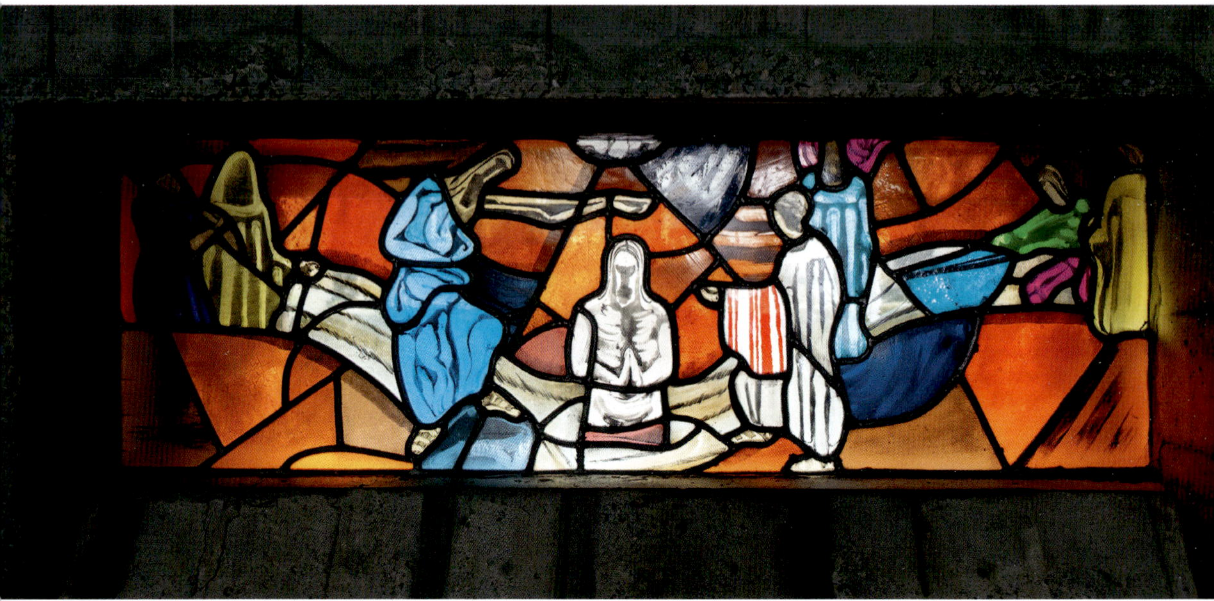

Patrick Pye, *The Baptism of Christ* (1972), St Michael's church

for him to use when he emerges from the river post-baptism. As with the figures in many of Pye's windows he dispenses with facial features and relies on gestures to communicate. In this window he selected shades of orange and umber glass as the dominant colours, evoking an arid, Middle Eastern landscape.

In addition to Johnny Murphy, Patrick Pye and Michael Biggs, other artists were employed by Pearse McKenna in the adornment of the church, among them Richard Enda King (son of the stained glass artist Richard King) who created the abstract tabernacle and sanctuary cross among other items, and Imogen Stuart, also working in metal, who created a large St Michael in beaten copper for above the main entrance, and depicted *The Last Judgement*, also in beaten copper, for the main entrance doors, as well as cast bronze handles.

The new church of St Michael was opened on 7 October 1973 by which stage Archbishop McQuaid, to whom modern architecture and art was an anathema, had died and it was his successor Archbishop Ryan who officiated.[14]

Presbyterian church

York Road, A96 D529

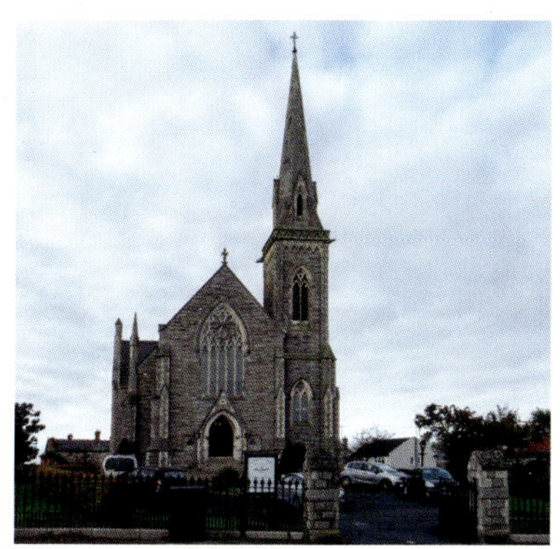

This landmark building was designed by the Scottish architect Andrew Heiton in Gothic revival style in 1861–3 and is virtually identical to his earlier design for Rathgar's Presbyterian church. Constructed of snecked rock-faced Dalkey granite with Portland stone trim, the sloped site allowed for the inclusion of schoolrooms, now a church hall, in the lower part of the building.

The church houses a fine series of three richly coloured 2-light windows full of visual interest created by Ethel Rhind over a number of years. All three windows were commissioned by members of the Beatty family who had originally come from Co. Louth and settled in Dún Laoghaire in the 1870s.[15] There were five siblings, none of whom married, and they lived together in a commodious residence at 3 Howard Place looking out to sea.[16] When the eldest brother, James, a banker, died suddenly in 1908 the remaining siblings placed an order at An Túr Gloine the following April to erect a window to his memory, and to that of their mother who had died almost three decades earlier.

Two parables were selected to be depicted, one in each light. In St Matthew's gospel *The Parable of the Faithful Servant* (left light) immediately precedes *The Parable of the Wise Virgins* (right light) and both have eschatological themes relating to being prepared for the Day of Judgement. In *The Parable of the Faithful Servant*, Rhind depicted the kneeling servant handing back to his master a bag of coins he had held

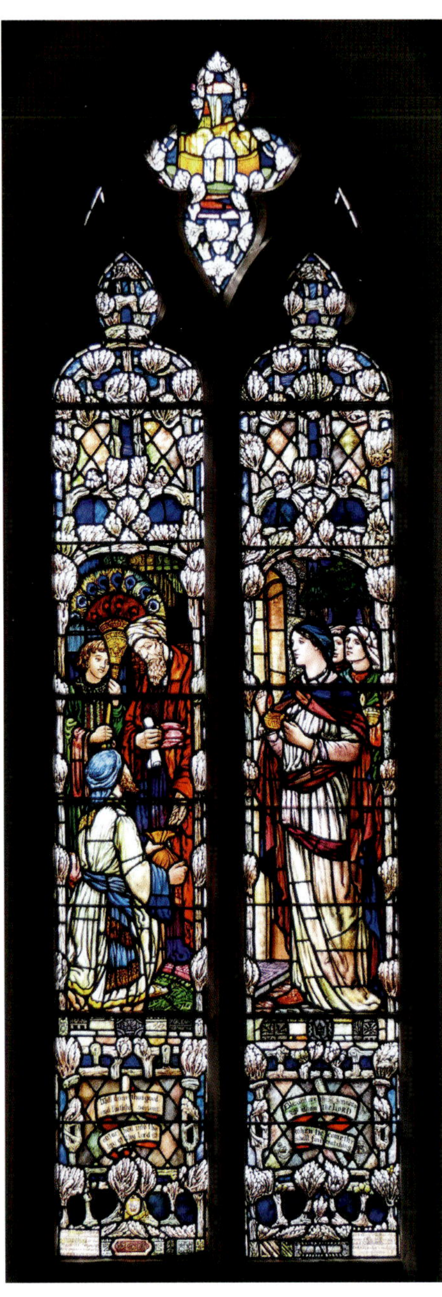

Ethel Rhind, *The Parable of the Faithful Servant*, and *The Parable of the Wise Virgins* (1909)

for safekeeping, while a young male servant holds aloft a large decorative fan made of peacock feathers, probably a reference to the master having returned from a distant land. It is noteworthy that the bag of coins indicates the master's trust, and the fact that it was returned intact demonstrated the probity of the servant, qualities one would want in a banker.

The corresponding light also features three figures; three of the wise virgins from the total group of ten, five of whom were wise because they had their lamps prepared, and five foolish because they were negligent in doing so. This parable was particularly popular in the Middle Ages though there are several instances of the subject appearing in nineteenth- and twentieth-century windows in Protestant churches in Ireland. Traditionally the virgins are depicted as lithesome young females, but Rhind, perhaps conscious that the window was in memory of a widow, has the trio as decorously dressed and with matronly figures. The irregular-shaped quatrefoil at the top features a golden city encircled by a high wall and accessible only via a large bolted door, presumably to suggest that entry to heaven is not an automatic entitlement.

Framing both lights and the quatrefoil are contorted branches sprouting oak leaves and occasional acorns, all painted in monochrome tones. These organic features were much favoured by A.E. Child, manager of the studio, who in turn was inspired by his master, Christopher Whall. Rhind's versions are singularly sturdy and rigid, to some degree negating their organic origins.

In 1913 a second brother, William Brooke Beatty, who had been a stockbroker, died and in due course it appears that the remaining three siblings, Dr Joseph, Elizabeth and Margaret, hatched a highly unusual plan; they would commission two more windows from Ethel Rhind so that the family would have three in row, and if each window carried an inscription in each light – as had been the case in the 1909 window – then all five siblings could be commemorated. This plan would mean the likelihood, which came to pass, that some of the inscriptions could only be added in years to come after the windows were erected when the respective siblings died. Additionally, when planning the second and third window it is clear that the siblings took their cue from the first window by choosing parables that featured men for the two brothers, and ones that featured women for the two sisters.

In September 1920 one of the Miss Beattys placed the order for the two windows at An Túr Gloine,[17] and although there may have been a certain eagerness to have the second window made that would commemorate their late brother William, there would be no urgency with the third one as those who would be commemorated in it were still very much alive. It is not recorded when Ethel Rhind started designing and making *The Parable of Drawing in the Net* and *The Parable of the Leaven* though it appears that the window was not installed until around September 1922, possibly a reflection on how busy the studio was due to the amount of ongoing war memorial commissions. *The Parable of Drawing in the Net* (left light) comes from the gospel of St Matthew and it refers to the final judgement – as did the 1909 window – and the gospel imagery is of fishermen separating edible from inedible fish caught in a net, referencing that 'the angels will come and separate the wicked from the righteous'. Ethel Rhind depicted two fishermen busy sorting through a catch while a third one pauses to scrutinize a particularly large fish. The young man on the left depicted bent over with neck straining resembles some of the faces painted by Rhind's friend and colleague, Wilhelmina Geddes. The dedication to William Beatty

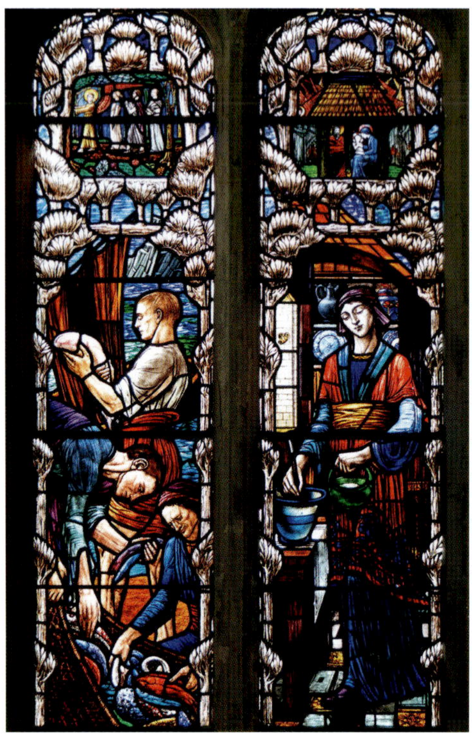

Ethel Rhind, detail of *The Parable of Drawing in the Net*, and *The Parable of the Leaven* (1922)

appears at the base of this light. Above the principal scene there is a vignette of an angel leading three figures into a forest or perhaps paradise, possibly meant to represent Mrs Beatty and her two deceased children.

The Parable of the Leaven (right light) refers to the impact a small amount of leaven has on a large quantity of flour when baking, alluding to the powerful growth of the kingdom of God from small beginnings. Rhind has depicted an image of domestic contentment as a woman stirs in a spoonful of leaven into a bowl. Behind her is a well-ordered dresser and through the open window a butterfly floats towards her; this can be seen as an attractive incidental detail but it may have a more profound meaning as the butterfly is a symbol of Christ's resurrection as it emerges from a chrysalis. The inscription at the base of this light was added much later, in 1936, after Margaret Anna Beatty, the last of the siblings died.[18] The vignette above the main scene depicts the Nativity with the stable guarded by attending angels. The quatrefoil above the two lights depicts a night time scene of the ocean with sailing boats and an illuminated lighthouse, no doubt referencing Dún Laoghaire, and in the foreground a newly harvested field of golden corn and an abandoned scythe. A single figure contemplates the view.

The third of Ethel Rhind's series of windows was installed in 1925 when the two siblings whose names would eventually be inserted were still alive; Elizabeth Matilda who would die in 1927, followed by Dr Joseph in 1929.[19] The subjects they chose for their window were *The Parable of the Good Samaritan* (left light), and *The Parable of the Lost Coin* (for the right light). The well-known story of the good Samaritan would seem to be an appropriate choice for a medical doctor as the man the Samaritan encountered had been set upon, beaten and left for half dead, and it is the Samaritan who attended to his wounds. Rhind depicted the bandaged young man slumped on a donkey while the Samaritan has one hand around his shoulder to steady him as he leads the donkey forward. It is a gentle image of understated compassion.

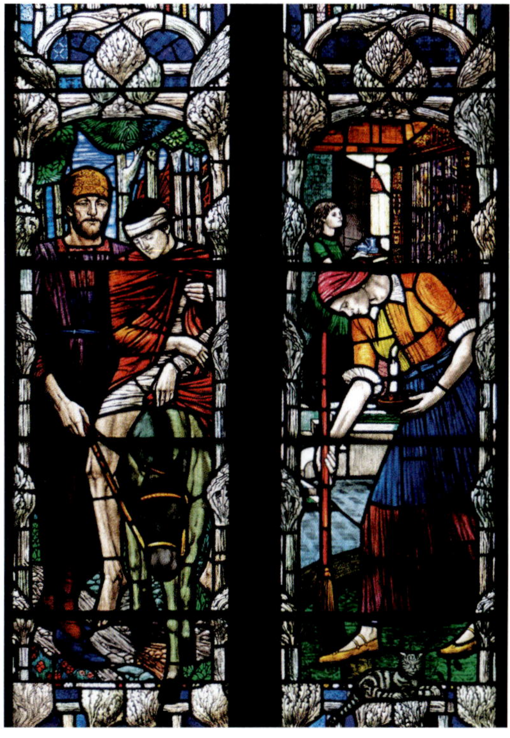

Ethel Rhind, detail of *The Parable of the Good Samaritan*, and *The Parable of the Lost Coin* (1925)

The corresponding light featuring *The Parable of the Lost Coin* presents a domestic scene, as did the right light in the second window; it would seem that neither Margaret nor Elizabeth Beatty had careers so probably keeping house (assisted by servants) was how they perceived their roles, and this may have reflected their choice of these particular parables. *The Parable of the Lost Coin* concerns repentance. Ethel Rhind depicted a woman gazing intently at where she is sweeping, while holding a candle for additional light, in her quest to find a mislaid coin, one of ten she owned. On finding the coin, St Luke's gospel states, 'In the same way, I tell you that there will be more joy in heaven over one sinner who repents than over ninety-nine righteous ones who do not need to repent.' At the woman's feet, indifferent to her sweeping, is a relaxing tabby cat who stares out at the viewer, and it would not be unreasonable to speculate that this is a portrait of a pet in the Beatty household. Rhind appears to have had an affinity for depicting animals and several appear in this set of windows, as in other ones by her. In the quatrefoil at the top Rhind depicted the burning bush which is the symbol of the Presbyterian church in Ireland.

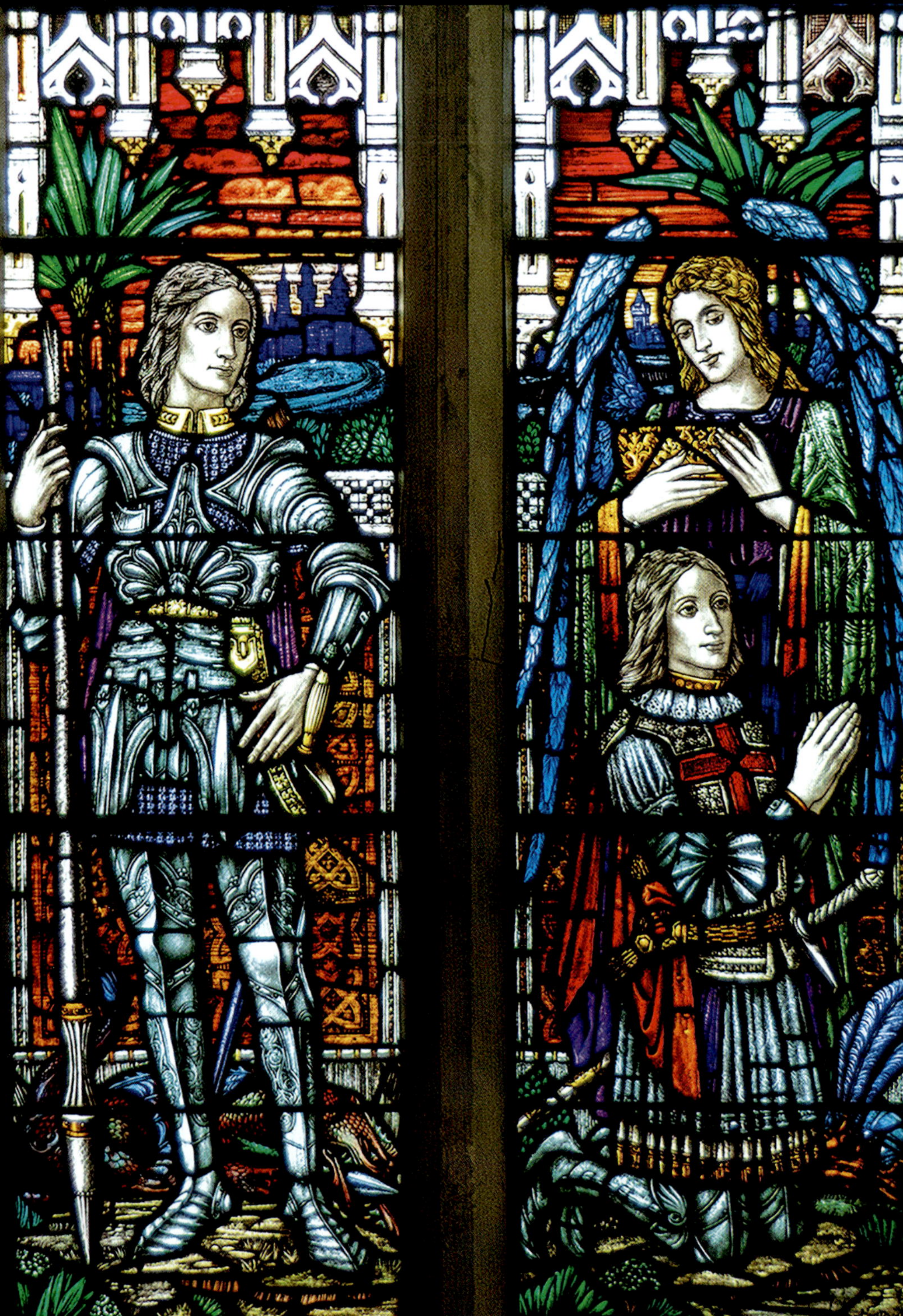

As with the previous two windows, Rhind framed the scenes and inscriptions with branches sprouting forth bunches of furled oak leaves with acorns attached. In this window, surrounding the inscriptions and elsewhere Rhind incorporated different pieces of glass, which she decorated with a variety of textures, evocative of a hand-crafted patchwork quilt, perhaps again, a deliberate hint of happy domesticity. These three windows make up a unique series and reflect the closeness of the five siblings and Ethel's Rhind's commitment to create bespoke windows to convey their love of faith and family.

Opposite the Beattys' windows there is a war memorial window to five men in the parish who died in the First World War. The minister at the time, Revd F. Stuart Gardiner, commissioned the window from Joshua Clarke & Sons in August 1920 at a cost of £217 and it was installed in September 1921. The Clarke order book and correspondence records the title as being *Conflict and Victory*.[20] It is not recorded who the artist was but one candidate would be the studio's senior artist, Dublin-born William Nagle (1853–1923) who had worked at Clarke's for several decades. The 2-light window depicts a knight holding a broken spear (*Conflict*), and in the adjoining light an angel crowning a kneeling knight (*Victory*). Both knights, who share identical facial features – perhaps to show that Conflict and Victory are two sides of the one coin – have long Renaissance-style hair and wear highly decorative armour that resembles theatrical costumes and lends them a dandified appearance. The background to both lights is particularly striking. The five soldiers being commemorated died in different countries, two in France, and one each in Belgium, Palestine and Turkey, and the background landscape features palm trees and exotic buildings set against a dramatic crimson sunset which suggests that the artist had either Palestine or Turkey, or both, in mind.

The same month as *Conflict and Victory* was installed Joshua Clarke died suddenly and thereafter Harry and his brother Walter assumed control of the burgeoning business.

(opposite) Joshua Clarke & Sons, detail of *Conflict and Victory* (1921)

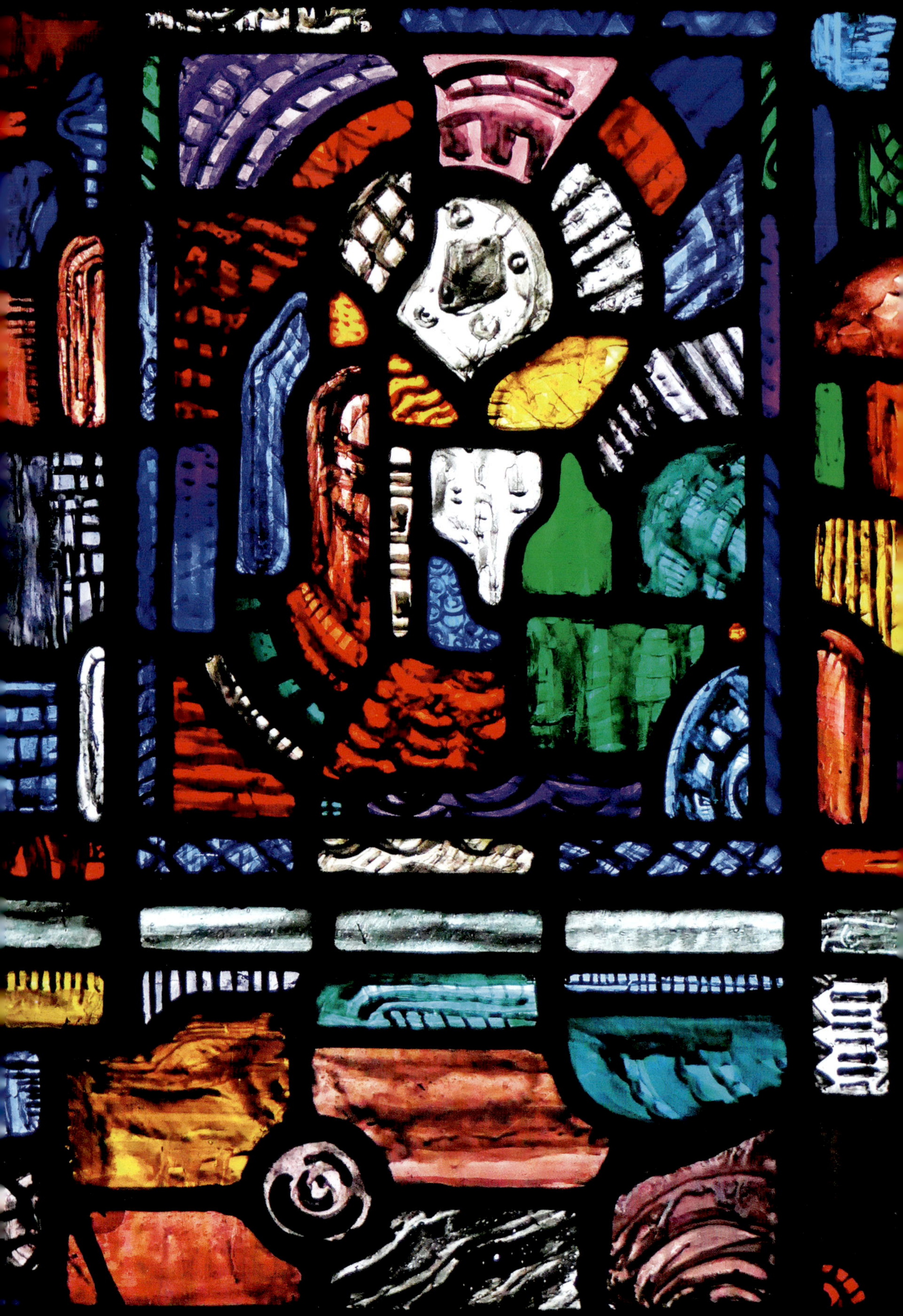

St Nahi's church (C of I)

Churchtown Road Upper, D14 V381

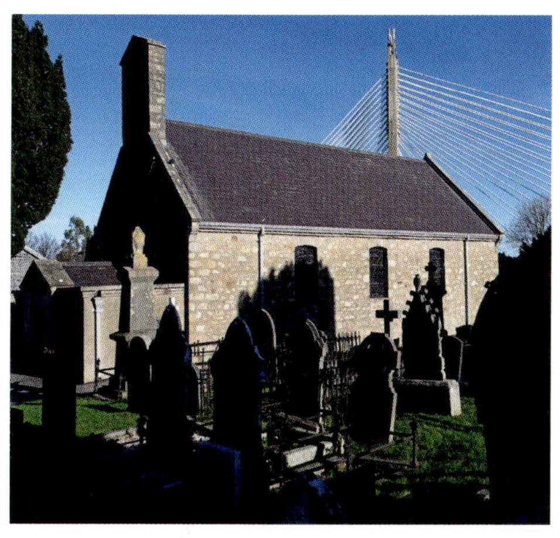

St Nahi's Church of Ireland church stands on a slightly elevated site just south of Dundrum village adjacent to Churchtown, where according to official records, a church was built about 800 probably on the ruins of a still older building. It was dedicated to St Nahi, a saint of the early Irish church who is thought to have lived in a monastery at Churchtown. The church was rebuilt several times and the present building, a simple barn-like structure, dates from 1750. The window opes are distinguished by the very shallow curve at the top of their near rectangular form.

(opposite) Evie Hone, detail of left abstract panel in *The Annunciation* (1933–4)

ST NAHI'S HOLDS A FINE collection of nine An Túr Gloine stained glass windows, all, it would appear, ordered by either the rector, Revd William Monk Gibbon (1864–1935), or by his widow and children. He had been appointed rector of Taney in 1901, a parish which included St Nahi's. It was then in a poor state of repair and he undertook its refurbishment. The first stained glass window was most likely installed in 1909,[1] and it is the only non-An Túr Gloine window. Erected in memory of Mrs Sophie Bond of Cheshire,[2] it depicts *Charity* and surprisingly it was ordered from Mayer of Munich, a company rarely patronized by the Church of Ireland but which was enormously popular with the Catholic Church, at least partly due to a papal endorsement. The figure of Charity is situated in an elaborately decorated neo-classical niche, totally at variance with the simplicity of the church's structure, and she holds aloft a piece of bread tantalizingly out of reach of a poor young girl who is on her knees begging for it – a curious image to represent Christian charity.

Charity, based on a generic design, made overseas in a large factory-like setting and taking no account of the environment it was destined for, was exactly the type of window that Sarah Purser and Edward Martyn had railed against at the turn of the century, and was the spur for their founding An Túr Gloine. One might speculate why, a few years after the Mayer window was installed in St Nahi's, Revd Monk Gibbon was converted to the hand-crafted, bespoke works created by the artists at An Túr Gloine. The answer probably lies in the long-established friendship between the Yeats and Monk Gibbon families.[3] In 1902 John Butler Yeats and his two daughters, Elizabeth (Lolly) and Susan (Lily), took up residence in a house in Churchtown not far from St Nahi's and it was where they attended religious service. The two sisters established the Dun Emer Guild with Evelyn Gleeson in Churchtown in 1903, specializing in hand-printing and embroidery, and the guild was grounded in a philosophy similar to that of An Túr Gloine. Lolly and Lily's brother, William, was an early supporter of An Túr Gloine and the Yeats family were friends of Sarah Purser (and also subjects of her portraits). It is easy to see how these connections ensured that orders for all windows subsequent to *Charity* were placed at An Túr Gloine.

The year 1914 marked the first An Túr Gloine window, the central light, and tallest, of a 3-light window above the altar. It was erected by George Wilson, the Portuguese

Consul who resided in Kingstown (Dún Laoghaire), in memory of his wife, Edith Frances Wilson.[4] Designed and made by Catherine (Kitty) O'Brien, it depicts *Christ with Martha*, and the influence of her teacher A.E Child, who in turn was influenced by his mentor Christopher Whall, is evident in the use of organically derived structures comprising branches and leaves which are employed as a framing device. This framing decision determined the overall design approach adopted by O'Brien for the four subsequent windows she made for the church. The focus of the window is on Christ's meeting with Martha. Two other women accompany her, also grieving for Martha's dead brother, Lazarus, and in the background the village of Bethany is visible where Mary has remained. The rector's son, also named William Monk Gibbon – who grew up to be the distinguished poet and writer – though only a boy at the time of its installation recalled years later his father's delight in O'Brien's window.[5]

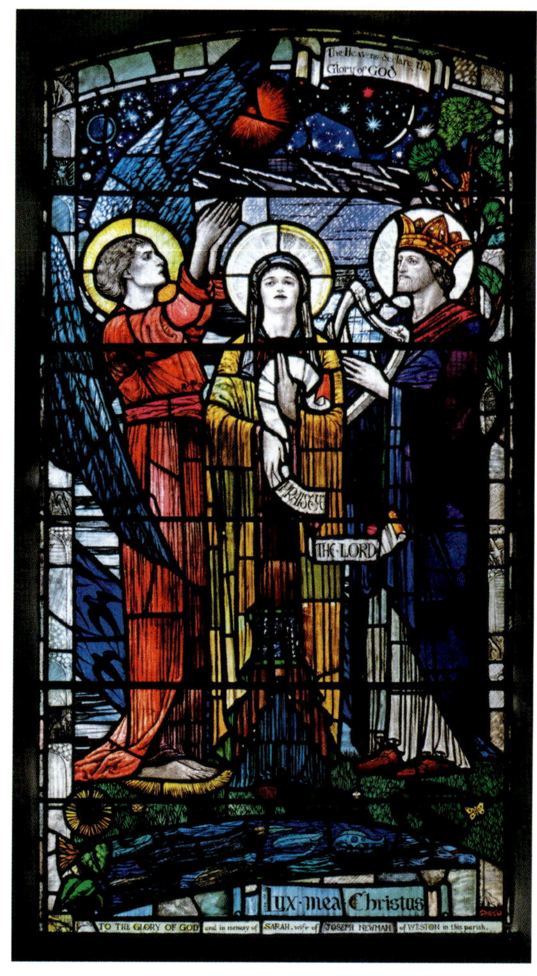

Ethel Rhind, *Praise Ye the Lord* (1916)

In 1916 Ethel Rhind created a window for the south wall of the church, and it is arguably the most charming and visually engaging window in the church. It appears that the theme is derived from *Benedicte*,[6] a canticle said or sung at the morning service in praise of all that God has created, though Rhind has specifically included short extracts from Psalm 19 ('The heavens declare the glory of God') and Psalm 150

('Praise ye the Lord'). As the scroll held by the central figure is inscribed 'Praise Ye the Lord' the window has been known by that title as well as *Benedicte*.

Praise Ye the Lord was erected in memory of Sarah Newman of Weston House, Dundrum, by her husband Joseph, a retired magistrate. Measurements of the window were taken by An Túr Gloine's glazier, Tommy Kinsella, in late March 1916 and Joseph Newman only got to approve Ethel Rhind's small-scale coloured design before his untimely death two months later. Ethel Rhind completed *Praise Ye the Lord* in November and it is perhaps surprising that the Newmans' daughter (who paid the bill) had not requested that the original inscription in memory of Sarah be altered so that the window was in memory of both deceased parents.[7]

Praise Ye the Lord features three figures, the one on the right identifiable as King David by his crown and harp, the one on the left an angel, and in the centre is an unidentified female saint. Above them Rhind has illustrated a dramatic night sky with the earth, moon, sun, stars and forked lightning. The three figures stand on the edge of a fast-moving stream teeming with different varieties of fish, with sunflowers and butterflies also visible. More small creatures painted in grisaille feature in the border. The Latin text near the base of the window, 'Lux mea Christus', translates as 'Christ is my light' which is the motto of the Newman family.

Three years later Revd Monk Gibbon placed an order for the two windows flanking Catherine O'Brien's *Christ with Martha* and these were erected in memory of two male members of the Barrington family,[8] wealthy tobacco merchants of Eden Park, Dundrum. Catherine O'Brien undertook the pair and they are so totally in harmony with her first (middle) window that one would not suspect that all three chancel windows had not been executed at the same time. The subjects this time were *The Miraculous Draught of Fishes* and *The Road to Emmaus*. As with the earlier window they depict encounters with Christ, though in the two flanking windows they depict episodes which occurred after Christ's resurrection and in which he is not initially recognized by those he meets. The subjects and placing of the three windows, presumably determined by Revd Monk Gibbon, were carefully thought through – the scene in the left light occurred in the early morning (with a rising sun on the horizon to indicate it), the middle scene, *Christ with Martha,* is clearly set during day time, and in the right light the incident took place at night (crescent moon and candle in window included). With only three or four figures in each window they convey an intimacy in the manner the individuals interact. It was Sarah Purser who selected which artist at An Túr Gloine would undertake which windows, and she believed that 'the gentle very "Irish" talent of Kitty O'Brien was ideally suited to the simplicity of village churches …',[9] and St Nahi's is the quintessential simple village church.

Ten years later, in 1929, Canon (as he had become) Monk Gibbon placed another order at An Túr Gloine on behalf of the Barrington family for a window to commemorate Richard Irving Williams Barrington who had died the previous year. The theme was *The Sermon on the Mount* and the order was undertaken by A.E. Child. It, along with a second window by Child made in 1934, *Our Lord Walking on the Sea*, and also commemorating a Barrington, have a different format with the subjects depicted in a central panel surrounded by small squares of almost clear glass, many decorated with delicate foliate motifs; this format allowed for greater light to enter the church which may have been a consideration as the earlier windows by O'Brien, and particularly Rhind's, featured a lot of deeply coloured glass. Child's pair of windows though excellently crafted are fairly conventional and lacking in originality or personality.

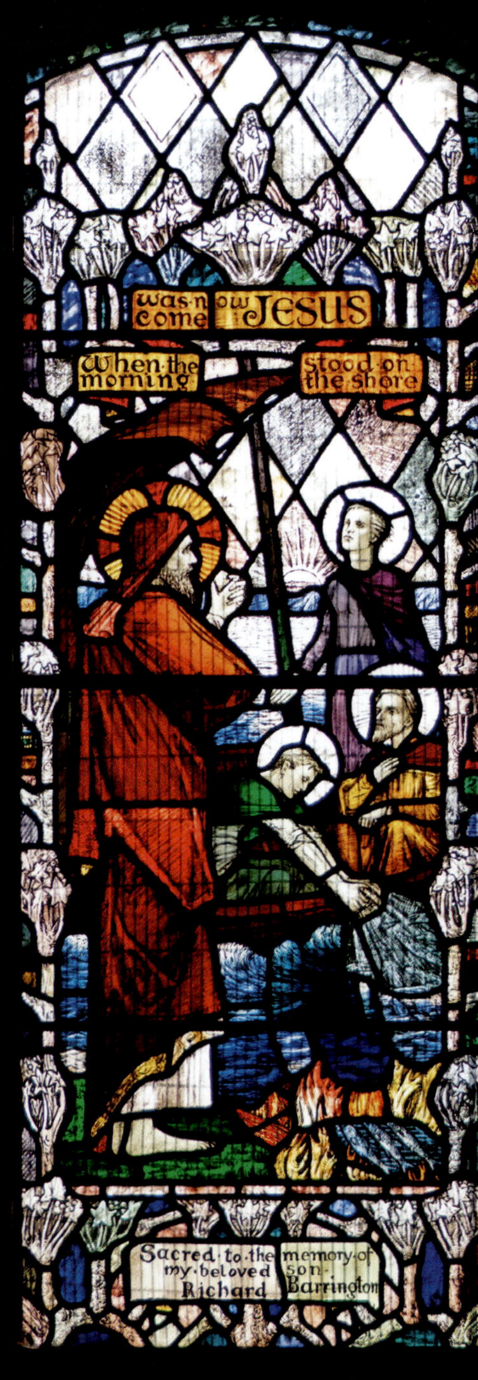

Catherine O'Brien, *The Miraculous Draught of Fishes* (1919)

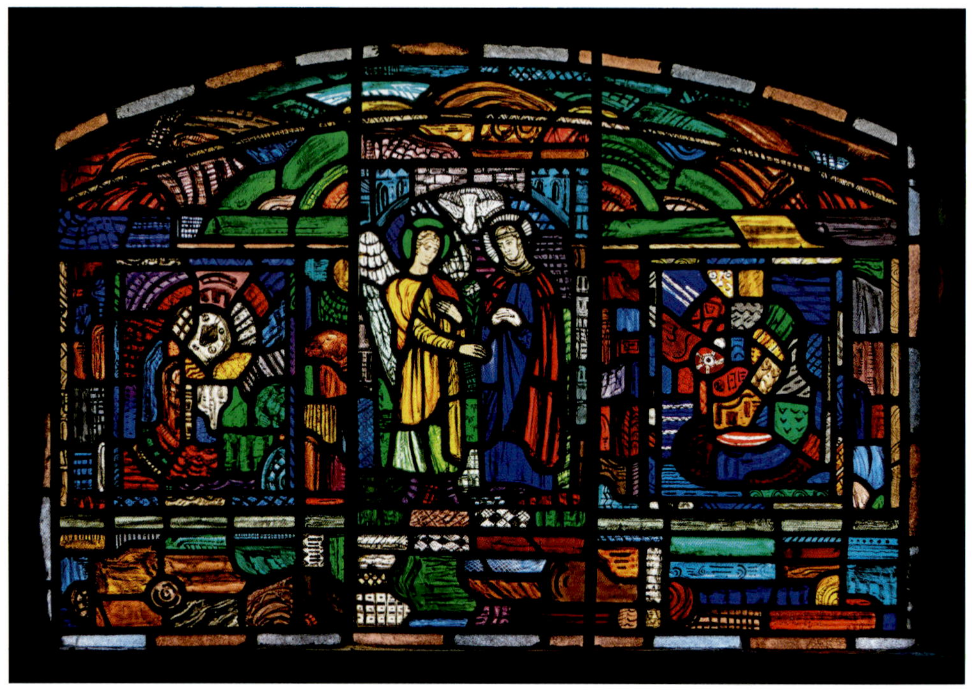

Evie Hone, *The Annunciation* (1933–4)

The same year as *Our Lord Walking on the Sea* was installed, another window, radically different in every respect, was erected also, though not in the main body of the church but in the tiny cell-like baptistry that Canon Monk Gibbon had had constructed to accommodate an historic font. *The Annunciation* was Evie Hone's first stained glass window and it comprised two small abstract panels (which she had made previously), and the central figurative panel.[10] In some respects this composite window can be viewed as an indicator of her moving away from abstraction, which had preoccupied her painting career for more than a decade, and re-embracing representational art. It was also a deeply personal window for her as the inscription indicates – it was created by Hone in memory of her older sister, Leland Hutchinson, to whom she had been especially close and who is buried in St Nahi's graveyard.[11] *The Annunciation*, which is intensely coloured, must have taken the other An Túr Gloine artists by surprise, so revolutionary and avowedly modern it was compared with what they were creating.

Catherine O'Brien, *After the Transfiguration* (1936)

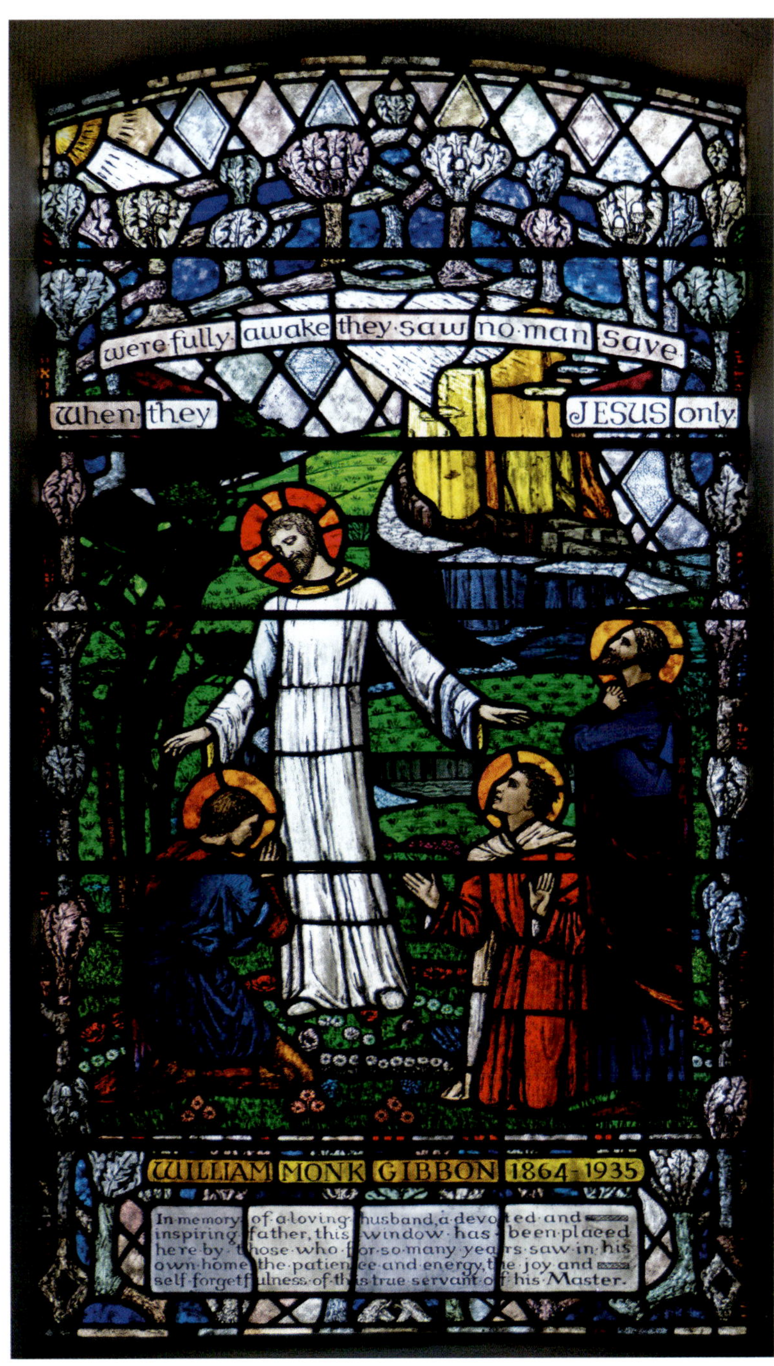

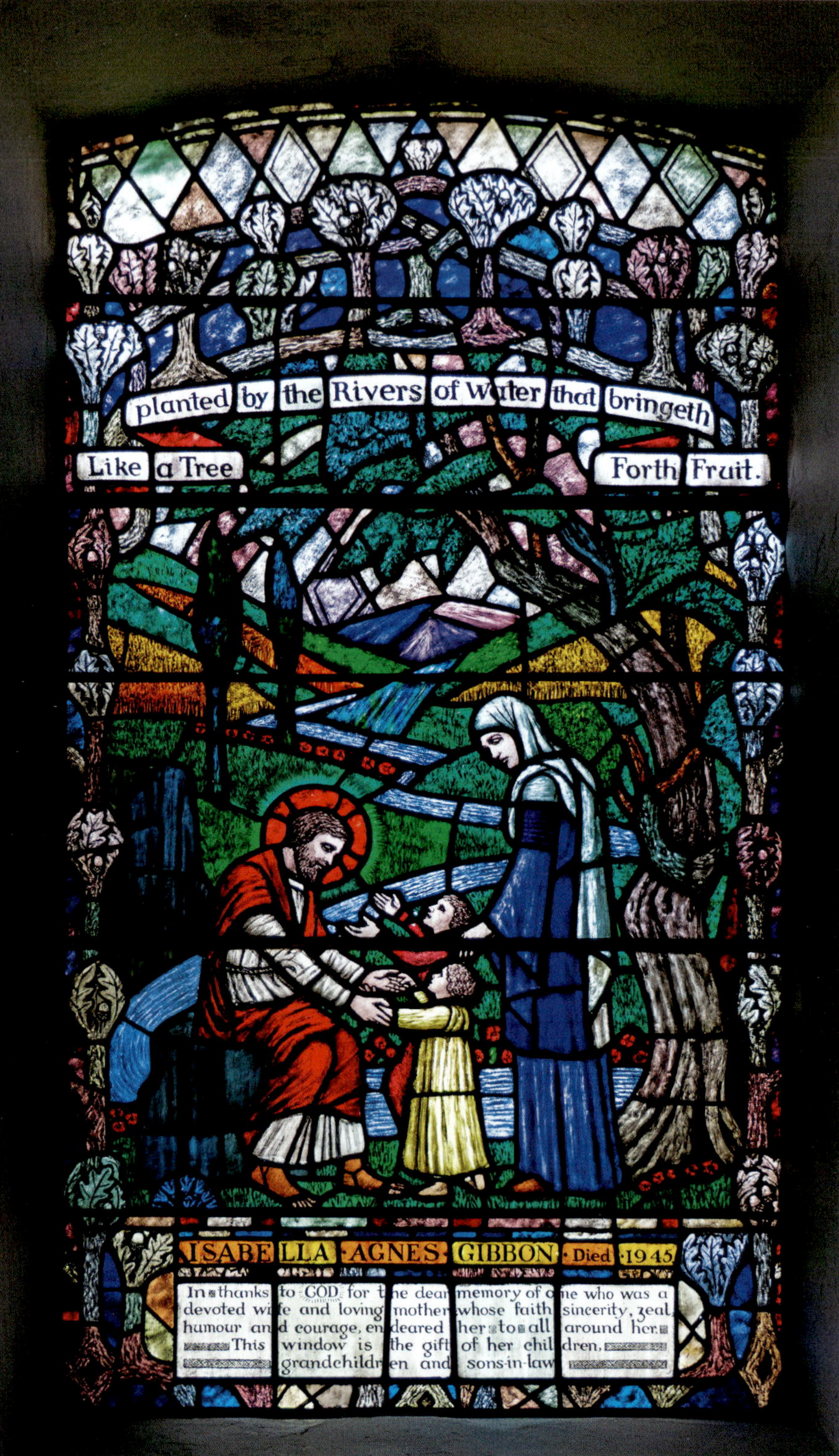
planted by the Rivers of Water that bringeth
Like a Tree
Forth Fruit.
ISABELLA AGNES GIBBON · Died · 1945
In thanks to GOD for the dear memory of one who was a
devoted wife and loving mother whose faith sincerity, zeal,
humour and courage, endeared her to all around her.
This window is the gift of her children,
grandchildren and sons-in-law

Around the time that Child's second window and Hone's *The Annunciation* were being made St Nahi's received a set of four beautiful embroideries – all landscapes featuring Christ – donated in memory of various deceased parishioners, and that was almost certainly arranged by Canon Monk Gibbon. They are framed and were installed behind the altar beneath Catherine O'Brien's trio of windows. All four were designed by Brigid O'Brien (no relation of Catherine) of the Cuala Industries (which grew out of the Dun Emer Guild), and worked by Lily Yeats, probably with assistants. Each is signed by Lily Yeats and two of the four are signed in monogram by Brigid O'Brien.[12] Lily, along with her sister, are buried in St Nahi's graveyard.

Canon Monk Gibbon died in March 1935 and in December Catherine O'Brien travelled to Dundrum to discuss a memorial window with his son, William Monk Gibbon.[13] The subject was *After the Transfiguration* and she made it the following year. William Monk Gibbon was thrilled with the outcome and wrote that his pleasure and appreciation of it 'is all the more increased by the thought of how much pleasure it would have given to him [his father, the late rector] to whose memory it now stands.'[14]

When Isabella, widow of Canon Monk Gibbon, died her family not surprisingly asked O'Brien to create a window to her memory, *Christ Blessing Children*, which would fill the last available ope in the church. O'Brien made it in 1947 and although the figures are a bit stilted and her use of colour had become less subtle, it and her other four windows in St Nahi's, which span a total of thirty-three years, are, from a visual point of view, remarkably consistent.

A short walk from St Nahi's one can visit Holy Cross church (RC), Main Street, Dundrum, which has a particularly fine 3-light by Michael Healy; influenced by Italian Renaissance painting it depicts, *St Dominic, Our Lady Queen of the Rosary, and St Catherine* (1919). There is also a framed cartoon, *Christ Among the Doctors* (1944) by Evie Hone, created for a window which she did not get to execute.

(opposite) Catherine O'Brien, *Christ Blessing Children* (1947)

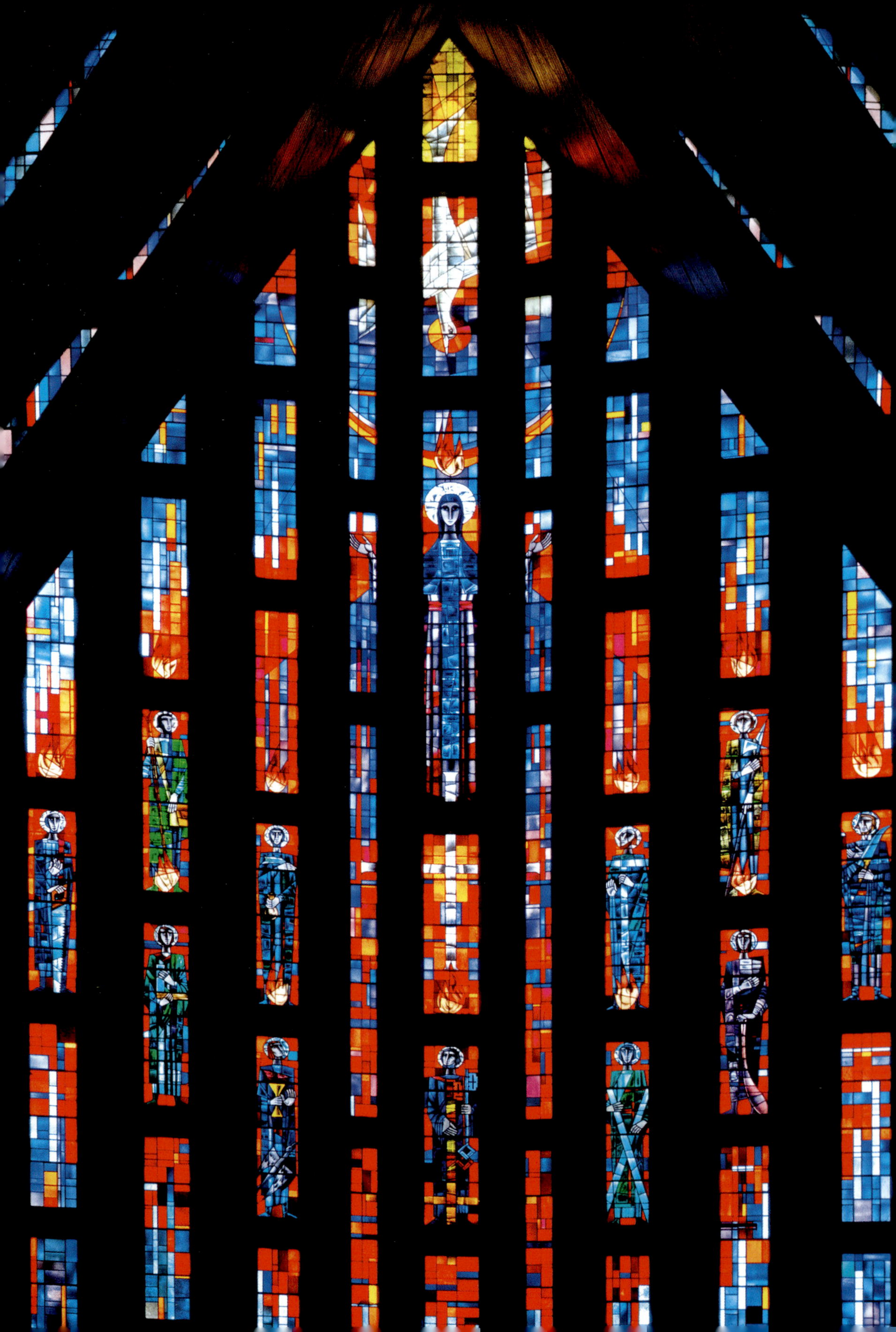

GREENHILLS

Holy Spirit church (RC)

Limekiln Lane, D12 YY0X

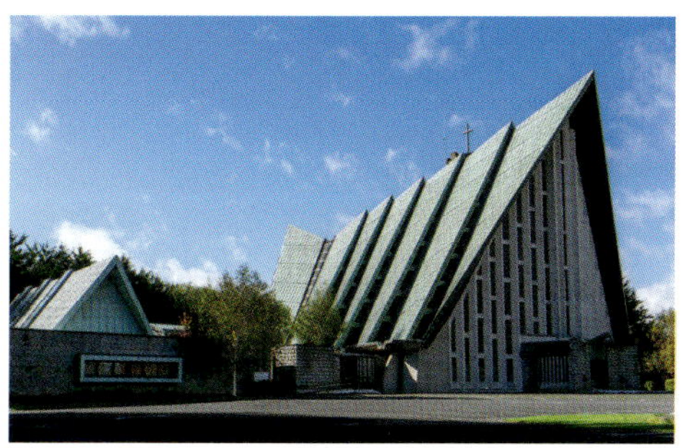

The church of the Holy Spirit was designed by architect Louis Peppard of Peppard & Duffy in 1967–71, and is one of the finest and most innovative twentieth-century churches in Dublin. The distinctive exterior is notable for its steeply pitched copper-clad roof comprising six staggered, overlapping segments like an armadillo's shell with a seventh segment above the sanctuary, the overall roof profile recalling the Sydney Opera House. The severe entrance porch of rough coursed granite rubble, with repoussé bronze doors by Peter Dowd, project out from the dramatic triangular-shaped front elevation which is constructed of a matrix of stained glass and concrete. The interior, bathed in colour from the profusion of stained glass and *dalle de verre*, has an elongated hexagonal nave and interlocking pentagonal sanctuary plan-form.

(opposite) Richard King, detail of *Pentecost* (1969–70)

Louis Peppard's earlier iteration for the church, made in 1964, was for a more conventional structure with a *flèche* and without a dramatic stained glass component. Peppard & Duffy had previously designed Our Lady Mother of Divine Grace church (1962) for Raheny parish which, like the revised plan for Greenhills, also features a distinctive triangular-shaped façade, though with *dalle de verre* rather than stained glass.[1] Dr John Charles McQuaid, archbishop of Dublin, who was avowedly antagonistic towards modern architecture, may have been reassured by Peppard during the design process for Greenhills church and was open to be convinced of the merits of a more creative solution.[2] Traditionally the main stained glass window in many churches is the east window ('liturgical east'), located above the altar, but in many modern Irish Catholic churches the approach was for a more restrained, perhaps less distracting, sanctuary with the focus on the altar and a suspended crucifix, and the west window became the principal stained glass window, located above the main entrance doors, as is the case in Greenhills.

Archbishop McQuaid had a particular devotion to Our Lady and during his episcopate, which commenced in 1940, he dedicated the majority of his new diocesan churches, over twenty, in honour of Mary. Even before Vatican II (1962–5) there was the beginning of a theological shift away from Mary and a move towards a more Christocentric church. The Second Vatican Council confirmed this, and with greater emphasis on the centrality of the paschal mystery in theology, other themes came to the fore including the role of the Holy Spirit. Dr McQuaid dedicated the church of the Holy Spirit, Ballyroan, in 1967 (see pp 325–31), and Greenhills' church of the Holy Spirit in January 1971, the latter featuring Richard King's finest work on the theme of the Holy Spirit.

Richard King began his stained glass career in the late 1920s as an assistant to Harry Clarke, remaining on after Clarke's early death and was subsequently appointed manager and principal artist of Harry Clarke Stained Glass Ltd from 1935 to 1940. He then took a complete sabbatical from stained glass returning to the craft only at the end of the 1940s at which point he built his own studio in the garden of his home in Dalkey, Co. Dublin, and it was here that his multi-panel *Pentecost* window for Greenhills' front façade was created. Peppard recounted

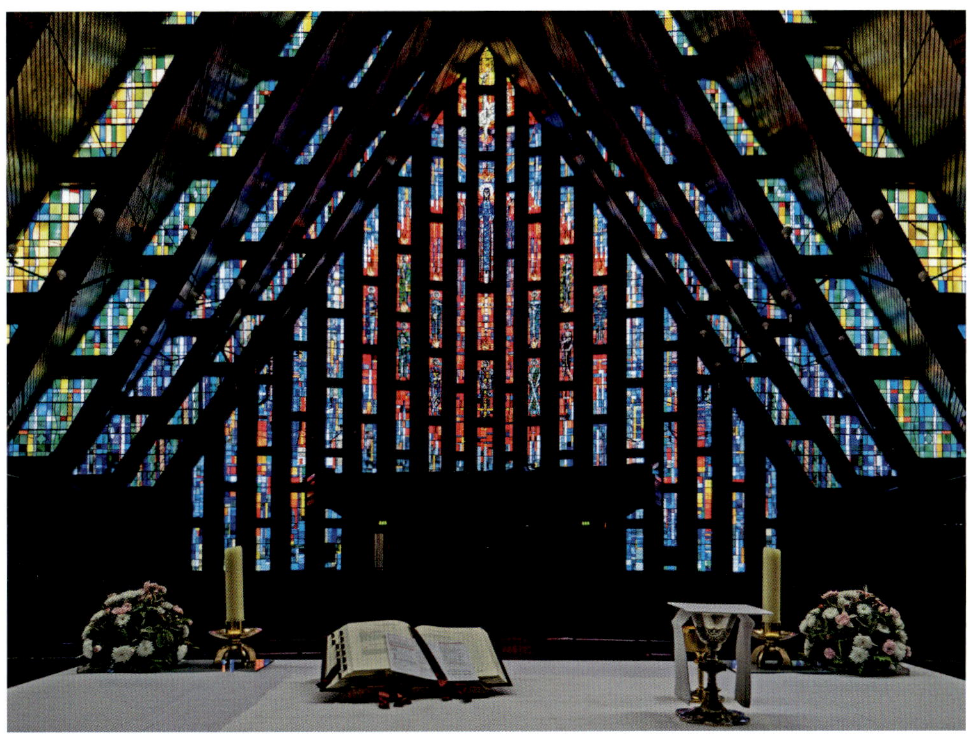

Richard King, *Pentecost* (1969–70), and Murphy-Devitt Studios, roof glazing (1969)

that he first made Richard King's acquaintance at his Dalkey studio when he had completed a very large window and was getting ready to despatch it to Australia.[3] This is likely to have occurred in 1957 when King was working on a series of seven windows that together created an expansive wall of glass for a college chapel in Perth, and this may have planted the seed for utilizing glass in a similar manner in Greenhills. Sharing a love of angling, King became a personal friend of Louis Peppard's, and it seems virtually certain that when Peppard was considering the prospect of featuring a vast gable wall of glass for Holy Spirit church, he had King in mind as the artist to create it, and discussed the project with him in some detail as the architectural success of the church would be largely dependent on this dramatic element.

The *Acts of the Apostles* is the principal source and describes the coming of the Holy Spirit on the Jewish feast of Pentecost –

When the day of Pentecost had come, they [the apostles] were all together in one place. And suddenly from heaven there came a sound like the rush of a violent wind, and it filled the entire house where they were sitting. Divided tongues, as if of fire, appeared among them, and a tongue rested on each of them. All of them were filled with the Holy Spirit and began to speak in other languages, as the spirit gave them ability. (Acts 2:1–4).

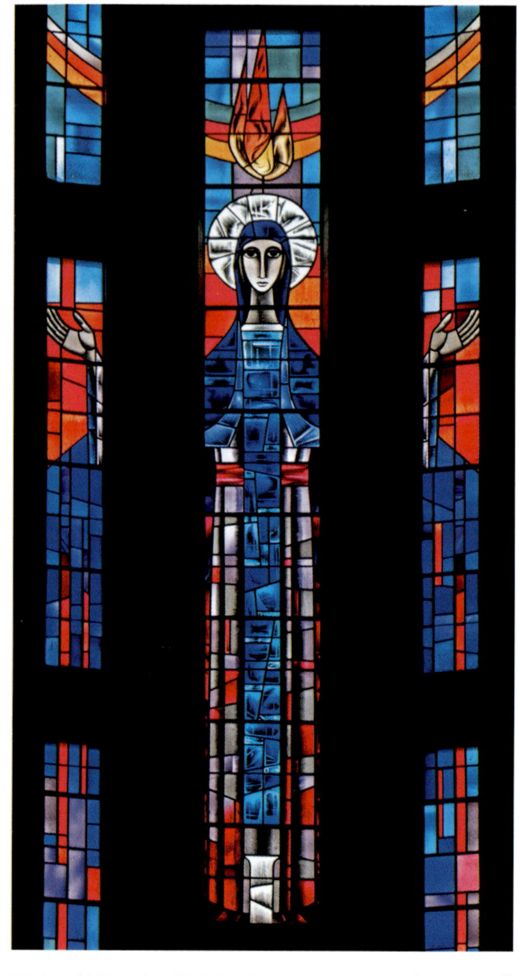
Richard King, detail of Our Lady in *Pentecost* (1969–70)

The Acts do not mention Mary being present, and her inclusion in Pentecost-themed works of art, including Richard King's *Pentecost* window, is seen as symbolic, personifying the Church itself or as spiritual mother of the apostles.[4] Unlike many other stained glass artists, Richard King maintained a keen interest in theological developments and read widely on the subject including the works of the contemporary theologian Pierre Teilhard de Chardin SJ,[5] so the challenge of how to present the theme of Pentecost visually to a contemporary congregation would have excited him. In his *Pentecost* window he did not attempt to suggest the interior of a house, nor to have the apostles seated; his approach being to communicate the meaning of Pentecost and the coming of the Holy Spirit, rather than illustrate the actual event as described in Acts. King's solution was to have a large ball of fire containing Mary and the apostles dominating the triangular gable wall, and above, descending from the apex, is the Holy Spirit in the guise of a dove. The dominant colours are shades of red and blue, redolent of medieval stained glass, the disc of red representing divine love and the surrounding blue representing heaven. Mary and each of the apostles have tongues of fire above their heads.

The figure of Mary, hands raised in blessing, has her cloak opened wide to suggest inclusion and protection. The apostles by comparison appear grave and stoic. St Peter, the first bishop of Rome, is beneath Mary, with a large white cross separating them which references Christ's crucifixion. There are five apostles either side of the centre light, each contained within his own stained glass panel; as Pentecost occurred post-crucifixion, Judas is not included but King has also taken the unusual step of omitting Matthias who replaced Judas due to his desire for compositional symmetry. The eleven apostles are shown with their attributes (from left to right, top to bottom) – St Simon the zealot with a saw, St James the Greater carrying the water gourde and staff of the pilgrim, St Thomas with a carpenter's square, St Matthew with a bag of money and quill, St John with chalice and eagle. In the centre is St Peter with keys and the inverted cross of his crucifixion. On the right is St Philip with cross, St Andrew with an X-shaped cross on which he was crucified, St Jude with halberd, St James the Less with the club with which he was beaten, and St Bartholomew with a knife to indicate that he was flayed. King's biographer, Ruth Sheehy, has written 'The symbolic identification is made between many of the apostles and Christ through their martyrdom and violent deaths which resulted from their preaching of the gospel. The association with Christ is also indicated by the aesthetic demeanour of the apostles which results from the spiritual purification of a life committed to prayer, ministry, and ultimately sacrifice. Some of the apostles are also wearing a stole which also links them symbolically to the priesthood of Christ.'[6]

By the time King made this window the enduring influence of Harry Clarke's signature style had entirely dissipated, and he was more influenced by contemporary German stained glass artists such as Anton Wendling and Georg Meistermann, whose severe angular figures and harsher aesthetic were the antithesis of Clarke's dainty ethereal creatures. King was influenced also by French artists who worked in stained glass such as Fernand Leger and Gabriel Loire,[7] and is likely to have seen the latter's scheme made in 1964–5 for the chapel of St Patrick's College (now DCU), Drumcondra – though unlike Greenhills, it is abstract and employs the *dalle de verre* technique (see pp 171–9). King, never a great enthusiast for overseas travel, did not visit Coventry Cathedral but is likely to have been aware of John Piper's wall-to-ceiling baptistry window (1962) made in partnership with Patrick Reyntiens, which has, like King's Greenhills window, a large disc of colour as the principal feature, though in Coventry it is gold, not red.

King's *Pentecost* is arguably the finest stained glass window made for a Dublin church in the second half of the twentieth-century. This monumental window which at its apex rises to 186ft, with a width of 80ft at the base, comprises a total of eighty-four panels which slot into the vertical apertures in the precast concrete frame.[8] It should be noted that during Mass the one person who gets to view the window in all its majesty is the celebrant standing at the altar whereas the congregation have their backs to the window; however thematically the window's theme benefits from this arrangement as when the faithful return to their pews having received the Eucharist they should feel enveloped by the joyful experience of the presence of God as revealed by the coming of the Holy Spirit at Pentecost.

Although King's Pentecost is the star feature of Greenhills church, it is by no means the only stained glass. The roof glazing by Murphy-Devitt Studios seamlessly merges with King's wall of glass. Johnny Murphy, who like King lived in Dalkey, clearly liaised with King so that the same colour palette and same mouth-blown glass (most likely coming from St Just in France) was utilized. Noteworthy is that of the six glazed roof panels, the ones furthest away from the gable wall are in lighter tones of yellow and green and slowly build up to the deep blues of King's *Pentecost* window. Likewise, the panels of *dalle de verre* at ground level replicate this approach, as they also escalate in intensity the nearer they come to the gable wall. Holy Spirit church is a holistic, 360-degree experience where one is best placed standing in the middle of the centre aisle to appreciate fully the architect's and artists' (King and Murphy-Devitt Studios) intentions to create something really special. The church was dedicated by Archbishop McQuaid on 24 January 1971.

Richard King, detail of *Saints Simon, James the Greater, Thomas, Matthew and John* (1969–70)

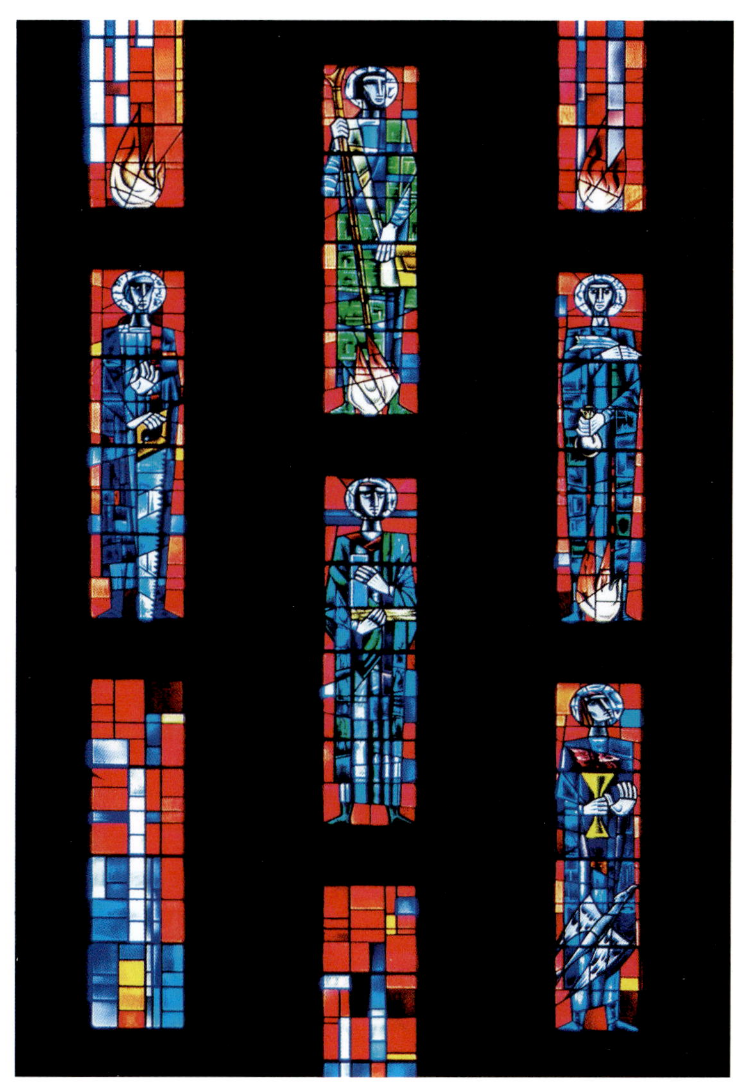

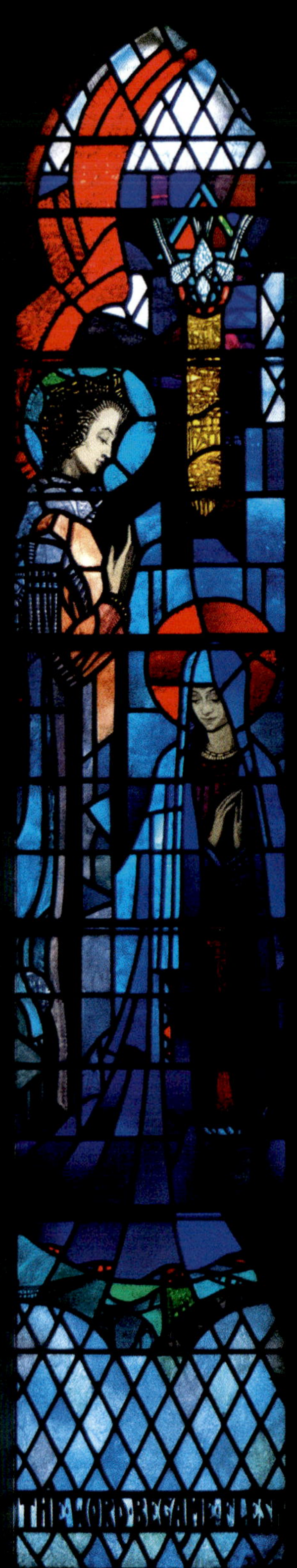
THE WORD BECAME FLES

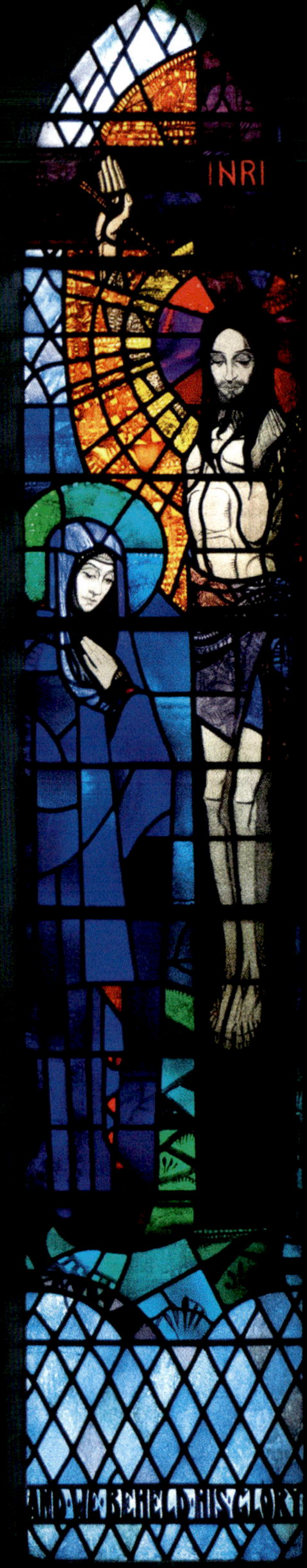
INRI
AND WE BEHELD HIS GLORY

KILLINEY

Killiney has two churches a stone's throw from each other – Holy Trinity and St Stephen's – and both have noteworthy stained glass.

Holy Trinity church (C of I)

Killiney Hill Road, A96 D990

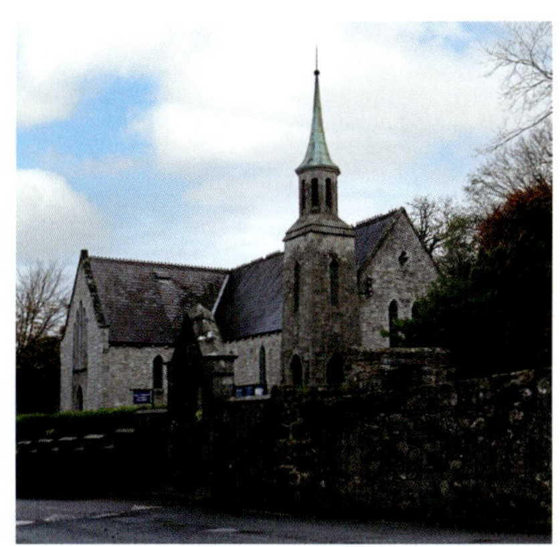

Killiney's Holy Trinity Church of Ireland church is located prominently on Killiney Hill Road at the base of Killiney Hill Park and, not surprisingly, is known locally as the 'church on the hill'. It was designed in the early English Gothic style by Sandham Symes who designed several Killiney residences and lodges, all constructed of locally quarried granite. It features a tiny copper-clad 'witches hat' spire atop the square tower. Holy Trinity church opened in 1859 by which time Symes had been appointed architect to the Bank of Ireland and in this capacity designed bank branches all over the country.

(opposite) Hubert McGoldrick, *The Annunciation and the Crucifixion* (1943–5)

The jewel of Holy Trinity church is a small lancet window by Harry Clarke which is quite simple in conception; it features an angel in profile holding a standard with the Flag of the Resurrection. Clarke himself referred to his window as both the Angel of Hope and the Angel of Peace, and for clarity the leading Harry Clarke expert Dr Nicola Gordon Bowe conflated the two so the usual title of the window now is *The Angel of Hope and Peace*.

The window was commissioned in memory of a local solicitor, Clifford Bartholomew Lloyd, by his widow, Edith, in autumn 1918. The Lloyds lived in the distinctive castellated Killiney residence, Victoria Castle,[1] and it is almost certain that Mrs Lloyd was introduced to the work of Harry Clarke by the Lloyds' near neighbour, Larkey Waldron, who was Clarke's earliest and most important patron.[2] Among the items which Clarke created for Larkey, Mrs Lloyd is likely to have seen the artist's set of nine exquisitely painted, etched and stained small panels illustrating John Millington Synge's poem *Queens* which he made for the bay window of the largest room in Larkey's home, his library. In many respects the figure of the angel in the Lloyd memorial window, aside from the wings and halo, would be perfectly at home among the majestic parade of Synge's queens, each decked out in her elaborate finery.

When Mrs Lloyd was seeking permission to erect the window she arranged for Harry Clarke to travel out to Killiney to meet with Holy Trinity's select vestry to show them his sketch design for the window, persuade them of its merits, and determine where it should be located in the church.[3] At this stage in his career, despite the success of his series of windows in Cork's Honan chapel (1915–17), his stained glass reputation had yet to be established in Dublin and he had no windows in the capital's churches to which he could direct people to view.

Following approval of his sketch design, Harry Clarke drew the full-scale monochrome cartoon for his Killiney window between 14 and 22 November in the garden studio of the house he and his wife Margaret were renting on Mount Merrion Avenue, Blackrock, to which they had recently moved from a flat above his father's stained glass works on North Frederick Street.[4] The background to the angel is composed of diamond quarries, one of the few times Clarke used this pattern in the early years of his career, and this decision may have been made to compliment similarly patterned windows of clear glass in the existing adjacent windows.[5]

Clarke and his friend, the art critic Thomas Bodkin (later director of the National Gallery), informally referred to the Killiney window as Clarke's 'Beardsley window', acknowledging the likeness of the angel to the ethereal figures in profile drawn by the popular English illustrator, Aubrey Beardsley, who worked in crisp black and white.[6] Clarke's sumptuously robed and winged angel stands in finely tooled leather footwear on a little grassy island, possibly meant to represent Ireland, and their windswept hair and flag gently rippling in the breeze are perhaps a nod to the elevated and coastal location of Killiney's church. The angel, with exquisitely fine, profiled features, gazes at a haloed dove, and although the window is not a war memorial as such, the dove with an olive sprig in its beak may represent the prospect of peace at the end of the Great War, and indeed by the time the window itself was completed the war had ended. Among the window's border are, in addition to abstract designs and assorted images, two tiny vignettes of lighthouses in stormy conditions, again perhaps a nod

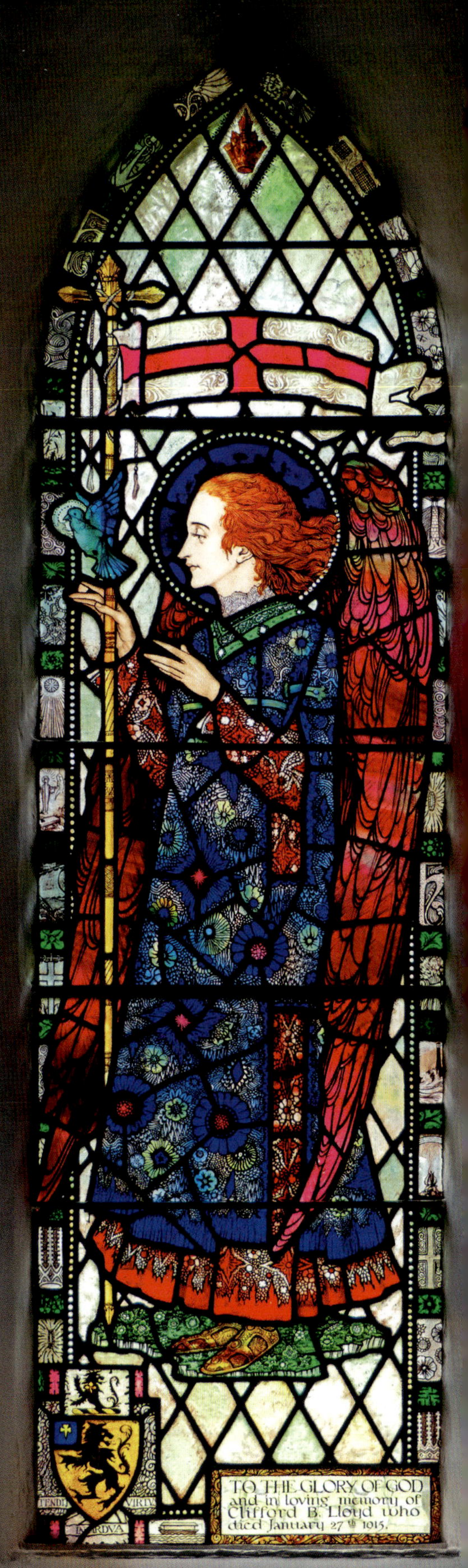

Harry Clarke, *The Angel of Hope and Peace* (1918–19)

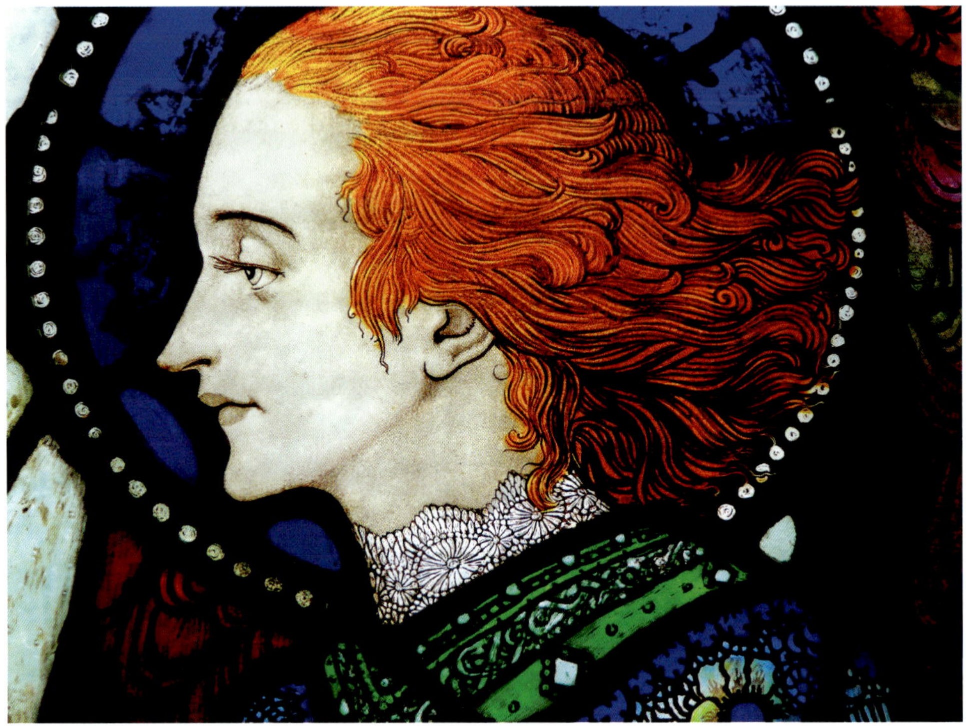

Harry Clarke, detail of *The Angel of Hope and Peace* (1918–19)

to Killiney's coastal location but possibly also to represent beacons of hope. Upon completion at the end of February it was exhibited in Clarke's studio for one day before being installed on 3 March 1919.[7]

Around the same time as Clarke's window was installed, Holy Trinity's select vestry decided to commission a set of three new windows, depicting Faith, Hope and Charity, for the chancel as a memorial to parishioners who had died or had fought in the First World War; regrettably they passed over Clarke – for whatever reason, possibly cost was a factor – and went instead to the long established 'trade' firm of Shrigley and Hunt of Lancashire. The sequence of negotiations and arrangements with Shrigley and Hunt is unclear but the perplexing outcome is that a window depicting *The Ascension* was placed in the centre (likely it had always been there) with *Faith* and *Hope* placed either side, and with the memorial inscription traversing all three lights, while *Charity*, with an inscription in memory of the rector's late wife, is isolated from her sisterly Virtues and ended up being located in the nave. Like Clarke, the designer of the Shrigley and Hunt trio of windows employed a diamond patterned background as a foil to the allegorical figures which are painted in a conventional style with muted tones and are in marked contrast to Clarke's daring ashen-faced, sharp featured and androgynous angel with trailing red hair.

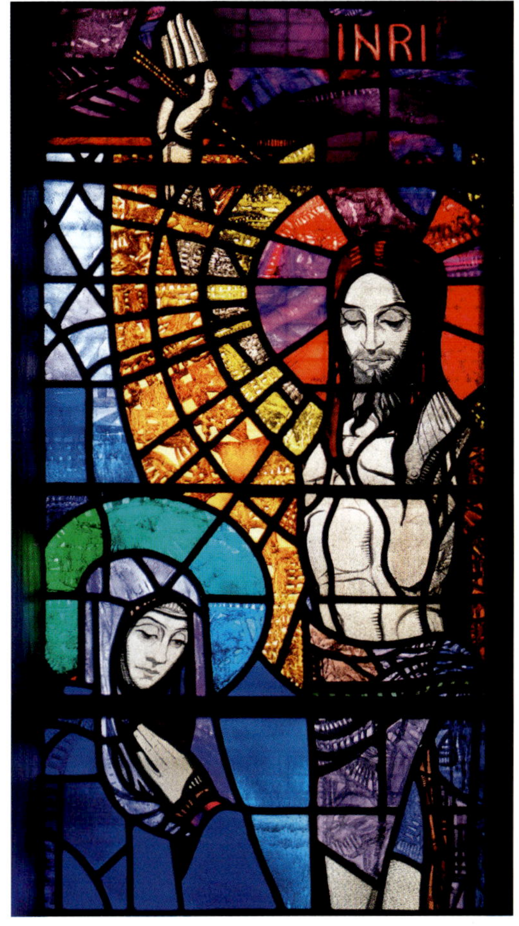

Hubert McGoldrick, detail of *The Annunciation and the Crucifixion* (1943–5)

In September 1942 Canon Ernest Barker was delighted to announce to the select vestry that an anonymous donor had gifted £500 to commission stained glass for the pair of lancet windows in the west gable wall 'to the memory of all people of every race who have voluntarily suffered in causes whose aims are the advancement of the good of humanity.'[8] It is thought that the donor was probably the distinguished railway engineer, Lt-Col. Henry Eoghan O'Brien of Mount Eagle, Killiney, whose only son, Lt-Cdr Brian Eoghan O'Brien RN, had died in the war in August 1940.[9] Having found English artists/studios too expensive due to import duties and war risk insurance the rector asked two Irish artists to prepare designs, and on 21 January of the following year the select vestry approved Hubert McGoldrick's designs for the pair of lancets to depict the Annunciation and the Crucifixion.[10]

Hubert McGoldrick had joined An Túr Gloine in 1920 when the studio was flush with war memorial orders but he seemed to have slowly withdrawn from the studio by the late 1930s; this may have been at least in part related to the diminishing number of orders being placed. Although still only in his mid-forties, his two lancet windows for Killiney would be his penultimate works in stained glass. McGoldrick's commission for Killiney did not progress smoothly; there were issues getting the right coloured glass, undoubtedly a result of the ongoing war, but the rector also became increasingly frustrated with what he perceived as McGoldrick's lack of diligence. Ultimately the completed lancets were not installed until the summer of 1945.

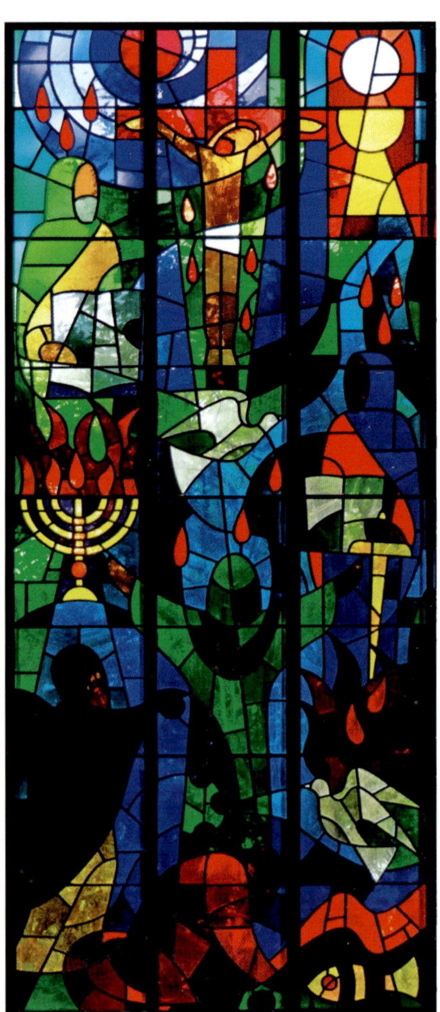

Helen Moloney, *Christ Crucified with St Stephen and Saul, with Symbols of the Life of Christ and the Redemption* (1982)

Interestingly, as in the case of Harry Clarke's window and the three by Shrigley and Hunt, Hubert McGoldrick also chose to feature a prominent diamond patterned background of quarries and set his figures against it. Demonstrating his flair for design he managed to fit both scenes, each featuring two figures, into their respective narrow lancets and although there is a significant space between the two windows he united them visually by the dynamic overall composition. Shades of blue predominate, probably to reference the Blessed Virgin who features in both lancets, and one can see the enduring influence of Clarke on McGoldrick in the facial features. McGoldrick himself was pleased with the end result, particularly from a technical point of view.[11] After the windows were erected a plaque was placed directly below, and the inscription, which includes (in very small lettering) the date '1945', indicates that the windows are a Second World War memorial.

St Stephen's church

Killiney Hill Road, A96 EY61

In contrast to Holy Trinity's prominent position, St Stephen's Catholic chapel of ease, though located close by on the opposite side of Killiney Hill Road, is essentially hidden from passers-by in a secluded leafy hollow. This low-slung modernist church was designed by MacKenna Brock Architects and the most striking feature of the white walled interior is a large (60 square feet) floor-to-ceiling intensely coloured sanctuary window by Helen Moloney. It is among a small number of narrative windows by the artist, and in this instance the story is complex; it deals with the period after Christ's crucifixion and the incidents leading up to the stoning of Stephen, the first Christian martyr, which was witnessed by Saul.[12] As with all Moloney's windows, it features images which have been distilled to their essentials along with recognizable symbols, and relies entirely on vibrant colour and shapes to communicate, with a total absence of any painted detail. The window cost £5,000 and was in place for the church's dedication in March 1982. Sadly it was Helen Moloney's penultimate window; soon after which she seemed to have lost confidence and suffered a sustained creative block, despite offers of work from distinguished architects familiar with her achievements.[13]

The only other stained glass window in the church is located in a shallow alcove; it features a small roundel, *St Joseph with Christ as a Child,* which is set in a glowing honey-coloured rectangular window. The artist who created it, Margaret Becker, was a friend of Moloney's, though the two windows could not be more different in mood and technique. Imogen Stuart, a friend of both artists, supplied the wooden altar and associated furniture.

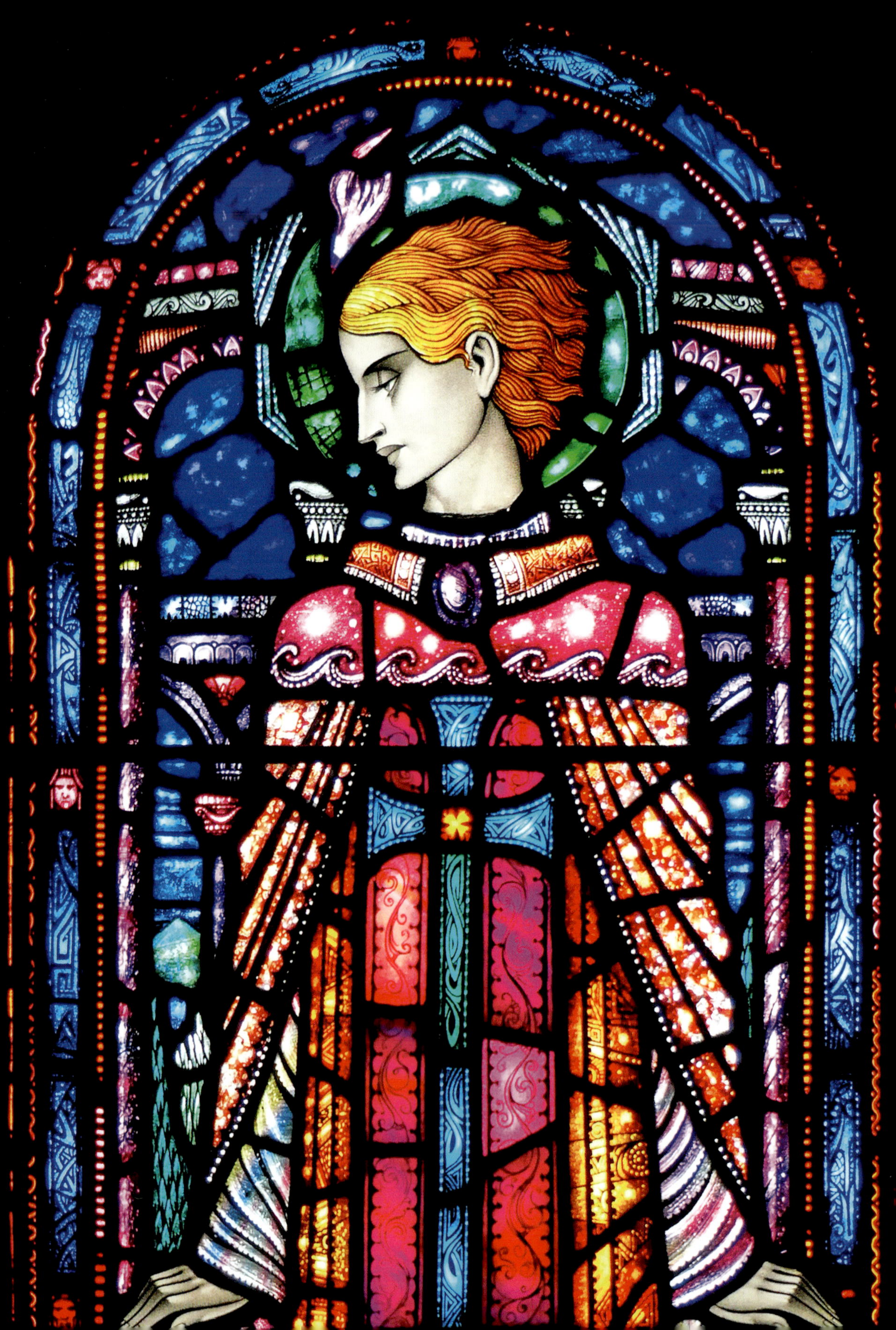

KIMMAGE

Holy Spirit church (RC)

Kimmage Manor, Whitehall Road, D12 WP44

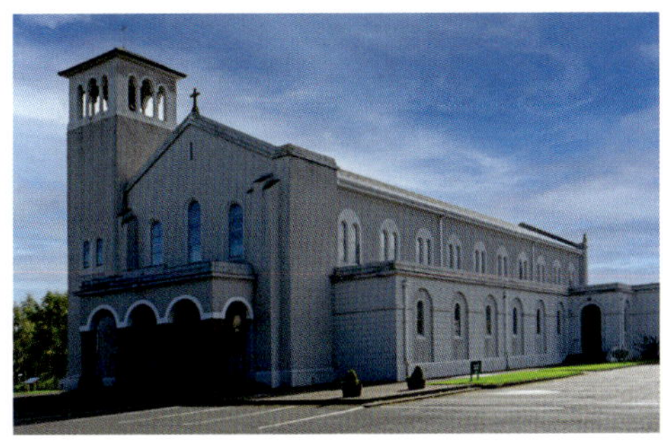

Kimmage Manor church, now part of Kimmage parish, is located off Whitehall Road in a residential enclave. It was designed by the Dublin architectural firm of Jones & Kelly in 1936–8 as a chapel for the Holy Ghost Fathers' (now Spiritan Fathers) seminary. The chapel was built in a straightforward Italianate style with an entrance featuring a Tuscan porch of coupled columns. The windows are all round-headed single lights, though the ones at clerestory level are paired. Inside one is struck by its scale and the arrangement of the long wooden pews in the nave facing each other collegiate-style, which reflect that it once accommodated large numbers of seminarians.[1] The original side altars in front of each nave window no longer exist, and instead the green marble front of each altar has been wall-mounted beneath the windows. The chapel was completed and blessed in October 1938 at which point stained glass windows had yet to be installed.

(opposite) William Dowling, detail of Angel Gabriel from *The Annunciation* (1940)

THE CHURCH HAS A remarkable collection of stained glass, twenty-six windows from Clarke's Studio and one window each from Earley's and An Túr Gloine; all were made between 1939 and 1942. Most of the Clarke windows are in the nave and transepts, eight are located in the sanctuary at clerestory level,[2] and there are two windows in separate rooms. It was an ambitious scheme to embark on, and to persist with, considering most of the windows were commissioned during The Emergency (Second World War), a time of uncertainty and hardship. Clarke's imported their glass from England; however, the consistent quality of the best mouth-blown glass and the expansive range of colours used in the Kimmage Manor windows suggests that the studio either had plenty of existing stock in place or were not hampered by importation issues. None of the windows carries a donor's name and it is understood that the windows, which cost £50 each, were paid for by ongoing fundraising.

There is quite a mixed bag of subjects, several Marian-themed windows, three of Irish saints, a plethora of popular and less well-known English and European saints, and several Old Testament subjects. Records show that the chapel's architects, Jones & Kelly, commissioned the first window in January 1939. This decision may have determined that the vast majority of subsequent orders also went to Clarke's. Two Holy Ghost priests, Fr Michael Kennedy and Fr Edward Leen, commissioned windows in nine different batches over the four years, occasionally a single window and another time a dozen.[3]

Only a small number of the windows are dated and trying to establish with certainty attributions for who designed which window during the decade following Harry Clarke's death can be challenging; in respect of Kimmage Manor it is understood that the vast majority of the windows were designed by William Dowling with a smaller number possibly by either Richard King or Terry Clarke.[4] For the studio the years 1939–42 was a period of transition; King, who had assumed the management of the studio in 1935, departed in May 1940 and his friend Dowling took over that role in a seamless transfer of responsibility.[5] Terry Clarke was only 23 in 1940, and unlike the other two, hadn't had the benefit of being trained directly by his uncle Harry. The majority of windows at ground level feature a single figure, or on occasion two, and a few include a predella scene, and though there is plenty of

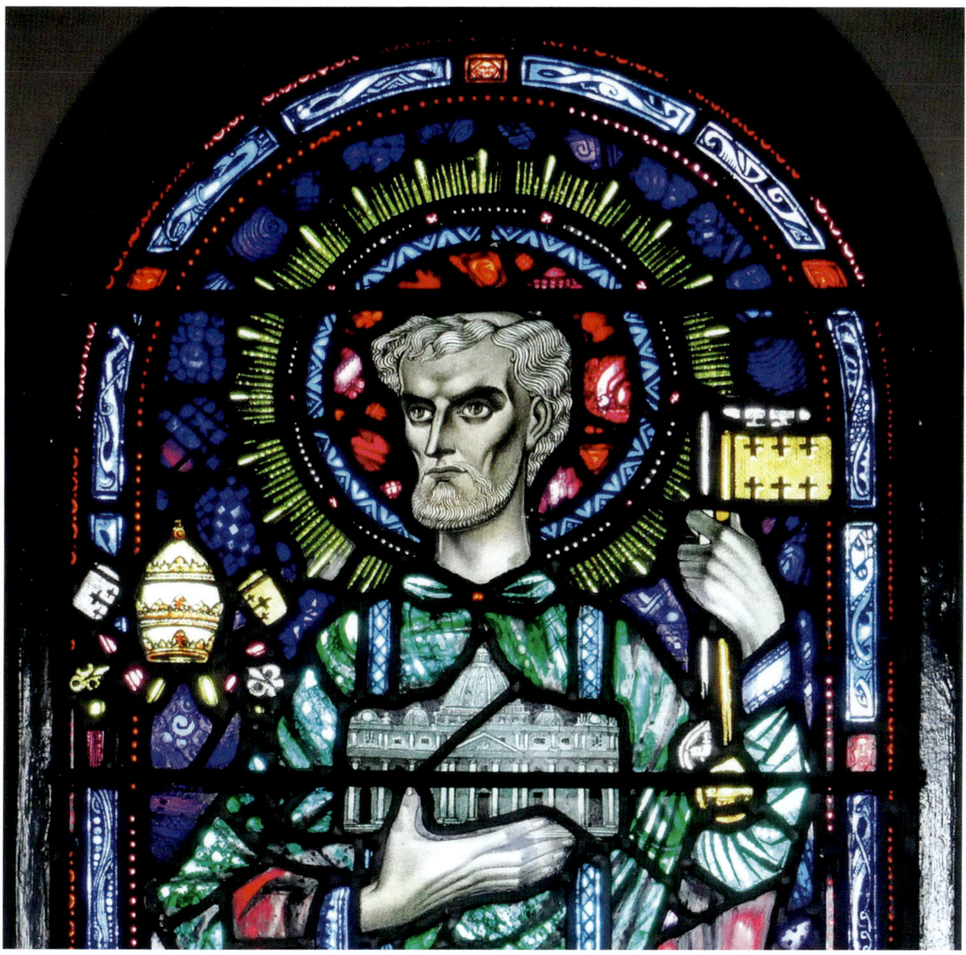

William Dowling, detail of *St Peter* (1939)

variation in composition the overall consistency of style, regardless of artist, makes for a satisfying viewing experience. With so many windows, it is possible only to highlight a few here.

The first window to be installed was *St Peter* which was destined for the north wall of the nave, and at the base it is just about possible to discern the date, August 1939, scratched into the glass. On a list compiled by Dowling in later years he included it as one designed by him.[6] Tall, manly, with trimmed beard, neatly parted hair, chiselled cheekbones and deep-set eyes, *St Peter* presents an intense, assured

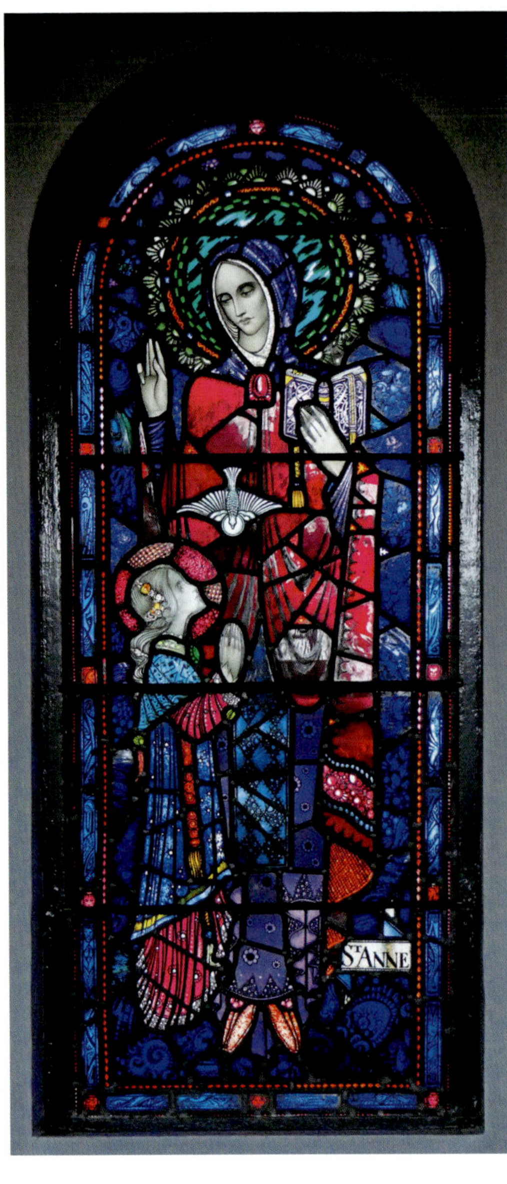

(left) William Dowling, *St Anne with the Young Mary* (1940)

(opposite page) Richard King, *St Thomas Aquinas* (1940)

figure, and possibly the depiction was calculated to inspire the callow young seminarians. In one hand he holds a detailed model of St Peter's Basilica, Rome, and in the other two keys, symbols of his authority and leadership of the early church. The papal coat of arms also features in the window as well as an unusual vignette of a fountain emanating from a dove (Holy Spirit) which nourishes two deer and two lambs which is derived from Psalm 42: 1–2.[7]

Possibly the most tender of the windows is St Anne teaching the young St Mary, which is located next to *St Peter*. It is beautifully composed so that the two figures while separate also harmonize as a single entity perhaps to suggest the intimacy of their relationship, which is mediated by the Holy Spirit in the guise of a dove. Noteworthy is the small volume that St Anne is using to instruct Mary which is covered with a delicate Celtic design. The window is signed and dated '26.8.40' on a small piece of glass at the base but it was leaded in upside down; this is perplexing and one wonders if this was the way it left Clarke's studio or the work of someone doing conservation work on it at a later date.

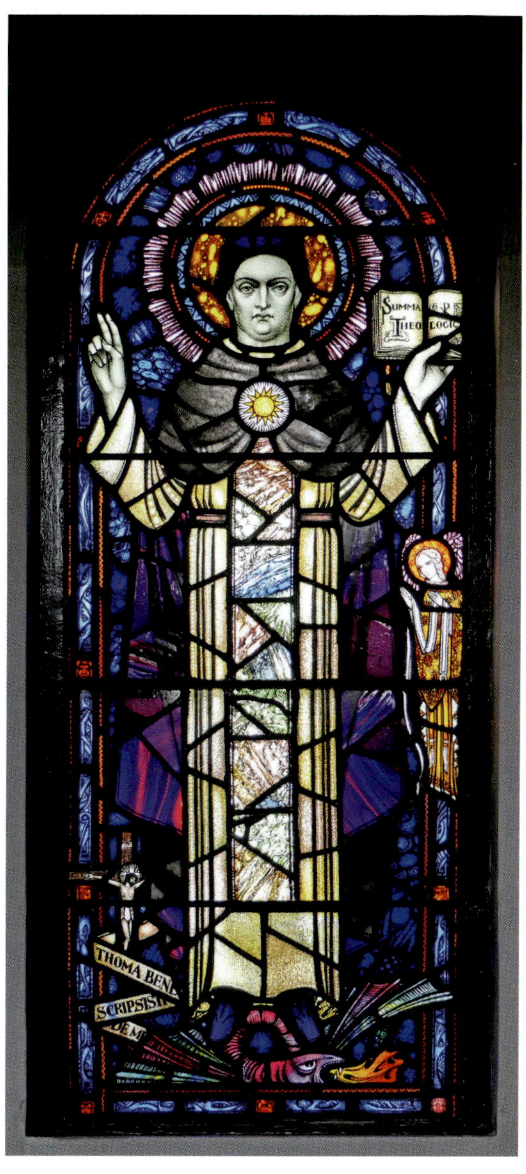

St Thomas Aquinas, the Dominican theologian and Doctor of the Church, can be found in the south wall. He has a distinctly dour and jowly countenance as he holds aloft his best-known work, *Summa Theologica* (Summary of Theology). A dainty little angel hovers at his side presenting him with a chastity belt that according to a medieval legend was dropped by Our Lady from the sky to him at the time of her Assumption; the belt possibly a subtle reminder to the seminarians that they had committed to a life of celibacy.

Next to St Thomas is *St Francis Xavier*, the sixteenth-century Spanish Jesuit missionary, included as Kimmage Manor's principal role was to train missionaries. Of noble birth, he has been depicted accordingly in striped doublet and hose, a length of emerald fabric fashioned around his middle as a stylish belt, and with a plush red and purple cape cast over his shoulders. The predella scene below depicts him on his deathbed with two people in respectful attendance, and although the saint died in China the male figure is wearing a turban, which might suggest a native of India from where St Francis had previously travelled.

In the south transept, three of the four windows are Marian-themed, and in one

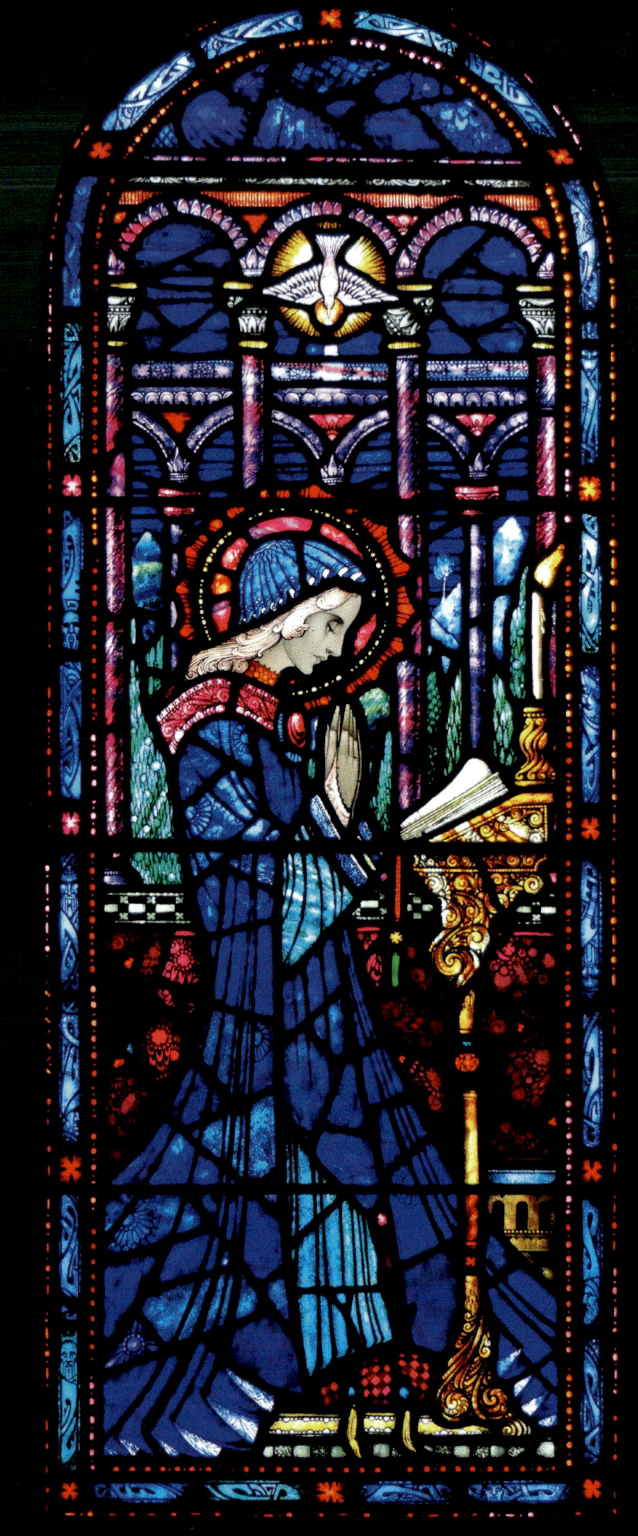

instance two windows have been paired together to depict *The Annunciation*, with the date '26.11.1940' scratched into the glass of the *Angel Gabriel* window. The window with Our Lady in profile kneeling at her prie-dieu is reminiscent of many depictions by Clarke's Studio of this subject, whereas the depiction of Gabriel is more novel; firstly he has no wings, and secondly he is shown opening his sparkling cape to reveal a jaunty short tunic emblazoned with a large decorative cross composed of pink and orange streaky glass. To complete his ensemble he is wearing elaborately tooled knee-high footwear that match his golden hair. If Dowling's *St Peter* window conveys an image of confident masculinity, St Gabriel presents a stylish, fey male. Unusually, Gabriel's name is written in Hebrew,[8] and the Latin words, *Ne Timeas Maria* ('Fear Not, Mary'), also feature.

One of the four windows in the north transept depicts *Edward the Confessor*, the eleventh-century Anglo-Saxon king and saint who is very rarely featured in Irish churches so his inclusion in Kimmage Manor would be confounding were it not for the fact that the president of the college at the time was Fr Edward Leen. William Dowling has depicted the saint with his kingly attributes – crown, sceptre, and ermine-trimmed cloak. There are few art historical precedents for depicting the saint though sometimes he is shown holding a ring which references a charitable deed with which he is associated. Dowling has resorted to depicting him holding a model of a humble church with square tower, which would not appear to represent any particular building but rather a general reference to his piety. He is also shown standing on a sword, presumably to convey that he was a man of peace – often a sword indicates martyrdom but Edward did not die in this manner – and the theme of peace is supported by a white dove which offers him an olive sprig.

The eighteen windows located in the nave and transepts are all by Clarke's, with one exception – midway on the south wall is *St John the Evangelist* by Earley & Co. which is a curious and inexplicable anomaly.[9]

The eight clerestory windows demonstrate some variation in style and treatment, and it is understood that they were designed by both William Dowling and Terry Clarke. The majority feature Old Testament figures, though among the exceptions

(opposite) William Dowling, the Blessed Virgin from *The Annunciation* (1940)

are *St John the Baptist* and his father Zacarias (side by side, south wall of sanctuary). Next to them, also paired, are Noah carrying a model of his ark, and Abraham about to slaughter his son Isaac. On the opposite side is Zechariah who foretold the Crucifixion,[10] paired with another prophet Malachi, though they look away from each other. The final pair of lights feature *God the Father* depicted as both blessing and pointing a finger towards the couple in the companion window, *Adam and Eve*; the latter are the antithesis of Harry Clarke's ethereal creatures and instead present a very robust couple. Noteworthy is the length of Eve's skirt made of heavy animal pelts, which goes well below her knees, possibly to shield seminarians from any impure thoughts. The design of *Adam and Eve* is likely to be by Terry Clarke. All these clerestory windows feature a lack of detail compared to their counterparts at ground level though this is apparent only when viewed with binoculars and arguably fine detail goes unappreciated at this height. Several demonstrate an interest in creative lettering that one does not often encounter in the windows by Harry Clarke Studios. Originally the intention was to fill all the clerestory windows with 'a long line of prophets extending to the choir gallery, telling the story of the Creation, Fall, Patriarchs and Prophets. However, it was feared that the completion of this plan would have darkened the church too much.'[11]

The separate rooms either side of the entrance each contain a window;[12] in the one on the right is *St Peter Claver*, who like St Francis Xavier was a Spanish Jesuit and missionary, now honoured as the patron saint of slaves. The other room has *St Columba* by Hubert McGoldrick which was ordered in August 1940 by Fr Kennedy at a cost of £50 8*s*. 0*d*. though not completed until the following September. It depicts the missionary as a young monk, not the more elderly bearded depiction that is more familiar, no doubt so that the seminarians could relate to him, and he carries a large bejewelled volume, presumably to convey his commitment to spreading Christianity.

In addition to the various stained glass windows, Clarke's also supplied two mosaics, the same size as the windows, which are set into the south and north walls nearest the junction with the transepts. These were designed by William Dowling and were created from what the studio referred to as 'opal glass', a glazed ceramic tile, utilizing the opus sectile mosaic technique; that is precise shapes were

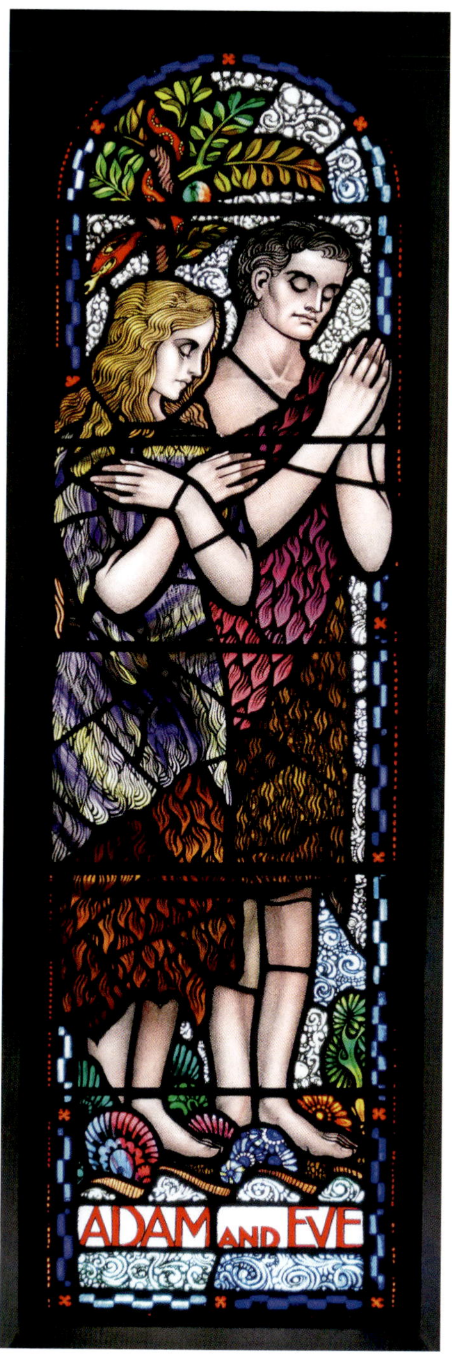

cut that slotted together in the manner of a stained glass window with minimal inclusion of tiny tesserae which are used exclusively in conventional mosaic production. One of the mosaics depicts *St Joseph*, the other honours the *Holy Cross* and the latter incorporates a small brass feature to contain a relic (presumably of the Cross), which is no longer present. Dowling also designed a series of *Stations of the Cross* in 1941 at a cost of £260. These square designs were also created in opal glass and feature realistic treatments of the fourteen Stations in a manner that references Harry Clarke's style while being less decorative and more understated to convey the solemnity of the theme.

Terry Clarke (attributed), *Adam and Eve* (1942)

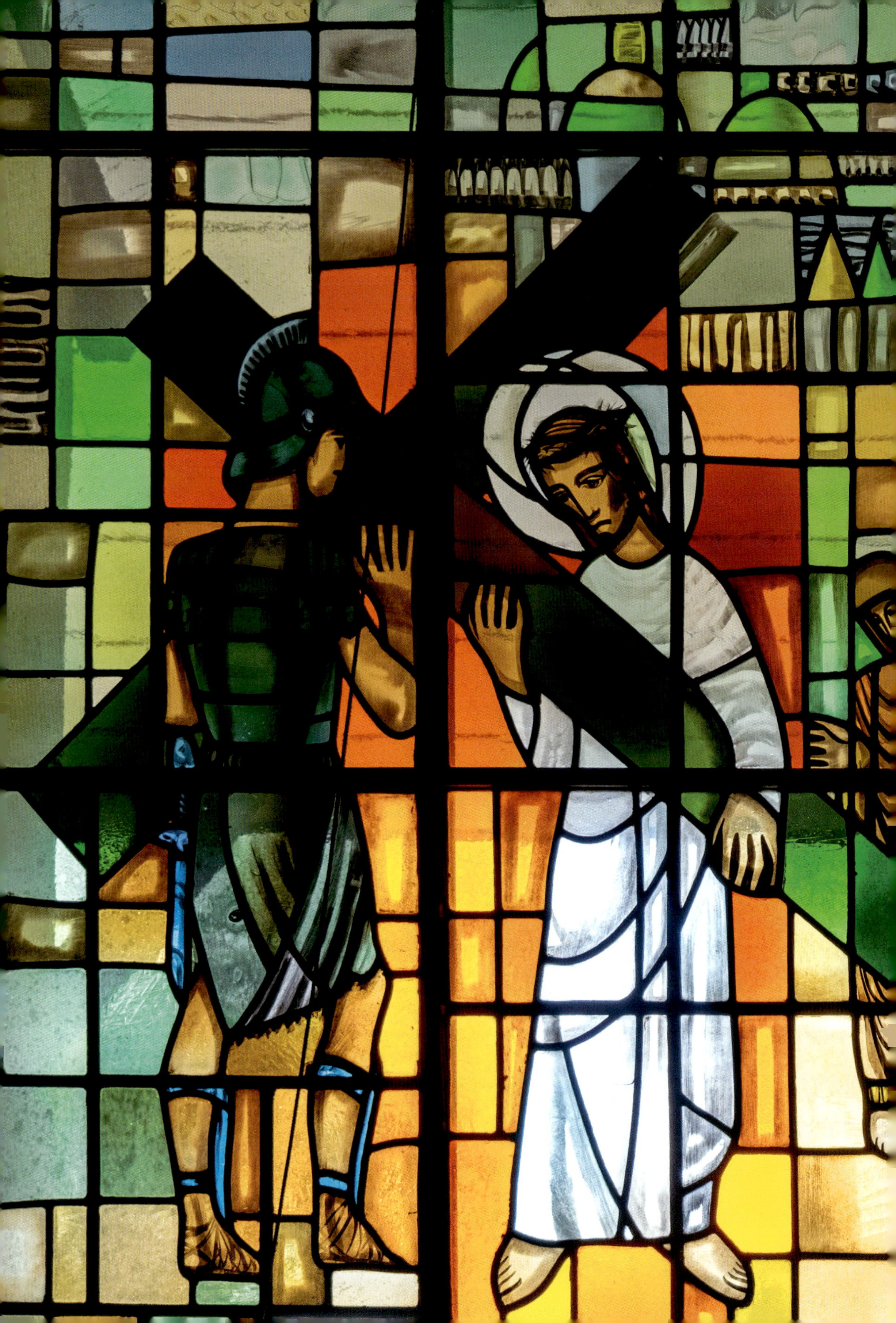

RATHFARNHAM

Holy Spirit church (RC) (Ballyroan Parish)

Marian Road, D14 VR68

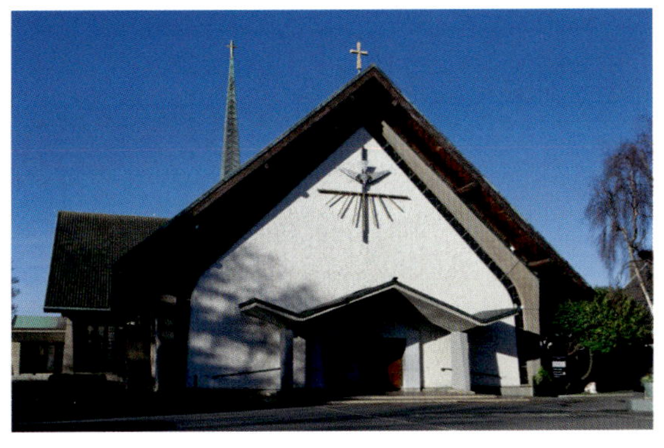

Designed by architect Raymond F. MacDonnell between 1963 and 1967, this large suburban church is of conventional cruciform plan but with an interesting roof structure that incorporates a lantern allowing light to flood in, and above which there is a *flèche*, a small copper-clad spire. The main entrance doors are copper-clad, the left one featuring repoussé lettering and the right one has an attractive rectangular bronze handle depicting the twelve apostles by Imogen Stuart; this hints to those entering the church that artists have contributed to its interior enhancement. It appears that Holy Spirit, Ballyroan, was the only church designed by MacDonnell though he designed a sizable extension for St Brigid's church, Blanchardstown, Dublin.[1]

(opposite) Johnny Murphy of Murphy-Devitt Studios, detail of *Station II, Jesus Carries His Cross* (1967)

BY THE MID-1960S, the two long established Dublin studios, Clarke's and Earley's, were struggling to secure commissions, their aesthetic largely perceived as being too old-fashioned by the younger generation of architects who sought an approach to stained glass that was intrinsically modern, sometimes abstract, and in sympathy with the buildings they were designing. Two new studios in particular, Murphy-Devitt Studios and Abbey Stained Glass, were ready and eager to respond to this opportunity.

Perhaps surprisingly, though Murphy-Devitt Studios were based in Dublin, after over a decade of successful operation, most of their projects had been for other parts of the country, with counties Cork and Limerick particularly fertile, partly due to repeat commissions from loyal locally based architects. The church of the Holy Spirit, Ballyroan, Rathfarnham, was significant as it was the studio's first time (1967) providing all the stained glass for a Dublin church (total cost £12,000),[2] though they had made an occasional window or undertaken schemes for smaller Dublin chapels (a hospital, school, and nursing home).[3]

What would have made the Ballyroan job a particularly attractive proposition to Murphy-Devitt Studios is that it combined figurative windows, symbolic windows, and abstract/decorative glazing; Johnny Murphy, the studio's principal artist/designer, excelled in all three individually but his real métier was combining them, like an orchestral conductor, within a single space. Arguably the most impactful are the series of windows located up high that depict the fourteen Stations of the Cross, and the narrative is spread across four bays on either side of the nave in unusual shaped windows as the confessionals, which are directly below, are surrounded by glass on three sides. One obvious challenge for Murphy was how to configure fourteen separate scenes across eight available windows; he achieved this by subtly blurring the edges of the individual scenes so there is a sense of a continual frieze; on closer inspection it is clear to see that there are two images per widow, and that two scenes (*Jesus Falls the First Time* and *The Crucifixion*) are allocated a complete window each.[4]

Stations of the Cross are an uncommon subject for treatment in stained glass but Johnny Murphy had previously created a series of the Stations – in this instance collaborating with his wife Róisín Dowd Murphy – for St Paul's church, Lurgan,

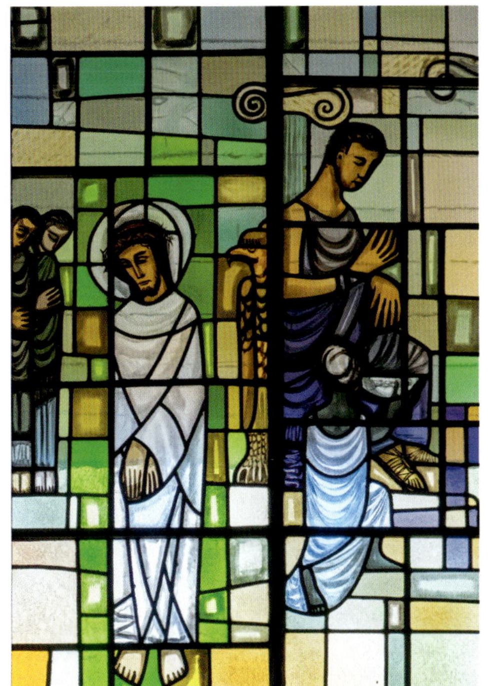

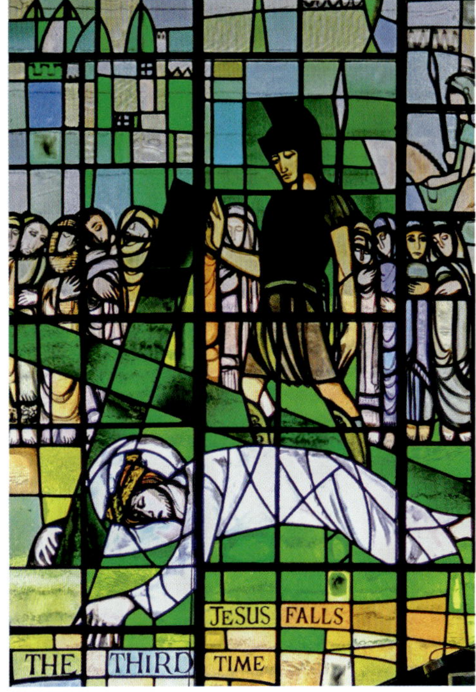

(left) Johnny Murphy of Murphy-Devitt Studios, detail of *Station I, Jesus is Condemned to Death* (1967)
(right) Johnny Murphy of Murphy-Devitt Studios, detail of *Station IX, Jesus Falls the Third Time* (1967)

Co. Armagh, in *c.*1965–6. The set in Lurgan, which are of rectangular format and considerably smaller than those in Ballyroan, feature dramatic close-cropping so that the focus is entirely on faces and hands; however for Ballyroan, Murphy took a diametrically opposed approach, visually pulling back to include not only the full-length key figures of the narrative but also a plethora of onlookers and a distant cityscape. It is difficult to determine his specific influences. Murphy was well versed in art history so possibly early Italian Renaissance paintings featuring large groups of figures in a frieze-like arrangement with shallow depth of field may have been a point of reference. Some of the groupings of the onlookers, closely bunched together, share some characteristics with Imogen Stuart's treatment of the apostles on the door handle. The geometric, modernist treatment of Jerusalem which features in the background, particularly in Station II, recalls the flat, abstract cityscapes of Swiss artist Paul Klee.

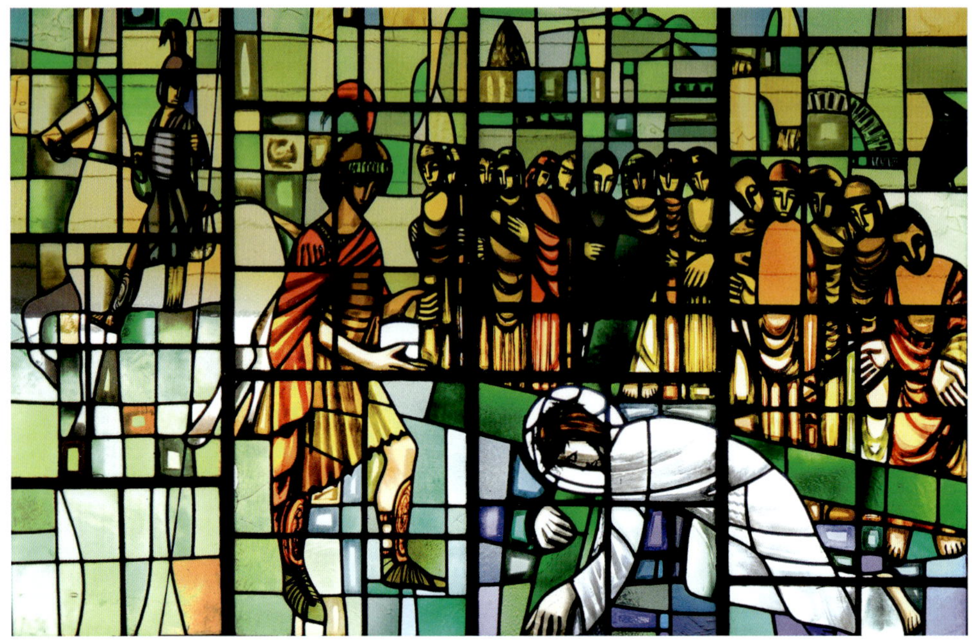

Johnny Murphy of Murphy-Devitt Studios, detail of *Station III, Jesus Falls the First Time* (1967)

One striking aspect of the fourteen scenes is the number of onlookers, not only adults but children and babies that Murphy has included. There is a real sense of Christ's humiliation being made a public spectacle; some of those present appear indifferent while most convey concern and empathy. Soldiers, some on horseback, feature too, some brutishly manhandling him, others carrying out orders with seeming disinterest. Because the scenes effortless blend from one to another across the eight bays, Murphy conveys a sense of Christ's ongoing journey from his appearance before Pontius Pilate at his court in Jerusalem to Christ's death at Calvary outside the city's walls rather than fourteen individual incidents as is the case with conventional individual Stations.

Although the narrative is clear to follow (commencing on the far left as one enters the church) Murphy included the standard descriptor to accompany each scene (though without roman numerals which are usually included). Notably the all-caps serif lettering style is in harmony with the lettering on the copper-clad entrance doors. The Murphys lived near Imogen Stuart and the two families were friendly, and it is quite possible that the treatment of the door's lettering was a shared vision of Johnny Murphy and Imogen Stuart. As the studio was busy at this point the Murphys' talented eldest daughter, Reiltín, not yet 12, was encouraged to undertake the lettering for the Stations. Reiltín Murphy remembers her father guiding her,

> homework was pushed aside and bits of glass covered in pigment were put in front of me: 'write this on that'. The try-outs were on tracing paper, I remember being told that they don't need to be on a straight line, some letters can be up or down from the line. 'Thick bits and thin bits' was another instruction. I was ashamed of them as I was old enough to want everything to be correct and well aware that I didn't know what correct was. I used carbon paper from the typewriter to transfer the letter shapes onto the pigment and then used a sharpened skewer to scratch away the pigment to leave the lettering. They were not written directly. I did a few at a time over days or weeks. The vision was Johnny's as always.[5]

The experience of hand-lettering at a young age paid dividends and in due course Reiltín Murphy became a professional fine art calligrapher and lecturer on the subject. Adjacent to each of Murphy's hand lettered titles a discrete three dimensional wooden cross has been adhered to the junction of horizontal and vertical glazing bars.

One challenge with the *Stations of the Cross* windows that Johnny Murphy had to contend with, which he would have been aware was unresolvable, was the roof's considerable overhang. This feature, popular with some architects of this period such as Andrew Devane, meant that the overhang, particularly in conditions of strong sunshine, would cast a deep shadow across the upper portions of the stained glass and frustratingly detract from the viewing experience.

As one walks down the nave, leaving the Stations behind, one is struck by two sizable floor-to-ceiling walls of stained glass, situated on either side of the sanctuary. While mainly in shades of orange, on close inspection they reveal that the upper reaches feature pale greens, greys and blues which gently merge into lighter tones and in turn a myriad warmer autumnal tones with a smattering of crimson squares. Scattered regularly throughout these glowing walls of glass are spindly little crosses, all of irregular form, a subtle reminder that this is a sacred space. This repeated cross motif was a favourite of Murphy's during this period and could have appeared clumsy or forced were the windows not executed by master glazier Des Devitt (who had trained at Harry Clarke Stained Glass, like Murphy) and his small team.

Located off each of the transepts there is a further room, both simple rectangular spaces with low ceilings, and each with one wall filled entirely with stained glass; one room designated as a baptistry, the other a mortuary chapel – these separate spaces a standard feature in churches of this period – though neither now used for their original purpose. The baptistry features a white dove swooping down, a symbol of the Holy Spirit,[6] and the mortuary chapel features a cross with symbols of Christ's passion. Murphy has utilized the leading in these windows to create a totally different mood to contrast with the calmness of the sanctuary; here he has captured an energy in the leading as it whirls around forming a vortex with the respective symbols, dove and cross, at their centre.

Non-stained glass features in the church include Imogen Stuart's crucifix, executed in polychrome and gilded wood, situated above the tabernacle. Particularly striking, partly due to their scale, are two paintings in oil and mixed media on board, one in each transept, by Seán Keating. He created them in 1967–8, by which time he was in his late seventies and still painting heroic figures in a realistic manner, as he had done throughout his long painting career. They depict *The Baptism of Christ* which features the artist as Christ and his wife May (who had died in 1965) kneeling, and *The Descent of the Holy Spirit at Pentecost*, with Keating as St Peter, along with one of his daughters-in-law.[7] Keating lived locally and regularly attended Mass in the church.

(opposite) Johnny Murphy of Murphy-Devitt Studios, *Abstract Sanctuary Windows* (1967)

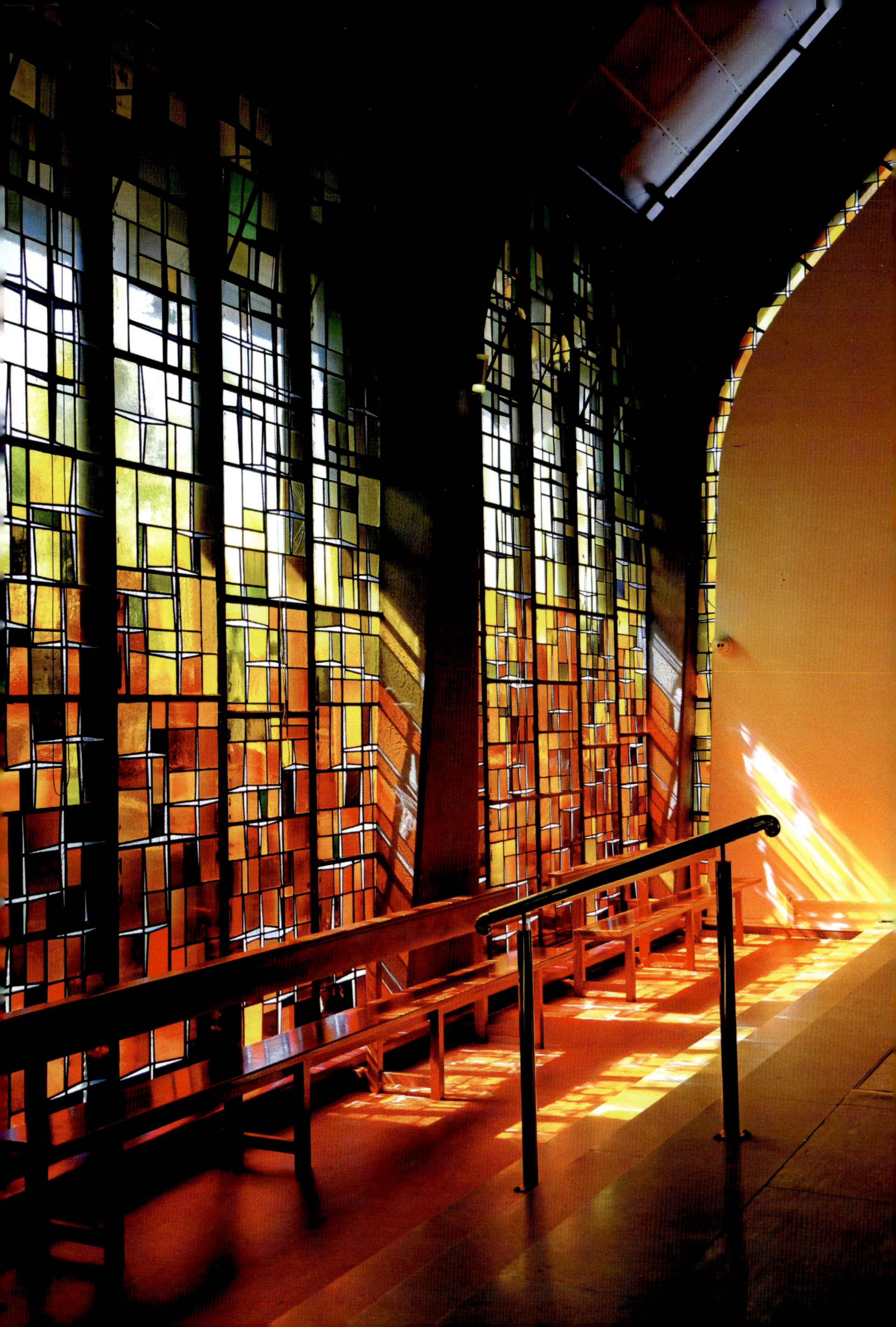

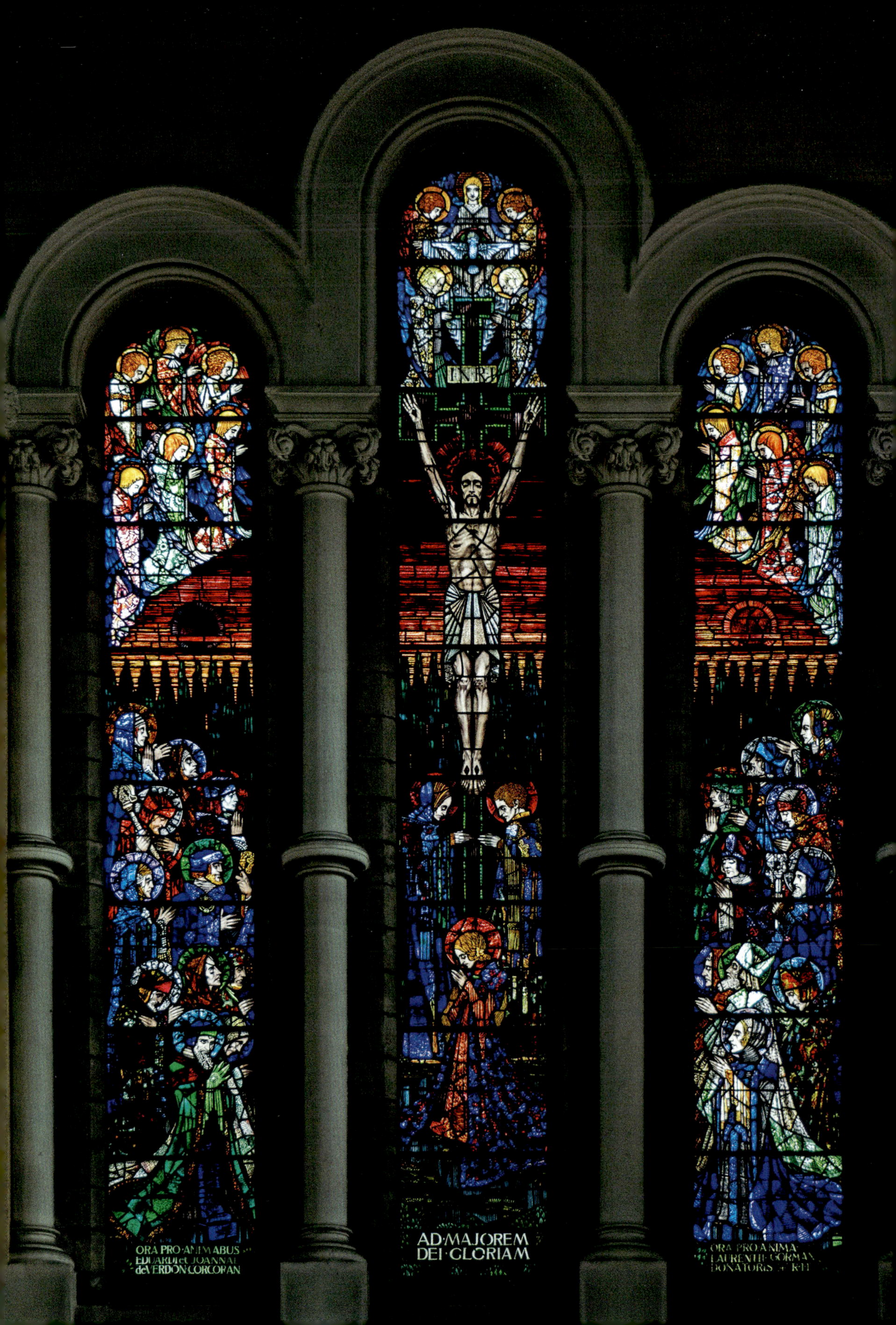
INRI
ORA PRO·ANIMABUS
EDUARDI et JOANNAE
de VERDON CORCORAN
AD·MAJOREM
DEI·GLORIAM
ORA PRO·ANIMA
LAURENTII GORMAN
DONATORIS

TERENURE

St Joseph's church (RC)

Terenure Road East, D06 CX23

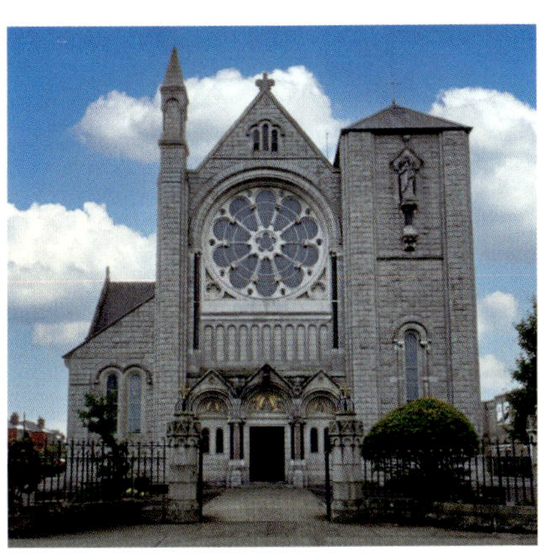

St Joseph's is a commodious Romanesque-style church of dressed Wicklow granite, the initial design by William Geraty Clayton of W.H. Byrne & Son and finished by W.H. Byrne himself in 1904. A spire rising to a height of 160ft was to follow. In time the priority for a soaring spire diminished and the focus moved to expand the capacity for the increasingly cramped congregation, and so in 1952–6 a substantial extension, this time designed by Simon Aloysius Leonard of W.H. Byrne & Son, was built to the rear with the result that the sanctuary in now located at the mid-point of an exceedingly lengthy nave.

(opposite) Harry Clarke, *The Crucifixion and the Adoration of the Cross by Irish Saints* (1918–20)

IF ONE HAD TO CHOOSE a single church in Dublin that demonstrates Harry Clarke's ability to tackle large scale monumental windows as well as small single-lights brimming with fine detail, it would be St Joseph's church, Terenure. The church also contains several windows by Clarke's most talented assistant, Richard King, a testament to the rigorous training Clarke's assistants received from him.

In February 1917 Harry Clarke began discussions about a 3-light east window with Fr John Healy, the parish priest of St Joseph's, who was described by the poet Austin Clarke as 'a man of culture, who met with much opposition in the parish but persisted'.[1] The theme was to be *The Crucifixion*, the subject having been stipulated in the will of the principal donor, Major Lawrence Gorman who had left the sum of £500.[2] At this stage Clarke was creating his own windows by arrangement in his father's studio, Joshua Clarke & Sons of North Frederick Street, though at times both father and son ended up being in competition for the same jobs, as was the case in this instance. Clarke expert Nicola Gordon Bowe surmised that Harry Clarke might not have been that keen on the commission initially either due to the price offered or because of its huge scale.[3] Joshua submitted a design proposal for the window 'of the richest colour' and assured Fr Healy that 'Harry has promised to superintend it, that is, if the work is not given to him',[4] however Fr Healy decided to entrust the commission to Harry. It appears that when the total cost became apparent a local resident, Miss Fannie Andrews, stepped into the breach providing an extra £200 which almost certainly accounts for why her sister's and brother-in-law's names, Edward and Jeanne de Verdun Corcoran, appear in the window too.[5]

Harry Clarke worked continuously on the design of the window from 15 August to 9 September 1918. He exhibited the coloured design in the following year's annual Royal Hibernian Academy exhibition.

Although the window does indeed feature Christ's crucifixion, that is only the centre light's subject; both side lights are filled with a profusion of Irish saints, some very obscure, and the window is correctly known as *The Crucifixion and the Adoration of the Cross by Irish Saints*. Though Clarke inscribed each saint's name on their halos, some are difficult to discern, even with binoculars. Brian Mac Giolla Phadraig has identified them as follows – in the left light, Saints Coga, Braccan, Erc, Conlaith,

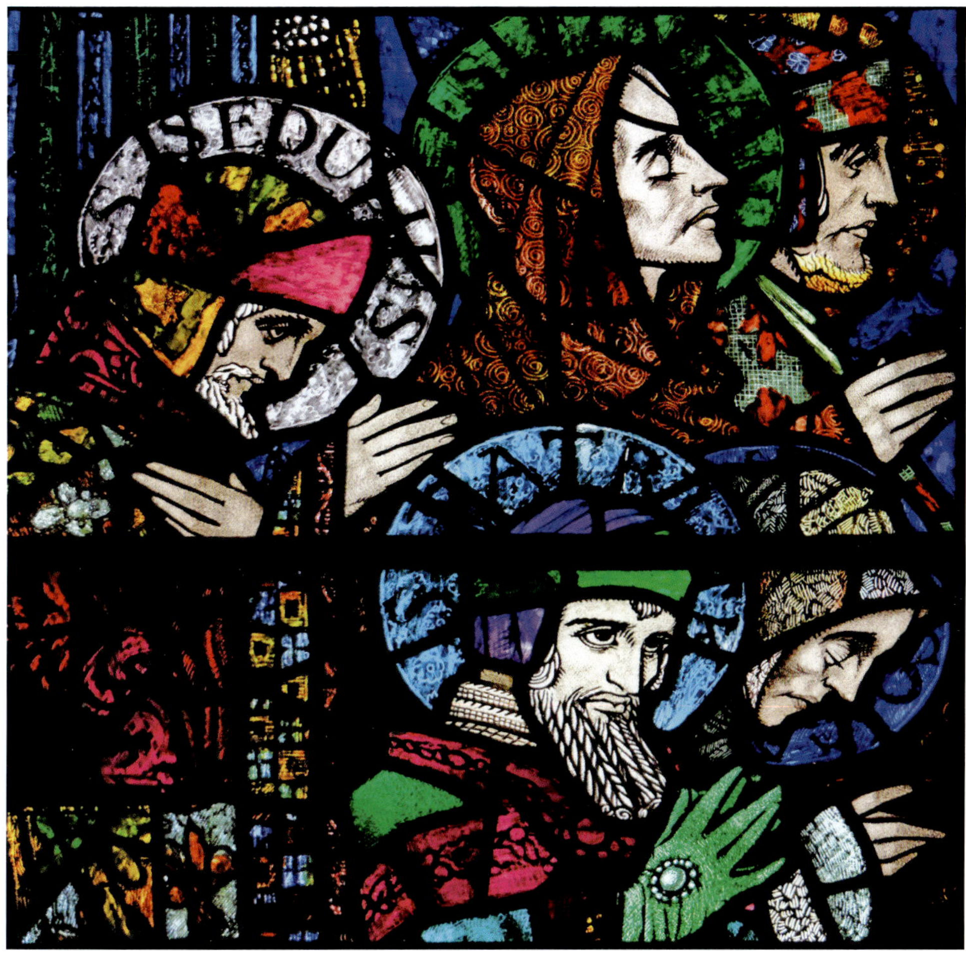

Harry Clarke, detail of *The Crucifixion and the Adoration of the Cross by Irish Saints* (1918–20)

Kevin, Ita, Sedulius, Fintan, Berac, Patrick and Colga; and in the right light, Saints Munchin, Albert, Gobnait, Attracta, Laurence, Brendan, Feichín, Colman, Finbarr and Brigid.[6] Saints from Leinster dominate but there are representatives from Munster and Connaught too. Curiously there are no saints with Ulster associations (except for St Patrick who naturally could not be omitted); St Colmcille would have been an obvious candidate.

Clarke had himself photographed in the pose of Christ, perhaps to ensure that it was feasible for both arms to be positioned upward rather than in the conventional

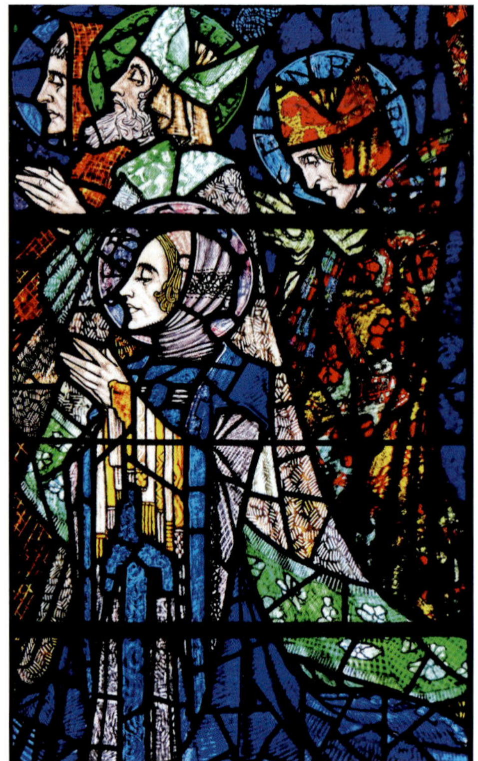

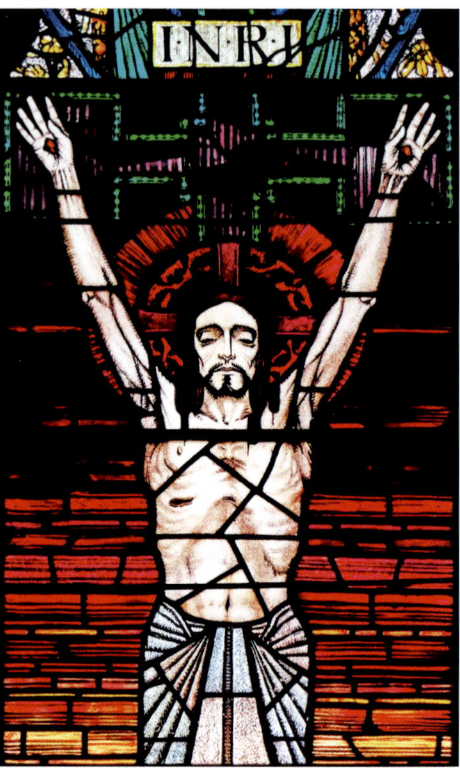

(left) Harry Clarke, detail of *The Crucifixion and the Adoration of the Cross by Irish Saints* (1918–20); (right) Harry Clarke, detail of Christ, based on a photograph of the artist, *The Crucifixion and the Adoration of the Cross by Irish Saints* (1918–20)

horizontal position and he used the photographs for reference when drawing the cartoon. While the pale, gaunt figure of Christ is the focal point, Clarke clothes Our Lady, the twenty-one Irish saints and the two groupings of angels in extravagantly embroidered garments. This results in a sea of highly textured multi-coloured fabrics with only faces and hands remaining visible.

The Crucifixion and the Adoration of the Cross by Irish Saints was located high above the altar reredos. Later, after the church was extended, it was relocated to the far end of the church, again at the same height. In its original location there were no adjacent clerestory windows which allowed the rich, deep colours to glow but in its new location it is detrimentally affected by surface light from nearby windows, something that William Dowling, manager of Harry Clarke Studios, lamented.[7]

Additionally congregants in the new part of the church now have their backs to the window whereas previously it would have dominated their view.

The window's scale is considerable (22ft x 3ft 11in. and the side lights 19ft x 3ft), and was Clarke's largest by far to date, and in time Harry Clarke would undertake a few more large 3-light windows,[8] though it seems he preferred a scale that permitted him to include more visible detail, and in which the viewer can have a closer, more intimate viewing experience. His next commission from Fr Healy afforded him this opportunity and an estimate was sent to Fr Healy for two single-lights in mid-February 1922.

Fr Healy's new windows were destined for the (former) Lady Chapel, to the right of the sanctuary, and have, unsurprisingly, Marian themes, though both are quite different in subject and treatment. On the left, in *The Annunciation* (1922), the Virgin Mary is depicted as a wide-eyed innocent young girl who has scooped up a handful of blossoms from the abundance of flowers which surrounds her and presses them to her chest. The companion window is *The Blessed Virgin in Glory* (1923), and in it Mary

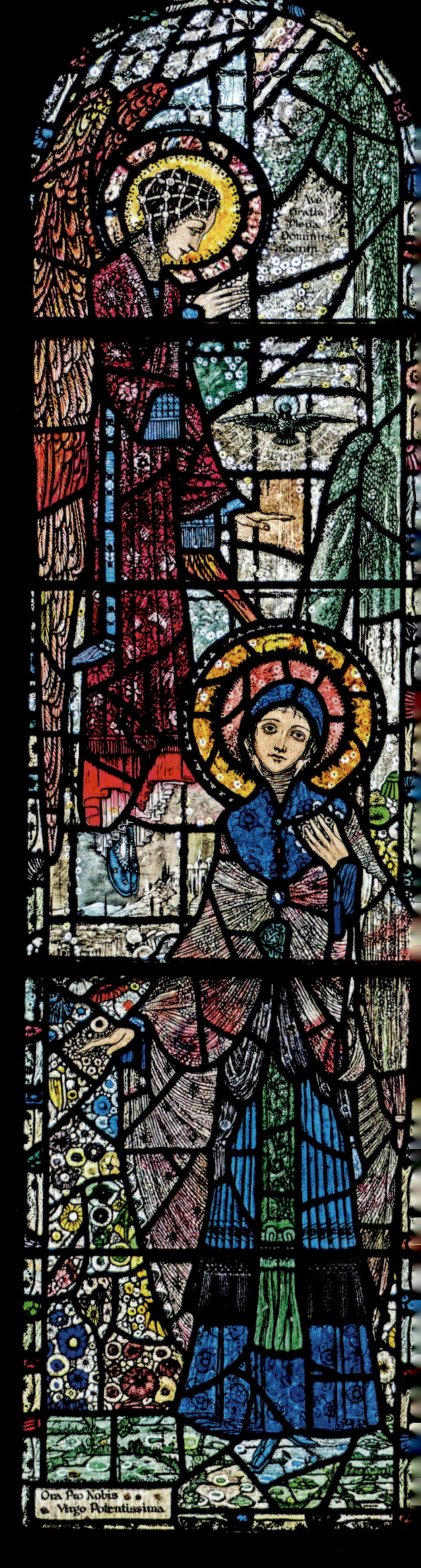

Harry Clarke, *The Annunciation* (1922)

gazes ahead with an inscrutable expression, appearing both gentle and regal while holding an orb and tiny sceptre, and with her feet delicately but firmly crushing a coiled serpent. Both windows contain a myriad details to relish, their treatment a reminder that Harry Clarke maintained a parallel career as a successful book illustrator.

In *The Annunciation* the Angel Gabriel, wearing pale blue ballet slippers, hovers above Nazareth rendered in a grisaille technique. Conventionally *The Annunciation*, one of the most popular Marian subject in Irish stained glass, is represented indoors but Clarke has chosen to depict Mary poised on a crazy-paving patchwork of limestone with tiny flowers poking through the crevices suggestive of a Burren landscape, or perhaps the Aran Islands where Clarke and friends used to go on sketching holidays. At the 1922 art competition held as part of the Aonach Táilteann, the Gaelic Revival festival, Clarke won first prize for *The Annunciation* in the stained glass section.[9]

The Blessed Virgin in Glory depicts the figure of Christ blessing the already crowned Our Lady. The background features vignettes drawn from Old Testament narratives, and mostly the figures wear elaborate costumes and headdresses – no halos included – which convey a secular, fantasy world which is more akin to *Arabian Nights* than traditional visualizations of biblical stories. On the left side in descending order are Ruth, Rachel with a lamb, Ahasuerus crowning Esther, Ahasuerus choosing a dancing Esther to be his queen. On the right side are Deborah with an owl, Rebecca with an urn, sword-wielding Judith holding Holofernes severed head, and below, Judith again, this time fleeing with her maid who grimaces as her blood-stained fingers clench a sack containing the head. What they have in common is that these are powerful, brave, wise, determined women who can be viewed as antecedents of Mary, though to celebrate them in this manner in the Lady Chapel may have seemed unusual to some in 1920s Ireland.

Clarke also used this window to introduce elements of the grotesque and macabre, genres that he was attracted to and which appear regularly in his illustrations, but religious subjects were less likely to accommodate them, and conservative clergy

(opposite) Harry Clarke, detail of *The Blessed Virgin in Glory* (1923)

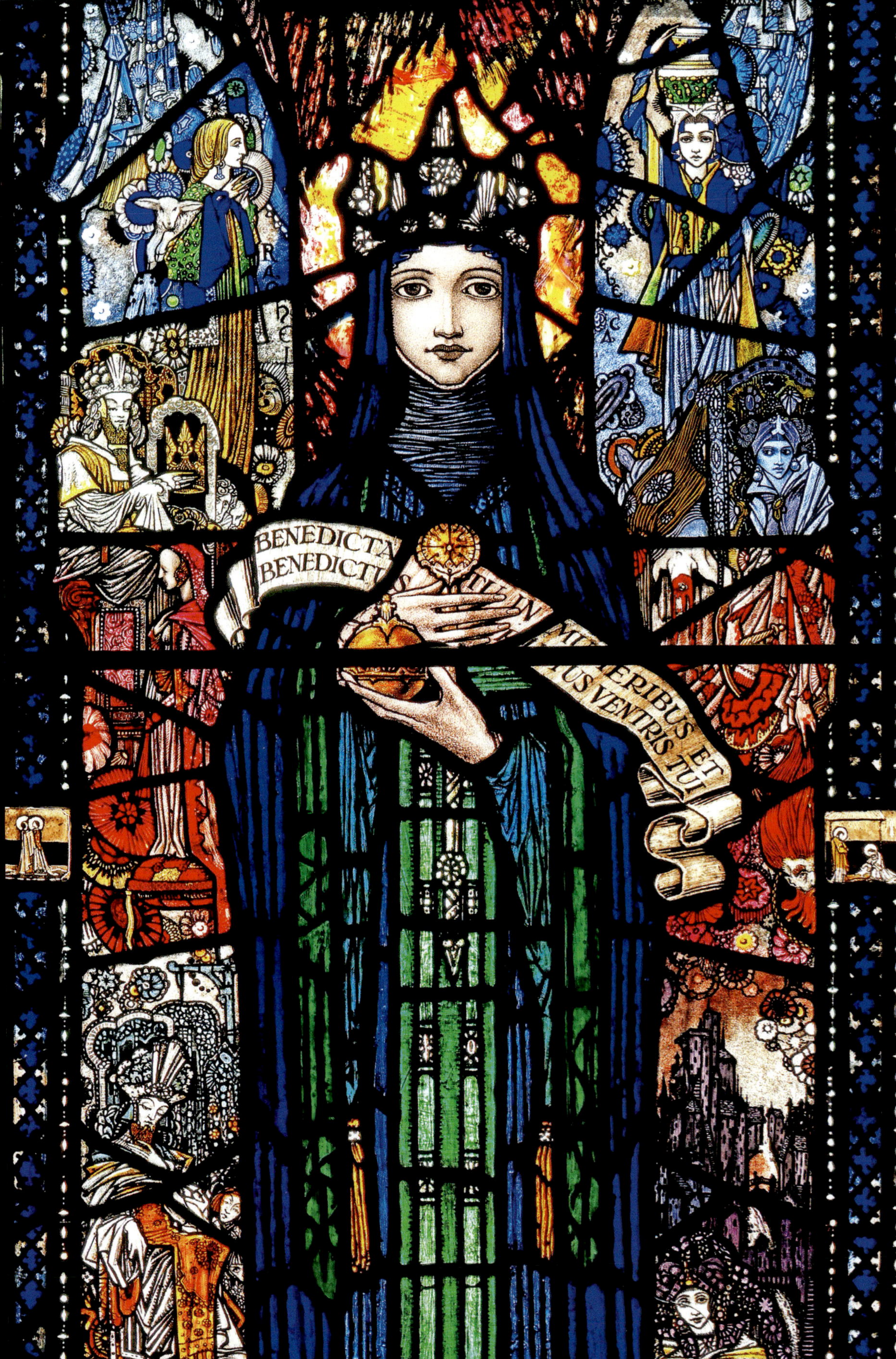
BENEDICTA
VENTRIS TUI

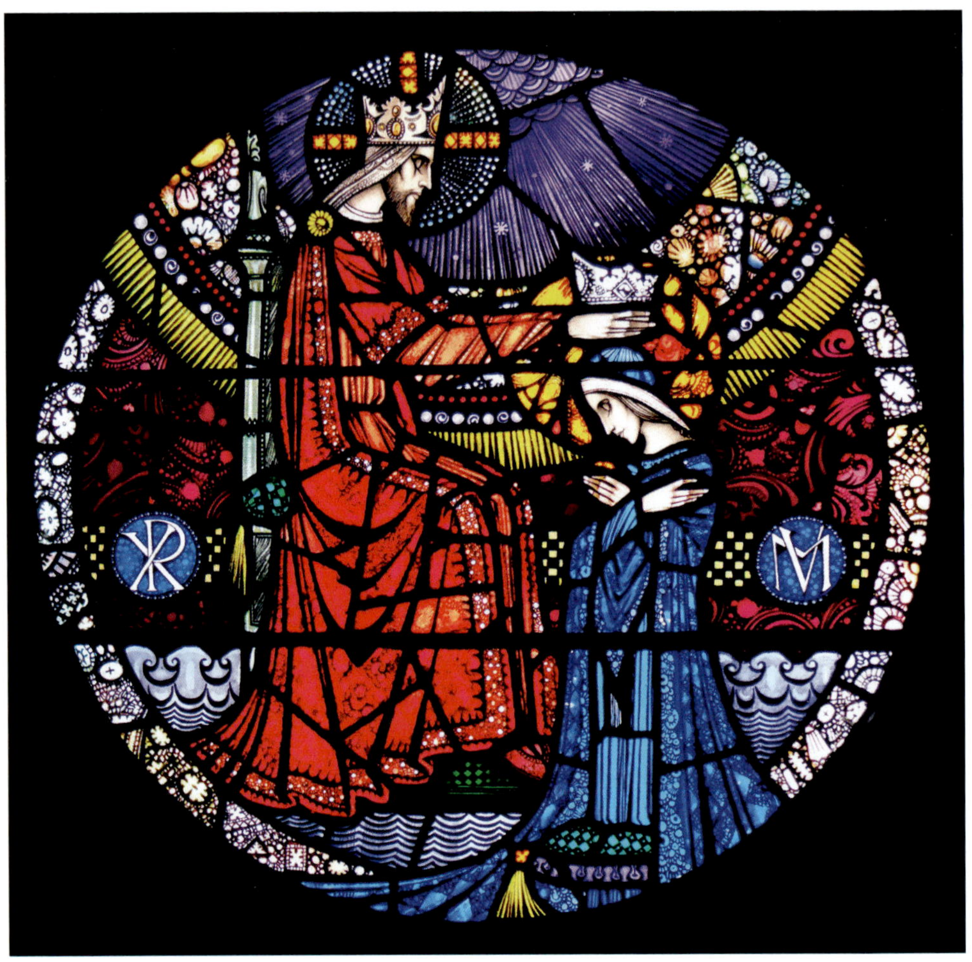

Richard King, detail of central roundel of *The Coronation of the Virgin* (1934–6)

less likely to approve them. At the base of the window are the pathetic cowering figures of Adam and Eve, their nakedness just about hidden by the Tree of Life.[10] There are odd juxtapositions too, no doubt deliberate, where the severed head of Holofernes, his wild red hair still gripped by his murderer Judith, ends up swinging next to a charming little nativity scene in the border.

Canon John Sheehan followed on as parish priest after Fr Healy's departure and he commissioned a pair of small six-petal rose windows, made at Clarke's in 1934–6. In the intervening years since the earlier 1920s windows Harry Clarke had

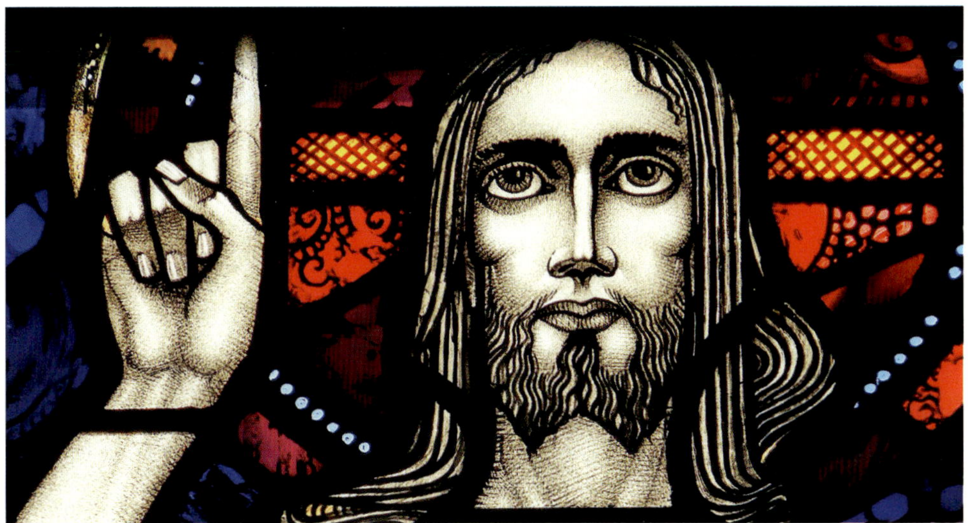

Richard King, detail of Christ from *The Resurrection* (1935–6)

died tragically young of tuberculosis, but the studio continued to champion his distinctive style. The two windows were designed by Richard King who had trained under Clarke and was his most talented assistant, and they depict *The Apparition of the Sacred Heart to St Margaret Mary* and *The Coronation of the Virgin*, the latter being positioned above the altar in the Lady Chapel. They were ordered by Mrs Davy of the Davy stockbroking family who lived locally. They are variations of popular subjects undertaken by Clarke's during this period.

The Lady Chapel had to be dismantled when the church was extended in the 1950s and the space subsequently became a transitional corridor leading from the existing church to the new part, the former altar now relocated to the adjacent transept. Richard King's two rose windows were moved to the new east wall, either side of Clarke's large 3-light.[11]

Of greater visual interest is a single-light, also by King, and made in 1935–6 for the west wall of the (former) mortuary chapel which was located in the base of the tower. The theme was God the Father, the Holy Spirit, and the Risen Christ (which was titled *The Resurrection* in the studio's order books). In the late 1980s, by which time the mortuary chapel was no longer in use, the bottom two-thirds of the window featuring the risen Christ was relocated to the south wall of the nave, though the top third – God the Father, the dove, and three cherubs – remain in their original location. The style of *The Resurrection* is quite a departure from King's two rose windows; as it was designed for a separate room which is far removed from the other windows, it meant that King could allow his own artistic vision some free reign.

In this window King's treatment of the human form is very different from Clarke's, his male figures in particular, as exemplified by his depiction of Christ and the two sleeping soldiers at his tomb, are sturdier and more assertively masculine. His preference of employing a more dramatically tonal treatment for the faces is also evident, but there are delicate decorative touches too such as Christ's finely patterned creamy white garment.

The next year, 1937, another order followed, this time for a 2-light, *The Baptism of Christ*, for the former baptistry, now used as a shop. It is a colourful and decorative window featuring a melange of energetic textures and patterns, some hinting at an art deco influence. King often imbues the faces in his windows, usually with large deep-set eyes, with an intensity of emotion but in this window both Christ and St John the Baptist appear surprisingly detached from the event that is taking place. The predella panels depict the young St John with Holy Family in the carpenter's workshop, and St John preaching to a crowd.

In 1939–40 Richard King made another pair of rose windows, for the same price as the previous set (£100); correspondence indicates that the cost of the windows was a recurring concern for Canon Sheehan.[12] Erected high up in the transepts they depict on the left, *The Little Flower before Pope Leo XIII*, and on the right, *The Virgin Mary and St Anne*. The former is the more interesting as it depicts a recorded event that took place in November 1887 when 15-year-old Therese pleaded with the elderly pontiff to allow her to enter a Carmelite convent at Lisieux. Roses, associated with 'The Little Flower', feature in the cusps surrounding the roundel.

The erection of the final window took place in 1946, after King had left Clarke's and William Dowling had taken over his role as manager and chief artist, and it was he who designed the enormous rose over the organ gallery. Some negotiations took place concerning the cost and treatment options, and the result, while impressive in terms of scale, is not one of Dowling's most memorable works.

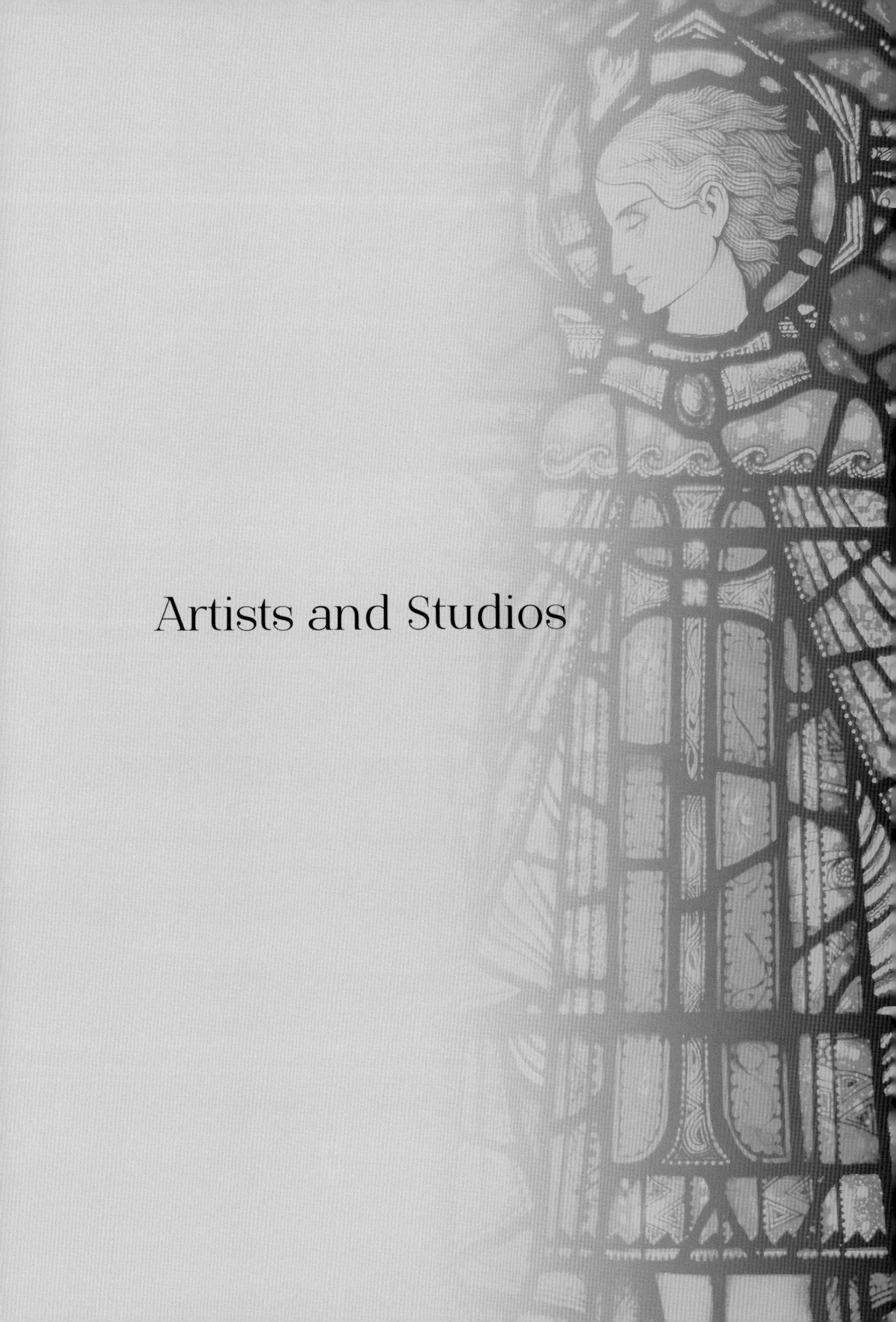

Artists and Studios

Abbey Stained Glass Studios had its genesis in the Dublin Glass and Paint Company which was founded in the late 1920s by Tom Ryan and was located at Middle Abbey Street. The company prospered providing glazing for domestic, commercial and ecclesiastical buildings. Ryan's nephew, Frank Ryan (1918–88), started attending the National College of Art in 1934 and joined the company in 1940; four years later he established Abbey Stained Glass Studios under the umbrella of the parent company with a mission to supply artistic stained glass for churches.

Patrick Heney, who had worked at Harry Clarke Studios from the early 1930s until 1940, was Frank Ryan's first recruit. Willie Earley, of the stained glass dynasty, had spent a few years working with his uncle William E. Earley in the family business before changing his allegiance to Abbey where he had become a full-time artist by the mid-1950s. Manus Walsh was also an early recruit. The most talented addition to the crew was George W. Walsh (see also separate entry) who had returned from working in the United States in the early 1960s. He brought with him a modern aesthetic and experience of new techniques such as *dalle de verre*.

Ryan, who relished the company of artists, knew the painter George Campbell from holidaying in Co. Galway and after Campbell's religious-themed works won various awards Ryan invited him to join Abbey despite his having no specific stained glass experience. Unlike Clarke's or Earley's, at Abbey Frank Ryan permitted each artist to design in their own style, encouraging collaboration where appropriate, so for instance George Walsh and Willie Earley regularly executed Campbell's designs. The 1960s and 70s were a particularly fruitful period for Abbey; during this boom in Catholic church building the studio supplied many churches with complete schemes of windows, often abstract or semi-abstract as well as figurative and symbolic. Designs were usually adventurously modern and the best of mouth-blown pot metal glass was used in conjunction with smaller quantities of factory manufactured cathedral glass.

In addition to the artists named above Ryan also facilitated independent artists who needed their designs fabricated by skilled glaziers, these included Richard King, George Stephen Walsh, Gillian Deeney, Helen Moloney and Sheila Corcoran. Among Abbey's large Dublin commissions was Our Lady of Victories church, Ballymun (1968), which features works designed by George W. Walsh, Moloney and Corcoran.

Frank Ryan was a skilled salesman and every two years would travel to the United States for a three-month period securing sufficient orders from clergy to keep the studio busy until the next trip. A year before Frank Ryan died in 1988, his son Ken took over the business and relocated it to Kilmainham where it still remains, and he appointed Kevin Kelly, who had joined the studio at the age of 14 in the early 1940s, as senior artist. Abbey Stained Glass Studios continues to undertake new commissions but in recent decades has increasingly specialized in conservation and restoration.

An Túr Gloine – In 1901 Sarah Purser, the established painter, arranged with Christopher Whall, the leading English arts and crafts stained glass artist and educator, to send his best apprentice, Londoner A.E. Child, to teach classes in the craft at the Dublin School of Art and in parallel establish a new studio that would employ the cream of his students, and so An Túr Gloine was inaugurated on 1 January 1903 at 24 Upper Pembroke Street. Purser funded the enterprise and for the next four decades played a key role in selecting artists, liaising with patrons and promoting the enterprise while Child held the role of official manager. Michael Healy and Catherine (Kitty) O'Brien were the first recruits, followed by Beatrice Elvery and Ethel Rhind, and in 1911 by Wilhelmina Geddes. All the artists were encouraged to develop their own styles and, as advocated by Whall, take sole responsibility for all aspects of their individual windows from inception to completion, with support from skilled glaziers. The studio soon established a reputation for creative and craft excellence, always using the best materials.

The studio was particularly favoured by wealthy Protestant patrons, partly due to the social circle Sarah Purser moved in and the many contacts she had made during her peak portrait painting days. An outcome of the First World War was many war memorial commissions, so much so that a new artist, Hubert McGoldrick, was invited to join the studio. Around this time the studio began to enjoy overseas success with orders for Britain, North America and New Zealand but it was not until the mid-1920s, largely due to its promotion by leading American stained glass artist Charles Connick, that it received several plum commissions in the United States.

In 1924 Geddes, who with Healy was one of the two most talented artists, departed An Túr Gloine and relocated to London. Although the studio operated on broad co-operative principles from the outset it was only in 1925 that it officially registered as a co-operative society with all the artists holding shares, and with Purser acting as chairperson and Child as secretary.

The final artist to join the studio, in the mid-1930s, was the abstract and cubist painter Evie Hone, despite an initial rebuff from Purser. Hone developed a close professional relationship with Healy, and immediately began creating daringly modern stained glass. She received commissions from the Irish state, the most important being a large window for the 1939 New York World's Fair. Despite her success and the injection of creative energy, the studio struggled financially during much of the 1930s. A.E. Child died in 1939 with Rhind retiring around the same time. The following year Purser, aged 92, announced her decision to discontinue her involvement in the studio. Healy died in 1941 and three years later An Túr Gloine was formally dissolved with O'Brien buying out the studio and contents while Hone established her own studio in Rathfarnham. Following a disastrous fire in 1958 O'Brien rebuilt An Tur Gloine.

Phyllis Burke (b. 1930) – Originally from Kildare town, Phyllis Burke began attending the National College of Art as an evening student in 1948. She studied drawing and painting under Maurice MacGonigal and Seán Keating, and sculpture under Domhnall Ó Murchada. At weekends she, along with a small group of fellow students, went sketching and painting and it was on one of these occasions in 1950 that she met her future husband, the architect Arthur Gibney. About 1954 she began attending stained glass classes run by Johnny Murphy (later of Murphy-Devitt Studios) at the School of Art, and by around 1958 she embarked on her first stained glass commission, a series of small square Stations of the Cross for a church in rural Nigeria at the behest of an Irish architect. However before being despatched, two of the Stations were exhibited at the Irish Exhibition of Living Art in Dublin which in turn led her to being commissioned by Liam McCormick, the distinguished church architect, to create three windows depicting Irish saints (1961) for the church he was then designing at Milford, Co. Donegal. This pivotal commission placed her windows alongside two much more established stained glass artists, Patrick Pollen and Patrick Pye. In fact she made her Milford stained glass windows with guidance from Pollen in An Túr Gloine, Upper Pembroke Street, where he was renting half of the studio space from the then owner, Catherine O'Brien.

Church building in Ireland was booming post Vatican II and Burke's experience was that one local commission often led to another such as her series of windows for several Galway churches. She often worked directly with priests and enduring friendships developed with various diocesan clergy and with members of the Carmelite order in particular. She also worked for several architects rather than one in particular. Like many stained glass artists of her day she moved comfortably between abstract leaded windows and highly narrative ones, and everything in between, always responding to the architecture of the location.

From 1974 onwards Phyllis worked with one particular glazier, Dermot McLoughlin, and they teamed up for what is perhaps her best-known commission, a series of twelve single-lights (eight of which measure 15.5ft x 6.5ft) for the Carmelite church in Clarendon Street, Dublin. These span the years 1990 to 2006. Phyllis Burke also designed two windows for the Carmelite community in Loughrea, Co. Galway, a window depicting Edith Stein (one of the windows she was most proud of, which was also a subject she returned to in her Clarendon Street series) and the other, the Good Shepherd. After Frances Biggs died in 2006 the Carmelites in Terenure College turned to Phyllis Burke to complete the final two windows for their school chapel, figurative single-lights depicting the Carmelites as missionaries, and the Carmelites as educationalists.

Phyllis Burke also worked in enamel from time to time, usually treating religious subjects. Stations of the Cross by her can be found in the Catholic church, Milltown, Dublin.

Alfred Ernest (A.E.) Child (1875–1939) – Born in London, A.E. Child studied at the Central School of Arts and Crafts. He joined Christopher Whall's stained glass studio, most likely as a paid studio assistant. Whall was by then a key figure in the arts and crafts movement, and Child has been described as his 'chief helper' and 'favourite pupil'. While there it is known he assisted Whall on his magnum opus, a magnificent series of windows for Gloucester cathedral.

1901 was a turning point for Child – early in the year he got married, moved to Dublin, and began teaching stained glass classes at the School of Art. On 1 January 1903 An Túr Gloine, a custom-built stained glass studio at 24 Upper Pembroke Street, formally opened with Child as official manager and his students would trail up to the studio with their glass to have it fired in the kiln.

The first entry in the An Túr Gloine order books was for a 2-light sanctuary window, the *Annunciation*, for Loughrea Cathedral which was designed by Child though closely adapted from a slightly earlier window by Whall, as was the case with the other two sanctuary windows. All were executed by Child with assistance from Michael Healy and Catherine O'Brien.

Child's importance in the history of twentieth-century Irish stained glass cannot be underestimated. He was an excellent craftsman, a dedicated and exacting teacher, and was solely responsible for instructing a generation of Irish stained glass artists in the craft including Clarke, Healy and Geddes. His teaching principles, his design philosophy and visual aesthetic were all closely derived from his mentor and he rarely deviated. Like Whall, he had a preference for large areas of pale quarries, loosely matted to diffuse the light, contrasted with rich, deep colours, always using the finest of pot-metal glass, and as with Whall, nature was a regular source of inspiration.

Aside from teaching the craft at the School of Art and managing An Túr Gloine during his career in Ireland he designed around 130 windows. Throughout this time his style and technique remained remarkably consistent. One of Child's weaknesses was his inability to instil much individual personality or expression into the faces he painted, many having a bland, generic quality to them. Following the First World War he undertook a significant number of war memorial commissions; these, and allegorical figures generally, suited him as they offered the opportunity to paint idealized, heroic figures, often in suits of armour which he was adept at rendering.

The window he considered his best was also his largest, a 5-light (1918) for the Unitarian church, Dublin, which consumed over a year of his life. Featuring five principal figures, including one with children (for which it is likely his own were the models), five predella panels and extensive tracery, it interprets the themes of discovery, truth, inspiration, love, and work.

Despite failing sight in his later years A.E. Child continued designing and painting windows apace, even completing three in his final year, 1939.

Clarke's studio – Joshua Clarke, originally from Leeds, established a church decoration business under his own name in 1886 at 33 North Frederick Street, Dublin. A natural entrepreneur, in 1892 he hired an English artist, James E. Pope, and added stained glass to the firm's services. After twelve years Pope was replaced by Dublin native, William Flood Nagle. Joshua clearly envisaged that his two sons, Walter and Harry, would follow him into the business, changing the name of the company to Joshua Clarke & Sons in 1900 before the boys had even entered their teenage years. Of the two, Harry demonstrated a prodigious talent and after leaving school aged 14 he started working in the family business. In due course, as his creative reputation soared, Harry began to make his own windows while paying his father for the use of materials, facilities and glaziers' time.

When Joshua died unexpectedly in 1921 both sons took over the running of the business, moving to larger premises across the street at nos. 6 and 7, and with increasing orders Harry began to train skilled assistants and progressively delegated the execution of the windows he had designed. In 1928, with his health deteriorating, he engaged two exceptionally talented young artists, Richard King and William Dowling, who would become key to the studio's future. Clarke spent much of 1929 and the early part of 1930 in a Swiss sanatorium for the treatment of tuberculosis but continued to design windows and liaise with the studio. In March 1930 a decision was made to split the business in two – Walter would manage the church decoration side, retaining the original name, and Harry would take over the stained glass side, naming it Harry Clarke Stained Glass Limited. To cope with Harry's declining health an English artist, Cecil (also known as Charles) Simmonds, was engaged as manager.

Following Clarke's death in January 1931 there were plenty of orders on the books and while Simmonds continued as manager, King and Dowling became the principal artists supported by a team of skilled glass painters such as George Stephen Walsh. For the studio to succeed it was deemed essential that Harry Clarke's trademark style was scrupulously adhered to, though over the 1930s it slowly evolved while remaining clearly recognizable. Simmonds departed in 1935 and King took over as manager with Dowling succeeding him in 1940 – all seamless transitions – and with Harry's widow, Margaret, steering the company throughout. Terry Clarke, son of Walter, became one of the key artists. By the 1950s the studio's signature style had become more mainstream with less focus on detail, and often not as readily identifiable with Harry Clarke. Although orders from Irish patrons began to diminish in the 1950s and 60s there was a significant increase in commissions from appreciative overseas clients, particularly among the Irish diaspora in the United States. During this period Harry's children David and Ann became actively involved in the studio while Dowling remained as manager and chief artist; however in 1973 a decision was taken to close the studio.

Harry Clarke (1889–1931) – Clarke's father, Joshua, operated a church decorating and stained glass business in Dublin's north inner city and from a young age there was an expectation that Harry would follow suit. Leaving school at 14, his talent for drawing and design quickly became apparent. In addition to working in his father's business he also attended A.E. Child's stained glass classes at the Dublin School of Art and many awards followed. In 1914 he married Margaret Crilley, a talented painter he had met when they were students. Clarke's first major commission was a series of windows for Honan chapel, UCC (1915–17), made by him at his father's studio, by which time Clarke had honed his signature style of ethereal, slim figures, usually adorned in elaborately embroidered costumes, headgear and shoes.

Clarke's windows for the Honan chapel heralded the start of the most fruitful period of his career which continued until around 1925; highlights to be found in Dublin include windows in St Peter's, Phibsborough, Saints Peter and Paul's, Balbriggan, St Joseph's, Terenure, and Holy Trinity, Killiney.

Throughout his career Harry Clarke drew on many influences – European Symbolists, Japanese and Celtic art, individuals as diverse as Beardsley and Durer, movements such as art deco and art nouveau, and theatrical spectacles such as Diaghilev ballets. Clarke was also a successful illustrator, usually choosing literary subjects, executed in both black and white and in watercolour, and by *c.*1917 he began to create small panels on acid-etched flashed glass for discerning patrons which essentially translated his minutely detailed illustrations onto glass with magical outcomes, three of which are on display in Dublin – two in the National Gallery, *The Song of the Mad Prince* (1917) and *The Enchantment of Titania by Bottom* (1922), and one in the National Museum, Collins Barracks, *A Meeting* (1918). On occasion Clarke created multi-panel windows of acid-etched flashed glass such as his beguiling interpretation of Keats's *The Eve of St Agnes* (1924), set entirely at night time and now on display in the Hugh Lane Gallery.

Following his father's death in 1921 Clarke took over the stained glass side of Joshua Clarke & Sons and trained a group of talented assistants to work in his style, moving to much larger premises on North Frederick Street in 1924. When the pressure of work became excessive he would escape to the Glass House, Fulham, where he made a small number of windows for British locations; he harboured an ambition to establish a studio in London where, less hampered by the demands of Irish clergy clients, he could undertake more secular commissions and work in a more experimental manner.

By 1925 Clarke was increasingly relying on his assistants to realize his small-scale sketch designs, sometimes with little direct input from him in the actual execution of windows. In 1926 a near fatal cycling accident accelerated a decline in his health and by 1928 he was displaying symptoms of tuberculosis. He died in Switzerland aged just 41 in 1931.

William Dowling (1907–80) – Born in Dublin, William (known as Willie) Dowling was initially apprenticed to become a printer but his artistic talent led him to enrol at the Dublin Metropolitan School of Art in 1925. Two years later Harry Clarke was looking for recommendations for assistants and his friend Austin Molloy put forward Dowling's name, along with Richard King's, and both men commenced training under Clarke in early 1928. Years later Dowling recalled Clarke's encouragement and found him to be 'fair and just, but severe at times and impatient of careless work'.[1] While Clarke took responsibility for the overall design of windows he encouraged his assistants to make changes if it benefited the design. In March 1929 Harry Clarke travelled to a Swiss sanatorium for treatment for tuberculosis and from this point onwards spent much of his time there until his death in early 1931; by now Dowling and others were beginning to take full responsibility for the design and execution of windows though the studio's policy was that individual artists were never permitted to sign them.

Throughout the 1930s Dowling and King, who became close friends, appear to have designed the majority of the windows and although the studio's style began to evolve very slowly in tune with contemporary tastes, the output was remarkably consistent and at times impossible to distinguish one artist from the other though King appears to have been drawn to a more angular aesthetic while Dowling had a preference for rounder, softer forms. Ultimately King departed in 1940, having managed the studio for the preceding five years, and Dowling succeeded him in this role.

The Second World War presented challenges due to difficulties importing supplies and with fewer commissions several staff were let go. By the 1950s the distinctive Clarke style had been watered down considerably with facial features becoming more generic and lacking individual character. Laborious techniques such as aciding and plating were phased out though the studio continued to use the best quality of imported glass. During this period the studio's colour palette became more heightened, arguably more cheerful and exuberant.

In the 1950s and 1960s an increased demand from overseas clients in the Anglophone world, often driven by Ireland's clerical diaspora, kept the studio buoyant. During these decades more than two-thirds of the studio's orders were from overseas patrons. However at home in Ireland, particularly post-Vatican II, architects who had become the main commissioners of stained glass, were drawn to a modernist aesthetic and often sought abstract designs, something that was alien to Clarke's. William Dowling remained as manager and principal artist until the studio finally closed in 1973, after which he continued to design a small number of windows, some of which he had fabricated by Irish Stained Glass.

Earley's studio – Ireland's longest-established stained glass studio, in its heyday Earley's employed the greatest number of staff. In addition to stained glass it also supplied a full range of ecclesiastical furnishings. Over its 114 years of existence, and with five generations of the family actively involved, the company underwent several name changes.

The first Earleys of note pertaining to stained glass were Thomas and John, born in Birmingham of an Irish father. Thomas was apprenticed to the great Gothic revivalist, Augustus Welby Pugin, and initially worked as a painter and gilder. From 1845, at the urging of Pugin, John Hardman of Birmingham entered the burgeoning industry of stained glass and both Thomas and John Earley became his employees. In December 1853, some months after the Great Industrial Exhibition was held in Dublin, Thomas Earley was charged with setting up a branch of John Hardman & Co. in Grafton Street, and in 1860 it expanded to no. 1 Upper Camden Street. Related to the Hardmans were the Powells and in 1864 Earley & Powells, ecclesiastical suppliers, came into existence at no. 1 Upper Camden Street. Following the successive deaths of Edward and Henry Powell and Thomas Earley, the business officially closed in 1893 though Thomas's nephew, John Bishop Earley, continued trading at the same location under the name, John Earley, Camden Art Works.

In 1903 the company underwent a further name change and Earley & Co. was established with John Bishop Earley as manager and he was joined by his younger brother, William. The studio's style at this time was fairly mainstream and arguably difficult to distinguish from some of their English and German competitors. In 1916 the company expanded into no. 4 Upper Camden Street which coincided with William E. Earley's appointment as manager; from an artistic perspective he was undoubtedly the most talented member of the family (see separate entry for him) and was single-handedly responsible for developing the aesthetically pleasing signature style, largely derived from classical and baroque painting, with which the company is readily identified. William's stewardship was responsible for the artistic high point of Earley's, which occurred between the early 1920s and the late 1940s.

Around 1930 William's nephews, Jack and Gerard Earley, joined the company and it expanded further into no. 5. By 1948 Jack's son, Leo Earley, continued William's stained glass work but also absorbed aspects of Harry Clarke's style, which on occasion led to misattributions of Earley windows. In 1953 Earley & Co. became Earley & Co. Ltd, with Gerard as managing director. At its peak Earley's enjoyed considerable success among Catholic clergy and lay clients – who were their target markets – both on the island of Ireland and in the anglophone world; however by the late 1960s with architects seeking a more contemporary approach to stained glass and competition from Murphy-Devitt Studios and Abbey Stained Glass Studios, Earley's closed in 1975.[2]

William E. Earley (1872–1956) – From the third generation of his family to work in the family ecclesiastic decoration business, commonly referred to as Earley's, and with two more generations to follow, William E. Earley was indisputably the most talented stained glass artist among them.

William Earley first attended the Dublin Metropolitan School of Art aged 12 in 1885, remaining for a year. Following an interregnum of three years, when it is likely he was an apprentice in Earley & Powells, he returned to the School of Art as a full-time student, remaining until he was 22. A high achieving student he, along with William Orpen, were the two Irish recipients of the Queen's Scholarships. Around the time Earley left DMSA the family business was undergoing an upheaval and he took up employment as a stained glass artist with William Martin & Son, St Stephen's Green. It is not recorded when exactly William moved into business with his older brother, John Bishop Earley, in Upper Camden Street, but it likely occurred around the beginning of 1903, and William's influence on the style of stained glass produced by the studio quickly became evident.[3] In 1916 he was appointed manager, a role he combined with principal artist.

Earley developed a pleasing aesthetic featuring a palette of rose pinks, ambers, emeralds, and most of all, blue. Subjects treated most regularly were standards such as *The Annunciation*, and all compositions were augmented with plenty of putti and billowing clouds with no area left unadorned. Intrinsically conservative, his artistic inspiration came from artists such Raphael and particularly Baroque artists like Murillo, but his deep Catholic faith also informed his approach. Of the studio's philosophy he wrote 'In our Stained Glass Designs we try to interpret the Spirit of the Church, when She calls on Her artists to illustrate the Written Word, bearing in mind that the Catholic work must first be devotional, and in every way worthy of its purpose ...'[4]

William Earley championed the style which became synonymous with the studio, particularly in the 1920s, 30s and 40s, and he was at his most creative when presented with an opportunity to undertake multi-light windows where he could treat all the lights as a unified canvas for his lush compositions. Examples in Dublin include his 5-light *Scenes from the Life of St Anne* (1933) for St John the Baptist church, Blackrock, and another 5-light, *God the Father, The Crucifixion, with Our Lady, St Patrick and St Brigid* (early 1940s) for St Patrick's church, Ringsend.

In the 1940s William Earley's grandnephew Leo became his apprentice, designing and cartooning windows, and in 1948 William suffered a stroke by which time his nephew Gerard Earley had assumed managerial duties. William Earley died in 1956. (See also entry for Earley's studio).

Beatrice Elvery (1883–1970) – Beatrice Moss Elvery was born in Dublin into a comfortably-off artistic and musical family. Following after her mother and aunt (Phoebe Traquair, a leading light in the Scottish arts and crafts movement), she started attending classes at the Dublin Metropolitan School of Art in 1896 and over the following years won many prestigious awards, mostly for life drawing and modelling. In 1902 she began exhibiting at the RHA which she continued to do most years for the rest of her long life. By 1904 she was tutoring at the School of Art, illustrating children's books, drawing dissections for doctors and archaeological finds, and it was around this time when Sarah Purser – who had provided her with a little corrugated iron studio in the yard of An Túr Gloine to do her sculpture in – suggested she enrol in A.E. Child's stained glass classes at the School of Art.

Beatrice Elvery's capacity for draughtsmanship, particularly of children and older male faces, is evident in *Christ Among the Doctors* (1907) for the Church of Ireland church, Mount Street, Dublin. This skill and her ability to capture emotion and humanity can be seen again in her window of the following year, *The Good Samaritan and the Prodigal Son*, for Tullow Church of Ireland church, Carrickmines, Co. Dublin, which she considered to be among her two best works. Elvery's other favourite stained glass work was her 3-light of 1910 for the tiny Catholic church on Tory Island which is full of rich colours contrasted with plenty of pale milky quarries which seems to sit well in this island location. In the same year she designed a huge rose window for Letterkenny cathedral depicting nine scenes from the life of St Colmcille with additional tracery. In it as in several others over the following years her natural talent as an illustrator came to the fore, though as she remarked about her windows generally, perhaps in a somewhat self-deprecating manner, 'They are rather like coloured illustrations to a child's book. I never got the right feeling for glass or the detached, austere quality necessary for ecclesiastical work.'[5]

Upon her marriage in 1912 Beatrice Elvery departed An Túr Gloine and moved to London with her barrister husband, Gordon Campbell, later 2nd Baron Glenavy. Henceforth, with the exception of a memorial window for her childhood parish church and one other, she ceased to work in the medium, though over an intense eight-year career she had managed to create about twenty-seven windows and a number of small domestic panels.

In 1918 the Campbells returned to Dublin and in 1934, by now styled Lady Glenavy, she was elected an academician of the RHA which coincided with the beginning of the final phase of a richly creative and diverse career; she now focused on painting and developed a unique surrealist style, often featuring still life compositions or stylized figures in Arcadian landscapes. She published her autobiography, *Today we will only gossip*, in 1964.

Wilhelmina Geddes (1887–1955) – Raised in Belfast, Wilhelmina Geddes attended the city's school of art from the age of 16 achieving successes in drawing, watercolour and graphic design. An illustration she exhibited in Dublin in 1910 caught the attention of Sarah Purser, and discerning a potential for stained glass she invited Geddes to An Túr Gloine to explore her suitability for the craft. The following year Geddes made a set of three small panels for Purser which confirmed how her confident drawing and painting style could easily translate to this medium. Two single-light windows for churches in Co. Fermanagh followed. Purser fostered her talent, bringing her to view medieval glass in Paris and Chartres in 1912 and 1914, though Geddes also found inspiration elsewhere including Gothic and Romanesque sculpture. Over the next few years Purser assigned her increasingly larger windows for prominent Belfast and Dublin locations. Her 4-light window for Belfast's Presbyterian assembly hall (Church House) of 1916, which depicts several parables, demonstrated her ability to skilfully interpret complex narrative scenes.

An Túr Gloine received many First World War memorial commissions and Geddes quickly showed her aptitude for depicting heroic male figures though without excessive idealization and this probably explains why Purser assigned her the most prestigious order to arrive at the studio to date – a window commissioned by the duke of Connaught, former governor general of Canada, to commemorate his deceased staff which was erected in St Bartholomew's church, Ottawa. Depicting *The Welcoming of a Slain Warrior by Soldier Saints, Champions and Angels*, it was Geddes most iconographically complex window and a major triumph for her and the studio. It was completed in 1919 and a few years later she undertook a 5-light war memorial for St Luke's church, Wallsend,

Tyneside. Depicting Christ's Crucifixion, it features considerably fewer figures than her Ottawa window but carries infinitely more raw emotional impact. It drew significant praise and is acknowledged as one of the finest twentieth-century windows in England.[6]

Wilhelmina Geddes never settled in Dublin, often retreating to the family home in Belfast to work on designs and cartoons, and her physical and mental health was frequently an issue. During a period of ill health Michael Healy executed designs for her trio of beautiful windows for Bardsea, Cumbria (1923–4). Geddes relocated to London in 1925, initially admitting herself to a psychiatric hospital for six months. Settling in London she took studio space at the famous Glass House, Fulham. The major success of the second half of her career was a monumental rose window for Ypres cathedral in memory of Albert I, King of the Belgians. It took her four years to complete (1934–8) and although lauded internationally her subsequent output began to diminish, partly related to deteriorating eyesight. After her death *The Times* in her obituary (16 Aug. 1955) referred to her as 'the greatest stained glass artist of our time'.[7]

Michael Healy (1873–1941) – Born into impoverished circumstances, as a child Michael Healy was noted for constantly drawing and a predilection to being solitary, two characteristics that would remain with him. He became a part-time student at the Dublin Metropolitan School of Art and, always devout, tried a stint as a Dominican lay-brother. A benevolent priest arranged for him to work in Florence for eighteen months and his exposure to Italian Renaissance painting had a lifelong influence.

Returning to Ireland, Healy was recommended, on the basis of his drawing prowess, to Sarah Purser then seeking recruits for her nascent stained glass studio, An Túr Gloine. From his first solo window, *Simeon* (1904), Healy demonstrated his ability to capture character and his natural affinity for the craft. Larger commissions followed such as *The Convention of Drum Ceat* (1910) with its heightened palette and panoramic cast of nearly thirty figures all with richly expressive faces. By now he was regularly employing the aciding technique to create a jewel-like effect, not dissimilar to Harry Clarke, which allowed windows to sparkle and come to life as the external lighting conditions changed.

Between 1918 and 1921 Healy designed six war memorial windows, some of which show his compassion for the plight of the ordinary soldier. In 1923 he created one of his finest windows, *St Thomas and Judith*, for Bridge a Crinn, Co. Louth, the two main panels of which demonstrate Healy's ability to depict highly charged scenes. *St Victor* (1930) provides an example of how Healy excelled at creating single-light windows which combined multiple small vignettes alongside the principal figure.

By the late 1920s one can discern an interest in Byzantine art evident in windows such as *Christ the King* and *Our Lady Queen of Heaven*, both for Loughrea cathedral, the latter a sumptuous symphony of pinks and mauves created by two layers of extensively acided flashed glass plated together. A few years later his style had evolved further, incorporating art deco-inspired influences as can be seen in his majestic *St Augustine and St Monica* (1934–5) for John's Lane church, Thomas Street, Dublin. His *St Joseph* (1935) shows his interest in conveying tender familial relationships.

Between 1936 and 1941, the year of Healy's death, he executed nine windows. There were two overseas commissions, for New Zealand and Arizona, the others comprising three distinct sets: a pair of 3-lights for Loughrea cathedral, the transcendent *Ascension* and apocalyptic *Last Judgement*, a pair of meditative Marian-themed 2-lights for Blackrock College's chapel, Dublin (one a homage to Fra Angelico); and the first three of the *Seven Dolours of Our Lady* for Clongowes Wood College's chapel, a series he hoped would be his magnum opus but his final illness intervened and which his friend Evie Hone then took over after his death.

In addition to his stained glass career Healy was a habitual recorder, mainly in rapid pencil and watercolour impressions, of Dubliners going about their daily business, often done on his lunch break from An Túr Gloine.

Evie Hone (1894–1955) – Evie Hone was born into a life of privilege and comfort, though one not without tragedy and misfortune; her mother died three days after Evie's birth, much of her childhood was solitary, and she contracted polio aged 12, and this was followed by periods of hospitalization. In 1912 she moved to

London to study at the Byam Shaw School of Art and while in London she met fellow Dubliner Mainie Jellett. Together they studied briefly under Walter Sickert and then travelled to Paris to study cubism, initially under André Lhote, and then with Albert Gleizes. Hone and Jellett became inextricably associated, at times their paintings almost indistinguishable, and together they championed abstractionism and cubism in Ireland for which they were roundly derided in the press.

In the mid-1920s Evie Hone sensed she had a vocation, took a sabbatical from painting, and entered an Anglican convent in Cornwall, staying nearly a year. By the early 1930s she began to explore the possibility of working in stained glass and approached Sarah Purser about joining An Túr Gloine but was promptly advised to enrol in A.E. Child's classes; this she did briefly but found the experience unsatisfactory and instead sought out Wilhelmina Geddes in London and Richard Ronald Holst in Amsterdam, both of whom were encouraging. Hone's first window combined two abstract panels with a small *The Annunciation* for St Nahi's church, Dundrum, Dublin which gave her the confidence to re-apply to Purser, this time successfully. Working alongside Michael Healy, who became a valued mentor, she created stained glass unlike any of her Irish contemporaries, windows that had a raw and compelling quality inspired by sources such as Irish medieval sculpture and penal crosses, and the contemporary French painter, Georges Rouault.

Hone's fresh, modernist approach was recognized by the new Irish state and commissions for two army barrack's chapels were followed by her large *My Four Green Fields* for the Irish pavilion in the New York World Fair of 1939, the same year she converted from Anglicanism to Roman Catholicism. When An Túr Gloine was being dissolved as a cooperative in 1944 Hone opted to establish her own studio at Marlay, Rathfarnham, and one of her first commissions was a series of five windows, which are now in Manresa House of Spirituality, Dollymount, Dublin, and which are rated among her finest. In addition to many commissions for religious settings Hone made approximately 150 small panels, examples of which are on display in the National Gallery and Hugh Lane Gallery. Her largest single order, which took her three years to complete, was *The Crucifixion and Last Supper* (1949–52) for Eton College's Gothic chapel which it dominates. Another prestigious commission from around this time was for the National Cathedral, Washington. Hone died unexpectedly on her way to Mass at her parish church in Rathfarnham. Following her death a major retrospective was mounted in Dublin and London.[8]

Richard King (1907–74) – Arguably Richard King had not one but two distinct stained glass careers, separated by a decade-long sabbatical from the craft. He was born in Castlebar, Co. Mayo, and when the family relocated to Dublin in 1926 he enrolled at the School of Art, studying illustration and design under Austin Molloy, a friend of Harry Clarke's, and when the latter got wind of King's prodigious talent he invited him, in 1928, to join his studio where he would learn the craft. Despite Clarke's ongoing struggle with tuberculosis, King was a ready student and quickly learned how to work in the easily recognizable style of his master. Clarke died in January 1931 and an English artist / manager was in place but much of the responsibility fell on King's shoulders, and those of his friend, William Dowling; together they diligently maintained the classic Clarke style while also slowly modifying it, almost imperceptibly, to contemporary tastes. When the position of manager became vacant in 1935 Richard King took the helm and for the next five years continued to design and oversee many major commissions without any compromise in the quality of artistry, design or craftsmanship. In addition to stained glass, King also created religious works such as Stations of the Cross in opus sectile mosaic made from opal glass.

The advent of the Second World War created problems with the supply of materials and King's dedication to maintaining Harry Clarke's distinctive style, albeit an evolved version, also came at the price of stifling his own creativity, and so he chose to depart, opting instead to focus on illustration and graphic design, for which he already had an established reputation. He was lauded for his many dynamic postage stamp designs and his illustrations for the popular *Capuchin Annual*, and both activities emerged from two of his principal interests – developing a visual identity for the new Irish state and celebrating

Ireland's saints and legends in a contemporary idiom.

By the late 1940s King was ready to return to stained glass, though this time on his own terms and he built a studio in his back garden in Dalkey, Co. Dublin. Although one can discern vestiges of Harry Clarke's distinctive style, what King seems to have mainly carried forward from his period at Clarke's was his deep knowledge of religious iconography. King's new aesthetic was mainly informed by modernism, and although he rarely travelled abroad, for inspiration he looked to German and French artists such as Georges Rouault, and later, Alfred Manessier, Gabriel Loire, Anton Wendling and Georg Meistermann.[9] Among the highlights of the second half of King's career are his wall comprising seven windows (1957–8) for the chapel of St Thomas More College, Perth, Australia, his gable wall, *Pentecost* (1967–70) for Holy Spirit church, Greenhills, Dublin, and his (now altered) windows (1969–70) for the chapel at Nazareth House, Malahide Road, Dublin.

William MacBride (1880–1962) – William MacBride was born in Ballymena in 1880. While employed by Ward & Partners, the stained glass company in Belfast, he was awarded a scholarship in 1901 to attend A.E. Child's stained glass classes at the Dublin Metropolitan School of Art. At some point over the next few years MacBride moved to London and worked for the large high-profile stained glass studio of Heaton, Butler & Bayne. By 1910 he was back in Dublin and that year Joshua Clarke announced he was delighted to sign on MacBride ('the greatest artist as a glass painter it was ever my pleasure to meet'[10]).

St Patrick's cathedral, Dublin, has a war memorial window (1917) by MacBride which he may have made while still an employee of Clarke's though it does not feature in the studio's records. It would seem that MacBride remained at Clarke's until late 1918 when The Craftworkers Ltd (sometimes referred to as the Craftworkers Guild) was established at 39 Harcourt Street, Dublin. The ambition of this co-operative was to foster closer ties between art and industry in a variety of media including sculpture, metal work and book binding, with MacBride supervising the 'department of stained glass', though it is unclear as to who else if any besides him specialized in this medium.

Possibly MacBride's earliest independent work which he made after he had formally left Clarke's was the Seaver war memorial (1918) for the Church of Ireland church, Malone Road, Belfast. At times MacBride incorporated portraits of deceased young soldiers in his war memorial windows – no doubt based on photographs provided by grieving families – which both humanize the windows and can create an unsettling visual tension between the 'real' and the allegorical; this is apparent in two of the other three war memorial windows he made around this time for the Malone Road church. When not depicting real people, his faces sometimes feature large eyes and full lips, a preference Harry Clarke had too, though in general they are of a much sturdier, robust build compared to Clarke's slim, ethereal creatures. In addition to an arts and crafts influence that he would have absorbed through A.E. Child, a Pre-Raphaelite influence can also be discerned at times.

In 1919 The High School, Dublin, commissioned a 3-light war memorial from MacBride which, like his earlier windows, is brimming with detail including elaborate Celtic strapwork designs in the border and on garments, along with Celtic-style brooches, not dissimilar to Celtic revival-inspired details found in many An Túr Gloine windows of this period.

In addition to stained glass, MacBride also created decorative schemes for churches, painted Stations of the Cross and portraits, and undertook illustrations for books including the Dublin Civic Week 1929 official handbook. Although he lived until 1962 it would seem that most of his stained glass output took the form of war memorials and when this demand decreased by the early 1920s his stained glass output diminished correspondingly.

Hubert McGoldrick (1897–1967) – Hubert Vincent McGoldrick was born in Rathgar, Dublin, and is first recorded as having attended classes at the Dublin Metropolitan School of Art at the age of 13. Two years later he joined Earley & Company, the city's longest established stained glass company. During his apprenticeship he continued attending A.E. Child's stained glass classes at the DMSA. In 1918 McGoldrick exhibited designs for stained glass at the RHA annual exhibition and two years later was invited to join An

Túr Gloine at a time when the studio was particularly busy undertaking commissions for war memorial windows. He was the first male and the first Catholic to join the studio since Michael Healy's arrival some fifteen years earlier.

His first window, *Sorrow and Joy* (1920), for Gowran, Co. Kilkenny, indicates a strongly developed personal style and choice of palette that would have been at variance to the prevalent house style at Earley's. Like Harry Clarke and Michael Healy, he revelled in rich detail, particularly evident in his works of the 1920s. One of his finest windows was produced early in his An Túr Gloine career, *The Sacred Heart Appearing to St Margaret Mary* (1925) for St Brendan's cathedral, Loughrea, a window that revels in rich colours and features little vignettes.

Perhaps his most outstanding window, and certainly one of the most unusual commissions to come to the studio, was a massive lunette, *The Spirit of Morning* (1926–7), for a private home in Singapore. Of all McGoldrick's works this one has the most sense of its period, possibly since the secular subject matter allowed a more contemporary representation of womanhood and he could tap into the flamboyant theatrical aspects of his personality. By now An Túr Gloine was receiving several substantial international commissions and McGoldrick was among six of the studio's artists whose work featured in a school chapel in Newton, Massachusetts. McGoldrick's final overseas commission, *Gethsemane* (1939), was for a crematorium chapel in Karori, near Wellington, New Zealand. In many of his later works, such as those for the Catholic church, Aughrim Street, Dublin, he eschewed the detail so prevalent in his earlier work for a simplified approach often using deep shades of blue and red and little aciding.

Worthy of note, is that alongside his stained glass career at An Túr Gloine, McGoldrick also occasionally worked in opus sectile mosaic, a type of mosaic that does not utilize the familiar tesserae but instead uses larger custom-cut pieces and in this manner resembles the structure of stained glass windows. He was also an occasional illustrator and his most recognized illustration, the *Magnificat Anima Mea Dominum*, was commissioned for the Legion of Mary.

Hubert McGoldrick appears to have withdrawn slowly from An Túr Gloine by the late 1930s creating fewer and fewer windows or mosaics. He did however exhibit four designs (two for stained glass, two for mosaic) at the annual RHA exhibition in 1942, and he made his final window *c.*1944–5.

Helen Moloney (1926–2011) – Helen Moloney was born in Tipperary town into a middle-class family that was steeped in the Republican movement on both sides. Leaving school at 14 she began attending the National College of Art in Dublin as a part-time student from 1942. In the academic year 1947/8 she changed to full-time status, graduating with a diploma in painting. The following year she departed for Paris to attend life classes at the Académie de la Grande Chaumière, Montparnasse, and while there viewed the stained glass in Notre Dame and the Sainte-Chapelle, which made a lasting impression. Returning to Dublin, she rented a top-floor flat in Ballsbridge where she would remain until her death. Initially working as a part-time art teacher in Blackrock vocational school, in 1957 she started attending Johnny Murphy's recently introduced stained glass classes at the College of Art, and exhibited stained glass panels at the Living Art exhibitions of 1957 and 1958. The major Evie Hone retrospective exhibition held in UCD in 1958 fired her enthusiasm for the art form. Upon graduating from NCA in 1960 she began to assist Patrick Pollen who was then renting space at the long established An Túr Gloine studio.

1964 marked a turning point for Moloney when she was commissioned by Liam McCormick to make eight stained glass windows for his church at Desertegney, Co. Donegal; this was the start of a fruitful relationship which amounted to twelve commissions over the following eighteen years. Her symbols of the Evangelists windows at Desertegney, though illustrative, demonstrate her keen sense of design and preference for strong colours with limited painted detail. Over the years she opted for increasingly simplified forms, often derived from early Christian symbols, and eschewed any painting, relying instead on the leadlines and dynamic colour choices. Among her particular achievements for McCormick were a continuous abstract band of clerestory glass for his most famous work, St Aengus's at Burt (1967), six small panels for St Michael's, Creeslough (1971), and six windows on the theme of light for Donoughmore Presbyterian church (1977), all in Co. Donegal. Although her flat also functioned as her creative space, Moloney's windows were fabricated, under her supervision, by skilled glaziers at studios such as Abbey Stained Glass, Dublin, and Caldermacs of Belfast.

Though based in Dublin she designed glass only for two churches in the city, a dramatic lantern for Our Lady of Victories, Ballymun, and her penultimate window for St Stephen's, Killiney, made in 1982, the same year she was elected a member of Aosdana having been nominated by her friends Patrick Pollen and Patrick Pye. Ironically thereafter, despite requests from prominent architects, she declined all commissions, seemingly having lost faith in her own creativity; she was only 56. In addition to stained glass, Moloney also created a few works in *dalle de verre*, in enamel, and made designs for altar and ambo textile hangings.[11]

Johnny Murphy (1921–2006) – Johnny Murphy was born in Cork and initially won a scholarship to attend the Crawford College of Art, transferring to the National College of Art, Dublin, in 1940 where he remained as a student of painting for four years. In 1947 he again won a scholarship, this one allowing him to spend an exhilarating year studying and travelling in Paris and Rome. Murphy joined the Harry Clarke Studios as a glass painter in autumn 1951 and in 1953 he married the painter Róisín Dowd whom he had known from their Dublin college days.

In 1954 Murphy was appointed a lecturer in stained glass at the National College of Art (now NCAD), re-establishing classes in the craft which had been in abeyance since 1938, the year before the previous instructor, A.E. Child, had died. Around 1955 Murphy joined forces with one of Clarke's master glaziers, John A. (Des) Devitt and they began undertaking stained glass commissions together, formally establishing Murphy-Devitt Studios in 1958. Johnny Murphy was the principal artist in the studio while Róisín Dowd Murphy played a key role in many of the commissions and also undertook solo windows.

During the 1960s and early 70s, which would have been the peak period of activity for Murphy-Devitt Studios, the studio was often called upon to create a 'scheme', or complete set of designs of windows, for new churches. This gave Murphy the opportunity to excel at what he did best – to devise an overall vision for a large number of lights, sometimes including clerestory windows and walls of glass, all contained within a contemporary space. He appears to have relished scale and drama, perhaps harking back to an earlier period when he had been employed painting huge cinema posters and theatrical backdrops.

Murphy's preference was for bold, graphic treatment of saints and other figures, regularly interspersed with passages of understated abstract glass. Like a composer, all elements would come together in effortless harmony though often with great visual contrast. His daughter Reiltín remembers his interest in music and his drawing an analogy with a fugue 'whereby the same melody / image is played in different ways – his abstracts are often flipped, turned, twisted to be similar but not identical ...' The selection and quality of glass was of paramount importance. 'He loved its kinetic effect in its flaws, its trees moving outside, its changing light and colours from passing clouds, its seeming to be alive.'

Throughout the decades working as Murphy-Devitt's chief artist he also, in parallel, ran the glass department at NCAD where he introduced new techniques and provided work experience for students and graduates at his studio. Following retirement from NCAD he relocated from Dublin to rural Co. Wexford where he and Róisín Dowd Murphy continued to undertake commissions in conjunction with Des Devitt up to 2004 under a loose arrangement covered by 'John A. Devitt and Associates'. Johnny Murphy, Róisín Dowd Murphy and Des Devitt all died in 2006. (See also separate entry for Murphy-Devitt Studios.)

Murphy-Devitt Studios – The two individuals who founded Murphy-Devitt Studios originally met in Harry Clarke Studios in the early 1950s; Johnny Murphy was employed as a stained glass painter and John A. (Des) Devitt was one of Clarke's master glaziers. Around 1955 they decided to set up their own stained glass enterprise, initially operating on a modest basis while Devitt remained as an employee of Clarke's. In 1958 they formally established Murphy-

Devitt Studios, working from a mews in Monkstown and later from a purpose-built studio in Blackrock, Dublin. Murphy and Devitt were well matched, the former was a creative force who embraced a modernist aesthetic and was equally comfortable designing figurative and abstract windows, while Devitt was an efficient studio manager, effective at soliciting commissions and excelled as a master glass craftsman. The third key person in the team was Johnny's wife, Róisín Dowd Murphy, who had trained as a painter and was taught by Johnny to translate her skills to stained glass. In time, the Murphy's eldest daughter, Reiltín, assisted with design work on occasion. The artists were supported by a small number of expert craftsmen, notably brothers Paddy and Dermot McLoughlin and Micky and Eddie Watson. Murphy-Devitt Studios encouraged students or young artists to work with them for short or extended periods, among them Celia Crampton Harriss, Terry Corcoran and Anne FitzGibbon.

The 1960s and 1970s were the key decades for Murphy-Devitt Studios when the Catholic church in Ireland had embarked on an ambitious building programme. For the most part Murphy-Devitt Studios undertook complete sets or 'schemes' of stained glass rather than individual one-off windows. Budgets were often tight and the studio had an impressive ability to maximize the visual effectiveness of costly mouth-blown pot metal glass combined with less expensive factory-manufactured cathedral glass. The studio's glass was usually sourced from Saint Gobain in France with additional glass from Pilkington in England.

Róisín Dowd Murphy often contributed windows, or painted significant aspects of windows in schemes which Johnny Murphy had devised and her style, while distinct, would always integrate effectively, sometimes almost seamlessly. If Johnny was in essence a designer, then Róisín was at heart a painter. Reiltín Murphy summed up her mother's windows as 'full of colour and movement, vigour and life. Róisín loved the Renaissance artists, such as Michelangelo and Botticelli, her images echo theirs with her love of flowers, of dressmaking, textiles, braided hair, of children and musical instruments.' The studio's vast job for Our Lady Crowned church, Mayfield, Cork (1962), exemplifies the unity of their joint approach. Later large schemes that are largely abstract, and entirely Murphy's designs, were for Our Lady of Consolation, Donnycarney (1968), and St Michael's church, Dún Laoghaire (1973).

Although Murphy-Devitt Studios undertook some overseas jobs (England, Wales, Pakistan, Philippines and Nigeria) the vast majority of their work can be found throughout the island of Ireland. The studio closed in 1980 though Murphy, Dowd Murphy, and Devitt continued to undertake occasional commissions thereafter (see also separate entry for Johnny Murphy).

Catherine (Kitty) O'Brien (1881–1963) – Catherine O'Brien was born in Durra House, near Ennis, Co. Clare, into a middle-class country Anglo-Irish Protestant family and enjoyed a comfortable, privileged upbringing until dwindling family funds forced her to move to Dublin to acquire training for a career. She is first recorded as being enrolled as a student at the Metropolitan School of Art in 1901 and she, along with Michael Healy, were the first two artists to be recruited by Sarah Purser when An Túr Gloine formally opened in January 1903.

Although the philosophy of An Túr Gloine was that one artist would be responsible for the entire creative process, in the early years O'Brien and the other new recruits were still very much learning their craft and often assisted in the painting of windows designed by Child and Purser. Her earliest windows which she designed and executed in their entirety show the legacy of Christopher Whall, as transmitted by his student A.E. Child to his own students. In these windows O'Brien regularly utilized plenty of pale quarries in the background, often with delicately painted designs, and characteristic 'architectural' canopy constructions of branches and leaves encasing saints. Not as talented a draughtsperson nor as imaginative as Healy, Elvery or Rhind, she was most comfortable with fairly straightforward representations of saints and narrative scenes.

By the mid-1920s An Túr Gloine had achieved significant international recognition and O'Brien was among the artists who designed and executed windows for prestigious overseas clients, among them a massive lunette, *The Spirit of the Night*, for a luxury villa in Singapore, and two windows each for school chapels in Newton, Massachusetts and Phoenix, Arizona.

Throughout her career smaller scale, intimate windows rather than large multi-light windows seemed to suit her style better and these often have a simplicity and modesty in execution and ambition which seem most at home in country churches, something that Sarah Purser recognized when assigning windows. Most of her windows can be found in Church of Ireland churches of which she was a committed member. Unlike most of the other An Túr Gloine artists she regularly signed her windows, either as 'K. O'B' or 'K. O'Brien', sometimes accompanied by a tiny tower.

In time O'Brien eschewed her preference for lighter, mellow tones in favour of a brighter palette and by the early 1930s had adopted regular use of pulsating intense oranges, reds, blues and greens, sometimes evoking a charming folk art quality in her windows. Some of her later windows are characterized by poorly drawn figures where attempts to capture gestures resulted in an awkward rigidity, along with faces lacking character and personality.

In 1940, on Purser's retirement, O'Brien took over as manager of An Túr Gloine until its closure in January 1944. She then bought out the studio and its contents, and from 1954 she rented out space to fellow artist Patrick Pollen. A fire in 1958 destroyed the premises though the studio was rebuilt a year later, a testament to her tenacity and commitment.

Patrick Pollen (1928–2010) – Born in London, Patrick Pollen was the son of two artists, sculptor Arthur Pollen and painter Daphne Baring whose parents owned Lambay Island, a happy retreat for Pollen family holidays. Patrick Pollen attended the Slade School of Art, London, and the Académie Julian in Paris where he was impressed by the stained glass in Notre Dame cathedral, but it was Evie Hone's recently completed magnum opus for Eton College's chapel (1949–52) that inspired him, aged 24, to move to Ireland to be mentored by the artist. Pollen rented half of An Túr Gloine from Catherine O'Brien, and his first significant commission was a memorial window for a chapel near Edinburgh (1954). Throughout his career Evie Hone's enduring influence is regularly evident, though his painting of his figures' features are often less expressionistic and done with greater finesse.

His largest single commission was for Johannesburg cathedral (1957–9); thirty-three windows amounting to 5,500 square feet of glass that feature symbols and pictorial scenes; the job put so much round-the-clock demands on the kiln that An Túr Gloine caught fire in October 1958 and was raised to the ground. O'Brien had it rebuilt promptly and Pollen facilitated emerging stained glass artists to avail of the new studio.

The distinguished church architect Liam McCormick commissioned windows from Pollen, Patrick Pye, Phyllis Burke and Imogen Stuart, with Pollen also undertaking the abstract glazing for St Peter's, Milford, Co. Donegal (1961), followed by a more imaginative scheme with large walls of glass, this time by Pollen alone, for St Patrick's, Murlog (*c.*1962–4), also in Donegal, which features his interpretation of the prayer, *St Patrick's Breastplate*. In 1964 also Pollen made a charming memorial window, *Madonna and Child, with St Luke*, in memory of Catherine O'Brien, and following her death he bought An Túr Gloine from her nephew. During this period Pollen married the Wexford-born sculptor Nell Murphy and they moved to Dundrum, south Dublin, where in 1967 he built his own stained glass studio.

During the second half of the 1960s Pollen was primarily occupied creating a series of single-light windows commissioned for the new Catholic cathedral in Galway city, twenty-six windows in total, mainly depicting Irish saints and scenes of Christ's miracles; collectively these windows can be seen as his greatest achievement though it is unfortunate that there were no multi-light windows available. With Pollen's strong English connections he regularly received orders in the country of his birth including one for the Jesuit church, Farm Street, London, which already had windows by Hone. By the late 1970s Pollen found it increasingly difficult to secure commissions and in 1981 he and his family emigrated to North Carolina, optimistic that there would be greater opportunities there, and although he was successful in securing some orders it was not the nirvana he had hoped for. In the late 1990s Pollen and his wife returned to Ireland, settling in Wexford, spending retirement revisiting the sites of many of his windows.

Sarah Purser (1848–1943) – Noted painter and first female full member of the Royal Hibernian Academy, Sarah Purser also played an unparalleled role in Ireland's cultural life for many decades. In her early fifties she, along with Edward Martyn, founded An Túr Gloine and her ongoing commitment over forty years to ensuring it was a success cannot be underestimated. Although A.E. Child was official manager of the studio, it would appear that it was Sarah Purser mainly who dealt with clients, a significant number of whom were known to her personally from her days as a society portrait painter; aside from this she was a supreme networker, whether at the popular monthly salons in her Dublin mansion or while traveling by rail, working her way through railway carriages to strike up conversations with ministers of religion. Taking a keen interest in the careers of her individual artists she took pains to match artists with commissions to which their artistic strengths were best suited.

It is difficult to be definitive as to which stained glass windows Purser herself designed, and particularly to what extent she was engaged in their execution. Although Purser had no formal instruction in the craft unlike the studio's other artists, she obviously would have acquired considerable knowledge by virtue of the amount of time she spent in the 'shop' each week and since she was not paid by the hour – as was the case of the other workers – the time she spent working on specific windows is not recorded in the studio's work journals.

Particularly in the early years of An Túr Gloine her name appeared prominently in the studio's publicity material and press reports regularly referred to it as 'Miss Purser's Stained Glass works' and likewise articles often erroneously gave her credit for windows designed and made entirely by other artists. In a slim ATG pamphlet, *List of principal stained glass windows executed in Ireland from 1903 to 1928*, it states that Purser was the 'artist' responsible for fourteen windows which again adds somewhat to the confusion; in reality these were mainly executed by other artists in the studio.

At a high profile reception to celebrate twenty-five years of An Túr Gloine in 1928, Sarah Purser somewhat self-deprecatingly told the audience 'I myself, though I hope I am some judge of glass, am not a stained glass worker in the sense we give the word … My only output is a tiny window in the porch at Loughrea, something in the nature of a curiosity. I designed … some of our early windows, but though the real artists obligingly painted them, we never found it satisfactory.'[12] Aside from her window depicting *St Brendan the Navigator* referred to above – and a small number of panels created as personal gifts – Purser produced approximately twenty designs for windows that were realized, though it is unlikely she drew many of the cartoons, nor did much of the painting.

Patrick Pye (1929–2018) – Patrick Pye was born in Winchester and moved with his mother to Ireland in 1932. At St Columba's College his art teacher was the sculptor Oisín Kelly and while there he first encountered, via a library book, the art of El Greco, which would leave a lasting impression on him. Pye attended the National College of Art from 1947 to 1950 studying under Maurice McGonigal. In the late 1940s he began to exhibit at the annual Oireachtas and Living Art exhibitions. A formative nine-month sojourn travelling in Spain, Italy, Germany, the Netherlands and France in 1954 brought him into contact with Romanesque sculpture and Giotto. He re-enrolled in NCA in 1955, this time to attend Johnny Murphy's stained glass classes.

Pye undertook his first stained glass commission, a somewhat abstract depiction of *St Brigid*, for St Brendan's cathedral, Loughrea, in 1957, most likely made in An Túr Gloine where his friend Patrick Pollen was renting studio space. In 1957–8 the Mainie Jellett Scholarship for Painting afforded him the opportunity to study stained glass under Albert Troost at the Jan van Eyck Akademie in Maastricht,[13] and while there he was commissioned by the monks of Glenstal Abbey, Co. Limerick, to create a 3-light window, one of four he would undertake for their chapel. The major Evie Hone retrospective exhibition held in Dublin in the summer of 1958 reinforced his vocation for the medium. Of Hone he appreciated the monumentality of her work and the Romanesque feel of it, particularly liking her small panels.[14] Pye characterized her work as acting as 'a goad and as an anchor'.[15] In the late 1960s he acquired his own kiln for his studio in Piperstown, located in the foothills of the Dublin mountains.

With a deep interest in religion and spirituality he converted from Anglicanism to Catholicism in 1963. Alongside his career as a painter and etcher of still lives, landscapes and religious subjects he created around thirty-four windows for seventeen locations, all but one on the island of Ireland, the last of which was in 1998. Responding to a question about the purpose of stained glass in contemporary churches he opined, 'I think it has the function of moving us, of touching our hearts, of making a world in the window which is very different to the world we live in. The colours are strong. It's a wonderful medium for expression …'[16] Although he considered himself a narrative artist, many of his windows are idiosyncratic and the viewer can benefit from any explanation he may have provided which reveals his personal vision and interpretation.

Patrick Pye was elected to Aosdána in 1981, and to the RHA in 1991 which held a retrospective exhibition focusing on his triptych paintings in 1997.

Ethel Rhind (1877–1952) – Ethel Rhind was born in India to a Scottish father then employed as an engineer in the Indian Civil Service and a mother from Co. Antrim. She acquired an art teacher's certificate at the Belfast School of Art then moved to Dublin and in 1902 took up a scholarship to study mosaic at the Metropolitan School of Art. By 1904 she was also attending A.E. Child's stained glass class though her particular aptitude for mosaic never left her. She scooped up many of the awards at the School of Art and Sarah Purser's invitation to join An Túr Gloine in 1906 must have been influenced by these achievements.

Ethel Rhind's earliest window is a small *St Eunan* (1906) for Raphoe cathedral, Co. Donegal, which she executed based on a design by Sarah Purser. A year later she painted a 2-light memorial window, *Harmony and Fortitude* (1907), for the Gore-Booths of Lissadell, again based on a design by Purser. Like Catherine O'Brien, even when she started designing and painting her own windows, the strong arts and crafts-influenced aesthetic of A.E. Child (passed on from his own teacher, Christopher Wall), remains evident for a decade or so, although she did demonstrate a preference for richer colours. One of the qualities distinguishing Rhind from both O'Brien and Child was an ability to instil greater individual character and personality into the characters she depicted.

Several of her 2-light windows are among her most successful such as the three (1909, 1922, 1925) for the Presbyterian church, Dun Laoghaire, Co. Dublin, and a pair for Townsend Street Presbyterian church, Belfast (1913, 1921–2). All revel in richly textured detail and a delight in decoration. Animals feature in her windows from time to time such as a variety of fish in 'Praise Ye the Lord' (1916) in St Nahi's, Dundrum, and a prominent tabby cat in her final window for Dún Laoghaire's Presbyterian church.

Parallel to her career in stained glass, Ethel Rhind also excelled in opus sectile mosaic, a type of mosaic that used larger, custom cut pieces of glazed ceramic tile (similar in approach to stained glass) rather than the conventional tiny square tesserae. Her greatest achievement in this medium are three sets of Stations of the Cross for West of Ireland churches. In contrast to her stained glass windows, her work in mosaic is more muted and restrained, with less detail and a reduced colour palette. Aside from her Stations, the majority of her fifty-plus windows can be found in Protestant churches.

Ethel Rhind was a member of the Guild of Irish Art Workers and exhibited designs for stained glass and opus sectile mosaic at the Arts and Crafts Society of Ireland (1910, 1917, 1921). Her tapestry, *Smuainteach*, was woven at the Dun Emer Guild, and is in the collection of the National Museum of Ireland. She appears to have retired from An Túr Gloine without any fanfare in 1939 and died in a Dún Laoghaire nursing home, aged 75, in 1952.

George W. Walsh (b.1939) – George William Walsh's father, George Stephen Walsh (1911–88), trained and worked at Harry Clarke Studios from the mid-1920s to mid-1940s. Following a stint in London he and his family relocated to Belfast in 1948. George W. Walsh studied stained glass under Edward Marr at the Belfast School of Art while commencing his seven-year apprenticeship under his father, then working at Clokey & Company, the city's principal stained glass studio, and when the family moved to Wisconsin in 1957, George

W. continued his apprenticeship under his father at Conrad Pickel Stained Glass Studio, Waukesha. The period at Pickel's was a formative experience for both father and son, introducing them to a fresh modernist aesthetic and an opportunity to work on extensive schemes for new churches. George W. then moved to Conrad Schmitt's Studio in Milwaukee where he learnt the *dalle de verre* technique.

Returning to Dublin in 1963, George W. took up employment at Abbey Stained Glass Studios, managed by the artistically inclined Frank Ryan who was happy for Walsh and the other artists, notably Willie Earley and George Campbell, to develop their own individual styles, sometimes collaborating as the need arose. In the years post-Vatican II church building was on the increase and architects were looking for studios that were willing to create dynamic abstract schemes as well as treating figurative images in a modernist manner; Walsh rose to the occasion and Abbey became the first choice for many architects and clergy.

During the 1970s Walsh reduced his involvement with Abbey in order to develop an independent career, building a studio in his back garden. Using the best of imported glass from England and France, he has had a prodigious output. Among his finest works from this period is his 4-light window featuring celestial symbols (1973) for the medieval Black Abbey, Kilkenny, evocative of medieval glass but resoundingly modern. Exuberant, expressive leadlines are a key feature in most of Walsh's works, such as those for the church of the Assumption, Tullamore, Co. Offaly (1986).

In many of his windows Walsh has introduced local references, historical and topographical, often juxtaposing the secular with the religious. Vignettes abound, populated with small figures and animals, often depicted in profile, engaged in any number of activities. Storytelling underpins much of Walsh's work and although brimming with vibrant detail they are always easy to interpret. Examples include his two windows for Dublinia (1993), Dublin, and his series of eleven windows for St Kentigern's church, Eyeries, Co. Cork (1996), which feature a panoply of images, everything from early Christian beehive huts to satellite dishes. Two of Walsh's greatest achievements are collaborations with architect Richard Hurley where he supplied all the glass for Hurley's two elliptical-shaped churches, the church of the Irish Martyrs, Naas, Co. Kildare (1997), and the church of the Holy Family, Belfast (2007). In recent years Walsh has increasingly worked in fused glass, creating smaller works suitable for domestic contexts.[17]

Notes

Dublin City

Bewley's Oriental Café

1 Swan Yard is a dead end lane, accessed off Harry Street.
2 Nicola Gordon Bowe, 'Harry Clarke 1889–1931, his life and work' (PhD, TCD, 1982), p. 761.
3 Nicola Gordon Bowe, *Harry Clarke, the life and work* (2nd ed. Dublin, 2012), p. 312.
4 Gordon Bowe, 'Harry Clarke 1889–1931' (PhD), p. 761.
5 Ibid.
6 'Quidnunc', *Irish Times*, 11 Jan. 1941.

Christ Church cathedral (C of I) and Dublinia

1 For a complete list of subjects, see David Lawrence's research compiled for www.gloine.ie
2 Christine Casey, *The buildings of Ireland – Dublin* (New Haven and London, 2005), p. 335.
3 It is not known what became of this window which is almost certainly by either Clayton & Bell or Hardman & Co. I am grateful to Dr Stuart Kinsella for his efforts attempting to trace this window and for information about the replacement commission.
4 The Mothers' Union is an Anglican charity that seeks to support families worldwide.
5 I am grateful to David Britton for drawing my attention to these panels in the IELA.
6 Private coll., Dublin. The colour design features different colours to the panel as executed.
7 I am grateful to George Walsh for information on the window.

Hugh Lane Gallery

1 Designs for both in the Brothers Kerr coll.
2 See N. Gordon Bowe, *Wilhelmina Geddes, life and work* (Dublin, 2015), pp 49–52.
3 Jessica O'Donnell, *Harry Clarke, the Eve of St Agnes* (Dublin, 2012), p. 6.
4 See Jessica O'Donnell, 'A gorgeous gallery of poetic pictures: Harry Clarke, Harold Jacob and John Keat's 'The Eve of St Agnes' in A. Griffith et al. (eds), *Harry Clarke and artistic visions of the new Irish state* (Dublin, 2019), pp 46–71.
5 Nicola Gordon Bowe, *Harry Clarke, the life and work* (2nd ed., Dublin, 2012), p. 348.
6 See Róisín Kennedy, 'The Geneva Window: a precious gift, never given' in A. Griffith et al. (eds), *Harry Clarke and artistic visions of the new Irish state*, pp 72–99.

St Augustine and St John's church

1 I am grateful to Dr Paul Donnelly for details concerning this order and those of the other Clarke windows in this church.
2 Church's website: www.johnslane.ie
3 In 1924 Clarke wrote to W.B. Yeats that Pope 'was in his time one of the finest stained glass draughtsmen in these countries'. Quoted in N. Gordon Bowe, *Harry Clarke, the life and work* (2nd ed. Dublin, 2012), pp 37–8.
4 The sketch design for the window (CSGSA, TCD) shows two options for ornamentation: Gothic or Celtic.
5 John P. White may have been responsible for maintaining the church's organ. I am grateful to Dr David O'Shea and Rónán Murray for sharing their knowledge of Dublin organ builders of this period.
6 'Dublin lady's death' *Irish Times*, 16 Sept. 1903, p. 6; I am grateful to Reiltín Murphy for her research on Alicia White.
7 Gordon Bowe, *Harry Clarke*, pp 276, 278–80.
8 The face of St Rita on the left is clearly a replacement as the flesh-toned glass is completely wrong.
9 The author has not succeeded in identifying the donor beyond his surname.
10 See D. Caron, *Michael Healy 1873–1941, An Túr Gloine's stained glass pioneer* (Dublin, 2023), p. 243.
11 For image of sketch design, see ibid., p. 285.
12 I am indebted to Dr Frances Gardner for her research on this window.
13 There is a sketch design for the window in the CSGSA, TCD, which was attributed to Dowling by David Clarke (son of Harry), and it appears to feature Dowling's handwriting. My gratitude to Dr Paul Donnelly for this information.

National Gallery

1 Nicola Gordon Bowe, *Harry Clarke*, a monograph and catalogue (Dublin, 1979), p. 111.
2 Will Schenck, *Harry Clarke's stained glass windows for the chapel of the convent of Notre Dame, Dowanhill, Glasgow: the architectural context* (Stained Glass Museum, Ely, 2013), p. 3.
3 Nicola Gordon Bowe, 'Harry Clarke, the Mother of Sorrows', lot essay for Christie's catalogue, the Irish Sale, May 2002.
4 Ibid.

5 There is a pencil drawing and a colour sketch design for the complete window in the Harry Clarke Archive, HLG.

6 See David Caron, 'Divine delights', *Irish Arts Review* (Winter 2020), pp 386–9.

7 Quoted in David Caron, *Michael Healy 1873–1941, An Túr Gloine's stained glass pioneer* (Dublin, 2023), p. 210.

8 Joseph McBrinn, '"The loveliest thing I have seen": Evie Hone's stained glass panels', *Glass Ireland* (Dublin, 2020), p. 23.

9 I am grateful to Sarah McAuliffe, NGI, for drawing my attention to this information contained in the gallery's archives.

10 I am indebted to Dr Joseph McBrinn for information on all five panels.

St Ann's church

1 *St Mark and St John* (1979) by James Cox replaced the original window destroyed by adjacent construction work.

2 An Túr Gloine order book no. 1, p. 260, job no. 372, CSIA, NGI.

3 Although not named in the window, like the figure of Charity, Nicola Gordon Bowe states their identities in *Wilhelmina Geddes, life and work* (Dublin, 2015), p. 67. Dr Gordon Bowe also elucidates several art history references that Geddes is likely to have drawn upon, pp 67–9.

4 Letter from W. Geddes to S. Purser, 9 Aug. [1915]. Quoted in Gordon Bowe, *Wilhelmina Geddes, life and work* (Dublin, 2015), p. 90.

5 'Sir Andrew and Lady Reed memorial window dedicated', *Evening Irish Times*, 3 Aug. 1916, p. 6.

6 I am grateful to Stephen Huws for details of the relocation. The non-figurative window (*c.*1860s), which was originally in the ope that Geddes's window was relocated to, was in turn moved and installed in the vestry.

7 Vestry Minutes, 29 Feb. 1916. RCB library.

8 Both men had been called to the Irish bar and Julian had been Reid Professor of Law at Trinity College since 1903.

9 N. Gordon Bowe, *Wilhelmina Geddes, life and work* (Dublin, 2015), p. 130. For further reading on this window see pp 124–30.

10 Quoted in Bowe, p. 130.

St Catherine and St Jame's church

1 The basic pose and attributes are the same as Sarah Purser's depiction of Hope (1905) in St Mary's church, Howth. See p. 193.

2 See Caron, *Michael Healy*, for all three windows in this church.

3 H. Thompson, 'The St Catherine window', *St Catherine's Parish Magazine* (Jan. 1924), p. 3.

4 Ibid.

5 Ibid.

6 *St Victor*, pencil and watercolour. NGI coll. A note on the sketch records the date it was sanctioned.

7 Hugh Thompson, 'The first vicar of St Catherine's'. Transcript of lecture originally delivered to St Catherine's Association on 2 Mar. 1914. Thompson MS, RCB library.

8 The inscription refers to 'Brownlow and Clara Thompson', suggesting that Brownlow was how he was known amongst family and friends. Curiously it omits his title 'Canon' or any reference that he was minister in the church.

9 Information from an unidentified newspaper clipping, 'Stained glass window as memorial', in Catherine O'Brien's scrapbook, p. 79, CSIA, NGI.

10 Ibid.

St Patrick's cathedral (C of I)

1 For a complete inventory of the cathedral's figurative windows, see www.gloine.ie compiled by David Lawrence on behalf of the Church of Ireland.

2 I am indebted to Peter Cormack for this information.

3 NGI coll.

4 'Royal Irish Regiment memorial unveiled', *Evening Irish Times*, 25 May 1907, p. 9.

5 John Alexander French of St Ann's, Donnybrook.

6 N. Gordon Bowe, *Harry Clarke, the life and work* (2nd ed., Dublin, 2012), p. 142. I am grateful to Paul Donnelly for reviewing the Clarke order books.

7 C of I Gazette, 2 Feb. 1917, p. 77.

8 Joseph McBrinn, 'Frank Brangwyn and stained glass; the earl of Iveagh memorial windows at Dublin and Elveden', *Journal of Stained Glass*, 26 (London, 2002), p. 33.

9 See D. Caron, *Michael Healy 1873–1941, An Túr Gloine's stained glass pioneer* (Dublin, 2023), p. 243.

10 Three designs are in the William Morris Gallery, London and reproduced in McBrinn's article referenced above.

11 Quoted by McBrinn in 'Frank Brangwyn and stained glass …'

12 I am grateful to Jasmine Allen for supplying me with photographs and her notes relating to this window.

13 McBrinn quotes Brangwyn's own words written to the church's rector in McBrinn's article, p. 39.

St Peter's church (RC)

1 Damaged windows included the rose, and windows depicting the Sacred Heart and St Joseph.

2 In 1920 and 1925 respectively.

3 See Nicola Gordon Bowe, *Harry Clarke, the life and work* (Dublin, 2012); she states that it was removed in the 1950s for reasons unclear (p. 164), but the relocation did not take place until 1972 (p. 316). Currently there is consideration to conserve, restore and reinstate the window in its original location.
4 Harry Clarke Archive, HLG.
5 Gordon Bowe, *Harry Clarke, the life and work*, p. 164.
6 For a very detailed description of the iconography, see Gordon Bowe, 'Harry Clarke, 1889–1931' (PhD), vol. 1, pp 269–336.
7 It is worth noting that the Victoria & Albert Museum, London, has, on permanent display, a variant of the central light of this window, which was made at Harry Clarke Studios in 1940.
8 Letter from Walter Clarke to Harry Clarke, 17 Sept. 1924, CSGSA, TCD
9 Bowe, 'Harry Clarke 1889–1931' (PhD), vol. 2, p. 611.
10 Gordon Bowe suggests that they were possibly painted by Clarke's assistant, Kathleen Quigly. See 'Harry Clarke 1889–1931' (PhD, 1981), vol. 2, p. 612.
11 These square slabs would have come from the base of a square bottle made in a mould.
12 Kilbride (Eneriley) Church of Ireland church, Co. Wicklow.

St Teresa's church (RC)

1 Made when the company was named either Earley & Powell or John Bishop Earley's Camden Art Works. I am indebted to Dr Michael Earley for this information.
2 I am grateful to Ken Ryan of Abbey Stained Glass Studios for this information.
3 Michael Earley, 'Devotion and tradition in stained glass in twentieth-century Ireland: Earley & Co. 1903–53', (PhD, NCAD, 2023).
4 Dr Michael Wynne was on the selection committee and correspondence relating to the commission is in his archive, NGI.
5 Author's interview with Phyllis Burke, July 2023. See also David Caron, 'Heavenly light', *Irish Arts Review*, 40:4 (Winter 2024), pp 84–91. For a list of all the subjects and dates of the windows see D. Caron (ed.), *Gazetteer of Irish stained glass* (Dublin, 2021).
6 Wilfrid Cantwell to Michael Wynne, 9 Dec. 1992. M. Wynne archive, NGI. In fact, St Patrick and St Brigid were retained and Edith Stein became the eight subject (replacing a copy of a window from Chartres by Willie Earley).
7 For a detailed analysis of the text and imagery in all of Phyllis Burke's windows, see Fr Nicholas Madden's *The new windows in St Teresa's church, Clarendon Street* (Dublin, 2008).
8 Author's interview with Phyllis Burke, Aug. 2023.

Unitarian church

1 For information on the previous windows, see D. Caron, 'A.E. Child's memorial window, 1918–2018', *Oscailt – Ireland's Unitarian Magazine*, 14:7 (July 2018), pp 9–19.
2 Ciaran O'Neill, 'The public history of slavery in Dublin' (Sir John T. Gilbert commemorative lecture, 2021. PDF document published by Dublin City Libraries), pp 16–21.
3 Ibid., p. 20.
4 Ernest Savell Hicks, 'Address on the occasion of the dedication of the Wilson memorial window', *What do these Unitarians really believe* (Dublin, 2010), pp 142–3.
5 Ibid.
6 Ibid.
7 Ibid.
8 David Caron interview with Norah Dungan, daughter of A.E. Child, Sept. 1981.
9 E.S. Hicks, 'Address on the occasion of the dedication …', p. 142.
10 Ibid.
11 Ibid.
12 David Caron interview with Norah Dungan, daughter of A.E. Child, Sept. 1981.
13 ATG order book no. 3, order no. 796. $1,000 draft received in August. CSIA, NGI.
14 Louise's name, along with those of Elizabeth and their parents, appear together on their shared gravestone in Cedar Grove Cemetery, Dorchester, MA.
15 Ten houses in Cork Street (later named Huxley Crescent) were funded by a donation from Miss Huxley, supported by members of Dublin's Unitarian Church.
16 There is a preliminary design in ink and watercolour for one of the trefoils, NGI.
17 Purser's executors paid O'Brien the cost of the window, £48. ATG order book no. 3. CSIA, NGI.

Dublin North, Suburbs and County

Artane – St John Vianney church / Our Lady of Mercy church

1 'Kilmore parish – planned giving campaign'. Brochure for parishioners, Sept. 1967 (copy in DDA).
2 Fiana Griffin, 'Thought-provoking stained glass windows in Artane', *Intercom* magazine (Oct.) (Dublin, 2020), pp 28–30.
3 I am grateful to Patrick Muldowney for information about the commission.

4 Theo Snoddy, in his *Dictionary of Irish artists – twentieth century* (Dublin, 1996), states that 'he worked for a period at Harry Clarke Stained Glass, Ltd.' though there is no record of this in the Clarke's studio records.

5 Information courtesy of Paul Donnelly.

6 It has not been possible to ascertain what I.A.G. stands for; it does not, for instance, appear to be the Independent Artists Group which Campbell did not exhibit with.

Balbriggan – Saints Peter and Paul's church (RC)

1 Canon Byrne to Harry Clarke, April 1923, quoted in N. Gordon Bowe, *Harry Clarke, the life and work* (2nd ed. Dublin, 2012), p. 221.

2 Harry Clarke to Canon Byrne, 9 Mar. 1924, quoted in Gordon Bowe, *Harry Clarke*, p. 221.

3 Both Dürer in his woodcut of *The Visitation* and Giotto in his Arena Chapel version of the subject include attendants with Mary. I am grateful to Dr Stephen Huws for drawing my attention to this.

4 Anna Brownell Jameson, *Legends of the Madonna, as represented in the fine arts* (London, 1890), p. 188. I am indebted to Dr Stephen Huws for drawing this to my attention.

5 In 1961 the Holy See ordered that the name of Philomena be removed from all liturgical calendars.

6 I am indebted to Dr Paul Donnelly, expert on Harry Clarke Studios and the work of William Dowling in particular, for making this attribution.

7 Ibid.

Ballymun – Our Lady of Victories church (RC)

1 Helen Moloney, single sheet titled 'Symbols used in windows for Our Lady of Victories, Ballymun'. Moloney coll., NIVAL.

2 Ibid.

3 Bart Felle, 'Helen Moloney, stained glass artist, her life and works' (MPhil, TCD, 2018), pp 43–4.

4 Author's conservation with George Walsh, Dec. 2024.

Dollymount – Manresa Jesuit Centre of Spirituality

1 Now on display at the top of a specially constructed staircase in Government Buildings, Merrion St.

2 Joseph McBrinn, 'Three kings', *Irish Arts Review*, 39:4 (Winter 2022), p. 105.

3 Anthony Symondson, 'A new setting for Evie Hone's Rahan windows', *Irish Arts Review*, 11 (1995), p. 205.

4 Ibid., p. 206.

5 McBrinn, 'Three kings', p. 107.

6 Ibid., pp 103–4.

7 James White, 'The Nativity in glass', *Catholic Standard*, 30 Mar. 1945, quoted in McBrinn, 'Three kings', p. 105.

8 McBrinn, 'Three kings', p. 107.

9 J. White, 'The Nativity in glass', quoted in McBrinn, 'Three kings'.

Donnycarney – Our Lady of Consolation church (RC)

1 Ellen Rowley (ed.), *More than concrete blocks, 1940–72*, vol. 2 (Dublin, 2019), provides an overview of the protracted development, with a description and insights into the building's design, p. 359.

2 Donnycarney Church was designed with an altar rail, albeit a slim one, which has remained in situ.

3 *Irish Builder and Engineer*, 17 May 1969.

4 Cathedral glass is textured translucent sheet glass made by casting and rolling, and despite the name, is unconnected with medieval cathedrals.

5 Ellen Rowley (ed.), *More than concrete blocks, 1940–72*, vol. 2, p. 359.

6 As recounted to Reiltín Murphy by Des Devitt, 2015.

Drumcondra – Our Lady Seat of Wisdom chapel (RC) and 'Quiet Space'

1 Thomas Kellaghan, 'Donal Francis Cregan', *Dictionary of Irish biography* (Dublin, 2009).

2 I am grateful to Colm O'Brien for his insights and knowledge of the campus's design.

3 Information on the symbols contained in the windows comes from an official leaflet, 'Chapel of Our Lady, Seat of Wisdom', no author and undated but post-1993. Copies in the chaplain's office.

4 Ibid.

5 Conversation with Fr Joe McCann, 14 Nov. 2024.

6 'Chapel of Our Lady, Seat of Wisdom', ibid.

7 Acts 2:1–4.

Dublin Airport – Our Lady Queen of Heaven church (RC)

1 See Ellen Rowley, 'Andrew Devane's Dublin churches: Catholic architecture in Ireland in an age of tentative radicalization, 1960–75' in (eds, *Modern religious architecture in Germany, Ireland and beyond* (London, 2019).

2 Michael Dunne (1921–2005), independent stained glass artist / craftsman.

3 Sheila Corcoran was born in 1943; in 1962 she exhibited at the Oireachtas exhibition.

4 'Light and colour', Brown Thomas Little Theatre, Dublin, June 1963.

5 Devane to Corcoran, 9 Mar. 1964. RKD archive. Corcoran made at least two trial pieces, one now in private coll., UK.

6 Devane to Corcoran, 9 Mar. 1964. RKD archive.

7 Corcoran to Devane, 29 June 1964. RKD archive. Devane kept the original version and later gifted it to a colleague. Now in private coll., US.

8 Devane kept the original version and later gifted it to a colleague. Now in private coll., UK.

9 O'Leary to McQuaid, 1 Jan. 1964 (dated 1964 but must be 1965). DDA. Fergus O'Farrell's (1918–2008) crib, paid for by airport staff, featured ten hand-turned wooden figures similar to sets he had previously made for churches in Britain and US.

10 McQuaid to O'Leary, Swords, 30 Dec. 1964. DDA.

11 In addition to write-ups in daily and Sunday newspapers, Gay Byrne was eager to do a segment on the Late Late Show, with O'Farrell and the recently appointed director of the National Gallery, James White, along with a representative from the archbishop's side. Typed unsigned memo from the archbishop's secretary(?) to McQuaid, 6 Jan. 1965. DDA.

12 She had been awarded the Henry Higgins Travelling Scholarship by the RDS.

13 Corcoran (Blackheath, London) to McQuaid, 3 Jan. [1965]. DDA.

14 McQuaid to Corcoran, 6 Jan. 1965, marked 'Personal'. DDA.

15 Devane to Barney Corcoran, 15 Feb. 1965, RKD archive.

16 Devane, to McQuaid, 19 Aug. 1967. In conclusion Devane suggested that the archbishop might ask his secretary to ring him indicating his approval or not of the Stations. DDA.

17 Also in 1967 McQuaid was engaged in protracted debate with Devane about a beaten copper figure of Our Lady by Imogen Stuart for the atrium, which was not resolved until 1969.

18 Devane to Corcoran, 9 Mar. 1964. RKD archive.

Howth – St Mary's church (C of I)

1 *List of the principle stained glass windows executed in Ireland from 1903 to 1928*, a slim booklet produced by An Túr Gloine to mark its twenty-fifth anniversary (Dublin, 1928).

2 Perhaps best known for the fine portrait of her with her daughter Margaret, titled *Mrs Noel Guinness* (1898), by Walter Osborne which won a bronze medal at the Paris International Exhibition and was widely reproduced at the time, coll., NGI.

3 *List of the principal stained glass windows.*

4 I am grateful to Reiltín Murphy for establishing the relationship between the MacDougalls and Mary Guinness.

5 Dr David Lawrence's research identified Hogan as cartoonist. See his entry for St Mary's, Howth, in www.gloine.ie

6 'Dedication ceremony in Howth Church', *Irish Times*, 29 June 1910, p. 8.

7 Ibid.

8 'Howth War Memorial', *Irish Times*, 31 May 1920, p. 4.

9 *Saints Patrick, Brigid and Berac – Kirkwood memorial* (1935), Ardcarne Church of Ireland church, Co. Roscommon.

10 It is difficult to be certain of the narratives depicted in the left light. In the top scene the two blind people appear to be female rather than male, the middle scene is ambiguous, and the bottom scene could be the *Raising of the Daughter of Jairus*, a theme Hone treated on another occasion.

11 I am grateful to Dr Joseph McBrinn for this information, and for his reflections on the complex iconography.

12 Dr David Lawrence's comprehensive survey of C of I stained glass for www.gloine.ie allows one to search by subject.

Lusk – St MacCullin's church (RC)

1 There are several variants of the saint's name. For instance, Clarke's order book records it as St Maculuid; other versions are St Maccuilinn or St Macculind.

2 I am indebted to Colm O'Brien for drawing my attention to these precedents.

3 Lawrence William White, 'Robinson, John Joseph', *Dictionary of Irish biography* (RIA online resource).

4 N. Gordon Bowe, 'Harry Clarke 1889–1931' (PhD, TCD, 1981), vol. 2, p. 590.

5 'A new church', *Drogheda Independent*, 25 Nov. 1922, p. 3.

6 Gordon Bowe, 'Harry Clarke 1889–1931' (PhD), vol. 2, p. 590.

7 Ibid.

8 My gratitude to Reiltín Murphy for identifying the window as a 2-light memorial to Fr William J. Donnelly and its original location. It appears that Clarke's were asked to remove this window when renovations/improvements were taking place including to the Lady Chapel, for which Harry Clarke created several oil paintings on canvas of angels in 1924 (now in NGI).

9 I am most grateful to Evan Connon for drawing this to my attention and allowing me to examine the windows in his studio prior to reinstallation.

10 A lantern may seem like a curious inclusion; it was used by the arresting soldiers at the time of Christ's betrayal.

11 This inclusion was something he had first tried in a small window for the earl of Wicklow earlier in 1924. On inspection of the Lusk windows it is apparent that Clarke plated a piece of clear glass to the amber

slab on which he deftly painted the perimeter area to enhance its glowing quality.

12 Much later, Harry's son David Clarke designed a small number of windows for the studio.

13 I am grateful to Dr Paul Donnelly for identifying the subject.

14 Attribution courtesy of Dr Paul Donnelly.

15 I am grateful to Reiltín Murphy for uncovering this information.

Malahide – St Andrew's church (C of I) / Presbyterian church / St Sylvester's church (RC)

1 The window was originally in the entrance porch but when the new entrance lobby was created (2006) it was taken out and reinserted so that it now faces into the lobby.

2 Marino was renamed Abbey Lea, and for information on it and the colourful Lady Joyce Talbot, see Pippa McIntosh, *Abbey Lea, a Killiney history* (Dublin, 2024), pp 123–31.

3 Murphy's first commission was in Pakistan (1955), and in 1956 he also undertook orders for two churches in Tipperary.

4 Now home to the Fry Model Railway Museum.

5 I am grateful to Reiltín Murphy for this information.

6 Author's conversation with Peter Young, 19 Aug. 2024.

7 A code is now required for access. Inquire from the parish centre.

8 I am grateful to Killian Schurmann for speaking about his work and explaining the process of its creation, Aug. 2024.

Santry – St Pappin's church (C of I)

1 A veteran of the Boer War, Capt. C.V.L. Poë was killed while leading an attack on a German trench, 1–2 Mar. 1915.

2 John Dugdale (former labourer, probably in Santry Demesne), gunner, died in France, 1 May 1915; Edward Harris (former postman), private in the Royal Dublin Fusiliers, killed in action, 7 June 1917; Stephen Rose (former botanical laboratory attendant), private in the Medical Corps, died at sea, 15 April 1917.

3 See N. Gordon Bowe, *Wilhelmina Geddes, life and work* (Dublin, 2015), pp 130–1.

4 See D. Caron, *Michael Healy 1873–1941, An Túr Gloine's pioneer* (Dublin, 2023), p. 157.

5 *St Michael* was the subject of another Geddes set of three archangel-themed war memorial windows in All Saints church, Blackrock.

6 Statistic based on research undertaken by Dr David Lawrence for www.gloine.ie

7 I am grateful to Reiltín Murphy for researching Muriel Poë and members of her family.

8 'Behold, we count them happy which endure. Ye have heard of the patience of Job', James 5:11.

9 'The Lord gave, and the Lord hath taken away; blessed be the name of the Lord', Job 2:21.

10 Turtle Bunbury, 'Leonard Hutcheson Poë (1888–1929)', *Turtle Bunbury Histories*, an online resource.

11 'Santry', *Church of Ireland Gazette*, 28 June 1935, p. 410.

Dublin South, Suburbs and County

Ballinteer – St John the Evangelist church (RC)

1 Drawings in IAA.

2 Apparently commissioned from him by John Quinn of William's supermarket, Sandyford Road. See framed account in church, and information also contained in Christopher Ryan, *The parish of St John the Evangelist, silver jubilee of the parish* (Dublin, 1998), p. 11.

3 See framed account in church.

Blackrock – St John the Baptist church (RC)

1 For details of these windows, see Michael O'Connell, *The church of Saint John the Baptist, Blackrock* (Dublin, 2014), pp 44–57.

2 Giotto depicted Christ as a seraph with St Francis about to receive the stigmata. I am grateful to Ruth Sheehy for information on depictions of the 'seraph'.

3 Three Carmelite communities were beneficiaries in his will.

4 *Irish Times*, 20 Dec. 1932, p. 14

5 Edward and Brigid Maguire's son was the distinguished painter Edward Maguire RHA (1932–86).

6 Information from Dr Jospeh McBrinn.

7 Cartoons for the window (coll. Clongowes Wood College) help interpret Hone's intentions. My gratitude to John Bird, archivist.

8 I am indebted to Professor John Turpin for alerting me to the fact that the window had been relocated.

Carrickmines – Tullow church (C of I)

1 Though designed by Beatrice Elvery they were constructed by Frank Browning and the panels were carved by the artist's mother, Therese Moss Elvery.

2 Nicola Gordon Bowe, 'The art of Beatrice Elvery, Lady Glenavy (1883–1970)', *Irish Arts Review*, 11 (1995), p. 171.

3 'Tullow parish church, Carrickmines', *Church of Ireland Gazette*, 13 Mar. 1908, p. 17.

4 ATG order book no. 3, order no. 955. Reference to 'porch window panel' costing £22 and 'rest of the

window' also costing £22. CSIA, NGI.

5 'An Irishwoman's diary', *Irish Times*, 12 June 1959, p. 6.

6 NGI coll., no. 19128.

7 'Exhibition in the Tower of Glass', J.[ames] W.[hite], undated newspaper clipping in Catherine O'Brien's scrapbook, CSIA, NGI.

8 'New window in Tullow church', *Church of Ireland Gazette*, 22 Sept. 1995, p. 6.

Donnybrook – Sacred Heart church (RC)

1 Roger Sweetman (1874–1954), barrister and later Sinn Féin politician. He chose not to be identified in the window's inscription which reads 'Pray for the donor and his kindred'.

2 Letter from Fr Michael Sweetman SJ (son of Roger Sweetman) to author, 4 Aug. 1988.

3 Healy most likely used Canon John O'Hanlon's *Lives of the Irish saints* as his source for hair colour.

4 David Caron, *Michael Healy 1873–1941, An Túr Gloine's stained glass pioneer* (Dublin, 2023), pp 221–2.

5 For further information on the window see D. Caron, *Michael Healy*, pp 124–8.

6 T. McGreevy, 'Healy window', *Parish of the Sacred Heart, Donnybrook* (Dublin, 1966), pp 133–4.

7 Based on her extensive research, Nicola Gordon Bowe, the expert on Harry Clarke, determined to what extent Clarke was involved in various stained glass commissions attributed to him, establishing three categories.

8 N. Gordon Bowe, *Harry Clarke, the life and work* (2nd ed., Dublin, 2021), p. 226.

9 St Gobnait is the patron saint of beekeeping.

10 Walter Clarke to Catherine Egan, 19 June 1924. Clarke MSS, TCD.

11 None of the windows carry an inscription though a plaque below indicates that they are in memory of Edward Egan and Bernard Martin.

12 I am grateful to Dr Paul Donnelly for drawing my attention to a black and white photo of the design for the window along with a colour pencil version (in which the right light is missing) in the Clarke Collection, TCD.

Dún Laoghaire – St Michael's church (RC) / Presbyterian church

1 Designs for these three windows, Clarke Collection, TCD. The subjects of the other two windows, for which there are no designs extant, were *Our Lady of Perpetual Succour and Our Lady of the Rosary*, and *St Joseph and St Patrick*. Information courtesy of Dr Paul Donnelly.

2 RTÉ news report by Mike Burns, 28 July 1965.

3 Pearse McKenna, 'Rebuilding St Michael's', *St Michael's parish, Dun Laoghaire, 150th anniversary* (booklet) (Dublin, 1979).

4 Ibid.

5 Stations of the Cross for St Benedict's Catholic cathedral, Ogoja, Nigeria. McKenna also commissioned *dalle de verre* in 1971 for the chapel of the Kiltegan Fathers (St Patrick's Missionary Society), Kiltegan, Co. Wicklow.

6 Letters and invoices, Pearse McKenna archive, IAA.

7 Madeleine Maher, *St Michael's church – art and artefacts* (Dublin, 2003), p. 13.

8 P. McKenna, 'Rebuilding St Michael's'.

9 Terry Corcoran, a talented graduate of the National College of Art, assisted Murphy on this job, working on the drawings and colour aspect.

10 M. Maher, *St Michael's church – art and artefacts*, p. 13.

11 Holy Cross (Dominican) church, Sligo town. Ireland's damp climate is not always ideal for *dalle de verre*.

12 Letter, P. Pye to P. McKenna, 15 Dec. 1969. Pearse McKenna archive, IAA

13 M. Maher, *St Michael's church – art and artefacts*, p. 29.

14 Dr Ryan returned to St Michael's the following November to celebrate the funeral Mass of 95-year -old Monsignor Patrick Boylan who had been deeply involved in the church project.

15 I am grateful to Reiltín Murphy for her research on the Beatty family members.

16 Since demolished, it was located beside the Royal Marine Hotel.

17 An Túr Gloine order book vol. 2, p. 1, order no. 485. The cost had risen to £300 per window.

18 Margaret Beatty must have left instructions for her inscription to be inserted after she died, perhaps with the minister. Judging from the style of lettering it was not done at An Túr Gloine.

19 The inscriptions' lettering styles and the colour of the glass differ in both to suggest that they were done by different hands at different times.

20 I am grateful to Dr Paul Donnelly for providing this information.

Dundrum – St Nahi's church (C of I)

1 The Vestry approved the design, subject to the inclusion of the word 'Charity', on 12 Oct. 1908. Vestry minutes, RCB.

2 As the Monk Gibbons had family connections in Cheshire she is likely a relative.

3 William Monk Gibbon, *The masterpiece and the man: Yeats as I knew him* (London, 1959), pp 13–14. I am grateful to Dr Billy Shortall for drawing this to my attention.

4 The ATG work journal no. 1 (job no. 380) indicates that a longer inscription was intended which stated that Mrs Wilson was 'the daughter of the late Rev Edward Arnold Carroll formerly of this parish ...' CSIA, NGI.
5 Newspaper clipping dated 25 Sept. 1936, Catherine O'Brien's scrapbook, p. 50. CSIA, NGI.
6 Dr David Lawrence, compiler of the www.gloine.ie survey of Church of Ireland windows, has identified the subject as *Benedicte*.
7 ATG work journal no. 1 (job no. 421). CSIA, NGI.
8 Richard Barrington and John Lawrence Barrington.
9 E. Coxhead, *Daughters of Erin: five women of the Irish renascence* (London, 1965), p. 145.
10 Cartoons for abstract panels, NGI; cartoon for complete window, Taney Parish Centre, Dundrum.
11 Hutchinson, who was then living near Oxford, died suddenly on a trip back to Ireland in March 1927 (though window inscription erroneously states March 1928). Canon Monk Gibbon, a friend of the Hones, facilitated her burial at St Nahi's. I am indebted to Dr Joseph McBrinn for information relating to this commission.
12 I am grateful to Dr Billy Shortall for this information.
13 ATG work book no. 2 (job no. 783). CSIA, NGI.
14 Newspaper clipping dated 25 Sept. 1936, Catherine O'Brien's scrapbook, p. 50. CSIA, NGI.

Greenhills – Holy Spirit church (RC)

1 Made by George W. Walsh at Abbey Stained Glass Studios, Dublin. It is thought to be the first work in *dalle de verre* that was made in Ireland.
2 There does not appear to be any extant correspondence relating to Greenhills church between Peppard & Duffy and Dr McQuaid, or any with Richard King.
3 Louis C. Peppard, 'In tribute to Richard King', *Capuchin Annual* (Dublin, 1975), p. 195.
4 James Hall, *Dictionary of subjects & symbols in art* (London, 1979).
5 See Ruth Sheehy, *The life and work of Richard King: religion, nationalism and modernism* (Oxford, 2020), pp 254, 280–5.
6 Ruth Sheehy, *The life and work of Richard King*, p. 337.
7 Ibid., pp 338–9.
8 According to Greenhills' parish website, the individual panels were installed by parishioner Michael Roche who worked for the Dublin Glass and Paint Company.

Killiney – Holy Trinity church (C of I) / St Stephen's church (RC)

1 Subsequently renamed twice, firstly Ayesha Castle and secondly Manderley Castle. The design of the castle is attributed to Sandham Symes.
2 Lawrence (Larkey) Ambrose Waldon (1858–1923), stockbroker, patron of the arts, Nationalist MP. See Pippa McIntosh, *Abbey Lea, a Killiney history; the life of Marino before it was the residence of the Australian ambassador to Ireland* (Dublin, 2024).
3 Select Vestry Minutes, Holy Trinity church, Killiney, 4 Oct. 1918. RCB Library.
4 The cartoon is in the collection of Dublin City Council.
5 The original windows either side of Clarke's window were replaced in 1986 with stained glass windows which came from the former C of I church, Collinstown, Co. Westmeath. One cannot be certain if the original windows were diamond-patterned but the large south transept window is.
6 Nicola Gordon Bowe, *Harry Clarke* (monograph and catalogue of exhibition in Douglas Hyde Gallery, TCD, 1979), p. 104.
7 Nicola Gordon Bowe, *Harry Clarke, the life and work* (2nd ed., Dublin, 2012), p. 156.
8 Select Vestry Minutes, Holy Trinity church, Killiney, 7 Sept. 1942. RCB Library.
9 I am grateful to David Millar for the suggestion that Henry Eoghan O'Brien was the probable donor, which was concurred by O'Brien's granddaughter, Olivia Robinson (née O'Brien).
10 It is not recorded who the other artist was.
11 Author's interview with Frank McGoldrick, the artist's nephew, 2 July 1987.
12 Preliminary designs and extracts from the Acts of the Apostles VI and VII are among Helen Moloney's archive, NIVAL.
13 See Bart Felle, 'Helen Moloney, her life and works' (MPhil, TCD, 2018), pp 72–3.

Kimmage – Holy Spirit church (RC)

1 In the 1930s there were 125 ordinations and in the 1940s there were 192. I am grateful to Margaret Bluett for these statistics.
2 There are also four more lead lights containing symbols at clerestory level by Clarke's.
3 I am grateful to Dr Paul Donnelly for information about who placed the orders, etc.
4 Again, I am indebted to Dr Donnelly for his insights and knowledge.
5 See Ruth Sheehy, *The life and work of Richard King: religion, nationalism and modernism* (Oxford, 2020), pp 112–13, 120.
6 Both William Dowling and Terry Clarke left partial lists of their windows, including those made for Kimmage Manor. I am indebted to Dr Paul Donnelly for this information.

7 I am grateful to Ruth Sheehy for identifying the source of this imagery.
8 I am grateful to Nora Tillman for the translation.
9 The records for Earley & Co. no longer exist but one could assume this window dates to 1939–42.
10 Inexplicably the name inscribed on the window is Zacarias, not the intended Zechariah.
11 'Our college chapel', *Tomorrow's labourers* (Kimmage Manor, 1953).
12 These rooms are now used for different purposes and usually not open.

Rathfarnham – Holy Spirit church (RC)

1 St Brigid's extension features a large window (1978) by Phyllis Burke.
2 Ledger, Murphy-Devitt Studios archive, NIVAL
3 National Orthopaedic Hospital, Finglas (*c.*1960), St Louis High School, Rathmines (*c.*1963), and Our Lady's Manor nursing home, Dalkey (1965).
4 A coloured sketch for Stations I and II is in NIVAL, along with cartoons all the Stations.
5 Reiltín Murphy to author, 8 July 2024. Several of Murphy's tracings for the Station's calligraphy are in the Murphy-Devitt Studios archive, NIVAL.
6 The dove as a symbol of the Holy Spirit was an image that Murphy featured many times in stained glass. See also Our Lady of Consolation, Donnycarney, pp 168–9.
7 Eimear O'Connor, *Seán Keating: art, politics and building the Irish nation* (Dublin, 2013), p. 276.

Terenure – St Joseph's church (RC)

1 Austin Clarke, *A penny in the clouds* (London, 1960), p. 191.
2 Major Gorman of Brighton Road, Rathgar, died in 1913 and his widow, Catherine, died in 1915; curiously her name does not appear in the inscription.
3 Nicola Gordon Bowe, *Harry Clarke – the life and work* (2nd ed., Dublin, 2012), p. 145.
4 Ibid. Letter, 19 May 1917.
5 Edward was an English wine merchant. Fannie lived with her sister and brother-in-law. I am grateful to Reiltín Murphy for researching the family.
6 Brian Mac Giolla Phadraig, *History of Terenure* (Dublin, 1954), pp 57–8. For further details of all the saints featured, see Patricia Curtin-Kelly, *Harry Clarke and his legacy – the stained glass windows in St Joseph's church, Terenure* (Dublin, 2017).
7 William Dowling, *Dublin Historical Review* (Old Dublin Society), vol. 27 (Dublin, 1962), p. 59.
8 Specifically *The Ascension* (1923) for Brisbane cathedral, Australia, and the final window Clarke designed, *The Last Judgement* (1930), for Newport, Co. Mayo.
9 Gordon Bowe, *Harry Clarke – the life and work*, p. 206.
10 Gordon Bowe has identified that Clarke based these on Paul Klee's engraving, *Two men meeting, each presuming the other to be of a higher rank* (1903).
11 There are architectural drawings in the W.H. Byrne & Son coll. of both the original designs and the extension, IAA.
12 See Curtin-Kelly, *Harry Clarke and his legacy*.
13 Ibid., pp 10–11.

Artists and Studios

1 Quoted in Paul Donnelly, 'Legacy and identity: Harry Clarke, William Dowling and the Harry Clarke Studios' in A. Griffith et al. (eds), *Harry Clarke and artistic visions of the new Irish State* (Dublin, 2019), p. 315.
2 Information on Earley's drawn from Michael Earley, 'Devotion and tradition in stained glass in twentieth century Ireland: Earley & Co. 1903–53' (PhD, NCAD, 2023).
3 Information on William Earley and the family firm drawn from Michael Earley, 'Devotion and tradition in stained glass in twentieth century Ireland: Earley & Co. 1903–53' (PhD, NCAD, 2023).
4 Quoted in Earley, 'Devotion and tradition', vol. 1, p. 203.
5 Beatrice Glenavy, *Today we will only gossip* (London, 1964), p. 40.
6 For a full account of Geddes's career, see Nicola Gordon Bowe, *Wilhelmina Geddes, life and work* (Dublin, 2015).
7 Obituary, *The Times*, 16 Aug. 1955.
8 Joseph McBrinn is currently preparing a major book on the life and work of Evie Hone.
9 The principal source for Richard King is Ruth Sheehy's *The life and work of Richard King: religion, nationalism and modernism* (Oxford, 2020).
10 N. Gordon Bowe, *Harry Clarke, the life and work* (2nd ed. Dublin, 2012), p. 48.
11 The chief source for Helen Moloney is Bart Felle, 'Helen Moloney, her life and works' (MPhil, TCD, 2018).
12 'Twenty-fifth anniversary celebration', a pamphlet (Dublin, 1928), p. 11.
13 Brian McAvera, *Patrick Pye, life and work* (Dublin, 2013), p. 16.
14 Ibid. p. 86.
15 Nicola Gordon Bowe, *Recent Irish art series, no. 3: stained glass* (Belfast, 1983), p. 16.
16 Brian McAvera, 'Vocation and vision', *Irish Arts Review* (Spring 2009), p. 75.
17 Finola Finlay is currently preparing a book on George Stephen Walsh and George W. Walsh.

Select Bibliography

Unpublished documentary sources

An Túr Gloine archive, CSIA, NGI.

Bowe, Nicola Gordon, 'Harry Clarke 1889–1931, his life and work' (PhD, TCD, 1982).

Church of Ireland archive, RCB.

Clarke Studios Collection, TCD.

Donnelly, Paul, 'The rise and fall of Harry Clarke Stained Glass Limited: an analysis of the main influences in the story of the company's success and decline' (MPhil, TCD, 2014).

Dublin City University archive.

Dublin Diocesan Archive.

Earley, Michael, 'Devotion and tradition in stained glass in twentieth-century Ireland: Earley & Co. 1903–53' (PhD, NCAD, 2023).

Earley, William, 'The stained glass work of Patrick Pollen' (MPhil, TCD, 2014).

Felle, Bart, 'Helen Moloney, her life and works' (MPhil, TCD, 2018).

Hugh Lane Gallery archive.

Irish Architectural Archive.

Moloney O'Beirne Architects archive.

Robinson, Keefe and Devane archive.

Thompson, Hugh, 'The first vicar of St Catherine's'. Transcript of lecture originally delivered to St Catherine's Association on 2 Mar. 1914. Thompson MS, RCB library.

Wynne, Michael, 'Stained glass in Ireland, principally Irish stained glass 1760–1963' (PhD, TCD, 1975).

Published sources:

'An Irishwoman's diary', *Irish Times*, 12 June 1959, p. 6.

An Túr Gloine – List of the principal stained glass windows executed in Ireland from 1903 to 1928 (booklet) (Dublin, 1928).

An Túr Gloine twenty-fifth anniversary celebration (booklet) (Dublin, 1928).

Anon., *Looking back, moving forward: Dún Laoghaire's Presbyterian church* (Dublin, 2013) (No author's name appears).

Anon., 'New window in Tullow church', *Church of Ireland Gazette*, 22 Sept. 1995, p. 6.

Bowe, Nicola Gordon, *Harry Clarke*, monograph and catalogue accompanying an exhibition of Clarke's work, Douglas Hyde Gallery, TCD (Dublin, 1979).

— *Harry Clarke, the life and work* (2nd ed., Dublin, 2012).

— 'Patrick Pollen, metaphysician in glass', *Irish Arts Review* (Summer 2011), pp 102–7.

— 'Stained glass', recent Irish art series no. 3 (Dublin and Belfast, 1983).

— 'The art of Beatrice Elvery, Lady Glenavy', *Irish Arts Review Yearbook 1995*, pp 168–75.

— *Wilhelmina Geddes, life and work* (Dublin, 2015).

Caron, David, 'A.E. Child's memorial window, 1918–2018', *Oscailt – Ireland's Unitarian Magazine*, 14:7 (July 2018), pp 9–19.

— 'Divine delights' (Harry Clarke's windows for Dowanhill, Glasgow), *Irish Arts Review* (Winter 2020), pp 386–89.

— (ed.), *Gazetteer of Irish stained glass* (Dublin, 2021).

— 'Heavenly light' (stained glass of Phyllis Burke), *Irish Arts Review*, 40:4 (Winter 2024), pp 84–91.

— 'In unison' (A.E. Child's window for Dublin's Unitarian church), *Irish Arts Review*, 38:4 (Winter 2021), pp 500–03.

— *Michael Healy, 1873–1941: An Túr Goine's stained glass pioneer* (Dublin 2023).

— 'Michael Healy's stained glass window of St Victor', *Irish Arts Review*, Yearbook 1993, pp 187–91.

Casey, Christine, *The buildings of Ireland: Dublin* (New Haven and London, 2005).

Curtin-Kelly, Patricia, *Harry Clarke & his legacy; the stained glass windows of St Joseph's church, Terenure* (Dublin, 2017).

Donnelly, Paul, 'Legacy and identity: Harry Clarke, William Dowling and the Harry Clarke Studios' in A. Griffith et al. (eds), *Harry Clarke and artistic visions of the new Irish State*.

Donovan, Katie, 'A touch of glass', *Irish Times*, 22 Jan. 1998.

Dowling, William, *Dublin Historical Review* (Old Dublin Society), 17 (Dublin, 1962).

Griffith, A., M. Helmers and R. Kennedy (eds), *Harry Clarke and artistic visions of the new Irish State* (Dublin, 2019).

Griffin, Fiana, 'Thought provoking stained glass windows in Artane', *Intercom* magazine (Oct. 2020), pp 28–30.

Hall, James, *Dictionary of subjects & symbols in art* (London, 1979).

Kennedy, Róisín, 'The Geneva Window: a precious gift, never given' in A. Griffith et al. (eds), *Harry Clarke and artistic visions of the new Irish State*.

McAvera, Brian, *Patrick Pye, life and work, a counter-cultural story* (Dublin, 2013).

— 'Vocation and vision', *Irish Arts Review* (Spring 2009), pp 69–75.

McBrinn, Joseph, 'Frank Brangwyn and stained glass: the earl of Iveagh memorial windows at Dublin and Elvedon', *Journal of Stained Glass*, 26 (2002), pp 30–44.

— ' "The loveliest thing I have seen": Evie Hone's stained glass panels', *Glass Ireland*, pp 23–5.

— 'Three kings', *Irish Arts Review*, 39:4 (Winter 2022), pp 102–7.

Mac Giolla Phadraig, Brian, *History of Terenure* (Dublin, 1954).

McGreevy, Thomas, 'Healy window', *Parish of the Sacred Heart, Donnybrook* (Dublin, 1966).

Madden, Nicholas, *The new windows in St Teresa's church, Clarendon Street* (Dublin, 2008).

Maher, Madeleine, *St Michael's church – art and artefacts* (Dublin, 2003).

McIntosh, Pippa, *Abbey Lea, a Killiney history* (Dublin, 2024).

O'Connell, Michael, *The church of Saint John the Baptist, Blackrock* (Dublin, 2014).

O'Connor, Eimear, *Seán Keating: art, politics and building the Irish nation* (Dublin, 2013).

O'Donnell, Jessica 'A gorgeous gallery of poetic pictures: Harry Clarke, Harold Jacob and John Keats's

"The Eve of St Agnes" in A. Griffith et al. (eds), *Harry Clarke and artistic visions of the new Irish State.*

— *Harry Clarke, The Eve of St Agnes* (Dublin, 2012).

'Our college chapel', *Tomorrow's labourers* (House of Philosophy, Kimmage Manor, 1953).

Peppard, Louis C., 'In tribute to Richard King', *Capuchin Annual* (Dublin, 1975).

Rowley, Ellen (ed.), *More than concrete blocks, 1940–72*, vol. 2 (Dublin, 2019).

— 'Andrew Devane's Dublin churches: Catholic architecture in Ireland in an age of tentative radicalization, 1960–75' in L. Godson and K. James-Chakraborty (eds), *Modern religious architecture in Germany, Ireland and beyond* (New York and London, 2019).

Sullivan, Kelly, 'Harry Clarke's natural world' in A. Griffith et al. (eds), *Harry Clarke and artistic visions of the new Irish State.*

Schenck, Will, *Harry Clarke's stained glass windows for the chapel of the convent of Notre Dame, Dowanhill, Glasgow: the architectural context*, Stained Glass Museum (Ely, 2013).

Snoddy, Theo, *Dictionary of Irish artists – twentieth century* (Dublin, 1996)

Sheehy, Ruth, *The life and work of Richard King: religion, nationalism and modernism* (reimagining Ireland series) (Oxford, 2020).

Symondson, Anthony, 'A new setting for Evie Hone's Rahan windows', *Irish Arts Review*, 11 (1995), pp 205–9.

Thompson, Hugh, 'The St Catherine window', *St Catherine's Parish Magazine* (Jan. 1924).

'Tullow parish church, Carrickmines', *Church of Ireland Gazette*, 13 Mar. 1908, p. 17.

W.[hite], J.[ames], 'Exhibition in the Tower of Glass', undated newspaper clipping in Catherine O'Brien's scrapbook, CSIA, NGI.

Index

of artists, studios and patrons

N

O

P

R

S